William Archer

WILLIAM ARCHER

A Biography

PETER WHITEBROOK

Methuen

To Anna and Mark Bennett

First published in Great Britain 1993
by Methuen London
an imprint of Reed Consumer Books Ltd
Michelin House, 81 Fulham Road, London SW3 6RB
and Auckland, Melbourne, Singapore and Toronto

A CIP catalogue record for this book
is available at the British Library
ISBN 0 413 65520 2

Typeset by CentraCet, Cambridge
Printed in Great Britain
by Clays Ltd, St Ives plc

Contents

List of Illustrations

Illustration Acknowledgements

1, 2, 4, 26, 29: Courtesy of Sir Anthony Parsons. 3, 31: Author's collection. 5: Courtesy of Mrs Karen Anderson. 6: W. Macqueen-Pope: *Gaiety: Theatre of Enchantment*, W. H. Allen 1949. 7: A. R. Caton: *Activity and Rest*, Philip Allen 1936. 8: Courtesy of Popperfoto. 9, 16, 17, 19: Courtesy of the Hulton Deutsch Collection. 10, 21, 22, 24, 30: From the collections of the Theatre Museum, by courtesy of the Board of the Trustees of the Victoria and Albert Museum. 11, 12, 14, 20: Courtesy of the Elizabeth Robins papers, Fales Library, New York University. 13: From *Black and White*, 25 April 1891. 15: From *Ally Sloper's Half-Holiday*, March 1891. 18: Courtesy of Mander and Mitchenson Theatre Collection. 23: Courtesy of the National Portrait Gallery. 25: Courtesy of the National Trust. 27: Charles Archer: *William Archer, Life, Work and Friendships*, Allen and Unwin 1931. 28: Pat Jalland: *Octavia Wilberforce*, Cassell 1989.

Front jacket: Courtesy of Sir Anthony Parsons. Rear jacket: Courtesy of the Elizabeth Robins papers, Fales Library, New York University; Courtesy of the National Portrait Gallery; Courtesy of Popperfoto. Author's photograph: Vivien Devlin.

Acknowledgements

Many people have assisted me during the writing of this book, and I am indebted to them all. I am especially grateful to Michael Holroyd, who gave me immense encouragement and generously gave up time while completing his own peerless biography of Bernard Shaw to discuss at length the complex association between Archer and Shaw. I have incorporated several of his ideas, but I naturally accept responsibility for the interpretation I have placed on them and the conclusions I have reached.

I also gladly thank Angela John. While unravelling the life of Elizabeth Robins for her own forthcoming book, she unreservedly shared her researches with me over many months. Once again, I accept responsibility for my own interpretation of the association between Archer and Elizabeth Robins, but our conversations were always enjoyable and useful and helped clarify my thoughts immeasurably.

At Methuen, I owe a great debt to Pamela Edwardes, whose commitment, encouragement, editorial advice and patience has been an invaluable strength throughout. I would also like to thank Briar Silich, Geoffrey Strachan and David Watson. I am particularly grateful to the Society of Authors, on behalf of the Estates of Bernard Shaw and Harley Granville Barker, for permission to quote from previously published and unpublished material, and to Mrs Roma Woodnutt, head of literary estates at the Society of Authors, for her work on my behalf. I am similarly indebted to Dan H. Laurence for allowing me to quote from previously unpublished letters by Shaw; and to Mrs Mabel Smith, trustee of Backsettown, for permission to quote from the letters and diaries of Elizabeth Robins.

For information, practical assistance, conversations and correspondence about Archer's life and writing, I thank Jonathan Abarbanel; Karen Anderson; James Ronald Archer; Jim Archer; Karin and Justus-

Henri Archer; Dr Simon Archer; Geoffrey Baskerville; Nicholas
Bridges-Adams; Bob Brown; Alma and Dr James Cullen; Vivien Devlin;
Dr Andrew Doig; Leon Edel; Sir Gerald and Lady Elliot; Robert
Ferguson; Don Finley; Richard Garnett; W. D'Arcy Hart; Bjørn
Hemmer; Tone Hoemsnes; Samuel Hynes; Barry Johnson; Joel
Kaplan; the late Ian Kinloch; Ann MacEwen; Michael Meyer; Margery
Morgan; Sidsel Marie Nilsen; Sir Anthony Parsons; Birgitte Possing;
Thomas Postlewait; Donald Scragg; Ann Thwaite; Murdoch Wales;
Stanley Weintraub.

I am extremely grateful for the long-term assistance of Claire Hudson
and the staff of the Theatre Museum, London; and of Frank Walker,
the curator of the Fales Library, University of New York.

I am similarly grateful to the staff of the following libraries and
institutions which hold manuscript material relating to William Archer
in their collections: The Beinecke Rare Book and Manuscript Library,
Yale University; Berg Collection, New York Public Library; Birming-
ham Reference Library; British Library Manuscripts Students' Room,
London; British Library of Political and Economic Science, London;
Bodleian Library, Oxford; Burgunder Collection, Cornell University,
New York; Cheltenham Ladies' College; Churchill College, Cam-
bridge; Columbia University in the City of New York; Dickens House
Museum, London; Ellen Terry Memorial Museum, Tenterden, Kent;
Folger Shakespeare Library, Washington DC; Harvard Theatre Collec-
tion, Harvard College Library, Cambridge, Mass.; Hove Central
Library; King's College, Cambridge; Merton College, Oxford; The
Manx Museum; National Library of Ireland; National Library of
Scotland; Nuffield College, Oxford; Reed International Books Library,
Rushden; Pierpont Morgan Library, New York; Shubert Archive, New
York; State Library of New South Wales, Australia; The Harry Ransom
Humanities Research Center, The University of Texas at Austin;
Trinity College, Cambridge; Trinity College, Dublin; University of
Birmingham; University of Calgary, Alberta, Canada; University Col-
lege, London; University of Edinburgh; University of Exeter; University
of Glasgow; University of Illinois at Urbana-Champaign; University of
Keele; Brotherton Collection, Brotherton Library, University of Leeds;
University of London; John Rylands University Library of Manchester;
University of Newcastle; University of Oslo; Van Pelt Library, Univer-
sity of Pennsylvania; University of Reading.

I also thank the staff and archivists at the Newspaper Library, the
Oriental and India Office, and the Scandinavian Department of the
British Library, London; Christ Church, Oxford; Commonwealth War

Graves Commission; Dulwich College, London; *Edinburgh Evening News*; Fawcett Library, City of London Polytechnic; the *Guardian*; The Honourable Society of the Middle Temple, London; Imperial War Museum, London; H. M. Kongens Kabinettssekretariat, Oslo; National Liberal Club, London; The *Observer*; Public Records Office, London; Reform Club, London; Scottish Records Office, Edinburgh; Shakespeare Birthplace Trust, Stratford-upon-Avon; Simplified Spelling Society, Croydon; Society for Psychical Research, London. I am grateful for the assistance of Inger Melhuus Raeder and the Ministry of Foreign Affairs, Norway; and Karl Gronlie and Arntor Blondal, Skien.

I am enormously grateful to the Author's Foundation, administered by the Society of Authors, which awarded me a grant enabling me to pursue researches in the United States; I am likewise grateful to the Scottish Arts Council for a similar award for research. Without their generosity, I would have found it very much more difficult to complete this book.

'We are intimate personal friends; and we roll
each other's logs with a will. . . . I imply that
Mr Archer is the best of critics . . . he insists
there is nobody like G.B.S. . . . He has the
reputation of being inflexible, impartial, rather
cold but scrupulously just and entirely
incorruptible. I believe this impression is
produced by his high cheekbones, the ascetic
outline of his chin and jaw, and his habit of
wearing a collar which gives his head the
appearance of being wedged by the neck into a
jampot. In reality, he is half a dozen different
men . . .'

—Bernard Shaw,
'Mr William Archer's Criticisms',
Saturday Review, 13 April 1895

'Have you never gone adventuring . . . in your
secret heart?'

—Harley Granville Barker,
The Secret Life, Act Two,
Scene Three.

I

Arrival

At the end of October 1883, William Archer returned to the fogs of damp and darkening London after a holiday in Norway. He was twenty-seven years old, a qualified lawyer who would never practice and the author of a book of startlingly original theatre criticism. A breakdown in his health had blown him off course, but he was now recovered and resuming his daily routine of taking the train from Dulwich to Charing Cross, from where he walked to the British Museum in Great Russell Street. Once there, he sat at a desk usually in the north-western quadrant of the Reading Room and continued writing articles for *Progress*, a subversive monthly paper for freethinkers.

For some time, Archer had been intrigued by 'a pallid young man with red hair and beard' who frequently sat at the next desk. He seemed reserved, dignified, and was evidently almost penniless. The frayed collar and cuffs and threadbare elbows of his green coat astonished Archer, who dressed as formally as all professional middle-class men, his dark tie knotted tightly around a stiff collar, his waistcoat and jacket buttoned. He adopted the same punctilious manner all his life. Strict Victorian rectitude was one of the many masks he presented to the world.

However, what convinced Archer that the pale young man was somebody worth knowing, was his choice of reading, which 'consisted of Marx's *Das Kapital* in French and a full orchestral score of *Tristan und Isolde*'.[1] And so William Archer met Bernard Shaw or, as Shaw gratefully remembered, 'Archer found me . . . and . . . took my affairs in hand.'[2]

Archer discovered his new acquaintance to be an unswerving vegetarian, teetotaller and non-smoker. But 'I think what I principally admired in him at first, was his knowledge of music in which, in an ignorant way, I was intensely interested. I interested him at first, I imagine, by talking about Ibsen.'3 The Norwegian playwright was almost unknown in Britain and certainly to Shaw, who saw that Archer was 'deeply under the spell of Ibsen . . . and he communicated the magic to me verbally. This and our anti-clerical views made a strong bond between us.'4 'We became fast friends,'5 agreed Archer.

Theirs was a friendship that was to last over forty years until Archer's death in 1924. Although often strained it was never severed because it was bound by unspoken but mutually acknowledged rules. Within them, they argued candidly and vigorously about the theatre, writing and criticism, each other's behaviour, that of friends and enemies, and the world in general. Personal matters, such as their immense regard for each other and their emotional relationships with women, were beyond the bounds of discussion. The breaking of this code caused awkwardness and sometimes pain and anger. Archer and Shaw were sensitive men, yet found it so difficult to describe their inner emotions that they sometimes chose to overlook the fact that the other had any sensitivity at all. At the same time, their relationship evolved into something more complex than the word friendship implies. It became a deeply-rooted alliance, sustained by the conviction that without the other to advise, encourage and denounce, neither would change the world in the way he planned.

The early nineteenth century had been kind to neither the Archers nor the Shaws. Once from Scotland, the Protestant Shaws had emigrated to Ireland. There, the line climbed as high in the social scale to reach the landed gentry before so many male Shaws were lost either to alcohol or the asylum that it careered down to land among the poorer middle classes. Such family influence that remained secured George Carr Shaw a sinecure at the Dublin Law Courts in the late 1840s, but failed to prevent the post being abolished shortly afterwards. He became a drink-befuddled partner in a corn merchant's business he had no idea how to run. In 1852, when he was thirty-seven, he married Elizabeth (Bessie) Gurly, the unprepossessing, twenty-one-year-old daughter of a profligate squire. Her mother had died, and Bessie was brought up by a tyrannical aunt who was determined that her niece should reclaim the family's social standing. Intimidated by her aunt and shocked by her father's impending remarriage, Bessie accepted a proposal from George Carr Shaw. He represented an escape of sorts. She noticed the slight squint, but possibly not the hint of epilepsy and was in no position to know about his churning, alcohol-soured stomach, for George assured her that he was a zealous teetotaller.

The couple moved into a poky terraced house at 3 Upper Synge Street, Dublin, a place their son would later liken to a kennel with primitive sanitary arrangements. There, over the next few years, George hid his empty bottles in the wardrobe, closed the door and fathered three children, the third, and their only boy, George Bernard, being born on 26 July 1856. Just over eight weeks later in Perth, a small, dismal town of grey stone in central Scotland, Grace Archer, the wife of Thomas, gave birth to her second and first surviving child. They named him William.

Like the Shaws, the Archers had tumbled in the world and were drifting. The Archer forbears arrived in England with the Norman invaders and their descendants became minor landowners in the midlands. According to family hearsay, Andrew, a soldier in a troop of horse fighting for Cromwell during the civil wars of the 1640s, was the first Archer to venture further north. Disillusioned by the destructiveness of the rebel army, he deserted and scuttled across the border for safety. By the late seventeenth century, the family had established itself at Perth, where successive generations of the family made a steady living as glovers. By the early nineteenth century, the Archers were prosperous timber merchants as Charles, William Archer's great-grandfather, became the proprietor of Charles Archer and Son, his sawmills overlooking the great River Tay.

However, the chill winds of economic depression following the Napoleonic Wars withered the timber and river trade and, by 1823, Charles had nothing to his credit but silent mills and unwanted equipment. The piercing gusts of bankruptcy fluttered the blank pages of the company's order books. His son, William, was then thirty-seven and his wife, Julia, thirty-two. They had seven children, all under twelve. The youngest, Thomas, William Archer's future father, was still a baby, having been born in Glasgow on 26 February that year. His future seemed uncertain as his father watched their livelihood blowing away with the dust in the family mills.

Then he had an idea. Having frequently visited Norway on business, he had been enchanted by Larvik, a small town on the south-eastern coast about sixty miles south of the capital, Christiana (since renamed Oslo). William declared the family would emigrate to Larvik, where he would begin a new timber business. With a generous proportion of his savings, he bought the *Pomona*, a three-masted schooner, to take them there, and refitted her. He took cargo on board to offset his costs, employed a crew, and one day in the autumn of 1825, when Thomas was almost three, they set out from Grangemouth in the Firth of Forth, launching themselves upon the blackly swirling waters of the North Sea and upon a new and uncertain future.

Several days later they put ashore at Arendal and unloaded the cargo before sailing on to Larvik, where they landed and paid off the crew. The town was little more than a huddle of timber houses in narrow, hilly streets between dense beechwoods and the rocky shores of the Larvikfjord. Having found rooms in a cramped, two-storey house in Rosendalsgate, William set out to begin his new career. He was not a good businessman. This was a trait that his son Thomas and his grandson William would inherit. When his timber business collapsed, he became an agent for an English fishing company, arranging the fortnightly export of lobsters and on this precarious basis, he began searching for a more spacious home. He found Tolderodden, a large, one hundred and fifty-year-old timber house standing in seven acres of ground at the tip of a low, rocky promontory. Partly shielded by trees and surrounded on three sides by the fjord, the property had unrivalled views across the water. Within a few years, William and Julia's family had increased to thirteen, nine of whom were boys. Such a number was not unusual then, but it was comparatively uncommon that all the children survived and grew up uniformly strong. They had to be robust, for life was tough. Almost inevitably, the lobster business failed and William was forced to branch out into exporting ice and tackling other hopefully remunerative and prestige-enhancing schemes. They managed to pay the mortgage at Tolderodden, but it was a struggle to make ends meet. Thomas was probably typical among the boys in that by the time he was fourteen, he had received only four years formal education. But one of the maxims that William pronounced from his chair at the head of the family table was that his sons should meet the challenge of the new age by learning a trade. And the most immediate prospect of the brothers accomplishing that lay on the other side of the world. In Australia. The Archers became economic migrants again.

By the 1830s, the new white settlers, many from England and Scotland, had developed the eastern coast of Australia and were nosing inland towards the vast and unexplored heart of the continent. As they did so, their convict and working-class labour sectioned off the bush plot by plot for sheep and cattle stations. Julia's uncle, William Walker, a Scottish banker, had done things in a marginally more sedate manner, arriving in Sydney in 1820 to become a director of the fledgling Bank of New South Wales. Then, with his brother James, a former marine artillery officer, he too foraged west, fencing off thousands of acres for sheep stations and developing a hugely profitable business selling Australian wool to the burgeoning English textile industry.

Alerted by Julia, the Walkers gave the Archers a helping hand. In 1834, Thomas's elder brother, David, left Norway to learn the sheep farming business. Three years later, in 1837, when it was decided that Thomas and another brother, William, should join him, he had become joint-superintendent at Wallerawang, one of the largest Walker stations and several miles north-west of Sydney. Thomas and William's voyage south took four months. They arrived at Sydney harbour at midnight on the last day of the year.

During the following decade, David, William and Thomas, together with other brothers who arrived one by one, became explorers and station owners in their own right. Driving five thousand sheep almost five hundred miles north, they set up a flurry of new stations before striking out further north and west, opening up much of what would later become central Queensland. Theirs was a formidable partnership, yet Thomas's heart was not in business but adventure. In 1849, he was off again, a sturdy, bright-eyed young man of twenty-six. This time he was heading for California where it was said the hills glinted with gold.

His was a life of high risk and extraordinary escapes. He survived shipwreck at Sacramento, rode with the Oregon Rifles in a raiding war against the Madoc Indians and eventually, after months of crawling across the earth shoulder-to-shoulder with hundreds of rival prospectors, discovered gold beneath the singing waters of Humbug Creek. In the spring of 1852, having earned almost two thousand dollars, he decided to go home. Travelling to Boston, he boarded a paddle-steamer and at the end of June disembarked at Liverpool. From there, he journeyed north to Perth to call on yet another brother before going on to Norway. Alexander was younger than Thomas and preferred an indoor life as a clerk in the accounting firm of J. and R. Morison. It was in Perth that Thomas met James Morison's daughter, Grace.

While the Archers had migrated from Perth to Larvik, it was hearsay in the Morison family that their far-off ancestors had arrived across the sea from Norway. For generations the Scottish Morisons were respected Perthshire booksellers and publishers, printing theological treatises and fine editions of the works of Pope and Goldsmith. Although he had sidestepped the family business and plumped for accountancy, James

Morison's family were still pillars of the society, powerful, God-fearing and abstemious; literary, home-owning and home-loving. They did not look kindly upon the grandson of a bankrupt and son of an unsuccessful emigrant, an adventurer who apparently lived from one day to the next, bewitching their Grace with tales of the outback. But at twenty, she was, in her way, as independent and as determined as Thomas. Slicing through Morisonian opposition, they announced they would be married on 29 June 1853 and that immediately afterwards, they would leave for Australia.

Once wed, Thomas and Grace visited Tolderodden before returning to board ship at Plymouth and at the beginning of December, arrived at Sydney. His brother Charles, together with a couple of Aborigine labouring boys, was there to meet them, and on a canvas-topped, horse-drawn cart they made the long and dusty journey into the outback to Eidsvold, one of the Archer sheep stations. For the first few months, everything seemed to go well. But within a year, the conditions had become too much for Grace and the higher the sun rose in her second summer, the more she wilted. She was exhausted and pregnant and at the beginning of November, after a long and painful confinement, she gave birth to a child so frail that he hardly breathed before dying. To a distraught Thomas it looked as though Grace might also die in the energy-sapping heat. She slowly revived, but there was no alternative but to return to Scotland.

Meanwhile, on one of their long expeditions further north, Thomas's brothers had discovered 'a perfect paradise',[6] a peninsula jutting into a lagoon near a bend in the Fitzroy River, a rich, fertile place and a sanctuary for birds. Once the sheep and cattle had been driven there and a new house built, they planned to make it the southern home of the Archers. In honour of their new sister-in-law they called it Gracemere, the name by which it is still known today.

Thomas and Grace's troubles were not over, however. On the voyage home, they were almost wrecked in the violent storms roaring around treacherous Cape Horn. Arriving at last in England, they made their way to Perth where they moved into rooms above a shop in the High Street. Thomas had hardly any money, but as the rooms were rented in the name of 'Mrs Archer', the Morisons presumably rallied round, possibly not without muttered reproaches, and paid the £4 15s annual rent. For Thomas, used to space and light, and for Grace, accustomed in Perth at least to a large and comfortable home, those dingy rooms must have been particularly oppressive. Perth was a town of weavers, lawyers, grain dealers and grocers, and Thomas the rover had difficulty in finding work. Little is known of the Archers during these months, but Grace's health improved and the marriage, if it faltered at all did not do so irretrievably, for in the spring of 1856, she announced that she was pregnant again.

William Archer was born at eight o'clock in the evening of 23 September 1856, not at the Archers' High Street rooms but just around the corner at 6 North Methven Street. This was a squat terraced house, squeezed between a bakery and a public house, and the home of Mrs McPherson, the midwife. This time, Grace was being professionally supervised. At the moment of William's howling entry into the world, a theatrical spectacle began at the City Hall a few streets away as with a dramatic flourish, M. Gompertz, a travelling showman, presented his 'Colossal Panorama of the WAR WITH RUSSIA'. The Crimean War had ended that year and heroic portrayals of the marches and battles, painted upon several hundred feet of cloth and gradually unrolled to present the illusion of action, were touring the country to enthralled audiences.

This was an imperial age in which an expanding British Empire fought a second opium war against China and crushed a mutiny in India. In 1856, Victoria had ruled for nineteen years and Palmerston been Prime Minister for one. Born three years before Darwin published *On the Origin of Species* and eleven before the first volume of *Das Kapital* appeared, Archer grew up in the shadow of Victoria's reclusive widowhood and became part of a generation daring to challenge the inherited orthodoxies in religion and social and moral traditions. He became a radical, and his battleground was the theatre. Archer lived until he was sixty-eight, by which time the carnage of war-ragged Europe weighed heavily on his heart. He saw Kings and several Prime Ministers come and go and witnessed the effective end of the Liberal Party. He transformed the English theatre and was as astonished as everyone else when one of his own plays blossomed triumphantly into an American motion picture. He knew both high achievement and corrosive disappointment, intimate love and tragic loss. Most of all, he knew continuous and often thankless struggle.

Both his parents were from unshakably religious but unrepentingly independent families. In searching for the closest possible communion with God, the Archers eliminated the filters of the established Church and observed instead the teachings of John Walker. He was no relation of Julia's, but a Bachelor of Divinity from Trinity College, Dublin, who defected from the Episcopal Church of Ireland in 1804 to found a sect which he named the Church of God, and which others called the Walkerites. The Morisons, on the other hand, were Glasites. This rather larger grouping was founded in the eighteenth century by John Glas, a former minister at a Church of Scotland kirk in Angus. His abrasive sermons advocating the disassociation of the congregation from its ruling presbytery resulted, inevitably, in his expulsion by the General Assembly of the Church of Scotland. Undeterred, Glas set off on a preaching tour which brought him in due course to Perth, where he found a receptive hearing and a financial generosity that enabled him to build a meeting house in the High Street.

As both Walkerite and Glasite doctrine agreed upon fundamental belief in the Bible and private consultation with God, there was talk of formal amalgamation, but as the Glasites were Sabbatarians and the Walkerites argued that each day was equal in holiness, the Separatists elected to remain separate from each other. At Larvik, rather than attend the Lutheran kirk, a brick building only a few yards from Tolderodden, the Archers held their own services at the house. Each member of the family, the children and, in time, the grandchildren, had his or her own Bible in which to follow the text read aloud by William senior. In Perth, Thomas submitted to the Glasite majority and when his son was a student, William was expected to keep up his attendances both at the Glasite meeting house and private family readings. Their meticulous devotion to these 'observances' instilled in him a fierce hostility towards religion and religious practice which he never lost. It became a vital component of a view of the world in which everything was subject to the test of Reason.

He did, though, salvage something from this purgatorial boyhood experience. During the 1880s in his capacity as drama critic, Archer frequently took Shaw along to the theatre with him. He enviously noticed Archer's ability not only to fall quickly but deeply asleep during a tedious performance, but to wake up instantly the curtain came down and offer an incisive comment upon what he had apparently blotted out. When he asked him about this, Archer replied that during the family readings, he would place a finger beneath the page of his Bible and, sitting bolt upright and seemingly attentive, close his eyes, training himself to respond involuntarily to the rustle of the others turning over their pages by following suit himself. At the end of the reading, he would wake up, with nobody any the wiser. Shortly before the end of his life, Archer claimed he had contentedly slept through dreary productions of most of the world's drama from Aeschylus to Shaw.

The pretence backfired, though, on more than one occasion. Once, during a revival of John Poole's comedy, *Paul Pry*, perhaps the one at the Gaiety in May 1884, the crack of a stage revolver being fired brought Archer springing to his feet with a shout of alarm. The shock also made him bury his hands in the elaborate coiffure of the woman sitting immediately in front of him. To his, and her, consternation, her hair came away and Archer was left standing, frozen by shame, clutching a large wig.

He was one year old when Thomas and Grace first took him to Larvik. William senior was seventy-two and Julia sixty-seven. Tolderodden seemed full of uncles and aunts, and mother and child were duly admired by one and all. Economically, things had improved. William had become British Vice-Consul in Larvik, and money regularly arrived from Australia. The garden bloomed with tropical plants and down at the shore, a wooden boathouse and a landing stage had been built. Two years later, when William was four and had two younger sisters, the family returned. This time, William promptly forgot the English he knew and began speaking Norwegian, only to forget that and speak English again once they were back in Scotland.

The family was prospering in Australia but not in Britain. Thomas tried farming for himself, failed, worked as a hired hand on other farms to save enough to start on his own again, and failed again. This evolved into a cycle lasting until his son was sixteen in 1872. During these years, as the family travelled the country tagging along in the wake of Thomas's search for work, William attended five schools including Perth and Dollar Academies in Scotland, the Solent Grammar School at Lymington in Hampshire, Reigate Grammer School in Surrey, and George Watson's College in Edinburgh. There were also stretches of private tuition, months at a time here and there. His progress was avidly scrutinized by his parents. When he was about seven and, like most small boys, able to sing in reasonable tune, Thomas and Grace proudly concluded he had an aptitude for music. In fact, William had no musical ability at all, but his parents' persistence that he did formed one of his earliest memories of 'a long series of wretched hours for myself, my governess and a poor domestic drudge of a piano'.

While he quickly developed serious literary tastes (admiring Dickens by the time he was ten, reading *The Pickwick Papers* and munching sweets on the daily two-mile walk home from Dollar Academy), he always preferred popular tunes to serious music, and comic to grand opera. As a student in Edinburgh, he endured the 'titanic tedium' of Beethoven's *Fidelio* before gratefully embracing the tumult of Gilbert and Sullivan. Domestic music continued to repel him. As a young man, he attended 'evenings' among Edinburgh's polite society, during which guests were often expected to listen to the daughter of the house playing the drawing room piano. Archer quickly came to detest 'young ladies who, by birth and training, were blankly incapable of any literary or artistic appreciation whatever', yet 'could perform with credit and criticise with confidence the greatest masterpieces of music'.[7]

It is difficult to say where his passion for the theatre came from. Neither the Archers nor the Morisons had any connection with nor interest in the stage. This was a time when, to some people, the word 'actress' was synonymous with 'prostitute' and when an actor could not possibly be thought of as a gentleman. But unlike many religious families, who fiercely disapproved of the theatre, the Archers do not appear to have checked their son's sudden enthusiasm. When he was in his thirties, Archer reflected that 'I cannot remember a time when the word "theatre" had not a strange fascination for me.' His interest may have been sparked by his reading of Dickens and the first theatrical entertainment he saw may have fanned it into flame. When he was ten or eleven, he saw a travelling mime performance of the Faust and Marguerite story which included a demonstration of Pepper's Ghost. This was a device whereby a sheet of glass was placed upon the stage to reflect the image of an actor standing on an understage and so produce the image of a phantom. For William, this exhibition of stage magic constituted 'an epoch in my experience', and from that moment he craved a toy theatre.

He never owned one, but in the spring of 1869, when he was twelve, he at last achieved his ambition of a visit to a real theatre. The Archers, now with seven children, had travelled over four hundred miles south in search of work and were in rooms in Lymington. William discovered a theatre in nearby Portsmouth, insisted that he be taken to it, and on Saturday 24 April, he entered a theatre for the first time as father and son took their seats at the Theatre Royal. The production was not a play but a popular opera, *Maritana*, a melodramatic love story set in Madrid. The music was by the Irish composer, Vincent Wallace, and the libretto by a jack-of-all-trades dramatist, Edward Fitzball. It was performed by the English Grand Opera Company, and Herbert Bond

('Primo Tenore of the Royal Italian and English Operas, Covent Garden') played the leading role of the swaggering Don Cesar. Sitting in the hot, dusty darkness, William was captivated. The Don's 'daring and wit . . . seemed to me incomparable – almost superhuman'.

Now there was no stopping him. One night in October on a visit to London, the family pushed their way along the Strand, a gaslit thoroughfare crowded with beggars and theatre-goers, raucous, evil-smelling and choked with hot air belching from restaurant doorways. Arriving at the Strand Theatre, they saw John Brougham's *Among the Breakers*, H. P. Gratton's *Toodles*, (starring the American comedian John S. Clarke), and William Brough's *The Field of the Cloth of Gold*, a farce, a comic melodrama and an extravaganza all in one evening.

But it was that Christmas, at the pantomime, that 'the full glory of the mimic world'[8] burst upon William Archer. Of all the great, spectacular pantomimes, none were more lavish than those at the Theatre Royal, Drury Lane, then under the bustling management of E. L. Blanchard. The 1869 production was *Beauty and the Beast, or Harlequin and Old Mother Bunch*, written, as usual, by Blanchard and designed by William Beverley, the leading scenic artist of the day. It was Beverley who pioneered the Lane's astonishing 'transformation scenes', in which successive gauze curtains rose to reveal vistas of increasingly fantastic virtuosity. At its most elaborate, this process could last up to twenty minutes.

Beauty and the Beast opened on 27 December, the advertisements promising 'extensive scenery and elaborate effects'. There were musicians, clowns, dancers and acrobats. Price's Christy Minstrels sang. Le Petit Rarey and his Performing Pony cantered across the stage, closely followed by Peterson's Performing Dogs, while The Tyler Family ('The Smallest Brass Band in the World'), blew a fanfare for the stars: the Vokes Family. The Vokeses were Fred, a dancer-contortionist ('The Man with the Elastic Legs'), his sisters, Jessie, Victoria and Rosina, and a comic, Walter Fawden. They would dominate Drury Lane pantomimes for the next decade.

Archer's admiration for speciality acts almost equalled his fondness of sentimental melodies. But as a thirteen-year-old at the pantomime, amid the excitement of good battling against evil, the music, the shouts and the squeals, he fell suddenly and heart-stoppingly in love. The object of his devotion was not the young and pretty Rosina Vokes, a defenceless, trembling Beauty before Fred's prowling Beast, but Kate Santley, a young member of the chorus. Eleven years later, on 9 June

1880, when he was twenty-four and theatre critic for *The London Figaro*, he recalled his adolescent adoration as he recorded her death in the paper. She was an actress, he wrote, 'not without ability of a certain order'.[9] Not surprisingly, for she was still very much alive and manager of the tiny Royalty Theatre in Soho, Miss Santley indignantly demanded a retraction. A week later, Archer frostily conceded that 'she has been very ill, but is now much improved in health'.[10] As manager of the Royalty, Kate Santley was later instrumental in the battle to establish a serious theatre of ideas.

His love of the stage was now well on its way to becoming 'a mania, a craze',[11] a passion which never diminished. Yet there was no more London theatre-going for the Archers were on the move again, back to Scotland and landing this time at Inverkeithing, a village on the northern coast of the Firth of Forth, from where William was packed off to the last of his five schools. George Watson's Boys' College in Edinburgh catered for the sons and grandsons of 'decayed merchants', a qualification William easily fulfilled, and was housed in a grim stone building on the south side of the city. As it was impractical to take the ferry across the river each day, William boarded with the family of an English master, James Balsillie, in a tall, narrow terraced house at 29 George Square.

As a 'classical' pupil, his studies concentrated upon modern and ancient languages with an emphasis upon English and Greek. There was no arts or science teaching, but to enable their smooth entry into Edinburgh society, the 'classicals' were energetically tutored in deportment and, by an elderly master sawing at the fiddle, in dancing the quadrille and galop.

He stayed at George Watson's for two years. It was an uninspiring education which, if he did not do so then, he later viewed with distaste. In 1905, when his own son had scraped through public school and was struggling at Oxford, Archer published a short book, *Let Youth But Know*, a strident and emotional plea for educational reform. Under the pseudonym of 'Kappa', he argued that the traditional, limited range of academic subjects had created an intellectually myopic vicious circle in which 'the system begets the masters and the masters beget the system'. In its place, he proposed a 'liberal education' in which all children would be bilingual in English and French by kindergarten age and subsequent learning be based upon an expanded concept of history and its relationship with the sciences. All academic subjects, he argued, were interdependent. The purpose was not to teach answers, but to 'teach youth to see, to wonder; then let it judge for itself . . .'[12]

Meanwhile, there had been changes in the family, both abroad and at home. In 1869, at Larvik, grandfather William, frail and senile, had died aged eighty-three. Two of his sons were also dead. The remaining brothers took it in turns to come home from Australia and look after Tolderodden, where Julia, now eighty-one, was living with her two unmarried daughters. Jane Anne and Mary, especially Mary, were formidable women. In her late forties, William's Aunt Mary owned and sailed her own boat, smoked cigars, wore men's suits and ties and was known as 'Mary Man'. She and Natalie Zahle, the Danish radical educationalist, were devoted friends, and for many years Natalie would arrive from Copenhagen to spend summer weeks at Larvik, while Mary travelled to see Natalie during the winter.

In 1872, it was agreed that Thomas should take his part in the management of Gracemere and, having fared none too well in Britain, the Archers decided to give Australia another chance. Thomas was now forty-nine, and Grace forty. Their family had increased to nine, five boys and four girls, William, the eldest, being fifteen and Francis, the youngest, only a few months old. They would have no more children. All except William sailed with them in March, for that autumn, having been awarded an annual bursary of twenty-five pounds, he was to begin a four-year course at Edinburgh University. He signed the matriculation record on 1 November, just over a month after his sixteenth birthday, enrolling in the Arts Faculty which, as well as offering lectures in English literature and moral and natural philosophy, ran supplementary courses in mathematics, agriculture and practical astronomy.

Before beginning his university career, he spent the summer at Tolderodden, as he would every summer for several years. That year, he had a nine-day break staying with family friends at Copenhagen, where he devoted himself to theatre-going. He saw eight plays, several at the Royal Theatre, including *Mascarade* by Ludwig Holberg who, although born in Norway, was regarded as Denmark's national playwright.

Archer himself was by now almost fluent in Norwegian. This, and his apparent self-sufficiency, made him seem a rather mysterious figure at Edinburgh University. He would take himself off for long walks across the tussocky hillsides bulking over the city, from where he looked down upon the Old Town of dark tenement buildings where families huddled in damp and unlit single rooms. Cheap alcohol was sold from barrows

in the streets. Disease thrived. Further afield, on the northern side of
the city, the New Town, home of the middle and upper classes,
expanded terrace by crescent by square, the houses, with their high,
corniced ceilings, separated from the pavement and prying eyes by
chest-high iron railings.

Archer rented a room at 21 Forth Street, nearer working-class Leith
than the New Town, and fifteen minutes or so walk from the university.
His room became stacked with books: Dickens, Carlyle, Tennyson,
Holberg, Schiller, Goethe and 'a couple of editions of Shakespeare'.[13]
In 1873, he made three profound literary discoveries. The first was
George Eliot, whose *Middlemarch* had just appeared. Absorbed by the
novel's combination of domestic realism and moral sensitivity, he went
on to read as many of her books as he could find. Even more
enthusiastically, he devoured John Stuart Mill's recently published
Autobiography as 'one of the most entrancing books I ever read'.[14]

A political psychologist, Mill had been educated by his father, who
shielded him from other boys and subjected him to rigorous cross-
examinations on their daily walks. Archer's upbringing had nothing in
common with this, but he was struck by Mill's admission that the
consequent neglect of his emotions had caused him intense misery as a
young man. Perhaps for the first time, Archer realised that his own
worries and depressions were not unique. Mill had learned to hide his
feelings from an early age, and Archer was following suit. Possibly this
was a result of the Archers and Morisons frowning upon displays of
emotion in males, and that as the eldest of the children, he was expected
to set an example of impregnable fortitude. Perhaps his parents were
becoming suspicious of their son's passion for the theatre. Whatever
the reason, he was becoming used to keeping his emotions to himself,
and was already on his way to becoming an expert dissembler.

Almost everyone who came across Archer in later years vouched for
his austerity. 'He was a cold creature,'[15] pronounced the playwright
Henry Arthur Jones. People thought of him as dry and remote, and
compared him to wood, most frequently to mahogany. It was part of the
mask he wore to face the world, but it has prevailed to become the
accepted view of William Archer. The real Archer was not like that at
all. He had hundreds of acquaintances and many friends, but only a
select few were trusted enough to become part of a privileged inner
circle. Those few knew him as sensitive, humorous, contradictory. 'If
you chaffed him by telling him that he took it [the theatre] solemnly, he
would laugh at that, for he was the least solemn of men,'[16] recalled

Granville Barker. Shaw also revelled in Archer's sense of fun but recognized that the more glacial he appeared, the more he was emotionally moved. He had perfected his art of firmly bringing down the shutters.

Archer's most crucial discovery in 1873, was Henrik Ibsen, the magician under whose spell Shaw discovered him a decade later. He was born on 20 March 1828 at Skien, a busy, prosperous trading town only twenty miles north-west of Larvik and standing above a natural harbour leading into the Frierfjord. There was a busy timber trade and by day the air was filled with the sound of over forty sawmills. Beyond the town were pine forests, iron ore mines and the stupendous homes of the mine-owners.

Like Archer, Henrik Ibsen was his parents' second son, the first having died when still a baby, and grew up the eldest of five children, only one of whom was a girl. His father, Knud Ibsen, imported wines from Bordeaux and yarns from London, and exported timber to Denmark and England, thereby becoming one of Skien's most prominent entrepreneurs. He expanded, buying a distillery and renting Venstøp, a farm nestling in sweeping green country two miles north of the town. Other rich families had country homes nearby, and the Ibsens hosted summer hunting parties, which ended with eating and drinking and dancing.

Then came catastrophe. Slump had bankrupted Charles Archer, and eleven years later, in 1834, economic depression rolled through Norway. The distillery failed and when Knud Ibsen fell behind with his taxes, the authorities hounded him relentlessly. The family had to stop entertaining and sell everything. This was a common enough occurrence and the newspapers were full of similar stories. To speculate and lose was in itself no social disgrace. Several failed speculators crop up in Ibsen's plays but only the criminals, like the banker John Gabriel Borkman, are castigated. It was not his losing money that ruined Knud Ibsen and shocked his friends, it was his furious resentment and his increasingly heavy drinking. In 1843, when Henrik was fifteen, the family abandoned Venstøp for a working-class area of Skien. After a few weeks, Henrik left home.

He went south, to Grimstad. He became an apothecary's apprentice, fathered an illegitimate son, deserted both mother and child, and wrote *Cataline*, a romantic verse drama set in ancient Rome. This was published in 1850, when he became a student in Christiana. A year later, Ibsen met the idealistic violinist Ole Bull, the founder of the Norwegian National Theatre at Bergen, a fishing town on the west coast. Danish and European plays routinely filled Norwegian theatres, but Bull, a fervent nationalist, longed to preside over the creation of a new and specifically Norwegian repertoire. Impulsively, he appointed the energetic, opinionated Ibsen as resident playwright and stage director at Bergen. During the next six years, Ibsen directed many plays, including four of his own, but had little success. In the light of his later realist plays, his early and mostly mythological verse dramas are undistinguished and best left on the shelf. Not that he was well served by his actors, who were used to the melodrama, comedy and folk-tales which, despite Ibsen's efforts, the Bergen audiences wanted to see. Defeated, he returned to the capital to become artistic manager of the Norwegian Theatre of Christiana.

However, like their counterparts in the west, audiences in Christiana preferred the light French comedies of Eugène Scribe to Norwegian drama by Ibsen. Now married to Suzannah Thorensen, a daughter of the Dean of Bergen, and the father of a legitimate son, these were years of poverty and depression for Ibsen. Audiences were meagre and morale at the theatre was low. In 1862, he completed *Kjærlighedens komedie* (*Love's Comedy*) his ninth play, a verse satire and his first to have a contemporary theme and setting.

The play is a study of modern love and marriage in which the leading character, a student named Falk, suggests the two might be incompatible. It was speedily rejected for production at the Norwegian Theatre by a board unnerved by reviews of the published text, several of which claimed the play was immoral. This final withdrawal of support threw Ibsen into profound despair. He was unable to write. He drank and, on the darkest days, contemplated suicide. By the end of the year, the theatre was bankrupt. Although he was made part-time literary advisor to the rival Christiana Theatre which, in 1864 staged his first real success, *Kongsemnerne* (*The Pretenders*), an historical prose drama, Ibsen's spirit was broken. Three months after the premiere, impoverished and bitter, he turned his back on Norway for self-imposed exile in Italy. He too became a migrant. He did not return to live in his home country for twenty-seven years.

In Rome, he was joined by his family. Almost destitute and alcoholic but supported by Suzannah, he revived sufficiently to resume writing. Two years later in 1866, he completed *Brand*, his eleventh play. It was an immense success in book form, although it remained unperformed for nineteen years. Its companion-piece, *Peer Gynt*, was similarly well received when it was published the following year, yet it too had to wait for production, this time for seven years.

Yet it was a new beginning. Ibsen was now thirty-nine. He could look back upon a family falling from grace; his father, deserted by his friends and retreating to a working-man's cottage, and then he himself being practically hounded from his country. But now, success and financial stability transformed him. He reinvented himself. People who were used to seeing him on the street with unkempt hair, worn shoes and holes in his only coat were surprised to see a man dressed fastidiously and formally, his hair and beard dark and sleek. He became a man of discipline and maintained a routine of daily walks one could set one's watch by. Even his handwriting changed, from a rapid, scratched italic to the deliberate, ornate backhand he assumed for the rest of his life.

Archer discovered Ibsen's work in Norway. None of his plays had been translated into English or performed in Britain, although he did have a self-proclaimed 'prophet to English readers'.[17] This was Edmund Gosse. Seven years old than Archer, he was the son of P. H. Gosse, an overbearing marine biologist praised by Darwin, and a fanatical member of the Plymouth Brethren. A twenty-three-year-old clerk in the cataloguing department at the British Museum, Gosse had taken his 1871 summer holiday in Norway and, in a bookshop in Trondheim, had stumbled across *Digte* (*Poems*), Ibsen's only book of verse.

Gosse nurtured hopes of leaving cataloguing and becoming a poet and a literary journalist. Having been advised to avoid writing about familiar authors as the field was far too congested for a new name to be noticed, he was looking for someone whose work he could claim as his own territory. He could not understand a word of *Digte*, but Ibsen seemed to be just the ticket. Back in London, he plunged himself into intensive language study and translated enough verses to write a review which appeared under the heading 'Ibsen's New Poems' in *The Spectator* on 3 March 1872. Encouraged, he published four more articles on Ibsen during the following year, including 'Ibsen: the Norwegian Satirist' in the *Fortnightly Review* on 1 January 1873, the first analysis in English of the range of Ibsen's writing.

Later on, Gosse's interest in Ibsen rapidly cooled as he became bewildered by the social and symbolic dramas and begrudgingly recognized Archer's unassailable position as the leading authority on his work. But he lost none of his pride nor pugnacity and, in a newspaper article written to celebrate Ibsen's seventieth birthday, peevishly staked his claim to a footnote in literary history. 'Mr Archer is the host, and his the guests and the dances; but it was I who swept the floor and lighted the candles; from this humble pre-eminence in time no one can depose me,'[18] he wrote, adding that it had been his initial articles which first fired Archer's interest in Ibsen.

'I first learned Ibsen's name through seeing his books in the booksellers' windows in Norway,' protested Archer. He had seen none of Gosse's articles, and the first time he heard Ibsen being discussed was one morning at Tolderodden in the summer of 1873. He was idly listening to the conversation of his aunts and their friends, when 'One of them, whom I never saw before or since, but whose face I remember as though I had seen it yesterday, said . . . "I think *Love's Comedy* is so brilliantly witty." "Hullo," I thought, "have they got anything . . . brilliantly witty in Norwegian? I must look into this" – & forthwith went and bought the book.'

With 'increasing delight'[19] Archer immediately read everything else Ibsen had published. What so enthralled him about the author of *Brand* and *Peer Gynt* was 'simply the great – one might already almost have said the colossal – dramatist . . . who knew how to extract from that wonderful instrument, the theatre, the intensest and most thrilling *emotional* effects'.[20] Already, it seems, he was visualizing the plays on the stage.

Archer responded to Ibsen instinctively, both intellectally and emotionally. He discovered a liberalism echoing his own and a sympathy for the individual similar to that which he found in John Stuart Mill. In *Brand*, the story of a fanatical priest whose congregation denounces him, and in *Peer Gynt*, the wanderer who thinks only of himself, Archer saw that Ibsen was debating the nature of God while delineating the two wings of the Norwegian sensibility, on the one hand driven by piety and on the other preoccupied by fantasy. Ibsen's imagination seemed to Archer to reach beyond the common human condition in search of something spiritually sustaining. Archer, though, had little time to ponder over such weighty matters, for he was about to set off on a tour of European capitals.

Before leaving Edinburgh, he had arranged his journalistic debut. Every town and village in Scotland had its newspaper and Archer persuaded James Lothian, the Presbyterian and staunchly Liberal editor of the *Alloa Advertiser*, a broadsheet serving the brewing town of Alloa in Clackmannanshire, to publish his impressions of European capitals. Under the heading 'Notes of Travel', his first piece appeared on 23

August and the fifth and final article on 11 October. They took their unobtrusive place among news stories rewritten from the national dailies, the results at local flower shows and such invigorating advice as the best way to brush a carpet. As was the custom, they were unsigned. Archer's first byline appeared as 'Written for the Alloa Advertiser'.

He reported from the International Exhibition at Vienna, where he saw the State Ballet perform 'alarming pirouettes' at the Opera House. The 'inferiority'[21] of the displays in the British section made him turn quickly to the American where, to his delight, he discovered that what appeared to be a model of a church turned out to be a machine for dispensing soft drinks. Arriving in Prague, he found narrow streets and shop signs in German, Bohemian and Hebrew. In the dingy Judenstadt, where he inspected the synagogue and the graveyard, he felt himself watched by dark, suspicious eyes. In Berlin, he was disconcerted to see that two years after the end of the Franco-Prussian War, there were so many soldiers still on the streets and that children wore spiked military helmets. At Dresden, he retreated quickly when a knot of people outside a house told him the terrible shrieks coming from inside was a woman dying of cholera. He hurried to a performance of Goethe's *Egmont* at the Interim Theatre, the temporary home of the Dresden Theatre, which was being rebuilt after a fire.

This was his first experience of a state-subsidized theatre, and the high quality of the design and acting astounded him. He had seen nothing like this before and he used his *Advertiser* letter to fire the first shot in what would become a lifelong campaign for a British National Theatre. 'When shall we in England have a national theatre, where the actors shall be government servants, and senseless burlesque shall be unknown?' he demanded. 'Then, and not until then, will public taste be roused to its proper level – or we should rather say, will the public have any taste at all.'[22]

2

Victorian Romances

In the theatre of Archer's youth, melodramas of women wronged, wills forged and poisons administered jostled with historical romance, filleted and prettified Shakespeare and farce and comedy preferably adapted from the French. This was not an age of seriousness on stage but of effect, not of playwrights but of actor-managers and neither they nor their audiences entirely trusted new English plays. In Edinburgh, Archer saw everything which came his way. His choice was limited, as in 1875 both the Theatre Royal and the Southminster Music Hall burned down and for a year until the Theatre Royal was rebuilt, he had no choice but to resort to the 'tawdry and grimy little Princess's'[1] Theatre in a seedy area of town, run by a man named A. D. McNeill.

Actor-managers like McNeill dominated the early Victorian theatre, both in London and the provinces. Of variable talent, they ran their theatres often in partnership with their wives, who were also their leading ladies. Picking the plum roles for themselves, either the leading or 'character' parts, they cast the rest from a resident stock company of actors engaged for their particular 'line' as a soubrette, first or second low comedian, leading man, leading lady or walking gentleman.

McNeill's company performed the usual melodramas and bowdlerized Shakespeare, *The Merchant of Venice* and *As You Like It* being especially popular. Goldsmith's *She Stoops to Conquer*, Sheridan's *The School for Scandal* and Edward Bulwer-Lytton's repertory warhorses *The Lady of Lyons*, *Richeleau* and *Money* were also guaranteed to fill the seats. Over a couple of seasons at the Princess's, Archer saw 'the whole standard repertory of the English stage' and came away convinced of 'the execrableness of the third-rate stock company actor'.[2] He sat in the pit, the cheapest seats, benches at the rear of the stalls where the floor, walls and ceiling were thick with grime. The Princess's pit was distinguished by a powerful stench from the drains which overlaid the smell of sweat, the sickly-sweet tang of the actors' make-up and even the noxious fumes emitted by the gaslights, clouding the air and hanging like a vaporous curtain between the actors and the audience.

Stock companies like McNeill's were regularly invaded by the 'touring combinations', usually elderly, well-known husband-and-wife actors specializing in Shakespeare or eighteenth-century comedy. Trundling indefatigably around the country, they would 'give' their Antony and Cleopatra or Sir Peter and Lady Teazle, supported at each stop by the lower ranks of the resident company. Not that the 'combinations' expected to be troubled too much by rehearsals. Provided the locals knew their lines and never upstaged the stars, all was well. Young and relatively unknown actors also formed 'combinations' and whenever he could, Archer saw Edward Compton and Ellen Wallis in *Romeo and Juliet*, *Much Ado About Nothing* and other Shakespearian plays. When he first saw them in 1875, Compton was twenty-one, a good actor from a theatrical family who would go on to form his own company. Nineteen-year-old Ellen Wallis, in whom lingered 'a good deal of the Macready tradition',[3] would become an actress of some standing.

Soon the 'combinations' were elbowed aside and the stock companies disrupted even further as the rapidly expanding railway network meant that entire London companies could be sent out on tour, steaming north, south, east and west and changing at Crewe on Sundays. Archer saw the Two Roses Company, one of the first fully-cast tours, which took James Albery's sentimental light comedies *Two Thorns*, *Apple Blossoms* and *Forgiven* around the country in 1875. Later the same year, the Craven Robertson Company toured T. W. Robertson's *Caste*, *School* and *Ours*. Robertson's plays were an enormous advance on Albery and anyone else in contemporary theatre. They were not without sentiment, but his characters were credible, his plots had a touch of serious social content and his settings were recognizable domestic interiors. Because of this, Robertson's plays became known as 'cup-and-saucer' dramas. In a world in which the alternative to blood-and-thunder melodrama was shrieking burlesque, Archer conceded that Robertsonian realism represented 'the hope of the dramatic future'.[4]

He was writing as theatre critic of *The Modern Athenian*, a newspaper born of impatience, for since his debut in the *Alloa Advertiser*, Archer had found it impossible to publish any journalism for almost a year. In the summer of 1874, *The Shadow*, an Edinburgh weekly newspaper, published a few of his reviews before fading itself into thin air, and, for several months, had nothing but his university work. But in the spring, he became a leader writer on the *Edinburgh Evening News*.

Hugh Wilson at the *Evening News* was one of several editors whom Archer hopefully bombarded with unsolicited articles. When the Edinburgh Free Kirk Presbytery solemnly declared the theatre to be a moral and social evil, he rattled off a piece mocking religious intolerance and to his surprise, it appeared as part of the *News* leader column on 10 April. Even more surprisingly, Wilson, a morose Scot whose ill-health had drained his face of any discernible colour, proposed that he should write regular leaders. Archer agreed, even though there was no mention of any payment. He was far too embarrassed to ask. This was a weakness successive editors would exploit.

His apprehension was resolved after a fortnight, when Wilson awkwardly pushed three grubby one pound notes into his hands and Archer calculated he was earning almost eighty pounds a year. He promptly sped off south, to stay with his Uncle David, who had left Australia to settle with his wife and ten children in Croydon. These sudden disappearances of Archer's became a lifelong habit. No sooner had he earned enough money to travel, than he travelled. In May, he saw a performance of *Trial by Jury*, Gilbert and Sullivan's first collaboration, during its premiere run at the Royalty. Then he journeyed to Paris where the most popular production at the Comédie-Française was Henri de Bornier's *La Fille de Roland*. Even sitting a long way back from the stage, he was mesmerized by the 'snow-white, willowy figure with lustrous eyes'[5] in the title role. This was Sarah Bernhardt. At thirty, she had become the undisputed star of the supposedly egalitarian Comédie-Française, a celebrity who, it was whispered, had several lovers and slept in an upholstered coffin in a bedroom draped in black fabric.

Returning to Edinburgh, the university, the Princess's and the *Evening News*, Archer planned his next move. He was now part of a quartet of friends which included Robert Lowe, a stocky, gregarious man three years his elder and a clerk at the Scottish Union and National Insurance Company. They probably met at the Watt Institute Literary Association, of which they were both members. Lowe had a passion for drama and regularly accompanied Archer to the theatre, but unlike him, he also relished appearing in the amateur productions of members's work at the Watt Institute's annual soirées. Archer never had the slightest desire to act, for he could not have faced appearing so publicly vulnerable.

Through Lowe, he met another insurance clerk, George Halkett, an effervescent personality and an incisive caricaturist. The fourth member of the group, the extravagantly named Edward Rimbault Vere Dibdin was, like Lowe and Halkett, born in Edinburgh. He was the same age as Lowe, and training for the bar. A wiry, dark-haired man with vulpine features, Dibdin's grandfather had been a manager of Sadler's Wells, and his father was an organist. He shared Archer's satirical, punning sense of humour and became his earliest close friend. As the *News* did not seem inclined to make him a theatre critic, Archer recruited all three as the staff of his own venture, a humorous and cultural paper to be called *The Modern Athenian*.

The first twelve-page issue went on sale at one penny on 16 October. Few contributions are signed, but the scathing review of John Oxenford's adaptation of Mrs Henry Wood's *East Lynne* at the Princess's ('a bad adaptation of a bad novel'[6]) is most likely Archer's. The paper's satirical element is represented by Brutus Blirt, possibly a joint creation by Archer and Dibdin who continued collaborating after *The Modern Athenian* stumbled and fell after seventeen issues on 5 February 1876.

When William Archer and Edward Rimbault Vere Dibdin juggled their initials, they discovered an alter ego. E. V. Ward made only intermittent appearances over the next six years, but he had an eventful life, rising from a satirical poet to become the librettist of a catastrophe-prone comic opera. His first creation, *Pictor Depictus, or The Daubers Bedaubed*, was a sixpenny pamphlet satirizing the Royal Scottish Academy annual exhibition of 1876. In about six hundred lines of rhyming couplets, Ward derides the sentimentality and provincialism of Scottish painting as:

> The self-same cotters in the self-same cots,
> The self-same scenes from Mary, Queen of Scots.[7]

Pictor Depictus, which sold well enough to earn Ward one pound, was the culmination of a winter of almost manic activity for Archer. In January, he completed writing a serial novel for *The North Briton*, a weekly paper published from the *Evening News* office in Old Fishmarket Close, a steep and damp cobbled alleyway adjacent to the city jail. *The Doom of the Destroyed, or Edinburgh in the Eighteenth Century* is a parody of Sir Walter Scott and a luridly sensational tale of love and retribution, and appeared between 28 September 1875 and 15 January 1876. At the same time, he completed his first play, a farce called *Mesmerism: or Quits* in which the central character was a roguish religious minister. It was given a single performance by the Watt Institute Literary Association at its March soirée, although no record of its reception appears to have survived.

There was his writing, his journalism and his theatre-going, doubled now that the Theatre Royal had re-opened. Friends wondered how he had the energy or time to devote to his studies. He found no difficulty with English literature, but other subjects were becoming a problem. One of his fellow students, Hector Mackenzie, later to become a pathologist at St Thomas's Hospital, recalled that Archer's mathematical incompetence was so profound that he coached him intensively for his final examination. Archer admitted that he passed solely because he had memorized the solutions to the questions Mackenzie predicted might appear and, by extraordinary good fortune, a good many of them had. On 20 April, he looked up to discover that he had graduated Master of Arts with a creditable if not spectacular degree.

There was now the question of what he was going to do next. He wanted to write plays and theatrical journalism, but as he was to a certain extent financially dependant upon his family, their support was crucial. Announcing that he hoped to go into 'press work and literature in general', he sent his father a batch of *News* cuttings for his inspection, stressing that the trick of leader-writing was 'first to find something to write about, second to conceal ignorance and not commit myself'.[8] He also canvassed the advice of Alexander Russel, the influential and eccentric editor of *The Scotsman*. An invitation to dine at Russel's home, arriving less than ninety minutes before he was expected, threw him into a panic and, by the time he had feverishly climbed into his evening clothes and scampered across town, he was very late. Russel quashed his apologies by growling that he would have saved valuable time if he had not bothered to change. Like Archer, Russel's other guests were turned out in their finery, but their host was in his office clothes, his shirt liberally bespattered with ink. He advised Archer to go to London and submit articles to as many editors as possible. He should also, he added, study Law, which would almost certainly come in useful, as he often wished he had some legal knowledge himself.

Armed with this information, and further encouraged when Dibdin confirmed that training for the bar left plenty of time for theatre-going, Archer travelled to Plymouth where he boarded the *SS Somersetshire*, a three-masted steamer. Soon, the cliffs of southern England were receding into the distance and at last, a thin line, they dropped below the almost invisible band of the horizon. He was on his way to Australia, where a family conference had been called to decide his future.

On the way, he discovered just how bad a sailor he was and resolved that he would never sail again without ample supplies of the strongest possible anti-seasickness mixture. He did not like life at sea and, except for the heat, he did not like life in Australia. At Gracemere, he felt equally out of place whether he was lazing on the verandah, knocking a croquet ball about the lawn or, dressed in a topee, blue shirt and moleskin trousers, learning to ride. He took part in a kangaroo hunt, which he enjoyed, but when he tried helping the fifty or so Polynesian, Chinese and Aborigine cattle workers, he merely got in the way. He felt he was wasting time. He and the family had not seen each other for four years and relations between them, which had never been particularly close, had drifted into a rather embarrassed formality. Neither side knew quite how to respond to each other and at Gracemere, like Tolderodden, it was as if he was a houseguest. The first Archer to go to university and the first to intend living by his intellect rather then his hands, he was turning away from his parents' world and to a realm of which they had no knowledge.

Thomas did try to make overtures. It was at his instigation that father and son made a trek on horseback into the bush, sleeping out at night, boiling tea in their billycans and visiting other sheep farmers. But if this was an attempt at comradeship, it seems to have failed. Thomas turned back early and Archer, clutching a map, carried on alone, eventually finding his way back to Gracemere. Later that summer a deal was struck. Thomas agreed that if his son trained for the Law, he would contribute to his expenses, and Archer sent an urgent message to Mackenzie to find out all he could about 'the amount of study and time that is *absolutely necessary* merely to pass or "to be called" or whatever they may call it'.[9]

He left Australia in the second week of April 1877. He would never return. Rather than take a long sea voyage home, he decided to travel to England by way of New Zealand, Hawaii and the United States. He sailed in the *RMS Zealandia*. After three weeks mostly spent cooped in the steerage cabin, perched on a bunk above the main engines, surrounded by the poor of several nations and a continual cacophony of many languages, he landed at San Francisco. It was twenty-eight years after his father came in search of gold.

He earned a few dollars by selling three travel articles to the *San Francisco Chronicle* and stayed long enough to visit all the city playhouses, including the Chinese Theatre, a tiny, shabby place in a bent-pin passage in the Chinese quarter. Here, he saw a performance of incomprehensible wailing and darting about, accompanied by a primitive string orchestra creating 'a tempest of indescribable discord such as I never before heard and hope never to hear again'.[10] It was his first taste of a theatre culture utterly different from his own.

Speeding east by train, he stopped off in Salt Lake City, Chicago and New York, which he was disappointed to find not as grand as he hoped. He preferred New England, Boston and Cambridge, and Philadelphia, where he admired the red brick buildings with their white doorsteps and at the Walnut Street Theatre saw a production of Offenbach's *L'Archiduc*, advertised as 'Elegant, Chaste and Complete'. Altogether, he saw twenty-five productions in the United States, but came away unimpressed. 'Dramatic art is low enough in England, but I should say that in America it is seventy-five per cent lower,' he informed his brother, Charles. Even the audiences were 'inexpressibly bad', having an 'unerring taste for applauding in the wrong places'.[11]

In the second week of June, he boarded the SS *State of Georgia* for his journey across the Atlantic. Having suffered steerage once, he took the precaution of booking a second-class cabin. The next month, he was back in England, his voyage around the world having taken just over a year.

As his legal training in London was not due to begin until the following autumn, he returned to Edinburgh, where he rented two attic rooms at 36 Hanover Street, at the summit of a hill descending into the New Town, and resumed writing leaders for the *Evening News*. No sooner had he done so, than Dibdin left for Liverpool, to take up a job as an agent for the Queen Insurance Company and to get married. They promised to keep E. V. Ward alive by post, although Archer's next publication, a twenty-four page, buff-covered pamphlet for which 'Lowe did the ideas ... I the writing, Halkett the illustrations',[12] was far too scurrilous even for a pseudonym. Written anonymously, *The Fashionable Tragedian: A Criticism* cruelly mocked Henry Irving, the most celebrated actor of the day.

Irving made his professional debut at Sunderland on 29 September 1856, just six days after Archer was born. He had since played hundreds of roles in far-flung theatres, slowly clawing his way up in the profession, divesting himself of an irasicible wife in the process, until making his name in 1871 at the Lyceum Theatre, just off the Strand. As Matthias in Leopold Lewis's melodrama, *The Bells*, who confesses while under hypnosis to murdering a rich Jew by throwing him into a lime kiln, Irving gave what would become one of his most famous and famously histrionic performances. He excelled in roles calling for a sustained tussle with inner torment, and Matthias is as tormented as they come. Irving was an actor of the grand gesture and rhetorical flourish. Tall and lanky, his long, dark hair framing high cheekbones, long nose and jawline, he contradicted the vogue whereby leading actors tried to look like gentlemen of leisure, by actually looking like a creative artist. Even though he had rooms in Mayfair, his heart and hopes were at the Lyceum, where his Shakespearian productions were already drawing the crowds.

Irving was redefining Shakespeare for the Victorian age. His lyrical, tender Hamlet was highly praised. He daringly omitted the usual stirring music from *Macbeth* and gave a controversial performance in the title role, suggesting that Macbeth is committed to murdering Duncan even before he encounters the witches. He therefore turned the play from a supernatural thriller into a study of the single-minded pursuit of power. Irving made an even more radical move when he announced he would abandon Colley Cibber's melodramatic version of *Richard III*, which had displaced the original for almost two hundred years. Cibber had butchered the text, inserted sections from the other histories and squeezed in a dash of his own dialogue, such as 'Off with his head! So much for Buckingham!' But Irving did not so much restore Shakespeare as eliminate Cibber. He still cut out much of the scene in which Clarence is murdered and most of those in which women were prominent. He refused to allow Lady Anne to spit at Gloucester, and excised lines which he knew would offend modern sensibilities, transposing speeches and scenes with such recklessness that for long stretches the play must have been incoherent. Nevertheless, Irving-Shakespeare, and the Lyceum, which he managed from 1878 onwards, became hugely fashionable for many years.

The preceding autumn, he stampeded through the provinces with *The Bells*, *Hamlet*, *Richard III* and *The Lyons Mail*, a melodrama of mistaken identity by Charles Reade, a successful but famously irritable novelist. Archer had seen Irving a few times and booked to see him again at the Theatre Royal. On 30 October, he notified Dibdin that he and Lowe were just off to 'the Eminent One's first night – I shouldn't wonder if we were to get kicked out of the theatre'.[13]

The Fashionable Tragedian, published two weeks previously, had created a furore. Archer and Lowe dismissed Irving as an actor of neither intellect nor originality, scorning the famous voice as skidding uncontrollably from bass to falsetto, and ridiculing his manner of breaking words and flattening and lengthening vowels. Halkett's caricatures emphasised his thin legs, shambling gait and satirized his facial expressions as stock poses of fear or frenzy. They attacked Irving as a purveyor of simplified Shakespeare. His cutting every speech from *Hamlet* which deliberated the Prince's state of mind, for example, meant that he simply ignored the vital question of whether Hamlet's madness is real or feigned. His Macbeth was no more than 'a Uriah Heap in chain armour' and his Richard 'a cheap Mephistopheles' which 'failed to convey any impression either of the tremendous mental power of Shakespeare's Richard, or of the dignity which should be apparent through all the bodily deformity.'

The pamphlet is a mass of sometimes immature barbs, but in presenting Irving as a symbol of the crisis in modern theatre, the authors were making a serious point. The only training available for actors was in companies such as McNeill's. Archer and Lowe argued that because profit-hungry managers demanded that a successful production ran until it was exhausted, an actor such as Irving, repeatedly playing the same role, inevitably became mannered and stale. Bad acting had made Irving popular, but his popularity was nothing but a measure of public ignorance and the dereliction of critical standards. The only remedy for the 'slovenly, haphazard training of provincial and minor metropolitan theatres', was the establishment of properly constituted schools of acting. Meanwhile, the creation of an informed audience was the job of 'a national theatre, with good endowment, good traditions, good government'.[14]

Neither Archer nor Lowe were ejected from Irving's Edinburgh performances, but within a few days of *The Fashionable Tragedian* appearing on the bookstalls, *A Letter Concerning Mr Henry Irving*, a pamphlet for the defence, was published simultaneously in Edinburgh, Glasgow and London. Its author, if not Irving himself then someone close to him, masqueraded under the name of 'Yorick', questioned their manners and derided their National Theatre proposals. Archer and Lowe launched a counter-attack in the form of a second edition of their own pamphlet with a four-page postscript, which George Taylor, a London printer with an eye for a quick sale, rushed into the shops by mid-November. Within days, rumours of legal retaliation from the Irving camp made him quickly withdraw the unsold copies.

Six years later, in 1883, when Irving was consolidating his partnership with Ellen Terry at the Lyceum, Archer published, under his own name, a judicious revision of *The Fashionable Tragedian*. But while the pamphlet attracted raised eyebrows in the press, *Henry Irving, Actor and Manager* had little impact.

Archer was now twenty-one and a tall, lean, big-boned man with a broad face and dark hair sweeping back from a high, wide brow above clear and confident eyes. He went to the theatre whenever he could, following the careers of Compton and Ellen Wallis, and flung himself into his writing. When he was not composing leaders for the *News*, he wrote satirical poems and fired them off to humorous papers which sometimes printed them. He laboured long hours over *Our Special Correspondent*, E. V. Ward's first play, written mostly by post, which the Watt Institute rejected, and his own second play which they accepted. *Rosalind*, a comedy set at the fictional Theatre Royal, Mudborough, was performed at the Institute soirée on 1 March 1878. Lowe played the leading role of Moncrieff, while Archer directed, carefully supervising the elaborate corking of moustaches and eyebrows. '. . . it went magnificently and was a great hit,' he reported to Dibdin. 'I take no end of credit to myself for the drilling of the company.'[15]

A couple of months later, he made his second visit to Paris, this time to cover the International Exhibition, again for the *San Francisco Chronicle*. On his return, he began stitching together articles for *The Globe Encyclopedia of Universal Information*, which was being edited in six large volumes by a local schoolmaster. In the summer, he bequeathed the *News* 'rot-riter-ship'[16] to his friend John Mackinnon Robertson, an aspiring journalist and freethinker, made a quick visit to Tolderodden and in the autumn arrived in London.

He moved into rooms at 180 Marylebone Road. He was joined by his brother Charles, five years his junior and who had returned from Australia to prepare for admission to Sandhurst Military Academy. Most of Archer's mornings were spent at the British Museum Reading Room, scratching out pieces on Shakespeare and Spiritualism for the *Globe Encyclopedia*. When his term of legal studies began on 2 November, he paid his ten pounds fee and was admitted to the Inn of the Middle Temple, where lectures were held in the afternoons. Afterwards, instead of eating in hall, where he soon fell behind in the number of dinners he was supposed to consume as part of the training, he headed off to one of the cafés in Museum Street where he bought a hot dinner for 1/2d. In the evening he went to the theatre. 'To a true lover of dramatic art, even a bad play has its interest,'[17] he reminded Lowe. The thing was, most of the plays he saw, the clockwork farces, comedies and melodramas, were worse than bad. The theatre was not taken seriously because, unlike the novel, drama was not considered a literary form. T. W. Robertson had died in 1871, but no successor had emerged to develop his realistic approach to the stage. Middle-class sensibilities and an alert official censorship, whereby each new script had to be sent to the Lord Chamberlain's office for approval before it could be produced, conspired to keep the theatre free of serious ideas and any contact, other than those permissible within melodrama or farce, with social issues, politics, religion or sex. The result, observed Archer, was that the theatre was 'incredibly puerile',[18] an empty diversion with no relation to real life.

In winter, London was made even more depressing by the obliterating, suffocating fogs. '2pm and positively without exaggeration as dark as the darkest night,'[19] he notified Dibdin one day in December. London was a city of flickering gaslight and acrid fumes, a place of vivid contrasts, of elegance and wealth and appalling destitution. There were balls and parties in Chelsea and Belgravia, while near the slums of Covent Garden and Westminster, slouched a grimy street-life of prostitutes and beggars with watchful eyes, ferrety, anxious faces and quick, thieving fingers. A third of the population of four million lived in appalling poverty. Social resentment was fermenting. Prices were rising, workers and tradesmen had recently come out on strike and socialist pamphlets would soon begin to rattle off the presses. The Victorian hierarchy was beginning to totter.

The theatre was pungent with gas, greasepaint and escapism. Archer was no killjoy, but he wanted a theatre to be pungent with life as it was lived, and a steady volley of urgent theatrical articles from Marylebone Road began landing on the desks of various editors. In December, the twice-weekly London Figaro published two of his letters, one defending the use of the word 'got', and the other describing his impressions of Albery's The Crisis at the Haymarket. Encouraged, Archer proposed he become the paper's theatre critic.

As it happened, James Mortimer, who edited the Figaro from offices near Ludgate Circus, was looking for a drama critic. He dispatched Archer to a revival of Hamlet at Drury Lane, in which the German actor, Herr Bandmann, was playing the troubled Prince and, coincidentally, Ellen Wallis was appearing for the first time as Ophelia. Archer began his career as a London theatre critic in the *The London Figaro* on Saturday, 14 December 1878. He devoted most of his review to the production rather than the play. This would be his usual approach to revivals. With new work, and especially the work he championed, he would far more upon the play itself. His *Hamlet* review, though, is sharply assured for a young man of twenty-two. 'Some actors,' he observed, 'illuminate Shakespeare, others may be said to play the part of annotators, and it is to the latter class that Herr Bandmann belongs.' He was similarly disappointed by his admired Ellen Wallis, although too polite to say more than the role 'comes well within the limits of her powers'.[20]

The *Figaro* was sympathetic to all things French, and in February Archer found himself back in Paris and staying at the Hôtel Gibraltar, a cheap place on the Rue St Hyacinthe St Honoré, run by a woman he surmised might be partially or even wholly Spanish and who appeared to speak scraps of most European languages but was fluent in none. Archer was researching a series of articles on the Comédie-Française and seeing the forty-one plays that the company, led by Sarah Bernhardt, were to tour to the Gaiety Theatre in the Strand in June. ('What we should have done throughtout this dull midsummer without the Comédie-Française it is difficult to say,'[21] he observed later.)

In London, life at the *Figaro* suddenly became hectic when Mortimer was flung into prison. He had run a series of articles by Georgina Weldon, an articulate, crusading and aggrieved woman who claimed her husband had her certified as insane and removed to an asylum in order to procure a divorce. This was not an uncommon resort for desperate husbands, but an angry William Weldon accused Mortimer of criminal libel and won his case. In November, Mortimer began a three-month sentence in the Debtors' Department at Holloway Prison. Neither was it unusual for editors to be snatched from their desks and convicted by the courts. Over the next few years, Archer worked for four successive editors who, having employed him, overstepped the mark and were bundled off to prison. 'I am beginning to think it unwise to mention this fatality, for fear editors decline to have me on their staff, believing me to have the evil eye,'[22] he would tell Charles nervously.

Mortimer's contravention of the law seriously impeded Archer's study of it as, apart from writing theatre criticism, he reviewed books, sub-edited and, in turn with other staff, edited the paper until Mortimer's release. While all this was happening, he suffered another shock. His family announced they were returning from Australia to settle in

London. 'I feel as if I were going to be married or imprisoned or buried or something . . .'[23] he complained.

Thomas, Grace and the remaining seven children arrived in May the following year, having begun the voyage from Sydney twice. The first ended after only two days when they were shipwrecked on a coral reef, forcing the Archers and the other passengers to scramble for the lifeboats and row through heaving seas to the nearest island, which turned out to be uninhabited. They ate periwinkles and waited to be rescued. The second voyage was successful, but once in England, the Archers transferred to Larvik, where Julia had died, aged eighty-nine. Finally, leaving Jane Anne and Mary in charge at Tolderodden, the family congregated in London. The letter Dibdin received from his friend at the beginning of June was far from cheerful. 'I am once more in the bosom of my family. There are moments when I feel rather as if my family were in, or on, my bosom, in the form of an incubus, or nightmare . . .'[24]

But for Archer, work was the solution. '. . . work is the supreme anaesthetic,'[25] he had tactlessly told Dibdin after his wife had died in childbirth the previous year. Since moving to London, besides reviewing for the *Figaro* and attending the sometimes perplexing lectures at the Middle Temple, Archer had blazed on with writing plays. Some were never completed. *Irina*, an intended romantic drama derived from Turgenev's novel, *Smoke*, which Archer read in German translation, did not progress far beyond a rough outline. Other pieces, such as the one-act farces, *Mixed: A Photographic Frenzy* and *Method in His Madness*, were no sooner finished than discarded as failures. Two plays had Norwegian sources. Mythology inspired *The Runic Ring*, while Ibsen's early, plodding melodrama, *Gildet paa Solhaug* (*The Feast at Solhaug*), about two sisters in love with the same man, became the basis of *The Feast at Felvik*. With this play under his arm, Archer went out in search of professional opinion.

Usually, established playwrights wrote at the request of actor-managers and new authors either sent or, if they were lucky, read their work to them. Archer avoided the managers and instead, on 20 December 1878, a week after publishing his restrained review of her Ophelia, he read *The Feast at Felvik* to his admired Ellen Wallis. He was given tea and plenty of sympathy. 'Miss W was gorgeous beyond all description,' he notified Dibdin the next day, adding that 'her opinions were splendid'. She turned the play down, but did so charmingly by suggesting he write a domestic drama for her. 'I think I shall try my hand at it,'[26] he reported. He got nowhere, for the actor W. H. Vernon, a compact, serious man with a short red beard and a distinctive, throaty voice, had intervened. He was far more encouraging, but about a different play altogether.

In Norway two years earlier, in the summer of 1876, Archer saw his first Ibsen play on the stage, a performance of *Peer Gynt* during its world premiere run at the Christiana Theatre. It was extensively cut and much use made of Edvard Grieg's incidental music and sadly, Archer appears to have left no record of his impressions. The run did not last long, as a fire destroyed the scenery after thirty-seven perform-ances, but seeing *Peer Gynt* may have given him the idea of translating Ibsen into English which, in retrospect, seems such an obvious step for Archer to take.

The impetus might also have come from Catherine Ray's translation of *Kejser og Galilæer*, Ibsen's epic Roman verse play, written over eight years, from 1865–73. As *The Emperor and the Galilean*, this became the first Ibsen translation into English to be published, appearing in London in 1876. A shadowy figure, Miss Ray subsequently published some undistinguished novels but never returned to translation. Archer read *The Emperor and the Galilean*, and may even have seen *Translations from the Norse by a BSS* (member of the British Scandinavian Society). This slim volume included a fragment of *Cataline* translated by a certain A. Johnstone, and was privately printed by the Society in Gloucester during the same year. But he would not have known that Edmund Gosse, who had published verse from *Love's Comedy* in 1873, had failed to find a publisher for his translation of the complete play.

Outside a small circle, Ibsen was entirely unknown in Britain when Archer sat down in Edinburgh in 1878 to read his latest play, *Samfundets støtter* (*The Pillars of Society*), which he had just received from Gyldendal, Ibsen's Danish publishers.

The first of Ibsen's prose dramas to have a contemporary setting, the play is a study of moral hypocrisy and the obsessive pettiness of provincial life. Bernick, a wealthy shipowner and a prominent figure in a small Norwegian seaport, has married solely to further his career. During his engagement, he was discovered in an actress's bedroom and allowed Johan, his future brother-in-law, to accept the disgrace and emigrate. Fifteen years later, as the play begins, Johan returns with Lona Hessel, a former love of Bernick's. After he threatens to expose him, Bernick allows Johan to go to sea in a ship that he knows is rotting and must sink. Too late, he discovers that his own son, Olaf, is on board. In a melodramatic ending, he learns the ship has not sailed after all, and in his relief, confesses the errors of his past and so redeems himself for the future.

Archer thought the play 'so tremendous that it made me shiver down my backbone'.[27] He wrote an article on it and sent it to *The Mirror of Literature*, a low-circulation paper which published his piece and promptly went out of business. Having 'dashed off a translation [of the play] in less than a week'[28] Archer sent it to several publishers, each one of whom sent it back. When Squire Bancroft, the actor-manager of the Prince of Wales in Tottenham Street, who had produced Robertson's plays, offered to read it, Archer immediately began 'skinning, chopping, disfiguring, cooking, spicing, & dishing up the finest drama that was ever written, so as to suit the vitiated state of the British public'. It was disheartening work, especially as 'the more I study *The Supports of Society* the more I feel convinced that Henrik Ibsen is the very greatest dramatist of the age'.[29] He would not make so great a compromise again, but in spite of his culinary manipulations, Bancroft rejected it. But once in London, Archer took a gamble and read the play to Vernon whom he hoped might be interested in the role of Bernick. He was. More than that, he promised to find a theatre in which to produce the play.

Archer had heard nothing for over eighteen months when Vernon popped up one day in the summer of 1880 and announced that he had arranged a single matinee performance at the Gaiety. The first British production of an Ibsen play would take place at 2.30 in the afternoon of Wednesday, 15 December 1880.

Vernon wanted the title changed to *Good Name*. Archer refused. They compromised on *Quicksands*, with the subtitle *The Pillars of Society*, the name which Archer subsequently preferred and by which the play became known. Once the Lord Chamberlain licensed the play for public performance, Archer publicized it in the *Figaro*, advising his readers that the production 'cannot fail to be of interest from the literary point of view'.[30] Vernon assembled a cast for a week of hurried rehearsals, with Archer assisting, checking lines in the text. 'Have just had a very fatiguing rehearsal,' he wrote to Dibdin.[31]

The matinee cost Vernon about seventy pounds, which included the rent for the theatre, nominal payment for the leading actors and a tiny budget for costume, scenery and advertising. The scenery consisted of canvas flats erected to hide those for the Gaiety's evening bill, which included a revival of Dion Boucicoult's rumbustious adventure, *The*

Corsican Brothers. In an attempt to add realism to the prediction of the storm at the end of the third act, Archer brought a barometer from Marylebone Road and hung it on the rear wall of their set. But as the sole piece of furniture on the stage, it merely distracted the audience, which comprised the actors' friends, several suspicious critics, a few curious theatre-goers and Dibdin. 'Its ludicrous effect in that absolutely bare room was a lesson in practical dramaturgy',[32] reflected Archer, who spent a good deal of the performance wondering how to avoid calamity in the fourth and final act.

Lack of time, money and actors meant that he and Vernon had failed to cast the delegation of townspeople who jostle into Bernick's room near the end of the play. So, during the second interval, Archer hastily mustered enough volunteers from the audience to represent a credible crowd but not entirely denude the stalls, with the result that, among others, Dibdin made his first and last appearance on the London stage. As the curtain came down, there was dutiful applause and even one or two calls for the appearance of the translator, 'a request', acidly observed a Danish critic, 'which was readily met, without any trace of embarrassment or reserve, by Mr William Archer'.[33]

The production was a milestone, but of the kind that is only recognizable as such when looking back from long distance. At the time, no one heralded the British advent of Ibsen. *The Times* conceded that *Quicksands* 'conveys the impression of being the work of a man of talent',[34] but *The Era* complained that 'the shadow of ruin and disgrace hanging over the head of the chief personage for four acts was by no means a lively entertainment'.[35] Even the usually loyal Charles Archer admitted that the performance was 'scrambling and ineffective'.[36] But Archer himself, writing anonymously in the *Figaro* and determined to accelerate the Ibsen campaign, claimed that the play was acted 'with a smoothness and completeness very unusual at [a matinee] performance'.[37] Yet even though Edmund Gosse had written over twenty pieces on Ibsen and had recently published a book, *Studies in the Literature of Northern Europe*, containing an essay devoted to the playwright, there were still no offers to publish *Quicksands*. The only English translation of Ibsen to appear that year was by a Danish schoolteacher called T. Weber and published in Copenhagen. Apparently with the aid of nothing but a concise English dictionary and a resolute absence of imagination, Weber produced a rendering of Ibsen's latest play, *Et dukkehjem* (*A Doll's House*), which he entitled *Nora*, after its leading character. It has the distinction of being unintentionally one of the most ludicrous translations of all time.

The Gaiety matinee also failed to create any interest for further productions. Archer managed to keep the playwright's name in print with two articles in the January and February 1881 editions of the *St James's Magazine*, but there, for the meantime, the battle for Ibsen rested.

Exasperated, he turned to Sydney Grundy, a thirty-two-year-old barrister in chambers at King's Bench Walk, close to the Middle Temple. From Manchester, which he disliked intensely, and where his father was prominent in local government, Grundy spoke in a soft Lancashire accent and was the author of several minor plays and sketches. Because managers demanded that he adapt from the French rather than write original drama, Grundy believed his natural talent was being thwarted and was becoming bitter as a result. In response to Archer's persistent stream of plot outlines and suggestions of collaboration, he had only four words of advice. 'You must write rot.'[38]

This is exactly what Archer did. He had kept in contact with his university friend Hector Mackenzie, who was now a fellow of Emmanuel College, Cambridge, and under the pseudonym of W. A. and A. G. Stanley, they ran off a brow-clutching, five-act melodrama called *Australia, or The Bushrangers*. It has an heroic hero, a palpitating heroine and desperate criminals; buildings burn, rivers run, railway tracks explode. The escapes are sensational and made only in the nick of time. It was snapped up by George Clark, the manager of the Grecian Theatre in Shoreditch. This was not quite so good as it might sound, for the Grecian had fallen upon hard times and was no longer fashionable. It was also a very long way from the centre of theatrical life in the Strand.

'Advance *Australia*!',[39] cried Grundy, after the first night on 16 April 1881, unaware that having watched the rehearsals, Archer was so appalled that he had stayed away. 'I have not seen it yet & probably never shall,'[40] he wrote to Dibdin on 22 April. Although the critic from *The Era*, one of the few to trail out to Shoreditch, pronounced that it was 'competely successful'[41] the play lasted less than a month. Even though he earned twelve pounds, Archer was greatly relieved, for although *Australia* appeared to be the kind of play he could write fairly easily, it was the exact antithesis of what he wanted to see on the stage.

Even worse was to follow. A couple of years previously, E. V. Ward had written the libretti for two comic operas, *The Khan of Kashgar*, loosely based upon Aristophanes's *Lysistrata* and with an Asian potentate as its leading character, and *Blue and Buff, or The Great Muddlesborough Election*. This was a one-act political satire in the manner of Gilbert and Sullivan, both in its subject and its metrical style of alternate and internal rhymes. The scene is the hustings at the market place of Great Muddlesborough (a refinement of the Mudborough of *Rosalind*). The Conservative candidate, Sir Snobley Snooks, and the former Liberal member, Pilate Pump, put their rival manifestoes before a citizens' chorus led by the mayor, Oylay Crabb, and his sister, Vinega. According to the patrician Sir Snobley:

> By right divine we rule who dine
> Each evening in a swallow-tail!!!

while for Pump:

> Religions, morals, monarchs, priests and judges,
> Will soon be set aside as useless fudges.[42]

Suddenly, Vinega intervenes to proclaim the natural superiority of women, and both she and Sir Snobley are elected. The mayor resolves the impasse by arranging that they marry, and Sir Snobley takes the seat only after agreeing to renounce Conservative principles and support Home Rule for Ireland.

With music by William Frost, a Liverpool composer and conductor of the local Amateur Operatic Company, *Blue and Buff* opened as a curtain-raiser at the city's Bijou Opera House on 24 January 1881. It played a week and disappeared. But on the last day of August, after *Australia* had closed, Archer picked up his newspaper and to his amazement read that it was to open at the Haymarket on 5 September. It appeared that Frost, hearing that a one-act piece was needed to complete the evening programme, had arranged for *Blue and Buff* to be performed. He and E. V. Ward had never got on well, and now they fell out entirely. There was less than a week for rehearsals, but despite being rather deaf, Frost insisted upon masterminding everything himself. At the same time he began re-scoring sections of the music and re-jigging lines of the libretto. The orchestra and the singers moved daily closer to mutiny.

Archer crept into the theatre on the first night and watched farce degenerate into fiasco. '. . . nothing could possibly be worse'[43] sighed *The Era*. Few of the singers were word-perfect, and neither was the prompter whose voice was frequently more audible. In the pit, and unable to hear quite how badly things were going, an increasingly angry Frost whipped on a struggling, or, as he thought, recalcitrant orchestra, which finally halted altogether when the singer playing Vinega Crabb stepped forward to complain. As she did so, Frost began humming loudly, stirring the baton in the air until cast and musicians despairingly battled on. After five dreadful performances, *Blue and Buff* was withdrawn.

Archer felt angry and humiliated as he walked back to his small room at 5 Sandland Street, off Red Lion Street. It was his fifth rented room in London. When his lease expired at Marylebone Road and Charles went off to Sandhurst, Archer moved to 7 Alfred Place, just north of Bedford Square on the edge of Bloomsbury, and from there to 8 Kildare Terrace, in Bayswater. When his family returned, they demanded he join them at their home in Croydon, near David's family. This lasted a year before he fled back to London, to a room at 353 The Strand, and finally to Sandland Street.

He was also restless and unwell. For two years he had been troubled by intermittent but severe headaches; to Dibdin he complained of heart palpitations and giddiness and to Grundy of persistent indigestion. 'Things are going very badly for me,'[44] he reported gloomily to Dibdin. 'The doctor calls it "liver dyspepsia",'[45] he notified Robertson on 21 October. His symptoms are consistent with a duodenal ulcer, with nervous stress caused by overwork and with depression. Certainly, he felt his career had plummeted. A measure of his anguish is revealed in an article he published under the byline of 'A Dramatic Critic' in the *St James's Magazine* in March 1881. Archer furiously attacked the theatre criticism written by his contemporaries as mediocre, expressing rather than leading public opinion. Castigating their timidity, he added miserably that fear of the vengeance of managers in possible collusion with editors had meant that in his own reviews he too moderated 'everything to an inoffensive grey'.[46]

There were also emotional problems. For three years, he had been immersed in a relationship with his cousin David's twenty-five-year-old daughter, Julia. The extent of their intimacy is unclear, but Archer was unsure of both his feelings for her, and hers for him, and the uncertainty worried him. At the beginning of the year, there seems to have been a crisis which may have involved Julia and which prevented Archer from going to Liverpool to see *Blue and Buff*: 'I am neither going to get married nor to get lugged up for breach of promise, but things have taken a turn half pleasant, half unpleasant,'⁴⁷ he told Dibdin mysteriously.

She was not the first woman to upset Archer's life. Before his voyage around the world, he fell wildly in love with a young woman he met at a relative's houseparty at Kabelvag, in the Lofoten Islands. She bewitched him; he called her 'Northland Sun' and they went for walks together and danced until one in the morning. He had also thought romantically of Ellen Wallis, his exact contemporary. Most likely, his listlessness was caused by both stress and emotional worries. But whatever the reason, it was clear he needed a change and a rest. His family offered to pay for him to go abroad. Archer suggested Italy. His parents agreed. He would winter in Rome.

He set off on 2 November, first to Paris and then to Marseilles from where he sent his luggage on to Leghorn by rail and, with a bag swung over his shoulder, followed it leisurely on foot. There was an ulterior motive in his going to Rome. Ibsen was living there, and Archer was determined to meet him. He tramped resolutely on.

By the end of the month he was in Rome and staying at the Hotel Laurati on the Quirinal Hill, from where he looked down upon dusty streets and a part of the ruined Servian Wall. 'Somehow you don't think of Rome as a city of dwelling houses, but as a city of temples and fora and theatres and amphitheatres.'⁴⁸ Delighted by the city and its soft colours, he became an energetically inquisitive tourist. With his copy of *Middlemarch*, he prowled the Vatican Museums until he located the statue of the Sleeping Ariadne where Will Ladislaw and Naumann glimpsed Dorothea, discovering to his satisfaction that everything was just as Eliot described it.

He moved into cheaper lodgings with a family at Via dell'Anima 55, near the Piazza Navona. It was an entertaining household. Among the inmates were his landlord, Signor Davide, and Elvira, his enormously fat and slovenly wife. There was a young servant, Rosina, even fatter and dirtier, two dogs and another lodger who claimed to be an advocate. Archer was known as Signor Guglielmo. For him, the worst thing about number 55 was the cold. Outside, the weather could be as warm as an English midsummer but inside, with its bare stone floors and no fireplaces, the house was like England in winter. In his room, he wore an Inverness cape over his day clothes and, when he read or wrote, swathed his legs and feet in a travelling rug and pulled a fez absurdly down to his eyebrows. He still suffered from headaches but, overall, his health was improving. He sent Grundy a Christmas card, with the parsimonious greeting of 'May you be as happy as you deserve to be, not more so,'[49] and assured him he was feeling much better.

At the Scandinavian Consul, Archer discovered that the Ibsens were living in an apartment at Via Capo le Case 75, near the city centre. Realizing that he had translated and produced *Quicksands* without asking permission, Archer decided the best approach might be a tactful letter. He composed 'a model of diplomacy', which produced an invitation to Via Capo le Case for Sunday, 11 December. But they met sooner than either imagined. There was a large Scandinavian community in Rome, and on Saturday, the 10th, Archer attended a reception at the Scandinavian Club at the Palazzo Correa. He had been there for no longer than fifteen minutes when the door opened and to his astonishment, in walked 'the great sight of Rome – Henrik Ibsen'.[50]

Having seen several photographs of him, Archer immediately recognized the domed cranium, glossy sweep of iron-grey hair and bushy whiskers almost meeting at the chin, the austere expression and small, gold-rimmed spectacles. Ibsen was fifty-three, and formally dressed in a long black coat with broad lapels. But what surprised Archer was how small he was. Because he held Ibsen in such respect, he had presumed him to be a big, broad man, yet the figure moving slowly across the room, hands clasped behind his back, was positively undersized. Archer asked Professor Ravnkilde, the Club president, to introduce them and, as he did so, cautiously watched Ibsen's unsmiling, thin-lipped mouth and the cold, blue eyes, the right slightly closed and the other beadily wide open, for signs of recognition and malevolence. There were none. Yet when Archer guardedly mentioned *Quicksands*, Ibsen admitted he had heard of it, and coolly accepted Archer's apologies for his discourtesy.

'His extreme quietness and reticence of manner have not been exaggerated – the only information of any importance I have yet got out of him is that he does not read French or Italian dramatists . . . & very seldom goes to the theatre,'[51] Archer informed Dibdin a few days later. But ' "the old min's [sic] friendly" and that's the main point'[52] he reported to Charles.

As they parted that first evening, Archer asked when a new play might be ready. Ibsen replied that *Gengangere* (*Ghosts*) was to be published in Copenhagen in four days' time. Immediately, Archer ordered a copy and waited with almost uncontrollable impatience for it to be sent from Denmark. When it arrived on 19 December, he retreated to his room, swathed himself in his rug, clamped his fez on his head, and read it at one sitting. 'It *is* a bombshell with a vengeance,' he wrote to Dibdin that night.

The action is set in contemporary Norway, in a large house above a fjord. The central character is Mrs Alving, a widow who knows her husband had several affairs and fathered an illegitimate daughter, Regina. Now a young woman, Regina works in the Alving household as a servant, but is unaware who her true father is. The Alvings' son, Oswald, a painter, returns from Paris and, to his mother's horror, a relationship develops between him and Regina. Later, the volatile Oswald reveals he has an incurable disease which the audience understands to be inherited syphilis. After Regina, whom he hoped to marry, rejects him and leaves to become a prostitute, Oswald demands that his mother administer a fatal dose of his morphine tablets when he becomes so ill he cannot fend for himself. As the play ends, Oswald sinks into incoherence and Mrs Alving is confronted by the dilemma of whether to kill her son or, by allowing him to live, watch him degenerate even further.

'. . . if it doesn't waken them up in the north I'm a Dutchman,'[53] was Archer's initial verdict. The play did indeed produce a jolt in Scandinavia. Theatre managers were too horrified to stage it and booksellers refused to stock it. Ibsen's legions of critics, shocked that he should write about venereal disease, furiously accused him of both defending free love and tacitly approving the possibility of incestuous marriage. For Archer, the play was 'the most refreshing slap in the face to all conventions in religion & morality', although he too was perturbed by 'the implied approval of consanguineous marriage'. He was none too sure of the genetic or psychological implications, but decided that 'Ibsen only means to protest against the "ghost-belief" that if the fellow had unwittingly married his half-sister there would have been anything to go mad about.'[54]

Over the next few days, while the Scandinavian controversy blustered, Archer and Ibsen met regularly, both at the Scandinavian Club and in the gloomy corner of a café near Ibsen's home. One day, Archer asked him whether, after the end of the play, Mrs Alving helped her son to die. Ibsen replied that he could never answer such a question and asked Archer his opinion. He suggested that if she did not, it would be because she retained the delusion that a miracle might happen. The playwright agreed that a mother would believe that while there is life, there is hope. He also agreed that, when proved wrong, Mrs Alving would kill Oswald and then herself. After a while, Ibsen remarked that it would probably be a long time before the play was performed. Archer said nothing. It was, he thought, 'a great achievement, with all its faults',[55] but 'too ghastly and hasn't enough action.'[56]

His introduction to Ibsen was not the only significant meeting of Archer's Roman winter. He came across Henry Bond, 'a thoroughly good fellow',[57] the son of a successful grocer and a law graduate of Trinity College, Cambridge. Only a few years older than Archer, Bond was on holiday with John Neville Keynes, a fellow of Pembroke College and the future father of the economist, Maynard Keynes. Bond became a close friend and once Archer returned to England, he often travelled down to Cambridge for weekends. Through Bond, he became loosely acquainted with a group of Cambridge intellectuals, including Keynes and Henry Fawcett, the Professor of Political Economy and follower of John Stuart Mill, who had been accidentally blinded by his father in a shooting accident. These weekends were important because Cambridge became an intellectual touchstone for Archer until he began creating his own circle in London. But the more decisive meeting for Archer in Rome was that with Frances Elizabeth Trickett.

With her elderly parents and Blanche Taylor, a friend from Paris, Frances had arrived in Rome earlier that autumn. She was twenty-six, a year older than Archer, and a small, animated, slightly plump woman with springy, dark hair which she wore tied back. Driven on by Frances's ailing and fractious mother, the Tricketts had descended upon Italy each winter for three years. They came in search of mild weather and suitable English people with whom to share it. They liked the English community in Rome, assiduously preserving its expatriate dignity even now the days of the Grand Tour had given way to middle-class canters of feverish inspection. Each year, earnest Victorians, gripping their Baedeker Guides, swept through Florence and Rome, examining anatomically vivid marble torsos and peering at flaking frescoes.

The youngest of eight children, of whom only three daughters survived, Frances was born on 17 March 1855 at the family home at 16 Tamar Terrace, Stoke Dameral, now part of the Devonport area of Plymouth. Her father, John Trickett, became chief engineer at the port at Keyham. She attended school at Malvern, but in common with the majority of middle-class women, Frances was not so much educated as accomplished. She spoke French, Italian and a little German, and in Paris had studied the piano to a standard at which she was thinking of giving lessons herself. Then, in 1879, her father retired and agreed that as Ann, his fastidious wife, was seldom in good health, the family should travel. Frances was summoned home. As her two elder sisters had long since married and moved away, she was required to abandon thoughts of teaching and shepherd her parents in their wanderings through Europe, translating their continual requests and caring for her mother.

In Rome, the Tricketts settled at Via de Babuino 29, in the midst of the English colony and, like their friends, spent their days peeping into churches and galleries, calling upon other expatriates and being called upon themselves. Both Frances and Blanche were members of the Unione Polyglotta, a social club led by a language teacher which held a twice-weekly *conversazione*, during which members were theoretically required to speak only the language of the country. During the evening of Tuesday, 20 December, Frances was introduced to a tall young man who spoke fractured Italian in what sounded suspiciously like a slight Scottish accent. This irritated her as she did not like Scottish people much. His name was William Archer.

His first impression was that she was 'by no means an imposing little person',[58] but she had an engaging personality and, more to the point, had read *Middlemarch* and greatly approved of it. By the following month, when Bond and Keynes had gone home to England, Archer and Frances were exploring Rome together, discreetly chaperoned by Blanche. They walked through narrow streets and ilex avenues and agreed that the gardens of the Villa Mattei were the finest in Rome. There they sat and argued contentedly about Ruskin. 'It has always been my luck hiterto to fall in love with stupid girls but this time I have fallen in love with a clever one and no mistake,'[59] Archer confided to Dibdin.

They attended a masked ball, Frances dressed as Day and Archer, inspired by *HMS Pinafore*, as An Englishman, 'that being the character I am most accustomed to'.[60] They stood in the Colosseum at night, gazing up at its ruined walls, imagining its gladiatorial past. Archer even put up with 'evenings' at the Via de Babuino, at which Frances and Blanche entertained at the piano, playing 'moosic [sic] from Mendelssohn to *Pinafore* . . . They both sing, though they haven't got a voice between them, & both play rather feebly . . .'[61] Frances would have been incensed if she knew what he thought, but in spite of the Thursday 'At Homes', they became a couple. 'The fact is, I never *lived* until now,'[62] he reflected.

However, his Roman adventure was nearing its end. On the afternoon of 4 March 1882, he said farewell to Ibsen, who presented him with a photograph of himself, inscribed 'To Mr William Archer, from your most friendly and grateful Henrik Ibsen'. The next day, he boarded the train to Naples. But within a fortnight, Blanche had returned to Paris and the Tricketts joined him in the south. In April, they travelled together to Florence, and then to Venice and the northern lakes.

The romance between Archer and Frances was that of two people who were often lonely, falling in love in a country that he at least thought idyllic. It was also the closest either had come to a meeting of minds with someone of the other sex. They were both intelligent and well-read, and within Frances there was a flinty seam of socialist feminism, although she could cling like a limpit to the rock of the conventionally feminine, bemoaning her intellectual prowess. 'I have only treacle for a brain,'[63] she repeated more than once. But, horrified by the zealous Catholicism of one of her brothers-in-law, she was as fiercely opposed to religion and religious teaching as Archer. 'I am sure mortal man never had a brighter, franker, kinder companion,'[64] he notified Bond.

Archer had been in Italy for almost six months. His time was over. He left the Tricketts on 13 May and, having negotiated with his father for an extension of his European tour, spent six weeks in Munich. From there, he complained about feeling lonely, badgered Bond to send him law books and flung himself into a round of theatre-going, discovering Wagner in the process. He had previously loathed opera, but was now emotionally extremely susceptible to tumultuous tales of love lost and found and men tormented and redeemed, and especially to *The Flying Dutchman*, with its Norwegian setting and theme of man's release from purgatory by a woman. He went on to see *Tannhauser*, *Lohengrin* and *Tristan und Isolde*, all of which were performed at the National-Theater within a fortnight. To the bewilderment of his friends, Archer proclaimed himself 'an out-and-out bigoted Wagnerite'.[65]

During the summer, he met Frances again when the Tricketts arrived at Hausen in Switzerland. When they moved on to Paris before turning back south, Archer followed, booking in at the Hotel Gibraltar while the Tricketts piled in to the Taylor apartment at 26 Avenue de Friedland, one of the grand boulevards fanning out from the Arc de Triomphe. Together, Archer and Frances wandered through the Louvre, saw plays at the Comédie-Française, ate late dinners in Latin Quarter restaurants and went dancing, walking home through the dark, tangy air. He stayed until he ran out of money. On the morning of 23 September, his twenty-sixth birthday, he called at the Avenue de

Friedland and reluctantly said goodbye. Catching the boat train to Boulogne, he crossed the Channel and late that night, steamed into Victoria Station. After eleven months, he was home.

'Surely we have been the happiest people in existence!'[66] cried Frances. 'It is so blank without you . . .'[67]

As *The London Figaro* had closed during his absence, Archer was wholly dependent upon his family for financial support. He had no choice but to join them at their new home, a large, modern house in Alleyn Park, Dulwich, which Thomas, now almost sixty and working as Agent-General for Queensland in London, had named Muirton after the area of Perth where Grace had grown up.

As it was five years since he had agreed to train for the bar, he decided to honour his promise and rid himself of the Law as quickly as possible. Closing the door of his room and propping his photograph of Ibsen on the mantelpiece, he began a crash-course of legal study in preparation for examinations after Christmas. He emerged only for two or three bouts of dentistry, agonizing gougings, drillings and tuggings in which several teeth were extracted. For some days after each ordeal, he existed on beef tea and bread without crusts. 'I wish I was around to cut off the crusts for you,' wrote Frances from Paris. 'I wish I could cut the sharp crusts off life for you, same as you do for me.'[68]

Archer's teeth were to be a recurring trouble, and the miseries of dentistry frequently crop up in his letters. Later, he had several false teeth, and even some of these were far from secure. Hiding the gaps and slightly jumbled appearance of his teeth was one of the reasons for his growing a drooping moustache, rather thin at first but emphatically bushy later on.

He sat his first Law examination on 27 December and the last two days later. In mid-January 1883, he learned to his immense relief that he had passed, but delayed being called to the bar until 17 November, which gave him several months, living if necessary at his family's expense, to revive his writing career. He was brimming with ideas for travel books and even one on Wagner, but failed to interest a publisher. In January, he became an upaid founder-contributor to *Progress*, a journal of freethought edited by G. W. Foote, an atheist, socialist and combative public speaker and writer. Damning the established church and the capitalists 'who wield the whip of hunger over their labouring tribes', Foote exhorted 'the warriors of freedom' to 'raise the standard of revolt . . . in a spirit of reform'.[69] Over the next eighteen months (during which Foote was temporarily imprisoned for blasphemy), Archer published fifteen articles in *Progress*, including one advocating the hygienic advantages of cremation which, although becoming legal in 1884, outraged fundamentalists as denying the literal interpretation of the resurrection of the body.

Archer was terrified his family would discover they were harbouring a vociferous freethinker. Before leaving for Italy, he had made Dibdin promise that 'in the event of my croaking suddenly'[70] he must instantly go to his room and destroy his letters, confessional poetry about Julia and all his papers and articles. As a further precaution, his *Progress* pieces appeared under the pseudonym of Norman Britton. Frances, who arrived in London with her parents in May and settled with them in Bayswater, rebelled at the deception, but after reading his work, agreed that using his own name while living at Muirton would be 'like going out in a heavy hailstorm without an umbrella'.[71]

And so Archer assumed a double life. At Dulwich, he accompanied his family to the observances, while in London he revealed his true self as a radical and freethinker, arguing with atheist friends and writing his articles at the British Museum.

It was there, after his usual summer holiday in Norway, that he met Bernard Shaw.

3

W. A. of *The World*

Both Archer and Shaw naturally gravitated to the British Museum Reading Room to work at desks arranged like the spokes of a wheel around a hub of catalogue racks. It was according to Archer, 'the jolliest place possible for either reading or writing'.[1] For them, and for several other young intellectuals, it became a kind of a club.

In recent years, three of the writers who most influenced Archer and many of his contemporaries had died, Dickens in 1870, Mill three years later and Eliot in 1880. Darwin followed in 1882 and Karl Marx early in 1883. Doubters, campaigners and radicals, they bequeathed the later Victorian years to a generation wondering how to take up their standard and fashion a new world.

Several members of this new generation of atheists, rationalists and socialists, many of them writers, journalists, civil servants and lawyers, were familiar Reading Room faces. Archer, from a family of Liberals and religious non-conformists, was drawn to those from a similar background, such as Ernest Radford, a young graduate of Trinity College, Cambridge, a barrister and acquaintance of Henry Bond. He would shake himself free of the Law in order to join William Morris's Socialist League, become secretary to the Arts and Crafts Exhibition Society and write irregular volumes of mundane verse. When, in 1892, he threatened to shoot an editor who had rejected some of his poems, he was consigned to mental and convalescent homes for a year. He never fully recovered.

Radford occasionally contributed to *Progress*, as did the woman he married, Caroline 'Dollie' Maitland. A vivacious personality, she assisted Eleanor, Karl Marx's dark-haired, clever but emotionally vulnerable youngest daughter, in her research for the New Shakspere Society, inaugurated by the philologist and oarsman, F. J. Furnivall.

Radford, whom impressionable women and even Marx himself thought resembled Irving, was a leading light of a discussion group called the Men and Women's Club. Others included his sister, Ada, as plain as her brother was dashing; Dollie; Karl Pearson, about to become Professor of Applied Mathematics at University College, London, and Clementina Black, a novelist and later social reformer.

Fortnightly Club meetings were held at members' homes, where the one inviolable rule was strict equality between the sexes. But although Radford introduced Archer, he did not attend many meetings and soon drifted away altogether. Intellectually, Cambridge was more important to him. Besides, he preferred to be independent of groups and so at this juncture did Shaw, simply because he was unable to find a socialist association worth joining.

By 1883, Shaw had been in London for seven years. He had followed his mother who had abandoned the decrepit George Carr Shaw and herself turned up in London in the wake of a piratical-looking music and voice teacher named George John Vandeleur Lee. While in Dublin, Bessie had become captivated by Lee as he applied his famous teaching 'method' and transformed her into a competent mezzo-soprano. In London, Lee took lodgings in Ebury Street while she found rooms a mile away, just off the Fulham Road. It was here that three years later, her son arrived, having fled from his father and his clerking job in a Dublin land agency. Lee would fall down dead in his rooms in 1886. In the meantime, Bessie supported her family by teaching the 'method' herself. As for Shaw, he was briefly employed as a land surveyor for the Edison Telephone Company before electing to become unemployed and devoting himself to several years of self-education and novel-writing at the British Museum.

For several months after his return from Europe, Archer watched the rising socialist tide of pamphlets and street-corner meetings with detached interest. He was sympathetic to socialism, but believed the theatre to be a potentially greater instrument of individual and social change. Shaw, however, had leapt without hesitation into 'the great Socialist revival of 1883'.[2] He joined various debating societies in order to polish up his oratorical skills and attended meetings of the recently-formed Social Democratic Federation, the first socialist organisation in Britain, to sharpen his blade as a revolutionary. Astounded to discover that hardly anyone in the Federation had read Marx, he stalked off up the socialist road in search of a new home. He found it, several months later, in the Fabian Society.

Archer and Shaw were vividly contrasting characters. Archer's back-ground was one of radical Liberalism, minor private school, university, the Middle Temple and journalism. By the time he met Shaw, he had travelled around the world and was as familiar with Norway as with Britain and knew Paris almost as well as London. He was confidently cosmopolitan whereas Shaw was shyly provincial, having had a scrappy academic career and never venturing more than a few miles from Dublin before arriving in England. But once Archer began enthusing about Ibsen, Shaw realized that he was far from the unyielding puritan that he appeared to be. For his part, Archer immediately noticed that Shaw's impishness and 'vivid, daring, fantastic' conversation hid 'a profound underlying seriousness'.[3] He took it upon himself to draw the serious Shaw from his clownish shell, while Shaw decided that he must strip the cloak of dreadful formality from Archer. To this end they counselled and hectored each other for a lifetime.

Yet their similarities outnumbered their differences. They had much more in common than immediate forbears falling upon hard times, a hostility to religion and a conviction of having something vital to contribute to the world. Both men were in the process of reinventing themselves. Archer never denied that he was 'a Scotchman' any more than Shaw deliberately concealed his Irishness and both were apt, when it suited them, to wave the flag of his national identity. But, for Archer, such occasions did not occur often. He was busily recreating himself as a Londoner and an Englishman at the centre of English-speaking culture, while Shaw was methodically transforming himself into GBS, the clowning genius of letters. Both were burying memories of the provincial capital cities of their youth.

Therefore, they could look each other in the eye, literally, Shaw being just an inch under Archer's six feet, and metaphorically, for both loved ideas, language and argument. Each was the intellectual equal of the other and in Shaw's presence, Archer had no need to conceal his radical thoughts and beliefs. Most significantly, both had campaigning minds, ruthless ambition and a sharp sense of humour. Although Archer's vision of the world was always darker than Shaw's, a spiky, ironic wit united them as allies and antagonists. 'To be devoid of a sense of humour,' thought Archer, was 'the only unpardonable fault in a companion.'[4] 'The way to get on with Archer,' Shaw quickly noticed, 'was to amuse him: to argue with him was dangerous.'[5]

There was, though, one vital difference between them. For all his literary and political hopes, Shaw had nothing to show for himself.

Archer had already begun to make his mark. His plays had been produced, he had written newspaper theatre criticism and the previous year had published his first book.

His Italian journey had not been wholly devoted to rest and romance. Most of the time he spent wrapped in his rug at Signor Davide's, he was reading plays and writing *English Dramatists of Today*, an assessment of contemporary writing. Henry Bond transported the manuscript back to England and delivered it to H. L. Braekstad. He was the Trondheim bookseller who sold Gosse a copy of Ibsen's *Digte*, and was now in London, working as a journalist and Norwegian specialist. Braekstad was acting as Archer's unofficial literary agent. 'The *aggressive* tone of the book constitutes its very *raison d'être*,'⁶ Archer hastily assured him. Braekstad placed it with Sampson Low who, on the basis of shared expenses and profits, published the book in the autumn.

English Dramatists of Today takes its impetus from both 'Will the Drama Revive?', the article which Archer had published in the *St James's Magazine*, and the critic Matthew Arnold who, following the Comédie-Française's London season, urged that a similar state-subsidized theatre be founded in England. 'The theatre is irresistible; organise the theatre!'⁷ he demanded. In time, this would become the rallying call for the entire National Theatre movement. Arnold's urgency thrilled Archer. 'I sometimes dream of a "great Perhaps" in the shape of an Endowed Theatre,' he agreed.

However, Archer realized that an Endowed or National Theatre, funded either privately or by the state, was a long way from becoming a reality. He pointed out that no English play for over a century, since the days of Sheridan, had been thought of as literature and therefore the first requirement was the creation of a modern drama fit for a National Theatre stage. At the moment, an unholy alliance of managers, critics, official censorship and audiences was smothering any hope of a drama of serious ideas with a blanket of sensational melodrama and comedy diluted from the French. If 'the drama of furniture and firearms' was really going to be bundled into the wings and replaced by plays of 'at least an undercurrent of seriousness', this alliance must be broken. If Victorien Sardou, Eugène Labiche, Eugène Scribe and Emile Augier were to be displaced as authors for the English stage, new opportunites must be created.

Archer argued that, for this to happen, the audience must be educated to expect higher standards and be broadened to include the range of social classes. At present, the theatre was 'supported by the most

Philistine section of the middle class, and by the worse than Philistine, the utterly frivolous section of the upper class'. Archer wanted to encourage plays relating to 'some moral, social, political – may I add religious? – topic of the day, or better still of all time'. But in a theatre in which even the audience had 'no taste whatever' a serious play, especially one 'to whose theme the word "unpleasant" might be applied', stood not the remotest chance of survival. The theatre had also to be liberated from the 'injustice, illogicity and futility' of official censorship. In Archer's eyes, the Examiner of Plays was as culpable as the managers, critics and audiences, people who 'talk of the theatre as an instrument of culture, but . . . take very good care it shall be nothing of the sort'.

It was easy enough to demand that the stage be cleared of 'frivolous irrelevance',[8] but far more difficult to achieve. Dramatists themselves appeared to live in fear of the managerial-critical-audience alliance. 'I have long itched to launch my thunderbolt,' whimpered Grundy, still protesting that managers prevented him writing seriously, 'but in my position I daren't. I have to be content with launching it at my wife.'[9] Poor Mrs Grundy; she must have endured much. It was simple for Archer in his book to compile a list of 'Playwrights of Yesterday', whose work might safely be relegated to the past, authors such as Bulwer-Lytton, T. W. Robertson (whose *Caste*, in the light of Ibsen, he now thought 'beneath contempt'[10]) and Dion Boucicault ('the supreme showman of the Victorian stage'[11]). Yet he was still confronted with the enormous problem of who to suggest might take their place. Most of those eligible for listing as 'Playwrights of Today' were unlikely to become the vanguard of new English realism. They included Alfred, Lord Tennyson; Sydney Grundy; W. S. Gilbert; F. C. Burnand, the old Etonian editor of *Punch* and prodigious author of burlesque and farce; and H. J. Byron, whose enormously popular comedy, *Our Boys*, he comprehensively ridiculed. It appeared to Archer that the only hope for the future lay in the little-known Henry Arthur Jones and Arthur Wing Pinero.

In 1882, Jones was thirty-one. He was a product of the non-conformist, provincial lower middle class, the son of tenant farmers in Buckinghamshire, a family in which 'dancing, card-playing and theatre-going were vices'.[12] He had left school at twelve to work in an uncle's drapery shop in Ramsgate, leaving six years later for London and life as a commercial traveller. Bright-eyed, bearded and spruce (as befits a man in the drapery trade), Jones discovered a liking for the theatre in London and began writing, learning structure and technique from the popular plays of the day. 'I used to hurry from the City almost every evening at six to see the same successful play for perhaps a dozen times, till I could take its mechanism to pieces,'[13] he remembered.

Having had several one-act plays staged in the provinces and *A Clerical Error*, a comedy, in London, Jones decided to become a full-time playwright in 1879. Three years later in *English Dramatists of Today*, on the meagre evidence of the 'commonplace' *A Clerical Error*, another comedy, *An Old Master*, and the melodrama, *His Wife*, Archer pronounced that Jones had 'done enough to establish for his future efforts a fair claim to respectful attention'.[14]

Jones had no connection with the theatre other than as a playwright, but Pinero, while writing, was also working as an actor and would do so until 1884. The son of a solicitor of Jewish-Portuguese origin, Pinero was born in Islington in 1855. He had matured into a clean-shaven, clear-featured, dark-browed young man, and would later be immediately recognizable by his bald, egg-shaped head, apparently incessant cigarette-smoking, and his habit of invariably wearing gloves. He had a rather sombre appearance. At his father's insistence, he had reluctantly followed him into the legal profession. As a clerk at a firm in Lincoln's Inn Fields, he began writing plays and sending them to managers, usually adding a covering note written on the company's headed notepaper, thinking it might create an air of authority. It did not. Neither did it impress his employer who one day inadvertently opened a letter reading: 'Dear Sir, Your stuff is no earthly use to me. For God's sake fetch it away as soon as possible.'[15] When his father died in 1874, Pinero was freed of his family obligations. The solicitors did not attempt to dissuade him when he left for the stage. He landed a job as a 'general utility', playing walk-on parts at the Theatre Royal, Edinburgh, during the years Archer was a student, but the two men did not meet.

In London, Pinero acted with Irving and continued with his writing, but by the time Archer left for Italy, only a handful of curtain-raisers and two full-length comedies, *The Money-Spinner* and *Imprudence*, had been produced. But in December 1881, *The Squire*, Pinero's first tentative attempt at serious drama, opened at the St James's Theatre off Piccadilly.

The theme was daring for its time, involving a young woman, Kate Verity, who rejects her lover, Gilbert Hythe, and secretly marries Lieutenant Thorndike whose child she is bearing, only to discover that his former wife, whom they thought dead, is still alive. Archer read a script, but Grundy, who saw the production and loathed it, reported with characteristic venom to Archer in Rome that Kate was 'the most brutal Philistine bitch in literature'.[16] Archer thought much of it sentimental and parts 'unutterably feeble', but nevertheless declared in his book that it was 'a great advance' on Pinero's previous work and predicted that here was 'a playwright of genuine talent, whose mature work will take a prominent and honourable place upon the stage in coming years'.[17]

Archer was taking an enormous risk in supporting Jones and Pinero, but on 16 November, within days of *English Dramatists of Today* reaching the bookshops, *The Silver King* opened at the Princess's Theatre in Oxford Street and Jones stepped into the front rank of English playwrights. Written (largely by Jones) in collaboration with Henry Herman, the story seems designed for melodrama on the grandest scale. Wilfred Denver, falsely accused of murder and pursued by both the police and the coolly villainous 'Spider', escapes London for the American West where he makes his fortune in the silver mines. A rich man, he returns to England to redeem himself and his family. But in its depiction of Denver as a flawed character, seduced by alcohol and the low-life, the foggy London underworld of petty criminals and the contrasting atmosphere of the Bromley middle-class villa-world of The Spider, *The Silver King* has the intermittent feel of observed real life.

The play settled in at the Princess's for a long run. In calling it 'the best of modern English melodramas'[18] Archer recognized that Jones and Herman were attempting a development from conventional melodrama as he defined it: 'illogical tragedy, in which the causes and effects are systematically disproportionate, and the hero is the plaything of special providences'.[19] He did, though, object to the 'idiot episode'[20] in which Denver reads in a newspaper that the train on which he is supposed to be escaping from detectives has crashed and burst into flames, killing all the passengers. He then thanks God for his escape. At this point, remarked Archer, the play's tenuous hold on real life is swept irrecoverably aside by a tide of melodramatics.

His confidence in Pinero took longer to be justified, and when *The Magistrate*, the first of his popular comedies, opened at the Royal Court Theatre in 1885, Archer admitted it lacked 'snap', but insisted it was 'one of the ablest and funniest plays . . . in our modern repertory'.[21] His faith was vindicated emphatically in 1893 when, with *The Second Mrs Tanqueray*, Pinero inaugurated the English 'problem play'. But the most important point about both *The Silver King* and *The Magistrate* for Archer, was that both were wholly original plays and relied on no imported material. With remarkable intuition and considerable luck, he had succeeded in identifying at the beginning of the decade the two playwrights who were to become the most influential English dramatists of the next fifteen years.

Both Jones and Pinero found Archer's early support crucial, although neither lived up to his expectations nor wholeheartedly committed themselves to Archer's campaign for realism. This precluded their membership of his select inner circle, but Archer and Pinero in particular became close friends. 'You are the only critic who has unvaryingly treated me with common fairness,' Pinero told him in 1923. 'But for you, I honestly believe I couldn't have managed to keep my end up.'[22]

Writing *English Dramatists of Today* sharpened Archer's resolve to be an active as well as a reactive theatre critic. He still thought his contemporaries to have 'no fundamental principles' and accused them of writing from 'considerations of personal friendship and enmity towards authors, managers and actors'. A new theatre, he noted, would only be brought about by a new criticism, one that encouraged authors to write seriously and educated a public to appreciate their work. 'I am convinced the "coming critic" ... must certainly precede the "coming dramatist," '[23] he wrote. This, in effect, was an advertisement for himself.

It worked. The newspaper reviews of the book were cautious ('a very thoughtful if sometimes too severe a critic,'[24] demurred *The Academy*), but when Archer wrote to Edmund Yates at *The World* proposing an article on Ibsen, he received the reply that 'Ibsen won't do, but if I'm addressing the author of *English Dramatists of Today* – you will.'[25]

Yates was the son of a versatile actor and one-time manager of the Adelphi Theatre in The Strand. A vigorous, imposing man in his early fifties, he was something of a gossip, had written theatre criticism, collaborated on several farces and produced a series of three-volume novels. He had known Dickens, and had a celebrated argument with Thackeray which resulted in his expulsion from the Garrick Club. He founded *The World* in 1874. Most sixpenny weekly papers were published on Saturdays, but Yates decided to publish every Wednesday instead, which meant that *The World* had plenty of visibility on W. H. Smith's expanding empire of railway station bookstalls. His 'Journal for Men and Women' became a success, with theatre, music and literary columns placed either side of several pages of social chit-chat and political speculation written by Yates himself in the guise of 'Atlas'.

In response to the summons, Archer arrived at *The World* office in Covent Garden on 21 February 1884, when Yates told him he was looking for a drama critic to succeed Dutton Cook and produce a light-hearted commentary on the West End theatre. Archer 'told him plainly that wasn't my line of business',[26] but finally accepted the offer of a three-month trial and a retainer of three guineas a week. He published his first *World* piece on 5 March, starting as he meant to continue, by writing lively but serious criticism, savaging a Shakespearian actor acclaimed as the equal of Irving. Having shivered for two nights in the draughty stalls at Covent Garden watching Tommaso Salvini's Italian company in *Othello* and the comparatively rarely-performed *King Lear*, Archer began his reign by acidly observing that 'One is inclined to pity Salvini, with his company of incompetents and his threadbare scenery . . .'[27] After his three-month trial was over, Yates asked him to stay on. In the event, Archer stayed for twenty-one years, but for ten of those at a salary of three guineas a week, because he could never find the right moment to ask for more. Signing his 'The Theatre' column with his initials, he became W. A. of *The World* and, as Granville Barker recalled, soon took his place as 'a power in and for the theatre'.[28]

Now he was a true metropolitan, Archer quickly divested himself of other incarnations. Norman Britton appeared no more and E. V. Ward, who had contributed poems to *Progress*, never wrote anything again. After eight years, Archer abruptly ended his collaboration with Dibdin by asking him to return the notes for *Votes for Vogan*, a satire of American politics which he had sent to Liverpool for comment. He had by no means lost 'a certain hankering after the rewards, if not the glories, of the playwright',[29] but had found a collaborator with whom there seemed a greater chance of success: Bernard Shaw.

Both Archer and Shaw were intrigued to discover that each had accumulated a cargo of unused manuscripts. Archer confessed to having written several original plays, while Shaw admitted to being the author of five novels 'of colossal genius, not one of which had yet been published'.[30] His dialogue, explained Shaw, was incomparable. What let him down was construction. Archer eagerly replied that, although unable to write dialogue at all, he was, as it happened, 'a born constructor'. The solution was so obvious it hardly needed saying. They must immediately collaborate upon a play, Archer supplying the characters and a plot which Shaw would then flesh out with his unsurpassable dialogue. In his youth, Shaw had written verse plays, but had

stopped once he began writing his novels. Now, at Archer's instigation, he abandoned novels to attempt his first full-length play in
prose.

Archer rifled through the stock of plotlines he kept at Dulwich and
selected one 'vaguely suggested' by *Ceinture Dorée*, Emile Augier's
'twaddling cup-and-saucer comedy', and which he was confident would
work up into something without too much trouble. Their play, he
informed Shaw, was to be called *The Way to a Woman's Heart*, and had
the romantic setting of a hotel garden overlooking the Rhine. There
were two heroines, one sentimental and the other comic. The hero was
to propose to the former, believing her to be the poor niece instead of
the rich daughter of the slum-landlord. He would then 'carry on in the
most heroic fashion, and was ultimately to succeed in throwing the
tainted treasure of his father-in-law, metaphorically speaking, into the
Rhine'.[31] Shaw listened gravely and, on 18 August 1884, sat down at
his desk in the Reading Room, opened his reporter's notebook and
wrote 'The Way to a Woman's Heart' at the top of a clean page. Archer
left him to it.

It seems hypocritical that Archer, who so vociferously attacked the
purveyors of second-hand French comedy, should propose that he and
Shaw invade the London stage with an Augier-inspired play. The
ostensible reason, as with *Australia*, was that it might make them some
much-needed money. But underlying this is the fact that Archer rather
liked melodramas, just as he enjoyed Gilbert and Sullivan and speciality
music hall acts. One of the several paradoxes of his nature was that he
was both a realist and almost absurdly romantic. He fought for realism
to become the dominant theatrical form but remained hypnotized by
the romance of the stage. He may also, by recruiting Shaw, have begun
to face the fact that he simply could not write the kind of play he
advocated in print. Perhaps Shaw might shovel some Fabian ballast into
a Rhineland fantasy.

Meanwhile, Archer's romance with Frances, sustained by almost
daily correspondence while she was abroad, resumed now she was in
London, on walks in the parks, tours around the galleries, occasional
dances and theatre outings. Shaw met her by chance rather than design.
One overcast day while he was walking down New Oxford Street on his
way to the British Museum, he saw Archer striding purposefully towards
him 'looking much more momentous than usual'. His impression that
Archer had grown even taller was due to his being accompanied by a
diminutive woman clinging to his arm and almost breaking into a run in

an effort to keep pace with him. This was Frances. Shaw observed that she had 'a small, comely face, winsome and ready to smile when not actually smiling . . . I feared the worst'. Sure enough, 'I was immediately introduced to the lady as his selection for the destiny of being Mrs Archer.'

They chatted briefly and as he watched them go on their way, Shaw reflected that if the couple had anything in common it was that neither was the person they appeared to be. Frances seemed 'dainty, unassuming, clinging', but really, he surmised, she was 'a woman of independent character, great decision and pertinacity, and considerable physical hardihood'.[32]

Shaw was not invited to their wedding, simply because Archer did not want any guests. He booked Kensington Register Office and immediately set about preventing the appearance of any well-wishers, including Dibdin. 'I need not excuse myself for not inviting you to the "waddin"', he wrote, concealing his brusqueness by mimicking a broad Scots accent, 'for there is to be none – that is to say no breakfast or cake or humbug . . .'[33] He was marginally more forthcoming to Bond: 'It is to be a civil marriage without the smallest attempt at festivity (only our two fathers and my sister present in all probability) and we are going to settle down at once in our rooms.'

So, on 23 October 1884, Thomas Archer, now sixty-one and retired, one of his daughters, possibly Julia, and John Trickett, apparently the lone representatives of the two families, watched as Archer and Frances were married. Even Archer's brother Charles, was absent. He had become an officer in the army and within a few months would arrive in India as a member of the Indian Staff Corps, and make his career there in the service of the Empire. There seems to be no evidence why neither Archer's nor Frances's mother attended the wedding, if, indeed, they did not, but the two families do not appear to have become friends nor had anything much to do with each other. Perhaps Archer entered his profession in the register as 'Barrister at Law' in yet another attempt to mollify his family. It was a perfunctory ceremony, after which husband and wife retreated to the rooms they had rented at 2 Queen Square Place, a small turning off Queen Square in Bloomsbury. There was no honeymoon as 'we have had more than one honeymoon already, under pleasanter circumstances than an English October'.[34] Instead, they set out their books, put up their pictures, sat down to tea using the Danish tea-set which Bond had given them, and began married life.

*

According to Shaw, 'the marriage seemed a great success. Mrs Archer fitted herself into the simple and frugal life of her husband quite naturally.'[35] This rather surprised him as he had warned Archer against marrying on the grounds that, as far as his literary future was concerned, he would be forced to sacrifice quality to income. But seeing no immediate deterioration, Shaw returned to his own affairs.

The Way to a Woman's Heart which, in deference to their shared passion for Wagner, they soon called *Rheingold*, and then anglicized to *Rhinegold*, was progressing quickly. By mid-November, Shaw had drafted the first two acts and twenty-three lines of the third when he claimed that he had exhausted Archer's plot and asked him for more. Explaining that his plot already constitued 'a rounded and perfect organic whole', Archer demanded that Shaw decipher his shorthand script and read what he had written. But the process was so 'lingering and painful'[36] that he pleaded with him to stop.

Shaw's problem with *Rhinegold* was one of form. Each time he settled down to write, it seemed increasingly evident that a French comedy, however strengthened, was far too weak a springboard for an incisive Fabian analysis of the iniquities of slum-landlordism. The play, and the collaboration, collapsed.

However, still determined to hoist Shaw on to some sort of financial footing and if possible launch him upon the world, Archer decided upon a change of tactics. Visiting his impoverished friend at the new lodgings he shared with his mother at 36 Osnaburgh Street, Archer had looked on in dismay as he heated his dinner of thick, glue-like porridge over a sputtering gas fire. He resolved to rescue Shaw from poverty by thrusting him into paid journalism. In the autumn of 1884, he harnessed Shaw's passion for music to freelance writing for the *Magazine of Music*. At the beginning of 1885, when Archer was approached by an Irishman, Edwin Palmer, to become a founder-contributor to his *Dramatic Review*, he had Shaw recruited as well. As Archer was reviewing books for the *Pall Mall Gazette*, and would do so occasionally for the next decade, he infiltrated Shaw into the paper's critical ranks, which already included Oscar Wilde. Like Shaw, Wilde was a Dubliner, although from well-to-do Merrion Square, a world away from Synge Street, and now lived with his wife, Constance, at Tite Street in Chelsea, all red brick and white stucco and a far cry from Osnaburgh Street. Meanwhile, Archer offered to lend Shaw money to tide him over, which he could ill afford to do, charging him 'the same rate of interest as I get at the bank – viz *nil*'.[37]

As he organized Shaw professionally, so Archer introduced him socially, to the Radfords, Clementina Black, Henry Arthur Jones (whom Archer decided was a man of 'flabby intellect, but no fool'[38]), and Robert Lowe, who had moved from Edinburgh to London. Married, fatter, balder, and still an insurance agent longing to write theatre journalism, Lowe would also benefit from Archer's generosity, covering for him in *The World* when he was away. As for Shaw, 'it was the easiest thing in the world to get him work,' remarked Archer, 'because whatever he did was brilliant'.[39] As Shaw obeyed Archer's directions and applied himself to his journalism, he 'suddenly began to make money: £117 in the first year'.[40]

It was not long before Archer was glad of Shaw's ability to turn his hand to more or less anything. During November 1885, the art critic of *The World* suddenly left and Yates coerced Archer into writing the exhibition reviews as well as the theatre column. When he protested that he knew nothing about painting, Yates retorted that ignorance had never impeded a critic before. In fact, Archer regularly visited galleries, particularly the Grosvenor where Whistler exhibited and Wilde was often to be seen, but he was still thankful that Shaw accompanied him on his rounds. 'He didn't know much more about painting than I,' wrote Archer, 'but he thought he did, and that was the main point.'[41]

Together they visited the Millais exhibition at the Grosvenor, stood before old masters at the Royal Academy and stalked after the moderns in Old Bond Street. Although he wrote the weekly reviews, Archer wanted Shaw to be paid his share and in December sent him a cheque for one pound, six shillings and eightpence. Shaw returned it by the next post. 'My moral ground is this,' he declared. 'If you are a competent critic you do not need my assistance. If you are not competent, you are imposing upon Yates, and I cannot be a party to a fraud. This, I hope, is conclusive.' Sensing an entertaining argument might be looming, he added, 'If not, I can easily find a fresh position equally elevated and unexpungable.'[42]

Archer took up the challenge, shoving the cheque into another envelope and contending that: 'Yates does not want a competent critic of art; what he wants is a man competent to write about art in a particular fashion, and that, with your help, I apparently am.'[43] Once again, the cheque bounced back, Shaw threatening that 'if you re-re-return it, I will re-re-re-return it again.'[44] From his socialist high ground, he informed Archer that, as he did not regard ideas as personal property, he could accept no payment for giving them voice. Archer was being paid not for ideas but for the labour of putting them on to paper, whether they were his own or not.

Archer's solution to this, their first and enjoyable postal tournament (there were to be many more and several far less good-natured), was to persuade Yates that the competent art critic was not himself but Shaw. Yates agreed and took him on. Shaw stayed for four years before handing on the post to the talented and formidable Lady Colin Campbell. Meanwhile, under his own steam, Shaw surfaced as Corno di Bassetto, the music critic for *The Star*, and when, in 1889, Yates found himself in need of a music critic, Archer 'secured it for Shaw, by the simple process of telling Yates the truth: namely that he was at once the most competent and the most brilliant writer on music then living in England'.[45]

Frances was now pregnant. In the summer of 1885, she and Archer left Queen Square Place and moved a few blocks to the east to 16 John Street, a neat little street of three-storey terraces. Number 16 was the former home of John Oxenford, the adaptor of *East Lynne* and a former drama critic of *The Times*. His ghost reputedly haunted the rooms, but in spite of having denounced his adaptation, Archer did not report any spectral vengeance. They had three rooms on the second floor and three on the top ('damage £75 per annum'[46]) and here, on 2 August, Frances gave birth to a son. Three weeks later, Archer issued Dibdin with a progress report. 'Frances and baby are both getting on capitally, the latter especially, though even maternal imagination can scarcely make a beauty of him.'[47] They named him Thomas after his paternal grandfather, and called him Tom.

Archer allowed neither marriage nor fatherhood to encroach upon his independence or disrupt his routine. While Frances managed the house, Tom's nurse and the visiting cook and housekeeper, he spent his mornings writing, either in his study or the British Museum. Each week, he wrote his review for *The World*, usually of about two thousand words. Most weeks (until the end of the year when Palmer went bankrupt) he completed an article for *The Dramatic Review*. He argued that French expressions such as 'ensemble' should be treated as English and no longer be written in italics, and proposed the founding of a society to publish modern plays. He called for an end to the convention that formal evening dress be worn in the stalls, boxes and dress circle of theatres, heading off the objection that a gentleman always dressed for dinner and the theatre by suggesting that, in London in the mid-eighties, 'Is it not nearer the truth that most men have no dinner to dress for?'[48]

There were book reviews to write for the *Pall Mall Gazette*, sometimes 'Occasional Notes' to be sent up to the *Edinburgh Evening News*, pieces for *The Theatre* magazine and as many other articles as he could place. He wrote on Norwegian life for the Liberal *Fortnightly Review*, on Robert Louis Stevenson for *Time* and published a short story in *Unwin's Annual*. The freelancer's life, he discovered, is one of chasing, chivvying, and long, tiring hours made all the more so if one's editor is in jail: in the wake of Mortimer and Foote, both Yates (convicted of criminal libel), and W. T. Stead at the *Pall Mall Gazette* (as a result of bad advice, found technically guilty of abduction while researching his sensational series on child prostitution) served short prison terms.

Guests might stay at John Street, but Archer was as impervious to them as to Frances and Tom. '. . . meals are on the table at certain hours – if you turn up, good and well, if you don't, good and well also'.[49] Although Archer was not vegetarian, Shaw was and they often lunched together at a cheap vegetarian restaurant, perhaps The Wheatsheaf off Rathbone Place or The Porridge Bowl in Holborn. In the afternoon, there was more writing, editors to see, proofs to check or a matinee to attend. Tea at John Street was more or less open house. Shaw came several times a week and they might be joined by Braekstad, Jones or Lowe.

In the evening, there was usually the theatre with Shaw. Over supper afterwards, they would discuss the play, Archer's last *World* review or Shaw's performance as speaker at one of the socialist meetings to which Archer occasionally accompanied him. He thought the debating societies 'an infinitude of twaddle' and preferred watching Shaw speaking from a public platform, on 'The Unemployed' at Hoxton, or 'Driving Capital out of the Country' at Hatton Walk. His lecturing 'lacked the warmth, the emotional thrill, without which there can be no eloquence',[50] but Archer thoroughly enjoyed watching him subdue hecklers with almost the speed and wit of a music hall comic. They made a vivid pair, Archer and Shaw, Archer neatly and correctly dressed, his hair vigorously brushed back and moustache combed and trained, and Shaw, in the rust-red stockinette Jaeger suit which matched his untamed hair and beard. Archer's disguise was his apparent conservatism; Shaw's his evident eccentricity.

Neither did the advent of family life cause Archer to abandon his habit of suddenly taking off on his travels whenever he could afford it.

As soon as they had celebrated Tom's first birthday, he installed Lowe at his desk at *The World* and disappeared across the Channel. It was the first time he had been abroad for three years. He headed for Paris, where he stayed a week, playing tennis and visiting the Comédie-Française. Then, joined by Henry Norman, a member of the editorial staff of the *Pall Mall Gazette*, he left for Geneva, where the recently retired Squire Bancroft challenged him to exhausting swimming contests in the lake. In September, they were in Italy and on the 20th, back in England. 'My wife met me at Folkestone at 4am on Tuesday, having come down to Sandgate with baby, who chose the opportunity of my absence to have an attack of English cholera or aggravated diahorrea,' he told Dibdin. 'Sum total, a very jolly four weeks which cost me about £35 – not dear at the money.'[51]

During the past couple of years, Archer had written enough theatrical articles for various journals from which to make a selection as a sequel to *English Dramatists of Today*. He revised nine, added an introduction, and published them in 1886 under the title *About the Theatre*. The book represents a compendium of his emerging obsessions and campaigns: critical ethics, the abolition of censorship, and the need for a National Theatre and a new repertoire.

It was not the job of a critic, he argued, to reflect the views of his editor, be a salesman for an actor-manager, or to be either a moral or political arbiter. The critic must be 'under no obligation to any one',[52] get to know as much as possible about the way the theatre worked, and be an open-minded judge of dramatic merit. 'If a play is amoral and dull, let him attack it because it is dull,'[53] he advised. His attack, or praise, must be informed and informative, written with honesty, energy, style and, most importantly, 'enthusiasm for the best interests of the English stage'.[54]

As newspaper theatre criticism was by and large a part-time occupation for amateurs, a resort of failed writers or an inconvenience for tired and irritable reporters, the best interests of the stage were often in fairly short supply. Playwrights could expect little in the way of a considered or consistent response to their work. It was part of Archer's achievement that, together with the obsessively Conservative Clement Scott at *The Daily Telegraph*, and A. B. Walkley, from 1888 the Liberal critic at *The Star*, he transformed theatre criticism into a profession with integrity at the top.

Most of the managers, such as Irving at the Lyceum or Beerbohm

Tree at the Comedy, were scrupulously honest in their relations with critics. But this was a time when susceptible critics might be intimidated or manipulated by devious managers, and Archer quickly earned a reputation for incorruptibility. During the first night interval, when managers anxious for good notices served chicken and champagne to critics in their private offices, Archer could be found sitting isolated in the stalls or wandering about the foyer. There were other, more subtle bribes. If a critic was known to have written a play, a cunning manager might ask to read it, praise it, murmur about a possible staging and perhaps even offer an advance of royalties. If the critic bit the bait, the manager put the script in the drawer and sat back, expecting effusive notices for his productions. Alternatively, he might ask a critic to advise on a translation and offer a fee for doing so, the translation itself never being mentioned again. As far as Shaw knew, nobody ever tried to bribe Archer. 'His integrity [as a critic] was unassailed because it was so obviously impregnable,'[55] he wrote.

Archer's concerted attack upon censorship began in 1886, when the Lord Chamberlain, on the recommendation of E. F. Smyth Pigott, the Examiner of Plays, prohibited a public performance licence for Shelley's verse drama, *The Cenci*. The office of the Lord Chamberlain had monitored theatrical entertainment since the late fifteenth century. But since 1737, when the post of Examiner of Plays was created, the Lord Chamberlain had statutory powers to forbid the production of any play 'whenever he shall be of the opinion that it is fitting for the preservation of good manners, decorum, or of the public peace so to do'.[56] He was not required to give any reason for his decision, nor was any appeal permitted.

The result of *The Cenci* banning was that the Shelley Society held a single private performance of the play at the Grand Theatre, Islington, on 7 May. As no money or tickets changed hands, this technically constituted a meeting of the society rather than a theatrical event, and established a loophole through which much would later pass. Archer thought that the play, set in the sixteenth century and dealing with incest and atheism, so negligible that in the third of the play's five acts, he gave up and closed his eyes. Shaw, sitting next to him, claimed that this time, instead of napping, Archer actually drifted off into a deep sleep, for he suddenly 'fell forward flat on his nose with a tremendous noise, leaving a dent on the floor of the theatre which may still be seen by curious visitors'.[57] Afterwards, Archer protested that staying awake for even three acts of *The Cenci* was a considerable achievement, but in print persisted that 'the English nation should be allowed to judge for itself as to whether the works of its great poets are fit or unfit for the stage'.

As a palpably bad play, *The Cenci* made a poor weapon for Archer's armoury. But for him, the real point was that unless state censorship was itself abolished, melodramas and comedies the Examiner had approved, relying upon sexual innuendo, a coy suggestiveness Archer thought near-pornographic, would continue to fill the theatres while plays by Ibsen and perhaps by Jones and Pinero, might never reach the stage. '. . . to say that he [Pigott] errs, frequently and ludicrously, is to say that he is mortal,' he wrote, 'and if he has erred ludicrously in the past, may he not err destructively in the future?'[58]

Yet the censor was fully supported by the managers. Moreover, Irving believed that the theatre should pay as a business before it had any right to flourish as an art. This idea of the theatre as a market-place, governed by 'supply and demand, the great "twin-Brethren" of modern mythology'[59] was anathema to Archer. But he was becoming an astute enough politician in his lobbying for a National Theatre to adapt his tactics to appeal to whomever he was addressing. In some quarters, he called for a state-funded theatre. In others, to appease the Conservatives (then in government and led by the Marquess of Salisbury), and to whom the word 'National' implied socialist state-control, he appealed to private enterprise, rich industrialists and the big-hearted patriotism of old money. 'Can we not, in short, conceive of a self-supporting National Theatre?'

This article, 'The Stage of Greater Britain', originally published in the Conservative *National Review*, comprises Archer's first substantial outline of his vision of a National Theatre. It was to be National in name but international in practice, as equivalent theatres would be built in London, New York and Chicago. Each would be equipped with extensive technical facilities and wardrobe departments, produce their own plays and receive productions from the others. The National Theatres would also have a large and fully-trained resident acting company, in the hope that the 'mechanical mimicry' he endured almost every time he went to the theatre might become a thing of the past.

Archer's National Theatre repertoire would be founded upon properly-restored Shakespeare, with the forgotten and less familiar plays being retrieved and the entire works being regularly performed and reassessed. Germany, France and Spain could be represented by Goethe, Molière and Calderón, and prominence should be given to new English and American plays. Cradled by the classical tradition and protected from the ruthless demands of commerce, contemporary English dramatists, he suggested, might then write plays combining 'technical skill with a serious "criticism of life" '.

The dominant form of the modern repertoire would be realism. Archer defined this not as an attempt by the dramatist to photograph life and present it in its entirety upon the stage, but to observe life and select moments from it in order to present a complex, essential truth within a dramatic framework. In 'Are We Advancing?' the introductory essay to *About the Theatre*, he observed that as burlesque appeared to be leaving the theatre for a new life in the music halls, there were signs that one or two dramatists were 'groping [their] way towards a drama of observation' and that 'on the whole, WE ARE ADVANCING'.[60]

This was written much more in hope than conviction, for even he had to admit there was precious little evidence to go on. 'The average English playwright,' he wrote elsewhere, '. . . is infirm of purpose and judgement.'[61] A case in point was George Sims. Four years earlier, Archer had identified him as a 'playwright of today'. Knowing that he was interested in the conditions of the working classes, Archer was hoping that he might produce a realistic drama of life in the docklands, the coal industry or the Westminster slums. But when Sims' *The Last Chance* opened at the Adelphi in April 1885, Archer realized within minutes that it was a lost chance, for instead of embarking upon 'the road of observation and nature', Sims had chosen 'the facile descent'[62] into melodrama.

It was a debilitating struggle and nobody stepped forward to support Archer in this or any other of his battles. He fought alone. But his increasingly provocative views were beginning to incite a backlash, particularly from melodramatists whose work he continually attacked. Grundy, who felt rejected by a maverick former friend, angrily scribbled 'No "Endowed Theatre"! No, damn it, no!'[63] across the bottom of a private letter to Archer. Now, he protested on behalf of Sims, bitterly informing Archer in the pages of *The Theatre* that 'It is not the paramount duty of every man to be a reformer, to starve himself to enrich others . . .'[64]

He was also coming under fire from Robert Buchanan, the touchy author of a raft of successful melodramas, including *A Sailor and his Lass* and *Storm-Beaten*. For Archer, Buchanan became a symbol of monumental mediocrity. 'It is inconceivable,' he wrote in *About the Theatre*, 'that he should be unaware of the crudity of his dramatic work,' demonstrating as it did 'a cynical contempt for his audiences'. Buchanan, concluded Archer, revealing the glinting seam of his puritan inheritance, was guilty of 'the most unpardonable sin a craftsman can commit – that of not doing his best'.[65]

Like Grundy, Buchanan was a highly volatile man addicted to writing open letters to the press. He was also a well-informed theatrical gossip and seems a likely author of the letter signed 'Inquisitor' which appeared in *The Era* on 3 July 1886, immediately following publication of Archer's book. 'Inquisitor' knew enough about the contents of Archer's cupboard to rattle a few skeletons and imply that his hostility was the result of his own failure as a playwright. Had he not written 'a gloomy adaptation of Ibsen?'[66] And might the W. A. who so loftily scorned melodrama not be one half of the mysterious W. A. and A. G. Stanley, the authors of *Australia*? And was he not also the author of other plays, rejected by successive London managements?

The letter stung Archer into a quick response. He had 'translated rather than adapted' *Quicksands*, he replied tartly, but after six years, admitted that it had been a 'melancholy performance'. But the fact that *Australia* was 'the feeblest play ever seen in the City-road' surely entitled him to be 'an authority on bad melodramas'. Agreeing that he was the author of several unperformed plays, he claimed that he had gathered them together, burned them all and 'strewed their dishonoured ashes to the winds'.[67] Nothing remained.

Archer's exasperation with his playwriting was compounded by his apparent failure to instigate a new movement in the theatre. Even though a small flame of interest in Ibsen had begun to flicker, there was no indication a fire might result. Then, in December 1882, he was sent two books to review for *The Academy*. One was a copy of *En folkefiende*, (*An Enemy of the People*) Ibsen's new play and the first since *Gengangere*, which was published as usual in Copenhagen.

En folkefiende is set in a small Norwegian town and tells the story of Dr Stockmann, a medical officer who discovers the water supply to the spa baths on which the town's economy depends, is contaminated. When he speaks out, he is acclaimed as a public benefactor, but when it emerges that the baths will have to be closed for several years, with a catastrophic consequence for local employment, he is vilified as an enemy of the people. The analogy between Stockmann and Ibsen himself, vilified after the publication of *Gengangere* for speaking the truth as he saw it, was evident to Archer who nevertheless soothed the sensibilities of *Academy* readers by assuring them the new play was 'not so startling as its predecessor' and contained 'no physical horror.' Stockmann, he predicted, 'will take his place among the most masterly' of Ibsen's creations.

The second volume in the post from *The Academy* was a translation into English of Ibsen's 1879 play, *Et dukkehjem* (*A Doll's House*) by Henrietta Frances Lord, and published in London. Like Catherine Ray, Henrietta Frances Lord was one of Ibsen's few British admirers and an enthusiastic but unfortunately inferior translator. A London dressmaker who had visited and loved Scandinavia, she had spent the past two years at home in Lambeth Road, stooped over her sewing, nursing her aged father and fondly recalling her holiday as she worked at her translation. Perhaps, like Nora at the end of the play, she longed for her freedom. Hers was the second translation of *Et dukkehjem* into English and with a plummeting heart Archer saw that, like T. Weber before her, she had entitled it *Nora*. The author was represented as Henry Ibsen. Any hope that she might have emulated Ibsen's style was quickly snuffed out. Archer's dismissal of Miss Lord's labour of love was swift and comprehensive. She failed to recreate 'the crispness and spontaneity of the dialogue' because she had 'neither a perfect knowledge of Norwegian nor a thorough mastery of English.'[68] His guess that instead of working from the original, she had used an inferior Swedish translation, provoked an injured response from Miss Lord the following week. She had indeed translated the play from the original, she said, and would 'rejoice'[69] to see it performed.

The world premiere of *Et dukkehjem* had taken place three years previously in Copenhagen, when its portrayal of a woman renouncing her marriage vows, her home and her family, created a sensation. Nora, the leading character, is married to Torvald Helmer, the newly-created manager of a bank in Christiana. They have three children. Some time before the beginning of the play, the family travelled to Italy, for Helmer to convalesce after a severe illness. He believes his father-in-law gave them the money to pay for the trip, but in fact Nora borrowed it from Krogstad, a clerk at the bank, and forged her father's signature as security. She has since made regular repayments, but when the play begins, Krogstad, who is aware of the forgery and suspects he might soon be dismissed from his job, threatens to reveal Nora's secret to Helmer if she does not ensure he stays at the bank. She confides in her widowed friend, Mrs Linde, but cannot face her upright, moralistic, patronizing husband. When he does learn the truth, Helmer angrily denounces her lies and hypocrisy and then, in a show of unctuous magnanimity, forgives her. But Nora has opened her eyes to his real nature and the imprisoning charade of their marriage and family life. Taking off her wedding ring, she leaves Helmer and the children. The final sound is the slamming of the door behind her.

It was not long before Archer saw a production of *Et dukkehjem*, but in Norway, not London. On his summer holiday that year, 1883, ('it's for the good of my precious health'[70]) he travelled as far north as the Lofoten Islands, where in August, 'night is ... unknown ... you see the glaciers glowing in the sunset at one moment, you turn around three times, & behold! they are gleaming in the sunrise'.[71] Turning south, he arrived at Tolderodden and spent each breakfast checking the theatre columns in the newspaper. One morning he saw a performance of *Et dukkehjem* advertised at the Christiana Theatre for the next night, 22 September. 'I at once packed my knapsack and started by the *Excellensen* [a coastal steamer] at 4 next morning,' he informed Charles.

The Christiana was the theatre where he had seen *Peer Gynt*, his first Ibsen production. *Et dukkehjem* was an equally unstable affair. Nora was played by 'a debutante from Bergen', and her husband by 'the beauty-man of the theatre'. His Helmer was so 'ludicrously feeble' that Archer wondered why Nora had not left him a long time ago. Archer's time, though, was far from wasted. From his reading of the play, he had concluded that the long scene between Nora and Helmer in the third and final act was 'not only psychologically but dramatically bad'. But when he saw it performed, its 'nervous force' soared above even the inadequate acting to create 'something new and genuine and powerful', a dramatic energy he had never experienced before. He came away convinced that the first two acts of the play, written in the manner of Scribe and Labiche whose work Ibsen had so often directed, were the final two acts of the old-fashioned drama of yesterday. The third, combining character, psychology and action in such a way that each appeared wholly a part of the others, was the first act of a new, invigorating, modern drama. He was more certain than ever of Ibsen's greatness, that 'The old min [sic] knows what he's about.'[72]

On 17 October, he was back in Christiana, this time at the Folke-theater to see the Norwegian premiere of *Gengangere* performed by a Swedish touring company led by a thirty-seven-year-old actor, August Lindberg. He was playing Oswald and had persuaded the renowned Hedvig Winter-Hjelm to emerge from retirement to play Mrs Alving. Archer arrived at the Folketheater early, paid three kroner 'for a capital place in the stalls' and waited impatiently while the house filled ('no music I am happy to say'), and for the curtain to rise.

He thought the set of the Alving home, with its sofa, chairs and table, a large painting on the rear wall and a massive glass backdrop of a conservatory, 'perfectly adequate', but he was dumbfounded to see the actress playing Regina padded out with obviously false breasts. Pastor Manders was 'too tall, bad wig', but things improved with the entrance of Hedvig Winter-Hjelm: 'middle-sized, not too stout, plainly-dressed – fine, intelligent face and fair hair slightly grey', she made Mrs Alving 'sympathetic and ladylike'.

Lindberg's Oswald was, however, a revelation. Archer had never seen a performance like it. 'Before he had been three minutes on the stage I saw it was going to be a masterly piece of playing,' he told Charles. 'The mere time he took it in was admirably conceived – slow, deliberate, dreamy, the manner of a man to whom the world has become unreal.'[73] Lindberg was so determined to achieve as psychologically realistic a performance as possible, that he had visited a Copenhagen hospital to study children certified insane as a result of inherited syphilis. The 'procession of the living dead'[74] he saw there became not only the inspiration of his performance but the cause of recurring nightmares during the weeks he played the role. Sitting in the stalls, Archer noted every aspect of his appearance, his 'short curling black hair and a small black moustache, a very pale face and those blinking, uneven, sort of lysraed [cowering] eyes one so often sees in broken-down debauchees'. He seemed wraithlike, reminiscent of portraits of Edgar Allan Poe.

Despite Lindberg's extraordinary emotional power, the final scene between anguished mother and deteriorating son eluded the actors. 'I don't think they sufficiently recognized that its utter untheatricalness is the very essence of the tragedy,' Archer remarked. 'They were not still enough . . . They relied too much on getting effects out of single speeches, instead of concentrating their effort on grasping the audience at the beginning and keeping what may be called the suppressed horror of the scene at a level height.' Even so, the production was undoubtedly 'a triumph'.[75] That autumn in Christiana, he realized for the first time how great an emotional force Ibsen's plays might achieve on stage, but also how dependent this was upon a new approach to acting and direction.

Although Ibsen was slowly gaining wider attention in Europe and there had even been tentative productions in the United States, 1883 was not a financially successful year for him. He earned the equivalent of £819, over four time less than Henry Arthur Jones who, fresh from the huge success of the long-running *The Silver King*, earned £3398, a considerable sum of money.

The partnership between Jones and Herman had been so successful that they decided to collaborate again, and on 3 March 1884, *Breaking a Butterfly*, yet another version of *Et dukkehjem*, opened at the Prince's Theatre in Coventry Street. Billed as being 'founded on Ibsen's *Nora*', Archer glumly commented that it would be more accurately described as 'founded on the ruins of Ibsen's *Nora*'.[76] Working from 'a rough translation from the German',[77] Jones and Herman conjured from the alchemy of psychological realism something their audiences found far more palatable, a melodramatic story of a frail, frightened wife and her heroic, protective husband. They transferred the action to England and from Nora created Flora, called Flossie by her husband, who became Humphrey Goddard. Krogstad was transformed into Philip Dunkley. The Helmers' children and Mrs Linde had disappeared, to be replaced by Humphrey's mother and sister. When Goddard discovers his wife's duplicity, he instantly shields her, taking the blame for himself. Flora does not, of course, leave her husband and home.

In 'The Theatre' Archer accused Jones and Herman of eradicating 'the supreme bitterness of the heroine's anguish' and tearing out the central moral issue of the play, which was 'a plea for women's rights', an entitlement to independent existence for a woman 'as a responsible member of society'. In making the play acceptable to Victorian standards of honour and respectability and reinforcing the conventional assumptions of marriage, 'they at once made it trivial'.[78] Dispiritingly, it seemed this was the only way to make Ibsen acceptable to a middle- and upper-class audience in a mainstream theatre.

Just over a year later, on 23 March 1885, Archer saw another version of *Et dukkehjem* in a tiny theatre at the School of Dramatic Art in out-of-the-way Argyle Street. Henrietta Frances Lord had been rewarded at last by having *Nora* performed, albeit by an amateur company. The Scribblers gave a single charity performance, ironically in aid of the Society for the Prevention of Cruelty to Children. Archer watched the 'travesty' in a pall of dejection, recalling that the last time he had seen an audience 'so hopelessly bewildered' was eight years previously at the Chinese Theatre in San Francisco. As he trudged home afterwards, he reflected that Ibsen and the English appeared irreconcilable. Ibsen was 'an idealist and we do not understand ideals; he is a moralist and we do not want ethics; worse than all, his morality savours of paradox, and, except in comic opera, we abhor paradox'.[79]

It seemed that Miss Lord's kind of Ibsen was in the ascendancy. In 1885, she published her translation of *Gengangere* as *Ghosts* in *To-day*, a socialist monthly magazine. But apparently convinced that 'Ibsen on the English stage is impossible',[80] Archer himself had made no further attempts at translation by the time he met Ibsen again, two years later, in the summer of 1887. On 24 June, the Archers left for a family holiday in Norway. When he learned that Ibsen was also on vacation at Saeby, on the coast of Jutland, he travelled from Larvik to see him one day near the end of July. At an hotel at Frederikshaven, where he stayed overnight, he met a businessman who agreed to give him a lift to Saeby in his trap. 'It was a delightful drive,' he wrote. 'A perfect summer day, the corn ripe all round, the wild flowers brilliant, the Cattegat dancing in the sunlight . . . at last we rattled over a bridge, past a lovely old watermill, into the quaint old main street of Saeby – one-storey houses, with great high gables, all brightly painted or at the very least white-washed. The moment we were over the bridge, I saw a short, broad figure ahead in an enormously long surtout and a tall hat made of silk looking too small for his immense head. It was Ibsen, evidently on the lookout for me.'

Ibsen was now fifty-nine and Archer thirty. During their conversation that day, Archer questioned him about his working methods, suggesting that the themes for each play must occur to him before the characters and situations. Ibsen admitted there was always a stage when his writing 'might easily turn into an essay as a drama', but insisted the characters soon took control, sometimes so much so that the finished piece bore little resemblance to what he originally intended. 'He writes, and re-writes, scribbles and destroys an enormous amount before he makes the exquisite fair copy he sends to Copenhagen,' Archer recorded. 'As to symbolism, he says that life is full of it, and therefore his plays are full of it.' As he listened to Ibsen talking, propounding the rights of the individual over the majority, it struck him that he was 'essentially a kindred spirit with Shaw – a paradoxist, a sort of Devil's Advocate, who goes about picking holes in every "well-known fact" . . .'[81]

At odd moments during the past three years, both at the British Museum and the new rooms he shared with his mother at 29 Fitzroy Square, Shaw had taken up *Rhinegold* again. On 4 October, he arrived at John Street, and left a parcel. When Archer opened it, he discovered the first two acts of their play, neatly transcribed in longhand. 'They are not supposed to be complete,' read Shaw's accompanying note, 'but they present a series of dialogues in which your idea is prepared and developed . . .' The crucial alteration was that 'my genius has brought the romantic notion which possessed you, into vivid contact with real life'. Knowingly or not, Shaw had put his finger on the flaw which Archer knew impaired his writing. But Shaw repeated he had 'no idea' of how the play should continue. 'Will you proceed either to chuck in the remaining acts, or provide me with a skeleton for them?'[82] he asked.

Two days later, he returned to John Street and read the first act aloud to Archer, after which, 'a long argument ensued, Archer having received it with great contempt . . .'[83] His constant tinkering, complained Archer, had demolished a perfectly usable plot into rubble. 'But this I did not mind,' reflected Shaw, 'as I classed constructed plays with artificial flowers, clockwork mice and the like.' Picking up the script again, he doggedly began to read the second act. This time, Archer appeared to fall asleep. Shaw stopped speaking. As Archer's eyes remained closed, he had little alternative but to pack up his things and leave. Several days later, still bewildered by Archer's behaviour, Shaw related the incident to Henry Arthur Jones, and asked his opinion of it. 'Sleep is a criticism,'[84] replied Jones.

For Archer, the end of *Rhinegold* was the end of a playwriting dream. The world of Ibsen, even of Jones and Pinero, was clearly beyond the range of his pen. Evidently, he was unable to express his emotions clearly and truthfully. This worried him just as much as it concerned him that he felt ill-equipped to write authoritatively about acting in *The World*. Intrigued by the new realist acting which Ibsen's plays demanded, he decided to try and penetrate the mysteries of expressing and controlling emotion. He planned a series of articles, later to be turned into a book, a sequel to Denis Diderot's analysis of acting, *Paradoxe sur le comédien*, which had been published over fifty years previously. His would be a grand pageant of actors and their art from ancient to modern times, inspired by the current debate between Constant-Benoît Coquelin, a comic actor from the Comédie-Française then appearing in London and who maintained that to play the extremes of emotion the actor must remain detached, and Irving, who declared that it was essential for the actor to immerse himself emotionally in a role.

In the guise of 'an amateur psychologist', Archer devised a list of seventeen questions and sent copies to several dramatists, including

Pinero (this resulted in their first meeting), and to leading actors including Beerbohm Tree, Ellen Wallis, Mary Anderson, Geneviève Ward and the Kendals (Mrs Kendal had played Kate Verity in *The Squire* and wept copiously as she burned Thorndike's love letters). 'In moving situations, do tears come into your eyes?' he wanted to know. 'Have you ever played a comic part while labouring under some sorrow or mental depression? If so, have you produced less effect than usual upon your audience?'[85] He asked whether actors 'lived' their roles outside the theatre, and generated a variety of responses broadly supporting the positions of Coquelin and Irving. The resulting articles were detailed and searching but laboured, the work of a man still fearful of his own emotions. As far as the stage was concerned, he concluded that great realist acting comprised a full emotional commitment tempered by a dispassionate technical approach.

At the beginning of 1888, Archer and Frances escaped from a foggier, smokier and more oppressive London winter than usual for a couple of weeks at Monte Carlo. On 30 April, they moved from John Street to more spacious rooms at 26 Gordon Square, a five-storied, terraced house overlooking plane trees in a central garden. Archer's book on acting, *Masks or Faces? A Study in the Psychology of Acting*, was published that autumn. It was 'favourably noticed', he told Dibdin, 'but I have not yet heard of a single person buying it'.[86] At the same time, he was battling his way through writing a biography of William Charles Macready, the famously brawling Shakespearian actor and finest Macbeth of his day, who retired in 1851 ending his many years of diaries with a heartfelt 'Thank God'. It was yet another attempt by a man who had repressed his own emotions to unravel the intricacies of the emotional life.

Intermittently, he returned to Ibsen. Having revised *Quicksands* as *The Pillars of Society*, he had started badgering publishers again and came across one with the formidably literary name of Walter Scott. A man in his early sixties, Scott specialized in monthly shilling volumes of lives of the poets, and agreed to publish three translations of Ibsen into English in his Camelot Classics series. *The Pillars of Society and Other Plays* appeared in the last few weeks of the year. Introduced by Havelock Ellis, a twenty-nine-year-old Ibsen enthusiast and former medical student, the book included *The Pillars of Society* and Archer's translation of *Gengangere* as *Ghosts*, which Ellis described as 'a most careful revision' of Miss Lord's version. This was a show of courtesy, for even Ellis, a line or so later, observed that the translation was 'practically new',[87]

Archer having worked entirely from the original. The volume was completed by a translation of *En folkefiende* as *An Enemy of Society* by Eleanor Marx, who had hyphenated on to her own name the surname of Edward Aveling, the socialist, hopeful dramatist and married rogue with whom she lived, in a forlorn attempt to create the impression she was his wife.

The book sold reasonably well, but had conspicuously failed to establish Ibsen as an irresistible dramatic force when, entirely unexpectedly, Janet Achurch and Charles Charrington, two virtually unknown repertory actors, approached Archer with a startling request. They asked him to prepare a new and accurate translation of *Et dukkehjem*. Moreover, they asked him to help them stage it. It seemed that dreams had not died after all.

4

A New Beginning

A is the ARCHER who booms in the *World*
B is the banner of IBSEN unfurled . . .

(From 'The ABC of Ibsenity',
Punch, 16 May 1891)

Janet Achurch came from a theatrical family, her maternal grandparents, the Achurch Wards, being well-known actors at the Theatre Royal, Manchester. Her mother had died at her birth, leaving Janet to be raised by an impractical and occasionally irascible father, and it was as much to escape home as to acknowledge her theatrical inheritance that she decided upon a life on the stage. In 1883, when she was nineteen, she made her debut in Geneviève Ward's company at the Olympic Theatre in Wych Street, just off The Strand. Within two years she had married an unknown playwright, St Aubyn Miller, and joined the touring F. R. Benson Company to play leading Shakespearian roles.

Frank Benson was twenty-five. He was an impetuous man with a mass of thick, dark hair, who had run his Shakespearian Company for two years, leaping into the breach after the previous manager absconded with the profits. A rumour that he was tenuously related to Edward Benson, the Archbishop of Canterbury, was untrue, but he was grateful for the air of mild respectability it gave him. An athletic but unnervingly erratic actor, members of his company were used to seeing him fail on Monday, score a remarkable success on Tuesday and revert to indifference on Wednesday. He ranted and roared his way through the lines but his productions had zest and his stage fights were thrillingly realistic. Unreliable in performance but unshakable in his conviction that audiences needed, indeed craved, Shakespeare, Benson valiantly marched his company up and down the country for the next thirty-three years, playing annual seasons at Stratford-upon-Avon from 1886 until his retirement in 1918. As he did so, he introduced thousands of actors and audiences to Shakespeare. By employing Janet Achurch, he also introduced her to Charles Charrington Martin, a quizzical-looking Irishman and fellow Bensonian actor in his mid-twenties, who dropped his surname and became her second husband.

Janet was an imposing presence, tall, open-featured, fair-haired. As she sailed across the stage, tossing her vivid golden hair and clutching her brow, Benson likened her to the statuesque beauties of Northern legend. They played several leading roles opposite each other, *The Theatre* reporting Janet's Lady Macbeth at Reading as 'youthful, with golden locks and a cajoling manner; but beneath this fascinating exterior she thoroughly expressed the relentless ambition and soul-subduing power ...' Great things were predicted for Janet. Soon she would 'make her mark as an emotional artist on the London stage'.[1]

Yet success in London obstinately eluded both her and Charrington. Their best, indeed only, chance to create a reputation, they thought, lay with an unknown but contemporary play. Aware of Ibsen, they called upon Archer for his advice on the best play to produce. Archer talked them out of producing *Ghosts* in favour of *Et dukkehjem*, a play with a good leading role for Janet and at least three substantial roles for Charrington to choose from. But he would only become involved himself, he told them, if they wanted a full and faithful text. The Charringtons agreed and while Archer sat down to prepare a new translation, they went off to find a theatre and production money.

They had such little luck that in the end they signed a contract to tour Australia and New Zealand for two years, beginning that summer at twenty-five pounds a week. After negotiating an advance on their salary, they booked the Novelty Theatre in Great Queen Street, Holborn, for a week in June. They also appealed through friends for more money and surprisingly Henry Irving, who to the end of his days vociferously opposed Ibsen and almost all modern drama, lent them a hundred pounds. Later, they discovered he had been persuaded to do so by Ellen Terry and was under the impression they were producing a light comedy.

The Charringtons and Archer had all the courage, naivety and optimism of true pioneers. With Salisbury's Conservatives still comfortably in government, it seemed hardly an auspicious time to try and re-launch Ibsen, yet, unlike 1880, there was a fresh nip of change in the air. People talked more about the 'woman question', one of the several political hot potatoes which the Fabians and socialists had seized in order to bake higher in the ovens of their own philosophy. The subject of increasingly heated debate, the 'woman question' became one of the most profound social issues of Archer's lifetime. It was intimately connected with the new drama he was promoting, and especially with the play he was now translating as *A Doll's House*.

Men such as Archer and Shaw considered women journalists, writers, reformers and the intellectuals prominent in British Museum Reading Room and Fabian Society circles to be their equals, but this was a point of view limited to socialist and artistic enclaves. When Archer was born, female students had only recently and begrudgingly been admitted to London University, but they were prevented from sitting degree examinations. It was not until 1879 that London became the first university to offer women degrees and prizes.

By the 1880s, women's colleges were established at Oxford and Cambridge, but the higher education of women was still an inflammatory issue that would divide families for years to come. It was acceptable for a woman to be decorously 'accomplished' in a language or music, but to be intellectually proficient was generally thought unfeminine. Education made women less 'womanly'. So did work. In the early 1860s, the Society for Promoting the Employment of Women had been founded by upper- and middle-class activists at Langham Place in London and was slowly making headway. The majority of women of their own social classes did not of course work. Their principal occupation, which continued far into the twentieth century, was marriage and motherhood.

Until the 1850s, a married woman had virtually no rights of her own. Legally, she was an appendage of her husband and any property and money she might have was owned wholly by him. Women could not divorce, and men could only divorce their wives by an expensive private Act of Parliament. In 1857, Caroline Norton, a granddaughter of Sheridan, successfully campaigned for a Matrimonial Causes Act, after which a woman could, in cases such as cruelty or desertion (although not adultery), divorce her husband. She could also retain most of her property but not gain custody of her children. A little more progress was made with The Married Women's Property Act of 1882, under which women were entitled to own and administer property in their own right, and a similar Act two years later established a married woman as independent and no longer a 'chattel' of her husband.

Many upper- and middle-class men and women married in virtual sexual ignorance. In polite circles, sex and discussion of sex was taboo and a matter solely for the procreation of children. But because it was recognized that men had sexual desires (a recognition not extended to women), it was accepted that many London husbands, with varying degrees of discretion, kept mistresses parked in small town-houses or regularly visited one of the city's numerous brothels. A middle-class woman might be ignorant of sex but she could hardly miss seeing the 'fallen women', the prostitutes and beggar-women clutching their babies in the streets of London's West End. For a respectable woman, sexual desire and enjoyment was tainted by guilt, and she was vilified if she demonstrated anything less than exclusive loyalty to her husband. It was a world of double standards.

Although the result of long and sustained pressure for change, the Matrimonial and Property Acts were more a symbolic advance than anything else, as their administration was labyrinthine and no amount of legislation could instantly sweep away the Victorian conception of the hierarchical social order. During the 1880s, if a woman divorced, she might retain her own money (if she had any) but she risked social ruin unless she was unusually resilient or rich enough to ride above gossip. Social ostracism forced many a divorcee to move to a new area and cower behind the fiction that she was a widow. If she had no income of her own, it was all too easy to slither into prostitution, either on the streets or in one of the London or continental brothels. A young single woman, seduced, pregnant and discarded, might suffer the same fate. The callousness of sexual betrayal is a central theme in many plays of the time. The melodramatic woman wronged re-emerged in later Victorian and Edwardian drama as the successful and dignified single mother hiding behind widowhood, such as Mrs Arbuthnot in Oscar Wilde's 1893 play, *A Woman of No Importance* and, sixteen years later, as Mrs Seagrave in St John Hankin's *The Last of the de Mullins*.

But the plays of Wilde and Hankin were still unwritten and the Victorian moral platform on which the family stood as the ideal symbol of society, and beneath which hypocrisy lurked, was still securely anchored. The spiritual centre was the woman. She was wife and mother; pure, radiant, compliant and uncomplaining. She was there to be protected and adored. Many women were happy. Many were not.

At the end of *A Doll's House* Nora takes her future into her own hands for the first time, whatever it might be. Nothing so shocking had yet appeared on the contemporary English stage. Neither Jones nor Pinero had created female characters who so defiantly broke convention. Yet they were gingerly pushing their noses above their burrows of melodrama and sprightly comedy, and sniffing the air of the more serious themes of morality, marriage and money. In September 1884, Jones followed the terrible *Breaking a Butterfly* with *Saints and Sinners* at the Vaudeville Theatre. The structure of the play, set in a dissenting community, and its themes of betrayal and retribution are wholly melodramatic. The characters, too, were familiar enough: Letty, the foolhardy, fallible daughter of Jacob Fletcher, the minister of Bethel Chapel, is seduced and betrayed by the cynical Captain Fanshawe and she and her father are blackmailed by the malicious deacon, Samuel Hoggard. But in his depiction of a nonconformist society, which he knew from his own upbringing, and his attempt, developed from *The Silver King*, to portray tradesmen, servants and the working class as real characters rather than caricatures, Jones began to edge away from strict melodrama and towards an observation of real life. In showing the hypocrisies of the fervently religious, he caused a minor scandal which produced angry letters in the newspapers and turned the play into a hit.

Archer thought *Saints and Sinners* badly flawed but worthy of a long *World* review in which he analysed the play scene by scene. In an effort to coax Jones into greater realism, he complained that too many characters were underwritten and grumbled over the lack of authenticity in the sets, in which study bookshelves were stocked with false book spines. But Jones was not easily drawn into Archer's campaign for absolute veracity. 'Nothing is so untrue and so unreal as ultra-realism,'[2] he warned.

He immediately reverted to melodrama. One evening in October 1888, he invited Archer, Shaw, William Morris and his daughter, May, to his north London home to hear him read *A Socialist Play*, of which he had high hopes. Under the much more innocuous title of *Wealth*, it opened at the Haymarket on 27 April the following year with Beerbohm Tree (who had played Dunkley in *Breaking a Butterfly*) in the leading role of Matthew Ruddock. A rich ironmaster, Ruddock is obsessed both with making money and perpetuating his name. But his daughter, Edith, refuses to marry his mercenary nephew, John Ruddock, announcing that she loves the socialist Paul Davoren. When he advocates a mild form of profit-sharing and Edith tells her father she cares not a jot for his gold, Ruddock begins to lose his reason. As he does so, the play subsides into familiar slapdash melodrama. It was a failure, explained Archer in *The World*, because it was neither truthful nor realistic. Jones had 'treated an original idea with little originality and less tact'.[3] Even though Jones thrust re-written snatches of dialogue into Tree's hands almost daily, *Wealth* quickly went out of business.

Also in April, Pinero's new play opened the grand new Garrick Theatre in Charing Cross Road ('lit entirely by electricity, gas available in case of a breakdown in supply, and entrance to the pit and gallery strictly by the new queuing system so successfully adopted at the Savoy'.[4])

Like *The Squire* eight years earlier, *The Profligate* is an outwardly melodramatic but seriously intentioned study of sexual and moral convention. The plot concerns Dunstan Renshaw, the profligate of the title, whose seduction and desertion of Janet Preece when he was a bachelor is discovered by Leslie, his new and morally upright young wife. In the original script, Renshaw commits suicide by taking poison before Leslie has time to forgive him. But John Hare, the manager at the Garrick, became so anxious that an audience already disconcerted by the play's seriousness might object to the suicide of a character whose remorse had won their sympathy that he pleaded with Pinero to alter the ending. For the only time in his life, Pinero agreed. In the performed version Renshaw realizes that suicide is another mortal sin and throws the poison aside as he and Leslie smother each other in mutual blessings.

Instead of reproaching Pinero for a 'feeble compromise', Archer concentrated on encouraging him in the hope of more substantial progress, adding that while 'the mere material of the play is trite enough', *The Profligate* remained 'by far the most direct and unflinching treatment of a moral problem that has yet been attempted by a modern English dramatist'.[5] It was also an unexpected success, running for almost a hundred and thirty performances.

Archer encouraged Jones and Pinero to create a bedrock for a new theatre and a receptive atmosphere for *A Doll's House* which, to his considerable surprise, Pigott had licensed for public performance. He and the Charringtons engaged a cast of eleven, including three children. Janet Achurch was to play Nora and Charrington Dr Rank, while the role of Helmer was offered to Herbert Waring, a tall, broad-shouldered, good-looking actor with dark hair and a small beard. He was thirty-one (Janet was twenty-five), interested in new plays and had the bonus of being sufficiently well known to be a modest draw. Initially, Waring was dubious of the play but after several readings discovered that 'the uninteresting puppets became endowed with an intense vitality; the dialogue, which I had previously thought so dull and unimaginative, became the cogent and facile medium for the expression of individual and diverse character. Every word of the terse sentences seemed to have a value of its own, and suggest some subtle nuance of feeling.' He was as impressed as Archer by the third act, which seemed to him 'more dramatic than anything which has preceded it'.[6]

Rehearsals began at the end of May for an opening night on 7 June. This time, Archer was keeping Ibsen informed of their progress in a succession of letters to Munich, where he was now living. 'It was a relief for me to hear that you have personally supervised the translation,' Ibsen replied. 'I can thus feel assured that it is both satisfactory and in a style that flows well. So much depends on that.'[7] On the *Doll's House* programme, Archer's name is given only as translator ('*With the Author's sanction*'), and the play was credited as being 'produced under the Direction of Charles Charrington'. In fact, Archer attended every rehearsal and shared the direction. 'I want to give the production as much chance as possible,'[8] he wrote to Charles.

The idea of an independent director assuming responsibility for a production, working with the actors, the stage designer and, if there was an orchestra, the musicians, was extremely new. Normally, rehearsals were conducted either by the actor-manager or the stage-manager, even the prompter, and any 'stage management' credit assigned to them. Rehearsals were perfunctory, often haphazard, the lowlier actors sometimes merely briefed on how to keep out of the way of the stars. It was still not uncommon, especially in the provinces, for actors to appear having had no rehearsal at all.

As Archer discovered while researching his biography of Macready, modern English stage direction began during the 1830s, when Macready instituted intensive rehearsals for his Shakespearian productions, especially for the crowd scenes which were noted for their detail and vigour. His contemporary, Madame Vestris, an actress and singer whose most popular roles included Macheath in *The Beggar's Opera*, and whose long and finely tapering legs became the subject of an admiring popular song, was among the first actor-managers to use historically accurate costuming. She also introduced the box set, complete with ceiling, on to the London stage.

Their ideas were developed by Charles Kean, the son of the frighteningly temperamental, often drunken Edmund, and the actor-manager of the Princess's on Oxford Street during the 1850s. As an actor, Charles was as unremittingly uninspiring as his father was intermittently brilliant, but he was a solid manager and a steady reformer, replacing many traditional fake stage props with the real thing. During the following decade, T. W. Robertson adopted the trend towards realism in set design and props in his contemporary 'cup-and-saucer' dramas, when he became the first modern playwright to direct his own work. In turn, Robertson encouraged W. S. Gilbert not only to write, but also to direct. Gilbert attended several of Robertson's rehearsals, learning how to break down a scene and rehearse short sections, adding detail to character, speech and movement as he did so.

Gilbert meticulously planned the staging of the operettas he composed with Arthur Sullivan and presided over exhaustive and often acrimonious rehearsals. A perfectionist and a martinet, he bellowed and threatened, regularly advancing from the darkness at the rear of stalls towards some hapless actor with a furious shout of 'What on *earth* do you think you are doing?'[9] For over ten years, Archer had admired the vitality and perfect timing Gilbert bullied from his actors, the fluidity he demanded of the ensemble, the realism he insisted upon for the costumes. For *The Mikado* in 1885, they were faithfully copied from Japanese originals and those Gilbert rejected were replaced by the originals themselves, some over two hundred years old. Other influential dramatists were following Gilbert's example and taking the responsibility for productions of their work away from the actor-managers. Since directing *The Magistrate* at the Court in 1885, Pinero not only directed all his own plays, but also approved the casting.

But one of the most forceful influences upon Archer both as a critic and aspiring director, was the European school of naturalistic ensemble acting to which he had been alerted in 1881 when the Meinenger Company made their London debut. The theatre-loving Duke of Saxe-Meinengen had been greatly impressed by innovations in London and created his own company, directing and designing most of the productions himself. When, in 1881, they presented ten plays in German at Drury Lane including *Julius Caesar*, *Twelfth Night* and *The Winter's Tale*, Archer saw for the first time how steps and rostra could be used to create multi-level action. More importantly, he noted that even in the so-called oratorical scenes the Meinenger actors actually tended to address each other rather than step forward and proclaim to the audience as Irving and English actors did. This was the most natural Shakespeare he had ever seen. The Meinenger Company, he claimed, was 'the dramatic sensation of the season'.[10]

It was inevitable that they should perform Ibsen, and their interpretations of *Kongsemnerne* (*The Pretenders*), *Gengangere* and *En folkefiende* were considered among the best in Europe. Unfortunately, Archer saw none of these, but he remembered the realism of Lindberg's *Gengangere*, and read that in 1885, in his production of Ibsen's new play, *Vildanden* (*The Wild Duck*), he had made even further innovations in naturalism. Instead of following the normal practice of cutting flaps from the canvas scenery to indicate doors, Lindberg had created a real room, with real, solid doors which opened and closed with handles. He had asked the actors to ignore the footlights and the audience, establish eye-contact with each other and move and speak as though they were ordinary people in an ordinary domestic room. This was an enormous advance. Suddenly, realism was flooding across Europe. In Paris in 1887, André Antoine, a Gas Company employee and amateur actor, opened the Théâtre Libre, from where he began plotting the overthrow of the Comédie-Française, romantic drama and the heroic style of Sarah Bernhardt. His example was emulated two years later in Berlin, where Paul Schlenther and Otto Brahm opened the Freie Bühne with a hugely controversial production of *Gengangere*.

In February 1889, four months before Archer and Charrington directed *A Doll's House*, the Théâtre Libre visited London for a short season at the Royalty Theatre, presenting *Jaques Damour*, an adaptation of a realistic novella by Zola, and Hennique's *La Mort du Duc D'Enghein*. This is a play divided into three scenes, the first showing Napoleon's generals planning to cross the Rhine and arrest the Duc d'Enghein; the second, his capture, and the third his court martial in the prison at Vincennes. Antoine had daringly lit the third act solely by candlelight. Even the house lights in the Royalty were turned out so as not to distract the audience's concentration upon the stage. Archer was profoundly moved by the austerity of the lighting and the simple, direct acting. This, he knew, was the way forward. 'It showed character in the grip of destiny, and showed it without any (actual or figurative) limelight effect,' he wrote. 'Now, is not this what we want in the drama of the future – a simplification of mechanism, a diminution of artifice?'[11]

Archer had spent much of the decade writing campaigning articles on the future of the British theatre, and in *The World* of 24 July 1889, he set out his manifesto as a director. 'Give me a deep stage,' he wrote, 'let me build the bright and airy scene according to the poet's directions, taking care to secure the different effects of light which ought to lend so much variety to the scene; let me revise the text carefully . . . let me choose a company, not of any unheard-of strength, but justly adapted to the task assigned it . . . give me a month for rehearsals, so that everything may go with smoothness and precision . . .'[12]

*

Archer's directorial contribution to *A Doll's House* was greater than that of *Quicksands*, but he refused to be credited on the programme. His preference for anonymity on this and six subsequent British premieres of Ibsen, and on other plays, resulted in his importance as a pioneer director being largely unrecognized even during his lifetime and eradicated in the years since. It has been assumed by several theatre historians that he was comparatively uninterested in performance. In fact, Archer was intimately involved with every stage of the process of production. Those copies of the texts which he used during rehearsals and which survive, are studded with his notes on line delivery and stage movement, while extant letters to actors, written usually late at night at the end of a long day's work, are full of encouragement, questions, demands and advice, and suggestions on props and lighting and costumes.

One of the reasons for his public reticence was that Archer wanted to build both a serious repertoire and an informed and critical audience, and believed that he could best accomplish that as a critic, a journalist and a translator. This was the base from which he ran his campaigns and the mulch from which a thriving drama of ideas and eventually a National Theatre would grow. He thought it essential that he preserve a position of critical objectivity, prompting and goading Ibsen into the national repertoire without too much identifiable self-interest. This apparent detachment was yet another of the masks he presented to the world. It concealed just how passionately involved he was. Of course, within the small and enclosed world of the theatre, the mask was transparent, but the fact that it was equally known that he accepted no payment for his directorial work nor royalties for his translations when they were used in the theatre, prevented accusations of conscious pretence or hypocrisy. (His only payment for his translations came from their sale in book form.) He may also have felt a certain lack of confidence, for he always directed in collaboration. Besides, he was not a vain man. He took pride in his translations, for which he accepted a programme credit, and that was that. These were his principles and perhaps his fears. If he had renounced and overcome them, he would have earned much more money. He chose not to.

The Novelty did not have a deep stage. It was small and square. But Archer had control of the text and influence in the casting. Despite Janet Achurch's Bensonian past, she leant away from the melodramatic gesture. Neither did she care for the modern, elegant but inconsequential drawing-room dramas that were little more than settings for beautiful actresses to wear the latest fashions. Society plays became a vogue during the 1880s and particularly suited actresses who were also society hostesses, such as Lillie Langtry, the former lover of the Prince of Wales, who ordered her costumes from Worth of Paris. In Archer's eyes, she could play just one role, 'to wit, Mrs Langtry'. The society play, which he satirized in the *Dramatic Review* as 'the fashion-play', having 'little or no plot, with no emotional crises, but full of delicate small talk, scandal, allusions to the topic of the day, quiet tea-table humour'[13], held little allure for Janet.

A serious though nervous woman, she seemed to think of almost nothing else but the theatre, telling Archer that wherever she was, she observed the behaviour of others, noting glances, movements, responses and memorizing them until she found an opportunity to use them in her acting. She was eager to help create the naturalistic style but alarmingly Archer found that the initial worry when rehearsals began was Janet's Nora. The first time he saw her rehearse the closing scene, the high point of the play in which 'every speech . . . rings like a clarion', he was aghast. '. . . she was deadly – querulous, whimpering, wretched'. He arranged an extra rehearsal for her, but when the time came, she was ill. Instead, he rehearsed the scene with Charrington who then went home and repeated everything to his wife. The next time she tried it, Archer sat in the stalls and watched closely. '. . . the thing was totally different,' he notified Charles. 'It gripped me line by line and simply thrilled me with intellectual pleasure and intense emotion.' At the end, Janet walked down to the footlights and peered out to him. 'How was that?' she asked. 'If that scene moves the audience half as much as it has moved me to-day,' he replied, 'the play's all right.'[14]

He must have wished that everything could be remedied so quickly. Waring and several of the others were afraid the audience might be so outraged by the scene in the second act in which Nora provocatively allows Dr Rank a peep at a pair of her silk stockings, and he confesses that he loves her, that they would be forced to abandon the play. Would the curtain have to be brought down in a hurry? Would the press brand them as pornographers? Archer could do little to dampen their apprehension except mutter reassuring nothings and conceal his own anxiety as much as possible.

They worked on, Archer bringing in bits and pieces of his own furniture from Gordon Square for the set of the Helmers' sitting room, a chair, a mirror and a vase supplementing what had been bought cheaply or borrowed from elsewhere. A real Lindbergian door was incorporated to provide an authentic slam after Nora left at the end, but realism could only extend so far, and Archer had to make do with cotton wool to simulate snow on the exterior window ledges. A week before the opening night, he was sending urgent requests to Braekstad, asking whether a Norwegian brass-mounted, white porcelain pillar stove could be found anywhere in London. Realism was exhausting. 'I scarcely know whether I am standing on my heels or my head,'[15] he exclaimed.

On the evening of 7 June, the British premiere of *A Doll's House*, rain fell unremittingly from clay-grey skies. By 8.30, when the performance was due to begin, a meagre audience of friends, sympathizers, intellectuals and Fabians, people unlikely at least to disrupt the performance, shook the rain from their coats and spread themselves dutifully among the Novelty's six hundred and fifty-one seats. Shaw was there, and a small knot of critics apprehensively watched the curtain rise. The Norwegian stove had arrived and even further realism was added by a few plaques by Thorvaldsen on the rear wall and a Norwegian newspaper lying on the couch. The door opened and Nora entered, wearing a long, pleated dress, its collar clasped at her throat by a large brooch, and a jacket edged in fur. The play began.

It was an extraordinary occasion. The one moment when Archer turned cold came in the momentous final act when Waring missed the line '. . . no man sacrifices his honour, even for one he loves', thereby cutting Nora's decisive accusation that 'Millions of women have done so', one of the most crucial lines of the play. 'I was mad at that,' said Archer afterwards and five years later, Waring was still doubting that he had been entirely forgiven. But at the end, the curtain fell to cheers. It was, after all, crowed Archer, 'a glorious evening'.[16]

For a year or so now, as well as writing for *The World*, Archer had been one of several critics contributing notices to the *Manchester Guardian*. He notifed C. P. Scott, the editor, that he could hardly write anything on *A Doll's House*, but had done as much as he could to guarantee a good review by fielding Shaw as his replacement. As Charrington stepped before the curtain to announce that news of their success would be conveyed to Ibsen, Shaw sped along to the *Guardian* offices in Charing Cross Road. 'The result was never in doubt,' he proclaimed. 'It is true that throughout the first act the house unconsciously accepted the husband . . . as a fine, manly fellow. [But] in the last act, [the audience] were in perfect sympathy with the situation and

Miss Achurch.'[17] His anonymous review appeared the following morning, 8 June. After lunch, he went along to Gordon Square with the
intention of having an Ibsen conference with Archer, only to find him
in bed, fully dressed and theatrically protesting that he needed rest.
Several more reviews had appeared, and more were to follow over the
next few days as the play became 'the great event of the week – almost
of the season . . . more talked about and written about than even *The
Profligate*'.[18]

Some reviewers congratulated Archer on his translation, although
only Frederick Wedmore in the *Academy* admitted that as he had no
knowledge of the original, his assessment was hardly authoritative. But
Wedmore had read *The Pillars of Society* and thought the dialogue of *A
Doll's House* smoother and more spontaneous, although time has since
made it sound formal, angular and perhaps rather stilted.

The critics were shocked and many angered by the play but the more
perceptive immediately saw, like Archer and the actors, that Nora was
the first woman's role of any substance in the modern repertoire. Janet
Achurch's performance was widely acclaimed as one of the finest in
London. 'Not even Ibsen or Mr Archer could have desired a better
Nora than Miss Janet Achurch, who entered into her difficult task heart
and soul,' reported the influential Clement Scott in *The Daily
Telegraph*.[19]

A bullish, forthright man, who adapted plays from the French often
under the absurd pseudonym of Saville Rowe, Scott was to emerge as
one of Archer's fiercest critical opponents in the Ibsen campaign.
Archer was thirty-two, seventeen years younger than Scott and from a
different generation. As an 'incorrigible Radical',[20] Archer's rejection
of religious and moral conventions in favour of freethought and
rationalism had led him to crusade for a new intellectual and emotional
honesty in the theatre, a new sense of moral worth and artistic freedom.
Scott, on the other hand, the son of a City of London vicar, a Christian
and stalwart Conservative, who genuinely loved the theatre but believed
it vulnerable to all sorts of immorality and odours, detected in Archer
and Ibsen social and moral irresponsibility and sedition.

In the first sentence of his *Daily Telegraph* review, he announced that
'Mr William Archer and the Ibsenites have had their grand field-day,'
so introducing the word 'Ibsenite' into the critical lexicon and giving an
indication of the intensity of his future bile. Yet he hoped the production
would last longer than its scheduled one week. 'Everything was well
done. The translation was that of a scholar; the play was perfectly

mounted; the acting was really remarkable,'[21] he observed. A. B. Walkley, who wrote as 'Spectator' for *The Star* unequivocally celebrated *A Doll's House* as 'the beginning of a dramatic revolution . . . The great intellectual movement of the day has at last reached the theatre,' he trumpeted. 'There is a future for the stage after all.'[22]

However, the rancour which Waring had feared in the auditorium soon broke in the press. 'It would be a misfortune were such a morbid and unwholesome play to gain the favour of the public,' warned the *Standard*. 'Unnatural, immoral and, in its concluding scene, undramatic', claimed the *People*. 'Pretentious inconclusiveness . . . dreary and sterilising', sneered the *Observer*. '. . . almost total lack of dramatic action', agreed *The Times*. 'Of no use – as far as England's stage is concerned', chimed the *Referee*.[23]

The most furious onslaught came from Scott, who had thought things over since his *Telegraph* review and within a few days was savaging Ibsen and his supporters in *Truth*, a radical Christian magazine, and in *The Theatre*, which he then edited. Here, he exploded with anger at the thought of a woman abandoning her husband and children. 'It is all self, self, self!' he cried. 'This is the ideal woman of the new creed . . . so unnatural a creature . . .' *A Doll's House*, he added, featured 'men without conscience and women without affection, an unlovable, unlovely and detestable crew'.[24] In the *Pall Mall Gazette*, Archer's old tormentor, the 'amazing lunatic'[25] Robert Buchanan, derided Ibsen as 'a Zola with a wooden leg stumping the north in the interests of quasi-scientific realism',[26] and a few days later expressed his disgust at the 'jaded appetites'[27] of men like William Archer. Even people whom Archer might have expected to support the play had their reservations. Neville Keynes, still at Cambridge, saw the play and could not forgive Nora deserting her family.[28]

In *The World* on 12 June, Archer abandoned critical detachment in an attempt to counter the hostility. He admitted that having translated the play and 'seen it take shape' made it impossible for him to judge it objectively. But 'history', he reflected, should not be unaware of 'the courage and the intelligence' of the actors who had achieved an 'unmistakable success . . . in a nervous and hazardous experiment'.[29]

The controversy sold tickets. The production became famous and played to full houses. There were queues at the box office. Edmund Gosse wrote with congratulations. Henry Irving came, but as he left was heard to mutter that 'If that's the sort of thing she wants to play, she better play it somewhere else.'[30] Despite Irving, *A Doll's House* became *the* play to see. On 11 June, Archer arrived at the Novelty with Shaw and Braekstad and met May Morris, her husband Henry Sparling, and Stepniak, the swarthy, sinister-looking Russian revolutionary who, after attempting to assassinate the chief of secret police in St Petersberg in 1884, had fled to Chiswick. The season was extended into a second and then a third week as the Charringtons delayed their departure for Australia as long as possible. Offers of work poured in upon Janet from managers and playwrights, for 'no actress for years has made such a success'. Archer turned up at several performances. 'She is really a delightful Nora,' he notified Charles, 'not ideal; her voice and tricks of utterance forbid that – but she *feels* the part right through, and is often very fine and even noble. In short she is *a* Nora and a very beautiful one, though not quite *the* Nora.' Once or twice, though, 'I have seen her play it *perfectly*.'[31]

He tried to interest Jones and Pinero in the play, but with only limited success. Jones was suspicious of Ibsen's supposedly radical views on women and told Archer tersely that by the end of *A Doll's House*, he had boxed himself into 'a cramped little pulpit of his own making'.[32] Archer was obviously confusing preaching with drama. 'You and Shaw don't know the difference between a taraxacum root and the Rose of Sharon,'[33] he cautioned. Jones was a complex man, genuine in his conviction that playwrights must seriously explore social and moral themes, but helpless to prevent his own plays becoming waterlogged by his innate conservatism. In his moral outlook, and especially in his attitude towards women, Jones was a man of his time and his class. He was also a depressive who wrote more to earn an income to support his wife and five children than forge new theatrical irons. His next play, *The Middleman*, which opened in August at the new Shaftesbury Theatre in Shaftesbury Avenue was, like *Wealth*, a cautious moral fable on the lure of money, swathed in a crude seduction drama. It was a substantial success but a setback for Archer's hopes. 'You'll write better plays someday,' he sighed, '& in the meantime I'm delighted with the success of this one.'[34]

Pinero received a copy of the *Doll's House* script in Ramsgate, where he had gone for the waters, read it carefully and replied that although he had 'enjoyed it very much',[35] he could not understand the relationship between Nora and Rank. With his next play, *The Cabinet Minister*, he retreated to the familiar territory of comedy and the Royal Court. *The Cabinet Minister* is an inversion of *A Doll's House* and redresses the balance which Ibsen's play so upset. Lady Kitty Twombley, the wife of

Sir Julian, the cabinet minister of the title, and thousands of pounds in debt through refurbishing and building a conservatory in their house in Chesterfield Gardens, is pursued both by guilt and social-climbiing money-leaders. Sir Julian manipulates their downfall and frees Kitty of her obligations, and at the end of the play, when she joins him in a dance, she assures him she will never be 'foolish, thoughtless, weak-headed' again. Archer '*did* enjoy it thoroughly', even though it was 'a series of episodes rather than a coherent play'[36] and one in which most of the characters were not as well written as they should have been.

On Sunday, 16 June, a celebration dinner was held at the Novelty, when the cast sat down with Archer, Shaw, Braekstad and two visiting actresses from the Christiana Theatre, one of whom told Archer that Janet Achurch was the finest Nora she had seen. Although overlooked by the theatrical press, the dinner was recorded in *The Star* by Shaw in his character of Corno di Bassetto. After the meal, Archer proposed a toast to Ibsen and, according to Corno di Bassetto, there followed 'a brilliant speech by Mr Bernard Shaw, a gentleman whose distinguished career I have followed from the beginning with unbounded interest and admiration'.[37] As Archer refused to improvise a satirical *World* review on the occasion, Shaw stood up instead and loudly sang a song. Then they all went down to the stage, inspected the realism of the set and left one by one, in imitation of Nora, slamming the door behind them.

Like Nora, the Charringtons could delay their departure no longer. Reluctantly, on 30 June, they bowed before their last audience and their impending obligations and on 5 July, caught a train from Charing Cross on the first stage of their long journey to Australia. As they settled sadly in their seats, they calculated that, as the production had taken about forty pounds a night, at the end of the day they had lost only about seventy pounds.

Back in London, Archer persuaded the publisher Fisher Unwin to print a limited edition of one hundred and fifteen copies of his translation of *A Doll's House*, complete with some photographs from the production. He sent one copy to Ibsen, for which the playwright was grateful, and in a long essay, 'Ibsen and English Criticism' in the July issue of *Fortnightly Review*, tried to steady the rudder on the Ibsen controversy. The social issues in the plays, he wrote, were secondary to Ibsen's overall aim, which was to represent real life on the stage. He was neither a sociologist nor a philosoper. 'He is not a Schopenhauer, and still less a Comte. There never was a less systematic thinker. Truth, is not, in his eyes, one and indivisible; it is many-sided, many-visaged, almost Protean.'[38]

Yet for Archer and for many others, 7 June 1889, when 'the first great and really noteworthy Ibsen performance'[39] was given in Britain, was to become 'unquestionably the birthday of the new movement'[40] in the theatre. The Ibsen campaign had begun in earnest and now, surely, there could be no turning back. This much he told Ibsen in Munich. 'I shall owe you a debt of gratitude all my life long,' Ibsen replied on 26 June. 'The movement in London marks a shining epoch in my life, and far surpasses anything I had dreamed of.'[41]

'Interesting young woman,'[42] Shaw noted in his diary, after sitting next to Janet at the *Doll's House* dinner. Besotted with her Nora, he ignored her chain-smoking and the speed with which she replenished her wine glass. He began writing her affectionate letters, and told Frances Archer of his obsession with her.

The friendship between Frances and Shaw was complicated. Women tended either to like or dislike Shaw almost immediately on meeting him, and initially Frances appears to have welcomed him as she did all her husband's friends. They often played piano duets and enjoyed trying out the new piano which Frances bought at the end of April that year. But Shaw's reason for knocking at their door was always to see Archer. Their association did not include her and she may have come to feel irritated by Shaw's frequent presence in their home and intimidated by his intellect and wit and his way of laying down the law. There was, for instance, the business of the novel.

During 1886, Frances completed a novel, a manuscript of over two hundred and fifty pages which now appears lost. The leading character seems to have been Edith, the daughter of a country rector, courted by rival suitors. Proceedings are complicated by a pair of presumably comic organ builders named Diapason and Reed. She asked him to read it, and his judgement was delivered in a twelve-page letter on 12 January 1887. 'Dont waste time bothering about publication,' advised Shaw, whose own novel, *Cashel Byron's Profession*, had been published that year, 'but start another book as soon as you can; and keep hammering away until you have learned the business in the only possible way – by practice.'[43]

Frances never attempted another novel, but Shaw's letter does not appear to have caused the rift between them. What did, was his sudden love for Janet Achurch. He dramatically confessed to Frances that he was in love with her. Knowing that Janet was married, Frances was deeply offended. Either she was less of an Ibsenite than Shaw supposed, or he deliberately set out to shock her. Choosing to ignore the fact that Archer had hung photographs of Janet as Nora on his study wall, Frances peremptorily banned Shaw from Gordon Square.

From Shaw's point of view, his fears that Archer was the kind of man for whom marriage and fatherhood would mean 'checkmate for years to come' were being realized. Things were looking very ominous indeed. He noticed his friend's attempts at saving money by making small and infrequent investments in Australian banks. One day, he read an anonymous article in a paper which was so badly written that he showed it to Archer and was about to criticize it clause by phrase, when Archer shamefacedly admitted he was the author. Sorrowfully, Shaw saw 'Tom Archer and the Australian banks in complete command of the situation',[44] and predicted that unless he 'broke loose' of his domestic obligations, he would become 'a lost man'.[45] Archer icily asked him not to mention Frances while he held such disparaging views of her. Shaw was not in the least perturbed. The unspoken code of their friendship meant that things were much clearer when women were not involved. The following Sunday morning, 23 June, they took a walk along the Thames Embankment as far as Blackfriars, discussed the Frances situation briefly and then moved on to the far less contentious subject of Ibsen.

Shaw's examination of the Archer marriage had an unexpected result. On 29 June, he began to sketch out the idea for a play, the first time he had attempted a drama since the end of the collaboration with Archer. In the notes for the new play, Archer appears as Kampenfeldt, 'the married man' and Frances in the guise of Mrs Lucy Kampenfeldt, 'pretty, affectionate, conventional but doesn't know it . . . an evil genius, her very sweetness making her the more dangerous'. Shaw steps forward as Hill, Kampenfeldt's 'friend, bachelor'. His intention was to write an astringent comedy of manners in which Hill, believing Kampenfeldt's marriage had clipped his wings, battles with Lucy for his 'soul'.[46] But although he scribbled away whenever he could, travelling to and from political lectures or the theatre, *The Cassone* obstinately refused to materialize as a drama. It remains a series of notes and a few disjointed fragments of dialogue. Shaw's second attempt at playwriting ended, like the first, in failure.

*

A Doll's House had a different but equally unexpected consequence for Archer. One of those who went to see the play was a young and ambitious American actress named Elizabeth Robins, who was earning three pounds a week as an understudy in *The Profligate* at the Garrick. Elizabeth was already intrigued by Ibsen, yet 'There was not a hint in the pokey, dingy theatre, in the sparse, rather dingy audience, that we were on the threshold of an event that was to change lives and literatures,' she wrote. But despite the theatre, the 'little-known actors' and the play's 'poverty-struck setting', this was the most thrilling and thrillingly produced contemporary play she had seen. Indeed, it seemed as if it was not a play at all, but 'a personal meeting – with people and issues that seized us and held us, and wouldn't let us go'.[47]

This was the inspiration she was looking for. It would lead, a year later, to the beginning of a collaboration with Archer that would change both their lives.

5

Domestic Moves
and a Fateful Meeting

A thunderstorm growled and flashed over Louisville, Kentucky on 6 August 1862, the day Elizabeth was born. She was the first child of Charles Ephraim Robins, a self-made businessman, and his second wife, Hannah Crowe. Beyond the house, the city was being bombarded and battered by civil war as the southern states fought for secession from the union. To escape the guns, the fires and destruction, Charles led his huddled family far away to Staten Island, from where he commuted to a Wall Street office which smelled strongly of Russian leather and cedar panelling. But Elizabeth's father, like Archer's, was not one of life's natural businessmen and several enterprises in which he invested fell by the wayside.

When Elizabeth was ten, she was packed off to her grandmother's in Zanesville, Ohio, to attend the Putnam Female Seminary and be spared the anguish of watching her mother slide helplessly into madness and be committed to the Oaklawn Sanatorium for the Insane in Illinois, where she would stay for several years. There were five children (two others had died in infancy) and Elizabeth became responsible for keeping her young brothers and sisters entertained. It was partly this which made her determined to go on the stage. In 1880, when she was eighteen, she defied her father and fled to New York to join the Monte Cristo Travelling Company run by James O'Neill, whose reputation as one of the most popular romantic actors of his day was largely based on his portrayal of the Count after whom his troupe was named.

As Clara Raymond, Elizabeth starred opposite O'Neill in a succession of romantic melodramas. Her father sat restlessly through one of her performances to deliver the kind of stage-door ultimatum with which parents and spouses throughout the centuries have singed the ears of hopefuls. 'If you must waste your youth and your splendid strength

play-acting life,' he told her, 'don't ask me to come and look on.'
Elizabeth's response was to join a stock company at the Boston Museum
Theatre where, as Bessie Robins, she appeared in almost three hundred
roles, doubling and trebling, in melodrama, comedy, French farce,
romantic drama and Shakespeare.

A gifted and hard-working actress and a beautiful woman, Elizabeth
soon found herself being ardently pursued by a fellow member of the
company, an aspiring matinee idol named George Richmond Parks. On
12 January 1885, she married him in a secret ceremony at the Episcopal
Church at Salem, Massachusetts, a town darkly notorious for its
seventeenth-century witchcraft trials. As if blighted by so ominous a
beginning, the marriage disintegrated almost immediately.

Elizabeth was a far better actor than her husband, who began
drowning his feelings of inferiority in increasing quantities of alcohol.
One night, when they had been married only two years, Parks walked
to the edge of the Charles River in Boston, methodically put on a heavy
suit of stage armour, and on the stroke of midnight jumped into the
rolling, freezing waters and sank quickly to the bottom.

Throughout her life, her husband's suicide remained a deeply
vulnerable fissure in Elizabeth's otherwise rugged emotional strength.
A widow at twenty-three, she left Boston to join a company led by
Edwin Booth and Lawrence Barrett, which specialized in large cast
plays with two leading male roles, such as *Julius Caesar*. She had spent
two seasons with Booth and Barrett, touring from the Canadian border
to the Gulf of Mexico, from the Atlantic seaboard to the Pacific, when
a friend from Boston invited her to travel abroad for the summer of
1888.

Sara Bull was the widow of Ole Bull, the musician who had founded
the Norwegian National Theatre at Bergen and given Ibsen his first job
as writer-in-residence. She was planning a sentimental return to
Norway, sailing first to England, then on to Bergen, taking her two
daughters with her. Elizabeth accompanied them as a ladies' companion. But at the end of July, when they docked at Liverpool, they
learned the ship to Norway had just left Hull. With the next not due to
leave for a week, Fru Bull whisked her daughters away for a tour of the
English lakes, while Elizabeth, still clad in her black, lustreless widow's
weeds, set off by train to London. Steaming south, she was delighted
by 'the unimaginable greenness of old England and the fabulous
strawberries bought at Crewe'. Arriving in London, she booked into a
private hotel in Weymouth Street, off Portland Place. Within days, she

had encountered such diverse characters as the actor and author William Poel, Stepniak and Oscar Wilde, the man, she remembered, who 'was to give me England for my home.'

Already famous for his aestheticism and his wit, Wilde had just published *The Happy Prince and Other Tales* and emerged, slightly incongruously, as the editor of *Woman's World*, which he transformed from a paper specializing in fashion to one containing charming fiction and articles on feminism and woman's suffrage. He was assiduously courted by those who had socially arrived, such as Mrs Langtry, those who intended to arrive and those terrified they were being forgotten. Shoals of invitations came through his Tite Street letterbox, which he either accepted or rejected with perfect judgement. Elizabeth too had a facility for receiving social invitations, and it was one afternoon at Lady Seton's 'at home' that she met Oscar Wilde. He was thirty-four and accompanied by his wife, Constance, whom Elizabeth thought looked pretty but unhappy, and his mother, Lady Wilde, then in her sixties, fierce, large-nosed and heavily rouged and veiled. 'You have a dramatic face,' she squawked at Elizabeth.

Her son, Elizabeth recorded, 'not only fixed my attention but that of everyone in the room. He was very tall and broad, and what my compatriots would uncomfortably call, fleshy . . .' His face was 'smooth-shaven, rather fat . . . rather weak; the frequent smile showed long, crowded teeth'. He was, she thought, 'a rather interesting presence in spite of certain objectionable points'. But despite the glossy, flabby appearance and beneath the posturing and the wit, Elizabeth saw a man of abrasive intelligence, great sensitivity and kindness. He was also one of the first men, and the first in England, to take her absolutely seriously as an artist.

Already she was hoping to act in London and she asked Wilde how she should begin. Select a play with a good leading role for herself, he replied, and spend a hundred pounds in producing it for a single matinee. 'Your social friends would make it a success.'[1] Elizabeth blanched. She did not have a hundred pounds. Wilde told her not to worry. While she was in Norway, he would see what he could do to help.

In early August, Elizabeth sailed for Norway with Fru Bull and her daughters. At the family home at Lyso, she met several former actresses who recounted their memories of working with Ibsen and the theatre at Bergen. This appears to have been Elizabeth's introduction to Ibsen's plays. The party sailed for England in September, when she left Fru

Bull and her daughters to return to London for another week and take lodgings at 10 Duchess Street, not far from Weymouth Street.

She found that Wilde had been as good as his word. He had mentioned her name to Beerbohm Tree, the actor-manager of the Haymarket Theatre, who invited her to a performance of *Captain Swift*, Haddon Chambers's dashing Australian melodrama in which he was playing the title role. She met him during the interval. Tree was in his mid-thirties, tall and of almost military bearing. Elizabeth thought him as English as the green fields and the strawberries at Crewe, but the faintly Teutonic timbre of his voice should have given him away. The son of a wealthy corn merchant, he was descended from German Balts from Lithuania. Tree was a stage name, possibly deriving from the pear tree on the Beerbohm coat of arms. He was optimistic, telling her that there were plenty of acting opportunities but never enough good actors. Encouraged, and captivated by the raffish Haymarket atmosphere and all of bustling London beyond it, Elizabeth returned to Duchess Street, more determined than she had ever been. The next morning, she cancelled her passage home.

It was extremely difficult for a young actress to make headway in the London theatre, especially one with no provincial experience and no British reviews in her scrapbook. Such a woman was a natural prey for the men hanging about stage doors with promises of nights out and spectacular leading roles. But Elizabeth was a woman of few delusions and impeccable moral standards. She was businesslike, forthright and ambitious, quickly made influential and watchful friends such as Wilde and Tree and listened carefully to their advice. In October, she made her London debut in a performance of Poel's *Chieromancy* at St George's Hall, Langham Place, an occasion entirely overlooked by the press. Anxious to use her Shakespearian experience, she wrote to Irving at the Lyceum, hoping for an audition, but received a courteous but emphatic refusal. Geneviève Ward, another American who was now fifty and described by Tree as 'Old Iron-Clad', fed Elizabeth ginger cake and tea at her St John's Wood home and gave her assessment of all the actor-managers. Benson, she counselled, must be avoided. He employed only novices and paid miserly wages, which was why his company always looked third-rate. Nevertheless, Elizabeth accepted his offer of a week's work in December as Portia opposite his Shylock. It was in Exeter, it paid only five pounds, but at least it was Shakespeare.

In January 1889, she took over from Mary Rorke on Saturday matinees, playing the American widow, Mrs Errol, in *The Real Little*

Lord Fauntleroy at the Opera Comique. Frances Hodgson Burnett's book had been adapted by the actress Mrs Kendal and the actor-manager Mrs Beringer as a vehicle for Vera, Mrs Beringer's terrifyingly precocious ten-year-old daughter. It was after Pinero saw her play Mrs Errol that he offered her an understudy's job in *The Profligate*.

On 5 July, she appeared in a trial matinee of F. F. Moore's *Forgotten* at the Islington Grand, a play which quickly emulated its title. Archer saw it, though. It was the first time he had seen Elizabeth and he observed in *The World* that she played 'the sympathetic heroine charmingly'.[2] Elizabeth read the notice but misremembered his name, assuming him to be called Herbert Archer.

It was not long after she had seen *A Doll's House* that she was offered her first Ibsen role. Mrs Beringer was so obsessed with establishing Vera as a serious actress that she actually proposed staging a benefit matinee of *Ghosts*, with her daughter, now aged twelve, as Regina. 'Don't,' cried Geneviève Ward. 'It's a piece of moral vivisection – fit only for an audience of doctors and prostitutes.'[3] Pale with alarm, Mrs Beringer backtracked quickly only to advance once more as the producer of a revival of Archer's translation of *The Pillars of Society*. This time, Miss Ward gave her consent. She would play Lona Hessel, W. H. Vernon agreed to repeat his role as Bernick and Vera would play Olaf, his thirteen-year-old son. Elizabeth Robins was cast as Martha Bernick, and the matinee was scheduled for the Opera Comique on 17 July.

Archer had no connection with the production. The text was severely cut but Clement Scott still thought it stuffed by 'an intolerable deal of mere pedantry and verbiage'.[4] Archer, he wrote, might be a scholar but he was certainly no dramatist. Even the mysterious occurence at the performance of 'an elderly chatterbox who dodged about the stalls to enthuse and give off opinions that nobody asked for'[5] failed to lift the heavy fog of tedium. The critical consensus was that *The Pillars of Society* was not only inferior to *A Doll's House*, but long-winded and boring. 'There are too many characters,' complained the *Daily Chronicle*.[6] 'Ibsen is no longer the Ibscene dramatist,' remarked the *Hawk*, but 'dull, deadly dull'.[7] Groans even greeted some of the longer passages, but a small band of Ibsen supporters loyally applauded at the end. There were 'loud calls for the critic-translator', wrote Elizabeth, 'but Mr Archer did not appear'.[8] He remained where he was, in the audience, sitting next to Shaw and scribbling notes for his review, in

which he wrote that 'the unaffected charm of Miss Robins's performance was quite memorable'.[9]

A few days later, he was travelling again. Rimbault Dibdin had
remarried and although earlier that year he had become the father of a
son, Archer insisted that it was essential he accompany him to the
Wagner Festival at Bayreuth, then under the direction of the composer's
widow, Cosima. It would also be absurdly cheap, he reasoned. The
second-class return fare was eight pounds and tickets to the productions
of *Parsifal, Tristan und Isolde* and *Die Meistersinger* were only one pound
each. They left in the last week of July and as soon as they arrived,
Shaw turned up, intent on gathering material for his music column in
The Star. This was not the first time that he had visited 'the Continong'[10]
as Frances put it, as he had toured the Netherlands in April, disliked it
intensely and 'fled howling'. The one advantage of being abroad was
the magnificient weather, but otherwise 'Nature conspires with you in
vain to palm off the Continent on me as a success,'[11] he informed
Archer.

The three of them attended the operas, ate at the cafés (Archer
leading them out of one mid-meal after an altercation with a waiter)
and bought photographs of Wagner and the theatre. On 2 August, on
their way home to England, they stopped off in Nuremburg, where they
visited the museum and silently inspected the displayed instruments of
torture before climbing aboard the cross-Channel steamer, Archer and
Shaw penitently submitting themselves to sea-sickness.

Soon after he arrived home, Archer and Frances began packing.
They were moving again, this time from Gordon Square to Queen
Square nearby, where they had taken rooms on the two upper floors of
number 40. In a large and comfortable study overlooking the square,
Archer put up his books and his pictures of Janet Achurch as Nora, and
spread out his papers and files. It was at Queen Square that, at the end
of the year, Frances revoked her explusion order upon Shaw, re-
admitting him after six months to the Archer dinner table and fireside.

Encouraged that *The Pillars of Society and Other Plays* was selling well,
Walter Scott agreed that Archer should edit Ibsen's prose dramas in
five volumes over the next two years. Archer was anxious that an
authoritative collected edition be produced as quickly as possible as
interest in Ibsen was growing, both in socialist and intellectual circles
and the eccentric literary fringe inhabited by Henrietta Frances Lord.
Since she published *Nora* eight years previously, Miss Lord had become

a devotee of the Indian philosophy of Karma, stressing the importance of harmony within and between souls. These principles she now sought to batten on to Ibsen and in a revised edition of *Nora*, claimed that the play was less a demand for dignity and mutual trust within marriage than a dramatization of the perils of imperfect karma. Once true spiritual harmony had been restored, she explained, Nora would naturally return to her husband and her children. Miss Lord also had a messianic interest in the healing practices of Christian Science and in her introduction to *Ghosts*, also published in book form in 1890, she explained that Mrs Alving could have saved her son from idiocy had she simply applied Christian Science methods.

The last few months had also seen an English translation of *Rosmersholm*, Ibsen's 1886 play, by Louis N. Parker, a music teacher at Sherborne School, Dorset. His dual career as a dramatist had begun hesitantly with *A Buried Talent*, a comedy, surfacing in the unlikely surroundings of a Sherborne hotel, but would later blossom into a consistent boulevard success. Clara Bell, meanwhile, was hard at work translating Henrik Jaeger's *Life of Henrik Ibsen* from Danish into English.

Archer worked quickly, revising his translation of *The Pillars of Society* and *A Doll's House*, and completed a translation of *De unges forbund*, written in 1869, which he first entitled *The Young Men's League* and later amended to *The League of Youth*. These three plays appeared in February 1890 as the first volume of *Prose Dramas*, bound in dark green cloth with gold lettering on the spine. The next three volumes appeared later in the year. For the second volume, he translated *Ghosts*, revised the translation of *An Enemy of Society* by Eleanor Marx-Aveling and re-named it *An Enemy of the People*, and supervised Frances's translation of *Vildanden* as *The Wild Duck*.

Frances had an efficient knowledge of Norwegian, but was not fluent, like Archer and Charles. Her translations and those by Charles, which he mailed from Baluchistan, where he was now assistant to the agent to the Governor-General, gave them work to fill the long hours and a feeling of taking part in a great literary enterprise, but meant hours of checking for Archer.

The third volume of *Prose Dramas* included three early plays: Archer's translations of *Haermaendene paa Helgeland* (1857) as *The Vikings at Helgeland*; *Kongsemnerne* (1864) as *The Pretenders* and Charles's translation of *Fru Inger til Østraat* (1854) as *Lady Inger of Østraat*. The fourth contained Archer's revision of Catherine Ray's *The Emperor and the*

Galilean as *Emperor and Galilean*, and was published in November. The fifth volume was scheduled for 1891.

He worked at great speed and long into the night. As well as translating Ibsen and writing for *The World* and as many other journals as would print his articles, he wrote lectures on modern drama which he delivered at the Royal Institution. He was also sending off regular columns of London drama news to the *Allahabad Pioneer*, India's leading English-language newspaper. Amongst all this, he still found time for a theatre-trip to Copenhagen in February and March of 1890. He stayed at Norrevoldegade 7, the home of Natalie Zahle, his Aunt Mary's friend, and saw almost twenty plays from which he manufactured a lengthy article for the *Fortnightly Review*. At the Royal Theatre, he saw productions of Molière, Holberg and Goldoni, and one of *Et dukkehjem*, in which Nora was played by Betty Hennings, the theatre's leading actress, then in her late forties and almost twenty years too old for the role. In the earlier, lighter scenes, Archer thought her better than Janet Achurch, but 'when the plot began to thicken Miss Achurch ... gradually pulled up' until, in the final act, Betty Hennings fell well behind. 'She simply scolded Helmer and became in reality the objectionable person of Clement Scott's imagination,' Archer exclaimed to his brother. 'I mean to speak or write to Fru Hennings about it.'[12]

A few weeks after his return from Denmark, Archer found himself flung into a repetition of the scene to which he had returned from Bayreuth. He and Frances began packing again. After only nine months at Queen Square, they had decided to rent two homes. From now on, Queen Square would become Archer's base, and Frances and Tom would spend most of their time at a cottage in the country.

The marriage had been tense for some time. Their relationship had begun as a fairy-tale in Rome and been conducted with romantic intensity in villa gardens, Neopolitan cafés, on an outing to Capri when they had stood on their hotel balcony one evening and watched Vesuvius flare red in the distance and on late-night gondola rides in Venice. It had even survived being relived through the trans-European post. But it had never wholly adapted to day-to-day London. Frances was a resilient woman, self-sufficient and adaptable. The Larvik Archers had even found her to be suspiciously socialist and 'full of fads'.[13] But she was also conventionally feminine, even childlike. Although her letters sent from Italy and France before her marriage contain the usual lovers' endearments: 'I think of you constantly ...';[14] 'I love you with all my heart',[15] she also turned their relationship almost into one of guardian and ward, reducing Archer to a series of diminutives, occasionally calling him 'Willie', but much more frequently 'little boy'. She called herself 'your old Godmother'.[16]

Even though it appears that Tom was conceived within days of the wedding, the sexual drive of their early marriage was soon extinguished. In the summer of 1888, when they were living at Gordon Square, it appears that Frances had a hysterectomy. Possibly before but almost certainly from this date, the Archers had separate bedrooms. It was a hard year for Frances. Her mother, fretful to the end, died in Bournemouth in April and in November 'after a week of trembling on the verge' her father also died. It was a year of comings and goings and, for Archer, of ladling out sympathy, and '. . . all this, as you may suppose,' he confided bitterly to Dibdin, 'has made ravages in my time'.[17]

He did his best to avoid it, but marriage and family relentlessly invaded his already crowded life. At times, it was awkward living in such close proximity to Frances and Tom. Archer had grown up emotionally and then physically independent, and now his wife, and in particular his son, demanded time and attention. Sometimes he was unsure of what kind of attention to give. When he returned from the theatre at night, Tom would be asleep, and possibly there were days when Archer did not see him at all. He brought him gifts occasionally, but they seem absurdly inappropriate. Once, when Tom was twenty months old, Archer returned from a short walking tour of the north and presented him with a bag of toffee. As Archer himself had withdrawn as a child, so Tom gradually retreated into a land of make-believe, a fantasy to which Archer was sometimes admitted, but to which the real key was held by Robert Louis Stevenson.

Archer met Stevenson in 1885, the year of Tom's birth, when his review of *A Child's Garden of Verses* as 'crisp, clear, vivid',[18] published anonymously (as was the custom) in the *Pall Mall Gazette*, produced a letter asking the single question: 'Now *who* are you?'[19] Archer revealed his identity and whenever he accompanied Frances to Bournemouth to visit her ailing parents, he slipped off to see Stevenson at Skerryvore, the cliff-top home which the tubercular author of *Treasure Island* shared with his wife, Fanny, and stepson, Lloyd. The two men would sit in the drawing room, with its wicker-work chairs and low divan of oak trunks covered with yellow silk cushions, and talk of their Edinburgh days, and of travel and adventure. As they reminisced and argued about Ibsen (whom Stevenson detested), Archer would watch him 'rolling a limp cigarette in his long, limp fingers' and sadly monitor the debilitating effects of his illness in 'the pallor of his long oval face, with its wide-set eyes, straight nose, and thin-lipped sensitive mouth, scarcely shaded by a light moustache'.[20] Sometimes, he reminded Archer of Buffalo Bill. The Stevensons left England 'for health, sport, bankruptcy'[21] in 1887, bound eventually for Samoa, where he died in 1894. From his travels and from the South Seas, Stevenson sent a stream of whimsical letters to the boy he called 'Tomarcher'.

Stevenson filled Tom's world with romance, but romance was something which had faded from his father's life. Ellen Wallis, who once symbolized to him the glamour of the stage and to whom he had read *The Feast at Felvik*, was married to John Lancaster, the owner of the Shaftesbury Theatre and was firmly entrenched in the mainstream repertoire. She was replaced on Archer's romantic pedestal by Mary Anderson, a beautiful young American actress, who had made her name in a revival of Gilbert's *Pygmalion and Galatea*. Three weeks after Tom was born, he was reporting enthusiastically on her 'ingeniously and effectively original'[22] Rosalind in *As You Like It* at Stratford-upon-Avon. Two years later he went to Northampton to see her become the first actress to double the roles of Perdita and Hermione in *The Winter's Tale*. That November, they enjoyed a long walk together across Hampstead Heath but in 1889, she too, had married and had retired from the stage to live with her husband in Broadway in Worcestershire.

Frances, meanwhile, was still complaining of the lethargy she had suffered since her hysterectomy. Her translations of Ibsen were probably part of an attempt to revive her energy and the marriage, and perhaps set her upon a career. If so, it did not work. But when it was suggested she might benefit from living in the country, they agreed to give it a try. Tom was now almost five years old and a rural school would be preferable to one in London. In May, they found a cottage in the small village of Cobham in Surrey, surrounded by tranquil country-side. As he was an admirer of Henry Thoreau, the Massachusetts essayist and gardener who built himself a hut in which to live a self-sufficient life by Walden Pond, Archer decided to name the cottage after him. Dibdin inscribed *Walden* on a piece of wood and presented it to them as a nameplate. They retained Queen Square, as there were no late-night trains to Cobham. It was an entirely amicable arrangement.

So began the routine that Archer would maintain for most of the next thirty-four years. While he lived in London, his family remained in the country and he travelled to see them on Sundays and odd days during the week. Yet, as Shaw realized to his astonishment, it was not Archer who 'broke loose' from his marriage in this way, but Frances. For after six years within what might be unkindly called her own doll's house, Frances stumbled upon a career.

The previous summer, around the time of Frances's hysterectomy, Archer received a letter from his friend Brander Matthews, an American law lecturer, critic, and sporadic dramatist. Matthews lived in New York and visited London regularly for the theatre and had met Archer at the British Museum. He wrote to alert him to Annie Payson Call, a teacher and amateur actress from Boston, who had been so impressed by *Masks or Faces?* that she was on her way from the United States with the express intention of meeting him. On 15 July, with Shaw in tow, Archer answered her invitation to meet her at the rooms she had taken in Devonshire Street. Sipping his tea, he listened while she told him that the alternative methods of portraying character he described in the book resulted in a terrific nervous strain for the actor. Surely there was a third and better way to great acting, she suggested, in which the actor was intellectually alert but physically relaxed? Archer was sceptical but suggested she put her ideas in writing. (She did, and her book, *Power Through Repose* was published in 1890.) But her vitality interested him, and in August he saw her again, this time accompanied by Frances who listened intently as she explained her theory that for true awareness, the mind must be in complete harmony with the nervous system. Frances came away convinced that she had found her calling.

In Cobham, she threw herself into studying psychology, the nerves and exercise techniques, keeping in touch with Annie Payson Call in Boston by letter. Meanwhile, the bracing country air and twisting lanes of Surrey induced her husband to take up a fashionable new pastime. 'I am performing as a champion cyclist,' he announced proudly to Dibdin on 2 June. 'This is only my fourth attempt, but I have done 15 miles today (safety bicycle) & am consequently feeling sore all over.'[23]

Since the invention of the safety bicycle and the recent commercial production of the Dunlop pneumatic tyre, cycling had become enormously popular. Despite Archer's enthusiasm, Shaw did not make his first serious attempts for another five years, when he wobbled about Beachy Head, but Archer practised zealously until, on 16 June, he completed a heroic but muscle-aching round trip of eighty miles. By the end of July he had persuaded Frances to take to the saddle. One day, they hired a tandem at Guildford and cycled 'along the Hog's Back almost to the Victory public house. It was a very pleasant run and I brought her down the hill into Guildford without having to call at the hospital in passing.'[24]

But cycling was only a rural diversion. If a new life had begun for Frances, so it had for Archer. And in his case it began with an innocent note from Elizabeth Robins.

That spring, Elizabeth was appearing opposite George Alexander in Hamilton Aide's long-running comedy *Dr Bill* at the Avenue Theatre near Charing Cross, when H. L. Braekstad told her that he was planning a matinee of *Ghosts* and asked her to play Mrs Alving. The problem from Elizabeth's point of view was, that although she was keen to appear in Ibsen, she agreed with Geneviève Ward that *Ghosts* was 'terrible and revolting'.[25]

On 29 May in Paris, André Antoine produced the play before an invited audience at the Théâtre Libre, appearing himself as Oswald. Archer was not there (Shaw had dragged him off to a piano recital by Ignace Pederewski at the St James's Hall), but he read an admiring article on the production in the *Pall Mall Gazette* on 5 June. Elizabeth also read it and was reassured by the fact that the performance had been well received and that in contrast to the first night of *A Doll's House* at the Novelty, a large number of women were in the audience.

She changed her mind, told Braekstad she would play Mrs Alving and promised to ask Tree whether they could use the Haymarket for their matinee. She saw him on 9 June. Most actor-managers would have recoiled with horror at the thought of being contaminated by Ibsen but Tree had no qualms at all. If anything, he was rather too keen, as he agreed to make the Haymarket available on condition that he play Oswald. Elizabeth prevaricated, knowing that he would not be Braekstad's choice. He also stipulated that, as they planned to use Archer's translation, he must be consulted.

The following day, having presumably checked Archer's christian name, she arrived at *The World*'s Covent Garden offices hoping to see him. He was not there. Redirected to 40 Queen Square, she pushed a note through the letterbox asking his advice on staging the play. Archer sent a message to the Avenue inviting her to Queen Square the following afternoon, or 'if the matter is urgent' they could meet later that evening, after the first night of Augustin Daly's Company of Comedians in *Casting the Boomerang* at the Lyceum. 'A note directed to me at Stall F8 (Lyceum) would find me and I could meet you (say) at

Gatti's Adelaide Gallery or anywhere else about the west end of The Strand.'[26] A Lyceum usher brought him her reply. She would meet him at Gatti's restaurant.

So, at about eleven o'clock that night, 10 June 1890, William Archer met Elizabeth Robins. She was a tall, slim, twenty-seven-year-old woman with fine features and an air of southern American grandeur. She no longer wore her widow's weeds but an elegant gown. Her clear, hypnotic eyes were the vivid colour of speedwell and she wore her long, chestnut hair curled up and around her head. With her was an older woman whom she introduced as Becky, her dresser from the Avenue. It was usual for a woman to be chaperoned in society, but less so in the theatre. Elizabeth, though, was a stickler for formalities.

Over supper, she outlined the plans for *Ghosts*. Her voice was well modulated with a just discernible drawl. The more she explained, the more flustered Archer became, repeating that Braekstad had said nothing to him about producing the play. When she told him that Tree wanted to play Oswald, he stared at her in astonishment and then suddenly roared with laughter at the thought of Ibsen's enfeebled artist played by one of the West End's leading romantic actors. From that moment, he and Elizabeth were collaborators and the atmosphere was so relaxed that she told Becky she could go home. Archer was warning her of the risks of producing Ibsen. Did she recognize the plays were for a minority audience and critics foamed at the mouth when Ibsen's name was mentioned? She assured him her heart was set upon playing Mrs Alving. Archer's commitment to absolute realism did not extend as far as pointing out that she was too young for the role. Instead, he told her he objected as much as she did to the prejudice against young women playing middle-aged roles. Later, outside in The Strand, he hailed a hansom cab, helped her into it and watched her rattle away.

Once back in her new rooms at 41 Marlborough Hill in St Johns Wood, Elizabeth confided her impressions to her diary. 'Archer is tall and dark,' she wrote, 'looks about 30, is probably 38, [he was thirty-three] has big honest eyes that win confidence & friendliness; is *most* courteous.'[27] As soon as Archer reached Queen Square, he wrote her a letter, suggesting a possible cast for *Ghosts*. They might try Fred Terry for Oswald and either Marion Lea or Gertrude Kingston for Regina. And perhaps they should book the Novelty Theatre. Then he hinted at a role for himself. 'Are you a good stage-manager?' he asked. 'You don't want a conventional stage-manager, but of course there must be someone to "boss the show."'[28]

However, Archer did not direct *Ghosts*, because within days the plans fell through. Tactlessly, Elizabeth left Tree in the dark and offered Oswald to Terry who, unaware of Tree's hopes of playing the role himself, innocently asked him for his opinion. Tree furiously informed her that on no account could she use his theatre. He was angry, but not vindictive. A week later, on the afternoon of 19 June, he honoured an arrangement for Mrs Erving Winslow, a professional reciter from Boston, to hold a public reading of *An Enemy of the People*. Mrs Winslow used a 'somewhat imperfect' and abridged translation, but as she impersonated all eleven characters and the crowd, and also read every stage direction in full, it turned into a very long afternoon indeed. 'Anything less enthralling,' commented Archer wearily, 'would be difficult to conceive.'[29] The Liberal leader, William Gladstone, conspicuously sitting in a stage-side box, fell asleep, suddenly awoke, and crept out. In the stalls, Elizabeth wished she could follow his example, but had noticed that Archer, who had arranged her ticket, was sitting nearby and every now and again, glancing at her intently.

Apart from his *Doll's House* review and dinner report, Shaw had written nothing on Ibsen. But on 18 July at the St James's Restaurant in Regent Street, he added his voice to the growing Ibsen-clamour by addressing a Fabian Society meeting for two hours, and 'in provocative terms',[30] on the relevance of *A Doll's House* to socialists. At the end of the month he braved the continent again, travelling through Germany where, in a violent rainstorm, he saw the Oberammergau Passion Play. He returned to England without attempting to see Ibsen. '. . . my total ignorance of Norwegian,' he explained to Archer, 'prevented my calling upon him during my stay in Munich to explain his plays to him.'[31]

It was a summer of comings and goings to and from Oberammergau. A few days before Shaw arrived home on 10 August, the Archers set out for a holiday in Switzerland. Frances and Tom stayed with friends while Archer went off to see the Passion Play for himself. Elizabeth Robins was also in Oberammagau for six days during August but there appears to be no evidence of their meeting. By the 23rd, Archer was in Munich, where he saw a production of *An Enemy of the People* at the Residenztheater, the first time he had seen the play on stage. He called on Ibsen at his spacious but austere apartment in Maximilianstrasse, their first meeting since Sæby three years previously. Archer thought he looked much older than his sixty-two years, but this was possibly because he spent most of the day grumbling that, as a consequence of

Shaw's lecture, he had been cross-questioned by a reporter from the *Daily Chronicle* on his views on socialism. He had never belonged to any political party, he complained, and probably never would. Archer pressed on to Frankfurt, where he saw a production of *Siegfried* at the Opera House on the 25th. The following day, he was back in London and a few days later, Frances returned from Switzerland. Elizabeth did not return until 3 September.

Archer plunged on with his reviewing, commentating and campaigning, seeing the *Prose Dramas* through the press and (to make money) translating Alexander Kjelland's *Tales of Two Countries*, for Osgood in London and Harper's in New York. It was an even more intensive than usual bout of late-night close work, resulting in recurring headaches and an alarming deterioration in the sight of his right eye. Anxiously, he consulted an oculist, who peered closely at his eye and diagnosed amblyopia. When Archer asked what exactly that was, the specialist explained that there was no apparent lesion or defect and to all intents and purposes the eye was perfect. The only trouble was that for some inexplicable reason, he could not see properly. Archer found the paradox so irresistibly funny he told the story to whoever would listen. Even Shaw thought it a curious subject for a joke.

Suddenly, after six months of inactivity, there were two Ibsen matinees in quick succession. On 27 January 1891, Marie Fraser, an actress, it turned out, of depressingly limited ability, played Nora for a single performance, directed by Fitzroy Morgan, of Archer's translation of *A Doll's House* at Terry's Theatre. Elizabeth appeared as Mrs Linde. On 21 January, a week before the performance, Shaw called at Queen Square to discover Archer deep in conversation with her, the first of several times he would see them together. The performance was a fiasco. 'There is no need to discuss Ibsen's *Doll's House* any more,'[32] wrote Clement Scott the next day in *The Daily Telegraph*.

Not one, but four directors converged like crows upon the next production, the British premiere of Charles Archer's translation of *Rosmersholm*. Two matinee performances were scheduled for 23 February and 5 March at the Vaudeville Theatre in The Strand. Archer directed and so did Shaw. The previous year, he had met the actress Florence Farr at William Morris's home in Hammersmith. She was a pretty, determined young woman whose husband of four years, an actor called Edward Emery, had emigrated to America, an event for which she was thankful. Florence was a feminist and a socialist and before the year was out, she and Shaw had become lovers. He convinced her that she must play Rebecca West in *Rosmersholm*. The third directorial force was Frank Benson, the unlikely replacement for Herbert Waring who had withdrawn from the role of Rosmer. On the programme, the stage-management was credited to Alfred Lys Baldry, but any influence he might have tried to exert was steam-rollered by the combined and conflicting forces of Archer, Shaw and Benson. John Todhunter, the Irish doctor and playwright whose *A Sicilian Idyll* Florence had turned into a minor hit, and who was putting up the money, looked on in bewilderment.

Rosmersholm is a study of guilt and the destruction of ideals, a tragedy of people of passion whose desires can find no outlet. John Rosmer is a pastor whose faith is thrown into doubt after his wife, Beata, drowns herself in the mill-race at Rosmersholm. He is loved by, and loves in return, his young housekeeper, the ruthless and ambitious Rebecca West, but learns that it was Rebecca who drove Beata to suicide by hinting that she was pregnant by him. Rebecca discovers that an older man whom she supposed to be her guardian and with whom she has had an affair was, in fact, her father. She is so ashamed that when Rosmer asks her to marry him, she refuses. Unable to be together in life they unite in death, following Beata by throwing themselves into the mill-race.

Benson and Florence Farr headed a cast of six. 'Very early differences of opinion became manifest between Archer and myself as to the right way of treating the story,'[33] Benson observed bluntly. Theirs was a clash of will, temperament and method. If Archer thought that he might persuade Benson to jettison all his rhetorical mannerisms and attempt a psychologically and emotionally accurate performance, he was mistaken. Benson was used to directing himself and acting in his own style. Rehearsals began in mid-February and before long, Benson had Archer marked down as an amateur, while Archer quickly became despondent at Benson's continuing failure to be word-perfect. Neither could Archer induce an adequate response from Florence, about whom Shaw flapped and fluttered and coached privately in the evenings at her home near Ravenscourt Park. On some days, Archer became so exasperated that he announced he was leaving the production. The next morning, he would arrive eager for rehearsal and with sheaves of notes for the cast.

But eventually, Benson, Florence and Shaw disheartened him so much that Shaw had difficulty in persuading him to attend the first performance. It was mediocre. Even Shaw admitted that Florence just about 'got through', but optimistically suggested that Benson 'did not distinctly fail except in the last act'.[34] *Rosmersholm* took ninety pounds at the first performance but only fifty at the second and mystified its audiences and the critics. Benson was paid twenty guineas for his efforts and the other actors between ten and three, with the exception of Florence Farr who was given Rebecca's dresses. But the winds of theatrical and social change which had made *A Doll's House* notorious had not entirely died down. Others were at last prepared to join Archer in his lonely campaign for a new repertoire. One was J. T. Grein, a twenty-eight-year-old Dutchman who combined journalism with a full-time job as a tea merchant in Mincing Lane.

Jacob Thomas Grein was born in Amsterdam in 1862, the son of a Dutch mother and a German father. A cheerful, neat little man with alert eyes and a full moustache waxed horizontally into points, Grein had been a theatre enthusiast for many years. He had written drama reviews for several Dutch newspapers and successfully lobbied for Jones's *The Middleman* and Pinero's *The Profligate* to be produced in Amsterdam. In gratitude, the playwrights presented him with an inscribed grandfather clock, 'an excellent timekeeper'[35] recalled his wife, until it stopped dead a week after Grein's death in 1935. Grein had established his Ibsen credentials by writing the introduction for a Dutch translation of *An Enemy of the People*. Having lost his job in a bank, he arrived in London in 1885, and as soon as he found himself a flat in Pimlico and his feet were under a desk at the offices of Wellenstein, Krause and Co., he devoted himself to founding and editing his own journal, *The Weekly Comedy*.

He was soon introduced to Archer, and at the end of 1889, with Archer promising his support, Grein wrote an attack on English actor-managers in the *Comedy* and proposed the creation of a Théâtre Libre in London. 'Progress,' Oscar Wilde would write, 'is the realization of Utopias,'[36] and Grein's utopia took its cue from both the French Théâtre Libre and The Shelley Society's private performance of *The Cenci*. It would be a theatre club open only to subscribers and therefore free of commercialism and the prying of the censor. The emphasis would be upon serious plays and their interpretation rather than their social acceptability and scenic decoration. Grein estimated it would cost about two thousand pounds to produce a season of five plays, each being given a single performance. As arranged, Archer published pieces in *The World* endorsing the idea, and further press support came from

George Moore, the Anglo-Irish author whose reputation for outspokenness had been established when *A Modern Lover*, his novel set in artistic circles, was banned by the circulating libraries.

By the spring of 1891, Grein was ready to launch the British Théâtre Libre. Archer appealed to him to change the title, advising that it smacked dangerously of free and, even worse, risqué entertainment. Grein hit upon The Independent Theatre instead, advertised in the press for subscriptions of £2.10s for the first season and booked the crumbling Athenaeum Hall in Tottenham Court Road in which to hold it. The inaugural production, he announced proudly, would be the British premiere, in William Archer's translation, of *Ghosts*.

The performance was set for Friday 13 March, only a week after the second dreary matinee of *Rosmersholm*. As it would be private, Grein did not waste time applying for a licence that would be refused, although the disquiet rumbling over Ibsen in the press immediately intensified into outright hostility. Critics were particularly incensed over *Ghosts*, testifying to its offensiveness and unabated moral degeneracy. Private performances had the acrid whiff of illegality about them and there were urgent calls for Pigott to take action. Ibsen began to be satirized in cartoons and parodies. In *Ally Sloper's Half-Holiday*, a comic weekly, a caricature of a Pears' Soap advertisement showed Clement Scott furiously scrubbing Ibsen's ears, while the ghosts of Archer, Grein and Gosse hovered in the background. The 'Ibsenites', identified as too-clever, dingy, morally dubious, socialist and anarchist, were discussed and diagnosed through many column inches. The *Daily News* provided an anthology of authentic Ibsenite sayings, advising its readers that by murmuring 'psychological insight', 'the symbolic side' and the 'bitterness of baulked individuality',[37] they would readily gain admittance to this rarefied club. The *Saturday Review* pleaded for someone to write a comedy of *The Ibsenites*.

On 10 February, Edward Aveling had read Archer's translation to the members of the Playgoers' Club, a circle of first-nighters. Four days later, a tight-lipped article in the *Saturday Review* hoped that as 'young girls continue to be the chief ornaments of English theatres' the reading did not imply that 'Ibsenites' were about to 'thrust themselves upon wholesome-minded people in decent places of amusement'.[38] Bloated by enthusiasm, Grein invited the entire Playgoers' Club to the Independent Theatre performance, with the result that the Athenaeum Hall proved too small for the number of subscribers and their guests wanting tickets. Frantically, he searched for another theatre and for fifteen pounds secured the Royalty in Dean Street, Soho, where the manager was Archer's adolescent pantomime-love, Kate Santley.

Ibsen agreed to Grein producing *Ghosts* providing that 'our mutual friend' Archer was there 'to watch over rehearsals and interpret the author's intention'.[39] Archer appears to have had about a fortnight for rehearsals, but not the free hand he wanted. Grein forged ahead and recruited the cast. The role of Mrs Alving went not to Elizabeth but to Mrs Theodore Wright, a stocky amateur actress and Fabian whose socialism did not extend as far as using her own name rather than that of her second husband, a prominent freethinker. Frank Lindo, Grein's business manager, was cast as Oswald and Edith Kenward as Regina. Archer shared the direction with Cecil Raleigh, whose previous experience was confined to melodrama.

The Royalty held six hundred and fifty, but *Ghosts* had created so many rumours and so much speculation that almost a thousand people applied for tickets and Grein opened the dress rehearsal on Wednesday, 11 March. On Friday, the night of the official premiere, most of the snow from the recent blizzards had turned to black slush. Theatregoers thronged Dean Street and surged up the Royalty's steps and through the doors into the tiny foyer. In the crowded auditorium, as Jan Mulder's nine-piece string orchestra played selections from Grieg before the heavily-brocaded curtain rose, the man from the *Licensed Victuallers' Mirror* looked nervously about and calculated that he was outnumbered by 'the Ibsenmongers' by 'ten to one at least'. Distastefully, he noted 'the long-haired, soft-hatted, villainous or sickly-looking socialists, well-known propagandists of atheism, iconoclasts and anarchists'. These were just the men, talking fervently to each other in high anticipation of the performance. Some of them were accompanied by 'spectacled, green complexioned, oddly-dressed females of unhealthy aspect . . . obviously priestesses of the cult'.[40]

Despite a full house, however, Archer was disenchanted. *Ghosts* had turned out to be another *Rosmersholm*. He had failed to overcome the different styles and mannerisms of the actors and persuade either Mrs Wright or Frank Lindo that unobtrusive, realistic acting was essential to the drama and absolute stillness the secret of its final moments. Where Archer had argued for less, the actors gave more. They created bedlam. In the last scene Mrs Wright took to pacing this way and that, shrieking wildly. Frank Lindo, having slouched gloomily throughout most of the play, suddenly threw himself into an eye-rolling frenzy which A. B. Walkley in *The Star*, a critic sympathetic to Ibsen and

Archer, thought merely farcical. Edith Kenward, he observed, played Regina as 'a pert Parisian soubrette, a thing of nods and becks and wreathed smiles and saucy pouts'.[41]

Not all the audience were sympathizers, or members of 'the fanatical sect'[42] of Ibsenites. 'Here were gathered together the faithful and the sceptical; the cynical and the curious', observed Clement Scott. The bristling tension between the two camps, the sniggering and the shushing, especially when the gas failed and the actors bumbled on for several minutes in the dark, was partly what made it for him such 'a great night'.[43] Yet the play still had an enormous impact. Many of the supporters who applauded loudly after the first act were startled into silence by the end of the second. After the third, the end of the play, there was mild pandemonium as the actors took their curtain call. Detractors hissed loudly and the advocates applauded tumultuously. Someone yelled 'It's *too* horrible!' and was greeted with a shout of 'Why don't you go to the Adelphi?'[44] When Grein, 'braving the opposition',[45] appeared nervously before the curtain to make a speech, a woman was heard querulously asking her neighbour whether he was Ibsen.

Rosmersholm, according to Archer, had been 'drenched with vitriol' by the critics. *Ghosts* created 'a frenzy of execration'[46] as over five hundred reviews, articles and satires hurtled from the presses. At the eye of the storm raged Clement Scott. In addition to his *Daily Telegraph* review, Scott (possibly assisted by Sir Edwin Arnold, the *Telegraph* editor), composed a leading article which has since become as celebrated as the play itself. *Ghosts* was 'an open drain', he cried, 'a loathsome sore unbandaged ... a dirty act done publicly ... a lazarhouse with all its doors and windows open ... melancholy and malodorous'. It was 'disgusting'; a 'dungheap'. But according to Scott, Ibsen's real iniquity was to portray every aspect of life as irretrievably corrupt. He invited his audiences 'to laugh at honour, to disbelieve in love, to mock at virtue, to distrust friendship, and to deride fidelity',[47] and this was unforgiveable.

Yet Scott was able to separate a play from its production and as he had done with *A Doll's House* and *Rosmersholm*, he praised the 'remarkable'[48] acting in *Ghosts*. But the vast majority of critics echoed only his contempt, so much so that the abuse overflowed to engulf both the audience and Ibsen himself. Only Walkley, who had opposed Scott over *A Doll's House*, did so again over *Ghosts*. 'One wonders whether these hysterical protestants have ever read anything, observed anything, pondered anything,' he exclaimed. 'Have they no eyes for what stares them in the face: the plain, simple fact that *Ghosts* is a great spiritual drama? . . . It is a cry for freedom.'[49]

Once again, Archer had not written a review but as the scandal threatened to sink the entire campaign for new drama, he decided to fight back. On 8 April in the *Pall Mall Gazette*, he published *'Ghosts' and Gibberings*, an anthology of critical 'delirium' divided into three sections. 'Descriptions of the Play' included 'naked loathsomeness'; 'dull dirt long drawn out'; 'garbage and offal'; 'foul and filthy . . . dull and disgusting'. There were 'Descriptions of Ibsen' as 'an egotist and a bungler'; 'a crazy fanatic'; 'a gloomy sort of ghoul, bent on groping for horrors by night', and 'Descriptions of Ibsen's Admirers' as 'lovers of prurience and dabblers in impropriety'; 'nasty-minded people'; and 'the unwomanly woman, the unsexed females, the whole army of unprepossessing cranks in petticoats . . . Effeminate men and male women'.[50]

By concentrating the abuse, Archer effectively parodied the abusers and demonstrated that British theatre criticism was less interested in the theatre and ideas than in sustaining the political, moral and sexual conventions of the day. He noted that Scott had endorsed several other critics by ending his *Telegraph* editorial by threatening 'author, actors and admirers alike'[51] with the law. But 'who', demanded Archer, 'can carry on a rational discussion with men whose first argument is a howl for the police?'

The tumult over *Ghosts* put a spark to the dry tinder of the theatre, divided the dramatic and literary community and filled Archer with defiance. Even before *'Ghosts' and Gibberings* was published, he was already working on the next Ibsen production. In a hasty note to Brander Matthews in New York, he announced that 'I am busily engaged in assisting two fair compatriots of yours, Miss Robins & Miss Lea, to produce *Hedda Gabler*.'[52]

Hedda Gabler
and Shavian Ambushes

Hedda Gabler proved to be the most difficult of the plays so far even to bring into the rehearsal room. Ibsen had completed it during the winter of 1890, sending the manuscript to Gyldendal, his Danish publishers, in November. But even before Archer received his copy, he found himself hurled into an air-blackening dispute with Edmund Gosse, Ibsen's former self-styled ambassador in England.

Archer assumed that he would translate the play himself to complete the fifth and final volume of the *Prose Dramas*, for which he had already translated *Rosmersholm* and Frances had prepared *Fruen fra havet* (1888) as *The Lady from the Sea*. But as interest escalated in Ibsen's notoriety, predators began swimming into Archer's pool. William Heinemann, a twenty-seven-year-old from Surbiton and in his first year as a publisher, was eager to capitalize on the Ibsen scandal. Having discovered that a new play was on its way to Gyldendal, he promptly offered Ibsen a hundred and fifty pounds for the British rights on condition that the proofs be sent directly from Copenhagen to Gosse, his chosen translator. Ibsen was easily lured by money while Archer, like Elizabeth, could often be astoundingly naive in trusting the motives of others. In an excess of the 'gentlemanly conduct'[1] with which Ibsen credited him, and on 'the explicit understanding'[2] that Heinemann would not impede Walter Scott and himself in publishing their own version of the play, Archer waived his rights to oblige Gosse.

As far as Heinemann and Gosse were concerned, Archer was now out of the running. To secure his British copyright, Heinemann published an edition of twelve copies of *Hedda Gabler* in Norwegian on 11 December, five days before Gyldendal published their own. By this time, Gosse was flying through an English translation and on 2 January 1891, sent Ibsen a contract for not only the first but the exclusive

British rights, which would prevent Archer from publishing and staging his own translation. Hearing of this, and incensed that he had been misled, Archer fired off an indignant letter to Ibsen. On 8 January, Ibsen wrote to Heinemann appealing that Archer be allowed to translate *Hedda Gabler* for Scott, so 'the great collected edition'[3] would be up-to-date. Heinemann ignored him. Archer was even more outraged. Sensing his fury, Ibsen deducted the *Hedda Gabler* fee from the seventy-five pounds Scott had sent him in payment for the *Prose Dramas* so far, and returned it as compensation. He then wrote twice to Heinemann demanding his one hundred and fifty pounds.

Heinemann rushed the English *Hedda Gabler* through the presses for 20 January. Archer read it the same day and immediately blasted off a corrosive attack upon Gosse, published in the *Pall Mall Gazette* three days later, denouncing his work as 'so inconceivably careless and so fantastically inaccurate as to constitute a cruel injustice to Henrik Ibsen.'[4]

Gosse had long since given up his cataloguing job at the British Museum and was now employed as a translator to the Board of Trade. He had also succeeded in his long-nurtured dream of becoming a literary authority, but it was an authority battered by bungling and mishaps. For his complete edition of *The Works of Thomas Gray*, Gosse claimed to have 'scrupulously printed' letters from the original manuscripts. But in fact, he employed a copyist who copied instead from editions already published and so perpetuated previous errors. Critics even discovered mistakes in the supposedly definitive text of 'Elegy written in a country churchyard'. Gosse's history of classical poetry, *From Shakespeare to Pope*, was shot down as 'a tissue of errors and absurdities'[5] by the scholar and University Extension Society lecturer, John Churton Collins. Gosse's glistening reputation was mildewed with an unreliability he would never lose.

Since withdrawing from Ibsen commentary in 1879, Gosse had contributed a piece on *Vildanden* (*The Wild Duck*) to *The Academy* in 1884, before falling silent on Ibsen topics for another five years. In 1889, he resurfaced with an essay in *Fortnightly Review* emphasizing his own importance as the first to publish Ibsen's name in Britain, and reviewing all the plays from *The Pillars of Society* to *The Lady from the Sea*. Now, with Archer mid-way through his edition of the prose dramas, Gosse had embarked on a similar three-volume project for a New York publisher. By translating *Hedda Gabler* for Heinemann, he was attempting to polish up his standing as an Ibsen expert.

But on the front page of the *Pall Mall Gazette,* Archer tarnished it even further, proclaiming that Gosse's Norwegian was ludicrously deficient and had been for years. He was infamous for having translated a phrase meaning 'distinguished himself on the battlefield' as 'always voted right at elections', and there were over twenty 'gross blunders' in *Hedda Gabler.* A sentence meaning 'She will never do it again' had become 'She is not in the habit of doing so'; 'I at last discovered his address this morning,' Gosse had transformed into 'I am really to see him tomorrow.' There were 'scores' of incidental mistakes: 'imorges', meaning 'this morning', was rendered once as 'tomorrow' and again as 'yesterday morning'. It all added up, proclaimed Archer, to 'one of the very worst translations on record'. As for the moral theft of his rights, he observed that 'To find a parallel for Mr Gosse's conduct in this matter, I need go no further than the play itself. Yet the parallel is not exact. It was by chance not through an act of courtesy, that Hedda became possessed of Lovborg's manuscript; and having become possessed of it, she did not deface, stultify and publish it – and then claim copyright. She did a much less cruel thing – she only burned it . . . "Traduttore, traditore," indeed!'[6]

This salvo provoked a letter from Heinemann claiming his innocence. Archer replied, agreeing that he had no argument with Heinemann but again accusing Gosse of shabby conduct. Gosse retreated to the sidelines and said nothing.

Following the row was the grave American novelist Henry James, who lived in London and sympathized with his friend Gosse as having fallen victim to Archer's 'extravagant malevolence'.[7] James knew what he was feeling as a fortnight previously, he had been the object of Archer's disdain himself. As part of his campaign to create a literary drama, Archer had been urging novelists to write for the theatre, and hearing that James had dramatized his own novel, *The American,* had asked for details. 'It *is* true that a play of mine is to be produced at a mysterious place, Southport, which I have never seen,'[8] replied James guardedly in one of his lugubriously baroque letters.

James was not a poor man but this did not stop him believing that his novels should be earning him more than they were. Therefore, he had responded eagerly to a request (and still more so to an advance of two hundred and fifty pounds) that he write a stage version of *The American.* The commission came from Edward Compton, the actor whom Archer had often seen on tour with Ellen Wallis and who had piloted his Comedy Company around Britain for the past ten years, occasionally landing in London to play short seasons of *The Rivals* or *She Stoops to Conquer*. Disillusioned by the rewards of fiction, James was grandly deluded by the theatre. Seduced by dreams of his name on billboards and of bowing from the stage before rapturous applause, James contemplated writing 'half a dozen – a dozen, five dozen'[9] plays and so earning a fortune. His delusions sprang from an intense loathing of the stage. Writing successful plays, he believed, was hardly the same as writing a literary novel but merely a matter of combining his technical proficiency with a grasp of what audiences wanted in London and New York. For Henry James planned transatlantic fame.

He soon discovered that things were not so simple. Compton accepted the script in the autumn of 1890, but demanded constant revisions. James was convinced that the actors required his 'zealous hand' at rehearsals, but as these were held wherever the company was playing, he was faced with many inconvenient rail journeys to grey, far-flung towns. He desperately wanted the Southport premiere to be a success, for he envisaged *The American* marching triumphantly upon London to be seen by serious critics and 'by yourself in particular', he told Archer. At the same time, rehearsals had sapped his confidence so much that he did his utmost to prevent him from coming to the first night at the Winter Gardens on 3 January. 'The place is far, the season inclement, the interpretation *extremely* limited,' he wrote. 'The circumstance *may* be definitely uncomfortable . . .'[10] But only hours before the curtain was due to rise, James was nervously telling Gosse that 'I believe Archer is to loom.'[11] Sure enough, that afternoon, Archer turned up in wet and windy out-of-season Southport, the only London critic to make the journey. Immediately the curtain came down that night, while James was still light-headed from the applause and calls for the author, Archer told him that although *The American* might succeed in the provinces, it would probably fail in London. James's sister, Alice, overheard and thought his remarks 'highly grotesque'.[12]

Archer would have been puzzled by this judgement. He was not an insensitive or malicious man but his honesty sometimes made him seem so. This reveals something of the complexity of his nature. He had little in the way of polite small-talk, but because he had the ability of emotional suppression and critical detachment, he often assumed that others could be similarly objective. Sometimes, he was unable to perform this emotional disappearing trick. As his various campaigns and close friendships were all emotionally as well as intellectually fired, he was often unable to tolerate those of whose work he despaired or views he opposed. Such was the case with Grundy, Buchanan, Scott and now Gosse.

Elizabeth Robins and her fellow American actress Marion Lea, were currently appearing at the Shaftesbury in Buchanan's new play, *The Sixth Commandment*, a melodramatic adaptation of Dostoyevsky's *Crime and Punishment*. Elizabeth, who thought Buchanan 'a lovely Viking of a man',[13] was playing Lisa opposite the Raskalnikov of the dashing Lewis Waller. Despite Archer's views of Gosse's *Hedda Gabler*, they were determined to produce the play in an improved form, with Elizabeth playing the title role and Marion appearing as Mrs Elvsted. At the end of January, after she had appeared with Marie Fraser in the revival of *A Doll's House*, Elizabeth asked Archer to join forces with them.

He appeared unimpressed when she told him that she and Marion had formed a partnership with the portentous title of the Joint Management. Neither did he seem perturbed by the rumours that the light dramatist and journalist, Justin Huntley McCarthy, planned to adapt Gosse's translation in the hope of providing a vehicle for Lillie Langtry. Elizabeth was aghast at his indifference. But she had known him less than a year, not long enough to realize that not only could he sink to occasional uncommunicative moodiness, but that the more interesting he thought other people's plans were, the icier the water he threw over them. The more Archer prophesied that Ibsen would never be accepted in England, the more resolute he became that his crusade would succeed. Pre-occupied with the forthcoming matinees of *Rosmersholm* and the Independent Theatre's *Ghosts*, he recited the litany of reasons why *Hedda Gabler* was too great a risk, in order to gauge Elizabeth's sincerity and stamina.

Elizabeth and Marion decided to go ahead. Like the Charringtons, they had no money of their own to fund a production, but they had jewellery and, using that as security, borrowed three hundred pounds from a friend. Once again, Elizabeth approached Archer, who this time agreed to help. As relations with Heinemann and Gosse were delicate, he advised they opt for a strategy combining caution and intrigue. He began preparing his own translation at the same time as establishing that, while Heinemann owned the British copyright of the play, the stage rights remained with Ibsen. Therefore, while Heinemann could not prevent them from producing the translation he had published, he could stop them from using any other. It also followed that they could, with the consent of Heinemann and Gosse, produce a new version providing they did nothing to indicate it was not Gosse's. 'This seems to be absurd, but I am assured that it is so,' he told Elizabeth on 17 February. After his onslaught in the *Pall Mall Gazette*, he thought it best that Elizabeth negotiate with Heinemann and Gosse, but remembering her tactlessness with Tree over the proposed production of *Ghosts*, he emphasized that 'you must on no account let Heinemann know that I have translated any part of the play . . .'[14]

The result was that Heinemann turned the decision over to Gosse, to whom Elizabeth explained that with previously unperformed plays, re-writing during rehearsals was common. She implied that she would vet for accuracy any changes in the script, explaining that she knew Norwegian. This was dangerously overstating the case, as she knew only scraps of Norwegian, less even than Gosse. She could not possibly work without a dictionary and was hesitant with simple conversational phrases. 'Tak for sidst [thanks for your hospitality] – does your Norwegian go as far as that?'[15] enquired Archer on 6 May.

It appears that Gosse declared that, if she wanted to produce *Hedda Gabler*, they must consult Archer. It was an extraordinary about-face. Perhaps Gosse intended this as an apology. Perhaps he thought that close association with Archer in Ibsen matters might repair his literary reputation. Archer apparently accepted it as a gesture of reconciliation, and although they were never close friends, relations thawed as far as the affable stage. The deal struck with Heinemann was that the Joint Management could produce Archer's version of the play but no translator would be credited in the programme. Instead, below the title would run the legend: 'By Special Arrangement with Edmund Gosse and W. H. Heinemann.' Archer could also publish his translation under his own name in the last volume of Scott's *Prose Dramas*, providing an acknowledgement was made to Heinemann on the title page.

Set in the Tesmans' villa in a fashionable area of modern Christiana, *Hedda Gabler* is the tragedy of an apparently conventional, happy marriage. Hedda, the daughter of a general and a fiery, passionate, bored woman, has married George Tesman, an amiable academic too absorbed by his work to take much notice of anything else. By their return from a long honeymoon, Hedda has become thwarted, restless and resentful. She is pregnant, but does not want the child; her vision of the world is romantic and idealized and the thought of sex and childbirth repulse her. One day, Eilert Lovborg, one of her former admirers, turns up. Once a writer of dazzling promise, he became an alcoholic but now, with the support of Thea Elvsted, a friend of Hedda's from schooldays, he has reformed, published one book and completed the manuscript of a second that seems even more brilliant. Jealous of their happiness, Hedda manipulates things so that Lovborg goes to a party with Tesman and Judge Brack while she and Thea stay at home. During the course of a drunken night, Lovborg loses the manuscript which Tesman discovers and brings home. Instead of telling the distraught Lovborg that the book is safe, Hedda gives him one of her father's pistols and commands him to go away and 'do it beautifully'. Later, she burns the manuscript page by page in the stove. Eilert does shoot himself, but accidentally, in a brothel. Brack, another of Hedda's admirers but more devious, recognizes the pistol as hers and blackmails her to become his mistress. Terrified of scandal, Hedda shoots herself.

While Archer wrestled with the Benson-Farr *Rosmersholm* and the Independent Theatre's *Ghosts*, he slowly translated *Hedda Gabler*. He was using his new typewriter, '& am like a child with a new toy', he informed Elizabeth proudly. Progress was difficult but he kept beating energetically and inaccurately away, obliterating his mistakes by hammering out strings of x's, so that his copy began to take on the ironic appearance of being heavily censored. He used the typewriter for translations and journalism but only occasionally for personal mail. Archer wrote letters most days but often when he was away from his desk, so that while he used formal notepaper (and in later years, large sheets of paper printed with his address and telephone number), he would also use postcards which he carried with him on trains or to the theatre, or pages violently torn from ruled notebooks. He used a fountain pen and black ink, and frequently a blunt pencil. As a young man, his writing was reasonably neat, curled and tightly-packed, but as he grew older it began to unravel and spread, so that by the time he was in his sixties it had become an untamed, looping scrawl.

Reading his progress reports, Elizabeth became impatient to book a theatre and begin rehearsals, but he refused to be hurried. In contrast to most English plays, there are no long speeches in *Hedda Gabler*. This was Ibsen's most austere work to date, composed of short, sharp, sometimes intricate exchanges, and 'my experience is that revising Ibsen takes a lot of time',[16] Archer advised her in mid-March. At the end of the month, 'a very speakable, very playable'[17] script was complete. On 28 March, they had an evening off from the new drama and saw an example of the old, *The Henrietta*, Bronson Howard's financial satire at the Avenue. At the end of the month, Pigott granted their application for a performance licence while admitting to Elizabeth that he was mystified as to why anyone should want to perform a play in which the characters appeared to have escaped from a lunatic asylum. 'You are evidently a born censor-tamer,'[18] Archer congratulated her.

The world premiere of *Hedda Gabler* had been given at the Residenztheater in Munich on 31 January. It was a failure, as were the half-dozen subsequent productions in Germany and Scandinavia. Archer and the Joint Management had everything to play for when they booked the Vaudeville for the British premiere on Monday, 20 April. This was the theatre where *Rosmersholm* had played, and cheaper than others on The Strand because it was currently thought 'unlucky'. This meant they could afford five matinee performances. After his experiences of *Rosmersholm* and *Ghosts*, Archer was adamant that nothing could be gained for the Ibsen campaign by under-rehearsed single performances. Like *A Doll's House*, *Hedda Gabler* would have at least a week's run.

With a capacity of seven hundred and forty, the Vaudeville was larger than the Royalty, although the stage was an inch or two smaller, hardly the deep and airy space he had hoped for in his 1889 manifesto. Rehearsals began on 6 April, when Scott Buist, Arthur Elwood and Charles Sugden (recently named as co-respondent in a sensational divorce case brought by the Earl of Desart), joined the company as Tesman, Lovborg and Judge Brack. This gave them only a fortnight instead of the month of rehearsals Archer would have preferred. But this time, he had far more confidence in the cast and in their stage-manager, George Foss, who took the credit on the programme. A thirty-one-year-old actor, Foss had previously directed plays for the Browning Society. He was from a well-connected legal family from Croydon, well educated and passionately interested in new drama. He and Archer became an effective partnership.

During rehearsals, Archer positioned himself in the stalls with his copy of the script beside him and a small pad of loose-leaf paper on his knee. Each time he filled a page with notes, he tore it off and slipped it behind the others, methodically patting the pad straight before looking up again, a fastidiousness which began to grate on Elizabeth. Every now and again, he stopped the actors, taking them phrase by sentence through the text, working on inflection, timing, pauses, silences, when to and how to move. This was the first time for two years that he had the chance of experimenting with naturalistic acting and, as Lindberg had done, he encouraged the actors to ignore the audience and think of the stage as an ordinary room. At the end of each day, he sat down wearily at Queen Square and wrote letters to the cast, giving suggestions which he expected to be absorbed in time for the next rehearsal.

At twenty-eight, Elizabeth was a year younger than Ibsen stipulated in his stage directions that Hedda should be. Her hair was more luxurious but her 'face and figure' had 'refinement and distinction' and her eyes, expressive, unflinching, not quite blue but almost violet, could, in a certain light, become the 'steel-grey'[19] of Ibsen's imagination. She imagined Hedda to be like many London middle-class and society women, 'a bundle of unused possibilities, educated to fear life; too much opportunity to develop her weakness, no opportunity at all to use her best powers'. She was 'pitiable in her hungry loneliness', a woman for whom 'marriage only emphasised what she was missing'. Hedda, according to Elizabeth, was ruthless, unashamedly selfish, determined to inject purpose into her life to the extent of dominating others, even if it meant that she destroyed lives and partly despised herself. This was the paradox that made Hedda a 'great acting opportunity'.[20]

In one of his post-rehearsal letters, Archer reminded her that the play was more than a feminist tract showing the tragedy of a woman suppressed by marriage and convention. Hedda was a complex character and Elizabeth should be careful not to court the audience's sympathy. She was indeed trapped, but the snare was partly one of her own making, and in many ways, she was her own worst enemy. 'I feel strongly that Hedda has the keenest sense of *irony* but no sense of *humour* – which I take to be the *enjoyment of irony*,' he told her. 'She knows this or that is ridiculous; if it concerns herself, it gives her pain; if it concerns others it awakens her scorn; in neither case does she get any pleasure out of it; consequently, I would never have her laugh as though she took pleasure in laughing . . .'

Archer understood Hedda's suppression of her emotions and sym-pathized with her isolation. '. . . there is scarcely a character in all fiction that I seem to have such an intimate and sympathetic knowledge of as I have of Hedda,' he notified Elizabeth. 'Hedda sees what a grim joke the world is, and she has not the power of enjoying a joke at her own expense – that's my idea in a nutshell.'[21]

Archer and Elizabeth apparently agreed on everything except one vital point. In the third act, after the loss of his manuscript and believing he has destroyed both Mrs Elvsted's future and his own, the despairing Lovborg promises to 'make an end of it all'. Archer had written Hedda's reply as '. . . will you not try to – to do it beautifully?'[22] as she hands him one of her pistols. Elizabeth changed the adverb to 'gracefully' each time it occurred. Archer insisted on its retention, but Elizabeth was obstinate. 'Beautifully', she argued, reeked of Oscar Wildean aestheticism.

Apart from this, Archer had the last word on everything. He and Foss designed a set to fit in front of that used for the evening production of Bulwer-Lytton's *Money*, a play which Archer had long ago consigned to the incinerator of drama. He rejected Hedda's pistol case because the wood was too dark and might not be seen clearly by the audience. For the same reason, he sent back a pair of black pistols and demanded they be replaced with white so they would gleam against the black dress she would wear in the final act.

But for all his attention to realism, he did not present the play precisely as it was written. The sexual sub-text was expunged. There would be no indication that Hedda was pregnant, Aunt Julia's leading questions to Tesman about grandchildren were cut and Brack's advances to Hedda were to be underplayed to the point of invisibility. Archer the anti-censorship campaigner was, with Elizabeth's agreement, censoring Ibsen. This was probably not as a result of his reticence on sexual matters, something which Elizabeth shared, but an attempt to counter the hostility to Ibsen by presenting a serious, realist drama uncluttered by anything too contentious. But despite their precautions, the press was glowering with apprehension and *Punch* continued to satirize Ibsen and Ibsenites. Anstey, otherwise the novelist Thomas Anstey Guthrie, one of the paper's leading humorists, parodied Archer's translations each week. Having completed *Rosmersholm*, he was currently half-way through *Nora; or The Bird Cage*. But as Shaw remarked, Archer was parodied because 'without Archer, the plays would not have bitten deep enough to be burlesqued.'[23]

Both Elizabeth and Marion gave press interviews attempting to diffuse anxiety by projecting themselves as demurely feminine. On 20 April, the day of the first performance, the *Pall Mall Gazette* recorded them as pleading 'Please don't put us down as Ibsenites! Because we *don't* cut our hair short, and we *don't* wear green bed gowns, and we *don't* rebel against baulked individuality and that sort of thing.' Elizabeth, though, rather punctured the pretence by volunteering the information that Hedda was 'absolutely and essentially a modern product . . . like hundreds of women'.[24] The previous night, 'Hedda-Eve', Marion Lea wrote to Archer: 'If we fail, it will be our own fault, but if we succeed we shall have you to thank . . . your very, very kind interest . . . has kept us up throughout these many weeks . . . Please put up an especial prayer for Ibsen and Liza and me tonight.'[25] Archer doubtless did no such thing.

At two-thirty the following afternoon, he joined the audience at the Vaudeville. Oscar Wilde was there, and George Moore, and Shaw, 'with a large and intelligent contingent of Fabians'[26] who at least filled a good part of the pit. The rest of the audience, and the critics, were dotted about here and there among the empty seats. Archer sat in the stalls and next to him, on one of her rare appearances in London and at the theatre, was Frances. The lights lowered and the curtain rose on the Tesmans' drawing room, with its couches covered in soft, copper fabric, the writing table to one side, the drapes pulled closed across the open doorway to the back room. The play began.

Presently, Clement Scott looked about him. The audience appeared startled by the play which, he conceded, had been 'rehearsed to perfection'.[27] Elizabeth swept on to the stage wearing a long, serpent-green gown decorated with flashes of bright orange silk which, in the opinion of 'Zingara', monitoring the dresses for her *Letter for Ladies* column in the *Leicester Daily Post*, gave the effect of 'a wild thing that could not be suppressed'.[28] She dominated the stage and 'fascinated every spectator', reported Scott, 'with her fine study of one of the most hateful, ill-disciplined, triumphantly wicked, and unwomanly women' ever written. 'Miss Robins evaded nothing;' she was feline, imperious, sensual, and 'sailed on triumphantly to victory. Her success was not a moment in doubt.'

Several critics echoed Scott's praise and the remaining actors, too, had some of the best notices of their careers. There was Scott Buist's wary, indecisive Tesman; Arthur Elwood's dissolute, failed scholar, Lovborg; Charles Sugden's cynically manipulative Brack and Marion Lea's pathetic, frightened Mrs Elvsted. 'So good was the acting, so devoted were the artists with their work' that 'the audience sat with their mouths open, gaping, staring . . . astonished that Art, the mistress of the beautiful, could give heterodoxy and ugliness so much power', noted Scott. For he was convinced that *Hedda Gabler* was Ibsen's ugliest play yet. It 'justifies the most appalling selfishness and sheds a halo of glory around self-inflicted death', he reported. 'It was like a visit to the Morgue.'[29]

Afterwards, in the corridors and the foyer, people argued over which scene was the most powerful. Some thought it in the second act when Hedda, wearing a dress of sapphire-blue velvet with white lace at the throat and wrists, sat close to Lovborg on the sofa as he whispered his

disbelief at her marriage. Others contended it was the scene in the third
act in which she appeared in a long, loose white gown and burned
Lovborg's manuscript in the stove. Then there was the terrifying
instance in the third act, when she handed the pistol to Lovborg, and
those chilling moments at the end when Hedda, wearing a sleeveless
black evening gown and black feather boa stepped into the back room
and pulled the drapes closed behind her. Archer had meticulously
rehearsed the final image of the play so that Hedda's suicide should be
seen as a defiant act of triumph. Once the audience heard the pistol
shot, Tesman flung the drapes aside to reveal Hedda, lying on a sofa,
her face averted so that her right temple was visible. Remembering the
macabre effect of the candlelight used in the Théâtre Libre production
of *Mort du Duc D'Enghein*, Archer had lit her by a single, low overhead
lamp. As he intended, the pistol still clutched in her hand gleamed
brightly against the black of her dress. The curtain slowly came down.

The performance had lasted three hours, considered long for a single
play, but according to the *Pall Mall Gazette* the next day, it was a
'revelation'.[30] During the applause, Archer glanced round to discover
that 'the heat and excitement were too much for my wife, whom I had
to take home half-fainting'. Furious that he was prevented from going
backstage to see the cast, he stressed in a letter to Elizabeth that evening
that 'I was really *moved* by the performance as I never expected to be.
The emotional interest fairly got the better of the intellectual. I shall
come and see you tomorrow.'[31]

The reviews the next morning hailed Elizabeth and admired and
condemned the play. 'Miss Robins is brilliant, no less; she is all
versatility, expressiveness and distinction,' cried the *Pall Mall Gazette*,
adding that the play's 'brilliant dialogue . . . sparkles in passage after
passage'.[32] In *The Star*, Walkley acclaimed it as 'the tragedy of a soul in
revolt' and Elizabeth as 'an intellectual actress of the highest order'.[33]
But the vituperation unleashed upon *Ghosts* was now directed upon
Hedda Gabler. 'It was like gazing on corruption,' spluttered Scott in the
Telegraph. 'There they all were, false men, wicked women, deceitful
friends, sensualist egoists, piled up in a heap . . . What a horrible story!
What a hideous play . . .'[34] Ibsen threw Scott into a dilemma. He was
too discerning a man and too perceptive a critic not to recognize serious
work by a substantial dramatist, yet Ibsen discussed ideas against which
all his sensibilities rebelled and which he could not bear to see on the
stage. Therefore, he accused Ibsen of using his artistry to make

immorality seductive. So good a writer was Scott himself, that his abuse was always more eloquent than anyone else's.

Only John Nisbet of *The Times* claimed to understand Hedda. She was, he explained, transparently insane. 'It is suggested in her inconsequent actions, in her callous behaviour, in her aimless persecution of all around her, and it is finally proved by her motiveless suicide . . . Hedda Gabler is manifestly a lunatic of the epileptic class.'[35]

Despite Elizabeth's acclamation in the press, Archer was at most of the remaining performances that week and sent her a battery of notes. She had begun darting at things, and must stop; she must remember that from the pit it was impossible to see the stage floor, so she should not crouch too low as she burned the manuscript. For her part, Elizabeth stopped taking her curtain calls. Somebody had written that her performance had been so realistic, that once Hedda had shot herself it was a shock to see the actress return moments later for her applause. 'I took the hint and have not allowed Hedda to come to life again,'[36] she explained.

At the weekend, the *Sunday Times* called the production 'one of the most notable events in the history of the modern stage . . . it marks an epoch and clinches an influence'.[37] But even with her personal success and audiences having improved sufficiently for the Joint Management to book the Vaudeville for another five matinees the following week, Elizabeth was irked by the poverty of critical support. Scott's notice, Archer agreed, was 'sheer mendacity'.[38] Elizabeth badgered him so much that he agreed to 'break my vow of abstinence from Ibsen criticism'[39] and write a piece for *The World*. A couple of days later, he published a spirited article in which he described her as greater than Bernhardt, a 'consummate virtuoso. . . I do not hesitate to call her performance in the last act the finest piece of modern tragedy within my recollection.'[40] He also seems to have given a highly partisan account of the critical response to Ibsen in Munich, who wrote to Archer on 29 April congratulating him on the play's 'unchallenged reception'.[41]

But Elizabeth was not only angered by slovenly reviews, she was also infuriated by Shaw. He had turned up at their final rehearsal, whispering and advising, a 'strongly-marked figure with . . . very long legs & [a] wide-brim hat over toffee-coloured hair, whisking about between stalls & stage for a word with Archer'.[42] He had written to her after the first performance, declaring that 'I have never had a more tremendous sensation in a theatre than that which began when everybody saw that the pistol shot was coming at the end . . . you were sympathetically unsympathetic, which was the exact solution of the central difficulty of playing Hedda.'[43] But then he complained that she was sometimes inaudible, that the omission of Hedda's pregnancy made her agitation meaningless, and that she should never have substituted 'gracefully' for 'beautifully'.

Elizabeth flared, dispatched 'a rude reply',[44] and demanded to know from Archer why a man who was neither an actor nor a critic assumed he had the right to pass judgement on their work. Archer did his best to soothe her, suggesting she had misinterpreted Shaw. 'He *is* an ass, and no one has told him so more frequently and emphatically than I have; but he has one of the keenest intellects I ever came across; he is a man who would starve and *has* starved rather than sell his soul; and as for humour, he is absolutely the wittiest man I know.'[45]

Despite Shaw and the critics, the production became so popular that on 4 May, *Money* was ousted and *Hedda Gabler* became the second Ibsen play in Britain to be given an evening run. The only successful production of the play so far, it also symbolized the first real advance for the new repertoire in London. 'You never played Hedda better than tonight,'[46] Archer congratulated her, as he typed up three pages of notes and the production began to sell out. A few of the appreciative critics reviewed the production again and there was even a wild rumour that Ibsen himself was about to arrive in London to see the play. But Ibsen never did visit England, reluctant to travel anywhere if he could not speak the language. 'I increasingly feel it is a painful lack in me that I did not learn to speak English in good time,' he confessed to Archer four years later, in 1895. 'Now it is too late.'[47]

As he kept up an almost daily stream of promptings and notes (the manuscript must be replenished and the backstage pianist seemed to have lost interest), Elizabeth caved in and dropped the word 'gracefully' in favour of 'beautifully'. 'I am really delighted,' he told her, adding that he would be coming to the theatre at random, alert for any regression: 'I shall sneak into the pit like a thief in the night and if you say "gracefully" I shall hiss.'[48] The notes began arriving with little endearments tagged on to the end. 'I'm afraid it will be a terrible strain for you to play it twice today,' he wrote before the first Saturday matinee. But evidently, she was not too tired to celebrate with him that night over supper at Gatti's. The restaurant became their regular late-night rendezvous, 'anytime between 11 and half past'.[49] Letters and even telegrams arranging meetings sped back and forth between them. One Sunday, he did not go to Cobham as usual but met her instead and the next day apologized 'that I had kept you talking for four mortal hours without an entr'acte'.[50] Work and success was bringing them closer together.

Hedda Gabler was the greatest test which Archer and the campaign for new drama had yet faced, yet it had no immediate effect on the theatre other than attracting attention to two dismal matinees, neither of which involved Archer. Edward Aveling's production of Eleanor Marx-Aveling's translation of *The Lady From the Sea* at Terry's Theatre on 10 May, turned out, according to Archer, to be 'out & away the worst Ibsen performance there has ever been'.[51] Another revival of his translation of *A Doll's House*, this time with the resolutely undistinguished Rose Norrys at the Criterion on 2 June, fared no better. Much more disheartening was the antipathy of Jones and Pinero.

Jones had equivocated over Ibsen for two years. Like Scott, he recognized the quality of his writing and, as a playwright, theoretically supported the freedom of the dramatist to write about whatever he wished. But for Jones, there were limits, and 'the sexual-pessimistic blizzard sweeping over North Europe'[52] was one of them. 'I protest against this with all my might,' he told the members of the National Sunday League earlier that year, assuring them that his kind of drama emphasized 'a balance of health, of beauty, and pleasure in life'.[53] To defend this balance, he was prepared, if necessary, to call up official support. The playwright should never, he wrote, 'offend against the recognized code of social decency, and here we have a sufficient safeguard in the censorship . . .'[54]

His new play, *The Dancing Girl*, had been running for four months at the Haymarket. Supposedly serious, it was wrecked by Jones's melodramatic timidity. Drusilla Ives is seduced by a Duke and then leaves him. In the final act, the Duke, hearing of her death after dancing one night in New Orleans, makes reparation for her ruined life by devoting himself to philanthropic works. 'Bravo! Bravissimo!!' Archer notified Jones. 'First three acts by far the best thing you have done, and about the best any Englishman has done in *my* time. Of course you know as well as I do that the fourth act is an anti-climax.' Again, he tried to be encouraging in the hope that next time, Jones might be 'logical & tragical to the end',[55] but Elizabeth was not prepared to be so generous. She loathed *The Dancing Girl* and told Archer so. Admitting the play was 'simply Ouida' (a popular novelist specializing in tales of love and intrigue), he urged her to be more tolerant. 'He *tries* to think, and he *tries* to write and that's more than most of them do.'[56] It was the second time within a few weeks he had found himself defending his friends to Elizabeth, but Archer's continued endorsement of Jones and Pinero, whether public or private, was looking increasingly precarious.

For Pinero was blaming Archer for blowing the theatre off course. 'A few years ago the native authors were working with a distinct & sound aim & with every prospect of popularizing a rational, observant & home grown play,' he told him heatedly. 'Then came the Scandinavian drama, held up by the new critics as the Perfect drama & used by them as a measure of discrediting native produce. Just for the present everything is knocked askew; the English dramatist has little influence & the public, urged to witness *A Dolls House*, patronises the Empire Theatre of Varieties.'[57]

Towards the end of May, Marion Lea resigned from the Joint Management. She was intending to marry the American dramatist Langdon Mitchell and thinking of leaving both the stage and England. Archer was secretly rather pleased, as he thought Marion held Elizabeth back. Besides, her departure made it easier for he and Elizabeth to consider a possible next production together. They looked at *Lady Inger of Østraat* and a sliver from a translation of *Brand* by C. H. Herford, a professor of English at Aberystwyth University, who was devoting 'all my leisure time'[58] to the work. One weekend in the country at Cobham, Archer re-read *The Duchess of Malfi*, promising Elizabeth he would 'report tomorrow night if you will come to Gatti's'.[59] But by 30 May, when *Hedda Gabler* closed after a six-week run, they had still not reached a decision.

Archer did not see the final performance. 'I hadn't the heart to face so melancholy an occasion,' he said. Instead, he promised Elizabeth that he would meet her afterwards for 'the last of our little suppers – you don't know how I shall miss them'.[60]

That afternoon, he was at Toole's Theatre at Charing Cross, to see a twenty-five-minute burlesque of *Hedda Gabler* called *Ibsen's Ghost*, written by a little-known Scottish novelist called J. M. Barrie, and at the end of which the cast shot themselves 'beautifully' with pop-guns. It was a fitting climax, Archer thought, to 'a piece of genuinely witty fooling which ought not to be missed'.[61]

On 23 July 1890, a few weeks after Archer met Elizabeth Robins, Shaw spent a day with him and Frances at Cobham. The two friends had a ramble as far as Ripley a few miles away, and returned to the cottage where, after lunch, they were joined by Walkley, who had a house nearby. Sitting beneath the elm trees in the garden, they listened while Shaw read the Ibsen lecture he had delivered to the Fabians at the St James's Restaurant.

Archer suspected that Shaw was less concerned with Ibsen the dramatist as Ibsen the social and moral reformer, and his reading that afternoon proved it. Neither man had read much Schopenhauer, the German philosopher who believed the essential creative force in human nature to be a covert and irrational will, but hearing Shaw appropriate Ibsen to celebrate impulsive will over rationalism, Archer began to use 'Shawpenhaurism'[62] as a stick with which to beat him. Walkley's thoughts drifted off to contemplating the Archer flower beds.

Throwing Archer's objections aside, Shaw expanded the lecture into a book. *The Quintessence of Ibsenism* (a 'loathsome title' in Archer's opinion[63]), Shaw's public entry into the Ibsen campaign, was published in October 1891. Reading it, Archer wearily discovered that Shaw was attempting 'an exposition of Ibsenism'. With Fabian intensity and considerable insight, he analyzed the plays from *Brand* to *Hedda Gabler*, most of which he had read in Archer's translations. Using Ibsen as a model, Shaw divided society into three classes: the idealists, the philistines and the realists. The idealists lived in a world of sentimental illusions, while the philistines were content with things remaining as they were. Social progress, Shaw insisted, depended upon the realists, who included both Ibsen and himself. It was their mission to expose the truth of the world as uncompromisingly as possible and proclaim 'the will to live'. *Ghosts*, he argued, was a 'realists' play, presenting ... an uncompromising and outspoken attack on marriage as a useless sacrifice of human beings to an ideal'. *The Wild Duck* and *Rosmersholm* demonstrated 'the power of ideals to kill'.[64]

The Quintessence of Ibsenism is the culmination of eight years of instruction by Archer on one hand and the Fabians on the other. Both parties grumbled over it, Sidney Webb bemoaning Shaw's emphasis on the individual rather than the socialist collective will. Archer reviewed the book in the form of an open letter to Shaw for the November issue of *New Review*. The essays on the plays, he acknowledged, were 'little masterpieces of dialectical and literary dexterity', and those on *Brand* and *Peer Gynt*, neither of which Shaw had actually read but had listened while Archer read, translating as he did so, filled him with awe. 'I have read and re-read these poems until I know them as intimately as Mr Ruskin knows Giotto's Campanile; you, on the other hand ... have merely picked up a vague, second-hand knowledge of their outlines, yet you have penetrated their meaning ... much more thoroughly than I have.' The reason, he hazarded, was that he became preoccupied with the detail of a play, whereas Shaw saw only the broad underlying brushstrokes.

However, this had made him tumble headlong into the deepest mires of Ibsenism, with the result that he was propping up the misconception of Ibsen as 'the showman of a moral wax-work'[65] rather than thinking of him as a writer portraying living people. Archer never denied that Ibsen was a didactic playwright whose 'originality lies in giving intense dramatic life to modern ideas', but he insisted that an idea should never be divested of 'the flesh and blood, the imagination, the passion, the style in which it is clothed'.[66] By this he meant the literary quality of Ibsen's writing, the light shone into the shadows of human psychology and the opportunities he gave to actors and actresses. Both Archer and Shaw agreed that Ibsen must revolutionize the English stage, but when he charged Shaw with reducing the playwright's ideas to 'diagrammatic definiteness',[67] Archer was accusing him of Fabianizing and Shavianizing Ibsen.

The open letter prompted the first skirmish in an autumn of tense ambush and manœuvre between Archer and Shaw. Once he received the article, Archibald Grove, the *New Review* editor, sent it to Shaw, suggesting he write a reply. Instead, on 25 October, Shaw wrote to Archer 'in hottest haste', advising him that his reputation depended upon him burning the review at once. Instead of recognizing that *The Quintessence of Ibsenism* was brilliantly and intricately reasoned, he had served up a disgraceful 'Noodle's oration'.[68] Archer replied he would publish regardless. 'An awful silence will fall on your little world when the *New Review* appears: your friends will breathe only by stealth,'[69] warned Shaw the next day. Thoroughly enjoying himself, Archer ridiculed his friend's majestic image of his own infallibility: 'I have always said you would end by being Pope, & now I'm sure of it. Better order your triple crown at once.'

These battles in which Archer took the literary and theatrical wing and Shaw the political, were integral to both their friendship and the campaign, for each tacitly acknowledged the interdependence of their views. 'The probability is that neither of us is anywhere near right, but it's very likely that you have the right end of the stick and I the wrong,' Archer reminded Shaw. 'All I want you to do is pull.'[70] But Shaw had dropped his end of the stick in surprised embarrassment, for Archer had unaccountably broken their prohibition on revealing their private emotions. He had ended his open letter with a declaration that it should be read in the light of 'the affection I have long felt for you'.[71]

For the moment, Shaw was disarmed.

When *Hedda Gabler* closed at the end of May, Archer had been living alone at Queen Square for a year, travelling back and forth most Sundays between London and the country. Elizabeth, meanwhile, moved from St John's Wood to top-floor rooms at 28 Manchester Square Mansions, just behind Wigmore Street. She would live here until 1900. In September, she opened in the leading role of Claire de Cintré in Henry James's *The American*, which Compton had brought into the Opera Comique. She had been recommended by James himself, who was impressed by her performance as Hedda while remaining decidedly ambivalent about Ibsen. '*Must* I think these things works of skill?'[72] he asked Gosse plaintively. *The American* created a small ripple of social interest (the Prince of Wales was lured along to see it), but floundered and finally submerged beneath hostile reviews in December.

'No letter from you,' Elizabeth wrote dejectedly to Archer, after returning home one Thursday night in October from the Opera Comique. 'I could tell you many things but I'm too tired & impatient to write . . .'[73]

She was exhausted, both physically and emotionally. While playing Hedda, she had stood 'at the peak – looking out over all the kingdoms of art',[74] but it was colder at the summit than she thought and during July she was left bedraggled by a vicious bout of influenza. During the summer, she and Archer continued to send each other little notes and meet regularly for supper at Gatti's. They also met at Queen Square and Manchester Square Mansions, where a climb of seventy-four stairs brought him to Elizabeth's sanctuary of two bedrooms, a dining-room and a study. Here, she kept her papers and books and collection of photographs, already including at least one of William Archer.

As Mary Anderson usurped Ellen Wallis in Archer's scheme of things, so Elizabeth had replaced the retired Mary Anderson and eclipsed both of them. Archer found something particularly erotic in American women, and Elizabeth was also a compulsive mix of intellect, romance and idealism, symbolizing everything he wanted to see in the theatre and his own life. The theatre had brought them together and *Hedda Gabler* had provided a tantalizing glimpse of how much they might achieve. Archer admired Elizabeth more and more, and she found herself responding to him. Yet both were wary of taking a step too far. It seems that for at least six months, their relationship was one of letters and late suppers for two, as they hesitated on the brink of the unspoken.

However, Archer was not the only one sending Elizabeth notes. William Heinemann had also taken a shine to her, writing and turning up every now and then out of the blue, announcing that he had reserved a restaurant table for supper. His appearances unnerved her, for she was generally suspicious of men and their intentions. The memory of her dreadful marriage and her husband's watery end was still distressing and when she arrived in London, she was dismayed that her black mourning dress failed to deter unwelcome advances. A male lodger at Duchess Street had barred her way on dimly-lit stairs; two men escorting her across a road began whispering lasciviously, and an incident had even forced her to change her seat at St Paul's Cathedral. She felt secure with the homosexual Wilde (who thought her Hedda 'a masterpiece'[75]), and the homosexually-inclined James, but at the same time she confided to her diary that she felt 'so alone ... There is no such want in my soul as the craving for love ...'[76]

Elizabeth and Archer were drawn to each other, yet she dithered as much as he did. Tiredness, exasperation at Heinemann's persistence, and her inability to decipher her true feeling for Archer or his for her, left her tense, unpredictable and 'perilously near a breakdown'.[77] The situation was delicate, for as well as angling for her affection, Heinemann was also negotiating to become Ibsen's British publisher in succession to Walter Scott, whose fifth and final volume of the *Prose Dramas* had just been published. As Archer wanted to prepare future translations and Elizabeth secure stage rights to the plays, it was essential that, throughout their emotional dodging and weaving, professional relations with Heinemann remained intact. There was much treading softly, although privately they vented their distrust of Heinemann by mocking his Jewishness.

The first emotional crisis between Archer and Elizabeth seems to have occurred over the fourth weekend in October. On Saturday, the 24th, he noted that she was looking 'like a ghost'. That night, she left the Opera Comique after *The American* and walked along The Strand to meet him coming out of the premiere of Pinero's *The Times* at Terry's. Later, at home, she found a note from him: 'I hope you're all right now.'[78] The next day, Sunday, instead of travelling down to Cobham, Archer arrived for tea at Manchester Square Mansions, bringing a copy of José Echegaray's *Madman or Saint* to discuss as a possible production. He was also bearing gifts of a box of bon-bons and a 'wonderfully fine' engraving of Elisa Rachel, the remarkable French actress who died early of consumption in 1858, mourned by many lovers.

It was an intimate afternoon. When someone, perhaps Heinemann, unexpectedly knocked on the door, they ignored it, not moving, holding their breaths like lovers in silence until the caller retreated down the stairs. But something happened to destroy their ease and the day ended in confusion. Elizabeth later typed a note for her diary which she left incomplete. 'Oh I'm a miserable changeable creature – he goes home to finish his writing after I've been about as unsatisfactory as I know how. I couldn't help . . .'[79]

The following day, Monday, she wrote 'a long letter to W.A.'[80] and on Tuesday, received one from him, neither of which appears to be extant. Nine days later, on 5 November, things had apparently still not been resolved. 'Horrible depression of yesterday deepened & more desperate today,' Elizabeth wrote in her diary. 'Even WA my strongest anchor to good good cheer & wholesome activity is coming to demand too much of me of time and of regard. It would not be hard for me to love this man not wisely but too well and I must guard my poor life against a curse like that. For soon after I had acknowledged him as the one being in the world for me he wd possess the supremest power to pain me; and unconsciously and inevitably he wd use his power. Not that he wd *wish* to, not that he wdn't try to avoid it, but he wd be as helpless as I.'

Elizabeth was simultaneously trying to distance herself from Heinemann and decide either how to prevent her affair with Archer from developing further than she thought wise or, if it had already done so, how to restore it to the close friendship of earlier that year. Under her diary entry of 5 November, she wrote emphatically that 'No man is my master.'[81]

One speculates whether Frances knew about the liaison and if so, how much. There is little direct evidence either way, but she met Elizabeth socially once or twice and it is doubtful that she was entirely in the dark. However, the question of Frances and Archer parting seems never to have arisen, for while they lived separately for most of the time, they never stopped watching over each other. The most likely answer is that Frances knew of a friendship and accepted it, or at least appeared to accept it. For his part, Archer was so practised at leading a double life that apart from the occasional rumour, his relationship with Elizabeth remained a secret. Elizabeth too was proficient at presenting a mask to the world. They were both so expert at subterfuge that in later years, members of the extended Archer family, Elizabeth's friends and various scholars have denied that any emotional relationship between them existed.

Meanwhile, Shaw was circling and was certain that something was going on. It was outside their code of friendship for him to confront Archer directly about Elizabeth, and besides, he had no moral grounds for doing so. He was still darting about town with Florence Farr, these days sometimes only a few steps ahead of Jenny Patterson, a vengeful widow fifteen years his senior, who loved him and felt jilted. 'However, no living woman shall turn my head as you have turned Archer's,'[82] Shaw taunted Elizabeth on 30 April, writing from the safe harbour of the Aereated Bread Shop on The Strand. This time, Elizabeth did not rise to the bait. But early in November, both she and Archer were dismayed to find themselves the victims of Shaw's indomitable passion for meddling in other people's business.

It started in September, when George Moore wrote to the *Pall Mall Gazette*, sneering at theatre criticism as the province of 'the idle, the sensual, and the unintellectual',[83] and hinting of cosy critical teas with pretty actresses in rooms decorated with flowers and shaded with pink blinds. Archer, whom he saw as a Don Quixote pitching against Scott's windmill, was, he reckoned, almost the only theatre critic worth reading. Finding himself the exception to a general charge of corruption, Archer might have ignored this outburst had not Shaw (echoing Archer's own article in the *St James's Magazine* several years previously) muttered in *The Quintessence of Ibsenism* that a critic 'may often have to choose between making himself agreeable [to managers] and forfeiting his post.'[84]

Archer reacted as if he had been punched. He valued his critical integrity over almost everything else and charged into print in the November issue of the *Fortnightly Review*, protesting that he had been a theatre critic for twelve years but 'no one has yet thought it worthwhile to make the slightest attempt to buy my goodwill. If I wanted to earn half-a-crown, or even a cup of afternoon tea, in exchange for a favourable "notice," I should positively not know how to set about the unholy traffic.'[85]

Unwittingly, he had wandered into Shaw's gunsights. On 7 November, Shaw launched his ambush, writing to Archer and accusing him of 'monstrous hypocrisies'. Had he forgotten taking Mary Anderson for a walk on Hampstead Heath? Were there not photographs of Janet Achurch as Nora hanging on his study wall? 'When I see you posing as the incorruptible Archer, assuring the public with an air of primeval simplicity that you would not know how to set about getting half a crown for a notice if you wanted to, and that no monk knows less of teas with pretty actresses than William the Anchorite, I really feel a moral revulsion,' he told him. 'How if I were to tell the world tha⁺ ˙ have hardly once dropped in on you unexpectedly at Queen Square without disturbing a tete-a-tete between you and some pretty actress or another . . . Marion la bionda today; Elizabeth la bruna tomorrow . . . Why, man alive, there is not an ambitious actress in London whose first move is not to get at William Archer.'[86]

Shaw did not 'tell the world', but he did the next best thing. On the 7th, at the same time as writing to Archer, he answered a letter from the editor of the *Fortnightly Review*. This was Frank Harris, an exact contemporary of Archer and Shaw's and a famously inveterate boaster, philanderer and gossip. Shaw was usually punctilious with his mail, but that day he put his letter to Harris in the envelope addressed to Archer, slipped the potentially scandalous letter to Archer in the envelope addressed to Harris, and posted them. Two days later, on 9 November, he wrote to Archer again, claiming this was a dreadful mistake. 'Horror on horror's head: I have put your letter into Harris's envelope – and such a letter!'[87]

On the same day, Shaw turned his fire upon Elizabeth, writing to ask whether she had read Archer's protestation of incorruptibility in the *Fortnightly*. 'What do you think of that,' he goaded, 'you, who put him in your pocket with one flash of your dark?!! eyes so ridiculously easily that I blushed for him? *Do* write an article entitled "How to get at William Archer: by one who has done it." The editor of the Fortnightly will pay golden guineas for it.'[88]

Elizabeth was angered and possibly alarmed, especially as the letter arrived so soon after her intimate weekend with Archer. She did not let him see it ('too outrageous even to be shown to WA'[89]), but unleashed a furious letter to Shaw by return of post, demanding he stop making insinuations. 'I did not mean that you deliberately took his scalp,' wrote Shaw the next day. 'But I assure you the scalp went all the same – walked spontaneously off his head and hung itself to your belt without the least help from you or conscience on his part.'[90] On the 11th, Harris returned to Shaw the letter written to Archer. It 'afforded me much amusement,' Harris told him. Shaw sent it on to Archer. 'Has anything more unspeakably awful ever happened than my sending this to Harris & his letter to you?'[91] he enquired disingenuously.

It appears that Shaw was deliberately attempting to sabotage the relationship between Archer and Elizabeth. He may have been trying to protect his friend from his own 'unconquerable innocence'[92] and thereby prevent him from perhaps making a fool of himself romantically and professionally. Less creditably, he saw that Archer and Elizabeth had formed an Ibsen alliance threatening to overshadow his own favourite actress, Janet Achurch, soon to return from her two-year tour of Australia.

Whatever the reasons, having made his point, he staged a temporary retreat. During the previous month's tussle over *The Quintessence of Ibsenism*, Archer had reminded Shaw how valuable their scuffling was and outflanked him by telling him how highly he regarded him. Now Shaw did the same, celebrating the fact that whenever a stick lay between them, they would instinctively pick up either end. In a reconciliatory letter of 13 November, he reflected that 'I sometimes, when a good side of you comes out by chance against a bad side of me, feel apologetic for the difference; but as we clearly could not stand the sight of each other if the difference were abolished, whether by the Archerization of Shaw ... or the Shawation of Archer, let us rejoice that it exists.'[93]

No sooner had he extricated himself from Shaw, than Archer found himself under attack from a pro-censorship alliance of Pigott, Clement Scott and George Moore, whose position on censorship had undergone a decisive transformation. As his third Independent Theatre production at the Royalty, Grein announced a programme of three short plays, *The Kiss* by Theodore de Banville, *The Minister's Call* by Arthur Symons and *A Visit*, a play in two acts which Archer had translated from *De Besuch*, by the Danish writer, Edward Brandes.

The play asks whether an unfaithful husband has the moral right to be rid of his wife, whose own infidelity has been exposed. Archer delivered his typescript and heard nothing further. It was not until the performance was advertised for 4 March 1892 that he discovered someone had tampered with the script and that an amended text would be performed. Suspecting that Grein had sent it to the Examiner of Plays for his approval and Pigott had ordered cuts to which Grein had agreed without consulting him, Archer retaliated in 'the only way left open'.[94] He had the officially deleted passages printed as a four-page leaflet and placed a copy on each seat in theatre.

A few days later, *The Daily Telegraph* revealed the excisions were not made by Pigott at all, but that the script had been 'corrected'[95] by Moore. Archer bounded into print in the *Pall Mall Gazette*, demanding to know whether Moore had 'merely held the blue pencil in execution of the Censor's express mandate' or whether he had been allowed 'a free hand'[96] in the mutilation of the play. Scott retaliated, defending Pigott as 'a gentleman and scholar' whose 'wholesome and friendly supervision' was appreciated by everyone in the theatre. By editing *A Visit*, Moore had done nothing more harmful than 'prevent a spade being called a spade in public'.[97] Again Archer blazed into print. The entire shabby episode, he cried, demonstrated 'the odious, dangerous and unconstitutional nature of censorship'.[98]

All this was partly public manœuvring in advance of hearings by a Parliamentary Select Committee into the regulation of the theatres and a review of censorship policy. Archer had ensured that he would be invited to give evidence and on 16 May, he told the committee that the Examiner suppressed serious work and denied the public its responsibility of self-censorship. Again, his was a lone voice, smothered by a battalion of critics and actor-managers led by Scott and Irving, who came to praise the Examiner and all his works. When Pigott himself appeared, he ridiculed Archer's 'very limited' experience of the theatre and declared that the reason he advocated Ibsen's plays was to make money from his translations. He himself had studied Ibsen's plays 'pretty carefully' and concluded that the characters were 'morally deranged'.[99] Then why, the committee asked patiently, had Pigott awarded performance licences to *A Doll's House* and *Hedda Gabler*? Because, Pigott stoutly replied, they constituted no threat to decency, for English audiences would laugh them into obscurity.

Immediately after the committee ended its deliberations by recommending no change, Pigott's 'stupid meddling' prompted Archer to come to the defence of Oscar Wilde. Archer liked Wilde and respected his intellect. Earlier that year, he had signalled his admiration of *Lady Windermere's Fan*, Wilde's first play to be produced in London, by advising in his review that it be substantially rewritten.

According to Archer, Wilde's wit held a dazzlingly high promise of seriousness. That summer, when Wilde told him about the rehearsals for his second piece, *Salome*, Archer slipped away 'looking forward, with a certain malign glee, to the inevitable suppression of the play by the Great Irresponsible'. Sarah Bernhardt was to appear in the title role wearing a flowing golden robe and her tumbling hair powdered blue. There was to be a violet cyclorama, and braziers of perfumed coals were to take the place of an orchestra but, as Archer predicted, Pigott suddenly descended, banning the production because the actors were portraying Biblical characters. Archer jumped into action, claiming that it was conclusive proof of the censor's 'petty tyranny'[100] that the work of a serious writer and one of the greatest actresses of their time should be prohibited, while Wilde's mannerisms were ridiculed each night by Charles Hawtrey in *The Poet and the Puppets*, a musical burlesque at the Comedy Theatre.

No one supported Archer. Wilde, who had escaped with Lord Alfred Douglas to wallow in the waters at Bad Homberg, sent a message thanking him for his 'courteous and generous recognition' of his work. 'We must abolish the censure,' he said. 'I think we can do it.'[101] Archer had little of Wilde's confidence.

On 18 August, Elizabeth took a train to Yorkshire, taking refuge from Heinemann, who was now pleading with her to marry him, secretly if necessary. She arrived at Redcar, the home of her friend Florence Bell. An aristocrat's daughter and the wife of Hugh, a successful ironmaster, Florence was an experienced but humdrum writer whose short play, *Karin*, derived from the Swedish, had been quickly revised by Archer and speedily produced by Elizabeth for an unsuccessful Vaudeville matinee in May. Elizabeth too, had begun channelling her feverish emotions into fiction. She was writing an autobiographical novella (which remains unpublished) called *The Coming Woman*, in which she figures as the actress, Katherine Fleet, and Archer appears as the critic, McBride, a name perhaps with some playfully melancholic significance. At the end, Katherine defects alone to Paris.

Elizabeth took her writing north with her. The same day, 18 August, Archer also left London. He took his bicycle and travelled 'alone due north'[102] to Lichfield, to visit the cathedral. Although he abhorred the Church, Archer liked churches, their gloomy, chilly, musty interiors, each one a history of its parish and, taken together, of England. He particularly admired Salisbury Cathedral, and once he had inspected Lichfield, he travelled on by train and cycle, across Derbyshire and Yorkshire to Westmorland, where he stopped at Kendal. He may have met Elizabeth; according to her diary, she and Florence were travelling the north, studying Norwegian. She arrived back in London on 9

September and Archer arrived in town on the 12th. The next day, he told Shaw he had been to Ireland.

The following month, Archer and Elizabeth went down to Brighton together, but this time there was no mystery about the trip. They had formed a precarious alliance with Janet Achurch and Charles Charrington, who had returned to England earlier that year. On 19 April, the Charringtons revived *A Doll's House* at the Avenue Theatre, where Archer and Shaw watched astounded as Janet put on a wildly unpredictable performance, her voice jolting from one register to another, while beside her, Charrington flailed miserably as Helmer. The reason for the deterioration was soon evident. Already prone to alcoholism, Janet was slithering into drug addiction. In Australia, she had almost died giving birth to her daughter and had since become dependent upon the morphia prescribed by her doctors. In July, she collapsed but rallied and carried on, determined to revive her career. Recklessly, Charrington booked the Theatre Royal at Brighton for the week of 3 October and announced that *A Doll's House* would play in repertoire with *Hedda Gabler*, in Archer's translations. Elizabeth agreed to revive Mrs Linde and Hedda, Janet Achurch would appear as Nora and Mrs Elvsted, and Charrington as Helmer and Lovborg. Archer was co-directing with George Foss.

The performances were terrible. The worst was *A Doll's House* on Wednesday, when not only Janet, but also Charrington was dulled by morphia, which he had taken to relieve the pain of neuralgia. Archer watched in anguish as they shambled through their scenes, whimpering and slurring their lines and once or twice even feeling their way about the stage by the furniture. Whenever they came off stage, he ran to the wings to keep them awake by walking them about. Henry James, who had come down to support them, sadly watched Elizabeth, 'a lonely, stranded figure ploughing through Charringtonian sands'. *Hedda Gabler* began on a surer footing but swung quickly into staginess as Janet 'ranted till you couldn't believe it'.[103] Frances had also arrived in Brighton and after the Thursday performance, Elizabeth invited the Archers, the Charringtons and Henry James to dinner at the Bedford Hotel, overlooking the grey and restless sea. The meal was strained and silent.

Returning to London on Sunday, Archer discovered that Shaw had sprung yet another ambush. He had answered Grein's appeal for a new British play for the Independent Theatre by exhuming *Rhinegold*, dusting it down and sprucing it up into 'an Original Didactic Realistic

Play in Three Acts' under 'the farfetched Scriptural title' of *Widowers'*
Houses. Laying 'violent hands' on Archer's 'sympathetically romantic'
plot, he recounted, 'I perversely distorted it into a grotesquely realistic
exposure of slum landlordism, municipal jobbery, and the pecuniary
and matrimonial ties between them.'[104] The play was scheduled for two
performances at the Royalty, the first being on 9 December.

'You made a plot for Widowers' Houses; and you can claim the
Rhine scenery of the first act, and the idea of the tainted treasure,'[105]
Shaw told Archer, but with his hands gripping the reins, the play had
bolted off into an altogether different direction than Archer originally
envisaged. Nevertheless, as Archer had thrust him into journalism, he
had nudged Shaw into the theatre by firing the engine of his imagination. The hero, Harry Trench still becomes engaged to Blanche
Sartorius, and still discovers her wealth to be derived from the rents of
her father's slum properties. But what Shaw did was to present her
father as not only a racketeer but part of a rotten social network in
which everyone, including the conservative Trench, either actively or
tacitly colludes. 'We're all in the same swim,' admits Trench. Shaw was
therefore able to reconcile Trench and Blanche, not in the sugary
romantic spirit of the drawing-room comedy but in embracing the
corruption of the real world.

Archer and Elizabeth went to see 'the great event'[106] together.
Florence Farr, Shaw's current favourite, played Blanche. By relentless
self-advertising, including publishing newspaper interviews with himself, Shaw had generated an audience of reasonable size. After a patchy
performance, led mainly by the prompter, Shaw, wearing his rust-red
Jaeger wool suit, scrambled on to the stage to inform them that they
had witnessed a regrettable but truthful slice of life.

Archer could not make up his mind whether the play was more
exasperating than tedious. Shaw had let loose his talent for soapbox
lecturing, but he evidently possessed no more instinctive aptitude for
drama than he had for painting or sculpture. He had simply not
observed society. 'If Mr Shaw would or could divest his mind of theory,
I think he would see that these lovers of his are not human beings at
all,' he pointed out in *The World* the following week. 'His world is
without atmosphere; no breath of humanity ... gets over the
footlights.'[107]

Shaw hit back the same day. 'A more amazing exposition of your
Shaw theory even I have never encountered,' he protested. 'Here am I,
who have collected slum rents weekly with these hands, & for 4½ years

been behind the scenes of the middle-class landowner – who have philandered with women of all sorts and sizes – and I am told gravely to go to nature & give up apriorizing [sic] about such matters by you . . . Get out!'[108]

The Master Builder
and Mrs Pat

'I have been pleasantly occupied this spring in losing the greater part of my humble savings in Australian banks,' Archer told Dibdin during the summer of 1893. 'I was a depositor in 3, two of which have busted.'[1] By chance, John Mackinnon Robertson, his friend from Edinburgh and now the editor of the *National Reformer*, had written a slim volume entitled *The Fallacy of Saving*, a copy of which arrived simultaneously with the news from Australia. 'I am already convinced of the fallacy of saving, thank you,'[2] wrote Archer in reply.

He had taken family advice in his investments and accepted his losses philosophically. He still earned three guineas a week from *The World* and made up his income from the *Manchester Guardian*, the royalties from his books and various papers and journals who would take his work. He was in his thirty-seventh year and although he was not well-off, he had sufficient income if he worked all hours, which he was happy to do. Like Corin in *As You Like It*, his watchword was that 'I earn that I eat.' This meant earning enough for books and papers, to pay rents and housekeepers in London and Cobham, to stock the larder in the country and buy Wheatsheaf lunches with Shaw and Gatti's suppers with Elizabeth. Frances seldom came up to town but when she did, 'we really *never* dine out'.[3] If there was enough left over for occasional travelling, Archer was happy. He took a Norwegian attitude to any surplus: to speculate honestly was fair enough and if one lost, then it was not a matter of shame. Shaw was surprised, when Archer told him the story of his Australian calamity, to see him 'chuckling with the enjoyment of a man who had just heard that his uncle had died in Australia and left him a million.'[4]

Far more important things than antipodean financial crashes were on Archer's mind in the spring of 1893. Chief among them were the darkly

mysterious currents swirling around Ibsen's new play and which had
their reaches both in London and Yorkshire. *Bygmester Solness* (*The
Master Builder*) was written in Christiana where Ibsen, now aged sixty-
five, had returned to live after an exile of twenty-seven years. The text
arrived in London from Gyldendal's Christiana branch, in batches
'projected across the north sea in a series of electric shocks'[5] during
November 1892.

The central character is Halvard Solness, a brooding, spiritually
unfulfilled master builder in his sixties, whose two children died young
and whose marriage to Aline has become loveless and bitter. One day,
he is visited by Hilde Wangel, a woman of twenty-three, who reminds
him that ten years ago he built a church in her village, climbed the
scaffolding around the spire and placed a wreath on the weather-vane.
Watching him was so enthralling that she believed she heard him
singing and that it sounded like harps in the air. Later, after supper at
her family home, Solness put his arms around her, kissed her on the
lips and said that in ten years he would carry her away to a magical
kingdom. She has now arrived to redeem his promise. Solness is
building a new house with a tower and Hilde implores him to climb to
the top again. He protests he has no head for heights anymore but at
last he climbs and reaches the summit. Hilde cries that once again she
can hear harps in the air. Suddenly, the master builder misses his
footing and, in an avalanche of scaffolding, falls to the ground and is
killed.

As he read each instalment, Archer became convinced it was 'one of
the most fascinating things that Ibsen had ever done',[6] but for Elizabeth,
who was hoping to produce the play, the signals from Norway became
increasingly scrambled. What on earth did *Bygmester Solness* mean?
Hilde seemed a disappointing, motiveless role. 'Think the old man's
stark mad,'[7] she commented gloomily to Florence Bell.

Archer was intrigued by the interweaving of realism and symbolism
and the play's psychological intricacy. The master builder embracing
and kissing Hilde, for example, was clearly fantasy, yet Solness is
persuaded that it happened. Archer saw him as a man whose loss of
faith and ambition had left him intellectually and creatively withered,
'sunk in bourgeois materialism, building towerless houses that are mere
breeding places for crude humanity'. In releasing him, Hilde emerged
as an avenging force of destiny whose idealism was so unyielding that it
destroyed other people's lives. Elizabeth, on the other hand, saw Hilde

as the emissary of an energetic younger generation demanding power in the world.

The play also deals with a young woman's physical and emotional awakening. The imagery of Hilde's fantasy, the towers, the embracing, the sounds in the air and the intensity of her pleasure suggest sexual arousal and orgasm. Archer and Elizabeth had muted the sexuality in *Hedda Gabler* in an attempt not to offend their audiences, but this would be impossible in *Bygmester Solness*. Certainly, Archer was fully aware of its eroticism. In an article in *The World*, he warned his readers that the new play was 'daring' even for 'these experimental days'. He pointed out that at the time of her fantasy, Hilde is 'at the age when the wonder of the world is beginning to dawn upon her'. In Archer's eyes, Solness is the instigator who, 'conscious of the woman in the child', imagines kissing Hilde; this thought 'flashes . . . from his mind to hers' and establishes an 'occult bond'[8] between them, which is broken only by his death.

Bygmester Solness was published in Christiana on 12 December. Several months earlier, Heinemann duly succeeded Walter Scott as Ibsen's London publisher and bought the British rights. He was then approached by Elizabeth, who wanted to strike out on her own as a producer-actress and who, without telling Archer, had hatched a plan that she and Florence Bell translate the new play. This was a case of ambition outstripping ability. Florence could translate moderately well from the Swedish but had never attempted Ibsen before and Elizabeth was hardly fluent in Norwegian. Heinemann acquiesced, possibly because he still nurtured hopes of marrying her. She told Archer of the plan in early August.

Archer had every right to feel he was the victim of yet another incomprehensible betrayal, but if he did, he concealed it. 'He takes it with amazing kindness,'[9] Elizabeth told Florence on 16 August. He tentatively endorsed the plan but advised her to keep her involvement a secret. When she asked why, he told her that to align herself so completely with the Ibsen cause might make managers reluctant to offer her other work. In reality, it was because he loved her too much to see her humiliated as an inept translator. And because he was determined to translate the play himself.

Elizabeth told Florence of his compliance two days before she joined her for their holiday in Yorkshire and Archer started out on his cycle tour. Whether or not events took another couple of turns in the north, by the beginning of November Archer had secured Heinemann's approval that he and Gosse translate *Bygmester Solness*. So it was that at least four separate copies of the text were dispatched from Christiana, one to Archer, another to Heinemann, a third to Gosse and a fourth to Elizabeth. On 6 December, Heinemann published twelve copies of the play in Norwegian to protect his copyright and, as a further safeguard, held a reading of the play at ten o'clock the next morning at the Haymarket. A single poster hurriedly put up outside announced the event to the London public. Four people turned up, one of whom was Archer, to watch Elizabeth read Hilde; Braekstad, Solness; Heinemann, Knut Brovik and Gosse, Dr Herdal.

After their public row over *Hedda Gabler*, Archer and Gosse worked together amicably enough on *Bygmester Solness*, although they communicated mainly by post. Gosse painstakingly observed every courtesy. 'I shall be very unwilling to contest any alteration that your taste & extraordinary knowledge of stage requirements have dictated,'[10] he assured Archer unctuously on 10 November. But then, Gosse admitted that the play baffled him. He could not understand Archer persisting that it was 'a drama which, while realistic in form, is in essence as poetic, as mystic, as fantastic, as *Faust*, or *Peer Gynt*;'[11] to him, it was 'the work of a majestic mind in rapid decline.'[12] Within a month, Archer had finished work, calling it *Solness the Builder*. 'Don't you think this sounds rather poor?'[13] murmured Gosse. Archer altered it to *The Master Builder*.

Gosse's contribution to the text was minimal. How much either Elizabeth or Florence made is unclear; probably very little, although Elizabeth and Archer frequently revised lines during rehearsals. Word of the new play spread quickly and intellectual London fizzed with curiosity. People cross-examined Archer as to what *The Master Builder* was about and arrived in rapid succession, avid for news, at Elizabeth's eyrie at Manchester Square Mansions. Henry James put his head round the door, and the social and religious novelist Mrs Humphrey Ward was followed by the sharp chronicler of country-house life, Rhoda Broughton. Sir Frederick Pollock, the jurist and keen advocate of amateur dramatics, made judicial enquiries. Tree and Oscar Wilde were equally curious.

Although the Joint Management was defunct and she had first thought Ibsen mad, Elizabeth had made up her mind to produce *The Master Builder* and play Hilde. Like Archer, she was frustrated by single matinees, but she was reluctant to raise her own money. The time had come, she believed, for Ibsen and herself to be welcomed into the fortress of the commercial West End. This Archer doubted. Undaunted, Elizabeth secured the stage rights and in December began the rounds of the mainstream theatres in search of an actor-manager willing to produce both her and the play under her authority. She was rejected at each stop except the Haymarket where, against all the odds, Tree's interest in Ibsen was unabated. This time, he wanted to play Solness. Elizabeth turned him down.

She was left with no choice but to find her own money and hire a theatre. Archer adopted his old tactic of prophesying 'certain disaster',[14] but by now, Elizabeth had learned to interpret his lack of encouragement as the precise opposite. By late January, she had persuaded Herbert Waring, the original Torvald Helmer, to play Solness and find a private backer who booked the Trafalgar Square Theatre in St Martin's Lane (now the Duke of York's) for five public matinees, the first being on 20 February.

The world premiere of *The Master Builder* had taken place simultaneously in Germany and Norway on 19 January. The production at the Lessingtheater in Berlin had been a disaster and closed after three performances. The version performed on the same night in Trondheim by a touring company led by William Petersen, who had daringly acquired the provincial rights, also failed, as did a later Swedish production in Finland. Archer, Elizabeth and George Foss, who once again joined them as credited stage-manager, found themselves in the same position as they had been with *Hedda Gabler*, with the chance of making the British premiere of *The Master Builder* the first successful production.

They assembled an 'ideal cast', including Louise Moodie, an actress of the old school but eager to experiment in the new, as Aline Solness, and John Beauchamp, a popular character-actor, as Dr Herdal. The programme announced the production to be 'under the direction of Mr Herbert Waring & Miss Elizabeth Robins'. This time, there was no programme credit for the translation, perhaps as a result of friction between the various hopeful claimants to the title, and as he took no credit for his co-direction, Archer's name does not appear at all. Yet Archer, 'the one man in the world', recalled Elizabeth, 'who could do most for our author, and . . . most for us', took up his place as usual in the stalls, pad of paper at the ready. 'Nothing escaped him, from the slightest inflection of voice, the significance of the smallest gesture and the most fleeting expression, up to the crescendo of a climax or the

1. William Archer
in his early thirties.

2. Grace Archer
in her early thirties.

3. Tolderodden, the Archer family home
at Larvik, Norway.

4. William Archer
as a boy.

5. William Archer in Edinburgh,
aged twenty-one.

6. The Gaiety Theatre,
Strand.

7. Frances Archer,
aged thirty-one.

8. Henrik Ibsen.   9. Bernard Shaw in the 1890s.

10. Janet Achurch as Nora, and Charles Charrington as Dr Rank, in *A Doll's House*, Novelty Theatre, July 1889.

11. Elizabeth Robins, aged twenty-nine, in the autumn of 1891.

12. William Archer, aged thirty-four. Inscribed on reverse to:
'Elizabeth Robins from William Archer 12 June '91.'
A further inscription by Elizabeth reads:
'You'll be sorry whatever you do.'

13. Elizabeth Robins
as Hedda Gabler, 1891.

14. Elizabeth Robins and Marion Lea.

15. In a caricature of Pear's soap advertisement,
Clement Scott attempts to disinfect Ibsen, as the ghosts
of Archer, Grein and Gosse hover in the background.

16. Henry Arthur Jones.

17. Arthur Wing Pinero.

18. Mrs Patrick Campbell as Paula and George Alexander as Tanqueray
in *The Second Mrs Tanqueray*, St James's Theatre, 1893.

capital crime of the smallest alteration of the text – nothing escaped that notebook.'[15]

Sniffing activity in the air and determined not to be left out, Shaw decided to mount another raid on the Archer–Robins partnership. In the afternoon of 4 February, he popped up at Manchester Square Mansions, ostensibly to interview Elizabeth for a preview of *The Master Builder* he planned to write for a newspaper. Still smarting from his previous interference in her affairs, Elizabeth flatly refused to give an interview without Waring present. Shaw persisted. He squeezed into her rooms, and what he said then so horrified her that in a frightening combination of Hedda Gabler and an imperious southern American woman, she picked up a revolver, pointed it straight at him and threatened that if he published one word she would shoot him. Shaw clattered down the stairs, her threats echoing in his ears. A clinical note dispatched later that evening rammed home the point that there would be no interviews. The next day, Shaw sent a 'promise not to play any more pranks on you'.[16]

Elizabeth swept him from her mind and concentrated upon *The Master Builder*. By the dress rehearsal, Archer was as usual near to despair. 'I have always found it quite impossible for anyone who has attended a long series of rehearsals really to *see* a piece of acting at a dress-rehearsal,' he confessed to the actor Bernard Gould. 'I myself never have the least idea how a thing is going to turn out at the performance.'[17]

He was even more apprehensive than before. None of the Ibsen plays so far performed in London contained any allusion to Norwegian folklore but in *The Master Builder*, Solness sees within himself the spirit of the troll, thought to be a race of curious dwarves living in mountain caves and representing the fantastic and evil forces in mankind. It was impossible to predict how an English audience would respond to this, or to the idea of an elderly woman still in loving possession of her childhood dolls. For the world premiere in Berlin, the dialogue between Aline Solness and Hilde in which Aline admits to having nine dolls, had been cut because the audience would have laughed. Archer decided to retain it, adamant that a full text should be played in London. 'I've no doubt the audience *will* laugh at the dolls,' he predicted to Clement King Shorter, the editor of the *Illustrated London News*, ' – if that is the only point at which they laugh in the wrong place they will be an exceptionally enlightened audience – but if you cut the dolls you cut the whole point of Mrs Solness's character – her abortive, atrophied maternal instinct – & you might as well cut the whole play at once.'[18]

At two-thirty on Monday, 20 February, the curtain rose on the first performance and on Solness's work room, with its sofa, chairs, table and bookcase. 'The blunder has been made,' intoned the *Pall Mall Gazette*. '*Master-Builder Solness* [sic] has been played on the London stage.'

The audience did indeed laugh at the doll speech. They smiled and shrugged their shoulders at the mention of a troll. Many were confused by what was supposed to be real and what was intended as symbolic and were perplexed and embarrassed by the characters' motives. As Hilde Wangel, Elizabeth wore a rough blue travelling dress with sailor's collar, gloves and a floppy cap. She carried a rucksack and an alpenstock and, once over the Solness threshold, she knocked the dust off her hobnailed walking boots. During her long (some thought interminable) conversations with Solness, she sauntered about the room, looking through his books, papers and drawing materials. It was all very odd. Actresses in plays usually wore a different dress for each act. Why, people wondered, had she intruded into his house? Was this unpleasant and nonsensical story about the kiss and the kingdom true, or was it all a fabrication? What did it all represent? Perhaps Solness was Ibsen himself and the towers were his plays. Was Hilde therefore an appalling spirit of the new age about to supersede even his excesses? Some noticed a sparkle in her eyes; she seemed demonically intense one moment and rippling with suppressed laughter the next. Was she, as the *Pall Mall Gazette* asked the next day, a nymphomaniac or a calculating murderer? Could she even be both?

As the critics emerged from the theatre into busy St Martin's Lane, they were as befogged as Elizabeth when she first read the script and the next morning they savaged the play with the vehemence to which Archer was becoming depressingly accustomed.

The mixture of realism and erotic symbolism antagonized everyone. Scott pronounced it to be 'a play written, rehearsed and acted by lunatics', while the *Saturday Review* cried that it was 'incoherent ... perverted'. 'Simply blasphemous,' shrieked the *Morning Post*. 'Dull, mysterious, unchaste,' rumbled the *Daily Graphic*.[19] Even the previously loyal A. B. Walkley poked fun, suggesting that asking after each other's troll would replace the weather as a suitable topic for tea-time conversation. 'I simply HATE obscurity,'[20] he protested to Archer. Following the lead of Nisbet at *The Times*, the *Evening News and Post* declared that not only was Hilde mad, but Solness and his wife were as well. Nisbet, as ever one step ahead, vouchsafed that is was probably Ibsen who was insane.

As with *A Doll's House*, *Ghosts* and *Hedda Gabler*, the play was 'spat upon', remarked Archer, by the critics who 'rushed whining to the Lord Chamberlain and implored him to protect them'[21] when Ibsen's name was mentioned. But again some garlanded the acting with superlatives. As usual, Scott led the way, praising Elizabeth's performance as glowing with 'something like the very spark of genius'.[22] In the *Illustrated London News* on 25 February, Archer himself highlighted her 'intense vitality', Waring's 'power and discretion'[23] and explained that the characters were far from mad. On the contrary, he argued, there were men and women everywhere unable to account for or resist the turbulence of their own emotions.

He might have been writing of Elizabeth and himself.

The production opened before small but attentive and sometimes mystified groups of serious drama and the independent theatre movement supporters. They were socialists, journalists, writers, a new and expanding body of social observers, chatterers and interpreters; and middle-class men and women free in the afternoons. But audiences quickly swelled and after another week of matinees, *The Master Builder* became the second Ibsen play to transfer to the evening bill at the Vaudeville. Archer and Gosse's names appeared on the programme as translators, Elsie Chester replaced the unhappy Louise Moodie, and the production ran another three weeks until 25 March. It was the most successful production of the play yet staged, and at five weeks, the run was only a week less than that of *Hedda Gabler*.

As he had done after *Ghosts*, Archer gathered the most vindictive reviews together and published them, with a commentary, in the July issue of *Fortnightly Review*. This time, he called the piece 'The Mausoleum of Ibsen', a title taken from a newspaper prediction that '*The Master Builder* bids fair to raise a mausoleum in which the Ibsen craze may be conveniently buried and consigned to oblivion.'[24]

It is a more opimistic piece than ' "Ghosts" and Gibberings', for, as the new century loomed, a quickening of life and imagination was becoming discernible. The political power which had swung back and forth between Salisbury's Conservatives and Gladstone's Liberals for the past decade now rested with the Liberal Party and would do so for the next two years, until 1895. Britain was rich and fat, nearing the height of its imperial power. Victoria had ruled for fifty-six years, yet the blanket of Victorian well-being was sliding even faster from the bed of social discontent, and the gathering intellectual struggle between the old conservatives and the new reformers.

Radical ideas were taking grip. The word 'new' began to be applied to the intellectual spirit, and to politics, humour, journalism and women. There was Art Nouveau, a style of decorative illustration marked by flowing lines and riotous foliage, and the black-and-white drawings by Aubrey Beardsley which began to appear in *The Studio* in 1893. Within months, Beardsley's dark-lipped, long-limbed, flowingly-gowned women would be gazing sensuously from the pages of *The Yellow Book* and *The Savoy*. The apostles of decadence stood beside the Fabians and the Socialists (who were to have a new magazine, the *New Age*), and alongside them stood William Archer, the pioneering voice of the New Drama. 'The critic, it seems to me, should not try to *express* the feeling of the audience, but to *guide* its judgment,' [25] he explained to the journalist Max Pemberton. Although the old-style critics, with their hostility to innovation and seriousness, commanded many more readers in their daily papers than Archer in his small-circulation weekly, his influence was demonstrably increasing. There was proof of this in the comparative success of his productions. *A Doll's House*, *Hedda Gabler* and *The Master Builder* had each achieved a respectable run and, between them, had taken over £4,600 at the box office. Since its publication in 1888, *The Pillars of Society and Other Plays* had sold 14,367 copies, while his five-volume *Prose Dramas* had already sold 16,834. These books alone, he suggested mockingly in the *Fortnightly*, would make 'a tolerably handsome mausoleum'.[26]

The Independent Theatre had survived into its second year and was now 'firmly on its legs',[27] Grein assured Archer. On 21 February, the evening after the opening of *The Master Builder*, he was at the Opera Comique to see *The Strike at Arlingford*, the Independent Theatre's ninth production and the first play by the unreliable George Moore. Grein had been forced to move from the Royalty where, just over a week after the second erratic performance of *Widowers' Houses*, Brandon Thomas's *Charley's Aunt* began a record-breaking run. Kate Santley might have sympathized with the New Drama but her cash box depended upon an Oxford undergraduate dressing up as his aunt from Brazil. Moore's leading character is John Reid, a socialist agitator leading a miners' strike and whose loyalties become divided between the cause of the workers and his former fiancée, who owns the colliery.

When the strikers reject him and she deserts him for the millionaire Baron Steinbach, Reid commits suicide.

Moore claimed that he was uninterested in politics. What he wanted to do was write a modern *Hamlet*, and portray a weak man pinned between two relentless and opposing forces. Despite his distrust of Moore, Archer peered through the murk of a monumentally appalling production in which, as Reid, Bernard Gould 'lacked everything', to pronounce that the strike-leader's dilemma was 'the large simplicity of really great drama'. That Moore had brought Fabian disdain tumbling down by confusing socialism with trade unionism and mixing up different kinds of capitalist, was, he commented, of no importance at all compared with the fact that he had observed human nature and tried to portray it truthfully. Even with its patchy dialogue, the play had 'ten times more flesh and blood' than the 'unimpeachable Fabianism but doubtful humanity' of *Widowers' Houses*.[28]

The most encouraging development in the fragile line of descent from *The Profligate*, was Oscar Wilde's *A Woman of No Importance* at the Haymarket. The play glinted with scathing wit, but by transforming the old melodramatic seduction-drama into an outspoken attack on sexual double standards and moral hypocrisy, Wilde proved to Archer that 'In intellectual calibre, artistic competence – ay, and in dramatic instinct to boot – Mr Wilde has no rival among his fellow-workers for the stage.'[29]

In Lord Illingworth's cynical eyes, the woman of no importance is the woman he seduced and abandoned several years previously and who now calls herself Mrs Arbuthnot. Horrified when her grown-up son, Gerald, who is ignorant of his father's identity, agrees to become Illingworth's secretary, she implores him to change his mind. When Gerald discovers his prospective employer to be his father, he demands that his mother absolve her shame by accepting Illingworth's begrudging offer of marriage. Contemptuously, Mrs Arbuthnot turns Illingworth down, while Gerald marries the puritan Hester Worsley, a visiting American. Unlike Ibsen in *Ghosts*, Wilde suggests that the sins of the father need not be visited upon the children, but emphasises that the parents are not necessarily redeemed. The unscrupulous Lord Illingworth earns his son's disgust, while Mrs Arbuthnot remains adrift from polite society.

Archer and Elizabeth attended the first night of *A Woman of No Importance* on 19 April. A Haymarket first night, and especially a Wilde first night, was a stupendous contrast to an Ibsen matinee or Independent Theatre evening where, Wilde observed, one was apt to discover the pit full of 'sad vegetarians and the stalls occupied by men in mackintoshes and women in knitted shawls of red wool'.[30] At the Haymarket, dignitaries, politicians and theatre people crammed the foyer and glittered in the stalls and dress circle. At the centre of it all was Wilde himself, thirty-eight years old, two years older than Archer, and wearing evening dress with a white waistcoat and lilies at his throat. This was the height of the era of the theatre as a social event, and people looked to the theatre for the latest fashions. Several papers (including the *Manchester Guardian*) required their critics to list prominent members of the audience. Weekly and women's papers provided their fashion correspondents with stalls tickets so they could meticulously describe the dresses the actresses wore. In *The Lady*, 'Thespis' wrote that no play could possibly be ignored if it offered a new idea for a hat. In *The Queen*, 'Miss Aria' debated waistbands and gloves, while, in *Black and White*, 'Virginia' discussed leg-of-mutton sleeves. It was part of Wilde's astuteness that he dressed moral arguments in morning suits and evening gowns.

However, Archer refused to be dazzled either by the overtures of the fashion industry or the velocity of Wilde's epigrammatic wit. 'That is one of the defects of his qualities,' he wrote in his *World* review of *A Woman of No Importance* on 26 April, 'and a defect, I am sure, that he will one day conquer, when he begins to take himself seriously as a dramatic artist.' It worried Archer that, although Wilde could produce 'the most virile and intelligent' writing in contemporary theatre, he was too often content metaphorically to lay on his back and blow soap bubbles to amuse his audiences. 'It is not his wit,' wrote Archer, 'that makes me claim for him a place apart among living English dramatists. It is the keenness of his intellect, the individuality of his point of view, the excellence of his verbal style, and, above all, the genuinely dramatic quality of his inspirations.'[31] These, he told Wilde, were too rare to squander.

At the end of the month, he returned to the Independent Theatre and working-class realism with two performances of *Alan's Wife*, a one-act play in three short and austere scenes set in the industrial north of England. The story of Jean Creyke was bound to be controversial. Widowed when her husband is crushed by machinery at work, Jean realizes that she cannot afford to bring up their crippled baby son alone and so baptizes him, and smothers him. This was the second piece which Florence Bell had adapted from a Swedish story. Elizabeth revised the dialogue and Archer gave it a final polish. Because of the subject-matter, they agreed it should be produced as being by an anonymous author.

This was probably just as well. The critics believed they were being asked to sympathize with a mother murdering her child and greeted both performances, in which Elizabeth played the central role, with howls of outrage. 'I am quite impenitent,' wrote Archer in the *Westminster Gazette*, confessing his part in instigating the production. He denied that Jean Creyke was either a victim of puerperal mania or clinically mad. (Madness was a brick frequently thrown at characters in realist drama, especially when the leading characters were women.) It was not up to the audience either to approve or disapprove of her action, reasoned Archer. In fact, the 'great tragic value of the theme lies in the fact that we can do neither with a whole heart'.[32] The first job of the new realism, he repeated, was to observe and dramatize truthful emotions. The first job of the audience was to accept them as the truth.

Ever since Pinero gingerly tested the waters of serious theatre with *The Profligate* in 1889, Archer had been urging him to jump in and start swimming strongly. He publicly acknowledged every step forward he made and ladled out his Ibsen translations as encouragement, but Pinero remained unconvinced. '*The Master Builder* is more shadowy to me than any dream.'[33] Yet in 1892, he completed his second serious play. He showed *The Second Mrs Tanqueray* to his old friend John Hare at the Garrick who, when he read it, dropped it like a handful of hot coals. Tree said it was far too risky for the Haymarket. Archer read it and recommended the Independent Theatre. 'I would rather throw the manuscript on the fire,'[34] Pinero retorted. In his opinion, a theatrical breakthrough was only worth making in a West End theatre before a large audience and over a long run. At last, George Alexander took a deep breath and agreed to stage the play at the St James's, a four-tiered theatre seating twelve hundred.

The central character in the play is Paula, a beautiful woman in her late twenties, who becomes the second wife of the wealthy, forty-two-year-old widower, Aubrey Tanqueray. His first wife was a strict Roman Catholic who, according to his male friends, was an 'iceberg' of a woman who 'kept a thermometer in her stays and always registered ten degrees below zero'. But Paula is no iceberg. She is a high-class prostitute, well known under a variety of names in London and on Mediterranean yatching parties. Because she is unacceptable to his friends, Tanqueray plans to leave London and live with Paula in the country. Before their marriage, she gives him a letter recording her past life, but he burns it unread.

The play deals with the sexual double-standard of promiscuity being tolerated in men but condemned in women, and whether it is possible for a 'fallen woman' to be socially as well as morally redeemed, for even in Surrey, Paula cannot escape her past. Aubrey's friends hover reprovingly. She is unexpectedly confronted by Ardale, one of her former lovers, an army captain who intends to marry Tanqueray's daughter, Ellean. To protect her, Paula confesses her affair with Ardale to her husband. For the first time, he realizes the consequences of having married her and all their illusions crumble. Paula goes to her room where she is later found to have killed herself.

Although the spoor of melodrama still clings as fast to *The Second Mrs Tanqueray* as it does to other serious English plays, Alexander took a risk in accepting the play and was right to be anxious, even though Pigott licensed the play without demanding any changes. Pigott may have thought that audiences would draw the simple conclusion that, once tainted, a woman can never regain respectability. From this point of view, *The Second Mrs Tanqueray* was a rebuke to those who lobbied for more liberal social attitudes. But seen from another angle, Paula is a comparatively rich and complex character, a woman without regrets or shame but nevertheless one of integrity, suffocated by an unforgiving moral convention and her own misjudgement of herself and others. It asks a middle- and upper-class commercial theatre audience to suspend its comfortable view of women as spiritually and sexually pure. The language is explicit for its time. Before their marriage, Paula visits Tanqueray alone at his apartment in the Albany late at night and it is clear they sleep together regularly.

As with the Ibsen plays, the success of *The Second Mrs Tanqueray* depended upon a brilliant leading actress. Someone exciting, somebody *new* had to play Paula Tanqueray. Alexander thought of Elizabeth Robins as, after all, Paula had something in common with Hedda Gabler. Meanwhile, Pinero had discovered a Mrs Patrick Campbell. She was young, tall, pale-skinned, dark-haired and appearing in *The Black Domino*, a Sims and Buchanan melodrama at the Adelphi, a play which Archer held in withering contempt. Mrs Campbell was virtually unknown, but that was in her favour and she was offered the role. She accepted immediately, but the *Black Domino* producers, who had just sacked her, declared that if she suited Alexander, she was indispensable to them, and reinstated her. Cheated of Mrs Campbell, Alexander signed a contract with Elizabeth. Mrs Campbell was promptly fired a second time from *The Black Domino* and hurried across town to the St James's to find that she had been replaced. Alexander and Pinero went to see Elizabeth to explain their dilemma. They would, they said, accept her decision as to who played the part.

Mrs Campbell was born Beatrice Stella Tanner, the sixth child of an English father and an Italian mother, in Kensington in 1865. Even as a baby, Stella was active and bawling. Her nurse declared she was a tiger. She was right. In 1884, when she was nineteen, she married Patrick Campbell who, four years later, left England in a bid to make their fortune in South Africa, informing her of his erratic progress in a series of letters and cables. Meanwhile, his wife headed for the stage. She tramped the provinces in repertory. She played hazardous Shakespeare in the open air with Ben Greet's Woodland Players on tours taking in five towns a week and two performances a day. She made and repaired her own costumes, fretting over Patrick in Africa and their two babies in the care of relatives. It was a tough life, but she pressed on, as far as the Adelphi, when on 1 August 1891, she caught everyone's attention.

It was the first night of a Buchanan and Sims melodrama, *The Trumpet Call*, and Mrs Pat was playing the temptress Astrea opposite Elizabeth Robins's innocent, deserted Constance. She was twenty-six and as beautiful as Elizabeth, who was comprehensively upstaged in the unscripted moment when Mrs Campbell's ragged black gypsy skirt slid gently down over her thighs and rested around her ankles on the stage. In the moment before she remedied matters, the audience glimpsed her long and shapely legs, and her drawers, which were decidedly scantier than most. But when her skirt fell, Mrs Campbell arrived. Two years later, she had become an actress not only of terrific profile but of extraordinary presence, playing the feeble role of Belle Hamilton, the discarded mistress of Lord Dashwood in *The Black Domino*, with, according to Archer, 'Bernhardtesque languor'.[35] But the problem, as she saw it, was not that she was being noticed, but that she was still playing melodrama. She desperately wanted to play Paula Tanqueray.

Elizabeth and Mrs Pat liked each other, and Elizabeth generously told Alexander and Pinero that the role of Paula should go to Mrs Patrick Campbell. 'From what I have heard read of the part,' she wrote to her 'it is the kind of thing that comes along once in an actress's lifetime ... You will play it brilliantly ... There is to my mind no woman in London so enviable at this moment, dear savage, as *you*.'[36]

Rehearsals became a battleground. Alexander, who was playing Tanqueray, was a quiet man in his mid-thirties. The spontaneous, uninhibited, disturbingly temperamental Mrs Pat chilled his natural reserve to ice. He had never worked with anyone like her. Neither had Pinero. She was charming, she was tense, she was vengeful, she was tearful. She took direction from Pinero, but told Alexander that acting with him was like acting with a walking stick. It was bewildering.

On the first night, on 27 May, Pinero spent much of the evening nervously pacing up and down the alleyway outside the theatre. Inside, Mrs Pat was similarly taut with nerves. Paula's first entrance is not until the end of the first act and when it came, she seemed subdued and ill at ease. But in the second act, she suddenly found her energy. Wearing a golden satin gown sparkling with sequins, her dark hair loosely gathered at the neck and her black eyes burning, Mrs Pat acted with such intensity that it seemed as if nothing else mattered. Everyone was riveted by her. Sitting in the stalls, Archer was gripped by a performance of such high voltage and emotional honesty that it seemed 'almost perfect in its realism'. This was indeed 'the haggard truth'. [37] But although she won him over, it was only when Pinero himself stood on the stage at the final curtain and the audience rose to give him and Mrs Campbell a standing ovation, that Archer, thought so cold and unemotional, felt tears swimming in his eyes.

The play itself had left him unmoved, because compared to Hedda Gabler or Hilde Wangel, Paula Tanqueray was woefully underwritten, and beside Tesman or Solness, Tanqueray faded into a shadow. Nevertheless, Pinero had achieved his breakthrough, English realism had come of age in the West End and, in *The World*, Archer lavished encouragement upon both author and actor-manager. *The Second Mrs Tanqueray*, he announced, was 'the one play of what might be called European merit of which the modern English stage can as yet boast'.[38] It was now up to Oscar Wilde, he added, to put an end to frivolity and write the second.

Serious drama had never had such consistent exposure or attention. Two days after the opening of *The Second Mrs Tanqueray*, Elizabeth opened in a fortnight's repertory of Ibsen at the Opera Comique, having raised five hundred guineas from subscriptions and a cast of seven guarantors including the faithful Wilde, Florence Bell, and the Home

Secretary, Herbert Asquith, and his future second wife, Margot Tennent. Elizabeth chose the Opera Comique with its claustrophobic, underground auditorium because, like the Vaudeville, it too had become temporarily unfashionable and therefore cheap to hire, and booked a week of six matinees and a second of six evening performances from 29 May until 10 June. The programme would consist of two performances a week of *Hedda Gabler, Rosmersholm* and a double-bill of *The Master Builder* and Act Four of *Brand*, the labour of love of Professor Herford who announced that travelling difficulties made it impossible for him to venture from Aberystwyth to see a performance.

Archer and Elizabeth had often talked of creating an ensemble of actors to work on a series of plays. For Archer, it would be a model for a future National Theatre. This was their first chance to discover whether they could make the idea work on a small scale. They had one advantage in that their growing reputation as Ibsen interpreters meant that reputable actors were interested in joining them, and a disadvantage in that Herbert Waring was not one of them. Waring had decided it would be more prudent for his career if he withdrew. 'I am afraid that by continuing to produce Ibsen plays without appreciable interval one runs the risk of being, most unjustly of course, put down as a "crank" or a "faddist",' [39] he apologized.

They assembled their strongest company yet, consisting of eleven actors, the majority of whom would appear in at least two of the four plays. Elizabeth would play Hedda, Hilde, and Rebecca West and Agnes in *Brand*, the last two being roles she had not played before. Lewis Waller, a thirty-three-year-old actor with a magnificently rich voice and whom she had known since they appeared in *The Sixth Commandment*, would appear opposite her as Lovborg, Rosmer and Solness. Scott Buist and Charles Sugden returned from the old *Hedda Gabler* company to recreate Tesman and Brack, and Marie Linden agreed to play her small role in *The Master Builder* again, as well as the more demanding Mrs Elvsted. Bernard Gould, who led a double life as Bernard Partridge, a caricaturist for *Punch*, joined them to play the title role in *Brand* and Brendel in *Rosmersholm*. Foss returned as stage-manager.

A basic box set was designed for all the plays. Archer achieved his ambition of having almost a month for rehearsals but this time had four pieces to rehearse. Most of the time was spent on *Rosmersholm* and, inevitably, the other plays suffered. At the first performance of *Hedda Gabler*, it was clear that not enough work had been done. There was enormous pressure on Elizabeth and even more on Lewis Waller, who had three leading roles to prepare in as many weeks. Even though Archer, Elizabeth and Foss had become a close team, they had tried to do too much in too short and too frenzied a time.

It is likely that Foss did much of the re-direction. Archer was here, there and everywhere. The pencil notes in his copies of *The Master Builder* and *Rosmersholm*, which he used during rehearsal, reveal him trimming lines to make the dialogue quicker, lighter and more colloquial and paying meticulous attention to movement and detail. 'Quick', 'no pause', 'too slow',[40] are scattered across the pages of *The Master Builder*. As always, he pelted the actors with notes, both at rehearsals and during the fortnight's run. On 2 June, the day of the first performance of *Brand*, he left a letter in Bernard Gould's dressing room. 'Do you do anything at your first entrance to indicate snow on your cloak?' he enquired. '. . . in strict realism, there ought to be something of the sort, for Agnes has just said, "Fast they fall, the softly sifted snow flakes" etc.'[41]

They played to small but enthusiastic audiences. Several critics renewed their attacks on the plays but more were now celebrating Elizabeth's performances, which were establishing her as one of the finest actresses of her generation. Mrs Patrick Campbell, who saw Elizabeth several times, remarked that her greatest quality on stage was the intensity of her intellect and the speed of her thoughts. Archer had no scruples over writing about the season in *The World*, where he recorded that Waller had achieved 'a genuine character-creation' in Rosmer; an 'excellent' Lovborg, and an 'admirable' Solness. Elizabeth's Rebecca West he called 'the largest, finest, most poetical' performance she had given, while her Agnes was 'singularly beautiful and true'.[42]

It seemed that everyone wanted to catch the growing momentum and produce Ibsen that summer. While the Archer-Robins season continued at the Opera Comique, the Italian actress Eleanora Duse led her company into the Lyric Theatre in Shaftesbury Avenue for a season of seven plays, including *A Doll's House*. Duse's London debut was an exciting prospect in a year of performances by great actresses. She had already demonstrated her modernist credentials by introducing Ibsen to Italy, playing Nora at the Teatro di Filodrammatici in Milan in 1891. In London, Archer thought her Nora 'masterly', if overall 'less satisfying than Miss Achurch's', noting approvingly that she cut most of the tarantella at the end of Act Two, 'Ibsen's last concession to the old technique'.[43]

As *La Dame aux Camélias* by Dumas *fils* was in her repertoire, Duse was inevitably compared with the legendary Sarah Bernhardt, who had made the role of Marguerite Gautier her own. Duse was thiry-five, thirteen years younger then Bernhardt, slender and spectacularly modern. Bernhardt still relied upon the elaborate facial make-up of the old school, but Duse came to the stage devoid of cosmetics. The difference between them was that between artifice and nature and for Archer in the new age of realism, Bernhardt in retrospect appeared reminiscent of 'an exquisitely-contrived automaton', and his allegiance swung to her younger rival. Duse's 'two great black eyes gazing, with a sort of pathetic intentness, from out a pale, sad, nervous countenance'[44] brought Marguerite heartbreakingly to expiring life, and made the production 'one of the landmarks of my theatrical experience'.[45]

A week after Duse's *Doll's House*, Tree finally overcame 'the most obstinate and rancorous [critical and managerial] prejudice recorded in the history of the stage' to become the first British actor-manager to present an Ibsen play. He played Stockmann in a revival of Archer's translation of *An Enemy of the People* at the Haymarket for three weeks, (interrupting the run of *A Woman of No Importance*) but as the prompter was heard as much as the actors, Archer found it impossible to work out 'how much was deliberately omitted and how much merely forgotten'. It was as much as he could do to prevent himself leaping up, stopping the action and redirecting it. Tree was 'too emphatic, too pontifical, above all too *slow* . . . I wanted to shout "Go on! Go on!. . ." '[46]

Things were becoming frenetically busy on the reviewing front. A huge company from the Comédie-Française moved into Drury Lane for a month with a repertoire of thirty-two plays. The Independent Theatre demanded attention. The impoverished Charringtons were performing five short plays in one evening. They were now familiar faces not only on the stage but to several pawnbrokers, and soon they were begging their friends for funds. 'Can and will you keep Charrington & myself with five pounds for a month or two,' Janet appealed to Archer. ' – I can't exactly say *when* we can repay it but we will do so faithfully as soon as possible . . . Help us if you can.'[47]

Charles Archer, who was visiting London on leave from India, told him he was overworking and dragged him off on a brisk walking tour of the west country for a fortnight to try and revive him. Shaw protested that his friend had transformed himself already. 'The restless energy with which you are throwing yourself into all manner of controversies suggests to me that you are going mad,' he exclaimed. 'Or rather, you have at last thrown off the restraints that used to keep up your character for sanity, and are recklessly exhibiting yourself to the public in your true character as a Nihilist.'[48]

8

Love Letters
and *Little Eyolf*

Archer was not a Nihilist, but Shaw was right in observing that his friend was humming with a new confidence. The events of the past years, meeting, working with, and loving Elizabeth, had refreshed his resolve. He felt that at last he was making headway in the battle for a serious drama of ideas. His writing took on a new urgency, dash, a sense of brio. Art Nouveau embraced Europe and even the United States, and, when Archer set out to define the New Drama, he too cut himself free of England and English tradition and aligned himself unequivocally with European psychological realism. The New Drama, he wrote, 'is not, like the Robertsonian movement of the sixties, or the Irving movement of the seventies, or the Pinero-Jones movement of the eighties, a thing of native growth. It reaches us from two quarters – from Norway and from France.'

The New Drama was by no means flourishing in England but over the past five years, Archer had done more than anyone to create the atmosphere for it. While Elizabeth looked with longing to the West End, Archer kept faith with the small theatre movement, 'free from the actor-manager, the upholsterer and the censor',[1] as the most likely to evolve into the National Theatre of his dreams.

The next three years saw a rush of activity and changing fortunes for Archer and his circle. Shaw's friend Florence Farr hoped that her first excursion into actor-management would transform the Avenue Theatre into the talk of theatrical London. Her sudden emergence in 1894 as the leader of a company was due to occult influence. Having been swept along by the current fascination for mysticism, she was a rapidly rising member of the Order of the Golden Dawn, a group sunk in the rites of an obscure blend of Hebrew and Egyptian ritual magic. Florence's sponsor was a fellow member, Annie Horniman, a thirty-four-year-old graduate of the Slade School of Art and the wealthy granddaughter of a Quaker who made a fortune by selling tea in packets instead of loose. Annie was an ardent smoker and a passionate theatre-lover who would later found a repertory company at the Gaiety in Manchester and build the Abbey Theatre in Dublin. Florence's season was her first investment but as the Hornimans fiercely disapproved of the stage, her involvement was conditional on absolute secrecy. Shaw promised Florence a play, but as *Arms and the Man* was not finished, she opened her season with *The Land of Heart's Desire*, a whimsical verse play by yet another Golden Dawnist, W. B. Yeats, and a curtain-raiser for John Todhunter's *A Comedy of Sighs*. The first night on 29 March was a catastrophe. From his vantage point in the dress circle, Yeats, wearing his customary black sombrero and cape over his evening clothes, sat snuffling with a cold, watching Todhunter sitting in sad dignity in his box and surrounded by his family as *A Comedy of Sighs* was remorselessly booed from first to last. The noise, and the Avenue's wilful acoustic, made the performance almost inaudible to Archer in the stalls. Florence was an actress who he knew lacked 'crispness of attack',[2] but that night she looked positively panic-stricken. Arrangements were made to replace *A Comedy of Sighs* as soon as possible with *Arms and the Man*.

Elizabeth was forging ahead with her writing, putting the last touches to *George Mandeville's Husband*, her first full-length novel which Heinemann published that summer. As soon as he had done so, she plunged into work on her second. *The New Moon*, published in 1895, is the first-person confession of Dr Geoffrey Monroe, unhappily married to the invalid Milly and in love with the intellectual Dorothy Lance. Monroe longs for Dorothy and sexual fulfilment but the more he desires her, the more guilty he feels, while she also craves physical love but shares his moral standards. She is frightened too of renouncing her emotional independence and worried that the insanity in her family is hereditary. The story ends at a Swiss health resort where Dorothy dies in a fire. Vividly sensational and rambling, but strongly autobiographical and symbolic, *The New Moon* reflects the continuing tensions embedded in the affair between Archer and Elizabeth, still disconcerted by the strength of their feelings for each other.

As Elizabeth had given Archer renewed confidence in his journalism and directorial work, so he encouraged her to become a novelist, reading and commenting on her work. That *The New Moon* was so close to home evidently caused him some foreboding. He said 'very nice things about it', recorded Elizabeth in her diary on 19 October, '& we haven't quarrelled at all this time'.[3] His reading her manuscripts became one of the clandestine bonds between them, made all the more so as Elizabeth guarded her identity as closely as she did her feelings for Archer. She wrote under the pseudonym of C. E. Raimond and hardly anyone, even Henry James, by now a close friend, knew of her new literary career.

Her writing reawakened Archer's interest in his own. It occurred to him that he might have been wrong in imagining he could write plays. Perhaps his real field was prose. Before long, he began deluging her with outlines for novels. Florence Farr's disastrous first night inspired him to write a synopsis for *The Efficient Person*. Even though Shaw was less enamoured of Florence these days and they would cease to be lovers at the end of the year, he had told Archer that she had withstood both the hostility of the Avenue audience and his decision that she would not be playing Raina, the leading role in *Arms and the Man*, with remarkable resilience. Archer said nothing, but confided to Elizabeth that, when the curtain fell on *The Comedy of Sighs*, there had been 'tears & hysterics & the devil to pay'.[4] The theme of *The Efficient Person*, therefore, was that of a woman's (Florence's) inability to become a man's (Shaw's) image of her as the enterprising, independent New Woman, and her eventual madness, perhaps even suicide.

Many of his plot sketches are transparently autobiographical and reflect moral themes borrowed from Ibsen and Pinero. Several involve a man confronting an emotional and professional crisis in which the alternatives are to follow his instincts or retreat into bland convention. Whether to risk or regret is at the heart of Elizabeth's fiction and Archer's notes, and in several plot outlines, he toys with the consequences of both.

He was looking for a way of reconciling his own public and secret lives. At least two of his surviving synopses are based upon the Parnell affair in November 1890, in which Captain William O'Shea divorced his wife, Kitty, naming as co-respondent Charles Stewart Parnell, the leader of the Irish Party in the House of Commons. Everyone had an opinion on the Parnell affair. A juicy scandal of high office, involving delicate public affairs and a beautiful woman, it had all the ingredients of a stage melodrama. It ended with Parnell hounded from office, his career in tatters and his sudden death a year later in Brighton, having been married to Mrs O'Shea for just five months. In his notes, Archer's

Parnell-inspired characters are men of imagination and integrity, and their opponents disreputable opportunists.

He wrote while on walks in the country, in the theatre and in the train between London and Cobham, filling pages from his notebooks and jumping out at stations along the way to post them at platform pillar boxes. Time and again, his plot summaries break off into proclamations of love for Elizabeth. 'Oh my darling, we were together this time last Sunday, & it was so sweet & so good to have you there . . . Oh my own love, when I cant be with you, I do nothing but think about you . . . I adore you my own.' Many times, he wrote from Queen Square at night. 'Dearest love good morning. How are you my blessed one?'[5] he wondered, having worked so late he had fallen asleep over his papers.

Between her bouts of writing, Elizabeth was resuscitating her bank account by appearing in melodrama and on 7 April, she opened in the title role of *Mrs Lessingham* at the Garrick, written by Constance Fletcher under the name of George Fleming. Mrs Lessingham is a widow who marries a young barrister, but once she discovers that he still loves the woman she manipulated him into leaving, she kills herself. (There was a disconcerting epidemic of suicide, especially female suicide, on the late Victorian London stage. For many men and women, though, caught between bitter unhappiness and social shame, death was the melodramatic but effective alternative.) Archer thought the play 'bent towards emotion rather than analysis', but that apart from the first act, it was 'beautifully acted by Miss Elizabeth Robins'.[6]

Even though he loved her, Archer was able to write about Elizabeth's acting with critical detachment, quibbling in *The World* over the impetuousness in her Hedda, her Hilde and her Mrs Lessingham as much as he praised them. It would never have occurred either to Archer or Elizabeth that he do anything else, for while they were experts in turning facets of themselves to face and fool the world, they remained people of instinctive professional integrity.

Mrs Lessingham ran for just over a month, until 16 May. During these weeks Archer and Elizabeth became more intimate, or as intimate as they had ever been, meeting at Gatti's, at Queen Square and Manchester Square Mansions. 'I love you my own beloved,' wrote Archer, '& thank you for the evening you were dear and beautiful to me my own Bessie.'[7] Every now and again, as he had done in the autumn of 1891, it seems that Archer would try and coax a greater commitment from her, either romantically or sexually. But to emulate one of his own plot outlines and dare to stumble forward in the wake of his instincts rather disconcerted Archer and panicked Elizabeth, who had written her version of the dilemma in *The New Moon*. Elizabeth also agonized over whether closer ties between them would impede her career. 'Believe me, darling,' he typed one Sunday night, 'the last thing I want to do is to hamper your work or stand in the way of your career, & in the meantime what you have clearly got to do is to devote yourself body & soul – and I am part of your body & soul – to *Mrs Lessingham*. So until that is over I shall try to remember nothing of yesterday except how dear & loving you were to me my own . . .' Exactly what took place the previous day is not known. He ended this his letter by declaring that 'My darling, my darling, I love you with all my heart . . .'[8]

Arms and the Man was the fourth play Shaw had written (in succession to *The Philanderer* and *Mrs Warren's Profession*) but the second to be staged. Set in the Serbo-Bulgarian war of 1885, the Swiss hotel-keeper's son, Bluntschli, fighting for the Serbs but who carries chocolate creams instead of ammunition, takes refuge in Raina's bedroom during a retreat. The daughter of a rich Bulgarian family, Raina is engaged to the dashing Sergius, but in the course of the comedy discovers her true love in Bluntschli, while Sergius finds his in Louka, the servant girl.

They had ten days in which to pummel the play into shape before it opened on 21 April. Following Archer, Shaw cast himself as director, although the dependable George Foss (perhaps summoned by the actors) soon appeared to help out. Alma Murray, who had played the leading role in *The Cenci*, signed to play Raina while the disappointed Florence had to make do with Louka. Bernard Gould appeared as Sergius and Yorke Stephens as Bluntschli. Shaw did his best to drum up an audience to make the Avenue the thinking person's equivalent of the Haymarket. He invited Archer, the Charringtons, Wilde, Henry Arthur Jones, Stepniak, and the Fabians Sidney Webb and Graham Wallas, and sprinkled them throughout the audience. As Shaw climbed on to the stage at the end of the performance to make a curtain speech, he answered the single jeer that pierced the applause by exclaiming, 'My dear fellow, I quite agree with you, but what are we against so many?'[9]

Although *Arms and the Man* had fifty performances before setting out on a provincial tour, the chocolate cream soldier failed to convince Archer that Shaw was a natural dramatist. He conceded that he had written a play as funny as *Charley's Aunt*, but *Arms and the Man* was worse than *Widowers' Houses*. It presented a mad wonderland, 'a fantastic, psychological extravaganza, in which drama, farce, and Gilbertian irony keep flashing past the bewildered eye'.[10] Shaw retorted that *Arms and the Man* was not in the least Gilbertian as Gilbert accepted conventional social and moral ideals, whereas he most emphatically did not. 'My whole secret is that I have got clean through the old categories of good & evil,'[11] he explained.

A fortnight later, on the evening of 4 May, the Independent Theatre staged the British premiere of *The Wild Duck* at the Royalty, two years after it was written. Apart from revising the translation by Frances published in *Prose Dramas*, Archer had no connection with the production which was directed by Herman de Lange. He theoretically supported the Independent Theatre but was increasingly irritated by Grein's inability to cast properly, and his persistent muddling through after insufficient rehearsal. This time, he was also doubtful of the play, which seemed a melancholic piece. In the character of the embittered and destructive idealist, Gregers Werle, Ibsen appeared to mock his own principles. He was dubious as well of his own translation. 'It is probably the most difficult of all Ibsen's modern plays to render satisfactorily,' he admitted. Gina Ekdal's vocabulary in particular, 'that of an uneducated woman of the small-shopkeeper class', was 'full of vulgarisms and Malapropisms'.[12]

At the first performance, the opening scene, set at a dinner-party at the Werle home, did nothing to allay Archer's doubts. As the guests ran on and off 'that bandbox stage' laughing and clinking their glasses, it was as if the curtain had gone up on a farce. Yet once the scene had transferred to the dingy attic room of the photographer, Hjalmar Ekdal, the production found 'that smooth, unhasting, unresting movement which is Ibsen's greatest invention in the technical sphere'. To his surprise, Archer discovered that, while it was tragic, *The Wild Duck* was far from gloomy. It was funny, ironic and absurd and this gave tragedy its air of reality. 'Hardly ever before,' he wrote in *The Sketch* on 13 June, '. . . had I seen so much of the very quintessence of life concentrated in the brief traffic of the stage.'[13]

Scott and his supporters were unanimous in dismissing the play as both eccentric and depressing. Unlike *Hedda Gabler* and *The Master Builder*, there was no continued flight for *The Wild Duck*, and 'yet again a heavy financial loss was the result,' Grein unhappily wrote to Archer on 8 May. 'I am £60 short. Of course, I tell you this only as an interesting fact . . .'[14] But Archer was too concerned about his own income to spare any money to help Grein, who had no luck elsewhere and was forced to cancel plans for any more productions that year. Archer was worried about the future of *The World*, which had suffered a sudden catastophe. On Saturday, 19 May, he was at the Garrick Theatre for the prestigious revival of Bulwer-Lytton's *Money*, the play which *Hedda Gabler* had replaced at the Vaudeville. Also in the audience were his editor, Edmund Yates, and his wife. 'The thing amused me more than I expected,'[15] Archer wrote cheerily to Yates the next morning, unaware that he had suffered a massive heart attack and was already dead in his room at the Savoy Hotel.

Returning from another holiday in the west country, from where he sent love letters to Elizabeth, Archer discovered *The World* had been taken over by a Major Arthur Griffiths, a journalist and an authority on the history of London jails. The paper continued without any perceptible change apart from the loss of Shaw as music critic. But Archer was now thirty-seven and had a dependent wife and a nine-year-old son. He was a controversial and respected critic, but poorly paid and when Frank Harris approached with 'urgent & flattering'[16] proposals, he sat up and took notice. Since the incident of Shaw's misdirected letters, Harris had been sacked from the editorship of the *Fortnightly Review* after revealing his support of anarchism. He left his home in Park Lane, where he lived as the husband of a woman he implied was socially well-connected and returned to Maidenhead, but that autumn, turned up again in London, having bought the almost moribund *Saturday Review*. Like many others, Archer thought Harris extremely shifty, but to be asked to become the *Saturday Review* drama critic at five guineas a week, was not something to be rejected out of hand.

Thinking he might turn this to his advantage, he reported the offer to Griffiths, hoping his three guineas-a-week retainer might be increased after ten years. Griffiths happily offered to match Harris's promise of five guineas, and Archer, congratulating himself on his shrewd tactical success, quickly accepted. Rebuffed by Archer, Harris approached Shaw, who told him bluntly that five guineas was not enough. Harris instantly offered him six pounds. Shaw agreed and in January 1895, became drama critic of the *Saturday Review*.

Defeated again by the inexplicable ways of men and money, Archer plodded on, making extra cash by translating *Eskimo Life* by the Norwegian explorer, Fridtjof Nansen, and *Hannele*, a symbolist play by the German dramatist Gerhardt Hauptmann. With Robert Lowe, now fatter and balder than ever, he began a two-year project editing three volumes of *Dramatic Essays* by Leigh Hunt, Hazlitt, and the biographer

John Forster and the writer George Henry Lewes. He spent long, back-breaking hours at his desk. 'I always seem to be struggling hopelessly after arrears of work,'[17] he wrote miserably. 'If my work was paying work, I should soon retire on my savings,' he told Matthews, 'but the greater part of it is connected with Ibsen, which does not pay . . .' He was paid royalties ('the merest trifle'[18]) on his translations and his other books, and in 1894, he published the first of five annual collections of his theatre reviews under the title *The Theatrical 'World' of* . . . Breezily, he predicted failure. '. . . like all my other productions: they get splendid notices & no one buys them'.[19]

Additional income was immediately absorbed by more domestic changes. Archer and Frances agreed that Tom should move from Ockham School, an experiment in educational socialism near Cobham, to a school in town. After a grim review of the faimily budget, he was enrolled that autumn as a dayboy at Alleyn's College of God's Gift in Dulwich, and the Archers took a house for the winter in nearby Upper Norwood. 'So now I have my town house, my country seat and my suburban retreat, like any Duke or millionaire,'[20] he reported to Dibdin in October.

Elizabeth, the Ibsen characters she played and one or two of the female characters Shaw wrote, were the kind of people being called New Women. There was a growing army of New Women, in favour of intellectual, social and moral equality and of winning the vote, and as such, they faced entrenched opposition not only among men but women too, including the influential Mrs Humphrey Ward. In her own way, for she was making her own career, Frances was a New Woman. Like Ibsen and Oscar Wilde, the New Woman was seized by the caricaturists on the page and the stage. On the 'woman question', as on many others, the mainstream theatre managed to protect itself from the assaults of Archer, Ibsen, Grein and Shaw at the *Saturday Review*.

Most male actor-managers were reluctant to play secondary roles, and parts which did not reflect upon themselves as being either romantic or authoritative. With the arguable exception of Paula Tanqueray, the New Woman made her appearance in the West End only so that she could be enlightened as to the error of her ways. The 'unwomanly woman' was depicted as temperamentally impossible, misguidedly and hopelessly battling against nature. This is the way Henry Arthur Jones decided to portray her in *The Case of the Rebellious Susan*, which opened at the Criterion on 3 October 1894.

Hearing of her husband's infidelity, Lady Susan Harabin is deter-mined to pay him back in kind and sails to Cairo intent upon an affair of her own. But, like Shaw, Jones could not write a play without speaking through at least one of his characters and giving him the loudest voice. In *The Case of the Rebellious Susan*, Jones appears in the the guise of Sir Richard Kato QC, Susan's uncle. Even after twenty-five years' experience in the divorce court, Sir Richard believes that conventional marriage, preferably one untainted by romance and in which a woman defers to her husband, is the natural and indeed perfect way to live. When his ward, Elaine Shrimpton, shows disturbing New Womanish tendencies over her money and plans to set up a Boadicean Society for the Inculcation of the New Morality, Sir Richard advises that she would be far better off taking cookery lessons.

Charles Wyndham, the Criterion manager who played Sir Richard, appealed to Jones to dilute the play still further, so that while Susan threatens to take a lover, a subsequent friendship need not be inter-preted as anything other than innocent acquaintance. Jones happily complied. Archer's response was to accuse Jones of wilfully reducing the play to a 'pure comedy' in which all the old assumptions about men and women and marriage were reinforced. It also provoked him into putting forward his own position on the 'woman question'. 'I am the very last to sympathize with the "fireside-and-nursery" ideal of woman-hood which the play appeared to enforce,' he wrote. ' "Nature's darling," says Sir Richard Kato, "is a stay-at-home woman, a woman who wants to be a good wife and a good mother, *and cares very little of anything else*." In that case, Nature and I differ, as we do, indeed, on a good many other points.'[21]

Five months later, on 13 March 1895, Pinero's *The Notorious Mrs Ebbsmith*, his second 'problem play' with a 'woman with a past' as the central character, opened at the Garrick. Archer had high hopes of this, for whereas Jones, with his virulent anti-Ibsenism, his mawkish senti-ment and appeals to the popular majority, had clearly subsided into a boulevardier, Pinero was visibly grappling with his prejudices in an effort to create something more dispassionate and closely-observed. It was what made his failure even more exasperating.

The Notorious Mrs Ebbsmith dramatizes a woman's attempts to break free of her past and assert her own independent identity. Agnes Ebbsmith is the lover of Lucas Cleeve, a man several years her junior who has abandoned his wife to join her in Venice. Agnes has survived an unhappy childhood and a dreadful eight-year marriage in which for twelve months her husband 'treated me like a woman in a harem, for the rest of the time like a beast of burden'. She has emerged a radical socialist and a campaigner for women's rights and she and Lucas plan to agitate for reform. But when she realizes that instead of a socialist intellectual, he wants a compliant sexual partner and social ornament, she betrays her principles in an attempt to keep his love. Agnes wears the daring dress he buys her and agrees that to be admired as a drawing-room hostess rather than as a platform orator is her, and all women's, true inheritance. To rebel against natural femininity is 'madness'. Like *The Second Mrs Tanqueray*, this new play could be interpreted equally as part of a daring challenge to moral convention or a tip-toeing regression into orthodoxy.

Mrs Ebbsmith was played by Mrs Patrick Campbell. Paula Tanqueray had made Mrs Pat a woman of importance and her opinion of Agnes was widely canvassed. Agnes, she replied, was a new type, 'the woman agitator, the pessimist, with original, independent ideals – in revolt against sham morals'.[22] Fashionable London adored Mrs Patrick Campbell and at the end of the first performance, she took curtain call after curtain call. Her husband, who had left his slight, anonymous, twenty-three-year-old wife to bring up his children while he went abroad to make their fortune, had arrived home the previous year having made next-to-nothing, and discovered to his astonishment that twenty-eight-year-old Stella had become a fabulous jewel dazzling London society. It was a considerable shock. Everyone seemed to have gone mad.

Archer, though, kept a sense of proportion. Mrs Campbell, he agreed, was 'beautiful', but she was also 'superficial' and so was Agnes Ebbsmith. Yet while *The Second Mrs Tanqueray* had been little more than a 'brilliant' portrait of Paula, the new play was far more coherent, 'a great advance' aiming 'straight for the universally relevant theme of marriage in general'. But better writing did not make a more successful play. *The Notorious Mrs Ebbsmith* failed because Pinero refused to observe clearly and truthfully. That Agnes Ebbsmith became known to audiences as 'Mad Agnes' proved that he had merely represented a woman's bid for emancipation as a symptom of neurosis. The play reflected Pinero's prejudices. 'I suspect him of holding "views" as to feminine human nature,' wrote Archer in his review. 'In this he is not alone. Nine-tenths of masculine woman-drawing is vitiated by "views" – and in these latter days about nineteen-twentieths of feminine woman-drawing.' There were still no English writers, he repeated, with the unflinching honesty of Ibsen: '. . . he looks straight at and through women, and draws them in their infinite variety'.[23]

While Archer with diminishing confidence tried to create a serious English drama by encouraging Pinero as 'a thinker and a craftsman',[24] Sydney Grundy (who had not written a worthwhile play in years) let loose another of his apoplectic tirades. 'We are marching to our doom,' he howled, in the March issue of *The Theatre*. Archer, he declared, had become a demonic Pied Piper of the theatre, luring Pinero away from mass popularity and towards the obscurity of small and cranky audiences who 'regard a play as a mere intellectual exercise'. Grundy's ideals were emphatically those of the market-place. 'A work of art which does not pay is only fit to be enshrined in a museum. It is not a question of taste, but economics. If you exhibit such works in a theatre, there will soon be no theatre.' Archer was presiding over the destruction of the theatre, and Grundy appealed to Pinero to 'fill your ears with wax, and bind yourself to the mast'[25] and set course once more for his real, commercial home.

Reading this gave Archer an 'exhilarating quarter of an hour' one evening, before battering Grundy in his next *World* column, pointing out that *The Notorious Mrs Ebbsmith* had (luckily) been Pinero's greatest financial success and that he represented the only future for English drama. 'If you insist on lagging behind and "marking time",' he threatened, 'your doom – fossilisation and oblivion – will inevitably overtake you.'[26]

It had already overtaken Oscar Wilde. On 25 May 1895, he was convicted at the Old Bailey of committing homosexual acts and sentenced to two years hard labour. His career was over. 'Open the windows! Let in the fresh air,'[27] cried Clement Scott. With public feeling against Wilde running high, *An Ideal Husband* had already been hustled off the Haymarket stage and *The Importance of Being Earnest* was quickly withdrawn from the St James's. His books were removed from bookshop shelves and most of his friends deserted him. Archer, one of the few critics to have penetrated the crackle and flash of Wilde's wit and glimpsed an incisively satirical observation at work, was horrified.

Archer was fascinated by Wilde, for clearly there were 'two men behind that enigmatic mask: Oscar and Wilde, the – I had almost said mountebank – and the artist'.[28] There was the ostentatious purveyor of trifles, but, as Archer pointed out, 'Man cannot live on trifle alone.'[29] The other Wilde, the intellect, the incisive social and moral critic, he hoped was the real Wilde. Each of his plays contained elements of both men, but leant towards one or the other. *A Woman of No Importance* was a work by the moralist, and demonstrated 'the one essential fact' that his work 'stands alone . . . on the very highest plane of English drama'.[30] But *An Ideal Husband*, which opened at the Haymarket on 3 January 1895, was evidently written by the mountebank. It derived, suggested Archer, from *The Pillars of Society*, in that a cabinet minister, Sir Robert Chiltern, 'renowned for his spotless integrity has committed a base action in his youth, is now ready to go to any length in crime rather than face the consequence of his error, is saved by the undaunted realism of a woman, and remains, at the close, on the pinnacle of prosperity'. The play, whether intentionally or not, had therefore a cynical edge to it. It was 'practically a "call to the Unconverted" – to become Cabinet Ministers'.

The Importance of Being Earnest on the other hand, which opened at the St James's a few weeks later, fell somewhere between the two but was obviously the work of a 'born man-of-the-theatre'.[31] It was 'entirely new and individual'. Archer saw nothing dark in the play. Instead, it was a magnificent entertainment that 'imitates nothing, represents nothing, means nothing, is nothing, except a sort of rondo capriccioso, in which the artist's fingers run with crisp irresponsibility up and down the keyboard of life'.[32]

Archer thought Wilde 'unique'[33] and Wilde thought as highly of Archer, writing to thank him for his 'luminous, brilliant criticism' of *A Woman of No Importance:* '. . . there are points, of course, where I differ from you, but to be criticised by an artist in criticism is so keen a delight and one so rare in England . . .'[34] But Wilde never did write the serious, great play which Archer believed that he could.

For Archer, Wilde's greatest flaw was his inability to live a discreet double life outside the theatre. He knew of course that Wilde, married with two sons, socially eminent and a fêted and flamboyant playwright, was also a homosexual. Most people in the theatre and social world did. But the cause of his downfall was not only his homosexuality, but his flouting the Victorian convention of presenting a formal face to the world and keeping his emotional and sexual preferences well concealed. It was as if the two Wildes stood side by side in public for all to see, the one intensely watching the strange fortunes of the other, an active spectator of his own tragedy.

While Archer agreed with the prevailing view that homosexuality was a psychological defect, he admired the 'extraordinary courage and nerve' which Wilde showed during his trials and, in contrast to Scott, he was deeply saddened by his fate. It was all such a waste. As long ago as 1890, when accusations of immorality had been raised against Wilde's novel, *The Picture of Dorian Gray*, in the *Scots Observer*, Archer had come to Wilde's defence and he had defended and championed him ever since. Yet Wilde had perversely squandered the talent which he, Archer, perhaps more than anyone else, had encouraged. 'Really the luck is against the poor British Drama,'[35] he notified Charles on 1 May. To Brander Matthews, now Professor of Literature at Columbia University in New York, he reflected sadly that Wilde 'has more brains in his little finger than any of the other men in their whole body'.[36]

Possibly, he also felt a gnaw of more personal betrayal. They were both men with double lives, but while Gatti's restaurant was hardly the most discreet of meeting places, being popular with theatre people and journalists, Archer's affair with Elizabeth was, for the most part, secret. Surely, for the sake of his work, Wilde could have played along with convention, and kept his own other life hidden?

On 25 May, the day on which Oscar Wilde was imprisoned, Queen Victoria conferred a knighthood upon Henry Irving, the first title given to an actor. In a peculiarly Victorian paradox, the theatre was simultaneously disgraced and honoured, at once outcast and recognized as being the centre of British life. After his eventual release, Wilde trailed off to Paris, to live in a succession of dismal hotels. In February 1898, he sent Archer an inscribed copy of *The Ballad of Reading Gaol*, and later, a copy of the first edition of *The Importance of Being Earnest* arrived 'with the author's compliments'.[37] The following year, 1900, Wilde was dead.

In March, the ailing Independent Theatre was revived at the Opera Comique to play host to Lugné-Poë's Théâtre de l'Œuvre from Paris. There had been no productions of Ibsen in London since *The Wild Duck* the previous year, But Lugné-Poë's productions of *Solness le Constructeur* and *Rosmersholm* 'did not stir my emotions'[38] wrote Archer. The reason for Ibsen's absence was not the lack of a new play, but because the attempts to produce *Lille Eyolf* (*Little Eyolf*) had run aground on the rocks of delay, confusion and interference.

On 24 October 1894, Ibsen reported to Archer that he dispatched the script of his first play since *The Master Builder* to Gyldendal and 'will not turn to anyone else until I know whether You are able and willing to accept the task of seeing to the translation.'[39] Archer assured him that he was, and the first instalment arrived at Queen Square on 8 November.

Eyolf is the nine-year-old son of Alfred and Rita Allmers, in whose house above a fjord the play is set. He is lame, the result of having fallen one day when he was a baby. Instead of watching him, Rita and Alfred were making love in the bedroom. Eyolf's paralysis has become the symbol of their mutual guilt, the cause of Alfred's impotence and Rita's consequent sexual frustration. The Ratwife, a tramp-like woman who exterminates rats, promises to rid them of 'any troublesome thing that gnaws here'.[40] The first of the three acts ends with the tragic news that Eyolf has drowned in the fjord. The remainder of the play is a conversation piece in which Alfred and Rita pick over their emotional wreckage. Part of Alfred's anguish is that he loves Asta, his supposed half-sister, yet when she learns they are not related and there is no moral impediment to their love, she rejects his suggestion they stay together. Rather than destroy the Allmers's marriage, she marries an engineer. Alfred and Rita decide to stay together and attempt to rediscover their old happiness by helping the local poor children. It is a delusion that will finally destroy them.

'It is certainly very strong, but how people will like it is another question,'[41] Archer commented to Matthews. He spent November working on the translation, while Elizabeth, who had the stage rights, began planning a production. She was drawn not to the role of the domineering, volatile Rita but to Asta, the quiet, steady voice of moral orthodoxy. At 3pm on 3 December, Archer invited Shaw and H. W. Massingham to Queen Square to hear him read Little Eyolf.

'His reading was clear, intelligent, cold, without a trace of emotion and rather wooden in the more moving passages,' recalled Shaw. Suddenly, a few pages from the end, Archer paused, froze, and, passing the manuscript to Shaw, icily asked that he continue, as 'my feelings will not allow me to proceed'. Shaw took the book and completed the reading. Nothing similar had happened before, but Shaw knew that the more outwardly glacial Archer appeared, the more distraught his emotions. 'We were face to face with a man in whom dissimulation had become so instinctive that it had become his natural form of emotional expression,'[42] he observed.

To Archer, the death of Eyolf was one of the most heartrending moments in all of Ibsen. It touched both his sense of the tragic and his deep sentimentality. He was also moved by the portrayal of the Allmers, people for whom the flame of love has been snuffed out. Archer sympathized with the literary Alfred, a man about his own age, inflexible, not sexless but sexually shy, preoccupied with his work, married and in love with another woman. It may also have occurred to him at the end of a year in which he and Elizabeth had again become intimate, that one day, like Asta, she might leave, perhaps even return to America.

On the morning of 7 December, Heinemann held his copyright reading at the Haymarket when Braekstad read Allmers; his wife took the part of Asta, and Elizabeth read Rita. Heinemann himself read Eyolf and published Archer's translation four days later, on 11 December. 'Don't you think the time has come when a proper production can be afforded an Ibsen drama?' Pinero asked him. 'The greatest prize,' he added, 'is the gaining of the great public.'[43]

Elizabeth, the optimist who still had far more confidence in the commercial theatre than Archer, trudged off to show *Little Eyolf* to Alexander and Wyndham, but came back with the predictable news that they had rejected it. She thought briefly of reviving the Joint Management and asking Marion Lea to play Rita, until Archer convinced her of 'the hopeless task of trying to force her into the front rank'.[44] Things now began to become complicated.

On New Year's Day, 1895, she agreed with Janet Achurch that if she produced *Little Eyolf* and played Asta, then Janet would appear as Rita. It was an extaordinary decision. Elizabeth was overlooking not only the débâcle at Brighton, but the increasing evidence of Janet's addictions. There was her perpetual restlessness, slovenly dress, heavy smoking, tendency to drunkenness and her latest and inexplicable act of dyeing her hair an extravagant yellow. Elizabeth was hoping that their names on the same bill might lure a commercial management into backing them, but the Charringtons, still in and out of pawnshops, were careering towards disaster. Then Shaw intervened.

He invited himself to Manchester Square Mansions on 8 January to read *Candida*, his new play, to Elizabeth. It was his sixth, following *Arms and the Man* and *The Man of Destiny*, and derived from his experience as interloper in several marital homes. It also circumnavigated the world of *A Doll's House*. The young, aristocratic and implausible poet Marchbanks infiltrates St Dominic's Parsonage, the home of the Christian Socialist clergyman, James Morell, and his wife, Candida. Marchbanks then informs Morell that he loves Candida far more than the clergyman does. Shaw's inversion of *A Doll's House* shows the husband and not the wife to be the doll in the home and the play ends as Morell clings to his wife in domestic security while Marchbanks steps outs to seek the lonely but higher spiritual fulfilment of the artist.

Certain to some extent of her affair with Archer and delighting in her show of implacability, Shaw taunted her by calling her 'Saint Elizabeth' and 'Holy Elizabeth'. Astonished that he seemed to have forgotten her threat to shoot him, Elizabeth quickly headed him off with a chilling letter. 'I . . . find myself prevented for hearing your play tomorrow,' she wrote, adding with all her southern American imperiousness that 'My name for you is Miss Robins; & I do not see the fact of my being an actress entitles anyone to call me by any other name. Please do not waste time discussing this.'[45] Once again, Shaw retreated.

On 12 January, the world premiere of *Little Eyolf* was held at the Deutsches Theater, Berlin, where it was a failure. In London, Archer was still hopeful of an early production. But suddenly, in February, after a few weeks of intensive activity when, in swift succession, Archer had completed a translation, Elizabeth had tried to interest Alexander and Wyndham, dallied with the Joint Management and negotiated with Janet, the momentum abruptly stopped. It was halted partly as a result of the rivalry between Archer and Shaw, for while Archer looked out for Elizabeth's interests, Shaw remained loyal to Janet Achurch. He was also, understandably, thinking of his own career. Having failed to secure a British production for *Candida*, Shaw suggested to the American actor-manager Richard Mansfield that he stage 'the most fascinating work in the world'[46] in New York, with Janet in the title role. In September, Mansfield had introduced Shaw to the United States by playing Bluntschli in his own production of *Arms and the Man* at the Herald Square Theatre in New York. Now, Mansfield agreed to produce *Candida* and on 16 March, Janet sailed for America. *Little Eyolf* was abandoned.

By this time, Elizabeth was in seclusion, having succumbed to one of the influenza epidemics scampering across England and taking several lives with them. During the early summer, she convalesced in Yorkshire but when she returned to London, neither she nor Archer resumed work on *Little Eyolf*. Instead, they began collaborating on their own play.

'Why the devil dont you write a play instead of perpetually talking about it?' Shaw demanded of Archer. 'You can do it well enough if you will only face making an ass of yourself in the preliminary trials, as you had to when you learned to cycle.'[47] Although Shaw knew that Archer had written plays before they launched upon *Rhinegold*, Archer probably kept the full extent of their incinerated remains a secret. Certainly he kept quiet about his collaboration with Elizabeth. *The Mirkwater* is the first original piece he had begun (and completed) since returning from Italy thirteen years earlier. It represented the rebirth of his dreams and the chance of symbolic marriage between Elizabeth and himself. 'Wouldn't it be good to have our names together on the same title-page, my own?'[48] he wrote to her wistfully.

The play is set in the country, where a young doctor, James Theobold, hopes to marry Felicia Vincent against the wishes of his superstitious and cantankerous mother. She suspects that Felicia is implicated in the unexplained disappearance of her elder sister, Mary, the previous autumn, and plans to frighten her into revealing her part in the crime. When divers dredge the River Mirkwater, Felicia admits to Theobold that her sister drowned herself after she was diagnosed as dying from breast cancer. A body is recovered, and as Theobold is required to make an examination, Felicia describes the scar on one of Mary's breasts and her sister's distress over their father's infidelity to their mother with a succession of women. The scarring therefore also symbolizes the psychological damage their father inflicted upon the family. As an accessory to her sister's suicide, Felicia feels guilty almost of murder, but is redeemed when Theobold defends her compassion against his mother's intransigence.

Archer and Elizabeth worked quickly and in the first week of June, as Shaw was beginning his seventh play, *You Never Can Tell*, she reported a completed first draft of the third and final act. Revisions took over another month. The play's themes of love and the impossibility of living by inflexible ideals were close to both collaborators and it is therefore difficult to tell what proportion of the ideas and the writing is Archer's and how much Elizabeth's. They wrote separately, exchanging notes and drafts, annotating and discussing before preparing a second draft, after which the process would begin again. Their handwritten comments run throughout the manuscript. 'Good idea,' she jotted in the margin at one stage. 'If you'll take my advice you'll let this stand,'[49] he scribbled at another.

The Mirkwater has some affinities with Ibsen. The drowning of the scarred Mary echoes that of the disfigured Eyolf. It also has much in common with British 'problem plays' in which moral questions are dramatized against the English upper-middle-class settings of the drawing room, rectory and study. It shares their atmosphere of melo-dramatic contrivance and as a play of its time, it tilts at the fascination for spiritualism and the spectre of the mendacious mother. Once more, Elizabeth returned to the commercial round, knocking on managers' doors, and back she came again, disappointed. Archer sent a copy of the script to Brander Matthews but he was unable to engineer an American production. They gave up. The play has never been performed nor published.

The failure of *The Mirkwater* diverted them into a short story, *Stall B25*, which returns to the themes of love unreconciled and the vogue for the supernatural. Written during July and August, the story is told by a young medical student from Guy's Hospital who one night goes to the theatre to see Dolly Cameron, a brilliant new actress with whom Darnley, a leading actor, is having an affair. As the play begins, a woman slips into B25, the seat next to the student. She is good looking, pale and dark-haired but her evening clothes are bespattered by mud. The student becomes fascinated by her stillness and apparent concentration on the stage. In the interval a child sitting in a stage-side box suddenly points at her and screams. Later that night he returns to the hospital to discover that a woman has been admitted after being thrown from a hansom on her way to the theatre. She died soon afterwards. In her pocket is a letter from Darnley insisting their affair is over. The student identifies the body as that of the occupant of B25, whom he now realizes to have been a ghost.

Elizabeth did much of the drafting, and Archer most of the revising. Collaboration, whether planning *Little Eyolf* or writing the play and the story, inevitably brought them as close, perhaps closer than they had ever been, both professionally and emotionally. At the beginning of September, he sent her revisions of *Stall B25* with one of his late-night love notes: 'I love you my own sweet & thank you for all your love Dear One I hold you to my heart & bless you & kiss you. 3.30 sweetest one – I kiss your lips and eyes . . .'[50]

In February, E. S. Pigott, the Examiner of Plays, died. Archer neither joined the procession of managers and critics laying tributes to his scholarliness and good taste, nor suspended his campaign to abolish state censorship itself. 'He was a timid and easy-going despot; he struck at the weak but winked at the strong,' he told readers of the *Daily Chronicle*. Then he pressed on, attacking the 'noxiousness and futility'[51] of censorship and deriding Pigott's hapless successor.

This was George Alexander Redford, who took up the post in mid-March. 'No one had ever heard of the alleged Mr Radford or Romford

– I forget the exact name – it was obviously borrowed from some novel of Anthony Trollope's,'[52] mocked Archer in *The World* a week or two later. In fact, Redford had not risen from a Trollopian saga but was a former bank manager, and Archer's article ruined the tranquillity of his holiday in Ayrshire from where he sent a plaintive letter wondering whether 'anything can be done to end the frivolous personal attacks which Mr William Archer continues to make'.[53]

In May, Redford arrived in London to take up his station inspecting scripts at St James's Palace. The following month, Janet Achurch stood on the deck of a steamer making her way back across the Atlantic from New York to London. Things had not turned out well for Janet. Once she landed at New York and Mansfield inhaled her powerful aroma of stale tobacco and alcohol, he decided that not only would she not be appearing in *Candida*, but neither would he produce the play. Janet was put on a ship home, where Archer and Elizabeth were working on *The Mirkwater* and Elizabeth was hoping to return to the theatre in the title role of a stage version of Thomas Hardy's novel, *Tess of the d'Urbervilles*. But Tess was more vivid, more daring and more fiercely determined than either Paula Tanqueray or Agnes Ebbsmith and the actor-managers quailed before her. 'The real, secret reason' that *Tess* failed to reach the stage,' Hardy told Archer, was because 'there was no *hero* in it.'[54]

Archer had known Hardy almost three years, since his enthusiastic review of *Tess* in the *Pall Mall Gazette* had prompted Hardy to send him an inscribed copy. At the end of September, Archer arrived for a long weekend at Max Gate, the novelist's home near Dorchester. Huddling into a long coat, he strode across wind-buffeted 'Egdon Heath', following Hardy's outstretched finger as he pointed out locations he had used in his work. The next week, he took the train back to London and a modern, brick-built villa in Dulwich.

When their Norwood tenancy expired at the beginning of the year, the Archers had returned to Cobham for the summer, but in October, when Tom went back to school, they took a long lease on 71 Alleyn Park in Dulwich. It was the same road in which Archer's parents had lived until they moved to nearby Sydenham. Frances thought number 71, a large, semi-detached house on two floors, 'rather ugly' but 'quite comfortable and *convenient*'.[55] During their sexless marriage and the Ibsen years, and between their two addresses, Frances sensed that she was adrift from her husband. She created a raft of independence in her work, learning all she could about Annie Payson Call's philosophy of intellectual and physical repose, and at Dulwich wasted no time in imposing her authority and dedicating herself to espousing the cause in England. Apart from Frances, Tom and occasionally Archer, number 71 also became home to a Miss Dietrick who arrived from the United States, and Kate Jorgensen, a young second cousin of Archer's who turned up from Norway, both to assist Frances in establishing the British branch of the Call method. She divided her time between Dulwich and town, renting a room at 9 Fitzroy Square where she gave nerve training consultations on three days each week. Watching from his window across the square, Shaw wondered and came to the conclusion that nerve training 'means simply petting a tired man'.[56]

Archer quickly discovered that living with three people professionally attuned to the radiation of mental harmony was immensely stressful, and took shelter at his rooms at Queen Square. He and Elizabeth continued to meet regularly, although with Frances sometimes nearby, caution was more than ever their watchword.

They had not forgotten *Little Eyolf*, but making plans involving Janet, or Charrington, or Shaw, was not an easy matter. As the Archers moved into Dulwich, Grein resigned after over four years as director of the Independent Theatre, and was replaced by his business partner Dorothy Leighton, and the battle-weary but resilient Charringtons. Suddenly, it became possible for Shaw to manipulate the company fortunes.

He lost no time in recommending on 7 October that Charrington announce a season of *Little Eyolf* ('if Elizabeth could be brought into the combination') and his own *Mrs Warren's Profession*. This play, in which a New Woman discovers the economic facts of life by discovering how her mother escaped suburban poverty by becoming a partner in a continental brothel, would, he promised Charrington, create 'a good scandal'.[57] Shaw also hoped Janet would play Vivie Warren. When the Independent Theatre approached Elizabeth, who still held the stage rights, she immediately suspected Shavian skulduggery. Besides, she was adamant that she could not work with a business manager who conducted his negotiations with pawnbrokers rather than banks. Further turmoil was caused when Janet fell ill with typhoid fever. Shaw scurried to her bedside at Onslow Square, provoking Charrington's jealousy by holding her in his arms and imploring her to renounce brandy for a diet of stewed fruit and brown bread. Again *Little Eyolf* was postponed.

By February the following year, 1896, the plans were revived yet again, and once more Shaw muscled in on the negotiations on behalf of the Independent Theatre, spreading confusion and bitterness wherever he went. Mid-month, he discovered that, with Archer's approval, Asta would not now be played by Elizabeth (who had lost patience and withdrawn into her writing) but the stunningly beautiful Rhoda Halkett. Shaw was aghast, for he saw Elizabeth's involvement as crucial to the success of the play, which in turn was essential for the revival of Janet's career. Asta was 'flatchested', he protested to Archer, while Rhoda was nothing if not 'voluptuous'. This was clearly yet another case of his being seduced by pretty eyes and a dazzling smile. 'Can you be serious?'[58] he exclaimed. Archer assured him that he was.

On 18 February, Shaw tugged Heinemann into the fray, firing off a letter pointing out that Rhoda would be a disaster and that it was imperative he used his influence to 'recapture'[59] Elizabeth. When Heinemann read a second letter from Shaw accusing him of indecision, he concluded Shaw was manipulating them all so as to bring forward a play of his own and angrily cancelled the Independent Theatre's rights to *Little Eyolf* altogether. 'I think Janet Achurch & the Independent Theatre have lost *Little Eyolf* after all,' recorded Elizabeth in her diary, '*if so*, they've Shaw to thank.'[60]

The *Little Eyolf* saga infuriated and saddened Archer, who was depressed still further by the sensational success of Wilson Barrett's *The Sign of the Cross* at the Lyric, a horrendously syrupy melodrama of a Roman patrician in love with a young Christian convert. He was briefly perked up by Jones's *Michael and his Lost Angel*, which opened shortly afterwards at the Lyceum. Johnston Forbes-Robertson played the priggish, idealistic priest who spends a night with the beautiful and married Audrie Lesden, and subsequently confesses his moral failings from the altar steps. It was a glimmer in the darkness and, wrote Archer, 'far – oh very far – the best thing'[61] that Jones had done. It was also a shattering commercial failure and closed with a few weeks.

What also worried Archer was that Frances and her nerve treatment devotees, Dulwich and Fitzroy Square were absorbing almost every penny both he and Frances could earn. He threw himself into a pile of extra work, laboriously translating a Norwegian biography of Nansen into English, but by the summer, things had become so tight that he was unable to renew his lease at Queen Square. Instead, he moved into smaller rooms just round the corner at 34 Great Ormond Street. Here, he was a neighbour of Graham Wallas, Shaw's Fabian friend, a tall, amiable man who had become a lecturer at the London School of Economics. No sooner had he settled in, than he joined Frances and

Tom for the journey north to Yorkshire, where they were expected at palatial Castle Howard as the guests of Gilbert Murray and his wife.

Archer had met Murray the previous year. He was a shy, rather hesitant-looking man who was born in Australia and brought to England by his family when he was eleven. After a meteoric career at school and Oxford, he shocked the academic establishment in 1889 when, at the breathtakingly early age of twenty-three, he was appointed Professor of Greek at Glasgow University. He was a staunch Liberal, a teetotaller, intermittent vegetarian and hopeful playwright. In March 1895, he sent a play to Charles Charrington, who passed it on to Archer.

By now, he was used to being stealthily approached for advice by actors and producers unsure of what they were reading and besieged by novice writers eagerly seeking his blessing, many under the delusion they had written a masterpiece. One of these was the Cornish novelist Arthur Quiller-Couch, who fancied his name on billboards and to whom Archer complained that he was quickly becoming 'a sort of consulting physician to dramatists'.[62] But Murray's play, he told Charrington, was different. It was 'the most original and powerful play I have ever come across in MS'.[63]

Summoned to tea at Queen Square on 11 April, Murray listened while Archer told him that he thought *Carlyon Sahib*, a forthright attack upon British imperial rule in India, a remarkable piece which only needed drastic re-writing, a task which he would begin immediately. Archer might have been a thwarted playwright, but he was an effective collaborator. He also saw himself as an expert play-doctor, teasing sturdy and serious plays from their melodramatic shells, advising Jones and Pinero of the grey ordinariness of their views and pointing them towards the combative and the profound. 'I've sometimes thought, with Tesman in *Hedda Gabler*, that "arranging other people's papers is just the work for me",'[64] he told Murray, in the midst of cutting and re-writing the first act of *Carlyon Sahib*.

As Archer and Murray were both serious men, shared similar political views, a distrust of officialdom and a pronounced sense of the ridiculous, Murray quickly joined Elizabeth and Shaw in Archer's exclusive but seldom harmonious inner circle. Having extracted a promise that he would tell nobody of his part in *Carlyon Sahib*, Archer continued to operate on it for several weeks. But it remained unperformed until 1899, when Mrs Patrick Campbell staged it in Kennington, south

London, effortlessly reducing Murray to a quivering bundle of nerves in the process.

Gilbert Murray was married to Lady Mary, a daughter of Lord and Lady Carlisle, the owners of Castle Howard. Under Lady Carlisle's energetic stewardship, it had become a formidable outpost of traditional aristocratic opulence and modern liberal radicalism. British oppression of the colonies was denounced in rooms hung with a stupendous collection of old masters and contemporary paintings. Alcohol was banned and smoking only very rarely tolerated. The Archers joined the Murrays there on 4 August 1896. As Lord and Lady Carlisle were away, Archer was free to roam the corridors and rooms, informing Dibdin that 'I feel rather like the Czar of Russia living in a compound of St Paul's and the British Museum.'[65] On 10 August, he was back in London, and three days later set off for his second visit to Bayreuth. It was his first trip abroad for six years. That night, he arrived in Frankfurt, where he saw *Faust* at the Schauspielhaus and next day, travelled on to Bayreuth where, over a 'lovely week', he saw a complete *Ring* cycle. By the end of the third week of August, he was back in England 'to finish Nansen's life – the polar bears having omitted to do so'.[66] The view from Great Ormond Street was drab indeed. 'Things are depressingly dull in the theatrical world,'[67] he told Brander Matthews in September.

They would not be dull for very much longer, for by the autumn, he had at last persuaded Elizabeth to inaugurate a fund to produce *Little Eyolf*. As with the 1893 Ibsen season, they planned to stage more than one play. Archer had introduced her to the work of the contemporary Spanish dramatist, José Echegaray, and earlier that year she acquired the stage rights to James Graham's English translation of *Mariana*, a florid romantic tragedy. The appeal for the *Ibsen-Echegaray Performances*, advertised under Elizabeth's name, raised several hundred pounds, principally from subscribers of the still dormant Independent Theatre. It was enough to hire the Avenue Theatre for a series of five matinees for *Little Eyolf* beginning on 23 November.

It was a bitingly cold winter that year. Archer sat hunched over his spitting gas fire at Great Ormond Street, revising the text and choosing the cast with Elizabeth. She herself would play Asta. Courtenay Thorpe agreed to undertake Allmers. An actor in his early forties, eccentric but striking with dark hair and a neatly-trimmed beard, he had played a notable Oswald in New York. Janet Achurch, who was now recovered and available, claimed her role of Rita. This was a rash decision, as her alcohol and morphia addictions had progressed to the point where she was apt to peer at her fellow actors with eyes resembling twin moons in a wet fog. She was also six months pregnant. None of the previous Archer-Robins productions had employed understudies, but this time they brought in Florence Farr on a retainer of ten pounds a week to take over from Janet if, or more likely when, she buckled. As far as the box office was concerned, the partnership of Elizabeth and Janet was already irresistible, but it became even more so when Elizabeth offered the small part of the Ratwife to Mrs Patrick Campbell. '. . . temperament without skill,' murmered Archer, after watching Mrs Pat play a surprisingly prudish Juliet opposite Johnston Forbes-Robertson's elegant Romeo (who actually was in love with his Juliet) at the Lyceum. Archer thought her too reliant upon her 'gazelle-like'[68] glamour, but she was still determined to become a great actress. Although the Ratwife appeared only once in *Little Eyolf*, speaking a few lines in the first act, the character was eye-catching and her dramatic importance far exceeded her limited stage-time. There was no better way for Mrs Pat to begin climbing the Ibsen mountain.

Three weeks of rehearsals began at the beginning of November. The performances were billed as being 'Under the direction of Miss Elizabeth Robins.' Archer took the translator's credit while their old ally George Foss was this time billed as 'producer'. Archer's partnership with Foss, which had begun with *Hedda Gabler* over five years previously, and had continued through the calamitous Brighton performances, *The Master Builder* and the 1893 Ibsen season, would end with *Little Eyolf.* This was the last show they would direct together before work took Foss elsewhere. By now, Elizabeth was an experienced realistic actor but their methods were new to Thorpe, whose 'set tragic air'[69] Archer began to demolish in a river of letters from Great Ormond Street, promising him that he sent them in the spirit of 'one collaborator to another', and because 'I am so utterly powerless to convey any indication, in action, of what I mean.'

Enclosed with this letter on 8 November, were three-and-a-half closely and sometimes haphazardly typed pages explaining Alfred Allmers's character. 'Will you forgive me if at the outset I suggest you should be careful not to let your Oswald Alving creep into your Allmers?' he wrote. '. . . every now and then I seem to recognise intonations and especially a certain querulousness of tone, that would be excellent in Oswald, but seems to be less in keeping with Allmers . . . Oswald knows himself to be broken down; Allmers is in fair physical health, and is, theoretically at any rate, a strong-minded man, capable of looking life fairly and squarely in the face. He is *defiant* rather than querulous or lachrymose.'

There were notes on the text. ' "I know only this one terrible thing" – you dropped the "this" which is of some value,' Archer reminded him. 'By a slip of the tongue, no doubt, you said "A crazy old woman has only to come along" instead of "come this way." I think "along" is an Americanism and tends to be comic.'[70] A few days later, Thorpe received an injunction to 'be careful of folding the arms too much'.[71] Then there was a request to change the line 'that you may be sure of' to 'you may be sure of that' each time it cropped up. Archer cut, altered and refined constantly during rehearsals. In his own copy of the published text, he scribbled dozens of directorial notes: 'no pause'; 'not so quick'; 'no smile'.[72] On 19 November, four days before opening, another list of 'slips of the tongue' arrived for Thorpe. 'I daresay you think me a great bore with my suggestions but I let you off comparatively easily – I am sending ELEVEN slips to Miss Achurch.'[73]

Each day, he warily monitored Janet's demeanour for evidence of pharmaceutical sustenance. She appeared so subdued, that just before the production opened, he encouraged her to 'play up a little', the opposite of what he usually told his actors. Mrs Campbell's rehearsals appear to be relatively trouble-free as Archer gently coaxed her towards playing the Ratwife as a harbinger of death rather than a volatile village harridan. Finally, he and Foss had achieved all they could. 'I am confident you will have a great success on Monday,'[74] he told them, fervently hoping that Janet would brighten up once she was in front of an audience.

The three actresses drew crowds to the opening on 23 November. Archer, Heinemann, Charrington and the usual serious devotees were there. Shaw was accompanied by Charlotte Payne-Townshend, an Irish Fabian who had subscribed generously to the performance fund. Pinero had taken a box for the 'Little Eye-opener'[75] and Mrs Pat's name brought the adoring Johnston Forbes-Robertson to another, while several of her friends helped fill the stalls.

The curtain rose on the first new Ibsen play in London for two-and-a-half years to reveal the sombre, heavily furnished set of the Allmers's garden room. The audience, 'very many of whom were women',[76] were silent and attentive and there were no ripples of embarrassed laughter, as there were during *The Master Builder.* But anyone hoping that bringing together the three most brilliant actresses of the day would produce a memorably fiery performance was disappointed. It was ponderous and seemed to drag on for hours. Clement Scott called it 'sepulchral'. The play, which Archer thought the most tragic Ibsen had written, seemed beyond his reach. Perhaps it echoed too much of his own emotional vulnerability. He and Foss had also failed to weld the disparate personalities of the individual stars into an ensemble. Everything was knocked even further out of joint when, once her appearance as the Ratwife was over, Mrs Pat emerged at the first interval, refreshed and dressed in a spectacular gown, to join her friends in the audience and give a whispered commentary during the remainder of the performance.

As usual, the reviews the next morning ranged from the cautious to the caustic. In the *Daily Telegraph*, Scott thought the play 'grim',[77] while the *Pall Mall Gazette* declared it to be 'a picture of mental and physical disease' which was nonetheless 'powerful and interesting'.[78] Nisbet at *The Times*, reluctant to discard a durable explanation for Ibsen and all his works, described the effect as one of watching 'the patients of a madhouse exercising in their yard'.[79] The real disappointment was that Elizabeth appeared so muted. There was little to praise except Mrs Campbell's Ratwife, which the *Pall Mall Gazette* called 'a tour de force of weirdness and intensity',[80] even though the character's precise significance was in doubt. Symbolism was widely considered a euphemism for the wilfully obscure.

Shaw, who had come to the performance in his capacity of theatre critic of the *Saturday Review*, pronounced the play 'extraordinarily powerful' and the performance 'very remarkable'. He praised Mrs Campbell, congratulated Courtenay Thorpe, and confessed that it was 'difficult to say much' about Elizabeth's Asta before proceeding to award Janet one of the most superlative notices of her career. She was at her most moving, her most magnetically authoritative, producing 'almost every sound that a big human voice can, from a crack like the opening of a rusty canal lock to a melodious tenor note that the most robust Siegfried must have envied. She looked at one moment like a young, well-dressed, very pretty woman; at another she was like a desperate creature just fished dripping out of the river by the Thames police.'[81]

By this time, Archer was claiming he had given up reading critics, and especially Clement Scott. He himself acknowledged the actors in *The World* and apologized for being unable to provide his readers with a critically objective report. *Little Eyolf*, he wrote, 'moves me so profoundly that I am totally unable to estimate its merits as a stage play'.[82] But the glamorous cast provided a shield against critical boredom and reticence. *Little Eyolf* sold out. Elizabeth booked a second week of matinees and still audiences jostled at the box office, crowded into the auditorium and elbowed the theatrical syndicate who came knocking at Elizabeth's dressing-room door, flourishing contracts for an evening run.

Inevitably, Janet was sacked. Yet her downfall was neither drugs, nor drink, nor approaching maternity, but desperation born of near-poverty. Hearing that an evening run was in the offing, she approached the syndicate herself and demanded an increased salary and a share of the box office to continue playing Rita. When this news filtered back to Archer and Elizabeth, they persuaded Mrs Pat to underbid her for the role of Rita. Whether or not Archer and Elizabeth gladly took the opportunity of firing Janet, the syndicate were delighted to accept Mrs Pat's offer and present a more luminous and arguably more stable star in the leading role for less money. Just before the curtain rose on Friday, 4 December, Janet was told that she was no longer required after the Saturday performances. Florence Farr, with exemplary grace, agreed to play the Ratwife and during the weekend, Archer rehearsed Mrs Campbell in her new role of Rita. There was not enough time. By Tuesday evening, Mrs Pat was still not word-perfect and Archer watched despondently as she survived the first two acts, but for most of the third resorted to the book dangling at the end of a ribbon from her waistband. Afterwards, Archer endured 'a frightful altercation'[83] with Shaw until the early hours of the morning over the ethics of replacing Janet.

Little Eyolf lumbered along, playing to full houses but with Archer grumbling that Mrs Campbell's increasing showiness was turning a serious play into a West End ornament. It lasted until 19 December and at four weeks, the run equalled that of *A Doll's House* in 1889. There were no regrets on Archer's part when it was over. A few days later, poor Janet appears to have suffered a miscarriage.

The first few weeks of 1897 were taken up with *Mariana*. The second of the *Ibsen-Echegaray Performances* took place at the Court Theatre for five matinees from 22 February. In *The World*, Archer described the play as 'a love tragedy pure and simple'.[84] H. B. Irving, a son of Sir Henry Irving, was cast as Daniel de Montoya opposite Elizabeth in the title role. Mariana is in love with Daniel, but when she learns his father seduced her mother, she rejects him and marries an older man. On her wedding night, Daniel tries to persuade her to elope with him, when the new husband discovers them together and shoots Mariana dead.

Archer left most of the production work to Elizabeth and Guy Waller, the stage manager. In his eulogy of Janet Achurch, in the *Saturday Review*, Shaw had compared her favourably with Sarah Bernhardt. In *The World* on 3 March, Archer retaliated by announcing that Elizabeth had scored 'a great and decisive triumph',[85] and was now the equal of Duse. No one else was so emphatic but Elizabeth was now saying with Archer that she did not read reviews.

Mariana closed after playing five performances to thin houses, losing over a hundred pounds. It was a failure, both financially and artistically. But as the Independent Theatre had produced nothing for two years, Archer and Elizabeth had nevertheless emerged as not merely the only serious interpreters of Ibsen but the potential saviours of the entire serious theatre movement. At last, the stage was clear for the launch of their own company.

9

Endings and Beginnings

They had been contemplating starting their own company for several months, and after the apparent demise of the Independent Theatre and with a West End 'almost entirely given over to musical farce', Archer maintained the need was 'more than ever pressing'.[1] They thought of producing a short series of plays for a month's run each, or an annual or biannual festival with two or three plays performed in repertoire over six weeks. Finally, they reverted to producing matinees wherever they could find a temporary home. As money mystified Archer and they both had to earn a living, they looked for someone of 'leisure, enthusiasm & intelligence'[2] to run the business side of things for them. They discovered Alfred Sutro, a thirty-three-year-old, round-faced man who examined the world through small, oval pince-nez.

Sutro's father, a descendent of German Jews from near Heidelburg, had emigrated to England to become a successful businessman and install his sons in the City of London as tea and coffee merchants. However, after his marriage to Esther Isaacs, an aspiring artist, Sutro abandoned his account books for Paris, where they fell in love with the Théâtre Libre and the Théâtre de l'Œuvre and everyone connected with them. In the spring of 1895, they returned to England. His awe of the theatre undimmed, Sutro laid on a lunch at the National Liberal Club in honour of the Théâtre de l'Œuvre's visit to London and it was then that he met Archer. But Sutro was so nervous that he ate too little and drank too much, and later could not recall a word either of them said.

Two years later, Sutro had still not given up hopes of becoming a playwright himself. But as far as Archer was concerned, the most important thing about him was that he earned enough from the family business not to need paying for looking after their as yet unopened accounts. He and Elizabeth made him their honorary secretary and set him to work rustling up subscriptions for their first season. According to Archer, after the success of the 1893 Ibsen season and rockier paths of the *Ibsen-Echegaray Performances*, the new company would be another step towards the eventual creation of a National Theatre. As the performances of *Mariana* limped almost unnoticed to their end, he informed a nonplussed Sutro that 'Our aim is to give England a permanent artistic theatre and school of acting.'

Archer was a curious character, thought Sutro. Spindly, with dark brows, a penetrating gaze and a loping stride, he appeared to have an enormous number of acquaintances but few close friends. He was a bit of an enigma, both formal and eccentric at the same time. The umbrella he carried, for instance, was so battered that it seemed to bear out what everyone said, that he never spent any money on himself. He found Archer bewildering, but his energy was startling. He bubbled with ideas. Letters began landing on Sutro's doormat, each one with a suggestion, a plan, a reminder or an article of faith. 'I think that *as a matter of principle* we should quite formally appeal for donations,' wrote Archer. 'Even if we don't get any at all, the principle is right that people in this land of millionaires or rather thousandaires, should be told: "If you see an art enterprise striving to do good work and doing it in a non-self-seeking spirit and capable of large and fruitful development if only it had the funds, you *ought* to support it generously, and you should be ashamed of yourselves if you don't . . ." '[3]

First, there was the matter of the company name. Archer began firing off a barrage of suggestions. The Interim Theatre (which he recalled from his youthful visit to Dresden); The Arts Theatre; The Pioneer Stage; The Progressive Theatre; The Repertory Theatre; The Renascence Theatre . . .

'Aurion!' exclaimed Elizabeth, bright-eyed with enthusiasm, one day in March. 'Aurion', she explained, was Greek for 'tomorrow'. It was perfect. They would call their company The Theatre of Tomorrow and they would be the new Aurionists. 'I don't like this at all,'[4] Archer muttered to Sutro, wondering if the name carried spiritualistic undertones. The reluctant Aurionist countered with his own suggestion, stubbornly keeping up the bombardment until Elizabeth relented. Taking its impulse from the nineties idea of the new, the company would march bravely towards aurion under the banner of the New Century Theatre.

Archer flung himself into organizing their assault. They needed a board of trustees bulging with influential names. He dashed off a list including the novelists Mrs Humphrey Ward and George Meredith; the Conservative First Lord of the Treasury, Arthur Balfour and the former Liberal leader, the Earl of Rosebery: 'You see, we want to *root* the thing . . .' he counselled Sutro. In the end, he settled for a Managing Committee consisting of himself, Elizabeth, Sutro and H. W. Massingham, the Liberal editor of the *Daily Chronicle*. The sculptor George Frampton agreed to act as Honorary Art Advisor, and Gerald Duckworth who, within a year would begin his own publishing house, was elected Honorary Treasurer.

Democracy might be essential in politics, Archer told them briskly, but it had absolutely no place in art. He had seen how easily Shaw had caused havoc at the Independent Theatre and both he and Elizabeth were agreed that the New Century had to be constitutionally sealed against Shaw. The Committee must remain 'a close oligarchy', protected by a labyrinth of rules so ingeniously constructed that subscribers were convinced of its trustworthiness while denied 'any actual right of interference'.[5]

They unveiled a prospectus heralding 'a new departure . . . in English theatrical life'.[6] Both seriousness and vivacity were implied in a first season consisting of the British premiere of Ibsen's latest play, *John Gabriel Borkman* and W. E. Henley and Robert Louis Stevenson's *Admiral Guinea*, with the British premiere of *Peer Gynt* pencilled in for the future. Subscribers were invited to buy a seat for each production, ranging from ten shillings for a place in an upper box to one pound twelve shillings for a seat in the stalls. Any profits, they promised, would be ploughed into the staging of more plays. *John Gabriel Borkman*, published in Christiana in December, was scheduled as the company's opening production on 26 April 1897. 'It is enormously interesting, though not so strange & terrible as the first act of *Little Eyolf*,'[7] Archer reported to Murray.

A miner's son who became a successful and respected banker, Borkman was convicted of embezzlement and imprisoned for five years. When the play opens, eight years after his release, he is living as a virtual recluse on the top floor of his house, refusing to see Gunhild, his wife, who lives below, and still believing that one day the community will put its faith in him again. His only visitor is Foldal, a boyhood friend. As a young man, Borkman, like Bernick in *The Pillars of Society*, married not for love but to further his career. Gunhild's sister, Ella Rentheim, whom he loved but rejected, accuses him of having sacrificed love for capital. As Borkman left her own savings intact, she has raised Erhart, the Borkmans's son. He is now twenty-three and Ella demands that he be allowed to take her name instead of his father's. At last, Borkman agrees, but Gunhild is incensed. As the two women argue, Erhart arrives to announce that he has decided to live with Mrs Wilton, a divorcee twice his age. At the end of the play, Borkman dies, like Brand, alone in the snow on the mountainside.

It is a bleak, despairing play about people whose emotions have withered to resemble a winter landscape. Archer recommended it as a 'tragedy of wasted lives',[8] but he was disappointed. From *The Wild Duck* until *Little Eyolf*, with the sole exception of *The Lady from the Sea*, Ibsen had produced 'masterpiece on masterpiece', and although parts of *John Gabriel Borkman* showed Ibsen at his most hauntingly powerful, Archer noticed for the first time that his genius was beginning 'to flag a little'.[9] The emotional impact was weakening. After twelve years, Ibsen appeared to be tiring.

On 14 December, Heinemann held his copyright reading at the Avenue, where Elizabeth was still in residence with *Little Eyolf*, and published Archer's translation two months later. On 10 January, two moderately succesful world premieres were held at the Swedish and Finnish Theatres in Helsinki, but the better production came a little later, directed by August Lindberg at the small Norwegian town of Drammen, thirty miles from Christiana.

In London, rehearsals for the British premiere were faltering and the opening was postponed from 26 April until 3 May. The cast, mostly chosen by Elizabeth, was an uneasy mix of the old rhetorical school, and novice and experienced realists. Elizabeth was playing Ella Rentheim and Geneviève Ward, Gunhild. W. H. Vernon who appeared as Bernick in *Quicksands*, Archer's first Ibsen production, took the title role. Mrs Beerbohm Tree strode purposefully forward as Mrs Wilton and James Welch, who had survived the trials of *Widowers' Houses* and *Arms and the Man*, joined them as Foldal. Martin Harvey, on loan from Irving's company at the Lyceum, played Erhardt. This time, Archer was unable to fall back upon the faithful Foss as Vernon was not only playing the leading role but also co-directing. His name would appear on the programme.

Sitting in the stalls, Archer scribbled on his copy of the text, altering and polishing lines. He climbed on the stage to rehearse Borkman's restless pacing of his room in the second act, devising a slow march in time with the dialogue, from downstage right to upstage left. Vernon, meanwhile, complained that several of his lines made no sense. In Act Three, for example, what did 'It is the eye that transforms the action. The eye, born anew, transforms the old action', mean? Precisely? Archer explained. Vernon shook his head. No, he said, he still did not see it, but having no idea of what he was saying had never affected his performance yet. He mumbled and gestured away, and rehearsals stumbled on around him.

The appeal for subcriptions resulted in 'a respectable sum'[10] having come in, but far too much had gone straight out again. Independence, Archer discovered, was alarmingly expensive. There was the rent for the five matinees at the Strand Theatre, the actors' wages and printers' fees for press advertising and programmes. An Art Nouveau-inspired poster, with red lettering on a grey background, had been commissioned for the front of house and each subscriber was receiving an eight-page pamphlet including an article on the play by Emile Faguet, a professor of literature at the Sorbonne. Having paid the bills, there was hardly anything left over for a set.

When the curtain rose on the first New Century performance at three o'clock on 3 May 1897, it appeared that instead of living in the old-fashioned, faded grandeur envisaged by Ibsen, the Borkmans had been reduced to destitution. For the Act One set of Fru Borkman's living-room, Archer and Elizabeth had managed to scrape together only a stove and a few heartbreakingly elderly chairs covered in threadbare white and gold fabric. The furnishing of Borkman's room in the second act turned out to be equally meagre, and for the final act, set outside on the snow-covered mountainside, a painted cloth representing snowy slopes and a night sky hung forlornly at the rear of a bare stage. The desolation was intensified because Archer, in the face of Vernon's protests, had directed that the play be performed in consistently subdued light.

It was Archer's most ramshackle production since *Quicksands*, impoverished, miscast, under-rehearsed and sluggish. 'When I looked at that,' remarked Shaw indignantly, 'and thought of the eminence of the author and the greatness of his work, I felt ashamed.' Next time, he promised Archer, he would present the company with a ten-pound note or, at the very least, lend them a couple of chairs. The shoddiness was reflected in the acting. Ibsen had called for a Borkman of smouldering force and leaping imagination, but Vernon presented merely a disillusioned, kindly old chap who spent too much time with his back to the audience.

Shaw did not bear grudges, but he was still angered by the cruelty of Janet's sacking from *Little Eyolf*. He wanted to bolster her self-esteem and reclaim her for Ibsen. Neither had he forgotten the incident of St Elizabeth's revolver, and nor could he avoid her continuing hypnosis of Archer. In the *Saturday Review*, he continued to thrust barbs into the bouquets offered to her acting. She might mesmerize Archer and sway an audience, he implied, but she would never hoodwink him. There was 'no reality, no sincerity' in her Ella Rentheim. He saw through her techniques, pierced her carapace of realism and exposed the sham behind. 'The genuine and touching tone of self-pity suddenly turns into a perceptibly artificial snivel,' he wrote. To Ella's combative and anguished speeches, she brought only 'a pretty tone'.[11] She lacked compassion.

In the *Daily Chronicle*, Massingham, a member of the Managing Committee, loyally called the production 'the best representation of an Ibsen play which has yet been given to the English world'.[12] Scott thought it 'the worst possible specimen of the master's theory',[13] while Walkley declared it to be the finest tragedy of old age since *King Lear*. But the gloomy monotony of the perforance caused boredom to rise like damp in both critics and audiences. Nobody could find the energy to begin the kind of controversy which had lit up the old days only six years ago.

It was a crushing beginning for the New Century. *John Gabriel Borkman* rambled on and closed after its fifth matinee, losing precious money. As if to underline their failure, a matinee revival of *A Doll's House* opened at the Globe Theatre the following Monday, with Janet Achurch as Nora and Courtenay Thorpe as Helmer. Shaw and many others applauded loudly.

Archer went back to weekly reviewing, and was still mulling over the misfortunes of the New Century when, on 30 July, under Frances's direction, the Archers set off together for Gryon, in Switzerland, their first holiday abroad for seven years. Archer did not enthuse over family excursions: '... wish I were back again', he told Murray. But he brightened once he thought of an alternative plan, 'to take my cycle with me and try to get over the St Bernard to Aosta, and hear Italian again before I die'.[14] He did exactly what he had done on their last Swiss holiday. Brimming with impatience, he stayed long enough for Frances and Tom to settle in and then scuttled off by himself. It so happened that a few days earlier, Elizabeth had left London and was holidaying in Germany. She wrote to Archer on 25 August, and they may have met, for that night at least, it appears that he was not in Italy at all, but at the theatre in Frankfurt.

Archer arrived home on 28 August, shortly after Elizabeth and a fortnight before Frances and Tom, and resumed his reviewing of up to five plays a week. The dismal standard of most soon buoyed him up enough to ponder the New Century Theatre's second production. *Admiral Guinea* was a boyish pirate melodrama to which Elizabeth was coldly indifferent. But Archer insisted it would grip a public already besotted with maritime dramas and as a result, treasure would tumble into the company's empty coffers. As a companion-piece they chose *Honesty – A Cottage Flower*, a whimsical one-act play by Margaret Young about a landlady's love for one of her lodgers.

Neither are 'plays of serious value & interest'[15] which the New Century Theatre was founded to produce, but Archer liked adventure stories and particularly *Treasure Island*, from which the play is derived. Written in 1884, *Admiral Guinea* had become 'a little mania of mine', he told Murray. The blind beggar David Pew, who appears in only a few pages of the book but who, with his stick, tap-taps his way through the play, was 'such a refreshing scoundrel'[16] that he longed to see him come to life on the stage. In this he was nearly disappointed, for casting took weeks of pleading letters before they secured the character-actor and comedian Sydney Valentine as Pew and twenty-one-year-old Robert Loraine, 'a young actor of whom we shall see much in the future'[17] as the swashbuckling hero Kit French.

Producing *Admiral Guinea* was no easier than *John Gabriel Borkman*. As soon as the Avenue Theatre was booked for five matinees beginning on 29 November, Archer and Elizabeth fell out with Sutro. They had chosen him to look after their accounts partly because he was Jewish, which Archer thought an infallible sign of business acumen, but he had turned out to be 'the very worst businessman in the world – an Hebrew in which there is no guile'.[18] Disillusioned with theatre people, Sutro stalked off to his cottage in Dorset, leaving the paperwork and most of the direction of *Admiral Guinea* to an ominously simmering Elizabeth. Archer hovered nervously about, foraging for bits and pieces for the set, braving the mysterious interiors of East End chandlers' for rope and sailcloth and wondering how best to keep things on an even keel.

After a thinly-attended and immensely tedious first performnce, Shaw declared that he would rather be boiled alive than sit through *Honesty – A Cottage Flower* again. Archer awkwardly admitted that it was 'absolutely commonplace'[19] but so, according to almost everyone else, was *Admiral Guinea*. Henley had written a special prologue for the production, which Elizabeth delivered as though she wished she was a very long way away. After this, the play stood little chance. To have any hope of success, it needed to be played quickly and lightly. Instead, it seemed infected by the gloom of *John Gabriel Borkman*, grinding along so slowly that it overran its scheduled length by twenty minutes. Privately, Archer blamed Elizabeth's direction, but stoutly defended the play itself in *The World*. 'It is the perfection of dramatic writing,'[20] he sniffed.

Listing and sinking before sparse audiences, *Admiral Guinea* exposed the vulnerability in Archer's relationship with Elizabeth and the dilemma confronting the New Century Theatre. They worked best when he was directing and she acting. As co-producers, especially on plays falling so far short of their ideals, they bickered and snapped. Part of the problem was that most of the British plays available for matinee production were hardly worth the effort, while the European plays were beyond the means of the New Century Theatre. They had spent hours meticulously sketching out an ideal repertoire of almost thirty plays, including Hauptmann's *Die Weber (The Weavers)*, a grim account of the revolt of Silesian weavers in 1844. 'Possibly, *probably* money in this, properly done,' thought Elizabeth. There was Goethe's *Iphigenia* in a translation by Gilbert Murray, whose *Carlyon Sahib* was down for production. They added *Daughter of the House*, ('a stockbroking play – not militant, some merit'[21]) by Kate Terry Gielgud, a niece of Ellen Terry who had recently married a stockbroker and in seven years would become the mother of John Gielgud. There were plays by Turgenev, Alfred de Musset, Maeterlinck, and Arthur Schnitzler. All these seemed impossible now.

Archer was too downcast to begin calculating their losses, especially in the days after *Admiral Guinea* when Shaw was earning a hundred and fifty pounds a week in royalties from New York, where Mansfield had produced the world premiere of *The Devil's Disciple*, his eighth play. 'This will certainly mean more money in Charrington's pockets,' Archer predicted. 'Shaw will finance *Candida* & set them afoot again.'[22] He envisaged a phoenix rising from the ashes of the Independent Theatre while the still small flame of the New Century would be ignominiously snuffed out by debt. He was flooded by pessimism. 'I was misled by *Little Eyolf*,' he told Murray sadly. 'Of course I knew that that success was exceptional; but I thought one might write down 50% of it to the circumstances . . . & that the remainder might imply the existence of a steady working public for well-conducted experiments in rational drama. Experience has shown that there is practically no such public at all.'[23]

Murray offered to donate £250 towards a new production, or £1000 if Archer would relaunch the New Century and run it himself. But he refused. He was too despondent and as so often happened, his misery was exacerbated by such violent toothache he could think of nothing else but seeing his dentist as soon as possible. In an excruciating hour on 9 December, four of his remaining teeth were extracted.

In April 1898, Shaw published his first seven plays in two volumes of *Plays Pleasant and Unpleasant*. The first, unpleasant volume comprised *Widowers' Houses*, *The Philanderer* and *Mrs Warren's Profession*, and the second, the pleasant *Arms and the Man*, *Candida*, *The Man of Destiny* and *You Never Can Tell*. As someone who had long campaigned for the wider publication of plays, Archer acclaimed this as 'an event, literary and theatrical, of the first magnitude'. Reviewing both books for the *Daily Chronicle*, he attempted to cleave a path through the dense and tangled undergrowth of Shaw's trumpeting, preaching and clowning, and discover whether an essential Shaw lay beneath. Yet how could he reconcile the best of Shaw's writing with the worst? 'That the man who wrote *Candida* should have written *The Philanderer* and should proceed to write *You Never Can Tell* is a bewildering and saddening phenomenon,'[24] he wrote.

Archer was especially horrified by *The Philanderer*, even though Shaw had discarded an inflammatory third act advocating amicable divorce and substituted another which made the play more pleasant than unpleasant. In *Widowers' Houses*, he had unveiled the spiky, pragmatic Blanche as his first New Woman. Keeping Archer up-to-date with his writing, he promised him that in *The Philanderer*, his second play, he had taken 'a step nearer to something'.[25] As far as Archer could see, it was a step further away from anything. He did not object to a fleet of women in various stages of Newness but was enraged by Shaw's creation of an Ibsen Club, tolerating neither womanly women nor manly men, in the library of which a bust of Ibsen stared down at the members. Privately, he was also aghast that Shaw could ostentatiously portray his own philandering in the leading role of Leonard Charteris, and the women should also be based upon those with whom Shaw had had relationships. If this was his sense of ethics, there was no telling where the man might stop. He might even write something about him and Elizabeth! The thought made him turn cold with apprehension.

Mrs Warren's Profession on the other hand, a moral problem play set at Mrs Warren's home in the Surrey countryside, was 'not only intellectually but dramatically one of the very ablest plays of our time'. The character of Mrs Warren herself, the restless, vulgar manageress of a string of European brothels, was 'superb', and Shaw's indictment of the economic conditions forcing women into prostitution 'thrilling and crushing'. It was exactly the kind of play that Archer (and Shaw) wanted to see in the theatre. But in Archer's view, the flaw in the piece was Shaw's third New Woman, Mrs Warren's daughter, Vivie. Because she was a 'Girtonian paragon' instead of a real character, argued Archer, the crucial scenes in which Mrs Warren and Crofts reveal the true nature of her mother's profession were far less harrowing than they might have been. Yet the play was undeniably Shaw's 'masterpiece',[26] and beside it stood the 'ingenious'[27] *Candida*.

Archer welcomed Marchbanks as one of the few genuine characters Shaw had created. Elsewhere, he identified the same fault-line that ran through *Widowers' Houses* and *Arms and the Man*. Instead of writing plays, Shaw threw off mechanized Fabian tracts. He painted idealized self-portraits and called them Charteris, Bluntschli, and Valentine (in *You Never Can Tell*). 'Each is a quick-witted, un-illusioned, fascinating young man, entirely at ease with himself in the world,' Archer noted. 'Each has kissed the blarney-stone. Each is ready at a moment's notice with a psychological theory of the persons about him . . . And . . . each is engaged in the same agreeable task – that of disillusioning and dominating a beautiful but headstrong young lady.' A version of Shaw could even be seen peeping from behind Vivie Warren's skirts, while another masqueraded as her half-brother, the clever, happy-go-lucky Frank Gardner. The reason *Candida* was 'incomparably' the best play of the collection was simply because 'there is less of the Charteris-Bluntschli element in it'.[28]

Shaw blustered, waving at Archer a list of people whom he had used as models for his characters, carefully omitting Charteris and Valentine. Vivie Warren was based on Beatrice Webb ('an absolutely new type'[29]), and Bluntschli on her husband, Sidney. 'I want . . . good plays, not . . . assertions that such and such a character is taken from such & such a real person,' retorted Archer. If Shaw really wanted to 'mow down the critics', he should 'write a few more *Candidas*'.[30]

Shaw did not write a few more *Candidas*. Instead, after years of castigating Archer on the debilitating effects of his marriage, he ducked into the Registrar's Office in Covent Garden on 1 June and emerged a married man himself. He was forty-one and his bride six months younger. She was Charlotte Payne-Townshend, whom Archer had seen at the first performance of *Little Eyolf.* 'Ladylike woman with green eyes,' whispered Shaw, jogging his friend's notoriously bad memory. 'So when you meet her remember that you know her already.'[31] Archer apparently commemorated the occasion by sending them a review of the event written in Shaw's *Saturday Review* style. 'That is the wittiest wedding present of the century,' wrote a delighted Shaw after reading it. 'Only, confound you, I believe you never read a line of the *Saturday Review*, and dont know how clever youve been.'[32]

Archer's marriage had been celibate for over a decade. Neither he nor Shaw discussed this of course, but between close friends understandings develop and some things need not be said. It is a question of atmosphere, and Shaw's marriage did not alter the atmosphere of their friendship because his relationship with Charlotte was similar to Archer's with Frances. Taking advantage of an injured foot and a broken arm, Shaw quickly adjusted to married life as he (and Charlotte) intended it to proceed. He concentrated his energies into his work while Charlotte stood guard between him and the world. On 15 August, while they honeymooned non-sexually in Mrs Warren country at Haslemere, Archer set off for another tour of Europe. Travelling was a compulsion. As he preferred to keep his emotions to himself so he liked to take off abroad, preferably alone and independent, and be free of England, the grit and grime of London and Frances's regime of perfectly poised intellectual and physical repose. He made first for Norway, joining Charles and his aunts at Tolderodden before journeying on to Christiana where, having overseen the advent in book form of England's newest dramatist, he renewed his acquaintance with Europe's most senior. Ibsen was living in an apartment in the Arbiensgate, overlooking the gardens of the Royal Palace. It was extensive and modern although, typically, Ibsen had made it cold and cheerless. Earlier that year, Archer and Gosse had raised fifty pounds from his English admirers to buy him a seventieth birthday present of partly reproduction Georgian silver, and as he was ushered into Ibsen's study, he saw the cup and spoon glinting on a small table. The room was dark and cluttered with a writing desk, and chairs and a sofa in green leather, and dominated by Christian Krohg's large portrait of Strindberg. Ibsen had never met the unstable Swedish author of *The Father* and *Miss Julie*

but the two men shared a touchy, usually hostile long-range relationship. '. . . I rejoice in that portrait,' Ibsen confided to Archer. 'I think
he looks so delightfully mad.'[33]

By 25 August, Archer arrived in Copenhagen. Two days later he was
in Berlin, where he stayed several days and saw ten productions. On 6
September, he checked in to the Hotel Royal, Vienna, and two days
later saw a revival of *The Winter's Tale* at the Burgtheater. In Munich,
he met the Norwegian author Biørsterne Bjørnson, as ebullient as Ibsen
was reticent, and arrived home on 15 September with a copy of his play,
Paul Lange og Thora Parsberg, (Paul Lange and Thora Parsberg) which he
thought idly of translating for the New Century Theatre.

Unpacking his bags at Great Ormond Street, he took stock of his
bank account, blanched, and hastily revived his lecturing career. Over
the next few years, whenever he could spare the time, he careered
madly about the country, clutching a box of magic lantern slides
(carefully prepared and regularly repaired by Dibdin) and a bag of
lectures. He spoke to local societies on David Garrick, various nineteenth-century actors, modern drama and, at a real push, Chaucer ('a
rather poor performance.'[34]) He lectured at Leicester, and Newcastle
where, on 30 October, he stood on the stage of the Tyne Theatre and
addressed two thousand members of the Literary and Philosophical
Society. He went on to Glasgow and down to Highbury and up to
Altrincham, thankless work for which he was paid at the most ten
guineas a time. He diversified, instructing the Society of Woman
Journalists in modern poetry and, from November 1902, became a
visiting lecturer in poetry at the ladies' department of King's College,
London, teaching Yeats, William Watson, Francis Thompson and
Housman's *A Shropshire Lad* to 'about 20 sweet graduates of all ages
from 15 to 55'.[35] It was exhausting.

In May 1898, after three-and-a-half years, Shaw resigned as theatre
critic of the *Saturday Review*. Max Beerbohm, who took over from Shaw
the following week, was the younger half-brother of Herbert Beerbohm
Tree, a snappily-dressed, twenty-six-year-old Oxford graduate and
mildly malicious caricaturist.

It was Beerbohm who represented the *Saturday Review* at the New
Century Theatre's fourth production. H. V. Esmond's *Grierson's Way*
was performed for five matinees at the Haymarket between 7 and 13
February 1899. Henry Esmond was a thirty-year-old actor and playwright who would later become a celebrated dramatist and actor-

manager in partnership with his formidable wife, Eva Moore. He would also be blighted by alcohol. In 1930, eight years after he died of drink in a Paris hotel room, his daughter Jill would become the first wife of Laurence Olivier.

Grierson's Way is a realistic play set in the living room of James Grierson's flat in Chelsea, and borrows the sexual and moral themes previously given a serious edge by Pinero and Wilde. Pamela has become pregnant by her lover, Captain Murray who, being already married, deserts her. Philip Keen discovers her secret, but the gallant Grierson steps in to marry her and save her from social stigma. Even though Archer sighed that it lacked any 'reasoned criticism of life', he thought he might guide Esmond towards the New Drama. Esmond played Keen and shared the direction of the play with the stage manager, John Harwood. Archer took little part and Elizabeth, disillusioned with the New Century and concentrating on her fiction, looked in only occasionally. The reviews were mostly hostile, yet Beerbohm thought *Grierson's Way* 'in its genre, a better play than any which has been produced in London' and complained that it was being restricted to 'furtive'[36] matinees when it deserved an evening run. Despite Beerbohm's support, Esmond's play slid into obscurity.

The New Century Theatre had lived up to none of Archer and Elizabeth's dreams. There was no ensemble of actors and its productions had been terrible artistic and financial failures. Elizabeth argued they should begin again by recruiting a small company of unknown actors, train them in realistic acting and return to their list of thirty plays. Archer toyed with taking over a small hall and leasing it to an amateur company whose audience of family, friends and well-wishers might spill over to patronize his own professional serious drama group, performing on alternate evenings. But the scheme folded on the drawing-board. It was the end.

Peer Gynt did not receive its British premiere until 1911, but Archer had nothing to do with it. After *John Gabriel Borkman*, he never directed an Ibsen production again. The New Century Theatre, intended to establish a vital, contemporary British and foreign repertoire and lead to the creation of the National Theatre, had petered out before the new century had even begun. But sometimes with Archer, when one dream faded, another glowed, and it did so now. On 17 February 1899, he proudly told Dibdin that 'I am in all probability going to America for a couple of months at the end of next week.'[37]

*

Revisiting the United States, said Archer, was 'literally the dream of my life'. Even the very word 'America' he thought 'electric with romance'. In Italy, he had peered into the past, brushing his fingertips across ancient stones to decipher an old world worn brief by time, but in America, he was watching the stone of history being carved and felt that he too could chip at the present and bring forth the future. America was a leap into the unknown, a great imaginative experiment from which anything might spring.

It was George Halkett, one of his old friends from Edinburgh, who was responsible for this dream coming true. Halkett's cartoons for *The Fashionable Tragedian* had stood him in good stead and seven years ago, he had left the insurance buiness, first joining the *Pall Mall Gazette* and then becoming art editor of *Pall Mall Magazine*. Steering Archer's proposal for a series of articles on the United States before *Pall Mall*'s proprietor, the American millionaire William Waldorf Astor, Halkett recommended that William Archer was just the man to bring back a rich harvest.

So, he locked the door at Great Ormond Street, caught the train to Liverpool and on 25 February 1899, boarded the Cunard Steamship *Lucania*. He would be away eight weeks. On the ship, he had a huge state-room to himself, paid for by the social reformer, Mrs Laura Ormiston Chant. He swallowed his anti-seasickness mixture, lay in queasy luxury, gingerly tottered about the promenade deck and, before they docked on 4 March, distributed tips to the stewards according to the scale in his Baedeker guide. They steamed into New York Harbour wreathed in a damp grey mist, but as he glimpsed the Statue of Liberty and Staten Island glide past and saw the skyscrapers of lower Manhattan looming before him like the giants of Scandinavian mythology, he felt as though 'the gates of the western world are opening to me'.

Having shuffled through customs, he jumped on to the platform of a trolley-bus and clattered past buildings of coffee-coloured brick and saloon bars with their names picked out in fading gilt letters; past sidestreets dotted with impacted, blackened wedges of snow, the remnants of winter blizzards. They rattled on towards Fifth Avenue. For a few days, before he moved to a rented room on Fifth Avenue, he was staying (probably free-of-charge) at the Astor-owned Waldorf-Astoria Hotel at Fifth Avenue and 34th Street. He entered its glittering lobby, stepped into an elevator, and – dizzying experience – was whizzed up to a room on the thirteenth floor. And even then, he was nowhere near the top of the building: 'far from it'.

He spent almost three weeks careering about Manhattan, notebook in one hand and pencil in the other, struggling to keep track of all his impressions. He flew up and down in elevators and jolted in the trolley-buses. Clinging on to the passenger straps, he zipped along in the elevated trains darting this way and that on rails high enough over the streets for the trolleys to pass below them. Buildings he vaguely remembered from twenty-two years ago were now hidden by new ones soaring ever higher into the sky as New Yorkers added a new dimension to living: 'When they find themselves a little crowded, they simply tilt a street on end and call it a skyscraper.' As he explored from Herald Square to Central Park and beyond, he could imagine forests of new buildings, 'magnificent beyond compare'.[38] He romanticized everything, the allegedly corrupt municipal politics ('a temporary condition'[39]), and even the East Side slums, urban ravines hung with balconies and fire escapes where tenants sat and ate and draped their washing, and in the summer months of furnace heat, slept. In these canyons of silent, watchful faces, he was reminded of Marseilles and Naples.

He lunched at Columbia University with Brander Matthews and became a temporary member of seven clubs, accepting every daytime invitation and rejecting any for the evening, for in the evening he allowed himself to be engulfed by Manhattan's brilliant tide of life, its confident, garish clamour for the modern. 'At night,' he wrote, 'under the purple, star-lit sky, street life . . . is indescribably exhilarating. From Union Square to Herald Square, and even further up, Broadway and many of the cross-streets flash out at dusk into the most brilliant illumination. Theatres, restaurants, stores, are outlined in incandescent lamps; the huge electric trolleys come sailing along in an endless stream, profusely jewelled with electricity; and down the thickly gemmed vista of every cross-street one can see the elevated trains, like luminous winged serpents, skimming through the air.'[40]

On Broadway, the theatres and music halls, where the vaudeville shows played from eleven until eleven, were clustered 'as thick as bananas on their stem'. There was the Empire, the Knickerbocker, the Manhattan, the Madison Square and Sam T. Jack's . . . almost forty theatres squeezed into hotel blocks and tucked in the shadows of newer, taller buildings. Broadway, he noticed, was dominated not by actor-managers but a cabal of producers who owned the theatres, chose and cast the plays. While the commercial London theatre was sustained by the upper-middle and society classes, Broadway depended upon the office class and 'the matinee-girl . . . the half-educated young woman,

shop assistant, type-writer, telephone girl', whose tastes ran from
'romance, sentiment and cheap idealism' to 'the crudest, tawdriest
French realism and vulgar humour'.[41]

They packed the stalls and circles for shirt-sleeved chronicles of
ranch-life by James A. Herne, and for musical farces trotting out strings
of chorus girls. This sad display comprised the indigenous American
drama. Otherwise, Broadway relied upon English imports. *Trelawny of
the 'Wells'*, Pinero's affectionate evocation of Robertsonian back-stage
life, and Grundy's version of *The Three Musketeers* were the season's
leading successes. Richard Mansfield was giving a self-conscious performance in the title role of Rostand's *Cyrano de Bergerac*, but no other
leading American actor was appearing in a serious or classical role.

Rushing onwards, Archer stopped off in Washington to glance at the
'dignified'[42] White House before speeding on to Baltimore, and then
Boston, where he spent a bizarre afternoon at the B. F. Keith
continuous vaudeville theatre, 'a sort of garishly luxurious club'[43]
decorated in marble and alabaster, and furnished with Louis Quinze
writing tables. He lunched with academics at Harvard and hurried on
to 'marvellous Chicago',[44] where he thought the women even more
beautiful than in New York. He nosed through the dark, gothic
underworld of the slums, visiting the feminist and socal reformer Jane
Addams at her Hull House Settlement for the destitute immigrant and
black population. He saw burlesque shows of 'revolting hideousness'[45]
patronized exclusively by men, and reeled out on to glaring streets
clanging with trolley-cars to marvel at the 'heaven-storming'[46] architecture. The extremes of vulgarity and magnificence were so disorientating
that when he went on a day-trip to Buffalo to see a production of
Herne's *Shore Acres*, he discovered too late that he had caught a train to
Detroit instead.

'My time here has been amusing and not unprofitable, but fatiguing
to a degree. You can't imagine the rush I have been in,'[47] he informed
Dibdin breathlessly. He was also sending accounts of his adventures to
Elizabeth, who noted the receipt of each 'beloved letter'[48] in her diary.
He sailed on the *Cymric* on 26 April and by 9 May was back at Great
Ormond Street, elated by his visions of the future. Feverishly, he began
writing up his articles for the *Pall Mall Magazine* (later collecting them
into a book, *America Today: Observations and Reflections*), and pestered
Dibdin to rescue his hat-box which he had mistakenly left in the
clutches of the Liverpool customs officers.

*

As his income was again trailing his expenses, which now, following mishaps on his bicycle, included a life insurance policy arranged by Dibdin at three pounds a year, and annual fees of twenty-four pounds towards Tom's scholarship at Dulwich College, Archer was once more forced to move rooms. At the end of June, he moved out of Great Ormond Street and into a single room 2 Vernon Chambers in South-ampton Row, just off Holborn. His inexorably expanding library, wobbling piles of theatre programmes (bound by theatre and year), scrapbooks of press cuttings, boxes of manuscripts and slides, papers and pens and typewriter, made it a suffocatingly tight squeeze. But there was, he pointed out to Dibdin, the definite advantage of using a 'SUPERB'[49] bathroom.

On 23 July, he went down to see the Shaws at their rented house near Hindhead. While Archer had been deep in *Little Eyolf*, Shaw had written *The Devil's Disciple*, a robust debate between romanticism and puritanism, bound up in melodrama and set in Massachusetts during the American War of Independence. Having kept Archer informed of the progress of his new play, *Caesar and Cleopatra*, he now presented him with a completed script. He had written it for Johnston Forbes-Robertson and Mrs Patrick Campbell who had recently appeared together in *Hamlet* and *Macbeth*, and who were looking for all the world the heirs to Irving and Ellen Terry. Shaw plotted intervention and the subjugation of their world to his.

As he read it, Archer recognized Caesar as yet another idealized Shavian self-portrait. Yet at the same time, he has some equally Archerian qualities. He is unassuming, indefatigable, quick-witted in debate and fond of barley water. *Caesar and Cleopatra*, wrote Archer, was 'full of wit, whim, satire, penetration, flippancy, ingenuity, perver-sity, sophistry, sense and nonsense'.[50] It was exasperating, tedious and engrossing: there was 'an amazing cleverness in it'[51] he told Murray.

As *Macbeth* had almost broken Forbes-Robertson's bank, he protested that he could not possibly contemplate the play. Shaw still hoped to capture Mrs Pat, but although she ran through a copyright reading while touring in Newcastle earlier that year, she flatly refused to spend any more time with *Caesar and Cleopatra*. Shaw dived into writing *Captain Brassbound's Conversion* which he completed that July. Set in Morocco, the play is an eccentric odyssey spiced with a revenge melodrama, presided over by the fearless, unpredictable and interfering Lady Cecily Waynflete.

She did not know it yet, Shaw informed Archer, but Ellen Terry, who was now fifty and with whom he maintained a voluminous correspondence although they had never met, was going to play Lady Cecily. Archer, who had endured too many first nights imperilled by Ellen's increasingly inventive memory, leafed through the script and told him she would never be able to learn it. Shaw promptly passed on this remark to Ellen, hoping it might prod her into rising indignantly to the challenge, but, like Mrs Pat, she agreed only to a copyright reading. She also took the precaution of provincial obscurity, choosing Liverpool. Brief outings in the north of England were, for the moment, the closest that Shaw's ninth and tenth plays came to a life in the theatre.

On 26 August, Archer sailed for Christiana and the State opening, on 1 September, of the newly-built Norwegian National Theatre. Standing in a leafy square in the city centre, he looked up at an ornate building of yellow brick picked out with granite. It was a combination he thought 'anything but attractive', but once inside, he found the gilt-encrusted auditorium 'hit the happy mean between the bandbox and the barn'[52] and that the acoustic was perfect. He was covering the event for the *Daily Chronicle* and lost no time in converting the opening of one National Theatre into a protest at the continued absence of another. Norway, he wrote, was a country of fewer than three million people and one of the poorer of northern nations. Yet private enterprise had succeeded in building a National Theatre, something apparently inconceivable in Britain and the United States, the richest countries in the world.

Instead of choosing an opening night play by one of Norway's two leading dramatists, Ibsen and Bjørnson (whose relationship was always prickly), the theatre diplomatically opted for the safety of the eighteenth century and a compilation of scenes from Holberg. The next night, Archer was back to see a production of *En folkefiende* and noticed Ibsen, sitting alone in the manager's box, bolt upright, a fierce icon. The performance was 'vivid, racy and lifelike', reported Archer, surprised to find the play still so fresh. 'Every line of it went straight home, for every line of it bears upon the essential problems of democracy.' The curtain fell to thunderous applause and afterwards, as the audience poured into the corridors, Archer pushed his way towards Ibsen and offered his congratulations. Almost squashed in the crush, the elderly playwright peered up at him, the light flickering on his spectacles and, after a long pause, said: 'Don't you think it went very well?'[53]

A few days later, Archer called on Ibsen at Arbiensgate, where he learned that he was completing the third act of a new play. It was, explained Ibsen, a summary of his later work. He was seventy-one now, and was ageing quickly. Archer did not stay long and when he left, Ibsen slowly accompanied him downstairs to the street door where they solemnly shook hands. It was eighteen years since they first met at the Scandinavian Club in Rome and today, at the doorway of a Christiana apartment building, was the last time they would see each other. 'What I said I do not remember,' recalled Archer, 'but doubtless it was not the right thing.'[54] What he meant to say, was simply 'Tak for alt': thanks for everything; but at moments like this, he was unable to find the appropriate mask to wear. A few months later, Ibsen suffered a stroke which partially paralysed his right side. He was falling towards death.

Time was leaving its traces on all of them. One morning, Elizabeth looked into the mirror and found that what was once an occasional greying hair easily submerged beneath chestnut tresses had become a small flurry at the temples. As the century faded, so her spirits and Archer's dimmed too, for Ibsen's latest, most mysterious and, as it turned out, last play, seemed 'a sad fiasco'. *Nar Vi Døde Vaagner (When We Dead Awaken)* was not a dramatic summation at all, thought Archer, but 'a mere hash up of fifty-year-old ideas . . . utterly without dramatic fibre.'[55]

Ibsen called the play a 'dramatic epilogue'. The aged sculptor Rubek, unhappily married to the much younger Maia, returns after many years to Norway, where he encounters Irena, one of his former models. She has since become deranged and fiercely accuses him of having manipulated her and ruined her life. Together, they climb the mountainside as a storm rises, leaving Maia and the huntsman, Ulfheim, below. Rubek and Irena climb to what they believe is freedom and the others know will be death, for Rubek has turned his back upon love and by doing so, he has rejected life. As he and mad Irena die in the snow, like Brand and Borkman before them, Ibsen implies that only when the imagination is liberated and the spirit soars free of earthly concerns, will mankind truly awaken. Rubek is Ibsen's self-portrait of the artist as a dying man and the play, the briefest he had written, is a coda to a life. Its symbolic lyricism mystified Archer, its sadness troubled him deeply. 'The old man,' he concluded, 'has suddenly become an old man indeed.'[56]

On 16 December, Heinemann staged his usual copyright reading in Norwegian at the Haymarket. There were probably very few people in the audience, possibly no one at all, but this was a unique occasion as for the first time, Archer himself took part. Elizabeth, on the other hand, who had not appeared in a full stage part for the New Century Theatre since *John Gabriel Borkman*, was now playing her last Ibsen role. They sat ranged across the stage. Braekstad read Rubek, and his wife, Maia. Heinemann played the small role of the spa manager. Elizabeth read the tragic Irena, and Archer read Ulfheim. His stage debut was probably a result of somebody else, Gosse perhaps, being absent. It was a first time for Archer, but it was a last time for Elizabeth, for after this, she would never appear in an Ibsen role again. The performance, held before rows of empty seats in a cold theatre, makes a curious and touching close to this part of the story of Archer and Ibsen, so much of which had also included Elizabeth.

Reading the play in a theatre did not clarify it for him, and his progress on the translation was slow. Before Archer's realist eyes, Ibsen's elusive, poetic prose shifted like a mist. He scanned it for hours but could only decipher indistinct shadows and pushed himself through a translation because not to do would have appeared disloyal. *When We Dead Awaken* was duly published in the spring of 1900, but it seemed to Archer that, with almost the final breath of the dying century, the genius, whose work he had championed for twenty-two years, was dying too. For the first time in a decade, he and Elizabeth decided not to stage a new Ibsen play.

He began the new year by sending her a poem. *The First of January, 1900*, is one of Archer's more bashfully sentimental efforts.

> My sweet, the century that's past
> (despite all unpropitious powers)
> Saw, from its first day to its last,
> No friendship tenderer than ours,
> No love more passionate and true
> Than yours for me and mine for you.
>
> Nor shall the century to come
> See, as its fateful decades roll
> Towards the new millennium,
> A closer bond of flesh and soul
> Than knits, in utter unity,
> Me, love, to you and you to me.[57]

Elizabeth slipped it into her diary. It was, she thought, 'a dear & beautiful poem'.[58]

It was a season of endings and renewals and Archer's sincere if trite verses stand at the end of one phase of their affair and the beginning of the next. During the past nine years, he and Elizabeth had shared a grand romance, a passionate if awkwardly intermittent sexual affair and triumph and setback in the Ibsen crusade. Depending on how far they were inhibited by Archer's fear of public exposure and Elizabeth's terror of closer emotional commitment, the barometer of their love either soared freely or plunged to self-recrimination.

They kept their secret well enough. Indeed, secrecy was the sustaining flame of their love. The Ibsen campaign had brought them together, but with the apparent end of his playwriting career and of the New Century, their love lost its urgency and began to mellow. From now on, they would be the closest of companions.

Over the new year, they were collaborating on their second play. *The Mirkwater* was an attempt at realism, but *Benvenuto Cellini*, set in the late 1530s when Cellini, the Florentine sculptor, was working at the French court, is a lavish melodrama in which heroism triumphs over treachery. This time, Elizabeth's tour of West End actor-managers was successful and in March, she signed a contract with Tree, giving him a year's option on the exclusive production rights.

Archer did much less work than Elizabeth on the play, insisted on anonymity and agreed to a share of the profits only 'in the fantastic contingency of its becoming such a property that after you had made £5000 out of it, there remained other thousands to be made'.[59] She ensured her own anonymity by inserting a clause in the contract stating that if her identity as author became known, she could refuse a production. This is exactly what happened after the *Daily Chronicle* revealed that C. E. Raimond was none other than Elizabeth Robins. The play has remained neither performed nor published, but Elizabeth continued to write, from now on under her own name.

The new year was only three weeks old when Archer and Shaw renewed their skirmishing, energetically arguing over the theatre and its future. Shaw had now moved some of his things from Fitzroy Square to Charlotte's apartment at Adelphi Terrace, near the river. On 22 January, Archer wrote suggesting that the New Century Theatre produce one of Shaw's expanding catalogue of unperformed masterpieces. 'My one condition is that Miss Robins shall have the leading part in whatever we do,' he stipulated. 'Of course I can't tell whether she would care for the part in "Captain Brassbound"; but I know she would be delighted to play Candida. Failing either of these, haven't you another play in hand that we could do?' He paused, then added an emphatic postscript: 'N.B. NO PHILANDERERS NEED APPLY!'[60]

This was Archer's code, signalling that Shaw should neither send him *The Philanderer* (which he would return immediately), nor resume his meddling between him and Elizabeth. Instead, Shaw replied that 'Cleopatra would hardly do for Miss Robins; and Captain Brassbound could only be done by arrangement with Ellen Terry.' He derided the New Century as out of date and out of touch with real life. In any case, he reasoned, it was preposterous to think that he and Archer and Elizabeth could possibly work together: '. . . what is the use of entering into friction-creating relations when we know quite well we shall not be happy in them,' he appealed. '. . . *you* don't matter: your dunderhead-edness will only give rise to your national sport of argument; but with a woman such maladjustments create hatred'.[61]

This was a robust, newly confident Shaw, who could afford to repel Archer's overtures now he had swerved away from the defunct Independent Theatre and was channelling his plays towards the newly-formed Stage Society. Founded the previous summer, its chairman was Frederick Whelan, a thirty-two-year-old Fabian and an employee of the Bank of England. Like its predecessors, the Independent Theatre and the New Century, the Stage Society was a subscription club. Its managing committee included Charrington and the actor James Welch, while Janet Achurch and Charlotte Shaw sat on the reading committee. With several of his own people in place, Shaw at last had a company both receptive to his work and, with almost three hundred subscribers, the money to perform it. On 26 November 1899, at the Royalty (still managed by Kate Santley), Welch directed the Society's inaugural production, the world premiere of *You Never Can Tell*, Shaw's comedy of a reluctantly reunited family.

The Society defied convention both by their repertoire and their timetable. Performances were initially held on Sunday evenings and, in order to evade the law prohibiting Sunday production and the eyes of the Observance Societies, were given a vaguely religious air by being known as 'meetings'. Whelan thickened the air of secrecy by banning press reviews. Archer did not see *You Never Can Tell*, ('it never interested me much'), and, to begin with, avoided Stage Society productions. As his campaign for a new drama was also a campaign against censorship, he rebelled against supporting an organisation which prevented free public discussion of its work.

As the Stage Society's house playwright, Shaw read Archer's request for a play, and danced gleefully about him, denouncing Archer as a sentimentalist and proclaiming himself a shrewd, unblinking realist. For Archer had objected to Frank Gardner and Vivie Warren in *Mrs Warren's Profession* being half-brother and sister as irrelevant to the play and evidence of Shaw writing merely to provoke, 'a pleasure which I believe quite genuinely translates itself into your consciousness as a duty'.[62] 'You really are an impossible chap,' sang Shaw. Archer's 'Arcadian innocence' blinded him not only to the stinging realism of his plays and but led him into the 'colossal blunder' of failing to recognize that he was 'by a very great deal the best English-language playwright since Shakespear, and considerably *his* superior on a good many points.'[63]

'Never was black lead more hopelessly wasted than in this letter,' snorted Archer on 1 February. 'We have never agreed about plays, & we never will. There is not the least reason why we should.' Shaw, he repeated, was no dramatist, but a Fabian rabble rouser: '. . . the play has always been the first thing to me; it is the last thing to you'.[64]

And so they continued when Shaw's next volume of plays, *Three Plays for Puritans*, was published in the new year. Each used the other as a sounding board for his own ideas and to test the quality of the other's opinions. Their shared aim was the redefinition of drama. Sometimes they opposed each other; sometimes they said the same thing but used the language of argument in which to say it, while at others Archer became Shaw's public spokesman. Archer saw the Stage Society production of *Captain Brassbound's Conversion* at the Criterion on 20 December (not with Ellen Terry but with Janet Achurch), and announced in *The World* that it was 'from first to last an intensely exhilarating, stimulating entertainment, the work of a thinker and a humorist'. As the Stage Society still frowned upon reviews, Archer smuggled his views into an article challenging West End managers to begin 'competing for the honour of being the first to set in motion the inevitable Shaw "boom"'.[65]

In his letters and face to face, Archer told Shaw plainly that he could not write plays. In his journalism and to others, he loudly banged the drum on his friend's behalf. Seventeen years previously, he had launched Shaw as a critic and chivvied him into playwriting. Now, he began doing everything he could to help him become an established dramatist. He attempted to foist him upon the mainstream theatre and arranged to have him exported. One day in the spring of 1900, Archer

met Siegfried Trebitsch, a visiting Austrian critic, who enquired about
new British dramatists. There was only one worth bothering about, said
Archer, and that was Bernard Shaw, 'a dramatist to his fingertips'.[66]

This was the first time that Trebitsch had heard Shaw's name. He
went away, read his plays, and two years later reported to Archer that
he was ready to become Shaw's apostle in central Europe. Having
checked that Trebitsch properly acknowledged the supremacy of *Candida* in the Shavian canon, Archer supplied him with a letter of
introduction with which he accosted Shaw and duly became his German
translator. In later years, Archer would point out Trebitsch's errors to
Shaw in German editions of his work.

While Archer was offering Shaw to the West End and telling Trebitsch
to read his works, Britain was at war. The Boer War began in October
1899, and by the time it was over in May 1902, it had proved bloody,
controversial and expensive. Joseph Chamberlain, Salisbury's Colonial
Secretary, called for expansion in Africa, while in the Transvaal, Paulus
Kruger, believing Boer independence to be threatened, moved against
the British and attacked the garrisons at Ladysmith, Mafeking and
Kimberley. At home, the conflict united the Tories and divided the
Liberal opposition between those supporting Henry Campbell-Bannerman, the Party Leader, a natural progressive but an ineffective parliamentary speaker who denounced the war; Herbert Asquith, who
advocated British action, and David Lloyd George, heading a 'pro-
Boer' faction.

Archer reflected the Liberal dilemma. In Washington in April, he
had stood on the steps of the Capitol, gazed across the Potomac to
Arlington and seen the flags lowered for the public funeral of United
States servicemen killed in Cuba. 'Every war is a civil war,' he had
written, 'a war betwen brothers.'[67] He was instinctively repelled by war,
but also saw the Empire as the only effective means of political unity
and cultural progress. In 'A Plain Man's Politics' in the *Monthly Review*
of November 1901, he ventured into political commentary, hesitantly
setting out the case for a man of the middle ground who still clung to
the notion of fair play. The war, he suggested, was 'neither just nor
unjust, but the inevitable outcome of a state of things for which both
parties were pretty evenly to blame'. Kruger might hold the 'moral
advantage', but the threat must be contained for the sake of the Empire.
It was 'our duty', he wrote, '. . . to keep the Empire unassailable from
without, in order that it may develop freely from within'. Having taken

up this rickety position, Archer found himself condoning what he would have liked to have condemned. The British policy of burning farms, literally setting the veld ablaze, 'may or may not have been a necessary measure', he wrote. The reports of violence in the concentration camps into which Kitchener herded Boer civilians, might be 'one-sided and exaggerated', and the deaths 'due to circumstances over which we have no control'.[68]

It was all very unconvincing, but 'I am a man of this age'[69] he had advised Shaw, and as such, he believed that it was far better that the world was run from England than anywhere else. In the absence of a theatrical campaign, he was searching for a cause to fight for and he found it in simple patriotism, his love of rambling across the green hills above the cathedral towns of England and sitting outside with a good book on a hot summer's day. It led him to a decision which overcame the arguments of Shaw and Murray and left them shaking their heads in fascinated wonder: '. . . the British Empire has taken on a new lease of life,' he informed Murray on 5 February 1900, ' – I have joined the Volunteers!'[70]

He enlisted as a private in the Inns of Court Rifles, a band of 'extraordinarily good fellows'.[71] Dressed in his uniform and armed with his Lee-Metford rifle, he bungled his way through parades at the Temple and discovered that he was not a natural man of war. Even on parade in the middle of London, his sense of direction deserted him. Under the bawled commands of a solicitor's clerk, he swivelled this way and that, and always the wrong way. He turned left when he should have swung right, and found himself facing the front when he should be facing the rear. To get this last manœuvre right was vitally important, he advised Murray, otherwise in the panic of battle 'you might find yourself winning the Victoria Cross when your intention was to run away'.[72]

Archer's war bordered upon the ludicrous. Over the next three years, he joined annual military camps for a week in Kent and on Salisbury Plain, bedding down in tents 'among the rifles, jam-pots, candles, scrap, pipe-clay, knives, forks, rifle oil and butter'.[73] Rising at reveille at five, he spent his days drilling erratically and eagerly taking part in exercises, dashing about the fields attacking hedges and barns. '. . . England still [has] some kick left in her after all,'[74] he told himself.

Back in London, he sought refuge from a troubled world and on 31 October, he was elected to the National Liberal Club in Whitehall Place. Here, he found comfortably worn armchairs, a library strong on history and politics and a dining room in which he could find a reasonable meal. He looked in almost every day, reading the papers, writing letters, and contemplating the many changes taking place beyond the windows.

In 1897, his old adversary, Clement Scott, was toppled from power after confiding to *Great Thoughts*, a grim religious journal, that the theatre was so morally corrupt that it was 'impossible' for a young actress 'to remain a lady'.[75] Irving, the gentleman knight, led an outraged campaign which resulted in his resigning from the *Daily Telegraph* (where he was succeeded by W. L. Courtney), and leaving England for continental exile. He died in 1904. Another of Archer's antagonists, John Nisbet of *The Times*, was already dead, having never relinquished his opinion that Ibsen was insane. His place was taken by A. B. Walkley. And in 1898, abandoned by the duplicitous Edward Aveling, the unhappy Eleanor Marx-Aveling shut herself in her bedroom and swallowed prussic acid.

Peering into the twentieth century, Archer saw only uncertainty. He was in his mid-forties and no longer felt part of a younger generation inventing the modern world. In April 1900, he picked up the *Fortnightly Review* to read a wildly enthusiastic appreciation of *When We Dead Awaken*, illustrated with quotations from his own translation. The author was an unknown eighteen-year-old Irish student named James Joyce. Archer met him that summer, when he visited London on a round of editors and music halls. They lunched together on wild duck at the United Services Club and subsequently, Joyce sent him a play, *A Brilliant Career*, and poems for his comments. The play was impossible and the poems showed temperament rather than substance, Archer told him, but he undoubtedly had talent. In November 1902, Joyce enquired whether he should leave Ireland for Paris, and teach English. 'I cannot dissuade you too strongly,' warned Archer, at the same time sending him Blanche Taylor's address in the Avenue de Friedland, promising that she 'will give you any information she can'.[76] Ignoring the pessimist and heeding the optimist in Archer, Joyce set off for France.

Archer was also worried about Elizabeth. Her adored younger brother Raymond had abandoned legal studies for the Alaskan goldfields and in 1900, he announced that he had failed to find his fortune but would soon be ordained into the Christian church instead. Elizabeth dropped everything and in a bid to prevent him disappearing into the clergy, travelled over twenty thousand miles from the fogs of London to the ice wastes of Alaska. After an emotional reunion, she delivered Raymond to the famly home in Kentucky and then came down with typhoid fever. She recovered, returned to London that winter, and fell ill again. Archer rushed to her bedside and alerted Hector Mackenzie, his collaborator on *Australia*, and now a consultant at St Thomas's Hospital. Mackenzie prescribed immediate rest at a nursing home in Devon. These long months were the longest that Archer and Elizabeth had been separated.

One afternoon at the end of January 1901, while the country was still subdued in mourning following the death of the widowed Queen Victoria, Fredrick Whelan came into the Liberal Club, looking for Archer. Over tea, he suggested cooperation, even amalgamation between the Stage Society and the New Century Theatre. Archer demurred, explaining that Elizabeth was far too ill to cope with theatre business. Yet in the absence of the New Century Theatre, the Stage Society was keeping the lamp of serious drama burning and was planning not only *The League of Youth* at the Vaudeville on 25 February, the British premiere and the first Ibsen production in London since *John Gabriel Borkman* in 1897, but a revival of *The Pillars of Society*. Archer thought *The League of Youth* amusing but insubstantial, but gradually, Whelan drew him into the preparations for *The Pillars of Society*. He revised his text, approved the casting of Oscar Asche as Bernick and pleaded that as director, Asche would have 'plenty of time for preparation, *and a roomy stage*'.[77] But Whelan and Asche failed woefully, and the performance at the Garrick on 12 May was 'dreadful'. 'They really require to be sat upon if they insist on shovelling things on to the stage after four rehearsals,'[78] he told Murray. Back came Whelan. Would he join the Stage Society Committee? 'No,' replied Archer. 'I am no good as a committee man.'[79]

Later that summer, he totted up his earnings from *The World*, the *Manchester Guardian*, the *Daily Chronicle* and his new miscellany column in the *Morning Leader*. He added his fees from lecturing and the royalties from his books, compared them with his outgoings and concluded that he could not afford even his one room at Vernon Chambers. At the end of August, he moved into 71 Alleyn Park. This was the first time for eleven years that he and Frances had lived under one roof without his having a bolt-hole in central London, and never was he more out of place. There was hardly room for his things (especially almost fifty boxes of slides), and in addition to Frances, Tom, the maids, a cook and a cat called Dan Leno, nerve treatment patients had begun to take up residence and were glimpsed padding anxiously about the corridors. He would open a door to enter a room to find strangers exercising their voices or lying on the floor with their eyes closed, breathing restfully. Even Tom was undergoing something called harmony lessons. It was a nightmare.

After a year, Archer fled. At the end of May 1902, complaining he could not possibly afford it, he carried his boxes and books, papers and files back to central London and a small, spartan room at 1 Westminster Mansions in Great Smith Street, a narrow crooked road alongside Westminster Abbey. It was 'comfortable enough & there is a bathroom handy',[80] but as the landlady did not provide breakfast, he walked each morning to the Liberal Club and ate there. Those first few weeks, alone at his table, the waitresses might have thought he looked a remote, melancholy figure. On 30 June, he heard that his old friend Robert Lowe had died.

Lowe was forty-nine, and had been suffering from Bright's Disease for several months. His eyesight was failing and recently, he had become delirious. His death 'is a great grief to me,'[81] Archer wrote, remembering their weekly visits to the damp and dingy Princess's Theatre twenty-five years ago in Edinburgh.

He had arranged for Lowe's library of over nine hundred theatre books to be sold to Harvard University and the money to provide for his family, when Elizabeth announced that her next stage role would be her last. After playing the disturbed Alice Manisty in *Eleanor*, an adaptation by Julian Russell Sturgis and Mrs Humphrey Ward of her Italian romantic novel of the same name, she planned to devote herself to her writing and, increasingly, the women's movement. *Eleanor* opened on 30 October at the Royal Court. According to Archer, Elizabeth acted with 'intensity',[82] but the production ran for only fifteen performances. At the age of forty, Elizabeth turned her back on an acting career which had touched greatness. For Archer, it was the end of an era.

Nothing emphasized the absence of Elizabth so much as Ellen Terry informing him in December that she was about to produce the British premiere of Ibsen's *The Vikings at Helgeland*. Having dodged Shaw's Cecily Waynflete, she had decided to play Hjordis. Archer was stupefied. Never was there such spellbinding miscasting. Hjordis was beautiful and a warrior; Ellen was fifty-four and matronly. 'Poor old thing,' he wrote contemptuously to Elizabeth on 30 December, enclosing his usual new year's gift of a diary, 'what *can* she do except make a hash of it?'[83]

The thought of another Ibsen production filled him with something approaching loathing. Although he neither liked nor understood *When We Dead Awaken*, his faith was not so undermined as to believe the play was unactable, and he emerged from the Stage Society's British premiere at the Imperial Theatre on 24 January 1903, furiously complaining that it was a 'sacrilegious outrage'.[84] Ellen, he noted dubiously, was producing *The Vikings of Helgeland* in order to launch the professional careers of her children. Her son, Edward Gordon Craig, would direct and design the set while her daughter, Edith, was to design the costumes.

The illegitimate son of Ellen and the architect Edward Godwin, Craig was thirty, egotistical and already had a name as the radical director and designer of amateur productions. Like James Joyce, he seemed the harbinger of a younger generation. Archer believed the central creative force in the theatre was the playwright and the test of good direction to be its ultimate invisibility. Occasionally as a translator but always as a director, he looked for collaboration, or at least support. But Craig proclaimed the director to be supreme, the conspicuous and autocratic interpreter, synthesizing text, acting, design, lighting and music. Craig intended to write his signature across the event. His was an aggressively stark, twentieth-century vision. Archer asked Ellen whether her son would 'explain to me his principles'[85], but Craig kept to himself. Possibly, he thought Archer might sabotage his ideas or infiltrate himself as a spokesman for a cast who, apart from Ellen, were so mutinous that Edith was often required to act as intermediary between them and her brother. The two men seem never to have met, although Craig's smitten mother assured Archer that he was 'an admirable worker – molten enthusiasm fills his every cranny'.[86]

In February, Archer sent the revised first act of *The Vikings of Helgeland* to Ellen at Winchelsea, from where he received the disconcertingly reckless promise that 'I am ... going at this business like a bull at a gate – *At it!* – At it! & please believe it will all be a great success if we make up our minds & work that it shall be so – We may smash to pieces gate & Bull – but I don't care – much. Anything better than wobbling.'[87] When she had the complete script a month later, the effort of packing the lines into her memory made her howl in anguish. 'All Ibsen's women talk at *such frightful length*,'[88] she cried.

The production opened on 15 April at the Imperial in Tothill Street, the same theatre where he had seen *When We Dead Awaken*. Craig's designs were visually breathtaking and, because he used neither foot-lights nor painted backcloths, critically controversial. His Helgeland shoreline consisted of a monumental slope of rock and his banqueting hall a circular platform below a crown-like wrought-iron crucible of lights. In an unconscious imitation of Archer's *John Gabriel Borkman*, he contrived a sombre, tragic mood by directing subdued lighting from above, forcing the audience to lean forward to decipher Ellen Terry's Hjordis, wearing the long bearskin cloak and blue gown lovingly designed by Edy. Even in the Craigian twilight it was clear that she was embarrassingly miscast, and nothing could veil the silences in the third act as she groped for the lines. 'I was too frightful,' she cried to Archer later.

However, Archer saw none of this. Despite Ellen's entreaties: 'Do you think you'll come? Let me know *P-l-e-a-s-e*,' he scrupulously avoided both her and the Imperial, slipping off to the continent, paying for the trip with money sent by Dibdin, to whom he had been complaining about lack of funds. 'I shd have been so glad to hear from you – even a *curse* wd comfort me,' wailed Ellen.[89] In less than a month, she prudently declared the production would close. The fault, she told Archer, was Ibsen's women. 'They . . . *bore* one's ears.'[90]

When he left for Paris on 11 April, Archer was not only escaping from Ellen Terry. He was taking Tom with him and hoping the trip might begin to repair their disintegrating relationship. Tom was seventeen and approaching his final year at Dulwich College. In some respects, he was doing well. He was editor of the school magazine and captain of school. But the academic achievements Archer was impatient for were failing to materialize. For the past four years, he had covertly sent Tom's Greek and Latin examination question papers to Gilbert Murray, appealing for a confidential appraisal of their difficulty and an opinion on Tom's marks, which hovered at about fifty per cent. Archer's probing embarrassed Murray, whose cautious replies failed to alleviate his doubts. He desperately wanted Tom to go up to Oxford and so consolidate academically the return to a distinction which the mercantile Archers had lost, at least in Britain, during the nineteenth century. But Tom '*will not* throw himself into anything,'[91] he complained.

Archer had been a weekly visitor during much of Tom's childhood, and he had grown up his mother's child. Sometimes, when Archer looked at his son, a delicate, tall young man with soft, almost feminine features, he saw an unaccountably listless stranger who rallied only at the mention of sports or the Officer Training Corps, of which he was an obsessive member. When Archer joined the Volunteers during the Boer War, it had been partly at Tom's insistence. But now, he viewed his son's ebullient, Kiplingesque imperialism with considerable anxiety, and it was to instigate more cultural interests that Archer hauled him off to Paris. They based themselves at the Avenue de Friedland, from where Tom was whisked from a matinee of Hugo's *Hernani* at the Comédie-Française to an evening performance of Gounod's *Faust* at the Théâtre de l'Opéra; they walked briskly around the galleries, stopped off at a circus and admired Fontainebleau. They were 'quite pleasant' days, he reported uncertainly to Elizabeth when they got back a fortnight later, 'but it was trying work . . .'[92]

That autumn, Tom sat the scholarship examination for Balliol College, Oxford, and failed. In December, he battled with the examinations for Christ Church and was awarded a classics scholarship for the following October. To celebrate, and in an effort to fan the embers of Tom's classical appreciation, Archer took him on a winter holiday to Italy. In London, Archer lived as thriftily as possible but he was developing a taste when he was abroad for first-class hotels. When they arrived in Rome on 31 December, they booked in at the Grand Hotel Marini on Via del Tritone, brilliant with electric lights and an opulently decorated dining room. Even though the weather was appalling, with wind and heavy rain, Archer pronounced the holiday 'successful . . . though the stake was rather high for these hard times'.[93] In October, when Tom left for Oxford, Archer nervously awaited the results of his first examinations.

However, the past few years had drained his own energy and sense of purpose. The Italian journey with Tom was the third such trip in as many winters, an escape from work and a depressing, cold England where *The Tatler* was calling him 'a prophet of lost causes'.[94] The previous year, he had despondently joined Charles, on leave from India, and Alice Hayes, an American whom he had met on board a ship to the United States and subsequently married. Alice's presence only made him realize how much he missed Elizabeth. 'It is a mistake to have a woman around who does not happen to be *the* woman you want to have around,' he wrote sadly. And then, in an outburst of misery and frustration, he cried 'I am old, I am poor.'[95]

Enter Harley Granville Barker

Among the many manuscripts and typescripts of plays Archer was accumulating in his capacity as honorary literary advisor to unknown authors, was *The Weather-Hen*, an Ibsenesque drama written by Harley Granville Barker and Berte Thomas. Aiming for a New Century Theatre production, they had first sent the play to Elizabeth in January 1898, hoping she might be interested in the leading role of Eve Prior, but Elizabeth passed the script on to Archer. In April, when Barker wrote to him asking what had become of it, Archer fished it out and returned it, saying it was unplayable. Barker thanked him politely, adding that he and Thomas entirely agreed. Archer heard nothing more until 11 June the next year, when Barker equally politely invited him to a matinee of *The Weather-Hen* at Terry's Theatre on the 29th.

It was organized by Madge McIntosh, who played Eve Prior, an actress trapped in a sterile marriage, who, rejected by an older man, takes up with one much younger before regaining her self-respect and leaving her husband. In *The World*, Archer conceded that it was 'very clever',[1] but confessed he could hardly follow the fragmented, elliptical dialogue. Even so, the play transferred to the Comedy Theatre for a two-week run. Archer was intrigued. Along with his invitation, Barker had sent another play written in collaboration with Thomas. *Our Visitor to 'Work-a-Day'* deals with the spiritual and sexual awakening of Griselda Greenhayes. It owed less to Ibsen than *The Weather-Hen*, but its dialogue was even more diffuse. Yet seeing Barker's work on stage had suggested that it had more potential than Archer initially thought. He invited him to Vernon Chambers to talk over his work when, Barker recalled, Archer sat tapping his watch chain and 'repeating with real deliberation'[2] that if he made up his mind, he would be a great success.

*

Harley Granville Barker was a handsome, thoroughly modern young man. It may have been the Italian and Portuguese ancestry that accounted for the dark hair and piercingly dark eyes, and the English and Scottish for the chiselled features and sturdy bearing. Both his grandfathers were Church of England clergymen. He was born in Kensington, the only child of Albert Barker and his wife, Elisabeth Bozzi-Granville, on 25 November 1877. His father, plagued by tuberculosis, was referred to as an architect. In fact, he converted Victorian villas into flats before letting or selling them. He does not appear to have been very successful as the family was almost wholly dependent upon Mrs Elisabeth Bozzi-Granville. She was seven years older than her husband and earned the family exchequer by performing recitations and bird impressions in assembly rooms and upper-middle-class drawing rooms. Ambitious for her little boy, she dressed him in a sailor suit and incorporated him into her programme to declaim 'The Boy Stood on the Burning Deck'. In time, she put him into an Eton collar and taught him 'To be or not to be'.

Barker grew up in an atmosphere of mildly eccentric rehearsal and performance, in which his mother's enunciation of Dickens and Shakespeare was punctuated by her warbling and whistling as she practised her bird mimicry. By the time he was twelve, whatever formal education he might have had was over, and in May 1891, supervised by mother, he made his acting debut in a juvenile company at the Spa Rooms at Harrogate. Back in the south, he enrolled at Sarah Thorne's stage school at Margate, and there met Berte Thomas. The following year, aged fourteen, he made an unnoticed London debut as Third Young Man in *The Poet and the Puppets*, Charles Brookfield's mockery of the aesthetic movement which played to popular acclaim as the censor banned Oscar Wilde's *Salome*. Two years later, in 1894, he was understudying in Florence Farr's Avenue Theatre season and the following year went off on tour with Ben Greet's Shakespeare and Old English Comedy Company.

Mrs Patrick Campbell had once travelled with Greet and by the spring of 1899 Barker had joined her company, touring with revivals of *The Second Mrs Tanqueray* and *The Notorious Mrs Ebbsmith*, and taking part in the copyright reading of *Caesar and Cleopatra*.[3] On 19 June, he created the role of Selim in Mrs Campbell's production of Murray's *Carlyon Sahib* at the Princess of Wales Theatre, Kennington, and on 11 November, crowned his year in the title role of the Elizabethan Stage Society's production of *Richard II* at the University of London.

The Society was run by William Poel, a former actor and manager of the Old Vic and a man with a mission. Poel loathed the West End Shakespearian revivals in which the text was cut to make time for spectacle, a vogue soon to reach its glittering zenith with Tree's lavish productions at Her Majesty's. For *King John*, Tree devised a boomingly triumphant ceremony to liven up the signing of Magna Carta. In *A Midsummer Night's Dream*, a flock of terrified rabbits loped this way and that, dodging the actors negotiating the boulders and bushes of an enchanted glade, while *Twelfth Night* was enacted on a terraced garden with real grass and splashing fountains, surrounded by clipped box hedges. Set changes, accompanied by frantic hammering and violent scraping and thudding, took up to three-quarters of an hour each night, and seemed to take even longer with every production.

Poel ruthlessly avoided all modern excesses and returned to what he believed to be authentic Elizabethan convention. Inspired by recently published drawings of the Globe Theatre and his own scrutiny of sixteenth century texts, he led his sometimes amateur actors away from the West End's proscenium arches and into dusty halls and lecture theatres. A stickler for voice, he presided over rehearsals like a tyrannical conductor over an unhappy orchestra, relentlessly beating out the rhythms, refusing to stop until the actors had mastered his technique. Then he dressed them in Elizabethan costume and placed them on low platforms with a minimum of scenery, to the accompaniment of period music performed on ancient instruments by Arnold Dolmetsch, a fellow enthusiast whose speciality was restoring clavichords.

While Archer disliked Tree's garish, processional Shakespeare, he was equally sceptical of Poelian authenticity. He doubted his scholarship, disputed his textual cuts and protested that actors entering through the auditorium and clambering on to the stage was pushing historical fidelity too far. To Archer, Poel often appeared merely a Tree bereft of a forest of scenery, yet his approach influenced many actors, including Barker, whose performance as Richard brought him almost unanimous critical praise. Archer found his light, rather clipped voice 'rang false' in the opening scenes, but that his 'vivid' performance following the deposition showed 'real and remarkable talent'.[4]

Fifteen days after *Richard II*, the Stage Society produced *You Never Can Tell*. In February, Barker made his Society debut, playing Eric Bratsberg in *The League of Youth*. It is not clear who invited Barker to join the Stage Society. Archer may have recommended him to Whelan or to Charrington, who directed the production; equally Charrington may have asked Barker himself or heard his name from any one of the tight network of actor-friends orbiting the small world of matinees. Barker constantly popped up to ask Archer's advice about his career, sending him scripts and asking whether becoming a critic would help his writing. On 9 April, Barker sent him *A Miracle*, a verse play written with Thomas and 'the result of two days' work'.[5] Archer thought it as incoherent as the others. Three weeks later, on 29 April, Barker made his debut as a director with a Stage Society triple bill, perhaps at Archer's suggestion, considering that one of the pieces was his own translation of Maeterlinck's *Interior*. The others were Maeterlinck's *The Death of Tintagiles*, and *The House of Usna* by Fiona MacLeod, the pseudonym of William Sharp, the Society's president.

It was Charrington who told Shaw that Barker should play March-banks in the Society's production of *Candida* at the Strand on 1 July. Shaw hesitated, but on 10 June, he went to see him in *The Coming of Peace* (translated by Janet Achurch and Dr C. Wheeler from Haupt-mann's *Friedensfest*) and was so impressed by Barker, 'whom I certainly never saw before',[6] that he immediately agreed to his playing the young poet. Archer did not see *Candida*, but Barker, Shaw told him in a letter, was 'the success of the piece'.[7] Years later, Shaw (being Shaw) would imply that he himself had discovered Barker. In fact, everyone was discovering Barker, but that summer, he seems unaware that Archer already knew him, either at all or as well as he did, for he included a quick biographical sketch of him in his letter.

Marchbanks turned Barker into the first real Shavian actor. In December, he appeared as Kearney in the production of *Captain Brassbound's Conversion* which resulted in Archer demanding that Shaw be let loose upon the West End stage. On 29 March the following year, at the Comedy Theatre, Barker played Napoleon in his own matinee of *The Man of Destiny*, Shaw's Napoleoic harlequinade in one act, and on 5 January 1902, at the New Lyric Club, he appeared as Frank Gardner to Madge McIntosh's Vivie Warren in the Stage Society's private performance of *Mrs Warren's Profession*. Archer glumly watched a masterpiece diminished as the production squeezed itself on to a stage seemingly not much larger than a handkerchief, reducing the acting to 'little more than recitation'.[8] But the most important event in the remarkable rise of Harley Granville Barker came almost three weeks later, on 26 January, when he directed his own play, *The Marrying of*

Ann Leete, for the Stage Society at the Royalty. He was now twenty-four years old.

A bitter comedy set in an English garden at the end of the eighteenth century, the play deals with Ann's refusal to be manipulated by her father, the failing Tory politician Carnaby Leete, who hopes that her marrying the Whig politician Lord John Carp will enable him to cross the floor of the House and claim an influential position among the Whigs. Barker portrays the old order as ailing, while the new is young and vigorous. It is a lyrical, complex play, sometimes awkwardly symbolic and with patches of overlapping and interrupted dialogue. Archer, who read it before production, thought it as wilfully obscure as the others, and several years later was still pronouncing it 'the maddest play in the English language'.[9]

Barker had already joined Elizabeth, Shaw and Murray in the inner circle of Archer's closest associates. He was 'a particularly nice & intelligent young fellow,' he assured her on 13 March 1903. He added that he was spending almost every afternoon at Barker's flat at 8 York Buildings, in the Adelphi, a short walk from his own austere room at Westminster Mansions. There, he told her triumphantly, they were discussing momentous business: nothing less than 'the budget and program for a National Theatre'.[10]

With little confidence, Archer had once again taken up the standard of the National Theatre in the winter of 1901, and was astonished to see that the fresh wind of a new century also brought several encouraging articles on the subject from Henry Arthur Jones and the critic, Hamilton Fyfe. He rattled off a fusillade of articles for the *Morning Leader*, the *Clarion* and the *Monthly Review* and in February, began talking over tentative plans for a building with the theatrical architect Edwin Sachs. Most London theatres had been lit by electricity for fifteen years or more, but only four years previously, Sachs had applied electrical power to the working of the stage at Drury Lane, the first time this had been achieved in England.

On the 13th, Archer told Murray that he was 'trying to compile a sort of Blue Book on the question of a National Theatre'.[11] By the summer, a Theatrical Reform Committee had been founded, consisting of himself; Barker; Murray; Sidney Lee, a biographer of Shakespeare and editor of *The Dictionary of National Biography*; Hamilton Fyfe; and Spenser Wilkinson, the editor of the *Morning Post*. In June, Archer met A. C. Bradley and conscripted his membership. As Professor of Poetry at Oxford, Bradley was delivering lectures which two years later would be incorporated into *Shakespearian Tragedy*, one of the most influential books of Shakespearian analysis. The Committee met at Lee's office and Wilkinson's home, and talked. And talked and talked. The Committee was predominantly liberal, Shakespearian and academic, and it did not take Archer long to realize that this was exactly the reason for its impotence. He and Barker were the only members with any practical theatrical experience and after a few weeks, they could bear it no longer. He told Barker they were going to sit down by themselves and work out a plan for a National Theatre.

For weeks, months, they debated and argued, filling pages, then fistfuls, then stacks of paper as an entire book began taking shape. There were proposals on plays and programming; budgets for restaurants and cleaning, for front-of-house and backstage; notes on artistic objectives and management structures, lists of figures, costs and accounts. As the now forgotten Theatrical Reform Committee mumbled to a standstill, letters crackling with ideas chased and crossed each other betwen the Adelphi and Westminster Mansions.

Something remarkable was happening to Archer. From Italy that winter he had cried out in despair that he was old and poor. He had lost heart. 'England is *stale*,' he had told Murray. '. . . a general blight of ineffectualness, uneasiness, pettiness . . .'[12]. To Elizabeth, he admitted that 'I am vaguely unwell; vaguely conscious of a decline in my power of work . . . and at the same time pretty well convinced that I am losing my hold on the journalistic world, and likely in a year or two to find my income seriously reduced . . .'[13] But Barker's energy and enthusiasm more than reinvigorated him. It transformed him. He felt young again and ready to challenge the world. As for Barker, he had found a leader he could follow. 'It is helpful for me,' he wrote, '. . . to get under the wing of your knowledge *and* experience.'[14]

In temperament and ambition, Archer and Barker were as natural a partnership as Archer and Shaw. They had a parental aspect in common, as with all three of them it had been the mother who was the dominant parent and the father the more easily discouraged and unlucky. Between the three of them was a bracing atmosphere of candour. Part of the reason he was on 'a very fine footing' with Barker, Archer explained to Elizabeth, was 'I have consistently scoffed at his plays.'[15] But crucial to their association was the fact that Barker was twenty-five and Archer forty-six. Barker, in other words, was both young enough to be Archer's son and eager enough to require him to be his mentor. He had grown up in the first breath of the theatrical change for which Archer had fought. He had come of age in the years of Ibsen, Pinero, the small theatre movement, and reading W. A. in *The World*, and, like Archer, he wanted to change the world. For Archer, over the next few years as he worried increasingly about Tom, Barker would appear an ideal surrogate son.

He had a similar effect on others, noticeably Shaw, who could 'scold and schoolmaster, encourage and idealize'[16] him, and Charlotte, who became quite maternal over him. But central to all this was a sense of creative progress and excitement, and for Archer a renewed vigour and optimism.

They told only a few close friends about their National Theatre planning. Elizabeth knew, and so did Shaw, who warned them to beware of voice production teachers and phoneticians, as 'Acting cannot be taught.'[17] Archer wrote long letters recording their progress to George Pierce Baker, the assistant professor of English at Harvard whom he had met in America and was hoping to found his own theatre. Murray was also kept abreast of developments. Looking up from their latest budget on 8 April, Archer informed him contentedly that 'According to our calculations, we only require a perfectly-appointed theatre rent-free & average receipts of £166 a night to regenerate the drama – a mere bagatelle!'[18]

By the beginning of 1904, the tide of paper at Westminster Mansions and the Adelphi had retreated to leave one small, neat rock: the typescript of *Scheme & Estimates for a National Theatre*. It comprised twelve chapters and four appendices in which Archer's contribution, noted Barker, 'much outweighed mine'. But as they were both connected with New Drama and known as 'notorious Ibsenites, Hauptmannites, Shavians etc',[19] they decided against publishing the book commercially and risking their proposals being mocked by traditional critics and politicians. Instead, they elected to publish a few copies privately and send them to prominent people in the profession, so their views and hopefully endorsements might be incorporated into a later, trade edition. Heinemann agreed to guide the typescript discreetly through the press, quoting Archer an estimate of seventy pounds for about fifty or sixty paper-bound proof copies.

As the collaborators could not afford even this 'very reasonable'[20] sum, they resorted to issuing a leaflet appealing for donations. As a demonstration of good faith, they announced that Archer had already contributed five guineas, while the more impoverished Barker had put up two. The fact of subscribing, they pointed out, constituted an undertaking that the book was 'ON NO ACCOUNT TO BE COMMUNICATED TO, OR CRITICIZED OR MENTIONED IN THE PUBLIC PRESS'. This condition was repeated on the title page of *Scheme & Estimates*, which Heinemann delivered in the spring.

The book looked dowdy, bound in blue paper and with no publisher's colophon. But at 177 quarto-size pages it felt reassuringly substantial, and even a glance was enough to see that it contained the most comprehensive and far-reaching plans for a new theatre which anyone had yet devised. The partnership sent the books out to the names on their list, asking each recipient to read and return it 'with marginal criticisms and suggestions'.[21] Also included was an endorsement slip which the reader was invited to sign: 'Having read and carefully considered this scheme for a National Theatre, we desire to express our belief that such an institution is urgently needed, and that it could in all probability be successfully established on the general lines here indicated.'[22]

The collaborators proposed that the National Theatre should be purpose-built and house a single auditorium seating 1,350. They calculated the total cost to be £330,000 (equivalent to £5,132,790 in 1977, when the National Theatre, with three auditoria, was built at a cost of £16 million). The purchase of the site would account for £75,000, and all building work, the installation of a fully-equipped stage, wardrobe, property and music departments, a further £105,000. Ideally, the National Theatre should operate at a profit made through the box office, but the remaining £150,000 from the building budget would be reserved as the basis for a guarantee fund in the event of an unsuccessful season. With Arthur Balfour's Conservative government zealously non-interventionist, Archer and Barker admitted that approaching them for financial support would be 'a waste of time'. The National Theatre would have to be the gift of a group of wealthy individuals or private enterprise.

Archer was adamant the National Theatre must avoid the fate of the Comédie-Française, where the artistic director was chosen by the government and was thereby liable to state pressure. Instead, he suggested that the director be appointed by a board of fifteen independent trustees, one member being elected from the universities of Oxford, Cambridge and London and the Royal Academy; two by the London County Council, and the remainder recommended initially by the theatre's sponsors. (The partners evidently believed that any interference from private enterprise could be contained.) The trustees would meet perhaps twice a year and whenever one retired, his or her successor would be elected by the remainder, the influence of the sponsors therefore being slowly phased out. The artistic director would control everything except the actual choice of the plays, which he would share with a literary manager and a reading panel who would recommend revivals and new plays, and select foreign plays and their translators. The directorate was completed by a business manager and a solicitor. The artistic director's salary would be a generous two thousand pounds a year, the literary and business managers, one thousand, and the solicitor, three hundred pounds.

Throughout his National Theatre campaign, Archer had called for the establishment of a near as possible permanent acting ensemble. In the *Scheme & Estimates*, they budgeted for a company of sixty-six, comprising forty-four actors and twenty-two actresses, many on three-year contracts. Earlier that year, Archer had welcomed the founding of the Academy of Dramatic Art in London, and, ignoring Shaw's advice that acting could not be taught, incorporated a training school into the National Theatre, from which the pick of the students would be invited to join the company. The actors were to be paid a basic salary topped-up by a performance fee. Actors' salaries were set on a scale from £250 to £900 a year, and fees from 10/- to £5, while actresses (the National Theatre was not an equal opportunities organization), would be paid from £200 to £700, and from £1 to £5. Authors would receive ten per cent of box office income whenever their play was in performance, while in the case of revivals an equal proportion would be invested in a pension fund for actors and staff. While salaries were comparatively high, ticket prices of between 1s and 7/6d distributed across the stalls and three circles were intentionally set far cheaper then elsewhere, so that as many people as possible could afford a night at the National.

They had thought of everything and costed everything. There would be twelve ushers, ten cleaners, five secretaries, three firemen and a twenty-four piece orchestra. There was a wardrobe filled with costumes from all lands and ages, and an armoury fit to fight any battle in history. There were master carpenters, stage-managers, prompters, engineers, dressers, call-boys and door-keepers. Full electric lighting was budgeted at thirty pounds a week. Even the refreshment rooms would be dazzling emblems of the new Edwardian age. Gone was the usual dowdy 'drinking bar' with its perfunctory display of macaroons on a fly-blown counter, and in its place would be 'a comfortable and well-managed tea room – with a license'. Evening meals would be served in a separate restaurant where silver and glassware glittered on crisp white tablecloths. Their brave new National Theatre, they concluded, could survive on an annual expenditure of £64,980, which meant average receipts at each performance of almost £200.

If Grein, Whelan, Elizabeth Robins or the writers whom Archer and Barker championed imagined they might inherit the promised land of the National Theatre, they were mistaken. 'IT IS NOT AN 'ADVANCED' THEATRE WE ARE DESIGNING,'[23] warned the collaborators. They realized that the traditionalists saw the Independent Theatre, the New Century and the Stage Society as maggots eating away the body of the theatre and thereby society itself. They knew the Conservatives would look at a rent-free, tax-free National Theatre and see the spectre of government funding and state socialism, while the socialists would bridle at the thought of an art house for a cultured elite. Letters in the socialist newspaper, *The Clarion*, had already acidly suggested that a govern- ment-subsidized theatre would merely 'tax the multitude to supply a few super-refined specialists with ultra-subtle plays'[24] such as *The Marrying of Ann Leete*. Consequently, in *Scheme & Estimates for a National Theatre*, Archer and Barker hastened to assure potential sponsors that the new theatre would stand at the centre of national culture, of England and the Empire, and had no covert or controversial ambitions. 'The great subsidised theatres of the continent are not "advanced" theatres,' they explained. 'It is not their business to be far ahead of the time, but to be well abreast of it.' It was the job of the 'outpost' theatres to experiment, and theirs the right to fail. The National had to be something else. It had to be 'national, representative, and popular'.

Therefore, there was no trace of any 'disputable'[25] plays in their first-year repertoire. The only mention of Ibsen, Shaw, Tolstoy, Gorky, Bjørnson and Hauptmann was an assurance that they would not be performed. Instead, the core of the repertoire, as Archer assured the readers of *The Clarion*, was to be 'the works of Mr William Shakespeare, late of Stratford-upon-Avon, gent, . . . [and] other representative plays of our vast and various dramatic literature'.[26] Their first year of forty-six weeks was composed of thirty-four plays and 363 performances. Instead of plays running successively for a few weeks each, there would be several in the repertoire at any one time so that the programme could change almost daily. The National would open with the first part of the Shakespearian history cycle, *Richard II*, *Henry IV Parts One and Two* and *Henry V*, performed over four nights. If Archer and Barker's scheme had become reality, it would have been the first time this had been attempted, but as it was, it was left to Anthony Quayle to stage the four plays in sequence at Stratford in 1951. Five other Shakespeare plays were included in the first year: *Romeo and Juliet*, *Hamlet*, *The Taming of the Shrew*, *The Tempest* and, inevitably, Archer's favourite, *As You Like It*.

Shakespeare outweighed all other dramatists. Ben Jonson was the only one of his contemporaries to be represented, with *Every Man in his Humour*, while Congreve's *Love for Love*, Sheridan's *The Critic*, Robertson's *Caste* and Bulwer-Lytton's *Money* (which Archer had come to regard with some malign affection), were the only plays selected from the next two centuries of British drama. Of the nine modern plays, Pinero led the list with *The Benefit of the Doubt* and *Trelawny of the 'Wells'*. Wilde was represented by *The Importance of Being Earnest*, and Yeats by *The Countess Cathleen*. Five fictitious titles and authors indicated the as yet unwritten plays which the National Theatre would premiere. Molière's *Don Juan*, Brieux' *La Robe Rouge* and Sudemann's *Johannesfeuer*, were three of the six allocated foreign plays.

The Archer-Barker *Scheme & Estmates for a National Theatre* was, according to later commentators, 'quite simply, the best blueprint for a National Theatre ever written'.[27] In the effort to recruit the great and the good to their cause, they sent the book to Sir Henry Irving, who declared that the plans 'must appeal to every thoughtful lover of the drama'[28] and signed their endorsement. His recommendation compensated for several refusals. Swinburne, then in his sixties, was bewildered by the lists of plays and tables of figures but as his keeper, Theodore Watts-Dunton, explained, he had only been to the theatre twice within the past twenty-five years because he was too deaf to hear what anyone said. Thomas Hardy did not sign as he thought being deeply tucked into the countryside precluded his having an opinion upon national affairs. The playwright R. C. Carton, Edward Compton's brother-in-law, curtly pronounced himself firmly 'in the opposition lobby'.[29]

They soon found themselves correct in ruling out government subsidy when Pinero, a strong supporter, reported that at a private dinner he had methodically explained the plans for a National Theatre and acting school to Balfour. 'Englishmen can never be *taught* anything,' replied the Prime Minister. 'It showed the attitude such men take,' observed Pinero, adding that the discussion had degenerated into 'a wrangle'.[30]

Within a few weeks, Archer and Barker had seven supporters, Irving, John Hare, Squire Bancroft, J. M. Barrie, Helen D'Oyly Carte, Pinero and Henry Arthur Jones, willing to have their names appear below the formal endorsement printed in further copies of *Scheme & Estimates for a National Theatre*. These were published in the summer and sent to the remaining subscribers and a fleet of 'unsuspecting millionaires'[31] identified by Archer, who had heard a rumour that the industrialist Andrew Carnegie might be interested. (As it turned out, he was not.) Neither Archer's nor Barker's name appeared on the title page, although acknowledgement of 'the assistance rendered us by many expert advisors' was followed by the initials, W. A. and H. G. B.

The response to the second issue of *Scheme & Estimates for a National Theatre* was hostility, indifference, caution and enthusiastic support in almost equal measure. Margot, the wife of the former Liberal Home Secretary, Herbert Asquith, and a guarantor of the 1893 Ibsen season, wrote to register her support, which made up for Balfour's antipathy. But the partners were fiercely attacked by Shaw for reneging upon their New Drama principles. The 'censored' author told them bluntly that no director with the necessary youth and vision to run the National Theatre would consider doing so after being presented with so musty a repertoire. When Archer retorted that they had deliberately cut a prudent cloth so as to demonstrate the seriousness of their credentials, Shaw contemptuously told him that if they did not have the courage of their convictions they did not deserve to be heard.

He had a point, but Archer clung to his conviction that the National Theatre could best be achieved by his double strategy, one public, the other private, of noisily attacking the cultural Establishment in his journalism while quietly appealing to the rich, and influential, playing on their sense of philanthropy, sentiment and patriotism. There were words in ears, lunches with lords and even an appointment in an outer office at Buckingham Palace. But to no avail, for by the end of the day, nobody had come forward to reveal himself as a potential benefactor.

There was, though, one important development. At the end of the year, Pinero tipped off Archer that Mrs Humphrey Ward and Mrs Edith Lyttelton were planning their own repertory theatre company at the Scala Theatre, off Tottenham Court Road. This was intriguing news as Mrs Lyttelton was herself extremely intriguing. She was the wealthy second wife of Alfred Lyttelton, the Liberal Unionist Member of Parliament, currently Secretary of State for the Colonies and one of Balfour's closest Parliamentary friends. But more importantly, Edith knew people; her home was a formidable intellectual and literary salon.

She was an irrepressible theatre enthusiast, known to dash off in cabs on rainswept afternoons to see serious matinees.

She was also the author of *Warp and Woof*, a minor but sturdy social problem play exposing the appalling conditions suffered by workers at a Society dressmakers' studio. It was produced by her old friend, Mrs Patrick Campbell, at the astonishingly down-at-heel Camden Theatre on 6 June. Many of Mrs Lyttelton and Mrs Campbell's glamorous friends thronging into the theatre had probably never been to Camden before, and mounted police had to be summoned to prevent their being too closely inspected by an inquisitive crowd of north Londoners. Mrs Pat played the central role of Theodosia Hemming, the downtrodden fitter. The play sympathized with those standing outside and accused the very audience who paid to see it. But how many of these 'guilty creatures', the fashionably-dressed women in the audience, wondered Archer, would 'relax one iota of their exigency the next time they happened to need a new gown in a hurry'. *Warp and Woof*, he wrote, was 'a fable-play, a tract, a pamphlet', and as such, it was far more sincere than the 'inane . . . gibbering'[32] elsewhere in the theatre.

He procured an invitation to tea for himself and Barker with Mrs Lyttelton and Mrs Ward on 2 February 1905, to find out exactly what their repertory plans were. The result was that Mrs Ward withdrew, and Archer and Barker discovered in Edith Lyttelton a woman who would become an enthusiastic and powerful supporter in the campaign for a National Theatre.

There were now further changes. In Liverpool, Dibdin had finally left insurance and, having spent several years traipsing the northern galleries as art critic of the local paper, had become curator of the city's Walker Art Gallery. Gilbert Murray had left Glasgow, and was about to become a Fellow of New College, Oxford, a position from which, Archer suggested, he might keep an eye on Tom.

With Tom at Christ Church, and with her practice established, Frances decided there was no reason to remain in Dulwich. While Archer retained his tiny room at Westminster Mansions, they gave up the house at 71 Alleyn Park and on 20 September 1904, moved back to the country, to King's Langley, a Hertfordshire village of about a thousand people. They signed leases for two houses, Langley Rise and Hillmead, good-sized, neighbouring properties shaded by elm trees on Langley Hill, just above the village on its western side. Here, in the clean rural air, away from the grime and stress of London, Frances founded a residential nerve training colony, where patients could stay for a few days or even a few weeks. She began by importing five from Dulwich, distributing them to their various rooms, arranging singing and breathing classes and encouraging healthy walks in the grounds. 'I have no great faith in the success of the scheme,' Archer notified George Pierce Baker morosely, 'but we are bound to it for only 3 years.'[33] By that time, he confidently expected to be declared bankrupt as Frances's grasp of practical economics was as tenuous as his. The patients paid, but they did not always pay their way.

Archer and Frances gradually settled in. On the ground floor of Langley Rise was the family dining room and living room and on the top floor, Archer and Frances had their separate bedrooms. He made one room on the ground floor of Hillmead into a study, placing a large armchair on one side of the fireplace and moving in a desk, and a good many of his books, papers and pictures. It was peaceful here. The view from his French windows was like a picture postcard of rural England. The garden was large and surrounded by a hedge in which there was a gate to the footpath leading down to the railway station. Beyond the garden were fields, some of grass and others scarred by ploughing. In the summer, flowers dotted the rough grass of the banks and wild roses dappled the hedgerows. A copse of beech trees screened a chalk quarry and in the distance more trees partially hid a manor house built of red brick. He could just see a road, and would sometimes spot an occasional car, or bicycle, or the brewers' dray. Green hills flowed to the horizon and far away rose the needle-like spires of three churches, one marking the site of Harrow School.

In Christiana, Ibsen suffered strokes which left him paralyzed and devoid of the ability to remember words. In the winter of 1905, Archer began to sketch out an obituary, believing the playwright's death must be imminent. But the next death was not that of Ibsen, but of Archer's father. Weakened by influenza and pneumonia, Thomas's heart stopped on 9 December 1905 at the house at Sydenham where he and Grace had lived some fifteen years. He was eighty-two. They buried him at Crystal Palace Cemetery. The funeral does not appear to have brought Archer any closer to the rest of his family. He kept his independence. Five months later, on 23 May 1906, a few weeks after his seventy-eighth birthday and having been in a coma for several days, Ibsen died at his Arbiensgate apartment.

Of the almost two hundred reviews and essays Archer devoted to

Ibsen's work, eighteen were written in the year of the playwright's death. In the obituary he published in the *Daily Chronicle* on 24 May, he recalled 'a poet, a man of soaring and transfiguring imagination' and a man of the 'utmost kindness and geniality'.[34]

This last remark was rather an exaggeration. Ibsen thought highly of the English theatrical tradition and of Archer's pioneering work on his behalf, but outwardly he was as taciturn a man as Archer was formal, and when in each other's company the two men seldom wholly relaxed, and never to the point of geniality. They were courteous, even affable, but not close. Their meetings were appointments rather than reunions and they usually corresponded only when a new play had been completed, a translation finished or a production opened. Archer was always happier writing about the plays than the man who had written them, but once, in writing about Ibsen, he unconsciously revealed an aspect of himself. In 'Ibsen As I Knew Him', which he contributed to the *Monthly Review* in June, the recollections of his various meetings with Ibsen over the years prompted a letter from Shaw, surprised there were more aspects of his friend which he knew nothing about. 'Until I read the *Monthly Review* I had no idea that you had seen so much of him,' he wrote. 'It throws a light on the gross secretiveness of your disposition. Apparently the only person you tell anything to is Charles.'[35]

In the articles and lectures he wrote during the next twelve years, Archer strove to secure a permanent place for Ibsen's plays in the British theatre. He did this by remorselessly concentrating upon Ibsen the dramatic poet, and his understanding of human character and relationships, rather than Ibsen as a social reformer. In 'Ibsen's Craftsmanship', he described his achievement as creating a dynamic modern drama in which action and the psychology of the characters were inextricably linked, and which reached its height in the five great plays from *The Wild Duck* to *The Master Builder* in which 'psychology *is* the action'.[36]

This was also the theme of 'The True Greatness of Ibsen', Archer's final public statement on Ibsen and given as a lecture at the Deparament of Scandinavian Studies at University College, London, on 30 May 1918. For the last time, he attacked the notion of Ibsen as 'one of the tub-thumpers of the world – a vendor of ideas, of doctrines, of social and spiritual patent-medicines'. Ibsen, he repeated, was neither a great, nor even a particularly original thinker. His ideas on life, that 'opinions, prejudices, superstitions cling to us and hamper our conduct long after they are really dead; that all truth and wisdom do not necessarily reside with the compact majority; that if a man wants to ennoble the world, he had better begin by ennobling himself',[37] were no more than general maxims and hardly the words of a genius.

Really, Archer had always known that things were not quite so simple. 'People are *so* apt to sink the poet in the teacher,' he told Elizabeth during the run of *Hedda Gabler*, 'that I like . . . to pretend that in *Hedda* he is pure poet. I know he isn't, & I don't really wish that he should be . . .'[38] He recognized that Ibsen's dramatic power lay in his integrating a theatrical artistry with a range of vital and complex social and moral ideas. But social evolution, whether for better or worse, was a continuous process. As times changed and ideas changed with them, flourishing and fading in importance, Ibsen the moral and social reformer, thought Archer, might soon become outmoded. But however society changed, the observation and interpretation of human behaviour in the theatre was something of lasting value. Therefore, the only way to establish Ibsen's place in the vanguard of the British repertoire was to emphasize his stature as an artist. If he succeeded in this, he would also succeed in his campaign to have contemporary playwriting regarded as literature. 'What was Ibsen then, if not a great and original thinker?' he asked his audience at Uiversity College. 'He was a great poet, and, more specifically, a great dramatist. That is what people either do not realise or insist on forgetting.'[39]

During the summer following Ibsen's death, Archer began working on a new edition of the plays. The five-volume *Prose Dramas* published by Scott had ended in 1891 with *Hedda Gabler*, and the four subsequent plays, together with *Peer Gynt*, had appeared in separate volumes over the following nine years. Now he had the chance to revise all the translations for a definitive collection for Heinemann.

Of Ibsen's twenty-six plays, twenty-one, from *Lady Inger of Østraat* to *When We Dead Awaken*, are included in the Heinemann *Works of Henrik Ibsen*. The five omissions are the earliest pieces, from *Cataline* to *St John's Night*, written between 1849 and 1851, and *Olaf Liljekrans*, written in 1856. Ten of the published plays are translated by Archer alone and four in collaboration. Two of the remaining plays are translated by Frances, two by Charles, two by Herford and one by Eleanor Marx-Aveling, all of which Archer also revised. For each play, with the exception of Herford's translatins of *Love's Comedy* and *Brand* (completed at long last), he wrote a biographical introduction. The *Works of Henrik Ibsen* were published in eleven volumes, bound in red cloth with gold lettering on the spines, at four shillings each, at intervals from the end of 1906 until 1908. A twelfth volume, *From Ibsen's Workshop*, containing early drafts and fragments, translated by A. G. Chater with an introduction by Archer, appeared in 1912. Also published in the United States by Scribner's, the *Works* became the standard English language edition of the plays for many years.

'When Ibsen was translated first into the English tongue,/It caused a great disturbance that such a thing was done!'[40] wrote Arthur Applin in *A Song of the Ibsenites*, a satirical poem, in 1894. The consternation revolved mostly around the subject-matter of the plays, but Archer's translations were not immune from controversy. They were burlesqued, admired and criticized, although few critics had the authority fully to get to grips with his work. 'Let those who criticize him know as much Norwegian as he,' cautioned the *Saturday Review* in 1894.[41]

Whenever he was asked how difficult it was to translate Ibsen, Archer replied that it was both deceptively simple and almost impossible. 'It is extremely easy, in his prose plays, to realise his meaning,' he maintained, 'it is often extremely difficult to convey it into natural, colloquial, and yet not too colloquial English.'[42]

Nobody really knew Ibsen, Archer maintained, unless they knew *Brand* and *Peer Gynt*, but 'Having myself translated *Peer Gynt*, I am in a position to say with some confidence that those poems are untranslatable.'[43] With *Peer Gynt*, which he translated with Charles, their problems were not merely limited to tracking the author as he moved from reality to fantasy and back again throughout the five acts. They had to decide how to represent the fast-flowing vernacular of the original, whether to duplicate its complex rhyming system and attempt to reproduce in English octosyllabic and decasyllabic poetry incorporating five different metrical variations. 'We had no precedent – within our knowledge – to guide us,'[44] he wrote in the introduction. Their solution, to which Ibsen had agreed, was to translate the play neither into rhyming verse nor prose but into a blank verse which followed the original metres as closely as possible. 'Your version I do not falter,'[45] wrote the Dante scholar, Ibsen devotee and critic, Philip Wicksteed.

Coping with the huge breadth of Ibsen's writing, from *Peer Gynt* to the treacherous vernacular of *The Wild Duck*, was only part of the problem. He had to find effective substitutes for words and phrases for which no direct English equivalent existed. Often, he found himself forced to choose between meaning and tone, and reluctantly having to forego the sound of words, which he knew to be dramatically vital. In

Act Two of *The Master Builder*, Hilde describes how she shudders at the word 'duty': 'It sounds so cold and sharp and stinging. Duty – duty – duty . . .' In the original, she cries out, 'Pligt!! Pligt! Pligt!' and, wrote Archer, 'the very word stings and snaps'.[46] 'Duty' neither stung nor snapped, yet it was the only word that would suffice.

He was virtually alone in his field and was ploughing a longer furrow than any of the others. Many critics thought his work 'excellent'[47] and 'valuable',[48] but while several were content to watch him dispassionately from the other side of the hedge, some threw stones. The main complaint was not that Archer was an inadequate translator but that he was not an instinctive playwright. *The Pall Mall Gazette* detected bathos in his *Little Eyolf*. His work was 'not altogether "convincing" on the stage: we think he lacks a little the true dramatist's ear'.[49]

Other critics accused him of being too literal, but they meant the plays were too explicit; or that they sounded too brittle, or too colloquial, or too American, a grave failing as American was considered an irredeemably slovenly version of English. One of the most hostile attacks appeared anonymously in *The Speaker* on 10 July 1897, after the publication of *John Gabriel Borkman*. Archer suspected the author to be Karl Pearson, who knew Norwegian and who in 1885 had led a disaffected band from the Men and Women's Club to found their own, more exclusive debating society. Pearson, if he was the author, darkly declared that Archer's translations were 'not all they might and ought to be'.

He could identify no literal errors, but alleged that the speed at which Archer must sometimes have worked had resulted in his sacrificing Ibsen's pace and lightness to the familiar 'rough-and-ready dialogue' of the British theatre. Moreover, his work was a crude hotch-potch of linguistic contractions: 'shan't', 'won't', 'he's', and 'you're' appeared among an appalling confetti of Americanisms. Instead of visiting, people tended to 'look in'; otherwise they would 'stop at home'.[50]

A fortnight later, Archer protested that just as Ibsen was a pioneering playwright so his translators also ventured into unexplored territory. Ibsen's prose was often colloquial in its structure if not always in its vocabulary, and therefore his approach was to reflect the strength of the original without being too literary, and at the same time capture its subtlety without being too conversational. He tried to create a language that was both acceptable to read and fluent on stage, but where a choice had to be made, he used the phrase that would be most effective in the theatre. 'My aim has always been to make an audience, as the play proceeded, gradually forget it was listening to a translation at all.'[51]

Nevertheless, Archer was shaken by Pearson's assault and asked Murray to read his reply before he sent it. Murray thought his defence 'entirely convincing', but told him confidentially that the expression 'right upstairs' which he had used in *John Gabriel Borkman* was stridently American. Otherwise, '*I* can't think of any modern translation into English which I have read with as much satisfaction – so much feeling of ease and fullness and freedom – as yours of Ibsen.'[52]

Archer gathered influential supporters and detractors. Yeats said that reading Archer's Ibsen was like drinking from an hygienic bottle. Sutro, who became a translator of Maeterlinck, agreed that 'Archer certainly was no poet and Ibsen was.' But he added that 'Archer's fidelity to the text, his unswerving loyalty in giving the exact rendering, without trimming or embroidery, was of greater help to our understanding of Ibsen than would be the perhaps more flowery translations that his belittlers might have offered.'[53]

Foremost among his supporters was Shaw, who denounced the denouncers and proclaimed 'Archer-Ibsen' to be far and away the finest. He did not even have to visit Norway to recognize that 'the air of Norway breathed through his versions'. In 1927, when he was a much-translated and mistranslated author himself, Shaw insisted that 'Whenever a translation was produced without the peculiar character that Archer gave to his, it had no character at all, no challenge, at best only a drawing room elegance that was a drawback rather than an advantage.' The reason that his translations were superior to any others was simple. 'Archer understood and cared for Ibsen's imagination.'[54]

For forty years, from the 1890s until the 1930s, Archer's translations were the standard texts for the British theatre, although in later years, they were often extensively rewritten by directors and actors. Published at the beginning of the twentieth century, Archer's edition of the *Works* is still, as it nears its end, available in public libraries and his work often forms the basis for new translations. During the 1930s, the art of translation declined as a new generation, ignorant of Norwegian, adapted the English texts or re-translated from the French or German. It was not untl 1959 that Michael Meyer and J. W. McFarlane, both fluent Norwegian speakers and authorities on Scandinavian culture, began, independently, to prepare scrupulous new English translations which both reflected the world of the original and felt linguistically at home in the post-war era. These are still frequently used in the theatre. It is now also an accepted practice for new versions to be written by leading playwrights, such as Christopher Hampton, working from literal translations prepared by Norwegian scholars. Hampton, whose work includes English versions of *A Doll's House* and *Hedda Gabler*, combines textual accuracy with pace and lucidity and, like many translators, acknowledges the importance of Archer's work.

Meyer argues that, while Archer was a great champion of Ibsen, his translations are faithful 'only in the sense that they are painstakingly literal. The knifethrusts of Ibsen's dialogue are absent; so is the humour, so is the poetry.'[55] In common with others who criticize Archer's dialogue, Meyer suggests that Archer failed to reproduce the sharp, sprightly feel of Ibsen's language. Instead of translating the plays into their natural English equivalent, the racy dialogue of Shaw, Archer 'fell back into exactly the kind of Mrs Tanqueray dialogue from which Ibsen was trying to liberate the theatre'.[56]

Certainly, compared with Shaw, Archer's dialogue is formal and prim, but he is neither unemotional nor entirely without humour. He may be Pinero-esque, but then Pinero is a clearer writer and more of a stylist than most of his contemporaries. But time has inevitably made Archer's Ibsen unwieldly, perhaps more so than it really was at the time. Language and meaning expands, contracts and alters as sensibilities change, and it is doing so faster at the end of the twentieth century than Archer might have imagined at its beginning. Every age discovers its own interpretation of great drama and every age, perhaps every decade, needs its new translations. Archer's achievement is only partly that he was the first to translate a body of Ibsen's plays into English and to produce an influential collected edition. It is also that his own productions, the eight British premieres he co-directed between 1880 and 1897, from *Quicksands* to *John Gabriel Borkman*, irrevocably established Ibsen in the repertoire of the British theatre.

In 1908, after almost three years of laborious revision, writing introductions, complaining at the inaccuracy of Heinemann's printers and tirelessly checking the proofs, Archer completed the final long lap of editing the *Works* by writing the general introduction for the entire series. It was thirty years since his first attempted translation of *Samfundets Støtter* in Edinburgh. 'It has since cost me five or six times as much work in revision as it originally did in translation,' he reflected, 'and something like ten years elapsed before it slowly dawned upon me that the translating and editing of Ibsen's works was to be one of the chief labours, as it has certainly been one of the greatest privileges of my life.'

Then, he added simply: 'That task is now ended.'[57]

Life at the Court

'Do you think there is anything in this idea?' Barker asked Archer one day in April 1903, while they were working on *Scheme & Estimates for a National Theatre*. The idea, was that he take over the Court Theatre for six months or a year and run a season of plays by Ibsen, Shaw, Hauptmann, Sudermann, Maeterlinck and Schnitzler, opening a new production every fortnight. It could all be done, he reckoned, on a guarantee of £5000, and expenses could be kept as low as £250 a week if they scraped by with only the minimum of set, lighting and costumes. The advantage over the Stage Society would be that by having a permanent theatre he could present evening performances, and so expand the audience for serious drama to include the 'intellectual would-be playgoers who are profoundly bored by the theatre as it is',[1] but who were unable to attend matinees because they were at work.

Outwardly, Archer was as dubious of Barker's hopes as he was when Elizabeth told him of her Joint Management plans over a decade before. There was no doubting his sincerity, but 'he has not as yet weight enough or experience enough to stand alone',[2] he told Baker at Harvard. And neither did Barker himself have the courage of all his convictions, admitting that raising the money presented a 'practically insurmountable obstacle'.[3] Yet exactly a year later, as he was taking delivery of the first copies of *Scheme & Estimates for a National Theatre*, Archer presented Barker with his chance to work at the Court.

The original Royal Court Theatre in Lower George Street, Chelsea, where several of Pinero's farces had premiered, had been demolished in 1887. It was replaced by a new Royal Court, seating just over eight hundred and with a reasonably adequate stage, built next to the Metropolitan District Railway station on the east side of Sloane Square. Pinero gave the new theatre its first successes with *The Cabinet Minister* and *Trelawny of the 'Wells'*. In the spring of 1904, J. H. Leigh, a rich businessman and theatre enthusiast, took over the lease, intending to produce a series of 'Shakespeare Representations' featuring what he thought were the unfairly overlooked talents of his wife, Thyrza Norman. When the first two representations failed, Leigh nervously approached Archer for advice. Archer told him to send for Granville Barker at once to take over as director.

Since *The Marrying of Ann Leete*, Barker had directed four Stage Society matinees, including Shaw's love-match and boxing burlesque, *The Admirable Bashville*. At the Court on 8 April 1904, he produced a cut and re-ordered version of *Two Gentlemen of Verona* with Thyrza as Julia and himself as Speed. It struck 'very nearly the right mean between "Elizabethan stage" austerity and actor-manager prodigality',[4] remarked Archer. But when Barker agreed to direct Shakespeare, he also arranged to direct Shaw. His revival of *Candida*, in which a 'too vivid' Kate Rorke played the title role, opened on 26 April and ran for six matinees. Charlotte Shaw had secretly given Leigh a guarantee of one hundred and sixty pounds in case it should fail. That it did not, owed much to Barker's performance as Marchbanks, an 'exceedingly able' portrayal, which revealed 'the fantastic imagination, the hysterical mobility and the hyperaesthesia of the character' even if at times he tended to 'overdo the impishness'.

Several critics grumbled that *Candida* was 'too clever', but Archer claimed this merely exposed their own intellectual and emotional shortcomings. They had allowed Shaw's unpredictable effervescence to wrong-foot them and knock them into confusion. Far from being 'too clever', *Candida* was 'the most human of all Shaw's plays and the one in which he is most successful in concealing himself behind his puppets – or rather in distributing himself among them'. One of the reasons Archer liked *Candida* was because it reminded him of the depth of his friendship with Shaw and how much he enjoyed their arguments. Watching the play was like spending 'a delightful afternoon with a sometimes perverse, sometimes irritating, but always irresistible wit and humorist . . .'[5] In short, there was nothing else like it in the London theatre.

Working with Barker put Archer in such dazzlingly good heart that he decided to revive the New Century Theatre and produce Gilbert Murray's translation of Euripedes's *Hippolytus*. That Elizabeth wanted nothing to do with the New Century did not worry Archer at all. He would carry on without her. 'My only stipulation is *no Gordon Craig*,'[6] he informed Murray emphatically on 22 January. Their man, he told him, was Granville Barker.

This was the first time that Archer had been involved in the production of a classical play. But what interested him in Greek tragedy was not its antiquity but its modernity, its interweaving of domestic issues with great world events. In Euripedes lay the roots of the psychological realism of Ibsen. Within a few weeks, they had raised subscriptions of £250, sufficient to pay for four matinees between 26 May and 3 June at the Lyric Theatre on Shaftesbury Avenue. Their set would have to obscure as much as possible of that for Henry Hamilton and Ivan Carlyle's operetta, *The Duchess of Dantzic*, which was enjoying a melodiously long evening run. Archer, Barker and Murray assembled a company of twenty-nine, making *Hippolytus* the biggest New Century production yet. Edyth Olive was cast as Phaedra and the popular Ben Webster as Hippolytus. Barker cast himself as a henchman, while Florence Farr was assigned a Chorus of eight Trozenean Women.

Archer attended several of Barker's rehearsals, and by mid-May was 'overwhelmed with work'[7] on the production. 'Simple grandeur'[8] became their watchword. Costumes were modelled on period robes and Barker arranged the actors in classical groupings but avoided gesture and spectacle by encouraging straightforward, muted acting. When Murray published his translation of *Hippolytus* in 1902, academic critics pounced on him for transposing iambic Greek verse into rhymed couplets. Archer, with whom Murray had debated his style before he began work, leapt to his defence in his *Study and Stage* column in the *Morning Leader*, refuting all allegations and claiming that if Murray had retained blank verse, the result would simply remind British audiences of Shakespeare. By using 'flowing rhymed pentameters'[9] in the tradition of Chaucer, Keats and William Morris, he had succeeded in preserving the spirit of the original while giving Greek tragedy a new and contemporary English voice. There were, observed Archer, many translations of classics but few classics of translation. Murray's *Hippolytus* was one of them.

As Murray had given Euripides new rhythms, so did Barker, demanding the lines be spoken quickly and expressively. Like Poel, he imagined a play as a symphonic score and the actors as instruments. With the first performance looming, Archer began dispatching notes to the actors. 'Once or twice,' he commented to Florence Farr, 'it seemed to me, when you were not doing anything, as if you let your attention wander & were not *in* the scene'. Her aimlessness was doubly worrying as it infected the Trozenean Women who consequently lacked 'crispness'.[10]

It looked at though the New Century Theatre was tumbling towards another disaster. Even though the producers and actors bribed as many friends as possible with free tickets, the audience for the first matinee on 26 May still only numbered about fifty, a pitiful handful in a theatre seating over a thousand. But reviews applauding Barker's direction and exclaiming that the play seemed written for the modern stage, doubled the audience for the second performance and the third was sold out. On the fourth day, Murray turned the corner on to Shaftesbury Avenue and thought for one moment he had arrived at the wrong theatre, for a lengthy queue snaked from the box office. Word had got around that *Hippolytus* should not be missed. Many people had never seen tragedy performed with such a vivid, contemporary feel. 'At the end of it we were all moved to tears,' noted the diplomat and poet William Scawen Blunt in his dairy, 'and I got up and did what I never did before in a theatre, shouted for the author, whether for Euripedes or Gilbert Murray I hardly knew.'[11]

In fact, *Hippolytus* did so well that when J. E. Vedrenne, Leigh's business manager, looked up from scrutinizing the New Century's accounts, he announced a substantial profit of £400. At last, the New Century had both a critical and a financial success to offset its record of dismal failure. There was excited talk of a transfer and a longer run, but other plans were already afoot. With Archer's encouragement, Barker and Vedrenne decided to go into partnership at the Court and, with money contributed by friends and associates, including some by Shaw, produce a season of new plays. In October, as Tom began wrestling miserably with Classics at Oxford, Barker triumphantly re-directed *Hippolytus* as the season's first production. It was, wrote Archer, 'noble and beautiful'.[12]

So great was the transformation in Archer's spirits that he was no longer complaining that he was 'unspeakably sick of dramatic criticism'. Neither was he thinking of abandoning England altogether and beginning a new life as an academic in the United States. Several months previously, he had desperately appealed to George Pierce Baker to keep him informed should any American university want a Professor of Dramatic Criticism, or a lecturer on 'any subject not hopelessly beyond my range'.[13] He had no luck in America, but in November 1904, Sir Oliver Lodge, the scientist and principal of the new university at Birmingham, sounded him out, via Murray, about accepting the chair of English

Literature there. But Archer refused. By this time, everything had changed. *Scheme & Estimates for a National Theatre* had just been published and Barker was at the Court and co-directing a new play by Shaw. There was a zest in the air, eager and sharp, of fresh ideas and optimism and, suddenly, it was vitally important to be a theatre critic again.

As the first Vedrenne-Barker matinee season was due to last until the following May, it represented the greatest chance for serious drama since the creation of the Stage Society five years before. It seems that Archer had taken every chance presented first by Leigh and then by the staging of *Hippolytus* at the Lyric to ensure that *Scheme & Estimates* might be complemented by a practical demonstration of the potential for a National Theatre. Although his name does not appear as officially connected with the Court season, Archer acted privately as a literary advisor and was always on hand when Barker requested a conference. Publicly, he became the Court's leading critical ambassador, writing about each production at length in *The World*. As surely as he had changed the gears of Shaw's career, Archer was now guiding the twenty-six-year-old Barker in his. His biographer remarked that taking over the Court was 'the most important development in Barker's career'.[14] By engineering this, Archer was helping to instigate the Shavian 'boom' which the commercial managers had obstinately refused to set in motion.

Initially, Barker had hoped to run an evening programme, but with the fastidious Vedrenne perched protectively over the accounts book, he had to be content instead with Tuesday, Thursday and Friday afternoons. Each production, he decided, would run for six performances, irrespective of its critical and public reception. Vedrenne imposed a stringent budget of £200 for each play, which meant that Barker was unable to pay actors any fee for rehearsals and only a guinea for each performance. He planned a dozen plays, and on 1 November, opened his second production. This was the world premiere of *John Bull's Other Island*, Shaw's thirteenth play and a satire of English capitalism and Irish dreams.

In Thomas Broadbent, Shaw presents the robust, philistine English businessman who has little emotional sensitivity but an eye for efficiency and profit. Broadbent is the embodiment of English Imperialism, a one-man market force. His business partner, the Irishman Larry Doyle who came to London to find his fortune and hovers uncertainly between practicalities and dreams, accompanies him back to Ireland to settle a land deal. Once there, Broadbent falls in love with Doyle's girlfriend, Nora, is adopted as a parliamentary candidate and acquires the land for development. The former priest, Peter Keegan, symbolizing a romantic, mystical world, denounces self-interest and at the end of the play, walks away towards the hills, a solitary Shavian figure, while Broadbent and Doyle select the site for their new hotel.

Shaw steered the play through rehearsals with Barker, who was also appearing as Keegan, while the thick-set, chubby-faced Louis Calvert played Broadbent. They were rewarded with a cluster of excellent reviews. In *The World*, Archer claimed it was an impossible play to classify and then classified it as 'a philisophico-political prose extravaganza'. He detected echoes of *Arms and the Man* in that, superficially, it was 'one of those ridiculous stories of love at first sight and marriage the following morning of which Mr Shaw is so inexplicably fond'. But the real substance of *John Bull's Other Island* was 'a keen analysis of Irish conditions and a genial caricature of English liberalism'. Shaw had taken two great strides forward. First, the 'Buddhist-Catholic Keegan' had a humanity he had not achieved before, and secondly, instead of writing a soapbox oration, he had managed to bring successive characters into focus. Shaw had done 'nothing more original'.[15]

John Bull's Other Island instantly made both the Court and Shaw the talk of serious London. After Beatrice Webb took Balfour to the fifth performance, news of the play filtered even as far as the House of Commons tea-room, yet Barker dutifully took it off after the sixth performance to make way for Maeterlinck's *Aglavaine and Selysette* before reviving *Candida* and Marchbanks. At Christmas, he produced *Prunella*, a Pierrot play with music which he had written with Laurence Housman (the brother of the author of *A Shropshire Lad*), and which Archer loyally rather than enthusiastically supported. The first productions of 1905 were a triple-bill, on 28 February, of Schnitzler's *In The Hospital*, Yeats's *The Pot of Broth* and Shaw's *How He Lied to her Husband*, a one-act peroration on triangular love affairs, and a 'pure delight'.[16] But after *John Bull's Other Island*, the audiences stayed away, mainly because it was a bitter winter and word had got around that the Court's heating system failed to heat. Archer was all right, because the Murrays, knowing his susceptibility to winter-long colds and his reluctance to buy new clothes, had taken pity and presented him with an expensive new coat for Christmas. The heating was hastily repaired by the evening of 11 March, when the Court was socially crowned by the presence of King Edward VII at a command performance of *John Bull's Other Island*.

The management took no chances and hired a special chair to support the monarchal weight, but the play made the King laugh so much that he broke it and toppled towards the floor of the Royal Box. But to Archer, a displaced sovereign was hardly the most embarrassing moment of the evening. It was far easier to replace a king on a makeshift throne than it was to give a good performance of a play which had been off the stage too long and inadequately re-rehearsed. This was the second rush-revival of *John Bull's Other Island*. After the first, on 7 February, when the play had been out of the repertoire for several weeks, he observed that 'It is impossible, in the theatre, to pick up a thread where you dropped it.' In *Scheme & Estimates*, he reminded Barker, they had evolved a plan of alternating performances in which several plays were in readiness at any one time, and 'this is the only rational system on which a repertory theatre can be run'.[17] But it also required far more money at the beginning of a season than either Vedrenne or Barker could raise.

On 21 March, he directed *The Thieves' Comedy*, Christopher Horne's translation of Hauptmann's *Der Biberpelz*, a lowlife satire on the highlife in which a scurrilous Berlin washerwoman outwits Prussian bureaucracy. The play's social context alone made it 'an event of the first importance' in British theatre, wrote Archer. The Court was again proclaiming its difference by depicting on the stage a social class ignored by the traditional theatre, and by doing so it had achieved what the Independent Theatre had sometimes done, and what Archer had thought the New Century might do with *The Weavers*. For too long, he complained, the English stage had been both dominated and imprisoned by 'the eternal drawing room', and the sensibilities of English playwrights 'bounded on the south by Belgravia, on the north by Bayswater, on the east and west by the Savoy Hotel and Hurlingham respectively'.[18] If British drama was to survive and develop, he argued, then dramatists must explore all social classes and situations, observing them dispassionately and portraying them accurately. This was a call to arms that would be echoed fifty years later by Kenneth Tynan, bemoaning a 1954 London season of only three 'successes' (one of which was Peggy Ashcroft's *Hedda Gabler*). 'We need plays about cabmen and demigods,' he cried, 'plays about warriors, politicians and grocers . . .'[19]

Despite Archer's encouragement, *The Thieves Comedy* failed and the Court reverted from Berlin to Greece and another of Murray's translations from Euripedes, this time of *The Trojan Women*. Archer read the play in typescript and admired it, but counselled Murray not to give it to Barker. Its proper place was a lecture hall and it could only work on the stage as part of a Euripedean cycle. When Barker staged it, Archer repeated his objections in *The World*. It was now the end of April and already Vedrenne and Barker had agreed to produce a second season of plays from September. They finished their first with a celebratory hail of Shaw, reviving *John Bull's Other Island*, *Candida* and *You Never Can Tell* and, on 23 May, raising the curtain on the world premiere of *Man and Superman*.

In *Man and Superman* Shaw flourished his theory of the Life Force and the alternative religion of Creative Evolution. To Shaw, God did not exist, yet at the same time there was an energy in the world which had to be accounted for and which produced occasional supermen like Caesar, Shakespeare and Shaw himself. This energy was the Life Force, an expression of intellect and will pulsing through history and surfacing in the individual. If only the Life Force was recognized and harnessed for the public good, Shaw reasoned, if only the sexual instinct was sublimated in favour of the intellectual and the world had faith in its genius supermen, man could progress through Creative Evolution towards a finer future. Creative Evolution was a massive spooling together of ideas extracted from the works of Wagner, Schopenhauer, the writer Samuel Butler, the French naturalist George de Buffon, the German philosopher Fredrich Nietzsche and a host of others to provide a kind of socialist and mystical chart of ideal human progression.

The principal characters in *Man and Superman* and in several subsequent plays, reflect differing aspects of the Life Force and Shaw's deliberations upon Creative Evolution. The idealistic and wealthy socialist, John Tanner (whose name Shaw borrowed from Mrs Patrick Campbell's father), is appointed the guardian of the manipulative Ann Whitefield. When he discovers that Ann intends to marry him, Tanner fears his revolutionary ideals will be compromised by domestic and social convention, and attempts to escape to Spain. The plan collapses when Ann turns his flight into a motor tour with family and friends. In Act III, set in the Sierra Nevada, Tanner dreams that he is Don Juan and debates the theory of Creative Evolution and the rival merits of Heaven and Hell with the other characters metamorphosed into the Devil, Donna Elvira and the Commendatore. At the end of the play, Tanner is condemned not to Hell but to marriage, capitulating to Ann's demands.

Shaw called it 'a comedy and a philosophy', but for the first production, he and Barker removed most of the philosophy by cutting Act III, leaving an Edwardian comedy of manners in which a woman ensnares the eligible bachelor of her choice. The Court's serious drama enthusiasts were therefore confronted with something they recognized as representative of the mainstream theatre, rather than an alternative to it. Barker played Tanner, resplendent in a russet beard and eyebrows so that he looked just like Shaw, while the twenty-four-year-old Lillah McCarthy, a dark-haired, rather plain-looking woman with whom he had once toured in Ben Greet's company, appeared as Ann Whitefield.

Watching them, Archer decided that *Man and Superman* was neither comedy nor philosophy but an exasperating exhibition of the old Shawpenhaurism mixed up with a dose of Nietzsche. It was 'not a good play, or even a good play of Shaw's',[20] he notified Murray. It was merely a technical drawing, he commented in *The World*, and, as such, it effectively illustrated the depths of the waters of life, but it was not drama, which was supposed to illuminate the cross-currents. To see the Life Force portrayed in truly dramatic terms, the Court audiences would be better off reading the novels of Thomas Hardy.

On the other hand, he admitted there was something wonderfully liberating in the way that Shaw turned everything on its head and made the theatre a place of delightfully eccentric argument. Shaw infuriated Archer, but he also thrilled him and this continually divided response, coupled with his natural inclination to affect indifference over things he most passionately cared about, forced him to revise his assessment of Shaw's talents with every play he wrote. Shaw 'posesses in a very high degree the specific gifts of the dramatist',[21] was his verdict after *Candida*. 'He is not, and never will be a great dramatist,' he reported after *Man and Superman*, 'but he is something rarer, if not better – a philosophic humorist, with the art of expressing himself in dramatic form.' It had been a mistake, he concluded, to try and turn him into a serious playwright. Had he succeeded, the theatre would have been 'the richer by an inferior Ibsen, the poorer by an individual, inimitable, irritating, tantalising, incalculable, delightful Shaw'.[22] The theatre, in other words, would have lost its natural Court jester.

However much he enjoyed Shaw's sense of fun (for, being argumentative, it was also his own), Archer nevertheless thought it his duty to help Shaw find his own dramatic voice. After the text of *Man and Superman* was published in August 1903, he had claimed in an article in the *Morning Leader* that Shaw was not as advanced a playwright as

Pinero. This was bait to draw Shaw into the open so that Archer could lecture him on why, as a playwright, he was his own worst enemy. It worked. 'My business is to fight for the Grand School,' protested Shaw from Scotland, where he was reluctantly on holiday, ' – the people who are building up the intellectual consciousness of the race . . . who have, as you know, nobody to fight for them . . .'[23]

In a nine-page 'sermon' scrawled in pencil the next day, Archer told him that there was no better evidence of Shaw failing to do himself justice as a playwright than the 'Nietzschean motor-car' of *Man and Superman*. 'You say "*your* men are Wagner, Ibsen, Tolstoy, Schopenhauer, Nietzsche" – I should reverse it & say you are *their* man. Why should this be? Why should you be always flying somebody else's banner and shouting somebody else's war-cry with only the addition of your own Irish accent?'

The great flaw in Shaw's make-up, Archer pointed out, was his immense gullibility. He treated every scrap of 'transitory jargon', such as Nietzsche's idea of the superman as 'the last word of human wisdom', and instead of writing plays, produced 'a glittering jumble of untested, unweeded, unharmonized thought, devoid of perspective or proportion'. What he should do, recommended Archer, was sit down, think carefully, and then 'go beyond Nietzsche, Wagner & Ibsen, & especially beyond Shaw . . . towards clarity'. It distressed him to see Shaw knitting together other people's ideas instead of weaving his own. '[I]n no way are you making the mark either upon literature or upon life, that you have it in you to make. The years are slipping away . . . & you have done nothing really big, nothing original, solid, first-rate, enduring.' To terrorize him further, Archer invoked a fantastical literary doomsday. 'If you were to die tomorrow, what would happen? In the history of literature you would find a three-line mention . . . as an eccentric writer, hard to classify, whose writings a few people still remember with pleasure. I think it highly probable,' he added, firing his final shot, 'that for thirty years or so Shaw Societies would spring up from time to time, especially in Boston – & I can't imagine a more doleful way of going to oblivion.'[24]

'You really are a very curious character,' replied Shaw, who could not understand why Archer took up such apparently contradictory positions on his plays. 'All that you ask for is there, not only in Man & Superman, but in my early immature scrawlings.'[25] Shaw found Archer as perplexing as Archer found Shaw. He wanted to make Archer laugh at the world, but Archer was more pessimistic than he was and his vision of the world was sometimes too dark for laughter. There was a deep seam of despair in Archer which troubled Shaw. But he rallied enough to fling back his own verdict on his literary future. 'I am very much afraid I am destined . . . to be the curse of English literature for the next 300 years at least. It is really not my fault; it is that in the country of the blind the one-eyed is king.'[26]

One eyed or not, it was precisely that Shaw was king of the Court that worried Archer. In the *Record and Commentary of the Vedrenne-Barker Season*, a sixteen-page commemorative pamphlet published in June, he reviewed the achievements so far. The standard of acting was as high as any in London and within their budget, the plays were technically as well-staged as possible. He was unconcerned that Barker had directed the entire season except when he worked with Shaw, but suggested that the 'one disquieting feature' of the enterprise was 'the undue prominence of the works of Mr Bernard Shaw'. He did not for one moment begrudge his friend his success. After all, he was partly responsible for it, and took the opportunity to repeat his castigation of the commercial managers whose neglect had made Shaw 'the hero of a perfectly natural and in itself a welcome reaction'.[27] But he was impatient that the New Drama should finally gain more than a tentative foothold in the theatre. He wanted more Shaws, more new writers, so that instead of being a kingdom, the Court might be established as a republic.

A few weeks later, on 26 September 1905, and as if in answer to his appeal, a play by St John Hankin became the first world premiere of the second Vedrenne-Barker season. Hankin came from a different social background than Archer, Barker and Shaw, his family being well ensconced in the south of England middle class. Born in Southampton, he was sent to Malvern School and later graduated from Merton College, Oxford. He was a member of the management committee of the Stage Society and had largely given up a prolific journalistic career for playwriting when he delivered the script of *The Return of the Prodigal* to the Royal Court.

The play is a social satire and a modern re-working and reversal of the Biblical parable. Having squandered most of the money his father had given him to go to Australia, Eustace Jackson returns to the prosperous family home, threatening that if turned away, he will either take up lodgings in the workhouse or drown himself in the canal, jeopardizing his father's hope of a Parliamentary seat and his brother's chances of marrying into the aristocracy. He finally undertakes to stay away from the family in return for a £300 annual allowance.

Hankin's argument was that capital was creating an England of predators and parasites. Archer thought *The Return of the Prodigal* 'sketchy and superficial', but he was considerably heartened by the approving reviews written by other critics. 'Ten, or even five years ago, such a piece would have been received with bewilderment,' he remarked. 'Clearly we are advancing.'[28] They took a few steps backwards when Barker directed a 'woolly and indecisive'[29] production of *The Wild Duck*, but darted quickly forward again when Shaw unveiled his third premiere of the year, *Major Barbara*.

Shaw's theme in *Major Barbara* was weaponary and poverty, a timely subject in 1905 when Britain was building the first Dreadnought warship, a ship of such destructive superiority that it began a full-scale naval arms race. At the same time, almost a million people in Britain were claiming Poor Law relief. About 150,000 people in London were paupers, or one person in every thirty of the capital's 4½ million population. Britain was at the height of its imperial power, but huge tracts of her industrial cities were notorious slums. The Salvation Army patrolled the worst, held meetings at street corners and distributed food from their shelters. On his journeys across London each day, Archer saw the miserable army which the Empire had left behind, the destitute, and the vagrants who slept either in the workhouses or out on the streets.

Shaw's 'discussion in three acts' between Andrew Undershaft, a millionaire arms manufacturer, his Salvation Army daughter, Barbara, and her fiancé, Adolphus Cusins, turns on whether poverty can best be alleviated by the power of religious faith or material wealth. In the final act, Undershaft wins the debate and Cusins graduates from idealism to realism, marrying Barbara and inheriting his father-in-law's company, perhaps to use his acquired power wisely. Undershaft represents the Life Force and is a distillation of several European arms manufacturers; Barbara is a combination of Beatrice Webb and the actress, Eleanor Robson, while Cusins, a classicist and political idealist, is based upon Gilbert Murray. Having strikingly impersonated Shaw in Tanner, Barker now stepped into the role of Cusins and assumed Murray's small steel-rimmed glasses and earnest, sometimes bemused expression.

On 29 November, the afternoon of the first performance, the theatre was crowded and hundreds more had to be turned away. A troupe of Salvation Army Commissioners in full uniform sat like sentries in a stage-side box. Balfour, in the last week of his Prime Ministership was accompanied by Beatrice Webb, whom he had appointed to sit on the Royal Commission for the Poor Law. Several seats away sat Archer who, once the curtain finally came down on the 'discussion' threw up his arms in exasperation. He was not surprised that the plot was another 'negligible figment of unconditioned fantasy, which neither Mr Shaw nor anyone else takes seriously for a moment', but angered that Shaw had ignored his appeals to break free from his masters and speak with his own voice. He had a chance to write a play of real political, social and moral importance, yet his characters were no more than shuttles loaded with single-colour yarns, which Shaw at the loom had set rattling in motion merely to weave 'the somewhat violent tartan of his humanitarian-Nietzschean life-philosophy'.

The play inspired scintillating performances, both from Barker on the stage and Archer in *The World*. In his column on 5 December, he cut out and pasted pieces of the play in their appropriate places in the biography of Shaw himself. *Major Barbara* was clearly autobiographical and featured past, present and ethereal Shaws. Barbara herself represented the optimistic socialism of the youthful Shaw, delivering half-a-dozen lectures in neighbourhood halls each week, fondly believing the proletariat could be marched to economic and political freedom on a diet of platform oratory and Fabian pamphlets. His Jaeger cap in which he used to take the collection was symbolized in the play by Barbara's Salvation Army tambourine. Undershaft stood for the Shaw of the present day, believing benevolence came through the acquisition of power rather than the discovery of love, while Cusins, the 'Euripedian ironist', in love with Barbara, hypnotized by Undershaft, depicted 'the fundamental, contemplative Shaw'.[30]

This review, 'the worst you ever wrote,' exploded Shaw, on 1 January 1906, 'delighted me. The complete success with which I wrecked your mind and left you footling – simply footling – was really the greatest proof of your fundamental sensibility to my magic . . . It is a MAGNIFICENT play, a summit in dramatic literature.'[31] But for Archer, a far higher peak had been conquered three weeks before *Major Barbara* opened.

The Voysey Inheritance was the first play by Barker which he refused to read, and therefore when it burst upon the Court stage on the afternoon of 7 November, he was all the more astonished by it. Since *The Marrying of Ann Leete*, the opacity of Barker's dialogue had cleared to reveal the kind of incisive austerity which he had been demanding from Shaw. In its realistic depiction of a professional Edwardian family and its criticism of capitalism, *The Voysey Inheritance* was a monumental play for their times. When the curtain came down, Archer ran to his typewriter and excitedly tapped out the news, beginning his review on 14 November with the proclamation that 'With *The Voysey Inheritance* a new force enters the dramatic field.' At long last, the new English realist dramatist had arrived.

The world of the play is one of men, capital, business ethics and moral values. Its settings are the dining-room in the home of the wealthy, self-satisfied and silkily-rancorous Voysey family in Kent, and the Lincoln's Inn office of the highly-respected Voysey and Son legal practice. Here, Voysey tells his son, Edward, that for years he has used the trust funds in the firm's care for personal speculation, appropriating the sometimes very high returns for himself while paying his clients' interest at the ordinary, low rate. The fraud, he explains, began with his own father. Soon afterwards, Voysey dies and Edward is left with his dubious inheritance.

Young, idealistic and somewhat priggish, Edward Voysey is hardly a man who naturally makes things happen but rather someone to whom things occur. His initial impulse is to confess, relinquish the assets and accept prison if necessary. But Alice Maitland, whom he loves and who has previously rejected his tentative marriage proposals, persuades him that if he can devise a way both to restore the defrauded money to his clients and preserve the company name, then, by overcoming himself he might also win her. But to try and win everything, he is forced to act illegally. The play closes as Edward and Alice discuss their future together.

Barker had written a sharply stylish metaphor of a corrupt England, a state-of-the-nation play. It showed, wrote Archer, 'how worship of respectability, measured by money, entails moral and intellectual degradation, and deadens, even in persons who think themselves perfectly honest, anything like an acute perception of the difference between right and wrong'. Nobody else in modern English drama had written such completely rounded characters as the six adult Voysey sons and two daughters. There was the 'cynical worldliness' of Trenchard, a barrister; the 'domineereing density' of Booth, an army officer; the 'impotent discontent' of Hugh, an artist; the 'stupid self-devotion' of Honor and the 'commonplace frivolity' of Ethel. Only Edward, it seemed, might escape the 'heritage of philistinism' crippling both the Voyseys and England.

Archer was astounded by Barker's sudden emergence as a dramatist of such authority, but he was even more astonished by a critical consensus placing Barker in the shadow of Shaw. GB, it was claimed, was merely GBS without the S. In *The World*, Archer went to great lengths to repudiate his colleagues' claims. He conceded that Hugh Voysey, an artist, and his wife, Beatrice, were loosely 'Shawesque' Fabians but, in 'the originality of its outlook, its technical methods', the play soared above Shaw. *The Voysey Inheritance*, he pronounced, was 'one of the sanest, largest, most human and vital plays of our time'.[32]

As far as Archer was concerned, Barker set a new standard for English writing and the production, which Barker directed but did not appear in, established a new authority for the Vedrenne-Barker performances. Gradually, the Royal Court was reflecting the kind of theatrical ambitions which he and Barker shared. There was still no real repertory system, but successful matinees, especially of Shaw, were moving to the evening bill. The theatre was beginning to be associated with a certain kind of playwright, a particular method of production, and a distinct audience. New and important plays were beginning to emerge. Although several actors came to the Court for a single production, a loose ensemble was already forming, including Louis Calvert, Lewis Casson, Lillah McCarthy, Nigel Playfair and Dennis Eadie. These were actors of intellect and versatility, and it was partly upon them and upon Barker's meticulous casting of actor to character that the Court's burgeoning reputation rested.

The Court also symbolized the growing reaction against more than two hundred years of dominance by actor-managers, from Thomas Betterton at the end of the seventeenth century to Alexander and Tree at the beginning of the twentieth. Modern West End actor-managers ran their theatres as extensions of the fashionable drawing rooms from which they drew their dress circle audiences. But the people who came to the Court were different. Like the audiences for Ibsen and the Stage Society, they were intellectuals; socialists and politicians, writers and artists, radicals and reformers. There was a high proportion of young, educated women. Broadly speaking, mainstream audiences went to the theatre to see their friends and their host and hostess, while Royal Court audiences went to see the play. Barker proudly told a story which exemplified the ensemble ethics of the Court. One day, influenza prevented him from playing Tanner in *Man and Superman* and a notice to this effect was placed at the box office. When one man asked who Barker was, it was explained he was the actor who usually played

Tanner. 'But I suppose somebody will play it?' the man asked. 'Yes,' the box office clerk assured him. 'Then take my half-crown, young man,' came the reply, 'and don't make such a fuss.'

Unlike most actor-managers, Barker began rehearsals by initiating long discussions about the personal history of each character which, if not explicit in the text, was devised between the actors and himself. He became famous in the profession for the seemingly absurd lengths to which he sometimes went, but he maintained it helped the actor discover more about the character and develop a psychologically accurate performance. These were methods developed from those which Archer and Elizabeth had employed for their Ibsen productions, and which Archer had seen August Lindberg using in Scandinavia. They were similar to the techniques being introduced at the Moscow Art Theatre by Konstantin Stanislavsky, who was attempting to replace the traditional Russian declamatory style of acting with a European simplicity. Like Archer, Stanislavsky had been enormously impressed by the pioneering work of the Meinenger Company. So, through Archer, Granville Barker came to stand at the centre of a European revolution in theatrical production.

His reviews of *Major Barbara* and *The Voysey Inheritance* were among the last Archer wrote for *The World*. Hearing rumours that the owners were about to sell the paper, he relinquished his column to Hamilton Fyfe and accepted an offer to become drama critic of *The Tribune*, a Liberal daily to be launched in the new year. 'I have felt for long that in writing for a sixpenny paper one had practically no influence; whereas if *The Tribune* is successful, it might become a power in the theatrical world,'[33] he told a colleague. After twenty-one years W. A. of *The World* became W. A. of *The Tribune*. For his last column on 16 January 1906, he covered Madame Rejane's season at the New Royalty; *Almer Mater*, a four-act play by Victor Stephany at the Great Queen Street Theatre, and an 'undistinguished'[34] *As You Like It* at the St James's, with Lillian Braithwaite as Rosalind. The previous day, a review of the same production inaugurated his new reign at *The Tribune*.

As Archer settled in to a daily instead of a weekly routine, Barker directed Murray's translation of Euripedes's *Electra*, two desultory double bills, and on 20 March, co-directed with Shaw the first public London production of *Captain Brassbound's Conversion*. The Court temporarily set aside its ensemble policy and imported Ellen Terry to play Lady Cecily Waynflete, the role Shaw had written expressly for

her. Sir Henry Irving, her long-time stage partner, had died the previous
year and in 1906, Ellen was fifty-eight ('you look 25'[35] Shaw told her
graciously) and celebrating fifty years on the stage.

Unfortunately, she was even more forgetful than she had been three
years previously in *The Vikings of Helgeland*, and kept her fellow actors
in constant fear of which lines she might forget or omit next.

At the beginning of April, Frances took Tom to Italy for a holiday to
help him recover from the rigours of Classical Honour Moderations,
the second-year examinations he had sat at Oxford at the end of the
Lent Term. Two weeks later, she urgently wired Archer that he had
fallen ill. He left London on the 15th and arrived in Venice two days
later. Tom's temperature was over a hundred degrees and they feared
typhoid, but the fever abated and although he was still weak, Archer
thought him fit enough to be told the results of his examinations, which
he had brought with him. Tom had hardly attended any lectures and
achieved only a second-class pass. Archer's bitter disappointment set
immediately into a cold pragmatism. 'He has not got a first because he
is not a first-class mind,' he told Murray bluntly.

Within a few days, Tom was pronounced well enough to travel. They
went to Paris and on 25 April, Archer travelled on to London by
himself, arriving at Westminster Mansions later that day. No sooner
had he done so than he was in high agitation, firing off a letter to
Murray. 'What's this about Barker's marriage?' he demanded. 'I have
heard nothing of it.'[36]

Hardly anyone had. Barker and Lillah McCarthy, Jack Tanner and
Ann Whitefield, the serious theatre's most celebrated couple, had
married quietly at the West Strand Register Office the previous day.
Coincidentally, as Archer arrived home, the Barkers were leaving on
the first stage of their German honeymoon. Initially indignant that he
was in the dark about the wedding, Archer kept his feelings about the
marriage to himself. He probably realized that neither Barker nor Lillah
were deeply in love, but both of them enjoyed the social aspect of
marriage which entailed being a brilliant host and hostess, or equally
brilliant weekend guests at country houses, and this sustained their
companionship. Theirs was a marriage which would produce no
children.

The friendship between Archer and Barker, like that between him
and Shaw, did not substantially change after Barker's marriage,
although, Lillah being an actress and the marriage a professional union,

Archer saw much more of Lillah in his working day than he did of Charlotte. He liked her and, from a distance, watched over them both while turning his attention to theatre-going for *The Tribune* which 'keeps me busier than ever; but I am fairly fit'.[37]

That summer, he emerged from Benson's *Henry VI* trilogy at Stratford more convinced than ever that Benson was 'an incorrigible despiser of verbal accuracy',[38] while Lewis Waller's *Othello* at the Lyric was 'the best that we have seen in London for many a long day'.[39] At the Criterion, he encountered Edith Lyttelton's *The Macleans of Bairness*, a ludicrous 'Scottish romantic problem play'[40] in which Mrs Patrick Campbell and Harcourt Williams struggled valiantly to make sense of Margaretta Sinclair and Bonnie Prince Charlie but admitted defeat after five nights when the play closed. After Archer had tried to be kind in his review, Edith wrote asking for advice on improving her writing. 'Unfortunately,' he replied, remembering perhaps, his own attempts at serious work, 'there is really no method, so far as drama is concerned, of "learning to swim without going into the water." '[41]

That autumn in Oxford, Tom abandoned his Classical studies for the School of Jurisprudence, raising several academic eyebrows, as it was unusual for a scholar to make such a switch. Once in his new surroundings, he 'adopted, almost wilfully, the average athletic Englishman's attitude of absorption in play and slightly bored indifference to the things of the mind and spirit'.[42] At the Royal Court, meanwhile, Barker was beginning his third season, again of matinee and evening performances, and had discovered another new writer.

John Galsworthy was a fastidiously dressed, sombre-looking former lawyer who a few months earlier had published *The Man of Property*, his first Forsyte novel. He was the son of a wealthy solicitor and, like Hankin, had been educated at public school (Harrow) and Oxford and was disaffected with English upper-middle-class life. Now thirty-nine, he had been galvanized into writing by his wife, Ada, who had become his lover a decade earlier while married to Galsworthy's cousin, Arthur, a reserved, sexually inhibited man with a strong dislike of music. More surprisingly, perhaps, Arthur's reticence extended to complying with Galsworthy's suggestion that Ada's defection should be kept secret from their respective fathers. His reason was that revelation of the affair would upset his elderly parent, a point upon which Arthur agreed, but it appears that Galsworthy may have been equally concerned that a family scandal might adversely affect his inheritance.

His first play reflects his life-long theme that in a society governed by a class corrupted by money and property, there is one law for the rich and another for the poor. *The Silver Box*, therefore, neatly represented Court politics. As the play opens, Jack, the son of John Barthwick, a Liberal Member of Parliament, returns to the family home late one night with James Jones, an unemployed workman and husband of the Barthwicks' charwoman. Both are drunk. Jack offers him drink and cigarettes, invites him to take anything he wants, and collapses on to a sofa. Jones helps himself to a silver cigarette box and a purse, which Jack himself has taken earlier that evening from a non-compliant girlfriend. The indignant girl is successfully paid off but poor Mrs Jones is charged with theft when the silver box is discovered at her home. Her outraged husband assaults a police officer and finds himself beside his wife in the dock of a magistrate's court. Having instructed his lawyer to protect his son's reputation, Jack appears as a witness, commits perjury and is mildly reprimanded for a youthfully unwise escapade while Jones is sentenced to a month's hard labour.

The Silver Box opened as a matinee on 25 September 1906. It was a 'studiously unemphatic' play, thought Archer, which 'skirted pathos a couple of times and hastily sheered off again', but what was remarkable was Barker's 'perfect'[43] staging in which the realistic low lighting and projected shadows of the opening scene contrasted with the noise and bustle of the magistrate's court.

Archer was establishing himself on *The Tribune*, as he had done on *The World*, as the champion of the new. Having reported on Barker, Shaw, Hankin and now Galsworthy, he set off for Berlin in mid-October to see productions by Max Reinhardt, the much-talked about new director of the Deutsches Theater. Reinhardt, who had also staged naturalistic plays and, earlier that year, *Caesar and Cleopatra* (which Barker saw on his honeymoon and reported savagely cut) was exploring an anti-naturalistic style that in a few years would evolve into Expressionism. Archer saw Reinhardt's productions of *The Winter's Tale* ('a vague suggestion of Kate Greenaway'[44]) and *Erdgeist* and *Die Büchse de Pandora*. The central character of these plays, written by Frank Wedekind, an actor and cabaret singer, is Lulu, a young, married, and avidly sexual woman who destroys several lovers, descends into degradation and is eventually murdered.

The plays were hugely controversial and Wedekind widely feared to be an anarchist and a libertine. It was Wedekind himself whom Archer saw stride on to the stage at the Deutsches Theater dressed in a circus ringmaster's uniform of red coat, white trousers and leather boots.

When he commanded a serpent to appear, a workman emerged, bearing in his arms Lulu dressed in a white Pierrot costume. This was Gertrud Eysoldt, a beautiful, thirty-five-year-old actress who had appeared with the Meinenger Company and already created a sensational reputation in Berlin as Salome, and in various Ibsen roles. As Lulu, she was 'the incarnation of soulless femininity'. Archer had never seen plays quite like these, 'an assemblage of horrors', a bewitching mixture of bleak realism, raucous eroticism and unpredictablity. Neither had he seen such acting, controlled but 'recklessly realistic'.[45] In *The Tribune*, he confidently predicted that if staged in England these plays would provoke a far more vitriolic response than *Ghosts* and make even the Stage Society's hair stand on end with fright. (Nobody rose to the challenge: as *Lulu*, the plays were not performed in Britain until 1970.)

He returned to London for Shaw's new play at the Court in which Granville Barker expired of consumption as Louis Dubedat, and Lillah McCarthy mothered and defended him as Jennifer. *The Doctor's Dilemma* owed its inspiration partly to Shaw's vaulting distrust of the medical profession and partly to Archer's challenge that he could not write a convincing death scene.

In an article in *The Clarion* earlier that year, Shaw accused Ibsen of being preoccupied in his work by death. Archer saw this as yet another opportunity to direct Shaw on to the path of becoming a better dramatist and on his new Blickensderfer 'compact' typewriter, purchased at Shaw's recommendation, ticked out a response which he published in *The Tribune* on 14 July as 'Death and Mr Bernard Shaw'. Shaw, he remarked, was so 'fatally at the mercy of his impish sense of humour' that he was incapable of writing truthfully about death. 'It is not the glory but the limitation of Mr Shaw's theatre that it is peopled by immortals.'[46] 'Stung by this reproach from an old friend,'[47] Shaw promised that he would not only write a play about death, but that it would be his funniest yet, in five acts and with the death scene correctly placed at the end of the fourth. On 19 November, a day before the new play's opening matinee at the Court, he assured Archer that *The Doctor's Dilemma* 'will not puzzle you: it is a Child's Guide compared to Major Barbara, which I now hardly understand myself.'[48]

From one point of view, the play is a melodrama in which Sir Colenso Ridgeon, who has discovered an antidote to tuberculosis, must decide between treating Blenkinsop, an uninspiring but virtuous East End doctor, or Louis Dubedat, an immoral but talented artist and a self-confessed disciple of Bernard Shaw. From another, it is a medical farce lampooning the bizarre pet theories of dangerously bumbling surgeons and from a third, it is a variation upon the Shavian triangular relationship. But in this case, when Dubedat dies, Sir Colenso's infatuation for his widow is rejected.

In a virtuoso 2,000-word *Tribune* review (written, like all his *Tribune* reviews, overnight), Archer acclaimed the play as Shaw's most brilliant. Never was he 'more witty, more penetrating, or . . . more human'. Wit, penetration and humanity had carried Shaw victoriously into the fourth act and almost as far as the death scene itself, which was 'enormously clever in an uncanny fashion'. But the point was that Shaw had not noticed that he had entirely run out of steam. Instead of ending the play at Dubedat's largely ineffective death, he had pointlessly kept it going into an excruciatingly dull epilogue, 'explaining all over again things that we knew by heart'.[49]

Archer knew that Shaw was notoriously long-winded, but he was alarmed, as he watched the production, to see a curious transformation in Lillah McCarthy. Having taking a month's course in posture and muscle control with Frances, Lillah McCarthy was confident her acting was more natural. 'I learned to move more easily and, when standing still to remain if need be, quite immobile.'[50] But her Jennifer Dubedat was the most unnatural performance Archer had ever seen her give. Somehow, either by Frances or by Shaw (perhaps both), the 'truth and feeling had been staged-managed out of her', while Barker's long course of Shavian heroes had led him into a disturbingly 'unreal, peachy'[51] delivery which Archer implored him to drop if he was to retain any credibility whatsoever as an actor. Yet these were minor complaints in the light of the fact that as Dubedat died, Archer had felt not one flicker of emotion, and neither, he suspected had Shaw or anyone else. His challenge still stood.

So did the insoluble problem of Shaw's merits as a dramatist. There was 'no doubt' that posterity would have to come to some sort of decision about Shaw. 'Will he be remembered as a really great writer,' he wondered, 'or only as the most brilliant journalist who ever lived?'[52] At the moment, he had no answer.

That winter at King's Langley, heavy snowfalls turned the garden, the quarry, the copse and the fallow fields white to the horizon. Archer sat in front of the fire, read, caught up with his work and took stock. He was now fifty and it seemed that already he had completed a lifetime's work. He had been a theatre critic for twenty-seven years and, according to Barker, was 'one of the chief formative influences in the English theatre'.[53] But with Ibsen's death and Elizabeth's retiral from the stage it seemed as though a line had been drawn beneath the nineteenth century. Shaw, of course, was a constantly invigorating and irritating presence, and as Ibsen and Elizabeth faded professionally into the background, Granville Barker emerged into the foreground. Archer's life and work entered a new phase and took on renewed energy. That the New Drama, for which he had been relentlessly campaigning for years, was being finally and confidently established at the Court was 'by far the most hopeful symptom in our theatrical life'.[54] He looked forward to the future.

The Shaws were now his near neighbours, for in November they moved into the old Rectory at Ayot, a village about twelve miles away. Over the years, they became regular visitors, especially when Shaw took to motoring. Like Archer, they kept a place in London, in their case the flat in Adelphi Terrace. On 2 February 1907, Archer escaped the bitter cold of Hertfordshire and headed for the palm-fringed promenades of the French Riviera, visiting Boulouris and Mentone before crossing the Italian border for four days at St Remo. Before he left, Barker had asked him where he might be able to get hold of a bust of Ibsen. 'If you are tactful you will not ask for what.'[55] Archer was thankful to be off. He had no wish to be present at the first public performance of *The Philanderer*. When he returned at the end of the month, the furore had quietened and Barker was preparing to direct Mrs Patrick Campbell in *Hedda Gabler*.

Archer conceded that the production 'came out well on the whole', although Barker (who was rather frightened of Mrs Campbell) had entirely misdirected the scene in which Hedda burns Lovborg's manuscript. The 'fatal mistake', Archer told him, was that once Hedda had thrust Lovborg's manuscript into the fire, she had closed the stove door. His reasons were perfectly logical. 'Even though she might draw back,' he pointed out, 'Hedda would never take her eyes off the manuscript until the last shred of it was consumed.'[56]

Having directed a play in which Elizabeth had once starred, Barker turned to directing one that she had written. Elizabeth had become absorbed into an increasingly militant women's movement. She became a committee member of Emmeline and Christobel Pankhurst's Women's Social and Political Union, made frequent speeches and in two years would become the first president of the Women Writers' Suffrage League and a founder-member of the Actresses' Franchise

League. She joined rallies in Trafalgar Square, demonstrated outside the Houses of Parliament and became caught up in running scuffles with mounted police. In the autumn of 1906, writing 'at white heat,'[57] she completed a new play in which Vida Levering, persuaded to have an abortion by her lover, Geoffrey Stonor, achieves moral compensation several years later when he becomes a successful Conservative Member of Parliament. Vida, a woman's rights activist, persuades him to support women's suffrage in the House. Nine years earlier, Barker had sent *The Weather-Hen* to Elizabeth; now, Archer having read a copy, she sent her play to him. It was a sprawling script which, with her approval, he cut, re-wrote extensively and entitled *Votes for Women!* after the slogan on the banner at the suffrage rally in Trafalgar Square during the second act.

Votes for Women! was Elizabeth's first play to be produced and the first performance on the afternoon of 9 April was received with tremendous applause by the usual Court audience and by the ranks of Women's Social and Political Union members who filled the stalls, cheering and drumming their feet on the floor. As Archer was travelling, he did not see it on its first outing, but when it was revived the following month. Elizabeth had described it as a tract, and yet while Archer ('a convinced adherent of women's suffrage') agreed that 'the English stage, even with Mr Shaw in full blast, stands greatly in need of tracts', he doubted *Votes for Women!* would interest anyone who was not already a supporter. It was loosely written and badly acted, he remarked, but 'a play that says something, and says it with vigour and conviction, is an exceedingly welcome rarity'.[58]

It was yet another of his enthusiasms which took Archer abroad that spring. In his early love letters to Frances he had proposed a modest spelling reform, mostly consisting of dropping the 'u' from words such as 'favour'. He had never gone to the extent of joining the English Spelling Reform Association, one of whose members, the phoneticist James Lecky, determinedly signed his letters 'jeemz leki'. But neither had he lost interest and recently, with varying degrees of success, he had been introducing his refinements into his weekly *Study and Stage* articles in the *Morning Leader*.

The previous year, the Simplified Spelling Board had been founded in New York and had immediately swung into action, recommending three hundred departures from conventional English usage. This was just the sort of thing Archer enjoyed, as it appealed irresistibly to his sense of the rational. Simplified spelling was modern, labour- (or labor-) saving, and smacked of American good sense and practicality. He envisaged a rationally written English becoming the dominant international language, binding disparate cultures together and perhaps even replacing the Empire as an agent for world peace and development. In the *Morning Leader*, he called for an international commission of eminent scholars to refine English spelling and produce a Rational Spelling Book as the official handbook of the Simplified Spelling Board, whose job it would then be to encourage newspapers and magazines 'by bribery and corruption'[59] if necessary, to translate at least some of their articles into new spelling. In time, he promised, it would be sure to catch on. This was the message he took with him to New York when he was invited to address the Board on 3 April 1907 at the Waldorf-Astoria Hotel.

His invitation to speak came from the Board chairman, none other than his old friend Brander Matthews, now Professor of Drama at Columbia. 'We pay your expenses over and back,' Matthews assured him, 'and hotel bills here also for a week or a fortnight.'[60] Archer sailed on the *Lucernin* on 23 March and arrived in New York in time to see an 'admirable'[61] production of *Mrs Warren's Profession* at the Manhattan Theatre and a 'very interesting'[62] performance of Ibsen's *The Pretenders* by the Dramatic Society of Yale University, to which he was invited by William Lyon Phelps, the Lampson Professor of English Literature.

America was welcoming him again, and installed him, free of charge, at the Hotel Belmont, a huge monolith rising ponderously above 42nd Street and Park Avenue. The hotel was an adventure in itself. There was a choice of five elevators to waft him up and down to and from his fifth floor room where a central heating system growled and gurgled in the night. There was a telephone and a complicated method of ringing the reception desk. He had a private bathroom, equipped with soap and toothpowder and a curious implement for heating curling tongs. Downtown, at the Waldorf-Astoria, he gave his speech to the Board, his proposals were approved, and off he plunged into 'the Great White Way' of Broadway, theatre-going. He sped on to Pittsburg, where he saw an 'execrably acted'[63] *Man and Superman*, and then to Boston for a week and to New Haven to stay with the Phelpses. On 30 April, exhausted, he sailed for England on the *Ivernia*. In London, the third Vedrenne-Barker season was fizzing to its close with a double-bill of *Don Juan in Hell* (from *Man and Superman*): 'a brilliant freak'; and *The Man of Destiny*, which 'bored'[64] him.

*

The three-year experiment was over. Vedrenne was eager to brave the West End and so they moved out of the Royal Court, took their manuscripts and programmes and papers, and said farewell to the actors. The 'inordinate prominence of Mr Bernard Shaw'[65] had occasionally made Archer wonder whether the Court should be renamed the Shaw Theatre but nothing could mar the fact that the experiment had been an outstanding success. *The Clarion* was calling the Court the 'Theatre of Ideas'[66] and *The Referee* was claiming that the Vedrenne-Barker management was 'the best thing that has happened to the stage in our time'.[67]

The record over the three seasons was impressive. They had given 988 performances of thirty-two plays. They had established Shaw and introduced two susbstantial new English writers, Barker and Galsworthy, and a New Drama, symbolized for Archer by *The Voysey Inheritance*, which closely observed their times and especially the property-owning upper middle classes, from a radical, realistic point of view.

The Court years were ceremoniously brought to an end by a dinner at the Criterion Restaurant on 7 July. It was Archer's idea but he artfully persuaded Whelan and several others to organize it, with two menus as Barker, Shaw and several Courtiers were vegetarian. After the meal, Lord Lytton, the chairman, proposed a toast, hoping that one day Vedrenne and Barker would be leading a National Theatre. Barker briefly paid tribute to the pioneers, to Grein, Poel and Archer himself. Then Shaw got up to speak on behalf of the dramatists and talked for so long that by the time he at last sat down it was almost midnight and the police were advising the management that their licence permitted them to stay open no longer. The guests were hastily dispersed into the night. Archer, who was to have given the vote of thanks to the chairman, put his short speech back into his pocket unread, and made his way sadly through the dark streets to Westminster Mansions.

In *The Tribune* of 16 November, Archer recorded that only ten years ago it was required by law that all motorcars be preceded on the road by a man carrying a red flag. In ten years' time, he wondered, would the drama have driven past, or over, its own man with the red flag? For that year, the censor had waved his flag with more vigour and irresponsibility than usual. Redford had refused a performance licence for *The Breaking Point*, a play by Edward Garnett in which a woman, pregnant by her lover, drowns herself. He subsequently published the play in a volume which included a protest letter to the Censor written by Archer but signed by Garnett. More importantly, in October Redford banned *Waste*, Granville Barker's new play.

This was a catastrophe, as *Waste* had been promoted as the main production at the Savoy Theatre, where Vedrenne and Barker were resuming their regime of matinees and short evening runs. The season, which began in September, was not doing well. Neither *Joy*, Galsworthy's second play, nor *Medea*, Murray's new translation from Euripedes, repeated the success of *The Silver Box* and *Hippolytus*. Their audiences were also uncomfortable in a West End theatre which had once been the home of Gilbert and Sullivan, and especially now that Vedrenne had for some bewildering reason observed the rules of the commercial theatre and begun playing the National Anthem at performances.

Waste, which again cut deep into the moral and political fabric of Edwardian society, was intended to bring their audiences back. The leading character is Henry Trebell, a prominent and successful lawyer who is being wooed by the Conservative Party, thought likely to win the next election. Trebell offers to join them if they guarantee him a cabinet seat and a chance to put his new education system into operation. At a political houseparty, he seduces Amy O'Connell, a young woman estranged from her historian husband. Later, to Trebell's horror and just as he seems to be accepted by the Tory hierarchy, she informs him that she is pregnant. Although he promises to stand by her, she undergoes a backstreet abortion and dies. Out of respect for Trebell, Justin O'Connell agrees not to reveal the paternity of the child at the inquest, but the Conservatives, aware that Trebell's uncompromising political views might split the Party, use his private misfortunes as an excuse to reject him. Emotionally and politically isolated, Trebell commits suicide. Barker assumed Redford objected to the seduction scene which closes the first act, in which Amy submits to Trebell's kisses and allows herself to be literally swept off her feet and carried into the garden. This, and the subsequent references to abortion, were considered shockingly explicit. Barker, who a few months earlier had directed *Votes for Women!*, which Redford licensed and in which Vida's abortion was openly discussed, was infuriated but hardly surprised. With all his old campaigning spirits burning brightly, Archer plunged into organizing protest action. He and Galsworthy composed a letter demanding an end to 'the menace hanging over the head of every dramatist of having his work ... destroyed at a pen's stroke by the arbitrary action of a single official neither responsible to Parliament nor amenable to law'. It appeared in *The Times* on 29 October over the signatures of seventy-one playwrights including Barker, Jones, Murray, Pinero, Elizabeth Robins, Shaw, J. M. Synge and Yeats.

Archer followed this by planning a protest march from Trafalgar Square to Downing Street. This was an eccentrically Archerian mix of agitation and patriotic fervour in which Barrie's address from Nelson's Column to the assembled dramatists would be followed by the Savoy Theatre orchestra defiantly striking up *Rule Britannia*. 'The procession will then form, & will be headed by Pinero and Shaw walking arm in arm,' he told a bemused Lady Mary Murray on 1 November. 'Immediately behind them will come Garnett & Galsworthy, each bearing the pole of a red banner with the inscription "Down with the Censor!"' An effigy of Redford, constructed by the Savoy property department, was to be carried by Frederick Harrison and Yeats, while Murray had been delegated to wave a banner bearing the legend 'Ecrasez l'Infame!' The Liberal Prime Minister, Henry Campbell-Bannerman, would be accosted outside Number Ten by the disturbing sight of the deaf and elderly Swinburne declaiming a specially written *Ode to C-B*, and regaled with speeches by Ford Madox Hueffer and Desmond MacCarthy, 'dramatists', Archer explained mysteriously, 'who cannot be suspected of interested motives, as they have never written any plays'.[68]

On the day, however, this fearsome protest crumbled, for the simple reason that Campbell-Bannerman was ill, and so could not see the dramatists, nor listen to Swinburne's poem, nor be intimidated by banners and effigies. Instead, Archer hastily organized a substitute delegation consisting of Barrie, W. S. Gilbert, Pinero and Murray and lobbed them towards the office of the Home Secretary, William Gladstone's son, Herbert. But in spite of Archer's elaborate rehearsals, once closeted with the Home Secretary, the playwriting ensemble disintegrated. For some reason, Barrie read extracts from the works of Charles Dickens, which perplexed everyone. Pinero later assured Archer that his own contribution, recounting the iniquities of censorship, was 'tear-compelling'. But Gilbert's anecdote was 'almost Georgian in its remoteness from the present day'[69] and Murray abandoned his prepared piece and shamefacedly apologized for the embarrassing poverty of the entire proceedings.

Although Archer's campaign ignominiously fizzled out, two private performances of *Waste* were stealthily held by the Stage Society at the Imperial Theatre on 24 and 26 November, when Barker both directed and played Trebell. *The Atheneum* acclaimed the play as 'the most important event of our recent dramatic history'.[70] But the increasingly Conservative Walkley declared in *The Times* that it was precisely because the play was 'the most vivid and probably the most authentic presentation we have yet had on the English stage of great social and political questions' that the Censor had a moral duty to prohibit its public performance. *Waste* was far too disturbing, he warned, to be put before 'a miscellaneous public of various ages, moods, and standards of intelligence'.[71] Even several of Barker's supporters wavered. Archer, so used to suppressing his own emotions, squirmed with embarrassment at the seduction scene. It was 'unnecessary', he murmured in *The Tribune* before hurling himself into the fray as the play's leading advocate. '*Waste* is a great play. It not only stands on the highest level of modern drama – it stands on that level and in a place apart.'

As a ploy to provoke Shaw a few years ago, he had compared him unfavourably to Pinero. Now, in all seriousness, he declared him inferior to Barker. The 'fundamental difference' between them, he wrote, was that 'Mr Barker sees life squarely through a clear atmosphere; Mr Shaw looks at it aslant, through the strong refracting medium of his own personality'.[72] Pinero agreed. 'The great difference between the two, I take it,' he volunteered, 'is that one means every, and the other not a single, word that he says.'[73]

On 28 January 1908, a copyright reading of *Waste*, incorporating Redford's officially-required deletions, was held at the Savoy Theatre. As a gesture of their support, the cast was comprised of Barker's friends and as such, made one of the most eminent (and unlikely) gatherings on a British stage for some time. Laurence Housman read Trebell, and Charlotte Shaw, Amy O'Connell. Galsworthy appeared as Russell Blackborough and Lillah McCarthy as Simson, the maid. Shaw read the Earl of Horsham. Hankin, Murray and H. G. Wells joined in. Archer himself, in his first stage appearance since his performance in *When We Dead Awaken* eight years previously, read Justin O'Connell. A programme was printed, with the readers' qualifications in parentheses after their name. Archer's promised that this would be 'His Last Appearance on any Stage'.

Archer never saw *Waste* professionally performed in public. The play which he would call 'our greatest modern tragedy'[74] was not licensed until 1920 nor publicly performed until 1936, twelve years after his death. If in 1907, it re-ignited the campaign against censorship it did so only by a long fuse, for it was not until almost two years later that the government acted. The credit went neither to Archer nor Barker but to

Robert Harcourt, whose *A Question of Age* had been a notable failure in the early days of Barker's reign at the Court. Since becoming a Member of Parliament, Harcourt had lobbied strenuously for the anti-censorship cause, and finally manœuvred Asquith, the new Prime Minister, into appointing a Joint Select Committee to review the position, and which examined forty-nine witnesses between 29 July and 24 September 1909. Giving evidence, Archer repeated much of what he told the 1892 Select Committee. Should 'the sexual problem' be discussed on the stage, he was asked. 'Decidedly,' he replied. 'As a serious subject?' enquired Colonel Lockwood, incredulously. 'Yes,'[75] said Archer.

This time, his was not the only voice opposing censorship. Archer was supported by Barker, Shaw, Pinero, Galsworthy and Murray who ranged themselves opposite Walkley, George Alexander, Bram Stoker – Irving's former business manager, biographer and author of *Dracula* – and Lena Ashwell, the actress-manager of the Kingsway (formerly the Novelty). The playwrights argued that the Censor prevented the development of serious drama; their opponents protested that in these permissive days, the Censor was an essential protection for managers and actors against the indelicacies of writers. Again the abolitionists failed. The Committee's Report, published in November, recommended that it become optional to submit a play for licence and legal to perform an unlicensed play, but that provisions should be made for the prosecution of the authors and producers of offensive material. It was stalemate. Yet Parliament was as weary of the struggle as the combatants themselves. No legislation was enacted and the following year the government appointed an advisory committee to assist the Censor in his work. Archer lost his battle. Official censorship of the theatre was not abolished until 1968.

When the Royal Court seasons closed, Archer and Barker attempted to revive the National Theatre campaign by publishing their book in a trade edition. The text remained unchanged, but the title was reversed to read *A National Theatre: Scheme & Estimates*, and their names appeared on the title page. At Archer's instigation, Barker wrote a preface, in which he declared they should include in their repertoire 'every author whom we so carefully excluded four years ago – Ibsen, Hauptmann, d'Annunzio, Shaw and the rest'.[76]

Then New York beckoned.

Travelling Years

After the turbulence of his various theatrical campaigns, Archer again looked beyond London and Hertfordshire to the wider world, and during the eight years from 1907 until the war turned the lights out across Europe, he became an insatiable traveller. He made seven visits to America. He saw the new canal being built into the mud of the Panama, bought a sombrero in the punching heat of Havana and walked the snowy imperial streets of Moscow. He returned to Norway. He went to Spain, Mexico, Jamaica, Ceylon and Capri; he made his second round-the-world journey, stopping off in Japan, where he discovered he was famous, in China, where he was not, and in India, where he was known as the 'Burra Sahib'.

In March 1908, he was back in New York, summoned by a consortium of theatre-loving millionaires led by the German-born banker Otto Kahn, whose dream project, the New Theatre, was rising on Central Park West between 62nd and 63rd Streets. Kahn had read *A National Theatre: Scheme & Estimates*, and decreed the New Theatre should go by the book. He offered Barker such a mouth-watering salary to run it that Archer reckoned that after three years he could return to London twenty thousand pounds the richer. Barker suggested it would be 'the correct sequel' to their book if they built Jerusalem on the edge of Central Park together. He would be the artistic director and Archer the dramaturg, 'with a professorship at Harvard or Columbia . . . you *have* had enough of criticism.'[1]

Barker was right. The triumph of the past five years had deflated with the troubled Savoy Theatre season. On 25 November, the 'glittering hotch-potch'[2] of *Caesar and Cleopatra* briefly invigorated a programme devoid of all the energy of the Royal Court. All that remained for Archer to look forward to was the never-never land of

Peter Pan at the Duke of York's. 'Nothing can keep me away from *Peter Pan*.'[3] At the beginning of January, he angrily stalked out of Brookfield's marital farce, *Dear Old Charlie* at the Vaudeville, when Barker was mocked as a Mr Bleater who had written a play called *Sewage*. A few weeks later, *The Tribune* closed having lost money and readers. Archer's last article appeared on 1 February, just two years after his first. He had already given up his occasional work for the *Manchester Guardian* and so for the first time in almost thirty years, he was without a regular drama column. With his journalism reduced to weekly commentaries in the *Morning Leader* and book reviews for the *Chronicle*, his voice, like Barker's, was suddenly diminished. There was nothing to keep either of them in London. Or England, for that matter.

They sailed for New York on the *SS Celtic* on 19 March, Archer having arranged to address the annual meeting of the Simplified Spelling Board and thereby ensuring his passage and hotel bills would be paid. The ship was buffeted by gales and, although Archer kept himself just about on his feet with large doses of Mothersill's anti-seasickness mixture, Barker was relying on stuff prescribed by his own doctor and was ill and bad-tempered. Radio messages from Kahn beckoned them onward, crackling and fuzzing through the wind and the rain, and they arrived in New York on 28 March. One look at the New Theatre convinced them that it was far too cavernous for non-commercial plays relying upon detailed, realistic acting. Leaving the 'Muddled Millionaires',[4] a penniless Barker sailed home to Court Lodge, the Elizabethan house he and Lillah rented in the Kent countryside. Archer stayed on at the Belmont. He had not been offered a professorship, although he did lecture on *The Elizabethan Playhouse* at Yale. Instead, he addressed the Simplified Spellers and then set off on his first assignment for the American monthly *McClure's Magazine*.

The editor of *McClure's Magazine* was Cameron Mackenzie, a Law School graduate and former *New York Sun* staffer. Under his leadership, the magazine published sensational fiction and anecdotal features, and readers soon encountered Archer deliberating upon whether it was possible to foretell the future (yes, perhaps), and pondering on the pleats and tucks of Paris fashions. But *McClure's Magazine*'s reputation was founded upon lengthy documentary essays for which Mackenzie paid staggering fees of between £200 and £500, far more than the editor of an English journal expected to pay for the entire contents of a single issue. Over the next few years, he commissioned several pieces from Archer, promoting him as 'the experienced English observer of world affairs'[5] and pitching him into a series of remarkable adventures.

First, he was commissioned to travel through the southern states of America and report on what was then known as the colour problem. From a prodigious amount of background reading, Archer learned that of the ten million black people in the United States, nine million lived in the south where they constituted one third of the population and in some areas outnumbered whites. Although slavery had been abolished for forty years, most black adults remained illiterate and their children benefited from only one sixth of the national education budget. Even the few who had made any headway in the professions had virtually no voice in municipal and political life. The south boiled with racial tension. There were riots, lynchings and the death count was rising. Britain, with its Empire over which the sun never set and with its own ghettoes forming in the smoking shadows of its ports, watched America warily. On both sides of the Atlantic, integrationists and segregationists battled in print. 'These are questions which the coming century will have to answer,' Archer noted, '[and] not only in America . . .'

On 16 April, he left 'the shrewd, bracing blasts of New York' for a few days in Chicago, from where he caught a slow train to Washington. 'In Indiana, rain; in Ohio, torrents; at Pittsburg, a deluge.'[6] The next morning, he awoke to see from the railroad car window that spring had arrived. Sunlight flickered and flashed across the rich Maryland woodland of blue-green pines, silver-green poplars, golden-green birch and dashes of red maple. It danced across the faces of the young couple, one black, one white, who sat opposite him and who told him their home-state laws prevented marriage between the races. The train pulled into Washington. Archer alighted and made for the White House, where he had an appointment with the President. Eight years previously, when he was Governor of New York, Theodore Roosevelt had read *America Today: Observations and Reflections*, and written Archer an admiring letter. As he was also a keen simplified speller, Archer had got in touch, with the result that they had 'an amusing talk',[7] if somewhat inhibited by the intrusive James Bryce, the British ambassador. Afterwards, Archer went out on to the White House steps and from there, began his descent into the deep south.

At a resort hotel at Virginia Hot Springs, he spoke to the rich white guests putting their way across the golf course, and moving soundlessly across the deep-pile carpets in the lobby towards telephones linking them to their Wall Street stockbrokers. They warned him of no-go areas in southern towns, of drink and drugs corroding the black communities. He went to Louisville, Kentucky, and then Memphis, Tennessee, where he discovered only whites could hold readers' cards at the public library. At the local bookshop, the owner leaned across the counter and whispered that the Ku-Klux-Klan was saving America. A black lawyer vehemently told him that no white man understood the black man because no white man wanted to.

Everywhere Archer went, he talked to shopkeepers, waiters, lawyers, doctors, teachers, and passengers on the railroad. White segregationists told him they zealously instructed their children to believe in their own racial superiority, and at the very least to ignore all black people. The black male, they explained, was innately over-sexed. 'Outrages' had been perpetrated upon innocent white women and to prevent more, blacks must be kept at bay in parks, public buildings, streetcars and trains. Liberal integrationists told him how they tried to build trust and found schools, and then despairingly described the shootings and lynchings. Sometimes a man was lynched for a crime he had not committed, or even when there had been no crime at all. The nation was going mad.

On bright, clear days, a passenger-segregated train took him snaking along the Mississippi valley, through deep green forest reflected in clear waters. Each station was freshly painted and each divided into separate areas for white and black passengers. At Vicksburg, he got out and in the still air of the midday heat, went for a walk. The sloping streets, dimly lit shops, and lounging, outdoor life reminded him of an Italian hill-town. But Vicksburg was his first real taste of the south, the first place where the black population appeared to be in the majority. Although most of the blacks he saw seemed unassuming, rural people, dawdling in the heat and preoccupied with reading the local newspaper, Archer was acutely conscious of being a long way from London and so conspicuously in the minority. He climbed back on to his whites-only car and, with a hooting and jolting, the train moved forward once more.

'What I *think* about the colour question may be superficial, and may be foolish,' he wrote, 'but there is evidential value in what I *feel* . . . There are some negroes (so called) with whom I should esteem it a privilege to travel, and many others whose companionship would be in no way unwelcome to me; but frankly I do not want to spend a whole day in the Mississippi Valley cheek by jowl with a miscellaneous multitude of the negro race.' This was an uncomfortable realization. Archer wanted to approach his investigation with an open and above all rational mind, but in common with most of his contemporaries, including Shaw and Elizabeth, he believed that each race had its innate characteristics and intellectual abilities, which meant that some were compatible with others and some were not. 'However fallacious may be the boundaries between this and that European race, the boundary between the European and African is real, and not to be argued away,' he maintained.

They were roaring across the low, flat Mississippi delta, towards New Orleans, a loud, blustery, ragged city in which the only architecture of any distinction was behind cemetery gates in the form of magnificently decorated tombs and headstones. The clanking, bumping streetcars swaying this way and that, their rear seats marked 'For Colored Patrons Only', made the knotty network of city-centre streets resemble a dilapidated railway yard. In the French Quarter, 'a rookery of grimy and dismal slums', Archer made his way along the Rue Royale, where he found a restaurant, sat down and ordered Creole Gumbo, a local speciality soup of ham, chicken and seafood. Placing his notebook by his plate, he tasted tentatively, made a note, and then tucked in to a delicious meal. Through a patchwork of contacts, he had arranged all his lodgings in advance, and early one Sunday morning, his suffragist hostess in New Orleans took him to see a boot-blacking factory. In the gloom of a long gallery, he saw a scene reminiscent of Dickens, a dozen small boys bending unhappily over their work, pasting labels on to the pots of blacking, and packing them in boxes. There was a law against employing children under twelve, his guide told him, but nobody bothered. These children were Greek, considered better workers than black children who reputedly fell asleep too quickly and had been demoted to night-time messenger work. She and Archer stood, filled with helpless dismay, watching the exhausted children silently pasting and packing.

North-west now, to Montgomery, Alabama, with its rich red soil; Birmingham, a place of iron and steel where laundries promised that all their clients were white; to busy, windy Atlanta, Georgia, to see the scene of a race riot in which several black people died; and to Charleston, South Carolina, where an elderly banker and philanthropist, every tooth in his head capped with gold, took him visiting well-to-do black and mixed-race families. Every home seemed to have a piano, and several families were stalwarts of the local whist club. One proudly showed him their picture of the Houses of Parliament.

In Charleston, he attended church, something which until now he had never voluntarily done in his life. Sitting among an African Methodist congregation dressed in their garish Sunday best, he prepared to watch the proceedings as if he were stationed in the stalls at the Court, having no idea that here the audience would participate themselves. The Minister had been preaching for only a few minutes when someone near Archer mumbled 'Oh yes! Praise the Lord.' A few seconds later, it happened again, only louder and from another part of the church and to nobody's surprise except his own. These apparently random interjections prompted others, gathering quickly in frequency and volume until they became 'quite inarticulate, passing over into wails, moans, and now and then a sort of wild maniac laughing and yodelling'. He was captivated. Nothing, he noticed, put the preacher off his stride. Quite the reverse. The noise seemed to galvanize him into even greater oratorical extravagance, just as he in his turn inspired the congregation, until the church reverberated to 'sounds not unlike the yelpings of a large kennel'.

South to Jacksonville now, and on to St Augustine, Miami and the Florida Keys where the train thundered along a sweeping causeway, leaning into the curve on the edge of a vast and glittering ocean. A ruthless sun flared down upon mangrove swamps and beat through dense, vine-contorted trees to lagoons from which he sometimes glimpsed heron rising, flapping long wings. It was the first week of May and he was nearly the end of his American journey. He had made pages of notes on the conditions and the attitudes of whites and blacks, yet the problems, he reflected, were too 'dishearteningly difficult' to be resolved by 'happy-go-lucky humanitarianism'. Nothing other than 'an almost superhuman wisdom, energy, and courage' would ever overcome all those years of mutual distrust, fear and hatred.

He resigned himself to the 'sheer *unlikeness*' of the two races. For Archer, innate racial strengths and weaknesses, combined with a cultural heritage, determined how far each race could climb the ladder of civilization. The Afro-American, in Archer's eyes, was simply not capable of the sophistication of the white American, and 'the fact of this inferiority seems to me as evident as it is inevitable'.[8] It was a defeat for liberal idealism. 'The whole thing is a pitiful tragedy,'[9] he wrote to Murray. Later, in *McClure's Magazine*, and in a book, *Through Afro-America: An English Reading of the Race Problem*, Archer examined the cases for intergration and segregation, and proposed the establishment on the American mainland of a separate state for the black population, but one with all the constitutional rights of the union.

19. Oscar Wilde
in 1894.

20. Elizabeth Robins
as Hilde Wangel.

TRAFALGAR SQUARE THEATRE,

ST. MARTIN'S LANE, W.C.

Sole Proprietors and Lessees ... ... Mr. and Mrs. FRANK WYATT (Miss Violet Melnotte).

Under the Management of Mr. YORKE STEPHENS and Mr. E. W. GARDEN.

MATINEES

FEBRUARY 20th, 21st, 22nd, 23rd and 24th, at 2.30,

Henrik Ibsen's Latest Play,

THE MASTER BUILDER

FOR THE FIRST TIME IN ENGLAND.

Halvard Solness	...	...	...	Mr. HERBERT WARING
Mrs. Solness ...	...	...	...	Miss LOUISE MOODIE
Dr. Herdal ...	...	...	...	Mr. JOHN BEAUCHAMP
Knut Brovik ...	...	...	...	Mr. ATHOL FORDE
Ragnar Brovik	...	...	...	Mr. PHILIP CUNINGHAM
Kaia Fosli ...	...	...	...	Miss MARIE LINDEN
Hilda Wangel ...	...	...	...	Miss ELIZABETH ROBINS

UNDER THE DIRECTION OF

MR. HERBERT WARING & MISS ELIZABETH ROBINS.

21. Programme, *The Master Builder*, Trafalgar Square Theatre, 1893.

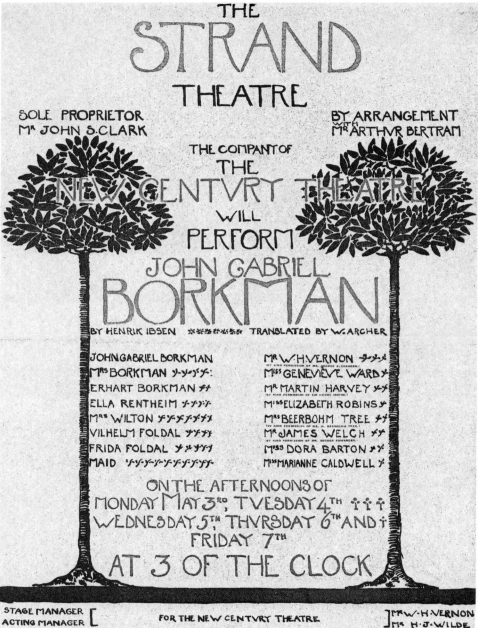

22. New Century Theatre poster for *John Gabriel Borkman*, Strand Theatre 1897.

23. Bernard Shaw and Harley Granville Barker, 1901.

SAVOY THEATRE,

STRAND, W.C.

Lessee - - - - - Mr. J. E. VEDRENNE.

ON TUESDAY, JANUARY 28th, at 11 o'clock,

WASTE

A Tragedy in Four Acts, by GRANVILLE BARKER.

(*As Licensed by the Lord Chamberlain*).

Lady Davenport	.. .. ..	Mrs. W. P. REEVES (Of New Zealand)
Walter Kent	.. .. ..	Mr. GILBERT CANNAN (Of "The Manchester Guardian")
Mrs. Farrant	.. ..	Miss MAGDALEN PONSONBY (By kind permission of LORD ALTHORP)
Miss Trebell	.. ..	.. Miss CLEMENCE HOUSMAN
Mrs. O'Connell	..	Miss CHARLOTTE PAYNE-TOWNSHEND (Mrs. SHAW)
Lucy Davenport	.. .. ..	Mrs. H. G. WELLS
George Farrant	.. .. ..	Mr. ST. JOHN HANKIN ("The Campden Wonder")
Russell Blackborough	.. ..	Mr. JOY GALSWORTHY (his First Appearance)
A Footman	.. .. ..	Mr. ALLAN WADE (his Original Character)
Henry Trebell	.. ..	.. Mr. LAURENCE HOUSMAN
Simson	.. ..	.. Mrs. GRANVILLE BARKER (her First Appearance in this Character)
Gilbert Wedgecroft	.. .. ..	Mr. H. G. WELLS (Of the Theatre Royal, Sandgate)
Lord Charles Cantelupe	..	Professor GILBERT MURRAY, LL.D.
The Earl of Horsham	.. ..	Mr. BERNARD SHAW (Late of the Theatre Royal, Dublin)
Edmunds	.. .. ..	Mr. ARTHUR BOWYER
Justin O'Connell	.. .. ..	Mr. WILLIAM ARCHER (his Last Appearance on any Stage)

Neither the Costumes nor the Scenery have been designed by
Mr. CHARLES RICKETTS.

**24. The programme of the special reading of Barker's *Waste*,
28 January 1908. The cast includes William Archer.**

25. Lord Howard de Walden, William Archer, J. M. Barrie, G. K. Chesterton
and Bernard Shaw, dressed as cowboys for a silent film comedy by
Barrie and Granville Barker. July 1914.

26. Tom Archer.

27. William Archer, Frances and Alys.
King's Langley, 1924.

28. Elizabeth Robins, probably in her fifties.

29. William Archer in his sixties.

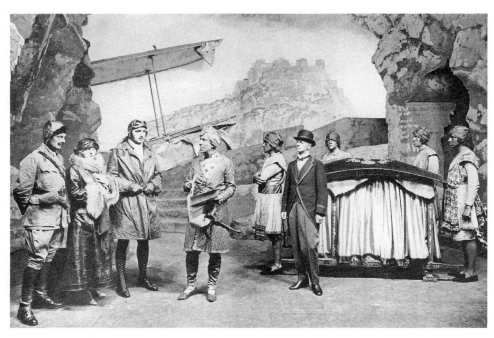

30. George Arliss as the Raja in *The Green Goddess*,
St James's Theatre, September 1923.

31. William Archer's grave,
All Saint's Churchyard, King's Langley.

He had reached Key West, the very tip of America. Deciding that the fee from the article he had not yet written would pay for some travelling, he decided to take the long route home. He boarded ship and a day later, sailed into Havana.

Whenever he was abroad, Archer preserved the formal dress of the Englishman, wearing his usual dark suit, stiff collar and tie. But in the island heat of Cuba, he was horrified to discover that the starch in his collars melted, making him feel as if a clammy hand was gripping his already burning skin. The situation clearly called for a desperate remedy. Once he booked into the Hotel Telegrafo, he went out, bought a sombrero, took a deep breath and placed it on his head, hoping it would save both his neck and his laundry.

It was early May, and Havana's 'arcaded side-walks; its huge windows, all barred with ornamental iron-work . . . its cool green patios' swarmed with festively bright life. The Americans were busy modernizing and Archer squinted approvingly at new roads threading off into fields from which new factories rose. Travelling across Cuba's rich red plains, he arrived at Santiago, where it was painfully hot and naked children shrieked in the street. Boarding the depressingly ramshackle *SS Oteri*, he lay wide awake in a poky cabin, on guard against bugs, and sailed across a sapphire sea to Kingston, Jamaica.

He wasted no time in escaping both the ship and dust and dilapidation of Kingston to travel inland. Here, rivers tumbled through valleys of banana and orange groves and the temperature was 'perfection . . . very warm yet beautifully cool'. In Port Antonio, where he conceded to the heat by recklessly wearing 'the airiest of attire', he sat on the verandah of the Waverley Hotel, writing up his travel notes. In the evenings, he watched a purple twilight slowly veil the palm-fringed bay below him until a tiny lighthouse on the furthest tip of the headland began blinking through the darkness. Jamaica, he recorded, was 'a fragment of Fairyland'.[10]

Before returning home, he sailed to Colon to inspect progress on the building of the Panama Canal. The Americans ran the Canal Zone territory five miles either side of the works, but what he saw there diminished his faith in benevolent America. Rows of hastily-built huts slouched in the mud, housing drinking dens for the black American and the local workers, paid in almost worthless Panamanian dollars, while beyond the works area, the white Americans lived in spacious, well-built accommodation and collected their pay in United States currency. With this grim insight into the divisive empire of capital, he set sail on *RMS Trent* for England on 22 May, arriving on 15 June.

Opening his mail at King's Langley, he discovered that King Haakon VII of Norway had awarded him a Knight First Class of the Order of St Olav, in recognition of his work in introducing Norwegian writing to English-speaking people. The Order is the highest civil honour the Norwegian monarch can bestow upon a foreign citizen, and Archer felt 'several inches taller in consequence'.[11] Yet no sooner were his spirits raised than they were crushed by Tom graduating from Oxford with a meagre third-class degree in law. Retreating to the sanctuary of the Liberal Club, he wrote to Elizabeth, apologizing that 'I am passing through one of those periodic fits of depression that always come upon me when Tom comes down from Oxford ... There is absolutely no sort of sympathy or point of mental contact between us, & the failure of a *possible* companionship makes me feel doubly lonely.'[12]

To pick himself up, he saw Shaw's *Getting Married* at the Haymarket and in contrast to most of the critics, found it 'brilliant and entertaining'.[13] He busied himself with his lectures and weekly *Morning Leader* column, no longer published under the title *Study and Stage*, but the more utilitarian *Things In General*. He urged that Greek should continue to be taught in schools and decided that of all the people he had met, the Americans were both the politest and the rudest. He mused on the nature of fame, the pleasures of reading aloud and reasserted his support of women's suffrage. He lobbied for the abolition of the death penalty and for a campaign against poverty, 'the social conditions in which the vast majority of crimes have their root'.[14] On 8 September, he was in Merionithshire, in Wales, speaking to the Fabian Summer School, an experiment in communal living, in which sturdy lectures were interspersed with even sturdier country walks.

His subject was 'Fabianism and the Drama', a warning against the sterilizing consequences of idealism. By fabianizing 'our ill-organised, ill-educated, ill-sanitated, ill-mannered, and ill-tempered world', he told the collected socialists, the grey-haired disciples of Sidney and Beatrice Webb and the younger followers of Shaw and H. G. Wells, they were cutting out the very roots of drama. The Fabians found this disturbing news, as Shaw was relentlessly impressing upon them how important drama was. But Archer argued that the equal distribution of wealth and the abolition of the class system, laudable and perhaps ultimately inevitable objectives, would also kill off serious New Drama, which thrived upon class and family conflict. The Fabians imagined a collectivized society without 'fuss', but the 'diminution of fuss', he explained 'means the atrophy of drama'. Theatre in a Fabian world would be reduced to 'exquisite spectacle, beautiful music, beautiful dancing'.[15]

Being a knight in Norway did not guarantee an income in England, and financially, he was still only bumping along. But as so often with Archer, something came along to save the day. He became a co-founder of the Simplified Spelling Society, an English counterpart to the American Simplified Spelling Board. At the inaugural meeting on 10 September, Walter Skeat, a Chaucerian scholar from Cambridge, was elected president and Archer secretary on a salary of two hundred pounds a year. A week later, owing to lack of volunteers, he was appointed treasurer as well. Renting a tiny office at 44 Great Russell Street, opposite the British Museum, he equipped it with a desk, typewriter and typist, and applied for funds from Andrew Carnegie, who was underwriting the American Board. Carnegie sent a cheque for £1000 but cautioned that 'I make no further promises, because everything depends on results. Frankly, we expect some work to be done in the old home.'[16]

He had hardly begun his secretarial duties when, on 7 November, after nine months without a drama column, he became theatre critic for *The Nation*, a Liberal weekly paper edited by his old friend H. W. Massingham. But no sooner had he put pen to paper, denouncing Jones's *Dolly Reforming Herself* at the Haymarket as 'moonshine',[17] than he dropped everything and rushed over to Dublin.

Four years ago, when Yeats had invited him to the opening of the Abbey Theatre, Archer had confessed that 'my heroism does not run to facing the Irish Channel in mid-winter'.[18] What changed his mind was that Barker, paying off his Savoy Theatre debts by touring in Shavian revivals, had fallen desperately ill. As he lay in his hotel room, the strength ebbed from him and the doctor diagnosed typhoid fever, the result of drinking infected milk in Manchester. It was even feared that he might die. Archer responded as instantly as if Barker was his own son, arriving seasick and shaken in grey and greasy Dublin, to be at his bedside. Lillah McCarthy joined them, and there Archer stayed until his protégé revived.

Immediately Archer returned to London, he plunged into a bitter dispute with one of the former Court dramatists, St John Hankin. *The Last of the de Mullins*, Hankin's new play, was produced by the Stage

Society at the Haymarket on 6 December. Lillah McCarthy, back from Dublin, played Janet, the eldest and unmarried de Mullin daughter, mother of an illegitimate son and the owner of a successful London hat shop. Even though she has set up the business on a legacy from an aunt and masquerades under the name of Mrs Seagrave and the fiction that she is a widow, Janet is represented as a New Woman, lecturing her family on the importance of women's independence. In *The Nation* on 12 December, Archer applauded Lillah's performance but dismissed the play as weak, the characters flat and Janet de Mullin sub-Shavian. In the next issue, on 19 December, Hankin retaliated, angrily accusing Archer of having 'ratted' on 'the great days' when he led the campaign for Ibsen. According to Hankin, Archer had slithered into conservatism and it was time for him to move over. It was 'Tchekof and the moderns round whom the battle now has to be fought', he cried. 'For that we need leaders somewhat more abreast of the times than Mr Archer.'[19]

The ferocity of this attack upon his authority winded Archer. Although the Stage Society had produced translations of Gorky's *The Lower Depths* and Tolstoy's *The Power of Darkness*, no play by Chekhov had yet been seen in Britain. (The first would be George Calderon's production of his own translation of *The Seagull* for the Glasgow Repertory Company in almost a year's time, in November 1909.) But already Hankin and several other dramatists were buzzing with enthusiasm about him. They had heard reports of the Moscow Art Theatre productions and read Constance Garnett's unpublished translation of *The Cherry Orchard*. Archer had not, and Hankin rebuked him for drifting so far from the centre of things that he had become a campaigner without a cause. On 9 January, Archer dismissed Hankin's claims as 'preposterous nonsense', insisting that he had fought unstintingly for serious drama, even to the extent of being 'laboriously civil to the thin, shrill cleverness of Mr Hankin' and his 'very insignificant productions'.[20] Hankin, he remarked, was one of several Court dramatists whose reputations lay in boasting about what they intended to achieve rather than actually achieving it.

Hankin's assault was especially unwelcome now that the New Drama appeared to be deep in one of its regular hibernations, and it was with some relief that Archer left a snow-mantled south of England, where Barker was recuperating by tobogganing down the slopes surrounding Wells's home in Kent, for a holiday in Norway. A few weeks later, he was back in New York.

*

By the Spring of 1909, Archer had written three Simplified Spelling Society pamphlets, or 'pamflets', urging the use of a 'fonetic alfabet' and had become the Society's ambassador to its sister organization in the United States, speaking at its annual general meeting in April. Somehow, he prised Frances away from her nerve patients and persuaded her to join him for the 1909 event. It was her first visit to America, and at the end of March they stepped off the *Lusitania* and took up residence at the Belmont. His speech spoken, they had a fortnight of intensive theatre-going before visiting Columbia and Yale, Montreal and Boston ('the cradle of nerve training'[21]) and finally Washington, arriving home at the end of May. An exhausted Frances burrowed back into the colony at King's Langley, but Archer returned briefly to New York in November for the official opening of the New Theatre. Winthrop Ames, the son of a railroad entrepreneur and one of the original investors, had become the artistic director and Lee Shubert the business manager. Archer was appointed advisor for European plays and on 8 November, he saw Ames's opening production of *Antony and Cleopatra*, staring the beautiful, tousle-haired Julia Marlowe and her future second husband, the small and dignified E. H. Sothern, whose father Archer had seen on stage in Edinburgh.

Just before he left London, he moved out of his room-without-meals at Westminster Mansions. His combined salary from the Simplified Spelling Society and *The Nation* meant that he could afford more spacious surroundings, and he moved into rooms on the ground floor of 27 Fitzroy Square. It was the other side of Tottenham Court Road from Bloomsbury, and rather dishevelled, but the rent was not expensive. The house stood in the middle of an impressive, grey-faced, four-storied terrace which had seen better days, and was two doors down from number 29, where Shaw had lived for eleven years until his marriage, and where Virginia Stephen (later Virginia Woolf) now lived with her brother, Adrian. Number 27 was owned by a Mr and Mrs Morgan, who lived on the upper floors. Archer had a good-sized study at the front of the building, looking out on the trees in the square, and two other rooms leading off a narrow hallway from the front door to the rear of the house. Frances exchanged her consulting room at number 9 for a room at number 27, which she used on Wednesdays and Saturdays, so that from now on, when Archer was in London, husband and wife saw a little more of each other. This would be his London home for the rest of his life. From here, he planned his last campaigns.

*

From here also, he set out for St Martin's Lane and the Duke of York's Theatre. In March, Charles Frohman, the theatre manager, had, with 'insight, courage and open-mindedness', produced *Strife*, Galsworthy's third play, dealing with the struggle between two political extremists, John Anthony, the chairman of the board of a tin plate factory and David Roberts, the leader of the striking workers. In the end, both men are defeated, Anthony being outvoted by the board and Roberts losing the support of the men. It was reminiscent of Moore's *The Strike at Arlingford* and still more reminiscent of the atmosphere of the Court. Archer hailed Granville Barker's production as 'one of the three or four events of the decade that distinctly marked a stage of progress'.[22]

Strife revived the careers of both Galsworthy and Barker, who had not directed a play for almost a year. Initially scheduled for six matinees, the production transferred to the evening bill at the Haymarket and convinced Frohman there might be both life and money in serious plays. Like Vedrenne, Frohman was a business man with ambitions of artistic credibility. An ebullient, portly American, he had first visited London in 1880 as the manager of a troupe of minstrels. Taking over the Duke of York's, he premiered *Peter Pan* in 1904, so making Barrie a household name and instituting what many generations would come to see as the traditional English theatrical Christmas. Encouraged by *Strife*, Frohman announced the creation of a Repertory Theatre at the Duke of York's for 'the production of new plays by living authors'.[23] He opened on 21 February 1910 with *Justice*, Galsworthy's sixth play, directed by Granville Barker.

Shaw, Edith Lyttelton and Elizabeth Robins had already used the theatre for explicit propaganda but Galsworthy intended *Justice* to be both a successful play in dramatic terms and an effective demand for penal reform, or what Archer called 'a liberal education in rational penology'. The central character, Falder, an inoffensive clerk in a law office, forges a cheque in order to emigrate with Ruth Honeywill, the unhappy wife of a drunkard. The forgery is discovered, Falder convicted and imprisoned for three years while poverty drags Ruth into prostitution. When he is released on parole, she discovers him sleeping rough in a park and asks his former employers to reinstate him at work. Falder waits in the next room. But their hopes for a new and respectable life together crumble when a detective arrives to arrest him for failing to keep them informed of his movements while on parole. Faced with the loss of Ruth and further imprisonment, Falder jumps from a window and is killed.

In order to recreate prison life accurately, Galsworthy visited Dartmoor Prison, not far from his home in Devon, and interviewed several of the inmates. As a result, the short, silent, third-act scene graphically showing the effect of solitary confinement upon Falder, austerely directed by Barker and compellingly performed by a crop-haired, panic-eyed Dennis Eadie, shocked the Duke of York's audiences who inundated Winston Churchill, the Home Secretary, with letters protesting that such torment was practised in their name. Churchill, who had himself been imprisoned during the Boer War, saw the play several times and instigated legislation to reduce the length of time prisoners might be kept in solitary confinement. Archer, for whom this was direct proof of the power of serious, contemporary theatre, celebrated Galsworthy and Barker as the vanguard of a drama which confronted public issues and transformed moral debate into literature. 'If there ever was a dynamic work of art, this is it,' he told the readers of *The Nation*.

Two days after *Justice*, Archer was back at the Duke of York's for Shaw's production of his own new play, *Misalliance*. John Tarleton, director of Tarleton Underwear and a comic confection of Undershaft from *Major Barbara* and the department store proprietor Gordon Selfridge, is surprised by an aeroplane crashing into the greenhouse at his country home. The Life Force alights in the shape of the passenger, Lina, a predatory Polish acrobat. A clerk claiming to be Tartleton's son emerges from a portable Turkish bath, brandishing a gun, while his daughter, Hypatia, throws over her fiancé for the pilot, and the young Lord Summerhays undergoes an unspecified initiation into manhood in the gymnasium. It is as if an Edwardian country house was suddenly invaded by anarchists. Critics were mystified and Archer enjoyed himself hugely. *Misalliance* was 'probably the most stimulating piece of nonsense ever presented', he wrote. 'Of course, like all Mr Shaw's nonsense, it abounds in sense, in suggestion, in thought and food for thought.'[24]

Shaw had written *Misalliance* having heard Granville Barker read his own new play, *The Madras House*, which opened a fortnight later, on 9 March under Barker's direction. Its theme, according to Archer, was 'the position and destiny of women in this queerly-ordered world'. In each of the four acts, Philip Madras of the Madras fashion house, is confronted by women of differing social backgrounds and by problems of business, marriage and family. In the first act, he visits the Huxtables, and their six adult, virginal daughters at Denmark Hill; in the second, set in an ante-room to his office, he listens to the appeals of Miss Yates, an assistant who refuses to reveal the identity of the father of her unborn baby. The only women who appear in Act Three are models parading fashions before Philip, his father, and an American store-owner (loosely modelled upon Gordon Selfridge) and yet, observed Archer, it is 'devoted to a discussion of female character and function, which I venture to call one of the most scintillating passages in modern literature'.[25] In the fourth act, Philip and his wife, Jessica, (like Edward and Alice in *The Voysey Inheritance*) discuss their future together.

As Barker had the misfortune to follow Shaw on to the stage with a play also using the metaphor of a fashion house to represent the state of the nation, he was again accused of simply imitating Shaw. This, persisted Archer, was 'one of the shallowest of critical errors'.[26] Shaw, he explained 'is not in any sense of the word a pioneer: he is not making a path which others can follow. He is a phenomenon apart . . . his aim is not to depict life but simply to express ideas.' This, for Archer, was not enough. He wanted plays which showed 'a true and significant picture of life'[27] and this is exactly what Barker and Galsworthy gave him. *The Madras House* was 'as solid and serious' as *Misalliance* was 'flimsy and flighty',[28] while *Justice* had established Galsworthy as 'one of the most original dramatists, not only of England, but of Europe'.[29]

However, this was not to say there was nothing wrong with *The Madras House*. Apart from Philip announcing his intention of becoming a reforming member of the London County Council, the play has no plot and there is no conventional beginning, middle and end. Rather, each act forms a variation of the theme of the status of women and the play as a whole becomes a series of fluid, overlaid conversations, which apparently have had a life before the play has begun and will do after it ends. Archer found these new techniques intriguing but warned Barker that the play 'drifts away into sheer talk . . .'[30] Instead of clarifying life, over three hours of talking left things as complicated as they were before. *The Madras House* was 'a brilliant and fascinating piece of work',[31] but it was neither another *Voysey Inheritance* nor another *Waste*. Archer was vaguely uneasy, wondering where the New Drama, which he had nurtured into the world, was going.

Immediately he filed his review for *The Nation*, he left on his travels again. This year, instead of going to New York, he decided to visit Moscow.

He journeyed by train across Europe, arriving at freezing Warsaw. From there, he sat for almost two days wrapped in his overcoat as the train clanked and rolled slowly north-east across a snowy plain so unbroken by trees or buildings that it seemed when he peered from the window he could see the curvature of the earth. Then came woods and then forests of dark pines and silver birch, and thatched cottages with whitewashed walls. But of the great estates described by Turgenev and Tolstoy, he saw not a sign. On and on they travelled, on and on; and then suddenly the train was screeching and shuddering to a stop. Doors were opening and the sharp air bit into this face. He collected his bags and climbed down on to the platform, turned up his collar and hurried through the crowds and the steam and the noise to the streets beyond and 'the clamor and glitter' of Moscow.

On freezing March mornings, Archer walked through snow-lined streets where four-wheeled droshkies, scarcely bigger than bath-chairs, driven by Falstaffian figures swathed in blue, swept in and out between clunking trolleybuses. Rich women swished past him in furs and fashions from Paris, while peasant women shuffled by in home-made sheepskin coats, the fur turned inwards and the outer leather stained a deep ochre. He toured the fabulously-decorated cathedrals of the Kremlin, their golden domes bright in the pale sun, their interiors dark and the air thick with the scent of incense. Moscow was 'a swift, fantastic dream'[32] from which he awoke with a jolt, when he arrived back in London and discovered the Duke of York's Repertory Theatre was failing. Like Vedrenne, Frohman was not prepared to buy artistic credibility with bankruptcy. When, on the night of 7 May, it was announced the King had died, Frohman took the opportunity of the general closing of the theatres to announce that with the end of the Edwardian era had come the end of his adventure in repertory.

Archer blamed the failure of this latest experiment in serious theatre on inadequate planning, the lack of a single artistic director (Barker, Shaw and 'Dot' Boucicault had each been given an even hand) and a badly chosen acting company. Barker was convinced the future for repertory now lay in the provinces, perhaps with Annie Horniman's Gaiety Theatre in Manchester, but Archer maintained that it could still succeed in London. Ten plays had been produced in seventeen weeks at the Duke of York's which was no mean achievement, but it was also clear to him that if a National Theatre based on his ideas was ever to materialize, it would have to be supported by a lot of money.

Meanwhile, he was preparing for his next *McClure's Magazine* assignment by learning as much Spanish in as short a time as possible. He was off to investigate the military execution the previous year, after a general strike and anti-clerical rioting, of Francisco Ferrer, a radical teacher who, in defiance of the Catholic church, had preached free-thought at the Escuala Moderna in Barcelona. Archer arrived in Spain in July, and toured Toledo, Madrid and Burgos, riding on trains steaming slowly through rich, golden countryside. In Barcelona, he interviewed legal officials and Ferrer's relatives, former pupils and friends, and in his articles and subsequent book, *The Life, Trial and Death of Francisco Ferrer*, concluded that, irrespective of his innocence or guilt, the State and clergy had colluded in 'malignant stupidity'.[33] One Sunday, he put on his straw hat and, notebook in hand, joined the crowd at the Plaza de Toros, a vast amphitheatre decorated with bunting, where he paid three pesetas for a seat in the shade. In the arena, a bull loped dejectedly this way and that beneath the burning sun, flicking its head dazedly from side to side as bandarilleros slid long, beribboned darts into its shoulders until they streamed with blood and the animal was weak enough to be safely killed by a prancing matador. Archer thought it 'contemptible'.[34]

He described all this to Elizabeth in Sussex. She had rented Backset Town House near Henfield, a fifteenth-century farmhouse with a garden where she grew roses. It was a quiet place where she could open the windows and still concentrate on writing, and where Archer frequently arrived by train to see her. In November, he told her that he had argued with Massingham, who objected less to his recurrent absences than he did to Archer's insistence that he, and not Massingham, select the plays for review. The result was that Archer wrote his final column for *The Nation* on 10 December.

He fell back upon his work as secretary of the Simplified Spelling Society, but as he now worked only part-time, he halved his salary to one hundred pounds a year. With Walter Rippmann, who took over as treasurer, he wrote the Society's handbook, *Proposals for a Simplified Spelling of the English Language*, outlining their phonetic principles and which, in a substantially revised form, is one of the publications still issued by the Society today. In April 1911, he was back in New York.

'Here I am again ... on my old mission of destroying the English language,'[35] he hailed Phelps from the Belmont. Accompanying him was Tom, now twenty-five, whom Archer and Frances hoped would be sufficiently inspired by America to take up some sort of enterprising career. But trailing his father on his next *McClure's Magazine* assignment was not part of the plan. Instead, he was diverted to friends at Yale, Harvard and Boston while on 18 April, Archer started southward to report the downfall of a Mexican dictator. 'What a marvel of youth and adventurousness you are!'[36] exclaimed Murray admiringly from Oxford.

The dictator was the eighty-year-old Porfirio Diaz, whose despotic, American-supported presidency had been tottering ever since he made the astonishing announcement after twenty-five years in office that he thought democracy was a very good idea. But when a reformist millionaire, Francisco Madero, stood for the presidency in 1910, Diaz changed his mind and imprisoned him. By the following spring, a cheated electorate was taking to the streets and violence was escalating. For over a fortnight, Archer holed-up at the Hotel Iturbide in Mexico City, 'wholly out of touch with the rest of the world',[37] and prowled the hot, turbulent streets, watching for the gunmen and horrified by the poverty in which most of population lived. Diaz' presidency looked as if it would survive only days at most and in his piece for *McClure's Magazine* he appealed to the United States, perhaps more in hope than expectation after his canal experiences, to support democracy even if it meant sacrificing its own financial and military interests.

His American adventures were only just beginning, however. At Santa Cruz on 4 May, he boarded the *Merida* for New York. It was an uneventful voyage and everything was still quiet when, shortly before midnight on the 11th, as Archer was dozing over a novel in his stateroom, there was 'a great crash, and a shock that sent a shiver through the ship'. He lay still: 'again a dead silence – ominously deader than before, in fact, for even the low pulsing of the engines had ceased'.

He scrambled out of bed, put on a jacket and trousers over his pyjamas and went up on deck. It was dark, deserted and eerily silent. Fog swirled in the electric lights swinging slowly from an awning and below them stood a row of empty deckchairs. A magazine or two lay about. Clutching the rail, he peered into the fogbound night, but could make out nothing. Then he looked downwards and saw a long gash in the *Merida's* side. Later, he discovered they had collided with the *Admiral Farragut*, a fruit steamer on its way to Jamaica. Clattering back down the steps to his stateroom, he dressed quickly and dragged the lifebelts from beneath his bunk, frantically trying to decide which of his belongings he should take with him in case they had to abandon ship. As he shoved his Mexican notebooks and 'a fragment of manuscript' into his pockets, wondering whether his writing would be decipherable after immersion in salt water, it suddenly occurred to him he might not actually survive to find out. He scuttled back up on deck, to find most of the other 350 passengers standing in small groups, some still in formal evening dress, others in nightwear and coats. Nobody appeared to know what to do. Then all the lights went out. 'That, I confess, was not a cheerful moment.'

Realizing that seawater must be swirling into the engine room, Archer groped his way back to his stateroom, rummaged through his trunk, found his little torch and returned to the deck. An officer was calling for women and children to dress warmly and take to the lifeboats. Seeing two Americans, a Mrs Seeger and her daughter, with whom he shared a dinner table, Archer gave them the torch and grappled his way to his stateroom for a third time to find them warm clothing. Fumbling in the darkness, he found his dress-coat, but 'even in a shipwreck one shrank from the grotesqueness of dressing a young lady in a swallow-tail'.[38] At last, he found an overcoat and a tweed jacket which he put around their shoulders before shepherding them to a lifeboat. He stood at the rail, watching as it was lowered into the black sea and cast off into the night.

Pandemonium broke out on the listing deck, officers and crew running this way and that, shouting orders and grappling with the lifeboats, and Archer lost sight of Cadwaller Washburn, another of his dinner companions, a deaf and dumb American artist whom he had met in Mexico. Suddenly, he found himself back at the rail, a rope hanging to a boat already in the water and a young man urging him to go. Not thinking twice, he swung himself over and slid down to outstretched hands which helped him into the crowded boat. They pushed off into the darkness. Within minutes, the fog obliterated the *Merida*, now sinking low into the water and slowly beginning to keel over. As the lifeboat was packed too tightly for anyone to work the oars properly, there was no alternative but to allow themselves to be carried along by the heaving sea. Too late, Archer realized he had forgotten to bring with him his precious supply of Mothersill's Anti-Seasickness mixture, and as they lurched up and down, forward and back, he resigned himself 'to complete misery'.[39]

After an hour, they transferred to the *Admiral Farragut*. The steamer had an alarming list to starboard, but the lights were working and someone said the wireless was being repaired. Archer located Washburn, who had got there ahead of him, and the Seegers who had found blankets and coffee. By dawn, distress signals had been sent and later that day, they abandoned the *Farragut* for the SS *Hamilton* which took them to Norfolk, Virginia. There, 'with nothing in the world but a suit of pyjamas, a jacket & trousers, 3 socks & a pair of Jaeger slippers',[40]

Archer gratefully booked into the Monticello Hotel. He also had his notebooks and a twenty-dollar bill, but the rest of his money, a substantial two hundred and thirty pounds, was locked in the purser's safe and was now at the bottom of the Atlantic. So was the camera he had borrowed from Dibdin, and all his film of Mexico.

He sent Frances a reassuring letter, hoping (correctly so, as it turned out), that she did not know he was on the *Merida*. He and Tom were going on to Jamaica, he told her. Murray was taken aback: 'Spain and Ferrer, then Mexico and Revolution, and then a shipwreck: and apparently no check to your wish for further and wilder experiences.'[41] But on board ship, the adventurer's stomach dipped in fear each time the lights momentarily dipped; he dosed himself with Mothersill's and tried once more to make some headway with Tom. In Jamaica, they stayed at the Hollymount Hotel at Mount Diablo, watching humming birds darting about the hybiscus flowers by day and the fireflies hovering by night, and gazing at the Blue Mountains in the distance. On 22 June, the Coronation Day of King George V, Union Jacks fluttered in the breeze.

The 'fragment of manuscript' rescued from the *Merida* contained notes for a book and during the voyage to England in July, and over the summer and winter at King's Langley, he worked on *Play-Making: A Manual of Craftsmanship*, which he intended as a textbook of serious playwriting. 'There are no rules for writing a play,' he began, and proceeded to contradict himself over three hundred and twelve pages as he analyzed the socially aware, well-made naturalistic play of ideas. He endorsed Ibsen, Barker and Pinero, emphasized the importance of narrative, and pointed out that 'the difference between a live play and a dead one is that in the former the characters control the plot, while in the latter the plot controls the characters'. The 'problem of the modern playwright', he concluded, 'is to make his characters reveal the innermost workings of their souls without saying or doing anything they would not say or do in the real world'.[42]

In September, as summer ended and the days turned colder, his mother died. Grace was seventy-nine. Theirs had been an affectionate though formal relationship, their differing religious views creating a division difficult to cross. She was buried beside Thomas at Crystal Palace Cemetery. Archer spent the new year at Tolderodden. In January, he lectured on simplified spelling in Scotland.

He was feeling at a bit of a loose end as, again, he had no regular dramatic column. His mission to the United States the previous year had been a success in as much that friends had offered Tom a job in a New York law firm. Frances was preoccupied by administering relaxation at King's Langley. Elizabeth was busy with her writing and her politics, while Shaw, Barker and Murray were these days often out of town or otherwise preoccupied. Shaw was being shuttled about the country by Charlotte, who declared he needed rest, and at the same time writing a new play, a harlequinade featuring Christian martyrs, as a result of which Murray received an extraordinary letter from Archer. 'I want to read the Holy Bible.'

For the second time in four years, there seemed nothing to keep Archer at home. Resigning as secretary of the Simplified Spelling Society, he planned his second trip around the world. The United States, of course, was first on the list, then Japan, China, and India. While he travelled, he planned to come to grips with the Christian religion in order to tackle Shaw when he returned. To Murray, he explained, 'I am taking precautions against conversion to Shintoism.'[43]

He left Liverpool on the *Mauretania* on 23 March 1912, and by 4 April, was back at the Belmont. Having ticked off the annual 'speling sinod' from his itinerary, he notified Elizabeth that he had eaten 'a not unpalatable'[44] lunch of tomato soup, fishcakes and baked beans, followed by lemon meringue pie, costing forty cents at the Political Equality Association on 41st Street and Fifth Avenue. That he was the only male intrepid enough to brave the Suffrage Lunch Room, where the crockery was emblazoned with the legend, 'Votes for Women', concerned him far less than the fact that his fellow diners were as fashionably dressed as the women shopping on Fifth Avenue. He could imagine a female president, he wrote, but not one more interested in hobble skirts and beehive hats than politics.

New York was fast and feisty, still the city of the future but after his trek through the southern states and his visits to Mexico and Cuba, he was wondering exactly what kind of future America might expect. Among the purposeful clerks in their featureless suits and the secretaries in their tight skirts, he glimpsed other, apprehensive faces. New York had become 'the toll-house of a continent', and through it were herding increasing numbers of immigrants demanding sustenance and a new life. 'But the limit is surely within sight,' he warned; 'the illusion of the "land of promise" cannot long be maintained.'[45]

'Now I am rushing across the continent to catch the *Mongolia* at S.F.

[San Francisco] on the 10th,'[46] he reported to Elizabeth. By 16 April, he had arrived at Honolulu, where he was horrified to find that the clear, tropical air he remembered from thirty-five years ago had become a toxic industrial smog. Where there was once trees there was a city of warehouses, cranes, candy stores and saloons. He stood on a street corner polluted by exhaust fumes and flicked through the local paper full of advertisements for American motor-cars and false teeth. A paradise had been turned into an Americanized Eden.

At dawn on 27 April, Archer sailed into Tokyo Bay, and from the ship's rail saw Mount Fuji appear through the mist, 'a sort of shimmering opalescence ... a pale pink ghost ... poised, as though utterly detached from the earth'.[47] Later, he walked through the mean and narrow streets of Yokohama, where the wooden buildings seemed flimsy, as if they might suddenly sag and collapse, and around him sounded the clack-clack of the peasants' wooden clogs and the tinging bicycle bells of the rickshaw men. He was noting down all his impressions for the travel articles he was sending to the newly-merged *Daily News and Leader*. Ostensibly, though, he had come here for *McClure's Magazine*. Japan was industrializing and its population expanding at an impressive rate. Wherever he went, chattering, black-haired, bullet-headed children swarmed around him like ants. *McClure's Magazine* wanted to know whether this new and ambitious Japan was likely to become powerful enough to turn against their former mentors and go to war against America.

He spent two 'extremely interesting and agreeable months'[48] in Japan, veering off the beaten track to tramp through the mountains, a land of trees, shrubs, blazing azaleas and hidden Buddhist temples flamboyant with bronze, lacquer and gold decoration. In the cities, the hotels were Americanized but in the country, he submerged into a culture utterly different to any which he had seen before. Each evening, after his day's journey, he arrived at a little family-owned inn in which each room, like those in ordinary homes, was separated from the next not by walls but by panels and paper screens. Usually, the only furniture in his room was a black-lacquer towel rail (which often fell apart when he touched it) and a curious shrine consisting of a porcelain jar containing an azalea branch. There was not even a peg on which to hang his hat. He exchanged his shoes for flat slippers and squatted with his hosts beside an 'hibuchi', or charcoal brazier and, muttering 'O cha' ('honourable tea') reverently accepted a tiny bowl of greenish-amber liquid. He tasted it, winced, and consoled himself with the thought that even Japanese tea was preferable to no tea at all.

Even more hazardous than the tea ceremony was his evening bath, often taken in a 'sloppy, steamy, dingy and uninviting' room where he was told to wash in a basin and only climb into the sunken bath when he was clean. Male and even female attendants emerged from the shadows offering to assist him, something to which Archer heatedly objected. Only once had he shooed them away and ensured they would not come back, did he undress, wash, and lower himself into the neck-high water which, to his supreme discomfort, was always scalding. The reason it was so hot was that he took care to take his bath early, having discovered that everyone in the house, the family, guests, waitresses, coolies and all, used the same water throughout the evening. Sometimes, people did not even wait their turn but actually joined him. 'Four or five people will crouch together in a tub which, to our notions, is none too big for one, and will seethe for an hour in water that would take my skin off,'[49] he wrote indignantly.

At dinner, he sat cross-legged at a foot-high table and picked at pieces of fish, vegetable and 'honourable rice' served in a glutinous mass so it could be held easily by chopsticks, an art which he eventually managed with some skill. At night, he lay between cotton quilts on the wooden floor of his screened room, and read by the light of a kerosene lamp until he fell asleep.

In Osaka he went to a puppet show, and in the shabby suburbs of Tokyo he knelt on small mats in Kabuki theatres, watching plays in which scenes of 'gobbling, gurgling, strutting, squinting romance'[50] were interspersed with broad slapstick comedy. Kabuki, he learned, was a popular theatrical form deriving from the seventeenth century, as opposed to the older and more formal Noh theatre of the court, still performed on a traditional stage and in a style unchanged since the fifteenth century. Archer saw two Noh plays in Tokyo, the more comprehensible concerning the widow of a murdered drummer going imperceptibly mad. 'But as she wore a doll-like, insipid mask, her features did not express frenzy; while her dance, which consisted of a shuffle, as though her ankles were chained together, was a miracle of calm restraint.' Four musicians, seated at the rear of the stage, kept up 'a terrible tom-tomming on two drums . . . and a monotonous shrilling of a single flute, eked out, at times, with an inarticulate vocal wail', while a chorus of eight squatting to one side joined in every now and then with a 'not quite unimpressive chant'.

Noh plays were not really plays at all, but semi-operatic dances in which the actual narrative seemed a minor consideration. Archer, who always wanted a performance to be lifelike and emotionally moving, found the unbending orthodoxy of speech and movement left him cold, but he was struck by the unblemished tradition, the delicacy of the choreography and the costumes, which were 'gorgeous beyond description'.[51] But what surprised him most of all about the Noh theatres in Tokyo and Kyoto were the buildings themselves. They were almost exact counterparts of the English Elizabethan playhouse. The one difference was that in the Noh theatre, the audience sat only on the ground level. Everything else, the thrust stage surrounded on three sides by the audience, the absence of scenery, the positions of the entrances and exits for the actors, even the square shape of the theatre itself, sometimes open to the air, corresponded to the kind of Elizabethan playhouse he had been researching with the theatre historian W. J. Lawrence in England, and with Baker at Harvard. 'I learnt more about the Elizabethan stage in Japan than I ever did from the performances of the Elizabethan Stage Society,'[52] he wrote.

Even more astonishing was his discovery that he was famous. Theatre people, academics, journalists, even shipping agents, nodded rapidly at the mention of his name which, it transpired, was synonymous with that of Ibsen. In Tokyo, they implored him to lecture at Weseda University on *The Future of Drama*. Newspapers clamoured for interviews, but while English was widely spoken, no editor ever sent a fluently English-speaking interviewer and so every conversation lapsed into a tiring system of halting speech and sign language. 'What is the difference between the folk-psychology of Japanese and English audiences?' one earnest questioner wanted to know. 'The nonsense I must have talked must have been appalling,' Archer confided to Murray. On 27 June, he sailed from Kobe to Darien, where his sister, Grace Stedman, and her husband ran a tea plantation. He felt rather self-conscious to hear that his fame had preceded him but was delighted to discover that the local missionary's wife had studied several recent articles about him, from which she concluded that he must either be a comic actor or a music-hall singer. 'Such is fame in the Orient,'[53] he observed contentedly.

'Avoid China,' was the urgent signal Archer sent home from Peking, where he arrived in early July. 'If I *could* describe the desolation, you would think I was exaggerating,'[54] he notified Murray from the hygienic safety of the Grand Hotel des Wagons Lits. He had arrived in China

only a year after Pu Yi, the five-year-old emperor had been overthrown
and with him 250 years of the Manchu dynasty. A tentative socialist-
nationalist republic had been formed, but as Archer mooched about
Peking, he was shocked by the dirt and despair, and repulsed by the
poverty and the sight of women whose feet had been so tightly bound
when they were young that they were now no bigger than a baby's.
Japan was a country with pride in its culture but here even the temples
were neglected and nobody appeared concerned. The 'gaunt, half-
naked scarecrows'[55] who unlocked the thirteen sets of gates of the
Temple of Heaven revealed a Hades of neglect. The Temple of
Agriculture was a wilderness of weeds, some of them eight feet tall, and
the Temple of Confucius was so dank and decrepit it reminded him of
something created by Edgar Allen Poe. It would not be so bad, he
exclaimed, if these were the ruins of a lost civilization. 'But not a bit of
it! All these filthy, weedy, mouldy institutions are supposed to be in full
swing.'[56]

It was only 'a stern sense of duty' which compelled him one day to
negotiate a filthy, vermin-infested street to get to what his guide assured
him was a very high-class theatre. Inside, it was shoddy, boiling hot and
packed with men, naked to the waist, jammed on benches at right-
angles to the stage and leaning on narrow tables bearing teapots and
sweetmeats. The noise, the heat, and the smell of sweat and food
knocked him back on his heels. Clenching his teeth, he squeezed
himself on to a bench between two hulking men glistening with
perspiration, noting that 'I really felt like a hero imperilling my life in
the cause of Science.'[57] On the stage, children danced badly to a
percussion orchestra as the audience talked, drank and threw large
white objects to each other. This mystery at least was solved when he
noticed a man moving slowly between the benches, distributing hot
towels with which men rubbed each other down before hurling them
back.

Archer left the infant republic as quickly as possible towards the end
of July. He sailed for Ceylon and once in Colombo, gratefully booked
himself into the Galle Face Hotel. The town was hot and dusty but the
hotel was cool, its linen crisp and its atmosphere colonially English.
Strolling out on to the private lawns, he stood beneath the palm trees
and watched the rolling surf. On the crowded streets, he studied the
Ceylonese, marvelling at 'their dignity and distinction'[58] and, writing to
Shaw on 7 August, remarked that 'we are a hopelessly insignificant and
vulgar lot in comparison with the extremely handsome and distinguished

people we rule over'.[59] This impression was reinforced at dinner at the hotel where, from his table-for-one in the corner, he watched the 'trivial mob' of English expatriates with barely concealed contempt. There they were, 'the dapper little men in their dinner-jacket uniform, and the overdressed or underdressed women, chattering about the day's racing or the morrow's hockey, and complacently listening to the imbecile jingles ground out by the band'.[60] To Archer, music at mealtimes represented the low-water mark of contemporary Western civilization.

He brought Shaw up to date with Shavian activity in Columbo, where a 'quite respectable' production of *Candida* was touring, which, on the night he saw it, was about half-full, 'not bad, considering the counter-attractions of Mr R. G. Knowles & his wife (described as "the Kubeliks of the banjo")'.[61] Here too, he wrote up his travel pieces and his article for *McClure's Magazine*, assuring America that as Japan had 'yet to prove her qualifications for holding her own in the industrial race',[62] the United States faced no immediate military threat.

Next stop was India, where he planned to stay with Charles and Alice in Baluchistan in the north-west, where Charles was now Officiating Agent to the Governor-General. Early one morning in mid-August, he crossed from Ceylon to Tuticorin and proceeded to Madura and 'plunged straight into the heart of Indian India'.[63] The sun flared down upon a vast land of shimmering colour, of exotic sights and smells. After a week in the south, he began the long rail journey north, to Madras, Poona, Bombay and Ahmadabad, steaming on through the vast, tropical Indus valley. On the journey from Hyderabad the sun was like 'a great furnace-door thrown open in heaven', the heat scorching the putty-coloured plains stretching into infinity either side of the railway. Archer had a first-class compartment to himself in which two overhead fans made no impression on the stifling air. Ice for his soda water melted as soon as he took it from the box. Reaching Sibi at five o'clock one morning, he climbed down on to an already sultry platform and drank 'chota hazri' in the refreshment room, a pot of tea made how Englishmen were supposed to like it, 'strong enough to blow his head off, ruinous to the nerves, and (one cannot but imagine) as destructive as alcohol to the liver'.[64]

From here, they climbed into the mountains of Baluchistan, the train hauled by two engines. Remote and tribal, Baluchistan was larger than Britain but home to a population of only 834,000, and divided between territory ruled by a native Khan under British authority, and that governed directly by the British themselves. As Officiating Agent,

Charles was the chief resident British official, responsible to the Governor-General. Archer looked from the train window across a desolate landscape. Higher still, and here and there he saw shrubs, the occasional drab, mud-walled village and a shepherd trailing a herd of brown sheep. India proper had been left far behind. Late in the afternoon, he alighted at a small station where a driver and dogcart, sent by Charles, was waiting to meet him. As soon as he piled his luggage aboard and jumped on, they set off, jolting and swerving into the hills, escorted by two Sikh policemen, dressed in khaki, with blue and white peaked turbans, rather comically carrying Enfield rifles with fixed bayonets. Thirty body-aching miles later, they arrived at Ziarat, a hill station eight thousand feet above sea level, where the Government of Baluchistan migrated from Quetta for the hot summer months. He saw a mud-plastered building bearing a placard reading 'GR', and deduced correctly that it was the post-office. There was a store selling a few European goods, an Officer's Library holding a sorry collection of eighty tatty novels and a native bazaar with half-a-dozen stalls. The only imposing house was the Residency with its parched patch of lawn, flag-pole and tennis courts. Archer stayed with Charles and Alice nearby, in a house in which each room opened on to the verandah. Mysterious 'back premises' proved to be the lair of a Genoese cook and a gang of servants, three of whom squatted each day on the verandah in the full blaze of the sun, patiently awaiting the summons of the Sahib or Memsahib.

Despite, or perhaps because of their isolation, Charles and Alice upheld the full domestic panoply of the Raj. At dinner on Archer's first evening, three more servants appeared, each one snappily dressed in a white turban, trousers and a long, full-skirted coat with a double row of gold buttons. They addressed him as the 'Burra Sahib', and he was told that 'burra' meant 'great'. Later he discovered it also meant old, and amused himself by speculating which meaning was intended by which servant. Life at Ziarat quickly bored him. Among the English adminis- trators, 'sub-currents of jealousy and tittle-tattle'[65] ebbed this way and that. Once, someone asked him how Bernard Shaw could be a socialist *and* own a motorcar. Archer occupied himself by reading government reports, learning a little Sanskrit and looking forward to 14 September when he watched his trunk, together with Charles and Alice's mountain of belongings, loading on to a caravan of ten camels, ready to leave for Quetta.

There, he sat in the shade of an apple tree to watch 'an amazing performance' in the open-air of *Gorahk Dhanda*, a Hindustani adaptation of *The Comedy of Errors* in which the opening scene was transferred to a coal mine which a gas escape causes to explode, and the villain was beheaded at the end. 'The management had collaborated with Shakespeare even more ruthlessly than Tree,'[66] he wrote to Baker. A few weeks later, he left Charles and Alice and struck out alone through the North-West Frontier before turning south to Lahore, then Amritsar, where he saw the Golden Temple, the holiest of Sikh shrines; and Simla, Hardwar and Delhi. The previous year, King George had announced the Indian capital would be transferred from Calcutta to Delhi. Archer approved entirely. Calcutta, he explained in the *Daily News and Leader*, was 'a creation of British rule and a monument to some of its worst features'. It represented the bogus 'realm of Anglostan' a discredited attempt to smother the culture of a subdued nation by imposing that of the conqueror. The British could ride their horses down streets bearing British names, trot past statues to British notables and post their letters in red pillar boxes. Calcutta, with its racecourse, polo club and English churches, was an artless fake. Delhi, he pointed out, was at least 'the very heart of Hindoostan'.[67]

For Archer, expanding trade and the likelihood that the economically developing and militarily stronger countries would soon pull away from the others in the material race, meant that the world was becoming smaller and potentially more dangerous. The idea of simplified spelling being a sufficient buttress against catastrophe was beginning to look frankly absurd. India, therefore, represented a final 'test case'[68] for the British Empire as a model of world unity. As he saw it, the continent had been intellectually and culturally impoverished for years by tyrannical religious doctrine, the 'ignorance' of the Muslim and the Sikh, and the 'barbarous and retrograde'[69] Hindu, whose humiliating rituals apparently included drinking a supposedly purifying mixture in which the principal ingredient was cow's urine. If the Raj ('a means not an end') could induce India to regain its place as one of 'the free and equal nations of the earth',[70] the British could go home, a job well done.

From Delhi he journeyed to Agra, where he ran into E. M. Forster. It was now late November, and Forster had been travelling in India with two Cambridge friends since October. Archer had vehemently disliked *Howard's End* which he had read the previous year, but they nevertheless got on very well. 'I liked him very much,' Forster wrote to his mother. 'We shared carriages with him several times, and on leaving he gave me some introductions for Hardwar that will be very useful.'[71]

In Bombay, Archer visited the Yacht Club, a gabled building on the harbour, a British enclave to which no Indian was admitted, unless he was a servant. 'Every club in India is a little England,'[72] he observed, adding that it was human nature rather than racial prejudice which made it so. Then he looped south, to see the temples at Madura and Trichinopoly before turning back to Bangalore and as far north as Benares and Allahabad, where he made a sentimental visit to the offices of the *Pioneer*. From there he went up to Lucknow and finally back to Bombay, where, on 7 January 1913, he set sail on the *SS Circassia* for England.

He had spent five months in India, travelling and meeting more people than most English officials did in a lifetime's service. By the time he arrived home, he had been away for almost a year. Once reunited with his friends and with Frances at King's Langley, he started work on the third book to result from his travels during the last five years. As he worked during the spring and summer, he developed his theory of the Indian civilization being essentially immutable and the European and American ever-evolving. As the agent of the more sophisticated mechanism, it was incumbent upon the Empire to detach India from its millstone of primitive Hinduism, convert it to Western dynamism and thereby release the suppressed but immense riches of its people. *India and the Future* took a long time to complete, and he did not deliver the typescript to his agent at Curtis Brown until 4 August 1914. That day, Britain declared war upon Germany. The book was delayed until the summer of 1917 when it was published to a mixed reception. Shaw thought it showed 'the right Ibsen impulse to get away from idolatry and get to the truth'[73], but many others, Indian and British, thought it outmoded and offensive. The world had changed.

Within weeks of his arrival in London, Archer was picking up the threads again, advising Frederick Harrison on the premiere production of his translation of Ibsen's *The Pretenders*, which opened at the Haymarket on 13 February. Ten months abroad had left him badly in need of money and he feverishly began buttonholing his editorial contacts for work. On 26 February 1913, he became theatre critic of *The Star*, the daily paper for which Walkley had once been theatre critic and Shaw had written on music. It was a post Archer was to hold for seven years. He began by hailing *The Schoolmistress* at the Vaudeville as the 'jolliest'[74] of Pinero's farces, went on to approve revivals of *Caesar and Cleopatra* and *Strife*, and reflected after a revival of *The Second Mrs*

Tanqueray that, although he may have over-emphasized its merits when it was first produced, it was nevertheless 'a landmark, a starting point'[75] for much that followed.

At the end of July, he was in Capri, interviewing an English eccentric for a possible article. Ten years previously, at the age of thirty-five, Mrs Roger Watts had lost all her money, discovered Capri, jujitsu, and what she described as the Homeric principles of Greek physical training. Archer watched Mrs Watts energetically demonstrating various forms of unarmed combat, disentangled himself, abandoned the article, and hastened to Italy to visit Max Beerbohm who, having married the American actress Florence Kahn, was living in an unprepossessing villa at Rapallo. He was back in London for 1 September for the opening of *Androcles and the Lion*, Shaw's new play which Barker and Lillah McCarthy were producing at the St James's.

Albert Rothenstein designed a series of painted hangings, giving a Post-Impressionist feel to a play set in ancient Rome. In the prologue, Androcles removes a thorn from a lion's paw and after many adventures, ends up in sharing a cell with a motley group of Christian prisoners at the Colosseum. Here, Lavinia (representing the Life Force) and a Roman captain debate the nature of faith and spirituality before Androcles is thrown into the arena. There, he finds the lion he has to fight is none other than his old companion and their embrace of friendship causes the Emperor to announce his conversion to Christianity. The play suggests that inner forces of courage and compassion portrayed by Androcles and Lavinia are more powerful than the doctrine of Christian legends. It was in order to square-up to Shaw's religious peroration, gladiatorially if necessary, that Archer had prepared himself by taking the scriptures with him around the world. He was glad he had, for it was widely rumoured that in the new play, Shaw 'mingled his wit and his strange religion in stronger doses than ever before'.

'But it was all a false alarm!' he lamented the next day in *The Star*. In the eight years since *Man and Superman* it seemed that Shaw had hardly progressed philosophically at all. *Androcles and the Lion* was still Shawpenhaurism surrounded by vivacious pranks. The message was 'simply . . . Mr Shaw's contempt for rationalism, and belief that it is by irrationalism that the world has been, and will be, saved'. It was a point of view diametrically opposed to Archer's, but by sticking tenaciously and entertainingly to it, Shaw earned his admiration just as much as his despair, for it meant that their marvellous, invigorating arguments would never expire. 'There is philosophy in the farce no doubt,' he added, 'but it is neither very obtrusive nor very baffling; and if you prefer to ignore the philosophy, you may simply yield yourself up to an hour-long revel of wit, humor and comic invention.'[76]

Apart from Shaw, it was a bleak season. Galsworthy's new play, *The Fugitive* at the Court, 'the tragedy of a sensitive soul immured in the prison-house of stolid upper-middle-class respectability'[77] harked back to early nineteenth-century romanticism, but compensation arrived in the form of *Hindle Wakes*, an ironic story of a working-class girl who refuses to marry the rich man's son who has seduced her. The author was Stanley Houghton, one of the dramatists encouraged by Annie Horniman at her enterprising Gaiety Theatre in Manchester. In September, the company performed at the Court, when Archer found the play full of 'the flavor of life' even though the last act (as they frequently did) 'ran entirely off the rails'.[78] It was not only dramatically but physically a hard winter. On 10 December, he reported himself 'an aching & ill-tempered cripple' after having been hit by a skidding motorbus. 'I spend half my time being bandaged and unbandaged,'[79] he fretted. But by 28 March 1914, he was fit and well, and once again steaming away from England, this time on the *Mauretania*, bound for New York and his room at the Belmont.

What took his breath away that spring was not the view from the top of the fifty-seven-storey Woolworth Building, the tallest building in the world, nor the partly subterranean splendour of new Grand Central Station. It was a dance-craze. New York had discovered the tango and 'never, never,' said Archer, 'have I seen anything more amazing'.

After the theatre one night, friends took him to a dance hall where two bands were playing alternately, one starting as soon as the other stopped. The noise was intolerable, 'barbaric rhythms' played 'with fiendish zest' which nearly drove him hot-foot out into the street again. Music at meals was bad enough, but this was the discordant howl of a new, angry and frightening future bearing down upon them all. It was 'the music of Pandemonium'. And the dancing! He watched dumbfounded as about thirty couples, all middle-aged and mostly obese, 'clinging on to each other in various unsightly fashions, went shuffling up and down the room with a grim seriousness at which one knew not whether to laugh or weep'. This pitiful, solemn waddling, interspersed with piston-like arm-movements was not the tango at all, he complained. There was no youth, no high spirits, merely the 'tragi-comic spectacle'[80] of people in thrall to the latest fashion. Bemused, he returned to England and his bizarre debut as a film actor.

It was the beginning of the silent film era, short, ricketty movies full of wild gesticulating, horrified expressions, swooning and chases. While Archer watched the tango in Manhattan, the first Charlie Chaplin films were being shown in London. Inspired, Barrie and Granville Barker planned a film arranged loosely along Keystone principles.

On 5 July, Archer, Shaw, the philanthropist Lord Howard de Walden and G. K. Chesterton, all dressed in cowboy costumes, gathered in the Hertfordshire countryside not far from Archer's home. As Barrie operated the camera and Barker shouted directorial instructions from behind the wheel of a car careering about behind them, they enacted 'a series of amazing adventures',[81] leaping on and off motorcycles, dashing across fields and crossing a river in a boat which sank beneath Chesterton's weight. Then rain stopped play. The film remained unfinished and seems to have been destroyed.

But as America tangoed and William Archer charged about the English countryside dressed as a cowboy, Europe stumbled into war.

War Work

The summer of 1914 was long and warm. In retrospect, English summers before the war seemed a succession of afternoons balmy with peace and security. 'One looks back upon last mid-summer as upon a sort of far-off Golden Age, when we lived in an earthly paradise & didn't know it,'[1] Archer wrote regretfully to Henry Bond, now a fellow of Trinity Hall, Cambridge, during the first, unsettling winter of war.

In reality, the Golden Age had been fading for a long time. In 1912, Archer left an England crippled by a coalminers' strike and battered by a guerilla war waged by women intending to force an obstinate government into extending the franchise. Members of the increasingly militant Women's Social and Political Union smashed the windows of shops and government buildings with toffee hammers, firebombed churches and the country house of the Chancellor of the Exchequer, David Lloyd George. The Actresses' Franchise League provided disguises for the more adventurous activists. Archer had already implored Elizabeth to persuade the miltants to '*Announce* a change of policy: announce that, till further notice, you will be active but strictly constitutional at propaganda.'[2] But the Union was not listening. An arson campaign resulted in Mrs Pankhurst being imprisoned and later forcibly fed. By the summer of 1914, suffragettes were marching and a general strike of miners and transport workers was threatened for the autumn.

Britain was at war with itself, socially and artistically. In 1910, the Italian artist and nascent fascist, Filippo Marinetti, visited London to deliver the gospel according to Futurism. Having once rejected the machine, art had finally caught up with industry and was preparing to celebrate it. 'Nothing is more incomprehensible to me than either a pietistic or an aesthetic shrinking from the future,' agreed Archer, surveying the Declaration of Futurism which condemned all that was past and embraced all that was new. But he was now old enough to wonder why the future could not grow from the past instead of break from it and Futurism seemed a 'brutal and truculent'[3] philosophy. In June 1914, one of Marinetti's few English converts, the painter and writer Wyndham Lewis, produced the first issue of *Blast*, a magazine violently proclaiming the supremacy of Vorticism, an uncompromisingly modern art breaking down and reforming modern life into jarring sweeps of colour and jagged edges. Everything seemed to be turning inexplicably towards anger.

There was even disturbing evidence that Shaw was masquerading as a graphologist. This news came from Beerbohm in Italy, who opened his newspaper one day to see an advertisement incorporating a photograph of Shaw. There was, though, no mention of his name. Instead, the reader was invited to send his or her birthdate, a sample of handwriting and eighty-five cents in stamps to a Professore C. Wallace of London, whereupon 'this wonderful and powerful man' would, free of charge, reveal intimate 'business, private or marital' secrets. 'This is really very sad,' wrote Beerbohm, sending the advertisement to Archer. 'I had thought that Shaw was still doing very well in England . . .'[4]

In fact, Shaw was just about to do very well indeed. He had at last achieved his ambition of luring Mrs Patrick Campbell into the Shavian world and symbolically raising the flag of Shavian drama over out-of-date Edwardian 'Pinerotics'. In 1912, blithely ignoring the fact that she was forty-seven, he had written the role of Eliza Doolittle, the eighteen-year-old cockney flower-seller in *Pygmalion*, expressly for her. Enormously flattered, Mrs Campbell accepted the part, clasped his hand in hers and pressed it to her breast, whereupon, madness upon madness, Shaw fell in love.

Mrs Campbell was now a widow, her husband having been mown down in a charge against Boer guns in 1900. To Shaw, she was a successor to Janet Achurch, his Elizabeth Robins. Archer did everything he could to keep his affair with Elizabeth secret, but Shaw, ballooning with pride and besotted by the magical Mrs Campbell, told everyone, even Charlotte, that he was in love with her. Archer was probably told not by Shaw (there was a background of embarrassment), but by the Barkers or perhaps Barrie. But Shaw would never have left Charlotte and so Mrs Pat turned to George Cornwallis-West, a good-looking but hardly intellectual army officer desperate to escape from his marriage to Jennie Jerome, the widow of Lord Randolph Churchill and mother of Winston. Shaw's year-long, unconsummated affair with Stella

Campbell ended elegiacally in the summer of 1913, when he followed her to Sandwich Bay on the Kent coast, and where she gently rejected him.

She threw over the author but not the play. Shaw called *Pygmalion* a romance but really it is a feminist Life Force fable. Having discovered Eliza one windswept night, huddled over her basket of violets in the portico of St Paul's, Covent Garden, the emotionally-repressed philologist Henry Higgins promises to transform her from 'a squashed cabbage leaf' to a lady in six months. But while his lessons prove a triumph of acquired pronunciation and social graces, Eliza is subdued into a mannequin of robotic manners, glazed eyes, and monotonous, pedantic speech until the Life Force, her own irrepressibly rebellious nature, changes her once again into an independent New Woman. An ironic parallel is played through Eliza's father, the violent and roguish dustman Alfred Doolittle who, on suddenly becoming a wealthy man, discovers that the abhorred middle-class dress of morning suit and silk hat brings with it an equally repugnant expectation of middle-class morality.

In the spring of 1914, Shaw was directing rehearsals at His Majesty's Theatre and exacerbating the temper of Mrs Pat and the anxiety of Tree, who was playing Higgins. One day, Archer bumped into an harassed-looking Tree, who admitted that rehearsals were 'spirited', and that his theatre manager had remarked, 'You know, Guv'nor, if you put a cat, a dog, and a monkey into a sack together, what can you expect but ructions?'[5] Time and again, Tree pleaded for Higgins to be turned into a romantic hero and that Shaw change the ending so that it is implied that the professor and Eliza might marry. This was the very opposite of Shaw's intention, 'a silly and vulgar gag',[6] he complained to Archer. But having survived Mrs Pat's tantrums, Tree's attempted sabotage and the additional trauma of Mrs Campbell suddenly marrying Cornwallis-West five days before the first night and vanishing for a three-day honeymoon in Kent, leaving Shaw and Tree doubting whether the production would open at all, *Pygmalion* indeed opened on 11 April. Mrs Campbell and Tree (who resorted to noting his more difficult lines on pieces of paper and secreting them about the set) made the play Shaw's first substantial West End success. Soon it was taking over £2,000 pounds a week.

'Mr Bernard Shaw has this time "backed a winner",' enthused Archer in the American edition of *The Nation* on 14 May. *Pygmalion* was 'one of his most human, if not most brilliant, productions', although hardly original. Almost fifteen years earlier, Barrie's *The Professor's Love-*

Story had featured a prototype Higgins in Professor Goodwillie, 'the absent-minded, unpractical, unworldly man-of-science, who considers himself an old bachelor and, when brought face to face with the devotion of the charming girl, cannot understand either her feelings or his own'. Nevertheless, Archer found the play so stimulating, moving and funny, that he devoted much of his review to advising Shaw how he should rewrite it. *Pygmalion* made Archer's translation fingers twitch.

The first scene, he noted, in which Higgins encounters Eliza, was picturesque but dramatically superfluous, although he admitted that Mrs Pat's cockney had been so uncompromising he had hardly understood a word she had howled. More importantly, the fourth act, in which Eliza rebels and 'shows her astonished Pygmalion the difference between a woman and a gramophone' was far too short, whereas the fifth and final act was too long and yet another blatant example of Shaw's incorrigible long-windedness. He should either build up the fourth and ruthlessly cut the fifth, or rewrite them as a single act.

However, it was the daring use of the 'crimson expletive' that made Shaw, and *Pygmalion*, notorious. The elegance of Mrs Higgins's at-home, already punctured by Eliza's laboriously-mannered English, is deflated entirely when she is asked whether she intends walking home across the park. 'Not bloody likely,' she replies. 'I am going in a taxi.' Was The Word necessary? became the question of the hour. Clerics pronounced, scholars debated and letters clogged the correspondence page of *The Times*. Archer joined the objectors' chorus, not on moral grounds, but simply that 'bloody' was illogical and dramatically ineffective. 'It is flatly incredible that Higgins . . . should not from the first have put an embargo on that word,' he reasoned. It would be far more truthful, and funnier, he suggested, if Eliza were to blurt out 'Not bl– ', clap a hand over her mouth, flounder, and hastily substitute a colourless, limply polite alternative.

Archer's revision of *Pygmalion* extended to the casting and production, both of which obscured rather than clarified the play. Mrs Campbell flowering from a bedraggled waif to a commanding vision swathed in the height of Bond Street fashion, stretched credibility to breaking point. 'To give the thing a moment's plausibility, Eliza should be an unripe slip of a creature, whom it is possible for men . . . to consider insignificant and negligible,' but neither description, he wrote, could possibly be applied to the mature and unavoidably formidable Mrs Campbell. As for Tree, he had 'long given up the attempt to subdue his personality to his author, and has adopted the opposite plan

... of subduing his author to his personality'.[7] Fourteen years pre-viously, Archer had campaigned for Shaw's invasion of the West End. But *Pygmalion* proved that it was easier for plays than ideals to make the journey from Sloane Square, for instead of Shaw usurping the main-stream theatre, the voracious West End had absorbed and subdued Shaw.

Meanwhile, the Stage Society was producing its second Chekhov play. Archer was abroad when the Society gave a disastrous *Cherry Orchard* in 1911, but on the afternoon of 11 May, he joined the matinee audience at the Aldwych to see *Uncle Vanya*. St John Hankin, one of Chekhov's English champions, did not live to see his work produced in England, for in June 1909, six months after accusing Archer of abdicating the battle for modern drama, apparently convinced that he would inherit the disease which had disabled his father, he drowned himself in the River Ithon at Llandrindod Wells in Wales. Had he lived, he would have treated Archer's perplexed response to Chekhov with contempt. 'So far as I could make out,' he wrote in *The Star* the next day, *'Uncle Vanya* is the tragedy of ... indecision, of drift.'[8] Chekhov irritated him for much the same reason as Ibsen's last play. He was irked by the torpor of these people sitting on their decayed verandahs and roaming their gardens, the embittered, drunken doctors, the decrepit landowners, the aimless women. He was exasperated by their indolence and indulgence, their sentimentality and priggishness, their inconclusive love affairs. He saw no poetry in Chekhov, only sloth and defeat.

Three days later, Archer and Gosse published a letter in *The Times* urging that Ernest Bendall, the former drama critic who had succeeded the hapless Redford as Examiner of Plays, lift the ban on *Ghosts* and award a licence for a public performance. He did, and the first public production, in Archer's translation, was staged at the Haymarket on 12 July with Bessie Hatton as Mrs Alving. It was 'infamously bad' and by now Archer was noticing 'some *very* weak points'[9] in the play itself. The sub-plot of the Alving orphanage was insubstantial, and how, he asked, when none of Oswald's artist friends in Paris could afford to marry, could they apparently afford to live with their mistresses and children? But its public production was a victory of sorts and in this last, unsettling, hot summer of peace, an era in censorship came to an end.

On 28 June, Gavrilo Princip, a Serbian nationalist, assassinated the Archduke Franz Ferdinand of Austria in Sarajevo. The shot reverber-ated throughout Europe, and was heard in countries connected by a complex series of treaties and alliances. Austria-Hungary declared war on Serbia; Russian mobilized against Austria and Germany, who in turn declared war on Russia and France. On 3 August, Germany invaded Belgium, and the next day, Britain declared war on Germany.

During the past few years, Archer had prepared not so much for war but for the preservation of global peace, by investigating the British Empire and simplified spelling as models of world unity. These had given way to his third and most ambitious scheme, the blueprint for which was published in a slim book in 1912.

Carnegie had written off the Simplified Spelling Society, claiming that the new spelling looked exactly like misspelling, and announcing that he was diverting his money into the building of a so-called Palace of Peace at the Hague. Archer's objection was that an international court of arbitration was 'a pitifully inefficient' means of diffusing global conflict, as it could only legally intervene once a world crisis had arisen. His alternative, which he set out in *The Great Analysis: A Plea for a Rational World-Order*, was the founding of an International College of Systematic Sociology. Composed of scholars and politicians from all nations, the College would monitor and interpret global affairs, its university anticipating the crises to be solved by its parliamentarians. Fearing the book would be scorned if it was known to be written by a theatre critic, Archer published it anonymously after persuading Gilbert Murray to lend it the authority of an Oxford Fellow by writing a signed introduction. In June 1913, he asked Carnegie to fund the College as an extension of the Palace of Peace to the tune of seven hundred and fifty thousand pounds, explaining that it would cost two hundred and fifty thousand to build and equip, while the remainder would fund up to twenty annual scholarships. Carnegie, 'that old duffer',[10] turned him down.

It was a grand scheme, one dear to Archer's heart and the muted interest from press, politicians and philanthropists depressed him. But once the war began, he set aside his model for a new world order and started looking for something to do.

At first, there seemed to be nothing. Newspapers were calling this a young man's war and he was one of the old men, almost sixty and well past military age. Finding no employment, he sat down to write poetry. Immediately the troops began to enlist, war poems began hurtling from the presses. On 5 August, the second day of war, Henry Newbolt's *The Vigil* appeared in *The Times*, and for the next few weeks over a hundred similar contributions swelled the paper's mailbags every day. The razing by German infantry of the small town of Louvain, a few miles east of Brussels and helplessly in the path of the invading army, appalled Archer. Hundreds of townspeople had died and over a thousand homes were burned to the ground over three days. By publishing *Louvain*, his own (not very good) war poem, in the *Observer* on 30 August 1914, Archer was joining what subsequently became a crowded field.

His impatience to do something other than compose verse was driven not only by patriotism, but by the conviction that German aggression would destroy both Germany itself and any hope of a united Europe and a world community. 'At least I find an occasional exhilaration,' he told Bond, 'in the sense that there never was a war in history which sane men, believing in democracy and progress, could go into with a better conscience, or with a clearer sense of its absolute necessity'.[11]

His chance came a few days after the publication of *Louvain*, when he was approached by Charles Masterman, a stocky, fleshy-faced Liberal Member of Parliament, married to a sister-in-law of Edith Lyttelton. As a former literary editor of the *Daily Chronicle*, Masterman appreciated the importance and influence of literature, and as a politician, recognized the necessity of having the press on his side. Having quickly convinced Asquith that to win the war abroad the government needed an effective propaganda machine at home, he founded the first Secret War Propaganda Bureau at Wellington House in Buckingham Gate, adjacent to the Palace. From here, in September, Masterman began recruiting the journalists and writers who would form his front-line troops in creating an infantry of articles, pamphlets and books, mostly for home consumption, giving the official view of the causes and progress of the war.

Archer was always both a realist and a romantic, and although he had no romantic illusions of the war, working for the War Propaganda Bureau both fulfilled his sense of realism and appealed to that side of his character which was naturally secretive. Within a fortnight, he had joined Barker, Barrie, Chesterton, Galsworthy, Hardy, Murray, Pinero, Wells and thirty-nine others in signing the *Authors' Declaration*, stating that 'Britain could not without dishonour have refused to take part in the present war.' It appeared simultaneously in *The Times* and the *New York Times* on 18 September.

The most prominent absentee from both Masterman's Wellington House battalion and the *Declaration*, was Shaw. When war was declared, the Shaws were on holiday in Devon, but by 11 November, they were back at Ayot St Lawrence, from where Shaw promised Archer that 'Next Saturday the *New Statesman* will contain my war supplement . . .'[12]

Published with the magazine on 14 November, *Common Sense About the War* outlined in over thirty-two closely-printed pages the complicated and sometimes contradictory Shavian position on the conflict. Shaw's view was that war had been avoidable, but as it had been deliberately fomented by capitalist-militarist junkers on both sides, neither the British nor the Germans had the right to claim a moral superiority.

Like the Labour Party, sections of Cambridge, where Bertrand Russell was now teaching, and the literary and artistic coterie of Bloomsbury, *Common Sense About the War* was generally seen as at best unwise and at worst treacherously pro-German. It was just the kind of thing against which Masterman and Wellington House were fighting, and its publication created a whirlwind of protest. *Pygmalion*, which had temporarily closed because Tree wanted a holiday, did not re-open. Shaw's new-found popularity was instantly eradicated and would not recover for ten years, until *Saint Joan* in 1924. Even socialist newspapers and many of his friends deserted him. Archer did not. He wished that Shaw had more sense than *Common Sense* but never doubted his friend's sincerity or intergrity. The war became another subject for them to argue over, but even after a particularly hard-fought lunch one day in November, when each went his own way wondering at the persistent obstinacy of the other, neither contemplated for one moment the ending of a friendship.

Archer and Shaw both agreed and disagreed about the war. They agreed its origins lay in militarism, but whereas Shaw saw militarism as a ruling-class disease which knew no geographical boundaries and therefore as representing a failure of civilization, Archer argued that it was a localized cancer which, during the past forty-odd years, had consumed the whole of German society. 'We are fighting the ghost of Bismark,'[13] he explained. Militarism, therefore, represented not a failure, but an attack upon civilization, and in this sense, Britain clearly had the moral advantage. But if Archer and Shaw disagreed on how and why the country had reached this calamitous position, they agreed that now it had, not only was a British victory essential, but it was vital that it brought social change. Shaw hoped Britain might be transformed into a socialist democracy and Archer, a British patriot with the added dimension of being a European democrat, speculated along vaguely similar lines.

In December 1900, the *Morning Leader* and the *New York World* had asked several 'notable persons' to predict the main danger which might confront the world during the twentieth century. 'I think the need of the coming century is some sort of Socialism,' replied Archer, 'while the danger is that it should take the form of a military socialism mechanically enforced, instead of a democratic socialism organically developed.'[14]

Increasingly, he saw democratic socialism as a foundation for a rational world government. Modern society was too fast, too mercenary for the old-style Liberalism which he had long supported and which he now saw crumbling. The Conservative Party, of course, was not an alternative for Archer. He had always considered the Conservatives bereft of intellect and ideals, and as underwriting the intellectual and moral conditions against which he and his troops of Ibsen, Barker and Galsworthy were struggling. His faith in capitalism, never very strong, had waned over the years. 'The present order of things is doomed,' he had told Fanny Stevenson as long ago as 1887, gloomily predicting they would have to endure 'some great Armageddon'[15] before a benevolent socialism could be introduced. If the present war was indeed England's Armageddon then at least it might result in social and moral renewal. By April 1915, he was reporting optimistically to Murray that in his daily scrutiny of the press, he detected a new spirit of 'public-mindedness' already replacing the old British 'private-mindedness': 'Of course public mindedness is Socialism in disguise; but I take it we are all socialists in *tendency*, though there is no definite form of socialism to which we care to subscribe.'[16]

Archer's formal response to *Common Sense About the War* was *Fighting a Philosophy*, a twenty-six-page pamphlet and the first of several which he would write for the Secret War Propaganda Bureau over the next four years. Masterman had persuaded several publishers, including Methuen and T. Fisher Unwin, to help the war effort by acting as a cover for Wellington House, publishing official propaganda under their own name and colophon. *Fighting a Philosophy* was published in January 1915, ostensibly by the Clarendon Press, Oxford. Although Archer makes no mention of Shaw, the pamphlet is both a reaction against *Common Sense About the War* and a late salvo against Shawpenhaurism and plays like *Man and Superman*. 'In a very real sense, it is the philosophy of Nietzsche that we are fighting,'[17] he warned.

Oh 26 May, Tom had left London to begin his new career in New York, but as soon as the war was declared he sailed home to rejoin the

London Scottish, a territorial regiment with whom he had trained during the past few years. It recruited clerks, bankers, civil servants, Scots or those of Scots descent, and alternated training exercises with social events like the annual Caledonian Ball. Coincidentally, their headquarters where Tom enlisted were near Wellington House in Buckingham Gate. There, he was given a medical inspection and issued with a uniform which included a kilt, a rifle, ammunition, field dressing and an identity disc. Within days, he was in France and promoted to Lance-Corporal.

After several weeks' general duties, the regiment transferred to St Omer, near the Belgian border, where, on 29 October, a fleet of thirty-four London buses complete with their drivers waited to take them thirty miles east through heavy rain to the fields of Flanders. The battle of Ypres, the western front marking the allies' last defence before the Channel coast, had been rumbling for over a fortnight. As Tom and the others lurched along in their incongruous procession towards the fighting, they passed coming the other way a continuous caravan of Red Cross wagons bringing the wounded back from the front.

The British, commanded by General Douglas Haig, were struggling to hold a ridge some miles to the south of the town. The morning of 31 October was chilly, but once the mist lifted it became warmer and the London Scottish took up positions behind the British lines to the east of the escarpment in what until recently had been farmland. By day, the Germans were shelling almost continuously and at night, the sky raged red with shrapnel. The first territorial regiment to land in France, the London Scottish became the first to be thrust into battle and that night in the noise and the mud they discovered how inadequately they were prepared. Most of their rifles were defective. Their kilts, shoes and spats, which looked so dashingly romantic on route marches through London, were tragically impractical in the sludge of battle. The chain of command broke down. They swung this way and that and when they flung themselves at the ridge, they flung themselves against enormous firepower.

It was a night of bedlam from which at last they were ordered to withdraw. The British had held their part of the ridge, but it was a much depleted London Scottish that regrouped in the thin light of morning. Over half their number, almost four hundred men, had been killed. Tom had survived. So too, had a good-looking young man called Ronald Colman who would soon be acting on the West End stage. On the German side, there was a young corporal whose bravery that night

won him the Iron Cross. He too had survived, but he was destined for
a far more terrible future. His name was Adolf Hitler.

A week later, Archer and Frances heard that Tom was well. Later in
November, they learned that he was at a convalescent camp in
Boulogne. A blister on his heel had become poisoned by the dye from
his sock.

The war affected everything. The kind of theatre for which Archer had
spent his life campaigning was all but wiped out. 'The intellectual
drama, which had been on the whole progressing before the war, was
stricken dumb in August 1914,'[18] he commented ruefully. Pantomime,
'that particularly English hotch-potch of spectacle and travesty,'[19] jollied
up a depressing Christmas. Otherwise, the winter reverberated with
revue and screamed with farce. Just before the war, large-scale 'international' revues had swept into London, lavish with French costumes
and scenery, and stuffed with Russian dancers, American singers, and
British singers hoping to be mistaken for American. *Hello Ragtime!* at
the Hippodrome was the kind of 'Anglo-Franco-Russo-American'
concoction in which Archer could discern 'no redeeming feature'[20] at
all. Once the war began, simpler, home-grown revues opened, one of
the first being *By Jingo, If We Do – !* at the Empire. Elsewhere, detectives
tracked down murderers while amateurs foiled spies. In Thomas Dott's
A Daughter of England at the Garrick ('not unamusing in its very
artlessness'[21]), an English-rose governess rebuffs the sexual advances of
her leering Prussian employer, escapes with secret papers and entrusts
them to a trained dog at the French border. In such plays, English
women stopped being New and started being plucky instead.

Sing-a-long revues and patriotic plays drew upon an open well of
sentiment and a will to see the British virtues of honour, fair play and
clean-living triumph over the enemy's criminality, deceit and lascivious-
ness. They provided comfort for a bewildered, anxious public and
became part of Britain's home propaganda war. But even as a member
of Masterman's army, Archer believed that propaganda should aim for
artistically high standards. 'I find it difficult to enjoy war plays,' he
admitted, conceding that his distaste would, in the circumstances
'perhaps be difficult to defend'.[22]

He found it easier to approve literature in battledress, as Shakespeare
and Thomas Hardy were pressed into government service. At His
Majesty's, he reported Tree's company 'doing their best to keep our
spirits up' with 'an ironclad revival' of *Henry IV Part One* in which

Tree's Falstaff told of brave deeds while standing beside a cannon, apparently 'exploring the sky for zeppelins'.[23] Over at the Shaftesbury, *Henry V* gave Benson the opportunity for a rousing display of 'patriotic declamation',[24] while at the Kingsway, Barker staged scenes from Hardy's *The Dynasts*, cutting anything which diverted attention from English heroism in the Napoleonic Wars and producing 'a night of triumph'[25] in the process. In these bleak days and bleaker evenings, Archer was grateful for Shaw, even if few other people were. On 13 February 1915, he went to the Kingsway to see a revival of *Fanny's First Play*, which he had missed when it opened in 1911. It is a play-within-a-play, the inset piece being a supposedly anonymous comedy of middle-class conventions, suggesting the younger generation are more likely realists than their elders. Four drama critics then squabble over its possible authorship. Archer, who enjoyed theatrical parodies if they were well done, 'laughed with a heartiness that almost recalled the Golden Age before the war'.[26]

Turning back to the tarnished present, he watched an air display at Farnborough, looking on with thrilled astonishment at the spectacle of two flimsy, stick-and-canvas biplanes looping-the-loop. On the ground, it seemed the war of words was going splendidly. There was 'an immense amout of sound & liberal & humane & penetrating thought'[27] about, much of it smuggled from the Propaganda Bureau through some of Britain's leading publishing houses to an unsuspecting British public. Archer himself distilled a pile of government documents into *The Thirteen Days*, destined for the Clarendon Press, in which he interpreted the political manœuvring from the Austrian Ultimatum of 23 July until the British declaration of war on 4 August in terms of 'a great historic drama' divided into five acts. Accusing the German government of behaving with 'criminal recklessness', he applauded 'the skill, the tact, the temper, the foresight, the unwearied diligence and the unfailing greatness of spirit'[28] of the British Foreign Secretary, Sir Edward Grey, a man who, despite Pinero's continued prompting, had for a decade maintained a sphinx-like silence on the subject of a National Theatre.

'Tom is all right,'[29] Archer informed Bond on 18 July 1915, adding that he was now a 2nd Lieutenant in the Army Ordnance Department at Abbeville in northern France, and was coming home on leave for his thirtieth birthday on 2 August.

*

Archer had been angling for a permanent staff job at Wellington House. But three days after Tom's birthday, when there seemed no likelihood of his being offered one, he wrote to Murray, who was also working as a propagandist and with whom he had written a short book, *The Foreign Policy of Sir Edward Grey*, and had the ear of government and particularly Foreign Office circles. 'I suppose you haven't heard of anything I could do?' he asked, adding plaintively that 'I should be quite willing to train for ammunitions work.'[30] But Archer never saw the inside of a factory. Instead, the War Office decided his proficiency with languages would make him an ideal censor of the overseas post and in October, he found himself stationed behind a desk in a grey building in Portugal Street at a salary of four pounds a week. He was grateful for the money but horrified at everything else. Not for one moment did he fail to recognize the irony of the leader of the campaign to abolish censorship of the stage being installed in an office, just around the corner from the theatre where he had co-directed *A Doll's House* twenty-five years previously, and examining other people's mail. But even worse was to come. He was told he would be transferred to Edinburgh in the third week of November. This was disastrous news. He panicked, and decided he must retrieve and destroy his love letters to Elizabeth.

Incriminating evidence of their affair existed in their letters. Archer had disposed of most of hers to him, but what concerned him was the fate of his to her. Elizabeth had instructed her family as early as 1894 that he was her 'artistic executor' and responsible for 'letters & papers relating to my life in London',[31] an instruction still in force when she journeyed to Alaska. Before going abroad himself in 1912, Archer appears to have asked Elizabeth to ensure that she could account for all his intimate letters to her, and keep them safely and separately from the rest of her private papers. On 23 April 1912, she put most of these letters in an old hatbox and stored this with Margaret (Zoe) Hadwen, a trusted friend, at her home at St Leonard's Terrace in Chelsea, asking her that if neither she nor Archer collected it, the letters must be burned unread.

This is how things remained until the first winter of war, when Archer apparently agitated for further precautions, possibly prompted by a fear of air raids and the thought of his precious letters being lost amid the rubble of a wrecked building. The Germans had already used zeppelins to bomb Belgian and Polish cities, and it was assumed it would not be long before bombs fell on London. Archer was so worried that he even dreamed of zeppelin raids. On 4 January 1915, he and

Elizabeth met for lunch. The next day, she may have retrieved the hatbox from Chelsea, as she 'read some of W.A.'s [letters] of former years'. On the 6th, it appears that she burned some in her garden in Sussex. Four days later, she took 'W.A.'s packet'[32] probably containing the remaining letters, to a bank, and the following day, 9 January, posted him the receipt for the safe deposit box. The first air raid on Britain came ten days later and the first on London, on 31 May. However, being transferred to Edinburgh renewed Archer's agitation over his letters. Instead of censoring other people's mail, he was desperate to censor his own, retrospectively. According to Elizabeth's diary, she received a letter from him on 18 November, just before he travelled north to Edinburgh. He had 'opened his box of records' (most likely the package from the bank), sifted through it and was 'knocked all of a heap' by what he had read. 'I *don't* know,' she wrote, ' – can't remember a 1000th part of what was there. Burnt now I suppose. 8 years 10 years & all "that" gone up in smoke.'[33]

If Archer indeed burned those letters in the grate in his study at 27 Fitzroy Square, he may have believed he had destroyed all his love letters to her. If so, he was wrong. Elizabeth had withheld several letters, notes and scraps and these are now among her papers, which include her diaries, at the Fales Library at New York University. Elizabeth, apparently, was determined to prevent at least some of 'that' from going up in smoke.

Neither she nor Archer had any regrets, for their love still inspired and sustained and comforted them. But it was a part of the fabric of Archer's nature, as well as of his moral principles that his infidelity be concealed, not only for his own time, but for the future. He not only took care to dispose of her letters to him, but knew that his brother Charles, whom he appointed as one of his executors, would also meticulously trawl through his papers and eliminate any oversight, any stray clue to their affair. He was concerned that posterity see him and Elizabeth only as professional associates in the campaign for a new theatre, and Charles, who learned of the relationship from Archer himself and who greatly respected Elizabeth, was in complete agreement. Only a version of the truth should be left to the family and presented to the world. Many letters from theatrical friends survive among Archer's papers which Charles presented to the British Library, but only one from Elizabeth, acknowledging the extent of his contribution to the Joint Management production of *Hedda Gabler*.

Only a few close friends knew of the affair. Charles and Frances may have suspected more than they actually knew, but were always loyal. If any other friends caught wind of it, they kept their counsel, even, in the end, Bernard Shaw, himself equally concerned that posterity would see him in the correct light. Everything was very private. But there was still a thin but persistent mist of speculation, both at the time and since. There was peripheral gossip, inference, and even, briefly and many years later, after Archer's death, hesitant whispers of there being a child.[34] But although Archer and Elizabeth shared an occasional sexual relationship, it appears that Thomas Archer is the only child of William Archer and that if Elizabeth was ever pregnant at all, it was while she was briefly married to the tragic George Richmond Parks.

Archer was eager to censor his own mail but doing the same for other people bored him. After a fortnight at the head Post Office in Edinburgh, he had read a meagre six business communications from overseas, four from Norway and one each from France and Italy. For the rest of the time, he notified Murray, he read 'letters from sailors & their sweethearts that any clerk at 30/- a week could read as well as I'. He had failed to discover any trace of subversion and was consequently 'making strenuous efforts to get recalled to London'.[35] He succeeded just after Christmas, reappearing briefly at the 'abode of imbecility'[36] at Portugal Street before diving into 'a sort of semi-official position'[37] at Wellington House in June 1916.

The Propaganda Bureau restored his self-respect and made him feel that he was making a solid contribution to the war effort. Most of his friends were also doing their bit. Elizabeth, though still an American citizen, was supporting her adopted country by volunteering for work at the Endell Street Hospital for Soldiers in central London. Later, she would lecture on nutrition for the Ministry of Food. Pinero was chairman of the United Arts Force, a volunteer home defence corps. 'We are about 1700 strong – art workers of all grades,'[38] he reported. At Wellington House, Archer dashed off another pamphlet, *To Neutral Peace-Lovers: A Plea for Patience*, and then attacked the neutrality of Norway and the United States.

As Europe sank lower into mud and carnage, Archer feared that Norway might drift to the German side of the divide. With Masterman's blessing, he planted strident articles in the Norwegian press attacking the fiercely pro-German novelist, Knut Hamsun. At the same time, he went to work on the more crucial battle of swaying American public opinion. In common with many others, Archer believed that if only the

United States would join the Allied cause, what otherwise looked like a long and bloody campaign might end quickly in victory. For the past two years, he had written a London theatre column for the New York *Nation* and in January 1916, he commandeered the death of a young playwright for his strategy of luring America into the war.

Harold Chapin, an American actor and writer who adopted England as his home, was killed in France in 1915. He was in his twenties. Archer had noticed the 'cleverness' of Chapin's *Art and Opportunity* at the Prince of Wales's in 1912, even though by making it a light-hearted West End vehicle for Marie Tempest's 'vivacious, showy talent', he had 'sacrificed some of his sincerity'. Four of his one-act plays were performed at a memorial for him at the Queen's Theatre in December. 'Can you wonder at the emotion with which I, who had watched Chapin and believed in him from the outset of his career saw the four little plays which remain perhaps the best witness to the promise sadly unfulfilled?' asked Archer. With the single exception of Rupert Brooke, he added, 'no English-speaking man of more unquestionable talent has been lost to the world in this world-frenzy'. Although few of his readers would have heard of Chapin, his was a name, he assured them, 'of which America may well be proud'.[39]

Then there was Alan Seeger, another American and, coincidentally, the son and brother of the two women for whom he had provided warm clothes when the *Merida* sank off the American coast in 1911. Seeger was living in Paris when war was declared and joined the Foreign Legion, to be killed charging into German gunfire at Belloy-en-Santerre in 1916. Later that year, Archer arranged for the publication of Chapin's letters. The following year, he did the same for Seeger's *Poems*. To each volume, he contributed an introduction.

Not content with conscripting an army of authors, the government brought up reserves of painters, and in the summer of 1916, Britain dispatched its first Official War Artists to the continent. Some, like the etcher Muirhead Bone, provided drawings of battlefields in the tradition of British landscape painting, free of carnage and designed to reassure rather than shock. But as the experience of war was giving soldier-poets like Siegfried Sassoon a new and uncompromising poetic language, so soldier-painters such as C. R. W. Nevinson began producing a new and disturbing war art.

He was the son of Henry Nevinson, a journalist colleague and exact contemporary of Archer who, as a *Manchester Guardian* correspondent, had sent home vivid reports from the fiasco of Dardanelles the previous year. Christopher Nevinson served as a Red Cross ambulance driver and then as a private in the Medical Corps in France before being invalided out with rheumatic fever. His paintings interpreted the war futuristically and showed angry columns of troops marching implacably onward, mechanized blocks of men defined by vivid force-lines. 'I was the first to paint war pictures without pageantry, without glory,' he remembered.

Nevinson's first exhibition, *Paintings and Drawings of the War*, opened at the Leicester Galleries in September and created a sensation. The Asquiths went, and so did Winston Churchill and Ramsay MacDonald, Shaw, Galsworthy and Joseph Conrad. Archer went along and closely inspected each picture. The energy, violence and emotional honesty pierced his reserve like an arrow. Suddenly, alarmingly, he knew that for once he was unable to freeze the emotions within him and as he stood there surrounded by the pictures, the tears began to course down his cheeks. For the first time in public, William Archer broke down and wept. When he heard about it, Nevinson admitted it was 'an exquisite compliment'[40] to his work.

By this time, Tom had transferred from the Ordnance Department to a second infantry regiment, the Seaforth Highlanders, and then once again, to the King's Own Scottish Borderers. By the autumn, he was in action at the Somme, a vast, hideously-scarred and diseased battle-ground, much of which was now waist-high mud. He was lucky to survive when an enemy bullet passed miraculously between his left ear and head. On 20 October, he was seriously wounded in heavy fighting at the Butte de Warlencourt, from which, according to their official history, the regiment withdrew 'tired but cheerful, despite the mud and the stench from the corpse-littered battlefield'.[41] Tom came home for several months convalescence and training with the regiment in Scotland and Ireland.

The shortage of newsprint in England meant that Archer's *Daily News and Leader* commentaries had been reduced from weekly to fortnightly. Later in the war, when the newspaper shrank to a single sheet, they were dropped altogether. Although *The Star* continued to publish his overnight theatre reviews, the space he was allocated contracted so much there was often no room for anything more than a perfunctory 'notice'. This was exasperating as once in a while, there was a more than perfunctory play to review, such as Harold Brighouse's 'enormously entertaining' *Hobson's Choice*, which opened at the Apollo in the summer of 1916. Like Houghton, Brighouse was one of Annie Horniman's group of writers at the Manchester Gaiety, and in its mixture of wry comedy and gentle social realism, *Hobson's Choice* is as well crafted as *Hindle Wakes*. Set in a Lancashire town, pragmatic Maggie Hobson, supposedly on the shelf at thirty, marries the shy but talented bootmaker Willie Mossop, makes him her business partner and triumphantly takes over her domineering father's bootshop. The theatre, Archer noted thankfully, could still occasionally reach beyond 'the parish of St James's'.[42]

Occasionally, but not too often, writers and managers were even more finicky than usual over where their shows were set. Brighouse's Lancashire settled in for a long run, but Germanic and mid-European operettas had been briskly removed from the stage at the outset of the war. In their place came *Chu-Chin-Chow* at His Majesty's, a musical conjured from the *Arabian Nights* and written by Oscar Asche, the actor who had played Sigurd opposite Ellen Terry in *The Vikings at Helgeland*. Asche, who also played *Chu-Chin-Chow*'s leading role of Abu Hassan, cleverly aligned the natural human desire when surrounded by a desert of gloom to search for an oasis of splendid fantasy, with the English fascination with the exotic. He spent only £385 on rehearsals and the orchestra, but an astonishing £1400 on dazzlingly spectacular costumes and sets, creating a show so successful that by the time it closed it had run a record five years and outlasted the war.

It was 'effective, bustling entertainment',[43] wrote Archer, although his own gloom evaporated not with the adventures of Abu Hassan but a charity revival of W. S. Gilbert's *Pygmalion and Galatia* at His Majesty's on 20 October. Over thirty years previously, at Stratford in the far-off autumn of 1885, he had been captivated by the young, glamorous and vibrant American actress Mary Anderson, playing Rosalind opposite Johnston Forbes-Robertson's Orlando in *As You Like It*. Shortly afterwards, she had married and abandoned acting. Now, in the second year of war, she emerged from over twenty-five years of retirement to recreate Galatia, the role which first made her name and for Archer, for a single, wonderful evening, the theatre became once more a place of magic and dreams. 'Was there ever,' he wondered, 'in theatrical history . . . such an event? . . .' When he saw her as Rosalind, he was twenty-nine and she twenty-six; he was now sixty and she fifty-seven, yet she appeared 'as lissom, as graceful, as charming, and (one would have sworn) as young as she ever was'. It was 'something very like a miracle'.[44]

Elsewhere, a dangerous clamour was rising. Pacifists, conscientious objectors, appeasers, negotiators, religious orators, artists and writers were raising their voices against the war. Many spoke through the pages of the *Cambridge Magazine*, edited by the left-wing linguist, C. K. Ogden, and which published news from the European press, including German papers, the words of dissenting serving soldiers, such as Siegfried Sassoon, and academics like Bertrand Russell.

To Archer, the *Cambridge Magazine* was the most formidable of the opposition journals because it was written and read by his own class and intellectual equals, whose appeals he recognized as sincere and carefully-argued. The *Cambridge Magazine* proclaimed that the war was the fault of self-interested and foolish old men, patrician Conservatives, military and political leaders, and newspaper proprietors, who had ruthlessly prevented the young men from gaining political and economic power and who now, equally ruthlessly, sent them into war. 'I say firstly that I know this to be untrue, & secondly that, if it were true, England would richly deserve her inevitable fate,'[45] Archer protested to Ogden in March 1917.

Clearly it was Germany who had invoked the demons of war and it was up to Britain to exorcise them. From his desk at Wellington house, Archer lobbed five short books and pamphlets into the attack in 1917, aimed at Scandinavia, Russia, German intellectuals and British men and women in the saloon bar and front parlour. Next spring, he collated newspaper reports of the sinking of civilian ships by German submarines to write *The Pirates' Progress: A Short History of the U-Boat*. In 1909, Archer and Frances had sailed to New York on the *Lusitania*; in 1914, it had brought Tom home from America, and a year later the ship was sunk by a German submarine. Among the twelve hundred victims was Charles Frohman. Archer denounced unrestricted submarine attacks as 'ruthless piracy', but it was partly this 'indiscriminate maritime murder'[46] which brought the Americans into the war at last. 'I thank Germany and her Kaiser for one happy day,' he noted, ' – that on which I saw the Stars and Stripes floating beside the Union Jack over the palace of the Mother of Parliaments at Westminster.'[47]

The war dragged on, poison gas drifted across the blackened battle-grounds of Flanders and revues sang and danced across the London stage. In 1916, audiences packed the Alhambra to see George Robey in

The Bing Boys Are Here and came away singing *If You Were the Only Girl in the World*. But on 17 March 1917, over at the St Martin's Theatre, just off St Martin's Lane, the musical comedy, *Houp La!* gave way to the most shocking piece of social realism to be staged for several years.

Eugène Brieux's *Damaged Goods*, a forthright study of indiscriminate sex and the effects of venereal disease, had caused a sensation similar to that of *Ghosts* when it was first produced in France in 1902. The Americans were already making films warning of the dangers of sexually transmitted diseases for the troops, yet the British had hardly confronted the problem. But now with soldiers roaming the streets and thousands of prostitutes in London, it was impossible to ignore. *Damaged Goods* is the story of a man who spends a night with a woman only to discover he has contracted syphilis. She had previously been seduced, infected and abandoned, and, having been refused treatment, sleeps with George to take revenge upon society. His doctor forbids him to marry for two years, but because he needs the money his marriage will bring, George ignores his advice, marries, and fathers a child suffering from syphilis. The London production, in which Ronald Colman, Tom's former companion in the London Scottish, took the leading role, caused a storm of controversy, and many found it too harrowing to watch. Archer defended it as 'a poignant and impressive dramatic tract', and as the profits were being channelled into researching the treatment of venereal disease, urged that 'Everyone who wishes to further a movement of vast importance'[48] should go and see it.

Otherwise, there was singing, dancing and laughter, almost as he imagined a collectivized, Fabianized theatre to be. At the Alhambra, another *Bing Boys* revue opened, *The Bing Boys on Broadway*.

Alys Morty was the youngest daughter of Scottish parents who lived with her widowed mother in Hampstead. A tall, dark-haired and rather plain woman, she was a cousin of a friend of Tom's who had been killed at Messines in 1914. His death brought them together. Alys was thirty-five and Tom three years younger when they married at the Emmanuel Church, Hampstead, on 23 February 1918. After the wedding, they moved into rooms at 48 Holmdale Road in West Hampstead and a few days later, set off for a three-week honeymoon in Ireland. They returned in the last week of March. 'Now I am under orders for the front again,' wrote Tom to Lady Mary Murray on the 27th, 'and go off on Friday. It is rather trying for my wife, but there is no braver woman than she.'[49]

Two days later, Tom, now a lieutenant, left with the King's own Scottish Borderers for the western front. After almost four years of struggle and massive loss of life, neither side had advanced nor retreated more than a few miles and Tom found himself fighting across the same desolate battlefield of mud and charred trees as when he joined up. The Germans were preparing to begin a furious, all-out offensive. The allies responded by spinning out a thousand miles of barbed wire, twisting and winding for 450 miles, 130 of which were defended by British forces sheltering in putrid, rat-infested trenches. Haig ordered that they fight it out to the end.

At home in Fitzroy Square, Archer cleared out his shelves and gave many of his books to sales in aid of the Red Cross. His library was still substantial and included his signed presentation copies of books by Shaw, Barker, Wilde and Mark Twain, his editions of Ibsen and Shakespeare, books on the theatre, and a few novels. On 17 April, he saw a shrieking bedroom farce called *Be Careful Baby!* by Salisbury Field and Margaret Mayo at the Apollo, in which three married couples clad in pyjamas chased each other through a bedroom, and which 'carries the art and mystery of stage undressing . . . to "the limit" ',[50] he observed coldly.

A week later, early in the morning of 25 April 1918, after five weeks of almost constant fighting, the Germans took Mont Kemmel, one of the strategic bastions of the front. The next day, the exhausted King's Own Scottish Borderers withdrew. Their losses during April were appalling. Four hundred and thirty four men were either dead or missing. One of them was Tom.

There was a chance he had been taken prisoner, but although Frances and Alys clung to this reed of hope, Archer realized there was not much chance of it keeping them afloat. There had been too many deaths to think that Tom might still be alive. During the war, he lunched regularly with Rosalind, Murray's daughter, and her husband, Arnold Toynbee, the satisfactorily freethinking historian. As he was working in intelligence at the Foreign Office, Archer had a direct line to the latest war news. From Toynbee, and from his own work at Wellington House, he was under no delusions that the cost of a British victory was almost incomprehensible carnage. Later, it was estimated that over ten million had been slaughtered during the Great War, over one million of whom were British.

Alys went back to Hampstead to her mother. Frances insulated herself in work, the only thing, she said, that would help her face uncertain days ahead. 'Life is one series of artillery just now; shock after shock and nothing to do but close the ranks and stumble blindly on.'[51] On 20 July, Archer told Elizabeth there was still no news. 'I don't think there will be any now . . .' Elizabeth was one of the very few people outside the family to whom Archer confided about his son. So successfully did he mask his anxiety that until they asked after Tom, few friends realized anything was wrong. As always, Elizabeth was his safety valve. 'I don't regard you as an outsider in what concerns me,'[52] he explained.

These were long, anxious days, days which became weeks and months as spring became summer and summer became autumn. Archer saw Elizabeth when he could, deriving comfort from her practical good sense and when it seemed the end of the war was in sight, he fell in love with her all over again. 'I have a letter from WA of the old times sort more or less,' she wrote in her diary for 17 September 1918. 'His relief at the prospect of victory throws him into moods of the past.'[53]

Anxiously, the family waited for word of Tom. None came. 'I *can't* think of him as dead,'[54] cried a distracted, terrified Frances.

The Consequences of War

With the news that Tom was missing, Archer withdrew into himself and his study at King's Langley, emerging in the third week of June clutching a manuscript. 'Would it surprise you to hear that I have written a play?' he asked Elizabeth. 'Such is the surprising truth.'¹ The announcement indeed astonished Elizabeth and everyone else. Shaw, who had been pestering Archer to write for years, exclaimed that it had taken a European catastrophe to 'knock a play out of him.'²

It was the first time since his early days in London that Archer had written a play alone, and the first time for eighteen years that he had worked on an original drama. *War is War* is in three acts and demands a cast of twenty-one and many extras. Its origins lay in the 'black oppression'³ which had descended upon him at the beginning of the war, intensified at the Leicester Galleries when he stood before Nevinson's paintings and which became almost unbearable now he realized that Tom might not be coming home. But he disguised his misery and his lack of confidence in the play by dressing it in the uniform of Masterman's army. 'It is a propaganda play – not a work of high art, but a talking cinema-film,'⁴ he explained to Elizabeth.

Subtitled *The Germans in Belgium: A Drama of 1914*, the play is a propagandist's interpretation of the destruction of Louvain. Archer's setting is the fictional village of Pirenne, a rural community 'injuring no-one, envying no-one, at peace with all the world', during the twenty-four hours from 8 am on 5 August until 8 am the following day. As the play opens, Burgomaster Decortis and his family read in the morning newspapers that the German army has crossed the border. Together with the village priest and the schoolmaster, they reassure themselves there is nothing to fear, for Germany has promised to respect Belgian neutrality and ensure that 'the war will be conducted chivalrously'.

Within hours, prisoners are taken and by the following morning, shops have been looted and houses set ablaze. *War is War* ends in Pirenne's main square as German troops massacre the villagers.

The colours of Wellington House reveal themselves in Archer's deployment of atrocity stories. Since the war began, rumours of appalling German atrocities had spread like an epidemic throughout Britain. Mostly spurious, they nevertheless helped to create the serum of outrage and moral justification with which to inoculate a nation sending its young men into war. It was said the Germans skewered babies on their bayonets and threw them into the air; that they charged into battle driving terrified women before them, and cut the ring fingers from dead British soldiers to pocket a sliver of gold. Similar allegations were made by the Germans. In these stories, the rings were on German fingers and it was the 'neutral' Belgians who hacked them off and gouged out the eyes of dead German soldiers. There was even, supposedly, a small boy, an urchin harpy of war, roaming the battle-fields, clutching a pail in which he collected gelatinous German eyes.

In *War is War*, Archer sets contrary rumours running among the German troops and Belgian villagers, but shows only the Germans drunk and looting. In a thirty-five-page epilogue, he claimed there was no foundation to the rumours of Belgian brutality but a mountain of testimony to German evil. Quoting from the popular blood-and-steel novels of Walter Bloem (who appears in the play, the only real-life character to do so, as a fanatical army captain), he railed against the German philosophy of 'war is war', the theory of war as both inevitable and necessary and therefore above statute law. The play, wrote Archer, was 'an almost literal transcript of fact' deriving from a 'prolonged study of documents',[5] with the massacre in the final scene being based upon that at Aerschot in Belgium.

He not only wanted to write good propaganda but a good drama, and submitted his ideas to the test of *Play-Making*. His principal rule was that 'The first step to writing a play is manifestly to chose a theme,'[6] and the theme he chose for *War is War* is that of the corruption and redemption of a good man. 'One point of originality it really can claim,' he advised Elizabeth, 'the sympathetic hero is a German!'[7] This good German is Karl Kessler, who previously lodged with the Decortis family and returns to Pirenne as a Lieutenant with the invading troops. But during the intervening months, Kessler has made so many imperceptible moral and political compromises that he is no longer the amiable young man who might have married the Burgomaster's daughter, Suzanne, but one who can excuse the peremptory arrest of an innocent priest as 'pure formality'.

Kessler represents cultured Germany infected by the malignant spirit of militarism, a fair-minded man who no longer has either the conviction or the courage to defy the extremists. Knowing that German infantry-men abuse and loot, he does not demand his superiors take disciplinary action. Kessler embodies the dreadful choice between principle and evasion which Archer imagined could face every soldier, and the question of whether, when the world is overrun by war, there is any use in continuing to believe in the rationality of man. When Bloem ridicules him for failing to understand that human nature is a jungle of paradox: 'You think men are rational beings', Kessler admits that 'I am beginning to find out my mistake.' Overwhelmed by convictions more fervently held than his own, Kessler protests to the Decortises that he is out of his depth. Suzanne retorts that no man is helpless and demands that he redeem himself. His chance arrives in the final scene, when the villagers are herded into the square and those about to be executed lined against a wall. Kessler is detailed to order the firing squad to shoot. Instead, proclaiming that 'I must cleanse my soul!' he shoots himself. As he falls, Suzanne's 'wild, almost triumphant laugh' breaks the silence.

With its naivety and its programmatic dialogue, the play never for one moment bears comparison to those he admired by Barker or Galsworthy. It is not inferior to the bulk of war-time dramas, and better than many, yet, as Archer himself pointed out, the war years produced no substantial plays. There are effective moments in *War is War*, including a pathetic procession of prisoners passing along the rear of the stage and, for its time, the final shooting at close range of the villagers as a military band plays *Deutschland über Alles* would have made graphic and sombre theatre. Archer confessed that the play was 'the outcome of a very real emotion . . .'[8] Ostensibly, this was his horror at the burning of Louvain. But really, it is his anguish at the fate of his son and the apparent death of moral decency. Kessler's dilemma and his pitiful end represents the crumbling of liberalism.

As soon as he completed the manuscript, Archer dispatched it to Barker. He was not impressed. 'The strength of the play is that it is a document,' he wrote guardedly on 28 June. The characters were weak and, apart from Kessler, did not develop: '. . . it should not be a three act but a three *scene* play'.[9] Severely stung, Archer replied by return of post. 'Of course your criticism of the great propagandist drama is perfectly sound from the artistic point of view,' he snapped. But: 'I do not imagine that much development of character took place in a Belgian village in the 24-hours between the arrival of the Germans & the massacre.'[10] It was useless Barker explaining that it was just this pernickety attention to rationalism which squeezed the drama from the play. Rebuffed, Archer asked Elizabeth whether she knew of anyone who might 'want to put about £3000 into what *may* be a goldmine' and stage *War is War* commercially. Given a chance, he suggested, the play might be 'an enormous success in all the allied countries & the biggest piece of propaganda the war has produced'.[11] But no money was found and the play has never been performed.

Instead, it was published in March 1919. 'Accept my congratulations on a fine, solid piece of work,' wrote Pinero, to whom Archer had sent one of the first copies. 'I envy the *ease* of the whole thing – though I know what pains have gone into the working of it.'[12] Shaw also congratulated him. 'I always told you . . . that you had the faculty. But you never really wanted to use it.'[13] According to Shaw, Archer had burst into creativity because he had discovered at long last that he had a social conscience.

He reviewed *War is War* in the *Daily News* on 9 May. It was a good play, he wrote, achieved by the only method which had ever produced a good play, that of having a story to tell and a conviction that it should be told. As a fellow playwright, he was generous, but as an author of vigoriously opinionated and lengthy prefaces, he could not condone Archer's documentary epilogue. It really was 'pathetically inadequate' stuff, he wrote. If Archer thought drunkenness and looting were restricted to German troops, then he was obviously wilfully averting his eyes from the real world and its incriminating facts. History clearly demonstrated the British army to be as barbaric as any other when it was the invading force. Archer had only to look at South Africa, and India, where the British routinely re-asserted their authority by dispatching 'punitive expeditions'[14] to burn hill villages.

The force of Shaw's contempt provoked Archer into writing to the *Daily News*, uncomfortably admitting there had been 'excesses' in India, but blurting out that 'the burning of a few mountain villages' could not be compared to the unprovoked ransacking of 'highly civilised and densely inhabited cities and townships'.[15] Recovering himself, he explained that cultural differences prevented armies from different countries behaving alike.

Shaw was not finished yet. The play became part of their four-year tussle over the cause and the course of the war and as Archer had rewritten *Pygmalion*, so Shaw remodelled *War is War*. According to Shaw, Archer was writing about the behaviour of invading armies, whichever country they might serve, and therefore his title should have been *Invasion*. Archer had also given the impression that the German complaint of their soldiers being picked off by snipers and vigilantes in a supposedly neutral country was a myth, which was untrue. In fact, Archer should have emphasized rather than diminished the vigilante presence. And surely it would be a far more effective ending if Kessler acknowledged that although terrible, the firing squad was 'militarily reasonable, militarily logical and militarily necessary as part of the general proposition that war is war'.[16] Rather than commit suicide, he should carry out the order to shoot.

Peace came at last, celebrated in London on 11 November by dancing in the streets. Archer did not dance, for there was still no news of Tom. 'If only the results should prove anything like worth the price!' he cried.

Several friends, and the loved ones of friends, were among the millions of deaths. There were Chapin, Seeger and Frohman; Mrs Patrick Campbell's son, Alan, and Barrie's godson, George Llewellyn Davies, one of Peter Pan's original lost boys. 'What a tragedy it has all been!' he wrote sorrowfully to Henry Bond.[17] Others were wounded but had survived. Denis, one of the Murrays' sons, had joined the Royal Air Corps, been shot down and interned. He would never fully recover. Robert Loraine, the dashing Kit French in the New Century's *Admiral Guinea* and one of Frances's voice production graduates, had also become an airman and was almost killed, but hobbled home to a long convalescence after which he would bravely go back on to the stage. Others had not fought but had not lived either. Sydney Grundy, one of his earliest theatrical friends and later most vociferous opponents, died of cancer in 1914, having spent many of his last years in Kent, studying astronomy and peering through his telescope. Nora, the daughter of Charles Charrington and Janet Achurch also died that year, aged twenty-four and in 1916, poor Janet died, aged fifty-two. In December 1918, George Halkett died. Of the three authors of *The Fashionable Tragedian*, only Archer remained.

There was little happiness. Even the uninjured were emotionally war-torn. During the conflict, Archer had been almost as concerned for Granville Barker as for Tom himself, for love and war had torpedoed his career and wrecked his marriage.

Like Archer, Barker had realized the war would put an end to serious theatre in London, and having been invited by the Stage Society of America to direct a series of productions at Wallack's Theatre in New York, he and Lillah set sail in early January 1915. That spring, Barker directed the American premieres of *Androcles and the Lion* and *The Doctor's Dilemma*, and met and fell passionately in love with Helen Huntington, a dark-haired woman of forty-seven, and a minor poet and novelist. She was also married to her second husband, Archer Huntington, the theatre-loving heir of a railroad millionaire and one of the guarantors of the New York season.

Lillah loved her husband and was prepared to fight to keep him. When the Barkers returned to England in June, they were £5000 in debt, £2000 of which was owed in royalties to Shaw who told them he did not want paying back. Barker assured Lillah his affair with Helen was over, but this was untrue. In London, he did no work, and became even more disillusioned. 'Barker has chucked the theatre,'[18] Shaw reported to Murray. At the request of the Red Cross, he went to France to research a propaganda book, but was back in America in September, lecturing in an attempt to pay off his debts, and seeing Helen. Instead of returning to England at the end of the year, he deliberately avoided London and Lillah and darted to France. From there, he sent her a letter, which reached her just as she was about to go on stage on the evening of 3 January 1916, briskly asking for a divorce.

Archer had noticed the unhappiness between the couple the previous summer, and when he arrived back in London from postal censorship in Edinburgh, his friends were humming with speculation about the marriage. Remembering how he and Elizabeth felt when Shaw began his prying into their affair, Archer dithered at first, then sent a worried letter to Barker in France, asking for explanations. '. . . so glad to get your message,' came the reply. 'Some day we'll meet! and I'll tell you all the whys and wherefores.'[19] It appeared that Barker did not want to confide in him yet. Things rapidly became even more complicated. Still skulking abroad, Barker asked Shaw to persuade Lillah to comply with his demand for a divorce. Shaw, as well as advising Barker, advised Lillah to get advice.

In France, Barker still laid low, then went back to America and Helen. The next Archer heard was when a letter arrived from Massachusetts in mid-April 1916. 'I feel a pig for not having written . . .' wrote Barker. 'But I didn't want to write to you without being quite open and telling you straight out of my separation from Lillah. To those

who impute faults over such things let it appear – and quite justly – as
my "fault." There is no use discussing it however – and there is no
"scandal" for mere busybodies to discuss – The thing is done – or
rather it is only half-done as yet.' It was a letter written by a lonely,
unhappy man, in which Barker recalled their first meeting at Vernon
Chambers when Archer told him he would be a success. He signed off
with an unprecedented declaration of his affection, 'My love to you
HGB.'[19]

Archer had always argued against conscription, thinking it might
begin a groundswell of popular opinion against the war, but when
conscription was introduced in 1916, Barker answered the pleas of his
friends to return to England and join up. He enlisted in the Royal
Horse Artillery, quickly transferred to an officer cadet school and in
October moved to Army Intelligence. Meanwhile, the emotional chess
game with Lillah continued until, at the end of the year, she reluctantly
began proceedings for the restitution of conjugal rights. The divorce
was made absolute in the spring of 1917. Helen's decree absolute came
through just over a year later and on 31 July 1918, when Archer had all
but given up hope of Tom and was hinting that Elizabeth might find
investors for *War Is War*, Barker and Helen were quietly married in the
Congregationalist Chapel in Grosvenor Square. On the marriage
certificate, Barker entered his age, correctly, as forty. Helen lied about
hers, reducing it by almost eight years to forty-three.

Archer was concerned for Barker, but he was also fond of Lillah and,
because he had been a victim of Shaw's meddling too often, he was
reluctant to join the chorus of advisors bobbing around the unhappy
couple. The result was that Archer kept his friends and made a new
one in Helen, while Shaw did not. Helen distrusted Shaw and slapped
an exclusion order upon him which Barker, tired and looking forward
to beginning a new life concentrating upon his writing, did not contest.
After his marriage, he and Shaw seldom met or corresponded again.
Their collaboration, which had been the powerhouse of the Vedrenne-
Barker Performances at the Court, and their friendship, was over.

By the time of Barker's marriage, Archer had discovered yet another
model for a rational world order. The League of Free Nations
Association was formed at the end of June 1918, one of a clutch of
societies promoting international understanding and which were proliferating as rapidly as the munitions industry. The Association was the
inspiration of David Davies, the wealthy and idiosyncratic Liberal

Member of Parliament for Montgomeryshire, a close associate of Lloyd George and the benefactor of a chain of tuberculosis sanatoria built in memory of King Edward VII. The Association did not aim as high as Archer's hopes for a College of Systematic Sociology, but was broadly sympathetic to the internationalism of the American President, Woodrow Wilson, whom he made the subject of *The Peace President: A Brief Appreciation*, his twelfth and final propagandist publication. Therefore, when Murray was elected Association chairman, he threw his support behind it.

Much of his professional life was a struggle, but occasionally, by strange Archerian luck, things fell into the right place at the right time. Just when he needed money a decade previously, the Simplified Spelling Society elected him their secretary. Now, in the summer of 1818, when his work at Wellington House came to an end, Murray and H. G. Wells offered him a part-time job as secretary to the Association's Research Committee. He simply moved a few doors down Buckingham Gate to the League of Free Nations Association's office at number 22, where he was given a desk, a supply of headed notepaper, and a salary of four hundred pounds a year. So fired was his enthusiasm that in August he was telling Murray that 'The more I see of this work, the more I feel that I ought to give my whole time to it.'[20]

Archer's committee included Wells as chairman; Murray; the former Foreign Secretary, Sir Edward, now Lord Grey; the political scientist, Ernest Barker, and the journalists J. A. Spender and Wickham Steed. Archer liked the neat symmetry of bureaucratic structure and admired its potential for smooth efficiency. What he loathed was everyone else's inefficiency and, in this sense, he was right when he told Frederick Whelan he was not a good committee man. Archer soon found himself engulfed in a storm of paper as he typed numerous letters to committee members, shuffling the dates and times of meetings so that a majority could attend, an agenda be drawn up and minutes made.

He also found himself typing plaintive letters on behalf of a shadowy body called the Sub-Committee on the Organisation of Will, and enduring the interminable meetings of committees to which he had been sometimes unwillingly co-opted. 'Oh, such a performance!' he cried one day, reeling from a particularly arduous session of the Press and Propaganda committee. 'I sat there for about $2\frac{1}{2}$ hours and suffered.' It was dreadful. People nominated him, recruited him, pursued him and pleaded with him to draft an appeal, submit a report, draw up petitions to Parliament and compose statements of principle and policy. 'They seem to have got it into their heads (not quite without reason) that I am the only man on the premises who can write,'[21] he complained. Soon, his headaches began to come back, violent migraines causing him almost to shout with pain.

The previous year, Archer had answered Wells's *God the Invisible King*, a book in which he outlined his idea of God as an inspired taskmaster, with his own *God and Mr Wells*, in which he set out his own position of virtual atheism. This renewed his assault upon religion ('I should like to get rid of it,'[22] he would inform the Norwegian academic Christen Collin, succinctly), and he continued the battle in articles for the *Rationalist Press Association Annual*. Although he was rather suspicious of Wells's brand of utopianism, Archer managed to work efficiently enough with him and Murray in engineering the amalgamation of the Association with the rival League of Nations Society, and in November, Lord Grey was elected president of a League of Nations Union with over 3000 members. Archer now typed his letters at the Union's headquarters at Central Buildings, Westminster, on notepaper declaring that its aim was 'to promote the formation of a World League of Free Peoples for the securing of international justice, mutual defence and permanent peace'. With Murray, he drafted the Union's new Covenant, or constitution. But just as everything seemed to be going well, it began to go wrong.

At the end of January 1919, Archer returned from Paris, where he had been due to speak at the Conference of League of Nations Societies, fuming that its organization was 'beneath contempt' and a sludge of procedural wrangling had resulted in his own speech being cancelled. Most farcical of all, 'the language difficulty was tremendous'.[23] Back at Central Buildings, the Union was sliding into chaos as 'money was being squandered at an incredible rate'. Drastic action was required. Diagnosing Davies, with his limitless industrial wealth, as a profligate dreamer, Archer took the audacious step of proposing that Murray, Spender and himself launch a coup against him and 'form a triumvirate to run the show' themselves. 'I would be the Executive head,' he explained to Murray, 'but I would be in daily contact with you & him by arranging an hour at which I could catch you on the telephone.'[24]

Among Archer's plans once they had taken power was the founding of *The League*, a weekly newspaper interpreting international events from a Union standpoint. For an editor, he had his eye on a fellow member of the new Research Department. This was Leonard Woolf, a

Fabian and the husband of his former Fitzroy Square neighbour, the novelist Virginia Woolf, with whom he had founded the Hogarth Press. Archer also envisaged a tight budget of £700 a month and the establishment of a League library and reading room. But the rebels were foiled and Davies clung tenaciously to his authority. At the end of March, the Research Department moved into offices at 171a Sloane Street, but because of a blunder over the lease suffered the humiliation of being shunted out into the street. 'I feel rather like a man in handcuffs on a sinking ship, unable even to work at the pumps,'[25] he cried, and at the beginning of May, Archer walked out of Central Buildings, and the Union, for good.

In 1916, David Lloyd George, backed by a powerful Liberal and Conservative coalition, had overthrown Asquith to become Prime Minister. Within days of the Armistice he announced a snap election for 14 December. There had been talk during the summer that Archer himself might stand as a Liberal candidate, but with traditional, Asquithian Liberalism in decline, he brushed the invitation aside. He thought Lloyd George an opportunist rogue, and stood by horrified as coalition candidates whipped up a roller-coaster of popular support, waving the banner for Lloyd George as 'the Man who won the War', and promising to extract huge financial reparations from the Germans: '. . . they are going to be squeezed as a lemon is squeezed – until the pips squeak,'[26] promised Sir Eric Geddes, the First Lord of the Admiralty. The coalition thundered back into power with a 516 seats, a thumping 340-seat majority. For the first time, the Labour Party became the official opposition as Asquith's Liberals were reduced to twenty-seven and even Asquith himself lost his East Fife seat. It was, said Archer, a 'Parliament of all the Ruffians'.[27] On the first day of 1919, he joined Murray, Wells and the novelist John Buchan in signing a letter to Lloyd George asking for the immediate release of the remaining 1500 conscientious objectors still held in British prisons.

Archer was now sixty-two. The strain of the previous year had left him exhausted, and soon after he arrived home from Paris he was sweating and shaking with influenza. He remained cooped up at Fitzroy Square for two weeks. The Morgans from upstairs monitored his progress. Frances fussed. Elizabeth looked in. Feeling 'as weak as a kitten & thoroughly abnormal',[28] he surveyed the peace and decided England looked shabby and uncertain. After eighteen years, he resigned from the National Liberal Club, as the place had become as dilapidated

as Liberalism itself. The furniture was tatty, the atmosphere melancholy, the food tasteless and 'the contempt of the waitresses' unbearable.
Spender and Wells came to his rescue and put him up for the Reform,
a 'nice Victorian haven of rest'[29] in Pall Mall, to which he was elected
on 27 March and where he was delighted to find civilized staff who
served 'capital fish'[30] for lunch. Yet, for a year there had been no news
of Tom. Alys placed an In Memoriam notice in the April issue of the
London Scottish Regimental Gazette, but refusing to think of him as
dead, recorded him only as missing.

For his part, Archer decided to consult a spiritualist medium. During
and immediately after the war, hundreds of parents whose sons were
missing or killed in foreign fields, sought comfort in spiritualism. There
was a hope, even a certainty that, bidden by specialist invocations, a
charged atmosphere might coalesce into a uniformed wraith or that
words of reassurance might spill out of the dim beyond. Mediums of all
kinds advertised consultations in Notting Hill, Bayswater and Padding-
ton. They sank into trances and relayed messages, or held pen to paper,
promising their writing to be spiritually guided, or asked their sitters to
lay their hands on a table and wait for it to begin mysteriously tilting.
Others performed publicly in damp East End halls. Some were
endorsed by influential figures. Sir Oliver Lodge, whose son Raymond
had been killed during the war, was certain the mind survived death
and that he was in communication with him. Neither was Murray
discounting the possibility of a spiritual existence, and had served as
president of the Society for Psychical Research for a year.

Archer was impressed that Lodge and Murray were prepared to take
mediumistic claims seriously, but Elizabeth was sceptical and told him
so. But this time, he ignored her advice. Although he and Tom may
have gone some way towards repairing their fractured relationship, the
grief he felt over his almost certain death was still compounded by the
remorse of a largely absent and too demanding father. Like others, he
wanted to learn exactly what happened to his son. He wanted to know
whether Tom was happy and whether he could think of himself as a
good parent. In March, he made up his mind. Saying nothing to either
Frances or Alys, he consulted a medium recommended by Lodge.
Nothing. Then a letter arrived from America.

It was from friends who had given some of Tom's letters to a
clairvoyant who, having examined them, pronounced that he was not
dead but had suffered a head injury which had affected his memory.
He was recovering in a camp in an unspecified friendly country and

would be contacting his parents in either seven weeks or seven months. Archer would have rejected this out of hand were it not for 'one or two curious details' he thought worth investigating. He took his sister, Julia, as well as Murray and Elizabeth, into his confidence. Julia was three years Archer's junior and married to a retired army officer, Major-General Sir Harold Parsons. They lived in London and although his sister was 'in no way occultly inclined', he informed Murray, she agreed 'that the matter ought to be followed up on the bare chance of there being anything in it'.[31]

The American clairvoyant had reported seeing the spirit of a young man named James standing near Tom. His son's closest friend, he told Julia, was a Jimmy Thomson, who was killed earlier in 1918. More significant was her suggestion that Tom was wearing a ring. Archer doubted Tom had ever worn a ring, but when Julia asked Alys, she said she had wanted to buy him one but they had finally decided against it.

Archer was still unconvinced, but agreed the investigation was worth pursuing. On 3 April, still keeping his enquiries secret from Frances and Alys, he consulted a second medium recommended by Lodge, and came away encouraged. 'She professed to get into communication with Tom (the whole thing was by daylight & she was in a quite normal condition) & she would have nothing to do with the idea of his being still alive,' he notified Murray the next day. Archer, too, was sure that Tom was dead, but he was wholly unprepared for the medium's announcement of there being 'Three friends – two passed out first – one later.' Apart from Tom, she said, there was Joe, and Monty. It seemed terribly thin evidence at first, but later, Archer remembered that a contemporary of Tom's who had died when he was twenty was called Joe, while Julia suggested Monty might have been a mistaken version of Morty, Alys's surname. Was it possible, she hazarded, that the name of the cousin who had introduced Tom and Alys and who later died at Messines, was Joe Morty? Yet when he asked Alys her cousin's name, she said it was Morrison. 'So *that* clue comes to nothing,' he thought. Then suddenly, she added, 'Monty Morrison,'[32] and Archer's scepticism cleared like a rising mist.

The medium had also said that Tom was showing her a coat that was torn on the right-hand side with papers in one pocket, and Alys confirmed that the only coat of Tom's which had been returned to her had a long rent on the right side and in the pocket was a copy of the London Scottish Regimental Gazette. But the most extraordinary moment of the sitting had come when Archer asked whether Tom had

any message for 'the two ladies who are interested in him.' He realized
the medium would guess the women were a mother and a wife, but he
was still surprised when she answered, 'Will you tell the younger lady
that he always answers goodnight – something to do with a picture or a
photograph.' He relayed this to Julia, whose job it was to prise evidence
from Alys under the pretence of occasional womanly chats. She reported
that Alys kept a photograph of Tom at her bedside and that 'Even now
I would never dream of going to bed without saying goodnight to him.'

All this was duly relayed to Murray, who understood the depth of
Archer's feelings but also knew him well enough not to strip away the
scientific wrapping in which he chose to bundle up his emotions. Archer
preferred to speak less in the voice of a bereaved father or a spiritualist
convert, than that of an amateur psychologist, the rationalist insisting
that his interest in clairvoyance was entirely 'impersonal'[33] and no
greater than if he had been following a detective story.

To some extent, this was true. At the beginning of the war, he read
Sigmund Freud's *The Interpretation of Dreams*. Although profoundly
disagreeing with the Freudian view that dreams, like neuroses, were
principally disguised manifestations of repressed sexual desires, he was
equally intrigued by his clarification of the subconscious mind, and had
since kept a record of his own dreams. He now yoked his spiritualistic
quest to an attempted analysis of the nature of the subconscious. 'My
study of dreams is bringing me to conceive our sub-conscious as a sort
of seething maelstrom of ideas, pictures, words, and what not, rotating
all the time, so that it is a matter of pure chance what may happen to
swim to the surface at any given moment *during sleep*,' he advised
Murray on 1 July.

During a seance, he suggested, it might be that the sitter's subconscious somehow played upon that of the medium in her sleep-like
trance, so guiding her to particular ideas which were then taken as
factual evidence of spiritual existence. But what exactly were the
subconscious impulses between sitter and medium, he wondered, and
who transferred what to whom? Could the apparently irrational be
rationalized? He read newspaper reports and scientific papers; he
peered at supposedly spirit photographs. Was it possible to photograph
a thought, or a memory? Perhaps; perhaps not. And what exactly was
the difference between the psychic and the psychological? 'This ragged
edge to the accepted & orthodox phenomena of psychology interests me
enormously,'[34] he wrote.

Meanwhile, he arranged a consultation with a third medium, again recommended by Lodge, to see whether she produced corroborative evidence of Tom's spiritual existence. On 28 April, he knocked on the door of Mrs Gladys Osborne Leonard's rooms in Maida Vale. She was an imposing, wide-eyed woman in early middle-age, given to wearing silks and scarves and her dark hair fashionably cut and curled so that it clung tightly to her head and ears. A highly respected medium, she had passed a series of stringent tests imposed by the Society for Psychical Research. She claimed to rely upon a spirit messenger, a young Indian girl named Feda, a vivaciously entertaining personality who had married Mrs Leonard's great-great grandfather in 1800 when she was thirteen and had subsequently died in childbirth.

For many months, Archer had regular sittings with Mrs Leonard and two or three times felt 'the sense of cold air on my face which is so often said to announce the presence of spirits'[35] and indicated that Tom was about to speak through Feda. Superficially, Archer managed to maintain the pretence of disinterest, but the conviction that his son was out there somewhere drew him on as if he was being guided across a marsh at night by a phantom beckoning finger. Experiment became moral duty. '. . . there is the feeling that if it *was* true that Tom was trying to communicate, it would be unkind not to respond,'[36] he explained to the still disapproving Elizabeth.

After the summer of 1920, his visits to Mrs Leonard abruptly ceased. One reason for this was that he was working on a new play. Another was that while for over two years there had been no official news of Tom, the unofficial bulletins from Mrs Leonard were so patchy that he sometimes did not know quite what to make of them. He believed he was in communication with his dead son, but still kept everything secret from the desperately unhappy Frances and Alys, promising Murray that he would tell Frances if he received a message for her. But in the end, he observed that 'all the communications are so *mixed* that I think they would only weary & unsettle her. I sometimes imagine that the striking *absence* of any direct message to her or to Alys purporting to come from Tom, may show that he takes the same view.'[37]

That spring, Alys had placed her second In Memoriam notice in the Regimental Gazette. This time, she admitted that her husband was 'now presumed dead'. The following year, she altered the wording a second time to 'wounded and missing'. She simply did not know what to think. She wrote letters to Berlin, appealing for information, but received no definite answers. Then, in early June 1921, the Ministry of Defence told Archer that a grave had been identified as possibly being that of Tom's. 'It is not *quite* certain,'[38] Archer told Murray, as there was more than one Lieutenant Archer on the Army's lists. He and Frances and Alys had already planned to go to Norway for a rest and they left on the 17th. They avoided Larvik and Christiana, and stayed instead near Sognefjord on the west coast, where Archer, who only had one pair of shoes, got badly chafed heels from walking too far and too long.

Within days of their return in the first week of July, the Ministry confirmed that Tom had been injured at Mont Kemmel, died of wounds in a German hospital and buried on 28 April 1918 in grave number 29 in Row C at the Communal Cemetery at Courtrai in Belgium. Just over three years since her husband was reported missing, Alys knew that she was officially a widow, and had already been a widow for longer than she was a wife. She had been married ten weeks before he died, and they had spent only six of those weeks together. '. . .we have had longer together than we might have expected,'[39] Tom had written before he left for France. At last his widow and his parents were able to cross the Channel to see his grave and say their farewells to him. '. . . it makes one feel that one has no right to be alive,'[40] Archer sadly told Dibdin, his old friend.

Alys never remarried. She died, aged 102, in 1985.

The war had brought deaths but also new marriages, and when she married the Oxford botanist Dr Frederick Keeble in the spring of 1920, Lillah McCarthy received an affectionate note of congratulation from Archer. From now on, she rarely appeared on the stage. Her second marriage whisked her away from the theatre and into the country. The same happened to Barker.

Helen was socially ambitious and rich, and within months she transformed Barker from an impoverished playwright, director and actor-manager, to a country squire. In the summer of 1920, they moved into Netherton Hall, an impressive Jacobean manor at Colyton, near Lyme Bay in Devon. There, he shrugged off his socialism to reappear as a liberal-conservative, hyphenated his name and became the employer of fifteen servants, including a footman in full livery.

Most of his friends thought Helen had mesmerized and virtually kidnapped him, but this was not true. His dreams for a new kind of theatre had withered into hopelessness and he decided that if he could not run a true repertory theatre, then he did not want to run a theatre at all. Instead, he concentrated upon writing. Loving Helen symbolized a new beginning and in Devon she created the peace for him to be able to work. Neither she nor her husband encouraged many visitors from his theatrical acquaintances, and especially from Shaw. But there was always a welcome for Archer, his old mentor. 'Say yourself when you want a weekend of Devonshire "air",'[41] Barker reminded him.

After the war, the friendship between Archer and Barker matured and became almost like that of an elderly father and a grown-up son. Affection (such as Archer and Shaw could never have expressed) bursts through their letters. 'I hope you are having a good time. Love to Helen . . .'[42] wrote Archer. 'Our love . . .'[43] ended Barker's reply. 'You are a brick,' he told Archer later, ' – you are a whole edifice of bricks . . . It is good to have such a letter and such a friend.'[44] 'Yours,' Archer signed off, 'in affection and admiration.'[45]

He was still reviewing for *The Star*, but there were few plays that interested him in those nervily uncertain few years between the end of the war and the whirling days of jazz and cocktails, fast cars and faster parties. Prices rose frighteningly, and as theatre rentals climbed, managers became more anxious than ever about their box office receipts, taking refuge in the safety of glamorous revues and tinkling comedies, or pleasant plays in which pleasant characters did pleasant things.

A. A. Milne's *Mr Pim Passes By* fitted the bill perfectly. It was slight, light and cheap to produce, having only seven characters and one set (the Morning Room at Marden Lodge, Bucks). A popular *Punch* humorist turned playwright, Milne knew Archer vaguely and thought of him as an austere Edwardian figure in a high collar and bowler hat. 'Archer had more gravity than any man I have ever met,' he recalled. 'One felt that humour in his presence would have as little chance of establishing itself as would some practical joke on a bishop during the final blessing. Nor was it more hopeful to be intelligent. Archer, one felt, knew it all and had rejected it.'[46] Milne's was the conventional impression of Archer. He was overawed by both him and Shaw, whom he thought to be the only writer who could get away with anything demanding in the theatre. What Milne did was to take the Shavian issues of political conflict and the marriage laws and whisk them into froth. After the war, theatre-goers wanted reassurance. They discovered it in *Mr Pim Passes By*, which opened at the New Theatre on 5 January 1920.

As the former wife of Jacob Telworthy, a fraudulent entrepreneur, and now married to George Marden, of old English Conservative stock and proud of it, Olivia is a woman with a past. But there is nothing remotely Ibsenish or even Pineroish about her. Olivia's social rebellion is restricted to disturbingly modern ideas on curtains. George's niece, meanwhile, plans to marry an amiable Cubist painter of mistily socialist sympathies, pointedly called Brian Strange. Olivia believes Telworthy to have died in the Australian outback six years previously, but to her and George's consternation, the passing Mr Pim reveals that far from having been a widow, she appears to be a bigamist, as he met a man called Telworthy on the ship to England. In the second act, Mr Pim remembers that Telworthy had choked to death on a fishbone at Marseilles, and in the third that his name was not Telworthy at all but Polwittle.

Archer thought *Mr Pim Passes By* almost unwatchable. Originally written for Lillah McCarthy, who wisely turned it down, the central role of Olivia was given to Irene Vanbrugh, who played it to roof-echoing cheers. Awakening from a snooze in the stalls, Archer conceded that it was 'a brilliant performance' but compared to the pre-war drama of Ibsen, Barker, Shaw and even Pinero, the play was 'a ripple in a teacup'.[47] Galsworthy's new play, on the other hand, was emphatically the opposite, a 'masterpiece'[48] which restored his faith in the theatre as a place for serious ideas.

The Skin Game, which opened at the St Martin's on 21 April, contrasts the old, complacent pre-war ways with the new, aggressive post-war ideas. The play opens in a large, baronial room in which Hillcrist sits surrounded by photographs of India and South Africa, and beneath foxes' heads mounted on shields. For well over 300 years, successive generations of Hillcrists have gazed from these windows across an uninterrupted rural landscape, but now the newly-rich Hornblowers, incomers and the purchasers of Longmeadow, plan to build a pottery that will ruin the view forever. Hillcrist instinctively recoils from the Hornblowers' brand of brazen capitalism. While he treasures romantic dreams of the family history, the Hornblowers strain towards the future. Galsworthy had written a state-of-the-nation play in which ruthless capitalist ambition confronts equally determined social entrenchment, privilege and snobbery. Behind it all lies the implication that the history of England is one of consistent exploitation by the strong and the rich of the weak and the poor. The sight of the Hillcrists resorting to emotional blackmail to defend themselves, disconcerted the St Martin's audiences. Galsworthy was both writing an epitaph for a morally bankrupt class and way of life, and lamenting the new Britain, with its heartlessness and greed.

Mr Pim Passes By and *The Skin Game* were offerings for a new era. Milne was assuring the nation that everything was all right, because the apparent threat represented by Brian Strange and modern curtains was really no threat at all in a world in which everyone is benevolent at heart. But Galsworthy was taking an altogether more despairing view, asking whether old England was really worth saving and whether the new was fit to be encouraged. Galsworthy looked at the present and the future and saw division and meanness of spirit.

However, *The Skin Game* was a play apart, and Archer was once again aching to have done with writing theatre reviews. Yet it was financially impossible for him to leave *The Star*. Indeed, he was so pressed for money that at the beginning of May, he began writing an additional weekly column for the *Illustrated Sporting and Dramatic News*, for whom he reviewed *The Cherry Orchard*, produced as part of Madame Donnet's Art Theatre matinees at the St Martin's on 11 July. Madame Donnet was a Russian émigré familiar with the work of the Moscow Art Theatre but she, like every other director who tried to introduce Chekhov into the British theatre, failed to explain the Chekhovian technique to her cast, who remained resolutely English and gave a hesitant and tense performance. 'Leading intellectuals "in the know",' Archer scrawled across his programme, pehaps having spotted Virginia Woolf and Katherine Mansfield among the audience. It was the kind of comment made over twenty years previously by Clement Scott about Archer, Elizabeth and their audiences for Ibsen.

Since *Uncle Vanya*, Archer had seen Madame Donnet's production of *The Seagull* in June 1919, when he had to 'recognise and "place" the characters'.[49] He was no further forward after *The Cherry Orchard*. 'I have not the remotest idea what types of character Chekhov intended to portray, and therefore cannot judge whether the English actors came anywhere near them,' he confessed. The problem with Chekhov was that 'Nothing whatever happens . . .' When the curtain fell on Firs disconsolately sitting in his lonely room, all Archer could say with certainty was that 'a number of vague people have wandered vaguely around'.

Even though Walkley at *The Times* agreed that Chekhov was a passing fashion, others were still bewilderingly hailing him as the life force of modern drama. Archer could not see why. There was surely no comparison to be made with Ibsen, whose writing was precise and poetic, and demanded intellectual and expressive precision from his actors. Chekhov's characters existed as if in a dream, actually requiring the actors to evade thought and emotion. Ibsen demanded the audience to engage with his characters, whereas Chekhov consciously prevented it. Plays such as *Rosmersholm* were closely-observed human crises in which lives were emotionally and psychologically substantially altered. But Chekhov's people bumbled and drifted and, having slid further into indecision, carried on much as they had done before. 'Ibsen writes dramas and Chekhov doesn't,' was Archer's conclusion. 'A "drama" is a thing done, and in Chekhov's plays, nothing is done.'[50]

However, he was so surprised to discover so many of his colleagues favourable to *The Cherry Orchard*, that he returned to the subject a week later, on 31 July. 'I cannot but ask myself whether it is they or I who ought to see a doctor,' he exclaimed, again echoing the critics who had so fiercely attacked his own championship of Ibsen.

His admission that modern drama was now charting waters which he was unable to navigate was, in effect, his public resignation as a drama critic. He tacked it on to his review of *I'll Leave It To You*, the first produced play by a nineteen-year-old actor and writer called Noël Coward, which opened at the New Theatre on 21 July. In this play, Uncle Daniel promises the indolent Dermott family that whichever one of them makes good will inherit his fortune. Each one becomes successful, but when it turns out that Daniel has no fortune at all, they are so grateful that he encouraged them to do well, they forgive him for having lied. Coward himself played Bobbie, one of the Dermott sons. The play was too sketchy even to justify the description of 'light comedy' in the programme, commented Archer, but as 'a romp or a rag' it nevertheless revealed 'a real power of character-drawing'.[51]

In November, he gave up newspaper theatre criticism for good, resigning from both *The Star* and the *Illustrated Sporting and Dramatic News*. His last review for *The Star* was of a production of *Romeo and Juliet* at the Hampstead Everyman on the 19th. The following day, his final article appeared in the *Illustrated Sporting and Dramatic News*, a pithy denunciation of the Phoenix Society, an offshoot of the Stage Society and dedicated to performing Elizabethan and Restoration dramatists. Archer was sixty-four, and after forty-one years of metropolitan theatre criticism, from Bulwer-Lytton to Chekhov, from Irving to Coward, he was tired, not of the theatre itself but of the drudgery of composing his few hundred words late at night immediately after a performance. Times, and theatre criticism, had changed. The lengthy, considered article had given way to the brief notice, to be swallowed along with a rushed breakfast, or a six o'clock cocktail. He was, he told Elizabeth, 'unspeakably thankful'[52] to be rid of it all.

During the past few years, Frances's Nerve Training Home and Colony at King's Langley had extended to include four houses, a couple of cottages and two or three chalets dotted across the lawns. She could accommodate about twenty-five patients, and as her work became more widely recognized, medical practitioners began referring patients to her care. Most were simply in need of a change of air and rest, but others were more demanding and the one or two who were seriously ill were redirected to a conventional hospital. Even so, there were sometimes distressing moments. A young woman patient was once discovered wandering naked in the garden, her breast bleeding from where she had tried to pin a brooch. As the Colony expanded, Frances took on more staff. Miss Spencer arrived to teach singing and help supervise voice production, while Miss Cross took exercise classes. Mr Goldring, blind in one eye, created superbly smooth lawns and lavish displays of roses in the borders. A succession of younger women, including Karen Archer, a second cousin of Archer's, shared the housekeeping and tidied the chalets, which could be revolved to catch the sun.

Now he had given up criticism, Archer usually spent each weekend at King's Langley and sometimes a day or two during the week as well. For several years, his usual routine had been to arrive on Friday, retreat into his study to write, hunched over his desk, or read, lying almost prone in his armchair, his feet on a stool. At lunchtimes, he would join Frances in the dining room, when they would frequently entertain guests. The Shaws regularly drove over from Ayot St Lawrence. Shaw and Frances tolerated each other, although Frances kept a sharp eye on him, once reputedly advising him that, 'Bernard, you will never be successful while you are so rude to people.'[53] The Murrays came down, and so did A. B. Walkey. Archer would sit at the head of the table holding vigorous debates lasting well into the afternoon. Relations would come, some with their families, and at times like these, the house and gardens would echo with chatter and life. In the summer there was birdsong and sunlight and walks across the fields, and in the winter, snow, drawn curtains and firelight.

In the evenings, Archer usually ate dinner alone in his study. He seldom appeared at the Saturday dances in the studio when Frances played the Steinway piano, a gift from grateful patients, and when

Maggie the laundress, in spite of being deaf and dumb, danced beautifully, claiming she felt the rhythm of the music through her feet. Sometimes, if there was a game of charades, Frances winkled him away from his reading, but he would lend his professionalism only as a critical audience. His performing days were over. Before he retired for the night, one of the housemaids would carry a jug of barley water up to his room and place it on a table beside his bed. On Sunday mornings, a man from the village came to read from the Bible at the Colony assembly, a ceremony Archer studiously avoided.

He left for town on Monday morning. Carrying his umbrella and bag of books and papers, he crossed the lawn, passing the chalets, opened the gate in the hedge where the footpath led down to the station and glanced back to see Frances silently watching him from the doorway of Langley Rise, and raised his hat. It always seemed such a sad, awkwardly formal leavetaking. Then, suddenly, he had turned and gone, back to Fitzroy Square, to the theatre, the gossip, his work and, if they were in town, his lunches with Shaw and Elizabeth.

At the beginning of October 1921, his brother James persuaded him to join him on a photographic holiday in Majorca. On the 18th, he sailed to Norway with Charles to deliver the inaugural address to the Anglo-Norse Society at the University in Christiana. He spoke on 'The British Empire', 'in the sense of drawing all the nations into closer friendship',[54] Frances told Dibdin, illustrating his talk, apparently to the delight of his audience, by quoting extracts from *Peer Gynt*. A reporter from *Tidens Tegn* interviewed him and described Archer as a typical Englishman, 'but with a considerably more vivid expression'.

However, he did not feel at all vivid. He visited Tolderodden, now occupied by a cousin and her family, and was more than usually weary by the time he arrived home. Since his influenza two winters ago, he had frequently suffered from catarrh and a tearing, rasping cough. That winter, he felt the cold terribly, and the Murrays, as discreetly watchful as ever, presented him with a muffler for Christmas. He mooched about Fitzroy Square and King's Langley and finally bowed to pressure to leave for a warmer climate. On 9 February, he sailed for the Balearic Islands, where he stayed for three weeks before going on to Rapallo and spending a fortnight with the Beerbohms, returning to the 'ice-box'[55] of London towards the end of March. Once at Fitzroy Square, he prepared himself for another onslaught in the campaign for a National Theatre.

The Longest Campaign

If modern drama was beginning to pass Archer by, campaigning still made him feel bracingly in touch. Ever since his *Alloa Advertiser* articles in 1873, he had never relinquished the fight for a National Theatre, and since the publication of *A National Theatre: Scheme & Estimates* in 1907, the idea had actually become popular. But Archer and Barker were only partly responsible for this unexpected surge of interest. The impetus was also generated by the unlikely figure of a retired brewer from Eastbourne.

Ever since his schooldays at Stratford-upon-Avon, Richard Badger had nurtured a particular interest in the works of Shakespeare. In the spring of 1903, when, unknown to him, Archer and Barker were putting the finishing touches to *Scheme & Estimates*, Badger wrote to *The Times* proposing a subscription to erect memorial statues of Shakespeare in both Stratford and London. By 1908, Badger had died, but his idea had spawned a Shakespeare Memorial Committee which in March launched an appeal for £200,000 to pay for the building of a monument in Portland Place in London. Its design would be the subject of a competition, but whatever it turned out to be, it would have an elegant backdrop of terraces designed by John Nash. This idea was vigorously opposed by Archer and many of the theatrical community. Archer and Barker, after all, were campaigning for only £370,000, less than half as much money again, for a fully operational National Theatre.

Within days of the appeal being announced, they were sailing to New York to inspect Otto Kahn's New Theatre. In their absence, some rapid shuttle diplomacy took place, spearheaded by National Theatre supporters Alfred Lyttelton and the Earl of Lytton (the grandson of Bulwer-Lytton, the author of *Money*). The result was that on 21 July, shortly after Archer returned to England from his trek through the

American south, the rival advocates of a Shakespeare Memorial and a National Theatre had united under the unwieldy banner of the Shakespeare Memorial National Theatre Committee. So began another train of committees, sometimes driven and sometimes derailed by Archer, and which would take him on an often ludicrous and exasperating journey until his death.

The Shakespeare Memorial National Theatre Committee was composed of twenty-one people and carefully constituted as to reflect both the Establishment and the radical, the academic and the theatrical. Tree and Forbes-Robertson faced Archer and Granville Barker; F. J. Furnivall, founder of the New Shakspere Society, and Israel Gollancz, a Professor of English Literature at King's College, London, sat opposite Pinero and the feverishly active Edith Lyttelton. Their number was completed by Gosse and Massingham, various academics, two Lords and a Member of Parliament. Gollancz, who loved committees, was elected honorary secretary and Alfred Lyttelton became honorary treasurer.

They discussed *A National Theatre: Scheme & Estimates* and wondered how their National Theatre could be made to sound commercially seductive while retaining a suitable British dignity. They produced an *Illustrated Handbook*, its pages decorated by laurel-leaf wreaths and busts of Shakespeare. Plates of the subsidized theatres in Dresden, Prague and Vienna pointed to absence of a similar theatre in the nation which had produced the world's greatest playwright. A new budget of £500,000 was struck and a public appeal launched, this time with the aim of actually building a theatre. Shaw commented that if they incorporated a racecourse and a football ground, they would have no trouble in raising the money. As it was, it proved impossible.

By March 1909, the indefatigable Edith Lyttelton had persuaded the wealthy businessman Carl Meyer to donate £70,000. Meyer was subsequently elevated to the peerage but the dizzy prospect of ennoblement lured nobody else to such generosity. Instead, Edith launched a succession of money- and morale-raising stunts. She cajoled her friends into hosting charitable At Homes, wrote a Shakespearian pageant and convinced Lady Sackville to stage it in the grounds of Knole, her splendid house in Kent. It was hardly her fault that on the day, torrential rain soaked everyone and forced Ellen Terry, as one of the Three Graces, to take refuge under a rhododendron bush. Undaunted, she commissioned a play from Shaw.

In *The Dark Lady of the Sonnets*, set one summer night on the terrace of the Palace of Westminster, Shakespeare encounters the cloaked figure of a woman whom he imagines to be his mistress. On discovering her to be Queen Elizabeth, he presses the case for a National Theatre until interrupted by Mary Fitton. It was performed at a matinee at the Haymarket on 24 November 1910, with Barker playing Shakespeare.

An increasing fascination with Shakespeare and perhaps more precisely, Shakespeariana, was one of the hottest coals stoking the interest in a possible National Theatre. During the Edwardian years, Britain reasserted its national identity and recruited Shakespeare's help to do so. In turn, Shakespeare was himself re-examined. In the theatre, the plays were being presented as fantastic, upholstered spectacles by Tree, and re-evaluated against modernist curtains and beneath severe white light by Granville Barker. Academics busied themselves re-ordering them into new chronologies, scribbling ever more extensive footnotes to individual lines, and arguing over who really wrote the plays in the first place. There was a *Shakespeare's England* exhibition at Earl's Court, featuring model theatres and installations and where, with a blithe disregard for historical accuracy, girls dressed up as Nell Gwynn and distributed oranges. Elsewhere, the merchandising industry was at full tilt, offering a bewildering range of hastily-manufactured souvenirs, including pottery, vellum scrolls and wax seals.

By 1913, the grand total in the Committee's coffers had risen by only £30,000, to £100,000. There were accusations of inactivity and incompetence, and even a demand that the statue should be built as originally planned, after which the Committee should declare itself redundant. Anticipation of a serious revolt prompted the search for a site on which to build the theatre. The Committee could then announce progress, even though it did not have the money to construct a building. The question of location had been debated for over a year when Archer intervened in early 1912 and revived a suggestion made several years previously. The National Theatre, he said, should be built on the south bank of the Thames, near Waterloo Bridge. This was greeted with much head-shaking by the majority, who thought the South Bank much too far from the centre of town and disgracefully scruffy. It was voted down, by Shaw among others, in favour of possible sites on the north side of the river. But time has revealed Archer's proposal to be a remarkable prophecy. Fifty-seven years later, in 1969, work began on building the National Theatre on the South Bank within yards of what he then thought the finest site in Europe.

Back in 1912, the arguments rumbled on. The following year, the

Committee bought a sight at the corner of Gower Street and Keppel Street in respectable Bloomsbury, and drew up important-looking plans for a long, low, pseudo-Elizabethan building to be ready for opening on 23 April 1916, the tercentenary of Shakespeare's birth. The embarrassment of thinking up excuses as to why building work was not beginning was saved by the declaration of war. Yet one day in 1916, a small prefabricated building suddenly appeared on the Gower Street site. Built by the Young Men's Christian Army, it was used to stage shows for the entertainment of wounded soldiers. It was known, ironically, as the Shakespeare Hut.

There were several absentees from the old Committee when Gollancz called a regrouping in the summer of 1918. Some former members had retired, lost money or simply lost interest. Alfred Lyttelton had died during surgery after being hit by the ball during a game of cricket, but Edith, his widow, was as determined as ever to carry on and was joined by her son, Oliver. There were other, and less reliable new voices, but during the coming years, as alliances formed and faded and ideas were hatched in enthusiasm and destroyed in acrimony, Edith and Archer, supported by Barker in Devon, became the powerhouse of the new Committee.

Edith thought it 'one of the most excitable collections of people ever flung together by different interests',[1] and it was not long before voices rose in rancour. Again, the cause was a plan of Archer's who was almost exploding with impatience. If they could not afford to build a National Theatre, he told them, they should use some of their money to support a new touring Shakespearian company. As usual, he had already discovered the man to carry the banner forward.

William Bridges-Adams was a twenty-nine-year-old actor and director, the son of socialists from south London. He had been educated at a progressive public school, acted in Dramatic Society productions at Oxford, and after graduating, worked as a stage manager and actor with Poel. In 1912, he appeared in Barker's production of *Iphigenia in Tauris* (another Murray translation of Euripedes), at the Kingsway. Later, he began directing in London, took over the Bristol Repertory Theatre and, in 1916, moved to the Liverpool Repertory Theatre, changing its name to the Playhouse.

A tall, loose-limbed man, Bridges-Adams was not physically robust and during the war had been rejected as medically unfit for the Army. But he was fiercely ambitious and capable of concentrated marathons of work. These were qualities Archer admired enormously, and in the summer of 1918, the two men began meeting regularly to discuss the future of the theatre. Since Barker had renounced acting and directing, Archer had been looking for someone of similar temperament and views to carry on their shared aims. Thirty-three years younger than Archer and eleven years Barker's junior, Bridges-Adams seemed the perfect choice to lead a new company 'fit to rank with that of Meinenger'.[2]

In November 1918, he supplied Archer with a budget for a Shakespearian company of forty actors, touring Britain for forty weeks of the year, estimating that he would need £10,000 for annual expenses and a guarantee of £12,000 over three years. When Archer presented this to the Committee, he was endorsed by those who thought it a daringly adventurous attempt to get things going at last, and fiercely condemned by others, including Shaw, who protested that subsidizing a Bridges-Adams company would be an irresponsible use of money raised specifically for a National Theatre. The Committee divided between supporters convinced that the crack Shakespearian ensemble Archer was advocating would prove once and for all the need for a National Theatre, and those who believed a building must precede the company. Archer had opened a wound which would bleed for many years to come, but after ten years of nothing but talk and delay, he was insisting that they act one way or another.

By May 1919, Bridges-Adams provided an alternative plan for a smaller company requiring a guarantee of only £5000. Archer, Edith and their supporters won their first battle, persuading the Committee to contribute a subsidy of £3000, exactly the annual rent of the Shakespeare Hut in Gower Street. This meant they need not dip into their capital. The reduced subsidy prevented the new company from touring, but Archer, keeping one step ahead of the game, was already negotiating for Bridges-Adams to be based at the Shakespeare Memorial Theatre at Stratford-upon-Avon. Stratford, Archer knew, was ripe for take-over.

For thirty-two years, Frank Benson had doggedly continued the old Victorian butcher-and-bluster school of Shakespeare and presented a spring and summer Festival at Stratford. His aged productions of *The Merry Wives of Windsor*, *The Taming of the Shrew* and *The Merchant of Venice* were so familiar that his company referred to the repertoire as *The Merry Shrews of Venice*. Archer had long thought him 'an impossible man, unless under the condition that neither he nor his wife should ever act'. As a director, he was 'slow-minded' and his ideas were 'execrable'.[3] It was a harsh judgement, but although Benson's commitment to Shakespeare and his loyalty to Stratford were unquestioned, even his most ardent supporters were hard-pressed to argue convincingly in favour of his productions. The revolution in text, acting and staging led by Barker and even Poel, had simply passed Benson by.

Yet Benson was a courageous man. Having staged his fervently patriotic *Henry V* in London as soon as war began, he had bravely but forlornly attempted to enlist in the forces. He was in his late fifties and looked older, but obstinately persisted that he was thirty-five. Politely turned away by successive recruiting officers, he went back to the theatre and in 1916, was knighted by George V in the Royal Box at Drury Lane during the interval of a tercentenary performance. Within weeks, he was running a canteen for the Red Cross in France where Eric, his only son was killed in action. Like Archer, Benson never fully overcame his loss, but in the spring of 1919, he returned to Stratford with a scratch cast and soldiered on for a week with a few scenes from *Coriolanus* and *The Merry Wives of Windsor*.

However, for Benson, it was the end. Archer and Edith from London, and Archibald Flower, the chairman of the Stratford governors and co-director of the local brewery, led 'a brief but glorious excursion into practical politics'[4] and formed an alliance between the Shakespeare Memorial National Theatre and the Stratford Memorial Theatre. Benson left Stratford and a Joint Committee of thirteen was elected to govern the fortunes of the Bridges-Adams company. Chaired by Forbes-Robertson, the members included Archer, Edith, Flower, Gollancz, and the actor E. H. Sothern.

When, in 1885, Archer had seen Mary Anderson play Rosalind at the Memorial Theatre, Stratford was a backwater, peaceful and rural. Now, increasing numbers of the summer charabanc visitors were American, and motorboats chugged along the Avon, leaking oil on to the water while cash registers rang in the shops. Day-trippers from Birmingham lolled on the river banks and actors and audiences dodged the cars speeding throatily along Waterside. The pace and bustle of the petrol age presented Bridges-Adams with his first decision. 'Our choice lay, so to speak, between Ye Olde Oake Shakespeare Bunne Shoppe and Beyreuth.'[5] He chose Beyreuth: 'straight Shakespeare played by a balanced cast'. He called them the New Shakespeare Company, 'a shockingly untradable name',[6] and began rehearsing six productions for the summer Festival.

Shaw was not a member of the new Joint Committee but nevertheless demanded that a clause be inserted into Bridges-Adams's contract stipulating that he produce the plays uncut. Archer furiously opposed this on the principle that once appointed, an artistic director must have a free hand. He also considered the fashionable drive to play unadulterated Shakespeare nothing but an extremist reaction to Victorian prudery. 'Holus-bolus Shakespeare', he explained to Edith, was a quirk of 'notorious cranks'[7] like Poel, and dramatists such as Barker and Shaw, who so implacably opposed any deletions from their own plays they were determined to accord Shakespeare the same protection. But while Archer successfully defeated him a second time, Shaw's intervention had so terrified Bridges-Adams that he not only decided to perform his first season plays virtually uncut, but meekly offerred his texts to the scrutiny of the Joint Committee. 'If I had been he, I would have told them to go to blazes,' Archer angrily told Shaw. 'It is instructive that (thanks to you) we should encounter ... such a glaring instance of the impossibility of committee-management in theatrical matters.'[8]

Archer was not advocating sweeping Bensonian cuts (Benson had reduced *Coriolanus* to one hour), but, clear, rational Shakespeare for the modern era. To illustrate his point to Edith, he deliberately chose one of the most obscure passages in the canon and commanded her to read Act One, Scene Two of *The Winter's Tale*. Three 'very large' pages of his New Variorum Shakespeare were devoted to analyzing lines 129 to 147, he explained, and the one thing on which all the commentators agreed was that their meaning was utterly irrecoverable. As the plays were written to be performed in the theatre rather than for the amusement of academics, it was therefore unforgivable pedantry to retain redundant lines. 'Shakespeare was not a pedant but a dramatist, &, if he were alive today, would have been the first to insist on cutting away absolutely dead wood.'[9] But when Bridges-Adams opened the first New Shakespeare Company summer Festival on 2 August 1919, *The Merry Wives of Windsor* was followed by *Julius Caesar, A Midsummer Night's Dream, The Tempest* and *Romeo and Juliet*, all at almost full-length, and *The Winter's Tale* was complete with lines 129 to 147. By the end of the season, he had earned the nickname of 'Un-a-Bridges-Adams'.

While the use of restored texts was innovative, the productions themselves had as much of the mustiness of the old as the fresh air of the new. This was partly the result of compromise. Bridges-Adams wanted to create an ensemble of equals but because he had hardly any rehearsal time, he had drawn the core of his new company from

Bensonian gestural actors such as Randle Ayrton, Baliol Holloway and Dorothy Green. Moreover, his staging echoed the decoration of Irving rather than the comparative austerity of Poel and Barker. As he liked a clearly-defined sense of location, Bridges-Adams retained the practice of playing incidental scenes before a closed curtain while a new set was being built behind it. Rather than emulating Barker's clean white light, which he thought cruel and antiseptic, he tried to achieve with electricity the kind of soft effects that Irving had created with gas. The results satisfied neither Poel nor Barker and nor, in time, Archer. Poel complained that *Romeo and Juliet* was intended to be played as one long scene, whereas Bridges-Adams had sliced it into twenty-three, lasting three and a half hours. Barker thought *A Midsummer Night's Dream* excellent until near the end, when he was appalled to see all 'the old obscene clowning',[10] which he had carefully eliminated from his own production at the Savoy, come flooding back.

Yet the New Shakespeare Company was well received and the Joint Committee twice renewed its subsidy. By 1921, the spring and summer Festivals had been extended and the company had undertaken short regional tours. But as he grew in confidence, Bridges-Adams began pruning texts and adding decorative flourishes in a manner which horrified Archer. In 1922, there was a *Twelfth Night* without the scene of Malvolio in prison, which he protested was integral to the play. Although he was considered 'the "patron saint" of the Stratford company',[11] Archer quickly moved on to the offensive and began the unsettling habit of bludgeoning Bridges-Adams with letters of advice, much as he had the actors in his Ibsen productions. After *Twelfth Night* opened, he notified him that the real test of a Viola was whether she could play the line, 'My brother he is in Elysium.' 'Miss [Ethel] C[arrington] makes little or nothing of it,' he commented drily, 'but I own it is difficult to speak it lying down.'[12] By the spring of 1922, after which the London subsidy was due to expire, Archer was agreeing with Barker that Stratford had 'degenerated' into 'old-Victorian ugliness.'[13]

Yet there remained one thing left for him to do. As a leading light of the Anglo-Norse Society, he lobbied for the New Shakespeare Company to be invited to the Norwegian National Theatre. From 20–22 June, the infamous *Twelfth Night*, *The Taming of the Shrew* and *Much Ado About Nothing* were performed in Christiana. For Archer, this tour was enormously important, partly to give Bridges-Adams international experience, as he was thinking of him as a potential director of a National Theatre. 'Of course the first Director ought to be H.G.-B,' he confided to Shaw, 'but if he shirks, then Bridges-Adams . . .'[14] But even more importantly, he was determined to complete unfinished Wellington House business. It had long rankled with Archer that Reinhardt's Deutsches Theater had visited Norway during the war to demonstrate the supposed German superiority in Shakespeare and while he had been at Buckingham Gate, he had failed to organize a counterblast. Now he could. The New Shakespeare Company tour was a huge critical and popular success, and Archer marched home satisfied that a company he had helped to found had 'induced a public sedulously nursed by Reinhardt and the German Ministry of Propaganda, to revise their opinion of the English stage'.[15] With the discovery of Tom's grave the previous year, and the Norwegian estimation of British theatre having been restored, Archer's war was finally over.

'The more I think of it, the more strongly do I feel there should be no delay in setting on foot a new campaign for raising funds for the SMNT,' Archer wrote to Lady Meyer in a burst of energy on 13 May 1922. '. . . if we can raise £50,000, we can raise £500,000.'[16] Edith agreed. 'We *must appeal for a National Theatre*!'[17] she cried. The disadvantage was that Archer had no confidence in his own abilities to prise money out of anyone. 'I'm afraid I haven't the art of making myself agreeable to microcephelous millionaires,'[18] he admitted. The most he could do was chivvy others, and this he did. He sent letters and stopped friends and acquaintances in corridors. He heard rumours, for instance, that two newspaper magnates, Lord Northcliffe of the *Daily Mail* and *The Times*, and Lord Burnham of the *Daily Telegraph*, might both be susceptible to arm-twisting and he passed on their names to Lady Meyer. In a flurry of morale-boosting memoranda, he outlined new strategies and tactics to the Committee. Disconcertingly, he found himself having to encourage Shaw as much as the others.

'Your able memorandum leaves me cold and weary . . . I cannot begin all that over again,'[19] sighed Shaw on 8 June. Like Archer, he was sixty-five, but unlike him, he was finding the protracted National Theatre discussions tedious and in a sudden reversal, wrote that he was more interested in developing the New Shakespeare Company. Archer was staggered. 'I think you better set about preparing your apology to posterity for this amazing note,' he exclaimed. 'Good heavens, man, why turn round and rend a project for which you've been working, & working well, for twenty years past! Why get cold feet at this point?' He was indignant and perplexed. Even when they were defiantly voting each other down across the Executive Committee table, they had been united in their fight for the National Theatre, but now it appeared that Shaw was just giving up. 'Come, come – take a brisk walk and warm your feet – this letter shows alarming symptoms of cerebral anaemia,'[20] he chided. 'Keep your hair on,' cooed Shaw. But he refused to change his mind: '. . . you are perfectly welcome to your NT if you can get it . . . But I have done more than my share for it; and now younger men may take up the running.'[21]

Shaw was both implacable and impossible. Archer turned to Barker who, having asked Archer to read and comment on the proofs of the preface ('say if there's anything you want altered'[22]) published a second blueprint for a National Theatre in 1922. *The Exemplary Theatre*, although not as thoroughly detailed as *Scheme & Estimates*, calls for a National Theatre with two flexible auditoria, and imagines a dialogue between a hypothetical Minister of Education and a Man of the Theatre, whom Archer warned was too 'resolutely high-browed'. The theatre, he reminded him, was also fun, 'a place – occasionally, & even frequently – of mere harmless, unpretending recreation'.[23] He was still hopeful of raising half-a-million pounds for a building, and in July sent Barker a Declaration he had written and had imposingly typeset, and which he proposed sending to influential people. *Towards A National Theatre: A Statement of Principle*, was designed to be a selective register of support. People like Henry Bond at Cambridge would sign it, he told Barker. 'Mrs Lyttelton could no doubt get some Goddam coalitionists. You & I could ourselves rope in some respectable littery [sic] and theatrical gents.'[24] But now it was Barker's turn to be disparaging. 'I believe the Declaration by itself will be of no use. Fine words butter no parsnips,' was the verdict from Devon on 24 July. The Declaration was far too woolly, he added, and needed a clause committing all those who signed it to donate at least £1000. Then they should send it to as many people as they could think of including 'the inevitable Lord Howard de Walden [and] the inevitable Lady Cunard.'[25]

Coming within six weeks of Shaw's rejection, Barker's nitpicking seemed gratuitously obstructive. 'I think you are wrong,' Archer retorted the next day, 25 July. 'Indeed I am so strong on the DECLARATION that if I could get any reputable & not quite ridiculous person to act with me, I certainly should. But you & I, as accomplices in the SCHEME & ESTIMATES, would have a sort of raison d'être that no one else would have. However, I don't want to force your hand against your judgement.'[26]

Determined not to be defeated by the defeatism of Shaw and Barker, he sat down, slipped more paper into his typewriter and tapped out a bundle of assessments of the social and cultural role of a National Theatre. He hacked out chains of statistics and calculations, appeals, forms of promise for the endowment fund and tasks for the alarmingly proliferating sub-committees clinging like burrs to the main Committee. These bureaucratic conclaves infuriated him because they were unfathomable. He could not predict who might vote with whom and for what. The Sub-Committee on Ways and Means in particular was proving a cauldron of anarchy, while the Committee itself was dividing and subdividing into a mass of small factions. Once again, the cause of the National Theatre was being rendered impotent by committee. In July, the Gower Street site was sold, which put more money in the bank but revived the old building-or-company argument. Archer, who was sympathetic to Bridges-Adams, now struggling on, unsubsidized, at Stratford, nevertheless felt that while they could give away income, they should not touch capital and that their purpose now must be to build the National Theatre. The situation was even more complex than it was in 1918, for while Archer had his supporters and opposers, still others were looking favourably on the claims of the Old Vic.

For several years, the Old Vic had been run by the formidable and eccentric Lilian Baylis. A plump-faced woman who wore round, tortoiseshell spectacles, Miss Baylis considered Shakespeare an enduring inspiration and in times of national crisis such an uplifting symbol of patriotism and defiance, that she had determinedly produced his plays throughout the war. Entirely unperturbed by air-raids, she expected similar fortitude from her company. The theatre was dusty and tatty and at one performance, Archer happened to glance down to see a rat purposefully making its way along his row towards him. Neither was it uncommon for the end of matinees to be permeated by a sizzling sound and the smell of frying fish or sausages as Miss Baylis cooked her meal on a gas ring just off stage. Both she and the Old Vic were held in such great affection that many saw them as the National Theatre-in-waiting. Meanwhile, Gollancz, whom Archer suspected would never be ousted from the honorary secretaryship except by dynamite, had come up with the wildly bizarre notion that they collaborate with the Young Men's Christian Army to produce amateur dramatics. Everything was becoming so complex and fraught that in desperation, Archer presented a bewildered Committee with a thirty-page typescript from which they deduced that he had finally gone mad.

The Foundation of the National Theatre, he told them, was Chapter XXIII of a putative *History of England After the Great War*, and comprised the story of the National Theatre as it might be written by a historian in 1950. It tells how an interim National Theatre Company was formed to play at an established London theatre and that its success encouraged a thousand rich men to contribute £1000 each to the creation of a new theatre. This prompted one crucial donation of £250,000, after which the government designated a site adjacent to Charing Cross station on which to build the National Theatre. Archer suggested they publish and distribute this fanciful document with the *Statement of Principle* to potential philanthropists. It was 'an attempt to loosen their purse-strings by stirring their imaginations',[27] but the Committee, which had no imagination, rejected it outright. Archer was driven almost to distraction. 'Really life is impossible with these people!'[28] he exclaimed.

The Interim Theatre was a serious proposition, and he canvassed Barker's support. Barker glanced at his budgets and told him that not only had he underestimated, the entire scheme had one great flaw. If it was successful, people would say the National Theatre was unnecessary, and if it failed, they would say it was impossible. Both ways, he would lose. Archer felt as if he was being spun round and round. His head ached; he was besieged both by migraine and the British expertise of apparently unending prevarication. 'My mind is a sort of Maelstrom of conflicting ideas & suggestions,'[29] he cried to Edith Lyttelton on 25 August. 'Mine is a shallow rather muddy pond,'[30] she sympathized. Archer was close to despair. 'I think we ought to send £100 to Germany (where it would be equivalent to several millions of marks) & in a few weeks they would ship us a National Theatre in sections, with Director & all complete,'[31] he told her bitterly.

The New Shakespeare Company had lifted his spirits at the end of the war but now, four years later, it returned to dash them. On 11 October, Bridges-Adams wrote to Archer, demanding the Committee renew his grant and increase it to £5000 a year for another three years, so that he could build a strong and ultimately self-supporting company. 'For four years you have had at your disposal an organisation capable of infinite development, but you have not made use of it,'[32] he said reproachfully. Archer replied with wounding honesty. 'I have always warmly appreciated your work in giving relatively good Shakespearian performances at a time when Shakespeare in the provinces had sunk to a dismal depth,' he said. 'Acting apart, I think we owe you a great debt ... But even with a subsidy of £5000 a year, you can't work miracles.

You can't give ... such conspicuously admirable Shakespearian performances that all the world will rush for its cheque-books, crying with one voice "We *must* have a National Theatre wherein to house this model company."[33]

Bridges-Adams's appeal had forced Archer into a difficult corner. He was obliged to present it to the Committee, but as he believed they should not encroach upon their capital, and as their interest did not amount to five thousand pounds a year, he could not personally support it. But at the meeting on 17 October, this dilemma paled into nothing when, to his utter astonishment, he was suddenly ambushed by his most trusted ally, Edith Lyttelton. Not only did she support the application, she 'went the whole hog' and to Archer's horror, suggested that they authorize Bridges-Adams to change the name of the New Shakespeare Company to the National Theatre Company. This was the most devastating blow anyone could have inflicted. The name 'National Theatre' was, for Archer, sacrosant. It was reserved and always had been, both for the building and the company that would perform in it. He had thought his closest friends were united on this, but unaccountably, they were turning away from him. Edith's was the most humiliating betrayal. When she spoke, he told Bridges-Adams, 'then burst my mighty heart – I said "Et tu Brute" and even at the base of Granville-Barker's statue which all the while ran blood – I fell!'

The longest campaign was over, destroyed in a welter of committee bickering and treachery. He felt as if his great ideal had been snatched from him, crushed and thrown aside. 'To tell the truth,' he informed Bridges-Adams bitterly, 'I don't care a damn what this Committee does with its money ... I must try to find somebody else to work with, though I have little hope.'[34] On the 18th, the day after the meeting, he wrote miserably to Edith Lyttelton: 'I am awfully sorry to part company with you. You have been splendid throughout – in fact it is only by & through you that anything worth mentioning has been done.' But the National Theatre, he added sadly, remained 'the one thing I care about ... and since no one will even consider the practicability of the methods I suggest for raising new money – I quit ...'[35]

He left London for Devon, to isolate himself at Fairbrook, a guesthouse at North Bovey on Dartmoor, not too far from where the Galsworthys lived and within reach of the Barkers. He had come here the previous year and found it the perfect retreat for peace and for writing. He stayed for a week, read no newspapers and took long walks across the moor. In London, Edith dashed to her typewriter. Everything was the most dreadful mess, she agreed, but they would sort it out. He must re-join them, and they would form a new Committee with a new constitution, which he and Barker could write. They would monitor Bridges-Adams, start all over again, raise the money and this time build the National Theatre. But Archer had had enough. To be so defeated after fifty years of struggle had left him feeling cheated and sickened. 'I quit,'[36] he repeated from Devon. But gradually, Edith managed to pacify him and bring him round, and on 18 December, he supported her in granting Bridges-Adams £1000 for 1923, provided he retained the name of the New Shakespeare Company. So Bridges-Adams carried on, and eventually stayed at Stratford until 1934 when, after a celebrated public dispute with Archie Flower, he left without a backward glance.

Archer never lost his conviction that the National Theatre would one day be built. Initially, he envisaged a theatre presenting literary rather than experimental work, classical and contemporary British, European and American plays. Now, enthused by Barker, he saw it also as a theatre of scenographic experimentation, where new ways could be found of presenting drama. But nothing made him more despondent than to reflect that after all his campaigning he had nothing more to show than a book of plans and a pamphlet of fantastic history. At Fitzroy Square, he gathered up his proposals, his appeals, his plans and reports, and stored them carefully, together with a large package of letters. 'Someday these things *may* have an historical interest,'[37] he muttered to Edith. This was one area of his life he was determined to preserve for posterity.

    That done, he turned his attention westwards. He had never quite shaken off the influenza he caught on his trip to Paris, and that winter he complained of the cold more than ever. One day in December, having succumbed to pressure from Frances and friends, he consulted a Harley Street specialist who told him to go away and spend the winter in a warm climate. 'I am therefore sailing on the 27th for that well-known health resort, New York,'[38] he told Gilbert Murray.

The Play of the Century

Archer had already visited the United States twice since the war. In 1920, he was there for a month during the summer and for three months during the following winter. The second visit was the most important (and perhaps most unlikely) he had ever made to America, for he went neither as a critic, nor a journalist, nor as an ambassador for simplified spelling, nor even a university professor. He arrived in New York as a playwright, and with a play about to go into rehearsal. Everything depended upon the previews in Philadelphia. Success there meant his name appearing on theatre billboards not quite on Broadway but literally only a few steps from it, outside the Booth Theatre on West 45th Street.

War is War had renewed old impulses and ambitions and during the next six years, Archer threw himself into a breathless bout of playwriting. A few years later, the gossip-journalist and spiritualist Hannen Swaffer claimed that at a seance at the Kingston Vale home of the writer Dennis Bradley, a spirit voice purporting to be Archer admitted that the idea for his next play had been spiritually transmitted to him by Tom,[1] but while he was alive, Archer maintained that it came to him in a dream. On 2 September 1919, a few months after the publication of *War is War*, he recorded that he awoke during the early hours from dreams 'vaguely connected with India'.[2] It seemed that he was travelling with the Galsworthys through a country resembling India when they heard gunfire. Later, they learned that several Europeans had been captured by highly-cultured Indians who treated them well before executing them in reparation for some unspecified action by the British government. When he read his notes the following day, Archer realized he had the makings of a drama. Over the next few days, he developed a storyline and reminded Shaw of his boast of many years ago that he was a master of dialogue. 'I want you to collaborate on a play!' he announced, describing his plans for 'a romantic melodrama, which only needs your cooperation to be infallibly THE PLAY OF THE CENTURY.'[3] While *War is War* had almost written itself, this play was different, for this time, his motive was money. 'I want an old-age pension,'[4] he explained to Elizabeth. Throughout his life, as his expenses perpetually threatened to outstrip his income, he fretted about money. He was not nearly as well-off as several of his friends, including Shaw, who, while at a low point in England, was nevertheless doing well elsewhere and was about to publish *Heartbreak House* in London and negotiate a production in New York. Too much depended upon 'the great melodrama'[5] for Archer not to take every possible precaution for its success. 'The object is . . . TO MAKE MONEY,'[6] he emphasized to Shaw.

He began writing in London, continued at King's Langley and on 9 October, had delivered drafts of three of the projected four acts of *The Raja of Rukh* to Shaw, recommending that he revise them, add the final act and sign his proposed agreement of collaboration.

Shaw refused, point-blank. 'Of course I could write your scenes in for you; but why should I?'[7] he demanded.

'If you let me down I shall have to fall back upon H. G. Wells – a sad anti-climax,'[8] Archer had warned.

Shaw was entirely unmoved. 'Your threat to go and ask someone else is quite dastardly in its incorrigible laziness,' he thundered. 'Have you no conscience, no shame?' Archer had nipped at his own playwriting heels for almost thirty years and now he had his chance to snap back. Archer's self-pitying pleas that he had not the talent to finish it earned no sympathy. 'You havent even tried,' declared Shaw. 'If you make an honourable failure, and I can help you out, I will; but there is not the slightest risk of this: the completion of the play is well within your powers, and may lead you to a fuller discovery of them.'[9]

Chastened, Archer went away. Rather than approach Wells he tried Pinero, but had no luck as he was assured again that the play was well within his grasp. He fleetingly considered appealing to Beerbohm in Rapallo but in the end, typed out the last act by himself. Despite the resemblance of its title and the leading character of a middle-Eastern potentate, *The Raja of Rukh* has little in common with E. V. Ward's comic opera, *The Khan of Kashgar*. Its true antecedent is the A. G. Stanley creation, *Australia*. It is an unashamed melodramatic entertainment in which British decency outwits foreign cunning and spectacular effects provide the backdrop to threats, bluffs and daring escapes.

The play opens at the shrine of the six-armed Green Goddess in the remote Himalayan province of Rukh, where a light aircraft has made an emergency landing, having run out of fuel. Clambering from it are the pilot, the handsome scientist Dr Basil Traherne, ('the Pasteur of Malaria'), and his passengers, Major Antony Crespin and his young wife Lucilla. They are on their way from India to a northern settlement where a native uprising endangers the British community and the Crespin's two young children. The Raja, summoned from the nearby palace, turns out to be a courteous man with a Cambridge degree in Moral and Political Science, a taste for dressing as an English country gentlemen and an enthusiasm for the works of Bernard Shaw. But, as in Archer's dream, instead of giving them fuel, he entertains them as his guests. Three of his brothers, he explains, have been condemned to death by the British for their part in the provincial uprising. His people believe the Green Goddess has delivered Traherne and the Crespins to be executed in revenge, and he has no choice but to accede to their demands if he hopes to retain his own political power.

Later, the Raja proposes a compromise to Lucilla. If she agrees to marry him, her children could come to live at the palace. She rejects him, but meanwhile, Crespin and Traherne discover the Raja is in wireless communication with the outside world. They bribe Watkins, the Raja's English manservant ('No-one can touch him at mixing a cocktail or making a salad'[10]), to send a distress signal. When he betrays them, they throw him out of a high window, but when Crespin attempts to send the message himself, he is shot dead by the Raja. Again, he offers to marry Lucilla, but again she refuses and, with great ceremony, the scene is set for the executions at the shrine of the Green Goddess. Just as it seems as though all is lost, aircraft are heard in the distance and bombs explode in the nearby valley. Crespin's valiant message got through. Seconds later, Flight Lieutenant Cardew, in leather flying suit, high boots and goggles, stalks fearlessly into the shrine, proclaiming himself to be the representative of His Majesty the King, and rescues Traherne and Lucilla. The defeated Raja concludes that perhaps everything has worked out for the best. Had Lucilla stayed, she might only have been a nuisance.

While Archer wrote *The Raja of Rukh* as a hopeful investment, the play also reflects some of his serious preoccupations. In India, he had decided that Hinduism was nothing more than a charade of barbaric ritual and in the play, religion is seen as both degrading and destructive. The Raja embodies Archer's growing conviction, deepened by the war, that civilized values are little more than a brittle veneer, easily cracked and stripped away. He might have a university degree and read the work of a socialist pacifist, but he remains so impervious to his ideas that he orders three executions and expects to watch them being carried out. The Raja is a debased Shavian superman, a Caesar brought down to size.

As for Crespin, the traditional upbringing of the English officer class has left him emotionally inarticulate and ill-equipped to face his own inadequacies, a reproachful wife and the rivalry of Traherne. He resorts to drink. In India and Baluchistan Archer may have seen several officers and their wives like Crespin and Lucilla. He completed the play by 29 December, promising to send Murray 'a quite legible manuscript' and urging him to 'read it *quickly* and with obs[ervations]'[11] as he wanted to have a copy typed to send to Barker, who was in New York. Murray was encouraging, and Elizabeth was sufficiently pragmatic to see that what it lacked in dramatic calibre it more than made up in commercial potential. '. . .that's just what I wanted to hear,'[12] he told her. In January 1920, he sent the script across the Atlantic for Barker 'to do what you think fit with – either place it in the hands of a more or less honest agent, or send it to Winthrop Ames . . .'

The former director of the New Theatre (which had become the Century and housed mainly musicals), Ames had since built the Little Theatre on 44th Street, between Broadway and Eighth Avenue. Here, he produced Shaw, Barker and Galsworthy, turning the Little into the New York outpost of England's New Drama. He now owned and ran the Booth Theatre, and, through Barker, was left in no doubt of Archer's intentions for the play. 'If I could make a little money – even two or three thousand pounds . . . it would ease the situation enormously,'[13] he wrote.

Barker liked *The Raja of Rukh*, but had reservations. Ames shared them and one night they worked until two in the morning breathing life into the fourth act. 'It contains no new idea,' wrote a sleepless Ames to Archer on 1 March, 'merely a re-ordering of the former material.'[14] He also offered an advance of $1000 for an American production. Archer was delighted, and once Barker returned to England, he scuttled down to Netherton Hall to discuss the revisions. On 4 April, he cabled Ames in New York. 'Amendments accepted. Terms accepted. Slight modification suggested. Letter follows.'[15] The 'slight modification' was that his advance should be doubled to $2000. 'Very willing to make it $2000'[16] replied Ames, apparently not put out at all.

Archer worked on the play during the spring and early summer. He was bursting with activity, still delving into spiritualism, and, also against Elizabeth's advice, re-writing Middleton and Rowley's *The Changeling* as *Beatriz-Juana*. This was an attempt to treat Jacobean themes in a modern manner, an act of transposition similar to Murray's Greek translations and one that might, he insisted, make him more desperately-needed money. He also hoped it might tempt Lillah McCarthy back on to the stage but when she refused, he put the script in a drawer and concentrated on *The Raja of Rukh*, incorporating all of Barker and Ames's suggestions, except those dealing with the Crespins.

Archer's portrayal of a marriage reduced to a stalemate of near-silence while Lucilla longs for release with Traherne is the most personal thread woven through the play. Crespin accuses his wife of being in love with Traherne and that her 'deadly coldness' towards him has driven him to drink. Lucilla retorts that his affairs with other women have made it 'impossible for me to be your wife again'.[17] Archer's love for Elizabeth made him sympathize with Lucilla and Traherne, and the intimacy between them pervades the play. But Ames was pressing him to delete this troubled triangular relationship. Instead of being her husband, Crespin should become Lucilla's father, perhaps initially objecting to Traherne as a suitable partner for his daughter. This would remove the 'unnecessary tension',[18] and allow the audience to concentrate happily on romance and last-minute escapes. But Archer refused to drop his portrayal of a desolate marriage and Ames reluctantly conceded defeat. But before he left for New York on 25 July to discuss the final draft, Archer made another alteration. He changed the title to *The Green Goddess*.

Ames's plan for *The Green Goddess* was to cast and rehearse from November, preview in Philadelphia just after Christmas and, if all went well, bring the production into the Booth in the new year. Archer readily agreed. He trusted Ames. 'I can't imagine what would have happened had I fallen into the hands of an 'Ebrew Jew like [the manager and dramatist, David] Belasco',[19] he remarked to Murray. Returning to London in early September, he threw himself into another classical reclamation, re-writing Philip Massinger's tragi-comedy *The Great Duke of Florence* as *Lidia*, and speculating about Sybil Thorndike for the leading role. 'Has she any intelligence?'[20] he enquired of Elizabeth. But in the event, neither she nor anyone else appeared in *Lidia*, and it too, was shoved away in Archer's desk drawer. It was now that he gave up writing theatre criticism. Everything, therefore, depended upon *The Green Goddess*.

Filled with his usual pessimism, he began explaining to anyone who would listen all the reasons why the play should never get beyond the rehearsal room, and if it did, why it would flop. The sets alone would prove much too expensive. It was asking far too much to have a crashed aeroplane and the rock face down which Traherne and the Crespins slither, the rooms in the Raja's palace, complicated-looking wireless equipment and the exotic shrine of the Green Goddess itself. But even supposing the sets were built, the cast would cost too much. In addition to the five main roles of the Crespins, Traherne, the Raja and Watkins, there were four minor parts and a large supporting company of tribesmen and bodyguards. When friends assured him that Ames would pay for spectacular sets and a full company, Archer countered that such a lavish production would only cruelly underline the flimsiness of the script. His final sally was that he could think of nobody to play the Raja. When he was writing the play, he had H. B. Irving in mind, but before he had finished, Irving had inconsiderately died. There seemed to be no one else. '[Henry] Ainley's too fat & much more of a tabby-cat than a tiger,' he told Murray. '[Arthur] Wontner is a splendid high-church curate, but hasn't got an ounce of the barbarian in him. [Norman] McKinnel – no, I *won't* have a Scotch Raja.'[21]

Nevertheless, on 29 November, he arrived in New York an anxious playwright, ready for the rehearsals of *The Green Goddess*. He stayed in style, not at the Belmont but the Pennsylvania ('The Largest Hotel in the World 2200 Rooms – 2200 Baths'), a massive stack blocking out the sun from Seventh Avenue between 32nd and 33rd Streets. Ames had found a Raja in George Arliss, a small, svelte, fifty-three-year-old Londoner whose long nose and jaw gave the impression that his head was slightly too long for his body. In London, and in the United States in 1902, he had appeared opposite Mrs Patrick Campbell in revivals of *The Second Mrs Tanqueray* and *The Notorious Mrs Ebbsmith*. When Mrs Campbell and the company left America and went home, Arliss stayed, having discovered an English accent to be an enormous advantage in New York. He was soon playing leading parts in Ibsen and Barrie and before the war appeared in the title role of Louis N. Parker's hugely-successful *Disraeli*. But although Arliss was a prominent actor, he was not a star and neither was he glamorous. He was a solid character actor in roles demanding sardonic insouciance. Ames would have preferred a real star, but he regretfully pointed out to Archer that American stars were reluctant to play anything less than an unblemished hero. 'They'd be wanting the Raja to reform at the end and marry the girl,'[22] he explained.

This put them behind in the game straight away and satisfactorily clinched Archer's expectation of humiliating failure. The remaining cast were known, but no better known. Archer's former Ibsen associate, Herbert Waring, came over from London to play Crespin, while the American actress Olive Wyndham was cast as Lucilla. Cyril Keightley, an Australian who had appeared in London, played Traherne, while the English actors Ivan F. Simpson and Herbert Ranson joined the cast as Watkins and Cardew. There was another familiar face in the company, that of the actor playing the walk-on part of a temple priest. It was Ronald Colman, who had fought beside Tom at Ypres, starred in *Damaged Goods* in London and had emigrated to New York earlier that year. Colman was so poor that he was living on a diet of soup and rice, and sleeping on park benches. The wages he was paid for *The Green Goddess* meant that he could at least buy adequate meals.

During the next few weeks, Archer watched *The Green Goddess* quickly taking shape for the Philadelphia opening at the end of December. Carpenters consulted electricians and conferred with scene painters. Stagehands dodged this way and that, carrying props. Guns, cushions, cigarettes, two Green Goddesses, table-lamps, an entire dinner service, writing materials, wireless equipment, the works of Bernard Shaw, incense and incense jars, flags, gongs and tom-toms were checked off against successive lists. Seamstresses wheeled racks of costumes this way and that, a fashion house designed Lucilla's dresses and actors were extracted from rehearsals for innumerable costume fittings. The Raja had three suits of clothes: exotic, European evening dress, and riding wear. Lucilla, Crespin and Traherne had fur-lined aviators' coats, goggles and caps; Lucilla had morning clothes and evening dress, Crespin an army uniform and Traherne a morning suit. Watkins had a tail-suit, the Raja's bodyguard were equipped with military uniforms and the priests with robes. Everybody, all the time, wanted a word with Mr Ames. At his shoulder, Archer began to feel almost ashamed that *The Green Goddess*, 'more trivial than it orignally was', now that he had 'sandpapered [it] to adapt it to the average American intelligence', had set such a huge juggernaut in motion.

Alarmingly, most of the cast were still hopelessly adrift by Christmas, and showed no sign of bringing the play into land. A dress rehearsal on

23 December left Archer more certain than ever of catastrophe. The worst was Cyril Keightley's Traherne. Archer thought Keightley 'a numskull',[23] but was quietly informed that he was particularly popular with American audiences. As for George Arliss, Archer could not fathom him at all. He mumbled and inserted long pauses between sentences. At first, Archer marked him down as a victim of 'the great vice of the star – always wanting to follow the line of least resistance and cut or alter anything he finds difficult', but slowly it dawned upon him that Arliss was not evading at all. This was his performance. Yet it was a performance almost exactly the opposite of what Archer imagined when he wrote the play. He thought of the Raja as mercurial, voluble, delighting in the sound of his own voice. Arliss contended that he was a quiet, devious man of infinite deliberation and Oriental subtlety. Once again, Archer began re-writing, pruning the Raja's speeches in an effort to prevent Arliss's delivery making them tedious.

He spent a solitary Christmas Day before joining friends for dinner in the evening. On Boxing Day, he left the Pennsylvania Hotel and travelled to Philadelphia, where *The Green Goddess* was to open on Monday, 27 December, and run for a week. He checked in at the St James's Hotel and on Monday night, walked the short distance to the newly refurbished Walnut Street Theatre. It was here that forty-three years ago on his first visit to America, he had seen a production of Offenbach's *L'Archiduc*! The Walnut Street was a large theatre, seating 1,700, and it was not quite full for the first night of *The Green Goddess*. Archer was smothering his nerves by declaring to friends that the play now bored him. 'I never felt less nervous in my life,' he proclaimed. After a few words with Ames, he sat down in the stalls and waited. The lights lowered. The curtain rose.

Now he realized why Pinero disliked seeing his own productions. Archer noticed every little mistake in performance, each slight slip from the script. At last, there was the sound of aircraft, of bombs falling and exploding, Cardew, the heroic Englishman, stalked on to the stage and Traherne and Lucilla were freed. The Raja spoke the last line and the curtain came down. Suddenly, there was tremendous applause, the curtain was rising and the cast were stepping forward to take their calls. The curtain fell, was raised again, and again as the applause and the calls continued. The next morning there were queues at the box office and Ames was jubilant. *The Green Goddess*, he declared, was on its way to New York. To Archer, it seemed as though this was all happening to somebody else. 'The whole experience,' he wrote, 'is weird and incredible.'[24]

As Ames hoped, radiant reviews heralded their arrival in Manhattan, and the first night at the Booth on 18 January 1921 was followed by a deluge of celebratory reviews the next morning. The New York critics were awed by the spectacle and admired the acting. They enthused over the wit and even the plot. The Booth was a small theatre, seating just over 760, but it was in a good location just off Broadway and Ames was banking on a sell-out in a small house being far better for future bookings than a big theatre being half-empty. He was right. The play immediately sold out until the end of March as *The Green Goddess* acquired a magic and momentum of its own, becoming the talk of Manhattan dinners and parties. People marvelled at the exotic shrine and shuddered when they recalled the sinister tribal chantings. The women loved the fabulous gowns, and everyone ran out of superlatives with which to describe the sumptuous dinner scene on the palace balcony with the snowy peaks of the Himalayas gleaming in the distance.

The Green Goddess made Arliss a star and his partnership with Ivan F. Simpson's broad-Cockney Watkins made them a favourite double-act. It was extraordinary. Archer was thrilled. 'You cannot be more surprised than I am to find me figuring in the character of a successful dramatist – but so it is!'[25] he gasped, writing home to Murray. '. . . behold!' he notified Max Beerbohm, 'it has been produced & is a success. . . . How amazed your brother would have been to see me . . .'[26] Each night the Booth reported standing room only. The run was extended and the play became 'the Dempsey of the occasion',[27] he told Barker proudly. To Elizabeth, he admitted that '*The Green Goddess* is quite the success of the moment & is playing to capacity every night. How *long* its moment may last is another question.'[28]

Meanwhile, Archer himself became a celebrity as journalists trooped into the lobby of the Pennsylvania anxious to record his thoughts for their readers. He was interviewed and profiled and photographed. New York thought him a wondrous, but odd phenomenon. He was the most important dramatic critic writing in the English language, who had introduced Ibsen to London and thereby New York, and who had championed the work of Shaw and Barker and Galsworthy. Yet here he was, popping up as the author of a melodramatic sensation. They asked him why he did not write like Ibsen or Shaw, and why, at sixty-four years old and with a life-time of drama criticism behind him, he bothered writing at all. Archer did not mention *Australia*, or *Blue and Buff*, and kept quiet about his impoverished bank balance, but told and re-told the events of his dream which made such a good story it was written and re-written. He found himself held up as an inspiration to elderly people. He was compared with William de Morgan, the English Pre-Raphaelite ceramicist who, in 1905 at the age of sixty-five, had abandoned his kiln and spent the last twelve years of his life writing whimsical Dickensian novels. Archer was the de Morgan of drama and 'there are a lot of people his story will buck up no end' [29] pronounced *The New York Times*.

At the beginning of February, Ames calculated that since their opening in Philadelphia, the play had taken over $100,000. Such astronomical sums made Archer feel vertiginous. 'When I realise that it is really I that have made such a success, I feel a sort of superstitious terror . . .'[30] he notified Murray. But in New York, success simply generated success. He was approached by the producer Sam H. Harris, who had just gone into partnership with Irving Berlin to build the Music Box theatre and meanwhile was looking for a play. On 25 February, Archer signed a contract for $1000 giving Harris the production rights to *Beatriz-Juana*. New York, it seemed, was his town.

He still loved ambling down Broadway at night, past the theatres and the movie houses with their sizzling electric lights. The New York *Evening Post* commissioned him to write seven articles telling New Yorkers what he thought about their theatres and with *The Green Goddess* as secure as a rock at the Booth, he plunged into as many of Manhattan's fifty theatres as possible. Over twenty years ago, he remembered, most plays in Manhattan were British. Now they were American, but to Archer, the most exciting new American voice was not to be heard on bright Broadway but in the dark shadows beyond Greenwich Village.

It belonged to a rangy thirty-two-year-old named Eugene O'Neill, the playwright son of James O'Neill, with whom Elizabeth had once toured. He was a graduate of George Pierce Baker's playwriting classes at Harvard and Baker had alerted Archer to his work the previous year. He had read *Beyond the Horizon*, O'Neill's first full-length play, the story of two brothers, one of whom goes to sea, leaving the other to tend the family farm and found it 'nothing less than a great tragedy of today . . . written with a stern sobriety, yet with deep poetic feeling'. At the Neighborhood Playhouse on Grand Street, he saw O'Neill's new play, *The Emperor Jones*, chronicling the downfall of a black dictator.

This was 'a monologue rather than a play', but one fuelled by 'a fine and original imagination'. It confirmed Archer's impression that O'Neill's demanding, invigorating and mysterious plays were 'the most original and significant things that have been done . . . on this side of the Atlantic'.[31] Yet the most curious play he saw was not in Greenwich Village but back uptown at the Garrick Theater on West 35th Street. It was a drama almost without recognizable characters or ideas yet it had nonetheless become almost as popular as *The Green Goddess* itself. It was *Heartbreak House*, Shaw's twenty-fifth major play, which had opened on 10 November 1920, and had yet to be produced in Britain.

The play is Shaw's dramatic response to the war and his indictment of the rarefied English social class who allowed it to happen, the intellectual idealists sealed within their own futile world. It is his 'Fantasia in the Russian Manner on English themes', for as he had once been enthused by Ibsen, Shaw had now taken up Chekhov and fully intended a Chekhovian comparison.

Full of melancholy and anger, *Heartbreak House* is set in Captain Shotover's rambling, disorganized home tucked into a fold of the Sussex downs. Shotover is an inventor whose restless intellect refuses to be caged by the mundane necessity to make money. At almost ninety, magisterial and eccentric, he has become a superman spiritually exhausted. In the same house lives his Bloomsbury-ish middle-aged daughter, Hesione Hushabye, and Hector, her husband, whose lethargy has reduced him to spinning spurious stories of his heroism to gullible young women. Hesione's sister, Ariadne Utterwood, arrives on an unexpected visit. Having married a colonial Governor, Ariadne represents Horseback Hall, the philistine alternative to Heartbreak House, peopled by a class who buy and ride horses, file dutifully into church, canvass for the Conservative Party and chatter of nothing else.

The talk, the illusions, flirtations and jealousies of Heartbreak House are complicated by the various arrivals of Ellie Dunn, and her gentle, naive father, Mazzini; by 'Boss' Mangan, the rich, pragmatic, bombastic industrialist and a burglar attempting to give himself up. It ends in a grand Wagnerian air-raid. By coincidence, both Archer and Shaw had plays running in New York which ended with the arrival of bombers. But when the bombs fall upon Sussex, Shaw evokes an inevitable apocalypse which Heartbreak House has brought upon itself. His is an unsparing and despairing vision, but Archer, unable to stare once more into the unbearable chasms of war, brings on his bombers as the jubilant fanfare of patriotic liberation. The war had prompted in Shaw his most serious and epic play, a cry of terrible anguish against England and the world. In Archer, whose vision was always bleaker than Shaw's, it had produced at first a deeply felt piece of propaganda and then a diverting melodrama. Such was the difference between them.

Heartbreak House opens with the arrival of Ellie Dunn, who, finding nobody to meet her, sits down and immediately falls asleep. It was all Archer could do at the Garrick to stop himself following her example, for he found Shaw's English fantasia as exasperating as his Russian model. Shaw had thrown plot overboard before, but now he had pushed character and action after it. The play was expertly directed, but nothing could disguise the fact that it was a structural shambles which lived, if it could be said to live at all, 'from moment to moment by the mere shillelagh-whirling of its dialogue'.[32]

Cautiously, he looked about him. Everyone else appeared captivated. It was baffling. It seemed that Shaw had transfixed Manhattan as effortlessly as Nellie Dunn hypnotizes Mangan in the second act. The astonishing paradox of the American audience, he concluded (and not for the first time), was that it could be both immensely sophisticated and intensely gullible. 'If you tell it there is something it ought to admire and enjoy, it will go in its thousands & never find out it is bored,'[33] he notified Murray. It was a chilling thought.

By the end of February, when he left for London, the queues at the Booth's box office were as gratifyingly long as ever. He arrived home to a welcome from Shaw. 'I am greatly pleased by your success,' he wrote. 'It proves that I was quite right all along . . . You can now go ahead with the original Widowers' Houses . . .'[34] With *The Green Goddess* heading into profit and his royalties set at ten per cent, the weight of financial worry was beginning to slide from Archer's shoulders, and the de Morgan of drama began thinking what he might do next. He briefly considered writing a wildly absurd fifth act, set in the distant future in which the Crespins's daughter, Iris, now grown up, accompanies Sir Basil and Lady Traherne on holiday to Monte Carlo. There, they unexpectedly encounter the Raja and, as a New Woman and faithful student of Shaw, Iris marries him in recognition of the service he did in shooting her renegade father.

In fact, there were several demands for a sequel. Beerbohm hoped for something with a happy ending and that autumn, after the discovery of Tom's grave and the family pilgrimage to Coutrai, Archer dived down to Dartmoor, spent ten days at Fairbrook, and returned with a new play. But *The Magician*, subtitled *A New Arabian Night in Three Acts*, does not involve the Raja. Instead, it is a caper of mistaken identity and fraud involving a portrait assumed to be by Leonardo. But Barker told him it had no dramatic interest whatsoever and Murray and Elizabeth expressed only cautious interest. All Ames wanted to talk about was the publicity splash to celebrate the four hundreth performance of *The Green Goddess* at the Booth in the new year. To Archer's horror, he planned to procure congratulatory telegrams from leading British dramatists and publish them in New York newspapers. This was embarrassing enough, but when Ames suggested approaching Shaw, Archer protested immediately. He knew Shaw to be irked by his 'significant silence' over *Heartbreak House*, which had just opened at the Royal Court, and feared a Shavian reprisal being published in New York. 'I BAR SHAW', he cabled. Instead, he drafted a message for Barker to send from Devon:

THOUGH HEARTILY ASHAMED OF EARLY COMPLICITY IN PIECE OF SHAMELESS POTBOILING, HOPE THAT GREEN GODDESS MAY RUN AS LONG AS CHU CHIN CHOW, TO WHICH, ON THE WHOLE, I CONSIDER IT SUPERIOR.[35]

Yet the play was almost at the end of its life in Manhattan and closed on 4 February 1922. But in New York at least, Archer had outlived Shaw. *Heartbreak House* ran at the Garrick for just over a hundred performances over five months, while *The Green Goddess* filled the Booth for 440 performances and for over a year. From the Booth, it set out to Boston and a long national tour, lasting until 5 May 1923.

In October 1922, following the National Theatre debacle, Archer again shut himself away at Fairbrook. He was working on yet another play, his sixth in five years. *Martha Washington*, he hoped, would establish him as a serious dramatist. Having been impressed by John Drinkwater's 'intensely interesting and often moving' [36] *Abraham Lincoln* at the Lyric, Hammersmith, he had decided to dramatize the American War of Independence from the point of view of George Washington's wife, and without any battles. He lifted the background from Sir George Trevelyn's *History of the American Revolution*, and worked at high speed, hammering what he imagined to be 'absolutely historical'[37] dialogue into eight scenes dating between 1759 and 1799. 'It is entirely a play of talk,' he informed Elizabeth, whom he was hoping might be coaxed into playing the leading role. Every so often, he tramped across blustery

Dartmoor to read long sections to the Galsworthys who 'seemed to like them',[38] and in December he had the entire play neatly typed.

When the Harley Street specialist banished him from the English cold, he agreed that the West Indies or Florida would be a suitably warm place for Archer to spend the winter. But first, as he told Murray, he intended stopping off in New York to present Ames with the production rights to *Martha Washington* and prod Harris into getting a move on with staging *Beatriz-Juana*. With *The Green Goddess* doing wonders for his bank balance, he booked his Atlantic crossing on the *Majestic*, the largest and most luxurious passenger ship in the world, and sailed on 27 December. It was not a pleasant trip. The sea was mutinous, whenever he tried to eat a jazz band started up, and his regular companion at the captain's table turned out to be Stanley Baldwin, the new Chancellor of the Exchequer in Bonar Law's Conservative administration, and 'about as unimpressive a human being as can be'.[39]

It was with heartfelt relief that he disembarked at New York, took sanctuary at the Pennsylvania and delivered *Martha Washington* to Ames. That done, he alerted old friends he was back and delved into a fortnight of theatre-going. Then: 'disaster'. Ames rejected the play. This was dreadful. He ran round to tackle the prevaricating Harris, who agreed to produce *Beatriz-Juana* on the condition the American actress Margaret Lawrence played the title role. But Archer detested her and refused. That was that. Catastrophe. He needed the money *The Green Goddess* was making, but equally, he wanted to be more than a quirky, once-lucky melodramatist. From his early days in Edinburgh, Archer had craved a reputation as a serious playwright and now it looked again as if those dreams were ruined.

Suddenly, he felt so exhausted that for once he was unsure of what to do next. His tiredness did not go unnoticed by his American friends, who saw that his brow appeared lined with worry, that he seemed to have lost weight and that he was tormented by a racking, mucous cough. Archer arranged to stay with acquaintances in Florida but after being turned down by Ames and reaching deadlock with Harris, he was so miserable he could not bear company. He thought idly about going down to Buenos Aires, which he had never visited, but instead, he booked a cruise on the Royal Mail Steam Packet *Orca* to Cuba and the West Indies. He assured his concerned friends that he would be all right. They let him go. He wanted to be by himself, think his own thoughts and retrace old travels for perhaps the last time.

It was a sad, lonely, sentimental journey. He left New York in late January 1923, and by the end of the month reached Havana. The place was unrecognizable. Like Honolulu, it was 'Americanized out of all knowledge', the screeching traffic and blaring motor horns creating a hell as raucous and as dangerous as Times Square. He turned back to the *Orca* and spent the rest of his time in Cuba sitting on deck beneath an awning, reading, snoozing and watching the sunlight flaming on the pink walls of the Morro Castle. 'If climate is going to cure my ailment (which it isn't) I have certainly come to the right shop,' he told Barker, trying to sound cheerful in one of his few letters. 'There is a breeze all day long & the shade temperature is ideal though the sun is hotter than in an English July.'[40] Occasionally, when he looked up, he spotted Lord Burnham, one of his fellow passengers and one of the press barons whom he had thought of approaching for a donation to the National Theatre, but he did not introduce himself. Having written a couple of letters to let his family and friends know where he was, he maintained his own company.

By the following week, the *Orca* had made its way to Jamaica where 'sad memories'[41] of his visit with Tom almost twelve years earlier again prevented him from leaving the ship. In Panama, he saw the completed Canal and thought grimly of its human cost, and then headed for the north and Bermuda, where he did go ashore and spent three hot weeks in February and March in Hamilton. Here, fanned by slow Atlantic breezes, he meditated upon death. It would be pleasant, he thought, to be buried here, beneath the palm trees in this little British outpost: ' – they have delightful, cool clean white coral graves, which they dig by the dozen in advance,'[42] he wrote to Granville Barker. This idea cheered him so much that he began to sketch out a play about a stock exchange gambler who comes a cropper and shoots himself dead. He sat on the seafront as he wrote, listening to a British military band, the blustering marches and patriotic melodies expunging the fiendish jazz of the *Majestic*.

In mid-March, he was back in New York, sufficiently revitalized to sign a contract giving Ames the English production rights for *The Green Goddess* in return for an advance of £400. He travelled south to Florida to honour his delayed promise to stay with his friends at Lake Alfred, and on 1 April arrived at Asheville, North Carolina, to spend what became 'two pestilential weeks at the most intolerable hotel I ever struck'.[43]

It was all the Corbins's fault. John Corbin had been the first literary manager of the New Theatre and was now an editorial writer for the *New York Times*. He and his wife Amy were two of his oldest American friends and had beseeched him not to leave their shores without visiting a health resort. They knew just the place, they told him. The Grove Park Inn at Asheville hugged the Blue Ridge Mountains, the air was clean and vibrant and the views of the tumbling waterfalls and valleys were some of the most inspiring he would ever see in America. It would put him right back on his feet again. They even knew the manager, so when he booked, be sure to mention their name. He did, and was promised a first-class room. From Florida, he travelled for two days and a night to reach Asheville.

The Grove Park was a large, rambling place of many wings, newly built in an overpoweringly ornate, sham-rustic style and surrounded by parkland. Archer was hot, dusty and ready to drop, but could not find anyone to deal with his booking. For ninety minutes he sat in a rocking chair in the lobby, surrounded by his bags and reading *Detective Story Magazine* before someone agreed to deal with his reservation. Having signed a declaration promising that he had no contagious diseases, he was allocated a room, but one considerably inferior to the kind he had reserved, where angry notices from the management hung from the walls and were propped on the tables. Some warned of penalties if he slammed his door or dropped his boots heavily on to the floor. Others extolled the purity of the water and the excellence of the soap. Downstairs in the restaurant, he discovered every dish on the menu to be introduced by a tribute to its tastiness and a description of the hygienic conditions of its preparation. Even the money the hotel gave in change, he read, had undergone a thorough boiling in ivory soap to ensure its absolute spotlessness. '. . . how could you find it in your heart to send me to this ridiculous, incredible, exasperating place?' he wailed in a letter to the Corbins. But, at least, he conceded, there was no jazz.

Then the music started. Organ music, music that was not music at all but a series of pianissimos, fortissimos and breathy whispers chased him about the lobby and corridors. He locked himself in the peace of his room, turned the notices to the wall and worked on his play about the stockbroker's suicide and as he did so, he realized that the very awfulness of the Grove Park was working on him like a tonic. Within days he felt marvellously fit. 'I am profoundly grateful to you for sending me here,' he reported to Amy Corbin on 3 April. 'It is an experience I wouldn't have missed for a great deal. I am doing some work that interests me, and rather enjoy being at enmity with my kind.'[44]

At the end of his two weeks, he left for New York and the Pennsylvania, where Ames found him and dragged him off to the eight-hundreth performance of *The Green Goddess* at Providence. 'Oh! How it bored me!' On 5 May, he boarded the *Homeric* for London, having been away almost five months. 'I have got rid of neither my cough nor of my plays,' he wrote to Max Beerbohm, 'but I have had a fairly interesting & amusing time.'[45]

Soon after *The Green Goddess* opened at the Booth, the Distinctive Pictures Corporation bought the film rights, snapped its fingers and disgorged hundreds of thousands of dollars in the creation of the most ambitious silent movie ever undertaken by an East coast studio. A cameraman was dispatched to the Himalayas to film aeroplanes flying above the mountains, while a 150 foot high cliff was built in New York for the scene of the crash. The sets of the shrine, the Raja's palace and the village covered over 100,000 square feet of studio floor-space, and over 2000 extras were employed to shuffle about as the goddess-fearing subjects. Everything, claimed the producers, was just like it should be. The palace was absolutely faithful to Indian architecture; the furniture and wall hangings were imported from the Afghanistan collection at the Brooklyn Museum of Art, and Roshanara, the 'interpreter of Indian dancing' solemnly vouched for the authenticity of 'Oriental details'.

George Arliss and Ivan F. Simpson were the only survivors from the Booth cast to appear in the film. The director was Sidney Olcott, noted for his deft handling of crowd scenes and drawing subtle performances from his stars. Archer had no part in this heady process, his script being adapted by Forrest Halsey, an experienced screenwriter. Neither did he attend the film's premiere, ironically at the Sam H. Harris Theatre on 14 August 1923. But there seemed no stopping *The Green Goddess*. The film was a huge success and eight years later it was re-made as a talkie. George Arliss again played the Raja and was nominated for an Academy Award.

In London, *The Green Goddess* was set to open at the St James's Theatre a few weeks later on 6 September. Arliss was returning after twenty-two years to play the Raja, but otherwise the play was entirely re-cast. Arthur Hatherton, who had made his name in musical comedy at the Gaiety, played Watkins. Owen Roughwood and George Relph, reliable Shakespearian and West End actors, appeared as Crespin and Traherne and Isobel Elsom, a singer and former Peter Pan, was miscast as Lucilla. Ames came from New York to direct. By now, Archer was thinking of having the play subtitled *An Anachronism in Four Acts*, but Ames decided to advertise it instead as 'A Play of Adventure'.

The magic of *The Green Goddess* survived its Atlantic crossing. The first night was sold out and rapturously received. Arliss was hailed and Archer cheered. It was his finest commercial moment, but it was dimmed by the fact that three of his closest friends could not be there to share it with him. Shaw was in Ireland, Barker in France and Elizabeth in the country. They had all sent their best wishes. 'A triumph for your green one and to you,'[46] wrote Barker. But it was not quite the same. Afterwards, Archer sent Elizabeth a telegram and followed it the next day with a letter reporting that the play 'fulfilled all reasonable expectations; & I think the press this morning is calculated to send people to it'.[47]

Even more than the American press, the English were dumbfounded by the Archer paradox. High-brow had suddenly become low-brow and was not frowning but laughing. Like a fabulous magician, the champion of the New Drama had suddenly exchanged his high collar and sober black suit for the multi-coloured dress of the theatrical illusionist. 'Whether Mr Archer has been laughing up his sleeve all these forty conscientious years I do not know,' admitted the critic of the *Pall Mall Gazette*, adding that *The Green Goddess* constituted 'a thoroughly well-knit bit of thrill-planning' which fully deserved its 'roaring reception'. The *Evening News* confirmed that the play 'pulsates action at a supernormal rate' and contained 'a hundred suspense-thrills'. The man from the *Evening Standard* proclaimed it 'one of the most thrilling and entertaining plays I have ever seen' and that the Raja and Watkins were 'every whit as good as the earlier and gayer creations of Mr Shaw'. St John Ervine, in the *Observer*, reflected that while Archer's dialogue was not particularly flexible, it was not wholly inflexible either, and praised Arliss's 'signally fine performance'.[48]

The critics debated, as far as it was possible, 'the Archer technique'. The story of the dream was recycled and a window at Selfridge's department store was given over to *Green Goddess* fashions. The name was conferred upon a steam locomotive at the Eskdale Valley small-scale railway in Cumberland. Largely as a result of the film, the name began turning up in all sorts of places. *The Green Goddess* became a cocktail in which crème de menthe is the principal ingredient, and a kind of lettuce salad. During the Second World War, it surfaced as the name of a military fire engine and even, during the 1980s, as the nickname of a female keep-fit instructor who appeared, wearing a bright green leotard, on breakfast television.

Meanwhile, in September 1923, letters of congratulation from actors and writers tumbled through Archer's letterbox. One took him back forty-five years and more to the Theatre Royal, Glasgow, and to his first playwriting days in London. 'I am indeed glad to read, not only how brilliantly you have scored, but, that which is better still, how very sincere is the gladness expressed on all sides that it is *you* carrying off all these honours.'[49] The note was from his once much-admired Ellen Lancaster-Wallis.

Two days after the play opened, Winthrop Ames stood at the dockside at Southampton, about to board his ship to the United States, scribbling a note to Archer. 'Good-bye for a little while, dear WA,' he wrote. 'I can't sail without telling you that I quite know what torture it must be to sit at rehearsals and see point after point go by unrectified. Thank you for your sweet patience. Now that it's all over, I realize that I've had a very good time! Good-bye.'[50] He slipped the letter into a pillar-box, and the ship sailed. Archer and Ames would never meet again.

The play settled in at the St James's to good business. It had a star attraction in Arliss, and curiosity value in that one of the oldest and apparently most austere of critics had become one of the youngest and most impish of dramatists. It was the critic of the *Evening Standard* who politely enquired:

> You are old, Father William, the young man said,
> And your hair is becoming quite white,
> But yet you exultantly stand on your head.
> Do you think at your age it is right?

17

A New World

Becoming an international playwright and the progenitor of a silent film was one of his more astonishing adventures, but by apparently standing on his head, he had fallen on his feet. 'The Green Goddess has secured me a moderate old-age pension, which is what I wanted,'[1] he told Elizabeth proudly, a fortnight after the London production opened.

He also signed a contract for $1000 for the Australian production, and with royalties from the United States and Britain began buying property for the first time in his life. Eventually, he owned most of the Nerve Training Colony at King's Langley. But the sudden increase in his income brought unforseen miseries. The Income Tax authorities instituted lengthy enquiries and Archer found himself closeted with financial advisors, staring incomprehensibly at tables of accounts as both sides conjectured his liability for tax. He had always been hopeless with money and while he had tried to keep abreast of changes in the law and pay what was due, Charles was later dismayed to discover that he had 'not chased up his business for 50 years' and that everything was in a 'fearful tangle'.[2]

While groping his way about his maze of income tax, he kept up his theatre-going, setting off from Fitzroy Square to see plays by Noël Coward, Somerset Maugham and Frederick Lonsdale, and revues starring Noël Coward, Jack Buchanan, and Jack Hulbert and Cecily Courtneidge. Plays by old friends were now being revived as vehicles for new stars. At the Avenue, renamed the Playhouse, Gladys Cooper was an acclaimed Paula in The Second Mrs Tanqueray. Twenty-two years previously, Archer had advised Pinero to give such a daring script to the Independent Theatre, but times had changed and burnished the play into a contemporary classic. There were also plays by new acquaintances. At the Royal Court, he saw Our Ostriches, an indignant tract attacking the Birth Rate Commission's condemnation of birth control and written by Dr Marie Stopes, who had opened Britain's first birth control clinic in 1921. He was 'favourable to her movement', he told Christen Collin, 'as tending to check two evils, namely the sterility of the cultivated classes & the over-fecundity of the unfit or less fit'.[3]

At the New Theatre an older friend, George Foss, appeared in the title role of *Cymbeline*, with Sybil Thorndike as Imogen. He travelled up to Hampstead where the energetic Norman Macdermott had converted a drill hall into the Everyman Theatre, covered the floors with prickly coconut matting and instituted a lively programme of revivals and instructive new plays. There, Archer saw new productions of *Candida* and *Major Barbara*, which he still thought merely a dazzling extravaganza. He also kept track of his own work. In 1921, the Everyman revived his translation of *John Gabriel Borkman*, directed and designed by Theodore Komisarjevsky, newly arrived from Moscow. The next year, he was shaking his head at the inept cuts in *Peer Gynt* at the Old Vic in which Russell Thorndike (Sybil's brother) played Peer.

Archer darted about here and there, a familiar face at the theatre and sometimes still on the lecture platform. Eager to stay in touch, he sniffed out company among younger writers, sometimes bearing down upon a solitary figure espied across the dining room at the Reform. One day in June 1922, Siegfried Sassoon was lunching there alone when Archer loomed up and asked if he might join him. 'And what did Archer say?' Sassoon considered in his diary that night. 'He conversed cautiously and his demeanor lacked liveliness. There is nothing sprightly about William Archer. But he is a nice man. He expressed extreme abhorrence for the Phoenix Society, which is a pity as I've just sent them three guineas.'[4] Among his younger friends was Rebecca West, the novelist who had taken her pseudonym from the heroine of *Rosmersholm* and was nearing the end of a ten-year love affair with H. G. Wells. She and Archer often walked together through Hyde Park. Rebecca, in her early thirties, thought him 'a dear'.[5]

In the early summer of 1923, he published his final book, *The Old Drama and the New*, a compilation of the lectures he had given in the autumn of 1920 and 1921 at King's College, London, on the history and interpretation of British drama between 1590 and 1915. The book represents the first systematic attempt to write the story of the English theatre from a dramatic rather than a literary point of view and to put contemporary realist drama in an historical context. Subtitled *An Essay in Revaluation*, it is also a summation of Archer's campaign for a realistic

theatre begun over forty years previously in *English Dramatists of Today*.
In the new book, he suggests that the non-naturalistic, lyrical strands of
Elizabethan and Jacobean verse drama slowly became siphoned off
during the eighteenth century, eventually finding a new life in opera
and operetta. Simultaneously, the realistic undercurrent had developed
with the rise of prose writing and the realistic novel, and in the theatre
reached its height in Ibsen and contemporary writers such as Barker.
The overwrought passions and rhetoric of the past had been replaced
by a cool, rational, psychological awareness, creating a modern theatre
where contemporary life could be objectively portrayed, analyzed and
criticized.

   The Old Drama and the New is also a sequel of sorts to *Play-Making*,
a volume of dramatic technique being followed by a reappraisal of
dramatic history. Busy with his own playwriting, Archer was disappointed with the book and regarded it as little more than a sketch for a
longer and more detailed work which he anticipated would take at least
five years to complete. But 'I have arrived at a time of life when one
does not lightly undertake such long engagements,'[6] he observed.
Nevertheless, it raised a flurry of argument, both in reviews and among
other critics and playwrights. Many welcomed it, although for others,
Archer's voice was no longer that of the theatrical revolutionary but of
the old guard. But most of all, *The Old Drama and the New* gave Archer
and Shaw yet another opportunity, after forty years, to lecture one
another on their great subject of the theatre.

   Archer never deviated from his belief that there were two problems
to be solved with Shaw, firstly, to make him discover his own dramatic
voice, and secondly, to make him realize what the point of drama was.

   His latest play, *Back to Methuselah*, a five-part religious epic, was a
case in point. They had been wrestling over this since it was published
in 1921. According to Archer, this sprawling 'Bible', delving back to the
Garden of Eden and hurtling forward through the centuries to 31,920
AD, was a monumental example of Shaw's 'tyrannous, irrepressible
idiosyncracy',[7] the eccentricity behind which he had hidden over three
decades of playwriting and which prevented him from becoming the
great dramatist he might otherwise have been. Archer's contention was
always that Shaw spoke in the voice of his masters and on 12 June
1923, he repeated what he had told him twenty years earlier. 'The
trouble with you ... is that you are incurably credulous ... Wagner
comes along & you are a Wagnerite; Ibsen, & you are an Ibsenite (I
never was); Nietzsche, & you are Nietzschean ... to my mind ... a

crack-brained poseur who was vastly over-rated in his little day.' The result was that after all these years, 'you are no whit nearer the real secret of things'.[8]

A week later, on 19 June, having inspected *The Old Drama and the New*, Shaw put pen to paper. 'Oblige me with a hammer, a saw, a beetle and a couple of wedges that I may operate on your all but impervious knowledge box,' he cried, explaining that part of Archer's 'colossal absentmindedness' was his overlooking the fact that he, Shaw, had developed drama far beyond the point ever conceived in *The Old Drama and the New*. Pointing to Archer's emphasis on the importance of dramatic structure, he argued that 'the plain fact is that there are two sorts of plays, natural growths and constructions, just as there are two sorts of flowers, natural ones and artificial ones (made mostly in France)'.[9]

'It won't do,' scoffed Archer the next day, 20 June. The artistic success of a play depended equally upon its technical construction and dramatic purpose, and whenever Shaw tried to justify the aimlessness of a play like *Heartbreak House*, a play redeemed solely by the phosphorescence of its dialogue, he succeeded only in tying himself up in excruciating knots. Archer tried attacking Shaw with a different metaphor. 'I say a cat is a quadruped, with a brain, a backbone and (unless of the Manx variety) a tail,' he wrote. 'You say, "Oh no – a cat is a round, mushy, iridescent object with long streamers, usually observed on the shingle at low tide."'[10] This was preposterous enough, but it was sheer lunacy for Shaw also to claim that since Chekhov, a jellyfish was not only a cat but the only sort worth keeping.

'You haven't got it yet,' taunted Shaw. 'The alternatives are not a cat and a jellyfish, but a clockwork cat and a live cat.' His dramatic technique, he reasoned, was really very simple. 'I write my dialogue (which involves creating the characters and doing all the vital work), as it comes. I then go over it and arrange it for the stage.'[11] This was not simplicity, countered Archer, merely simplistic. 'All drama is ... a product of two things: character & action: the person doing & the thing done ... Character is by far the higher element ...'[12]

He said it again: Shaw would never write anything really far-reaching until he threw away the clownish mask of G. B. S. Shaw laughed and repeated that Archer had never lived in the real world at all, but in one entirely of his own making. That they agreed so heartily on each other's fallibilities was one of the reasons their friendship was as firm as ever. Archer nagged Shaw because he knew him to be a genius and wanted him to reveal it to the world before it was too late. 'There have been deeper and more original thinkers than he,' Archer told an audience in New York in 1921; 'there have been greater dramatists; there have been as brilliant, though scarcely more brilliant wits. But I doubt whether there has ever been a more extraordinary and fascinating combination of gifts in one single human brain.'[13] But knowing that a mixture of facetiousness and self-satisfaction would prevent Shaw from writing a play worthy of his talent, caused him much anguish. Instead of becoming one of the great fixed stars of modern thought, he was destined instead to become an erratic, brilliant flash, a meteor flaring and dying. 'He will be regarded by posterity, not as a great dramatist, but as the greatest of dramatic lecturers,'[14] Archer predicted.

While Archer was fighting over the future of drama with Shaw, he was also conducting a similar contest with Barker, who in June sent Archer the proofs of *The Secret Life*, his first full-length play for thirteen years. On the 10th, Archer spent 'a very exciting day' reading it, 'with constant admiration for the bounding originality, wit and even profundity of the thing, but with despair at the pervading sense that I am at least three generations from it'.

The Secret Life is Barker's response to the war, as *Heartbreak House* was Shaw's, *The Skin Game*, Galsworthy's and *War is War* and *The Green Goddess*, Archer's. It is both an elegiac remembrance of things past and a cautious peering into the future. Evan Strowde, a former Member of Parliament, has lost his faith and ambition but looks at the new world with unflinching intellectual and emotional ruthlessness. A deeply sensitive man, he is one who can love completely yet whose capacity to love is frozen, suspended in the memories of his broken relationships with Joan Westbury and the Countess of Peckham. As the title suggests, the characters have interior as well as exterior lives and Strowde is eventually torn between private love and public duties as, giving in to his political friends, he stands for election again.

The inhabitants of Heartbreak House are idealists bereft of ideas, while Hillcrist finds himself and his world overtaken by developers and the acquisitve society. In *The Secret Life*, the guests at Braxted Abbey are the uncertain survivors of war. Patrician politicians, they are people faced with the governance of Britain in an age in which beliefs and ideals must be rediscovered. Strowde encounters Joan Westbury, the woman he loved eighteen years previously, lost and still loves and whose sons have been killed in France. He meets Oliver, his grown-up, disabled and illegitimate son by Lady Peckham. Later Joan leaves for America and while there falls fatally ill. In a desperate bid to reclaim his faith, Strowde abandons the election campaign and sails to be with her. Unknown to him, she dies soon after he leaves. It is a play of conversation, of dreams and regrets, in which Barker's themes of the meaning of love and loyalty and how men and women might cope in a world in which the realities fall so far short of ideals, are at their most profound and most lyrical.

Like Shaw, Barker was writing in the lightning-flash of Chekhov, and in its drifting talk and atmosphere of his world on the edge of change, *The Secret Life* is fleetingly Chekhovian, yet its despair is essentially English. It has the rhythmic sweep of a symphony, and it both absorbed and troubled Archer. 'I take it your theme is the importance of the undercurrents of life that never come to the surface,' he hazarded. 'Therefore, if I am right, the absence of outward visible drama is the very thing you set out to portray.' Yet just when he thought he had grasped the drift of things, they slipped from him again. 'I thought again & again in the brilliant second act that I was really getting the hang of the thing & saw the drama crystallising; but in the third act the crystals seemed to dissolve again, leaving behind them a sort of shimmering opalescence from which I could extract nothing solid,' he wrote. But then, he had found *The Wild Duck* baffling when he first read it, and now thought it one of Ibsen's greatest plays. 'That ought to make me humble,'[15] he remarked.

As someone who himself lived a secret life, Archer was fascinated by Barker's portrayal of hidden emotions and yearnings. 'Have you never gone adventuring ... in your secret heart?' Strowde asks his sister during the second act. As a man who had fought for his ideals and his vision of the theatre and of the world, Archer sympathized too with Strowde's admission in the third act, that 'I lived half my life in the happiness ... and unhappiness ... of a vision. One fine day, I find that the world I'm living in is nothing like the idea of the world I've been living by. It comes quite casually ... conversion to disbelief.'

This was the undercurrent of the hidden life which drew Archer back to the play time and again. *The Secret Life* was clearly a great imaginative achievement, and he took far more time over it than he did with plays by Chekhov and very often by Shaw, because Barker's voice was unique and his intentions were serious, which made him a better dramatist. 'The reason Shaw's plays cannot be ranked as serious is that he starts with an incurable bias towards laughter,'[16] he explained to

Murray. But rather than a Shavian conundrum for the present, *The Secret Life* was a challenge for the future. 'It is written for the next generation, if not for the next again; while I belong to the last generation and cannot hope to overtake it,'[17] he notified Barker, sadly.

Making strenuous efforts to become as young as its author, he sent Barker two closely-typed pages of questions. Who owned the cottage by the sea in the first act? What was the time difference between his affairs with Lady Peckham and Joan Westbury? Why exactly did the relationship between her and Strowde break down? He added comments on individual lines, criticizing the punctuation and identifying conjunctions which spoiled the rhythm. Quibbling with Barker had the same effect as bickering with Shaw. It rejuvenated Archer and put them both on their toes.

Despite his reservations over *The Secret Life*, Archer was convinced that Barker would come to be seen as the most important all-round man of the theatre to have emerged during the first quarter of the century. He devoted long hours to encouraging and cross-examining Barker, writing extensive letters from London and travelling down to Devon where they went for refreshingly blustery walks. They discussed ideas for a National Theatre, and at his request, Archer provided him with bundles of notes about the Elizabethan theatre as background material for the prefaces he was writing to *The Players' Shakespeare*, seven volumes of which would appear over the next five years. When he completed those for the first three volumes, *The Tragedie of Macbeth*, *Cymbeline* and *The Merchant of Venice*, Barker immediately sent them to Archer for his comments.

Once *The Green Goddess* opened at the St James's, Archer returned to *The Secret Life*, yet however searchingly he read, he never felt as if he had the play within his grasp. '. . . your people are too busy philosophising – generalising about life, ever to think about *doing* anything . . .' he cautioned. '. . . this reflective method is not for a moment to be confounded with Ibsen's retrospective method. Ibsen withdrew veil after veil from the *happenings* of the past . . .'[18] Yet Barker had provided neither sufficient past nor enough happenings.

That summer, he sent the same message to both Shaw and Barker: 'ALL THE PLAYS THAT HAVE HAD MORE THAN AN EPHEMERAL LIFE IN THIS WORLD ARE MORE OR LESS WELL CONSTRUCTED PLAYS.'[19] But then, he conceded, perhaps the fault lay with him. He would have never said as much to Shaw, but to Barker he confessed ruefully that 'Perhaps – indeed probably – I am only an old fogey falling behind the march of progress.' Many years ago, he had pinpointed the beginning of modern drama as being the third act of *A Doll's House*. Now he was sure he had tumbled upon either its end, or a new beginning which he could not understand. He was not sure which. '. . . my old fogeydom began at the fourth act of *The Madras House*. Up to the third act, I was in the foremost files of the time. But I now confess my slogan . . . is BACK TO THE VOYSEY!'[20]

Barker held his ground and in letters and on their walks, gently instructed Archer in the new modern drama. In 1914, he had visited the Moscow Art Theatre and been impressed by the subtle, lyrical way in which the actors performed Chekhov. This was how *The Secret Life* should be played. 'I protest I never have – I cannot – write an unactable play,' he promised Archer; 'it would be against nature, against second nature anyhow: I act it as I write it.'[21] At the beginning of October, Archer sat down and read the play yet again. '. . . poor patient WA!' sympathized Barker. This time, they were both rewarded. Where once all was obscure, Archer found clarity and Barker 'rejoiced'. Audiences, he assured Archer, would understand *The Secret Life* as they understood events around them in real life, 'by a *mixture* of explanation, apprehension, observation'.[22] 'But will you get even an audience of elite to see & accept this?'[23] Archer persisted. Perhaps the play was too advanced (or too obscure) for the minority audience they used to be able to call upon at the Court and the Duke of York's. Even they had been dispersed, for although the Stage Society had survived the war, internal acrimony had brought it almost to the edge of bankruptcy. *The Secret Life* it seemed, would remain secret. Barker was forced to agree. Until the National Theatre was built, it would be impossible to create an acting ensemble in England equal to that of the Moscow Art Theatre. Therefore, he withheld the play in readiness for the new theatre. In the event, neither Archer nor Barker ever saw the play performed, for the National Theatre was not built during Barker's lifetime and *The Secret Life* was not produced until 1988. Even then, the world premiere was not at the National, but a London fringe theatre, the Orange Tree, at Richmond, where it was directed by Sam Walters.

During his travels at the beginning of 1923, Archer had written two plays. One concerned the suicidal stock-exchange speculator and now appears lost. The other, written partly at the Grove Park Inn, was *The Joy-Ride*, a three-act farce-melodrama for which the situation and characters were inspired by his love of American detective fiction and the 'crook plays' he had seen in New York.

The play is set on a howlingly wet night in the kitchen of a remote north-of-England farmhouse belonging to a man named Grimbly. He is nowhere to be seen, but is being impersonated by an elderly man called The Gaffer. Molly, known to the police as Irish Moll, is cooking pea soup, while the sharp-suited Montague Taw and his associate Lemuel Nixon are in the cellar, busily forging high denomination bank notes. Not only the characters, but also the dialogue springs from American detective magazines. When the gang are tipped off that the police are on their way to arrest them, Molly looks at the lights and snaps 'Shall we douse the glims?'

The gang escapes as a car draws up outside but instead of the police, Captain Hugh Rimington and Lady Hermia Croyland enter the kitchen, seeking shelter after Rimington's car, like Traherne's aeroplane, has run out of petrol. Rimington is Royal Flying Corps, boyish and in love with Lady Hermia. She is aristocratic, sensible, and unsure of whether she loves him. He is modern, she is not. 'We can't foxtrot through life,' she sighs. Yet is seems unlikely they will marry even if she wanted to, for she represents the 'last negotiable security' of a peer who has gambled himself bankrupt and promised her in marriage to Orlando Buckingham. In *The Green Goddess*, Archer portrayed the desolation of a failed marriage. In *The Joy-Ride*, he creates the prospect of marriage as an emotional winter without even a preceding summer.

A conveniently passing telegraph boy takes a message for Lady Hermia's friends to send a car, but within moments, the police duly arrive. Unwilling to reveal their real names for fear of scandal, Rimington and Lady Hermia submit to being interrogated as Molly and Monty, a fiction substantiated when detectives haul in the Gaffer, whom they have arrested nearby. At the second act curtain, the real Molly and Monty, together with Lemuel, storm the cottage, free the Gaffer and lock the police in the scullery. In the final act, a third car arrives. The latest arrival in a crowded kitchen is Buckingham, who has come in place of Hermia's friends, furious at being dragged out on a wet night and even more incensed at discovering her with Rimington. The telegraph boy reports finding the murdered body of Grimbly thrust into a hollow tree as the police burst out of the scullery to arrest the forgers. The Gaffer tears off his disguise to reveal himself as Peters, Buckingham's former valet, and denounces his master as none other than Maurice Breitstein, a 'swindler, fence-smasher, usurer – and traitor',[24] and shoots him dead. The gang are taken away, and Rimington and Hermia left free to marry.

The Joy-Ride is Archer's eighth post-war play and far more contrived and less entertaining than *The Green Goddess*. Yet it became the second to reach the stage, although he did not live to see Robert Courtneidge's production at the Prince's Theatre in Manchester, on 18 May 1925. A local newspaper review described it as 'a thoroughly workmanlike and jolly play', which had 'a very cordial reception',[25] but it proved insufficiently jolly to move into London and closed after a week. It was revived by Jack de Leon at the tiny Q Theatre on the Thames at Richmond, on 8 February the following year, but fared no better, and has not been performed since.

In the autumn of 1923, Archer had just slipped *The Joy-Ride* into a drawer stuffed with the rest of his unperformed plays, and was 'feeling quite lost without a play to work on',[26] when he suddenly received his first commission. The request came from Sir Oswald Stoll, then at the summit of his power as the owner of a nation-wide chain of seventeen variety theatres. Stoll had decided to bring the Japanese film-actor Sessue Hayakawa on a tour of Britain, and now that *The Green Goddess* was doing roaring business at the St James's, it occurred to him that Archer was just the man to write a piece of Oriental hokum with a leading role for Hayakawa.

Quite by chance, Archer had an idea in mind. Earlier that year, it was predicted in the press that Edward, the Prince of Wales, would become engaged to be married to Elizabeth Bowes-Lyon. Buckingham Palace issued an immediate denial and ten days later, announced that it would be Edward's brother George, the Duke of York, who would marry Elizabeth. During the summer, Archer told Barker the case was 'a ready-made play',[27] but once the call came through from Stoll, he quickly adapted it into a seventeen-page sketch called *The Samurai*.

The setting is a splendid private room at the Hotel de Russie in Nice, during the 1910 carnival. Idzu no Kami, played by Hayakawa, is attracted to a Russian girl, the Countess Varvara Alexievna. While she is at the carnival, Kami draws her father, Count Alexis Korsakoff, into defending Russian atrocities during the Russo-Japanese war of 1904, especially an incident at Yalu when a Russian officer tortured a Japanese to learn campaign secrets. Kami has identified Korsakoff as the officer, but neither admits this, and nor is Korsakoff aware that Kami is his former prisoner's son. The Russian's response is to maintain that 'war is war'.[28] Kami leaves the room, to return in full Samurai dress to avenge the death of his father. The two men struggle, and just as Kami is about to plunge his sword into Korsakoff, Varvara appears on the balcony outside the window. Kami is unable to kill a man in front of his daughter, but neither, as a Samurai, can he allow himself to live after both failing his father in his mission of vengeance and disgracing himself before the woman he loves. There and then, he commits hari-kiri. '. . . It is of course awful rot,' Archer told Elizabeth, but he hoped nevertheless to earn about sixty pounds from it.

The play went into rehearsal in Manchester at the end of November, when he travelled north to find to his horror that Hayakawa was 'the most wooden actor that ever was'. He returned to London, regretting he wrote it and expecting to 'lose much more in reputation than I shall make in money'.[29] *The Samurai* opened at the Hippodrome, Bristol, on 4 December, and subsequently trundled through most of Stoll's theatres including the London Coliseum. As *The Green Goddess* was still running, Archer found himself for a few brief days with two pieces of exotic melodrama on the London stage at the same time, a coincidence representing the peak of his career as an original playwright.

At the beginning of 1924, he thought of another sequel to *The Green Goddess*. 'I am no sort of good at comedy or social drama,' he explained to John Martin Harvey, the actor who had appeared as Erhart in *John Gabriel Borkman*, and was now a manager, 'but . . . I have some knack of handling strong situation.'[30] In *The Maisonette at Monte Carlo*, the Raja has escaped Rukh before the arrival of a British punitive expedition, survived adventures in Bolshevik Russia and become the leader of an anarchist cell on the French Riviera. But Archer felt too weary to work on it himself and instead asked Judith, the daughter of the dramatist and poet, John Masefield, to 'furnish me with a plot'. In return, 'over & above my eternal gratitude', she would receive ten per cent of the royalties. 'I can't say no fairer than that.'[31] But, like Shaw, Judith was reluctant to collaborate.

It seemed that his career as a playwright was almost over. By the summer of 1924, the audiences for *The Green Goddess* were declining, even though an extra eighty pounds a week was being spent on advertising. Arliss persuaded the management to keep the play going until its anniversary on 6 September, when it closed, exhausted, after four hundred and sixteen performances, fourteen fewer than in New York. And so, three weeks before his sixty-eighth birthday, Archer suddenly and disconcertingly found himself once again 'without any visible means of support'.[32]

18

Final Days

He was looking much older now. His hair was thinning rapidly and receding to leave a severe widow's peak. His cheeks were sinking and his gaze was becoming loomingly melancholy. He stooped a little and the cough persisted, deeper and chestier. He had sufficient money on which to live modestly, but a lifetime as a freelance made him compulsively try to earn more. He dabbled in collating the notes on his dreams for publication in book form. He contributed to *The Literary Guide*, a rationalist monthly. He chaired meetings addressed by his friends and his friends invigilated those at which he spoke. At the beginning of 1924, Shaw was asked to chair an event in the City at which Archer was to talk on *The Decay of Decency*, but replied that in view of their age, it would be more appropriate if they meditated on the decency of decay.

On 26 March, he was at the New Theatre to see Sybil Thorndike in the premiere of Shaw's *St Joan*, and to see Shaw himself restored to his pre-war popularity. In October, he journeyed to Birmingham for Barry Jackson's production of *The Master Builder* at the Repertory Theatre, in which Gwen Ffrangcon-Davies was playing Hilde Wangel. Although they were using Archer's translation, the company had re-written long sections in an effort to enliven the pace, but as this had been done without his permission, it was with horror they learned that he had arrived for the performance. Afterwards, he went backstage and spoke to everyone, congratulating them and offering notes. Finally, he said gravely, 'Concerning the translation – ', and the company braced themselves – , 'I felt it stood up quite well to the passage of time.'[1] Either he had not noticed the revisions or he approved of them.

On 9 October he made his last will, witnessed by his solicitors at the Temple and appointing his brothers Charles and James as his executors.

He left the property at King's Langley to Frances, made small financial bequests to his family. Elizabeth was not mentioned. He asked that his collection of forty-five years of theatre programmes and theatrical library be given to a suitable institution.[2] Later, the gross value of his estate was calculated at £21,691 13s, (equivalent to £581,550 in 1993), and the net value £14,323 5s 2d. (£385,000).

He was gathering his life together, tidying things away as best he could while he was still able. He made a final attempt to set Shaw on to the right rails, preparing an article for a special Shavian issue of *The Bookman* in December. 'The Psychology of GBS' is partly a tribute and partly an appeal to 'the most uncompromising, not to say, fanatical idealist I have ever met.'[3] Shaw, he wrote, although 'a profound revolutionist, will revolutionise nothing' because he persistently miscalculated his audience, who had no idea as to whether they were supposed to take him seriously or not. His plays amused, but did not convert. He appealed to these audiences, assuring them that at heart, Shaw was intensely serious and that his ideals were both moral and humane. It was his last shot in a thirty-year campaign.

With Elizabeth, he shared thirty-four years of memories, and on 5 November, he spent an evening with her at her London rooms at Cambridge Terrace. She was now sixty-two. He arrived at seven, they had dinner and afterwards he went to give a lecture, returning later. 'He is tired and worn,' she noted in her diary. 'Coughs. Life is hard. I too am tired and worn but I do not as yet cough.'[4]

Meanwhile, he was pouring his strength into a new play. He had returned to Dickens, among the earliest of his literary favourites, and was planning a four-act dramatization of *Little Dorrit*. On 16 November, he wrote the stage directions for the first scene of *The Father of the Marshalsea*. The Marshalsea Prison, to which the Dorrit family is condemned (William Dorrit has been there so long he is known as the Father of the Marshalsea), is the predominant image of the novel. Archer's opening scene is set in the lock of the prison, a dowdy room in which the walls are painted with ochre distemper. Archer's notes cover less than a single sheet of paper and appear to be all that he had time to write.

A few days later, he left England, having been invited by an association of friendship societies on a lecture-tour of Scandinavia. At Copenhagen he spoke on 'Holberg' before the Anglo-Danish Society and on 'The British Empire' at the Students' Association, repeating this lecture at Lund, Gothenburg and Stockholm. There, the Crown

Princess came to hear him, together with Karl Branting, the Social Democratic Prime Minister who, as Archer had done many times in the theatre, slept soundly throughout. Those who were awake noticed that Archer frequently paused as if he was exhausted, and looked as though it was an effort to dredge up the strength and the will to carry on. From Stockholm he travelled to Christiana, where he spent a day seeing friends. On the 29th, he left Norway for the last time, and sailed home to London.

On 16 December, he went to a performance of *Fratricide Punished*, a Hamlet play originally performed by troupes of English Comedians during the late sixteenth century, and recreated by 'that arch-imposter' Poel at the New Oxford Theatre. Poel contended its author to be Thomas Kyd, who died shortly before Shakespeare wrote *Hamlet*, but after the performance, Archer wrote to Barker that it was 'manifestly post-Shakesperian'.[5] It was the last play he was to see.

Two days earlier, Shaw had written him a long letter from Ayot St Lawrence. He blustered a little about *The Bookman* article, but knowing that all their battles were underpinned by unbreachable affection, asked to see him soon ('I should be glad of a hail'[6]), and announced that he and Charlotte were due to sail for Madeira on the 26th, where they would stay for a month. But Archer had no time to see Shaw as Frances, shocked by his gaunt appearance, had booked him in at his doctor's for an immediate examination. On the morning of the 17th, he was subjected to a battery of tests, proddings, soundings and questions, diagnosed as having a tumour near the kidneys on the left side and told to prepare for an operation as soon as possible. Frances supervised. Instead of going into a hospital, he would go to a nursing home at 56 Hallam Street, a short distance from Fitzroy Square. It was 'a lovely new place',[7] she informed Dibdin, owned by an acquaintance of hers, a nurse by the name of Miss Fulcher. Once again, Hector Mackenzie was called upon, and recommended Cyril Nitch as the best surgeon to carry out an abdominal operation.

After he left the doctors, Archer kept a lunch appointment at the Norwegian Legation with King Haakon of Norway ('quite nice, without the least nonsense about him,'[8]) Prince Olaf and Paul Vogt, the Norwegian envoy to London. Returning to Fitzroy Square late in the afternoon, he spent the remainder of the day in his study overlooking the square, writing letters to Charles, and to his closest friends, Elizabeth, Shaw, Granville Barker and Gertrude Jennings.

A former actress and the author of several popular one-act plays and a full-length light comedy, *Young Person in Pink*, which Archer praised on its first outing in 1920, Gertrude Jennings was a comparatively recent acquaintance. She was forty-seven, single, and had a house just off the Old Brompton Road. As her father was once editor of the *New York Times* and her mother a former actress, their friendship was strengthened by a mutual affection for the United States. Archer and Gertrude frequently accompanied each other to the theatre. It appears that only one of their letters survives, from Gertrude to Archer and written in verse, in which she assures him of 'the pleasant amity/Which exists between the humble me and the noble W.A.'[9]

In each of the letters he wrote that wintery afternoon as the light faded over Fitzroy Square, Archer explained that he was due to undergo an operation, 'not I hope a very serious one, but not quite a slight one either',[10] he told Elizabeth. He assured them all that 'I feel as fit as a fiddle',[11] or at least had suffered nothing more than occasional discomfort. He tried to sound optimistic, but he was worried and frightened of surgery, as 'accidents will happen'[12] he admitted to Shaw and Barker. 'I ought to pull through all right,' he advised Elizabeth, 'but one doesn't always do what one ought to do'. To Charles, he confided that 'This means, of course, that you may enter upon your executorship sooner than we anticipated.'[13] He wished Gertrude success with her writing, and ended her letter with an attempted joke. 'Whatever happens, I shall escape the Christmas festivities, which is one consolation. Au revoir I hope – if not, adieu.'[14]

To Barker he added that 'Shaw has taken like an angel my article on him in *The Bookman*.' This was a profound relief, as he could not bear to face an operation if their friendship was strained. In 1891, following the publication of *The Quintessence of Ibsenism*, Archer had momentarily broken their pact of emotional reticence by declaring his regard for his old ally. Now, in his brief and otherwise formal note to Shaw, Archer awkwardly repeated how deeply he valued their friendship. 'This episode gives me an excuse for saying, what I hope you don't doubt – namely, that though I may sometimes have played the part of all-too candid mentor, I have never wavered in my admiration and affection for you, or ceased to feel the Fates had treated me kindly in making me your contemporary and friend. I thank you from my heart for forty years of good comradeship.'

Shaw read this letter, but was 'not seriously alarmed'[15] by the news of his friend's illness. With his letters to Gertrude Jennings and Elizabeth, he enclosed small Christmas gifts. 'I shall write to you as soon as I am allowed,' he notified Gertrude. To Elizabeth he sent a red-covered diary similar to those he had sent her on previous new years. He addressed her formally as 'My dear Miss Robins,' and did not allude to their past great love. 'Don't write,' he warned her, ' – my letters would be opened. You may of course take no news for good news, & as soon as I am able I shall let you know how I am getting on . . . Goodbye for the present, & in any case "tak for alt." [Thanks for everything.] Ever yours W. A.'

The next day, Thursday the 18th, he was at King's Langley, packing things to take to Hallam Street. Then he and Frances travelled to town and the nursing home, where a room was ready for him. That night, feeling 'very sick & empty to have left him', Frances caught the eight o'clock train from Euston back to the village. On the journey, she wrote to Dibdin in Liverpool, asking him to cancel Archer's lecture to the Dickens Society on 14 January. 'W says he feels quite well & has no idea of anything wrong with him – He *looks* pretty ill just now, poor dear,'[16] she reported.

He was suffering from a comparatively rare form of rapidly-growing malignant tumour of the left kidney. It had been present probably only a few months. On Saturday, 20 December, two days after he was admitted, Nitch operated. The surgery involved in the removal of a massive tumour and the consequent loss of blood was such a severe shock to the system of a sixty-eight-year-old man that Nitch doubted his patient would recover. Indeed, when Archer came round from the anaesthetic, he began coughing continually. 'Poor darling, he was really depressed tonight & no wonder,' a distressed Frances informed Dibdin the following night. '. . . all that skill and devotion can accomplish is being done for him . . . I see W twice a day, so does his surgeon.'[17]

By now the family had gathered in London. Frances had moved into Fitzroy Square. Charles was also there and James was at a hotel nearby. During the next two days, Archer slowly rallied and by midweek, they were even contemplating a full recovery. Apart from Dibdin, his friends were unaware of how critical things had been. Elizabeth was in Brighton, staying at 24 Montpelier Crescent, the home of Octavia Wilberforce, a young doctor friend, and had become confused with the dates, assuming that as well as going into the nursing home on the 18th, Archer was to have his operation that day. 'I think of him a great deal,'[18] she wrote in her diary that night. During the following days, perhaps encouraged by the absence of news from London, she continued planning a visit to America in the new year. On Thursday, Christmas Day, Archer suffered a sudden relapse. On Friday, knowing nothing, Shaw duly sailed for Madeira, and Gilbert Murray left Oxford for a holiday in Italy. Barker and Helen were already staying in Paris. Dibdin, in the north, was the only one of Archer's closest male friends remaining in England. Shortly before seven on Saturday evening, the 27th, he received a telegram. 'Willie died this morning 3 am. Mrs Archer well. Letter following. Charlie Archer.'[19]

For two days, Archer had suffered intense pain, and 'one could scarcely wish the struggle to be prolonged', wrote Charles later that day, 'so perhaps it is best for him that he is gone, though to others, it means much pain & sadness . . .'[20] The Dibdins immediately travelled to London, where Charles and James were making the funeral arrangements. At Hallam Street, Nitch diagnosed the cause of death as sarcoma of the kidney, complicated by a post-operative blockage of the mesenteric blood vessels, cutting off the blood supply to the gut and resulting in gangrene of the bowel. There was no postmortem.

Isolated in Brighton, ignorant of Archer's death, Elizabeth spent most of Saturday packing her luggage for America. That night, she could not sleep and the next day complained of influenza and an irritating cough. The following morning, Monday the 29th, she saw Archer's death notice on the front page of *The Times*. She was shocked and distraught, having muddled the dates, and was hoping that no news was good news. It was 'a strange day' during which 'I remember all I owed him'. Feeling 'bronchial' she ordered a wreath for the funeral. She read the *Times* obituary and later, Octavia brought her the evening papers, each one with an obituary. Letters arrived, including one from Charles. That night, there was a new moon. Elizabeth opened her bedroom window and stared out into the bitingly cold Brighton air. 'WA's new moon & mine,' she reflected. '*He thought too well of . . .*' She stopped, and wrote: '*Good night, my friend.*'[21]

The funeral was arranged for the following day, Tuesday, 30 December. That day, the Shaws arrived at Reid's Palace Hotel at Madeira and as they entered the foyer they saw a news placard announcing that Archer was dead. The shock catapulted him into 'a transport of fury', for in his grief, he rounded, as he always did, upon the surgeons. 'The operation had killed him,' he raged. Archer's final words to his old sparring partner were those ending his note of 17 December: 'All good wishes for 1925 – Ever yours, W. A.' Shaw felt cruelly cheated, as Archer's death had deprived him of his own opportunity to reciprocate his declaration of respect and affection. 'I never could get him to think as well of himself as I thought of him,'[22] he wrote regretfully. He tried to assuage his grief by working, swimming in the warm Gulf Stream waters, and learning to dance the tango with the wife of the Reid's Palace proprietor who had herself survived an operation for cancer. Following death by dancing 'would surely have impressed Archer as quintessentially Shavian',[23] wrote Michael Holroyd.

In his anguish, Shaw remembered Archer as a man of whom 'I have not a single unpleasant recollection, and whom I was never sorry to see or unready to talk to'. And now they would talk and argue no more. Archer's death prompted one of the few public outpourings of grief from Shaw, for when three of Archer's plays were published in a single volume in 1927, he wrote a long introduction, 'How William Archer Impressed Bernard Shaw'. In effect, it is a forty-page obituary, at the end of which he recalled that 'When I returned to an Archerless London it seemed to me that the place had entered on a new phase in which I was lagging superfluous. I still feel that when he went, he took a piece of me with him.'[24]

In the south of England, there had been torrential rain and gales for most of the previous few days. Low-lying ground near reaches of the upper Thames was flooded. On Sunday and Monday, the rain ceased and the wind dropped. Everything was quiet. Then on Tuesday, the storms returned, as violently as ever. Elizabeth spent the day of the funeral 'ill with cold', finishing her packing for America and travelling first up to London and then down to Backset. She did not go to the funeral; possibly she was not invited. Elizabeth caught the two-thirty-five to Victoria and as the train steamed through the wintery Sussex countryside, she sat miserably in her compartment, the fleeting rain streaking the carriage windows, and thinking that 'at King's Langley they bury William Archer'.[25]

A few minutes before three o'clock, unbroken cloud as dark as slate hung over the village. The unrelenting rain and the wind sweeping across the graveyard of All Saints' chased the mourners into the cold gloomy shelter of the church. The coffin stood below the altar. Flowers hung from pillars and stood on window ledges, surrounding a congregation of villagers and a full choir. Frances was joined by Charles and other members of the family, but Dibdin and John Mackinnon Robertson were the only old friends of Archer's. An acquaintance, the freethinking journalist S. K. Ratcliffe, arrived. E. A. Baughan, the drama critic of the *Daily News* alighted from the London train and presented himself, dripping wet, as the representative of the Critics' Circle, of which Archer had once been vice-president. There was nobody from the theatrical world.

Archer had reserved a burial plot in the graveyard, and the previous year he had prepared an Order of Service in which he replaced passages from the Book of Common Prayer with extracts from the works of Shakespeare. But this was still lying among his papers and the Reverend J. P. Haythornthwaite, 'a grey-bearded chap fairly free from churchiness', conducted the service according to the rites of the Church of England, but 'with more show of sincerity than is usual', Ratcliffe informed Shaw. Haythornthwaite spoke of Archer as the greatest drama critic of their time, the choir sang competently and the organist played the Dead March.

Outside, the light was fading and it was still raining and blowing. The coffin was carried to a new grave dug at the boundary of the churchyard, near the hedge dividing it from the main road through the village, and within a few yards of a war memorial on which the name of Tom Archer is engraved. Frances looked up at Robertson and murmured, 'It came too soon.'[26] As the coffin was lowered into the ground, rain flicked this way and that, blown by the wind ruffling and tugging at the three wreaths at the graveside. One was from George Arliss, another from the Rationalist Press Association. The third was Elizabeth's. Her card read simply 'From Hedda & Hilda in grateful memory.'[27]

As clods of wet earth thudded down on to Archer's coffin, the mourners turned and filed quickly away.

A stone edging, marked only with his name and the dates of his birth and death, surrounds William Archer's grave. Today, it is extravagantly overgrown and so sheltered by the overhanging branches of a tree that in winter it is protected from the worst of the weather and in summer lies deep within a cave of dark green foliage. There is no tombstone, but in an article for *TP's Weekly* written eleven years before his death, Archer wrote what seemed to him an appropriate epitaph. 'He was not, on the whole, a stumbling block to progress.'[28]

Notes

The majority of the reference notes refer to articles by, and letters written by or to William Archer. He is denoted throughout by his initials: WA. The names of other frequent correspondents are similarly abbreviated as follows:

ABW: A. B. Walkley.
AS: Alfred Sutro.
AWP: Arthur Wing Pinero.
BM: Brander Matthews.
CA: Charles Archer.
CC: Charles Charrington.
CS: Clement Scott.
EG: Edmund Gosse.
EL: Edith Lyttelton.
ER: Elizabeth Robins.
ERD: Edward Rimbault Dibdin.
FA: Frances Archer.

FT: Frances Trickett (later Archer).
GBS: G. Bernard Shaw.
GM: Gilbert Murray.
GPB: George Pierce Baker.
HAJ: Henry Arthur Jones.
HGB: Harley Granville Barker.
HI: Henrik Ibsen.
LMM: Lady Mary Murray.
MB: Max Beerbohm.
OW: Oscar Wilde.
SG: Sydney Grundy.
WBA: William Bridges-Adams.

The location of an unpublished manuscript is given in shortened form. The full name may be found by referring to the Acknowledgements, where there is a list of libraries I have consulted which hold Archer material. The larger collections are:

WACTM: William Archer Collection, Theatre Museum, London. In his will, Archer asked that his collection of theatre books and bound theatre programmes be deposited with a suitable library. His executors chose that of the British Drama League, London, which subsequently evolved into the British Theatre Association. When this closed in 1990, the William Archer Collection was transferred to the Theatre Museum at Covent Garden.

398 Notes

Other frequently cited locations are:

BL: British Library (CA, ERD and GBS papers).
Broth: Brotherton Library.
Cal: University of Calgary.
Col: Columbia University.

FL: Fales Library.
KC: King's College, Cambridge.
NLS: National Library of Scotland.
PC: Private Collection.
PM: Pierpont Morgan Library.

The locations of some published and of other unpublished sources are as follows:

CL1–3: *Bernard Shaw: Collected Letters.*
DT: *Daily Telegraph.*
GBS/PN: *George Bernard Shaw: Personal Notes* by WA, August 1911. TS at WACTM.
G of I: *The True Greatness of Ibsen*: a lecture by WA delivered at University College, London, 1918. Copy at WACTM. Also published in *Edda* magazine (Norway) 1919.
HWAIBS: *How William Archer impressed Bernard Shaw*: Introduction by GBS to WA: *Three Plays.*
LWF: CA: *William Archer: Life, Work, Friendships.*
NY/1921: *Galsworthy, Barrie and Shaw*: a lecture by WA delivered at the College Club, New York, February 1921. TS at WACTM.
PMG: *Pall Mall Gazette.*
WHI: *The Works of Henrik Ibsen.* (12 vols, Heinemann).

Chapter One

1. WA: *NY/1921.*
2. GBS: *Sixteen Self Sketches*, p. 39.
3. WA: *GBS/PN.*
4. Op cit, 2, p. 40.
5. Op. cit, 3.
6. Archer/Wales: *Recollections*, p. 293.
7. WA: *Groombridge's Magazine*, January 1891.
8. WA: Epistle Dedicatory, *The Theatrical 'World' for 1893*, pp. xi, xii, xiii.
9. WA as Almaviva: *The London Figaro*, 9 June 1880.
10. WA as Almaviva: *The London Figaro*, 16 June 1880.
11. Op cit, 8.
12. 'Kappa' (WA): *Let Youth but Know*, p. 57.
13. WA to Thomas Archer: February 1876. WA/ Stanley: *Tourist*, p. xxxii.
14. *LWF*, p. 39.
15. *Life and Letters of HAJ*, p. 98.
16. HGB: *Drama*, July 1926, p. 176.
17. Bredsdorff, p. 3.
18. EG: *The Sketch*, 23 March 1898.
19. WA to EG: 23 March 1898. Broth.
20. WA: *G of I.*
21. WA: *Alloa Advertiser*, 23 August 1873.
22. WA: *Alloa Advertiser*, 4 October 1873.

Chapter Two

1. WA: *The Student* (Edinburgh University), January 1901.
2. WA: Epistle Dedicatory, *The Theatrical 'World' for 1893*, pp. xv, xxii.
3. Op. cit, 1.
4. WA: *The Modern Athenian*, 30 October 1875.
5. Op. cit, 2, p. xviii.
6. WA: *The Modern Athenian*, 16 October 1875.
7. E. V. Ward: *Pictor Depictus*, p. 5.
8. WA to Thomas Archer: February 1876. WA/ Stanley: *Tourist* p. xxxiii.
9. WA to Mackenzie: 10 October 1876. *LWF*, p. 49.
10. WA: *The London Figaro*, 20 August 1881.
11. WA to CA: *LWF*, p. 61.
12. WA to ERD: 4 October 1877. BL.
13. WA to ERD: 30 October 1877. BL.
14. WA: *The Fashionable Tragedian*, pp. 19, 20, 19, 23, 24.
15. WA to ERD: 4 March 1878. BL.
16. *LWF*, p. 74.
17. Op. cit, 2, p. xxx.
18. WA: *TP's Weekly*, 21 February 1913.
19. WA to ERD: 16 December 1878. BL.
20. WA: *The London Figaro*, 14 December 1878.
21. WA: *The London Figaro*, 19 July 1879.
22. WA to CA: 12 November 1885. *LWF*, p. 143.
23. WA to ERD: 11 May 1880. BL.
24. WA to ERD: 10 June 1880. BL.
25. WA to ERD: 14 March 1879. BL.
26. WA to ERD: 21 December 1878. BL.
27. WA to ERD: 4 April 1878. BL.
28. WA: *WHI*, vol. 1, p. xiii.
29. Op. cit, 27.
30. WA as Almaviva: *London Figaro*, 8 December 1880.
31. WA to ERD: 13 December 1880. BL.
32. Postlewait: *Prophet of the New Drama*, pp. 28–9.
33. J. W. McFarlane: *The Oxford Ibsen*, Oxford University Press, vol. 5, p. 434.

34. *The Times*, 18 December 1880.
35. *The Era*, 19 December 1880.
36. CA: *LWF*, p. 82.
37. WA as Almaviva: *The London Figaro*, 18 December 1880.
38. SG to WA: 29 March 1879. BL.
39. SG to WA: 22 April 1881. BL.
40. WA to ERD: 22 April 1881. BL.
41. *The Era*, 23 April 1881.
42. Ward: *Blue and Buff*, pp. 13, 14.
43. *The Era*: 10 September 1881.
44. WA to ERD: 17 June 1881. BL.
45. WA to Robertson: 21 October 1881. *LWF*, p. 92.
46. WA: *St James's Magazine*, March 1881.
47. WA to ERD: 2 February 1881. BL.
48. WA to CA: 30 November 1881. *LWF*, p. 99.
49. SG to WA: 27 December 1881. BL.
50. WA to ERD: 10 December 1881. BL.
51. WA to ERD: 19 December 1881. BL.
52. WA to CA: 11 December 1881. *LWF*, p. 102.
53. WA to ERD: 19 December 1881. BL.
54. WA to ERD: 1 January 1882. BL.
55. WA to CA: 5 March 1882. *LWF*, p. 111.
56. Op. cit, 54.
57. WA to Robertson: 12 February 1882. *LWF*, p. 107.
58. WA to Bond: 15 May 1884. KC.
59. WA to ERD: 27 March 1882. BL.
60. WA to ERD: 19 February 1882. BL.
61. WA to ERD: 2 February 1882. BL.
62. Op cit, 60.
63. FT to WA: 1 October 1882. PC.
64. WA to Bond: 23 May 1882. KC.
65. WA to ERD: 15 July 1882. BL.
66. FT to WA: 29 September 1882. PC.
67. FT to WA: 6 October 1882. PC.
68. FT to WA: 18 November 1882. PC.
69. Foote: *Progress* editorial, January 1883.
70. WA to ERD: 10 March 1881. BL.
71. FT to WA: 5 January 1883. PC.

Chapter Three

1. WA to Thomas Archer: 6 November 1878. WA/ Stanley: *Tourist*, p. 105.
2. GBS to Hamlin Garland: 29 December 1904. *CL2*, p. 477.
3. WA: *GBS/PN*.
4. WA to ERD: 13 September 1880. BL.
5. GBS: *HWAIBS*, p. viii.
6. WA to Braekstad: 27 March 1882. Oslo.
7. Arnold: *The Nineteenth Century*, August 1879.
8. WA: *English Dramatists of Today*, pp. 17, 5, 4–5, 9, 8–9.
9. SG to WA: 11 February 1881. BL.
10. WA to ERD: 2 February 1879. BL.
11. Op. cit, 8.
12. Russell Jackson: *Plays of HAJ*, Cambridge, 1982, Introduction, p. 1.
13. *Life and Letters of HAJ*, p. 34.
14. WA: *English Dramatists of Today*, pp. 220, 225.
15. Griffin: *AWP and HAJ*, p. 123.
16. SG to WA: 28 January 1882. BL.
17. Op. cit, 8, pp. 287, 282, 271.
18. WA: *About the Theatre*, p. 47.
19. WA: *To-Day*, February 1884.
20. WA: *The World*, 8 April 1885.
21. WA: *The World*, 25 March 1885.
22. AWP to WA: 20 May 1923. BL.
23. Op cit, 8, p. 16.
24. *The Academy*, 25 November 1882.
25. Yates to WA: 19 February 1884. BL.
26. WA to ERD: 28 February 1884. BL.
27. WA: *The World*, 5 March 1884.
28. HGB: *Drama*, July 1926, p. 176.
29. WA: *The World*, 14 December 1892.
30. Op cit, 3.
31. Op cit, 29.
32. GBS: *HWAIBS*, pp. xvii, xix.
33. WA to ERD: 10 October 1884. BL.
34. WA to Bond: 7 October 1884. KC.
35. GBS: *HWAIBS*, p. xvii.
36. WA: *The World*, 14 December, 1892.
37. WA to GBS: 12 November 1885. BL.
38. WA to ERD: 10 February 1884. BL.
39. WA: *NY/ 1921*.
40. GBS: *Sixteen Self Sketches*, p. 39.
41. Op cit, 39.

42. GBS to WA: 12 December 1885. *CL1*, p. 145.
43. WA to GBS: 12 November 1885. BL.
44. GBS to WA: 14 December 1885. *CL1*, p. 146.
45. Op cit, 39.
46. WA to ERD: 16 July 1885. BL.
47. WA to ERD: 23 August 1885. BL.
48. WA: *The Dramatic Review*, 9 May 1885.
49. WA to ERD: 10 June 1887. BL.
50. Op cit, 39.
51. WA to ERD: 24 September 1886. BL.
52. WA: *About the Theatre*, p. 190.
53. WA: *Nineteenth Century*, February 1885.
54. Op cit, 52, p. 191.
55. GBS: *HWAIBS*, p. xxxiv.
56. Section 14, Theatres Act 1814.
57. Henderson, Archibald: *Bernard Shaw – Playboy and Prophet*, Appleton, 1932, pp. 258–9.
58. WA: *About the Theatre*, pp. 154, 138.
59. WA: *Fortnightly Review*, June 1886.
60. WA: *About the Theatre*, pp. 273, 258, 270–1, 17, 100.
61. WA: *The Dramatic Review*, 22 February 1885.
62. WA: *The Dramatic Review*, 11 April 1885.
63. SG to WA: 11 February 1881. BL.
64. SG: *The Theatre*, May 1885.
65. WA: *About the Theatre*, pp. 24–5, 27.
66. Inquisitor to *The Era*: 3 July 1886.
67. WA to *The Era*: 10 July 1886.
68. WA: *The Academy*, 6 January 1883.
69. H. F. Lord to *The Academy*: 13 January 1883.
70. WA to ERD: 22 July 1883. BL.
71. WA to ERD: 3 August 1883. BL.
72. WA to CA: 27 September 1883. *Edda* magazine.
73. WA to CA: 18 October 1883. *Edda* magazine.
74. Meyer: *Henrik Ibsen*, vol. 3, p. 27.
75. Op cit, 73.

76. WA: *The Theatre*, April 1884.
77. Jenkins: *The Making of Victorian Drama*, p. 134.
78. Op cit, 76.
79. WA: *The Dramatic Review*, 4 April 1885.
80. Op cit, 76.
81. WA to CA: 25–28 July 1887. *LWF*, pp. 152–7.

82. GBS to WA: 4 October 1887. *CL1*, p. 176.
83. GBS: *Diaries*, 6 October 1887, p. 304.
84. GBS: *HWAIBS*, pp. xiv, xv.
85. WA: *Masks or Faces?*, pp. 4, 213, 215.
86. WA to ERD: 28 December 1888. BL.
87. Ellis: *The Pillars of Society*, Preface, p. xxii, Note.

Chapter Four

1. *The Theatre*, June 1885.
2. HAJ: *The Renascence of the English Drama*, p. 167.
3. WA: *The World*, 8 May 1889.
4. WA: *Manchester Guardian*, 24 April 1889.
5. WA: *Manchester Guardian*, 25 April 1889.
6. Waring: *The Theatre*, October 1894.
7. HI to WA: 13 June 1889. BL.
8. WA to CA: 31 May 1889. *LWF*, p. 167.
9. Hayter, C: *Gilbert and Sullivan*, Macmillan, 1987, p. 147.
10. WA: *The London Figaro*, 4 June 1881.
11. WA: *New Review*, September 1889.
12. WA: *The World*, 24 June 1889.
13. WA: *The Dramatic Review*, 8 February 1885.
14. WA to CA: 13 June 1889. *LWF*, pp. 181–3.
15. Op cit, 8.
16. Op cit, 14.
17. Shaw: *Manchester Guardian*, 8 June 1889.
18. Op cit, 14.
19. CS: *DT*, 8 June 1889.
20. WA to BM: 28 September 1890. Col.
21. Op cit, 19.
22. ABW: *The Star*, 9 June 1889.
23. WA: *Fortnightly Review*, July 1893.
24. CS: *The Theatre*, July 1889.
25. WA to ERD: 25 March 1889. BL.
26. Buchanan: *PMG*, 11 June 1889.

27. Buchanan: *PMG, 14 June 1889*.
28. Skidelsky: *John Maynard Keynes*, vol. 1, p. 53.
29. WA: *The World*, 12 June 1889.
30. Irving: *Henry Irving*, p. 535.
31. Op cit, 14.
32. HAJ to WA: n/d [16] July 1889. BL.
33. HAJ to WA: n/d June? 1889. BL.
34. WA to HAJ: Wednesday morning n/d. Broth.
35. AWP to WA: 30 June 1889. BL.
36. WA: *The World*, 30 April 1890.
37. Corno di Bassetto (GBS): *The Star*, 21 June 1889.
38. WA: *Fortnightly Review*, July 1889.
39. WA: *WHI* vol. 7, p. x.
40. WA: *Fortnightly Review*, November 1891.
41. HI to WA: 26 June 1889. WACTM.
42. GBS: *Diaries*, 16 June 1889, vol. 1, p. 512.
43. GBS to FA: 12 January 1887. Cornell. Shaw's spelling is rather idiosyncratic. He tends not to use apostrophes in words such as 'dont', 'cant' and 'wont'. He also drops the final 'e' of 'Shakespeare'.
44. GBS to WA: 21 August 1893. *CL1*, p. 402.
45. GBS: *HWAIBS*, p. xviii.
46. GBS: *The Cassone, The Bodley Head Bernard Shaw*, vol. 7, pp. 533–4.
47. ER: *Ibsen and the Actress*, pp. 9, 11.

Chapter Five

1. ER: *Both Sides of the Curtain*, pp. 61, 3, 9.
2. WA: *The World*, 17 July 1889.
3. Op cit, 1, p. 198.
4. CS: *DT*, 18 July 1889.
5. *The Referee*: 21 July 1889.
6. *The Daily Chronicle*: 18 July 1889.
7. *The Hawk*: 23 July 1889.
8. Op cit, 1, p. 209.
9. WA: *The World*, 24 July 1889.
10. FA to ERD: 21 April 1889. BL.
11. GBS to WA: 18 April 1889. *CL1*, p. 208.
12. WA to CA: n/d 1890. *LWF*, p. 185.
13. Caton: *Activity and Rest*, p. 19.
14. FT to WA: 30 October 1882. PC.
15. FT to WA: 2 December 1882. PC.
16. Frequently in letters between October 1882 and May 1883. PC.
17. WA to ERD: 12 November 1888. BL.
18. WA: *PMG*, 24 March 1885.
19. Stevenson to WA via *PMG*: 26 March 1885. BL
20. WA: *The Critic* (USA), 5 November 1887.
21. Stevenson to WA: n/d [June 1888]. BL.
22. WA: *Manchester Guardian*, 1 September 1885.
23. WA to ERD: 2 June 1890. BL.
24. WA to ERD: 30 July 1890. BL.
25. Op cit, 1, p. 208.
26. WA to ER: 10 June 1890. FL.
27. ER diary: 10 June 1890. FL.
28. WA to ER: 10 June 1890. FL.
29. WA: *The World*, 25 June 1890.
30. Holroyd: *Bernard Shaw*, vol. 1, p. 197.
31. GBS to WA: 17 August 1890. *CL1*, p. 258.
32. CS: *DT*, 28 January 1891.
33. Benson: *Memoirs*, p. 297.
34. GBS to CC: 30 March 1891. *CL1*, pp. 287–8.
35. Orme: p. 68.
36. OW: 'The Soul of Man under Socialism', *Fortnightly Review*, February 1891.
37. *Daily News*, 24 February 1891.
38. *Saturday Review*, 14 February 1891.
39. HI to Grein: 20 February 1891. Orme, p. 85.
40. *Licensed Victuallers' Mirror*, 17 March 1891.
41. ABW: *The Star*, 14 March 1891.
42. *Daily News*, 14 March 1891.
43. CS: *DT* review, 14 March 1891.
44. Op cit, 34, p. 289.
45. Orme, p. 79.
46. WA: *Fortnightly Review*, July 1893.
47. CS: *DT* editorial, 14 March 1891.
48. Op cit, 43.
49. ABW: *The Star*, 14 March 1891.
50. WA: *PMG*, 8 April 1891.
51. Op cit, 47.
52. WA to BM: 10 April 1891. Col.

Chapter Six

1. HI to Heinemann: 8 January 1891. Meyer: *Henrik Ibsen*, vol. 3, p. 165.
2. WA: *PMG*, 23 January 1891.
3. Op cit, 1.
4. Op cit, 2.
5. Thwaite: *Edmund Gosse*, pp. 235, 277.
6. Op cit, 2.
7. James to Stevenson: 18 February 1891. *Letters of HJ*, vol. 3, p. 338.
8. James to WA: 27 December 1890. *Letters of HJ*, vol. 3 p. 309.
9. Kaplan: *Henry James*, p. 336.
10. Op cit, 8.
11. James to EG: 3 January 1891. *Letters of HJ*, vol. 3, p. 317.
12. *Letters of HJ*, vol. 3, p. 323.
13. ER: *Both Sides of the Curtain*, p. 281.
14. WA to ER: 17 February 1891. FL.
15. WA to ER: 6 May 1891. FL.
16. WA to ER: 10 March 1891. FL.
17. ER: *Ibsen and the Actress*, p. 17.
18. WA to ER: 31 March 1891. FL.
19. WA: *Hedda Gabler*, Prose Dramas (1891), p. 254.

20. Op cit, 17, pp. 17, 26, 20, 21.

21. WA to ER: Monday [April 1891]. FL.

22. Op cit, 19, p. 341.

23. GBS: *HWAIBS*, p. xxv.

24. *PMG*, 20 April 1891.

25. Lea to WA: 19 April 1891. BL.

26. GBS to ER: 20 April 1891. *CL1*, p. 291.

27. CS: *Illustrated London News*, 25 April 1891.

28. Zingara: *Leicester Daily Post*, 27 April 1891.

29. CS: *DT, 21 April 1891*.

30. *PMG*: 21 April 1891.

31. WA to ER and ML: 21 April 1891. FL.

32. Op cit, 30.

33. ABW: *The Star*, 21 April 1891.

34. Op cit, 29.

35. *The Times*, 21 April 1891.

36. *Illustrated London News*, 25 April 1891.

37. *Sunday Times*, 26 April 1891.

38. WA to ER: n/d [5 May 1891]. FL.

39. WA to ER: Monday evening [27 April 1891]. FL.

40. WA: *The World*, 29 April 1891.

41. HI to WA: 29 April 1891. BL.

42. ER: [n/d] note. FL.

43. Op cit, 26, p. 292.

44. Op cit, 42.

45. WA to ER: Tuesday evening [n/d 1891]. FL.

46. WA to ER: 4 May 1891. FL.

47. HI to WA: 27 June 1895. BL.

48. WA to ER: 21 May 1891. FL.

49. WA to ER: 9 May 1891. FL.

50. WA to ER: Monday [n/d]. FL.

51. WA to HAJ: 11 May 1891. Broth.

52. Jenkins: *The Making of Victorian Drama*, p. 163.

53. HAJ: 15 February 1891. *Renascence of English Drama*, p. 246.

54. Griffin: *AWP and HAJ*, p. 110.

55. WA to HAJ: n/d [16? January 1891]. Broth.

56. WA to ER: Saturday evening. FL.

57. AWP to WA: 25 May 1892. BL.

58. Herford to WA: 6 November 1889. BL.

59. WA to ER: 27 May 1891. FL.

60. WA to ER: 23 May 1891. FL.

61. WA: *The World*, 6 June 1891.

62. WA: *New Review*, November 1891.

63. WA to ER: 21 May 1891. FL.

64. GBS: *The Quintessence of Ibsenism* pp. vii, 30, 82, 109.

65. Op cit, 62.

66. WA: *Fortnightly Review*, July 1889.

67. Op cit, 62.

68. GBS to WA: 25 October 1891. *CL1*, pp. 317, 318.

69. GBS to WA: 26 October 1891. *CL1*, p. 318.

70. WA to Shaw: n/d [26 October 1891]. *CL1*, p. 319.

71. Op cit, 62.

72. James to EG: 28 April 1891. *Letters of HJ*, vol. 3, p. 340.

73. ER to WA: Thursday n/d [October 1891]. FL.

74. ER: diary note n/d 1891. FL.

75. OW to ER: 23 April 1891. *Letters of OW*, p. 291.

76. ER: diary 20 October 1890. FL.

77. ER: diary 19 July 1891. FL.

78. WA to ER: 24 October 1891. FL.

79. ER: diary 25 October 1891. FL.

80. ER: diary 26 October 1891. FL.

81. ER: diary 5 November 1891. FL.

82. GBS to ER: 30 April 1891. FL.

83. Moore: *PMG*, 9 September 1891.

84. Op cit, 64, p. 154.

85. WA: *Fortnightly Review*, November 1891.

86. GBS to WA: 7 November 1891. *CL1*, pp. 320–1.

87. GBS to WA: 9 November 1891. *CL1*, p. 322.

88. GBS to ER: 9 November 1891. FL.

89. ER: note attached to 88. FL.

90. GBS to ER: 10 November 1891. FL.

91. Harris to GBS: 11 November 1891, GBS ms note to WA on letter of 7 November. *CL1*, pp. 320–1.

92. GBS: *HWAIBS*, p. xxxiii.

93. GBS to WA: 13 November 1891. *CL1*, p. 328.

94. WA: *A Visit*, leaflet. WACTM.

95. CS: *DT*, 11 March 1892.

96. WA to *PMG*: 12 March 1892.

97. CS: *DT*, 16 March 1892.

98. WA to *DT*: 17 March 1892.
99. Report: *Royal Select Committee on Theatre and Places of Entertainment*, 2 June 1892, pars 5204, 5227.
100. WA to *PMG*, 1 July 1892.
101. OW to WA: 20? July 1892. *Letters of OW*, p. 319.
102. WA to ERD: 14 August 1892. BL.
103. James to Mrs Hugh Bell, 6 and 7 October 1892. *Theatre and Friendship*, pp. 70, 71.

104. GBS: *Widowers' Houses* preface. *The Bodley Head Bernard Shaw*, vol. 1, pp. 18, 17.
105. GBS to WA: 30 December 1916. *CL3*, p. 445.
106. WA to ER: 5 December 1892. FL.
107. WA: *The World*, 14 December 1892.
108. GBS to WA: 14 December 1892. *CL1*, p. 373.

Chapter Seven

1. WA to ERD: 7 August 1893. BL.
2. GBS: *HWAIBS*, p. ix.
3. WA to Braekstad: 21 January 1893. Oslo.
4. Op cit, 2.
5. ER: *Theatre and Friendship*, p. 78.
6. WA: *Illustrated London News*, 25 February 1893.
7. ER to F. Bell: 12 November 1892. FL.
8. WA: *The World*, 22 February 1893.
9. ER to F. Bell: 16 August 1892. FL.
10. EG to WA: 10 November 1892. BL.
11. Op cit, 8.
12. EG to WA: 2 December 1892. BL.
13. Op cit, 11.
14. Op cit, 6.
15. ER: *Ibsen and the Actress*, p. 42.
16. GBS to ER: 5 February 1893. *CL1*, p. 381.
17. WA to Bernard Partridge: n/d March 1893. NLS.
18. WA to C. K. Shorter: 20 March 1893. Berg.
19. WA: *Fortnightly Review*, July 1893.
20. ABW to WA: 19 May 1890. BL.
21. WA: *Fortnightly Review*, November 1891.
22. CS: *DT*, 21 February 1893.
23. Op cit, 6.

24. *Illustrated Sporting and Dramatic News*, 25 February 1893.
25. WA to Pemberton: 25 October 1892. NLS.
26. Op cit, 19.
27. Grein to WA: 13 July 1891. BL.
28. WA: *The World*, 1 March 1893.
29. WA: *The World*, 26 April 1893.
30. OW to Mrs Grenfell: n/d [late April 1891]. *More Letters OW*, p. 96.
31. As 29.
32. WA: *Westminster Gazette*, 6 May 1893.
33. AWP to WA: 16 August 1893. BL.
34. AWP to WA: 27 November 1907. BL.
35. WA: *The World*, 12 April 1893.
36. Peters: *Mrs Pat*, p. 73.
37. WA: *The World*, 31 May 1893.
38. WA: *The World*, 3 June 1893.
39. Waring to ER: n/d [May? 1893]. FL.
40. WA: annotations in *The Master Builder*. WACTM.
41. WA to Gould: 2 June 1893. NLS.
42. WA: *The World*, 7 June 1893.
43. WA: *The World*, 14 June 1893.
44. Op cit, 42.
45. Op cit, 37.
46. WA: *The World*, 21 June 1893.
47. Achurch to WA: 5 October [n/d] FL.
48. GBS to WA: 21 August 1893. *CL1*, p. 401.

Chapter Eight

1. WA: *Fortnightly Review*, November 1891.
2. WA to Florence Emery: 18 June 1891. University of London.
3. ER: diary 19 October 1894. FL.
4. WA: *The Efficient Person*, undated ms notes [1894]. FL.
5. WA to ER: undated ms notes. [1894]. FL.
6. WA: *The World*, 25 April 1894.
7. WA to ER: undated ms note [1894]. FL.
8. WA to ER: Sunday night [April–May 1894]. FL.
9. Holroyd: *Bernard Shaw*, vol. 1, p. 298.
10. WA: *The World*, 25 April 1894.
11. Shaw to WA: 23 April 1894. *CL1*, p. 427.
12. WA: *The Wild Duck*, 1890, p. v.
13. WA: *The Sketch*, 13 June 1894.
14. Grein to WA: 8 May 1894. BL.
15. WA to Yates: 20 May 1894. Beinecke.
16. WA to Griffiths: 5 November 1894. FL.
17. WA to ERD: 1 January 1894. BL.
18. WA to BM: 10 April 1894. Col.
19. WA to ERD: 1 May 1895. BL.
20. WA to ERD: 16 October 1894. BL.
21. WA: *The World*, 10 October 1894.
22. Peters: *Mrs Pat*, p. 105.
23. WA: *The World*, 20, 27 March 1895.
24. WA: *PMG*, 23 October 1893.
25. SG: *The Theatre*, March 1896.
26. WA: *The World*, 25 February 1896.
27. CS: *DT* quoted Ellmann: *Oscar Wilde*, p. 450.
28. WA: *The World*, 9 January 1895.
29. MB: *More Theatres*, p. 123.
30. WA: *The World*, 26 April 1893.
31. Op cit, 28.
32. WA: *The World*, 20 February 1895.
33. *PMG*: 1 July 1892.
34. OW to WA: 26? April 1893. *Letters of OW*, p. 338.
35. WA to CA: 1 May 1895. *LWF*, p. 215.
36. WA to BM: 24 May 1895. Col.
37. OW's inscription in WA's copy. WACTM.
38. WA: *The World*, 3 April 1895.
39. HI to WA: 24 October 1894. BL.
40. WA: *Little Eyolf*, Heinemann, 1895, p. 20.
41. WA to BM: 10 November 1894. Col.
42. GBS: *HWAIBS*, p. x.
43. AWP to WA: 29 November 1894. BL.
44. WA to ER: 26 November 1894. FL.
45. ER to GBS: 7 January 1895. FL.
46. GBS to Mansfield: 22 February 1895. *CL1*, p. 486.
47. GBS to WA: 11 May 1893. *CL1*, p. 395.
48. WA to ER: undated note. FL.
49. WA to ER: undated ms notes on *The Mirkwater* script [summer 1895]. FL.
50. WA to ER: undated ms notes with *Stall B25* script [September 1895]. FL.
51. WA: *Daily Chronicle*, 9 March 1895.
52. WA: *The World*, 24 April 1895.
53. Redford to *The World*: 25 April 1895. FL.
54. Hardy to WA: 17 February 1904. BL.
55. FA to ERD: 11 November [1895]. BL.
56. GBS to E. Terry: 5 November 1896. *CL1*, p. 695.
57. GBS to CC: 7 October 1895. *CL1*, p. 562.
58. GBS to WA: 19 February 1896. *CL1*, p. 602.
59. GBS to Heinemann: 18 February 1896. *CL1*, p. 600.
60. ER: diary, 22 February 1896. FL.
61. WA: *The World*, 22 January 1896.
62. WA to Quiller-Couch: 30 July 1894. NLS.
63. WA to CC: 28 March 1895. WACTM.
64. WA to GM: 13 April 1895. WACTM.
65. WA to ERD: 5 August 1896. BL.
66. WA to GM: 20 August 1896. WACTM.
67. WA to BM: 3 September 1896. Col.
68. WA: *The World*, 25 September 1895.
69. WA to Thorpe: 12 November 1896. WACTM.
70. WA to Thorpe: 8 November 1896. WACTM.

71. Op cit, 69.
72. WA: annotations in *Little Eyolf.* WACTM.
73. WA to Thorpe: 19 November 1896. WACTM.
74. WA to Thorpe: n/d [20/21? November 1896]. WACTM.
75. AWP to WA: 17 November 1896. BL.
76. *The Era*, 24 November 1896.
77. CS: *DT*, 24 November 1896.

78. *PMG*, 24 November 1896.
79. *The Times*, 24 November 1896.
80. Op cit, 78.
81. GBS: *Saturday Review*, 28 November 1896.
82. WA: *The World*, 25 November 1896.
83. GBS: *Diaries*, 8 December 1896.
84. WA: *The World*, 24 February 1897.
85. WA: *The World*, 3 March 1897.

Chapter Nine

1. Undated, untitled planning document. FL.
2. WA to James: 9 March 1897. FL.
3. WA to AS: 26 February 1897. FL.
4. WA to AS: 12 March 1897. FL.
5. WA to AS: 6 March 1897. FL.
6. New Century Theatre prospectus. FL.
7. WA to GM: 12 November 1896. WACTM.
8. WA: *The World*, 5 May 1897.
9. WA: *G of I*.
10. AS: *Celebrities and Simple Souls*, p. 189.
11. GBS: *Saturday Review*, 8 May 1897.
12. WA: *Daily Chronicle*, 4 May 1897.
13. CS: *DT*, 4 May 1897.
14. WA to GM: 28 July 1897. WACTM.
15. Undated, untitled planning document. FL.
16. WA to GM: 23 November 1897. WACTM.
17. WA: *The World*, 8 December 1897.
18. WA to GM: 6 December 1897. WACTM.
19. WA to GM: 23 November 1897. WACTM.
20. WA: *The World*, 8 December 1897.
21. ER: *Plays to Remember*, document. FL.
22. WA to GM: 3 December 1987. WACTM.
23. Op cit, 18.
24. WA: *Daily Chronicle*, 19 April 1898.
25. GBS to WA: 11 May 1893. *CL1*, p. 395.
26. Op cit, 24.
27. WA: *Daily Chronicle*, 21 April 1898.

28. Op cit, 24.
29. GBS to WA: n/d [21 April 1898]. *CL2*, p. 34.
30. WA to GBS: 30 April 1898. BL.
31. GBS to WA: 6 June 1898. *CL2*, p. 48.
32. GBS to WA: 3 June 1898. BL.
33. WA: *Monthly Review*, June 1906.
34. WA to ERD: 28 February 1901. BL.
35. WA to GM: 12 November 1902. WACTM.
36. *Saturday Review*, 11 February 1899.
37. WA to ERD: 17 February 1899. BL.
38. WA: *America Today*, pp. 9, 10, 18.
39. WA to CA: 19 March 1899. *LWF*, p. 244.
40. Op cit, 38, pp. 38, 39.
41. WA: 'The American Stage 1', *Pall Mall Magazine*, November 1899.
42. Op cit, 38, p. 60.
43. WA: 'The American Stage 2', *Pall Mall Magazine*, December 1899.
44. Op cit, 38, p. 83.
45. Op cit, 43.
46. Op cit, 38, p. 89.
47. WA to ERD: 7 April 1899. BL.
48. ER: diary 30 April 1899. FL.
49. WA to ERD: 14 October 1899. BL.
50. WA: *Daily Chronicle*, 16 January 1900.
51. WA to GM: 2 August 1899. WACTM.
52. WA: *Daily Chronicle*, 6 September 1899.
53. WA: *Daily Chronicle*, 8 September 1899.
54. Op cit, 33.
55. WA to CA: 14 December 1899. *LWF*, p. 261.

56. WA to BM: 31 December 1899. Col.
57. WA: TS poem. FL.
58. ER: diary 1 January 1900. FL.
59. WA to ER: n/d September 1902. FL.
60. WA to GBS: 22 January 1900. *CL2*, p. 136.
61. GBS to WA: 24 January 1900. *CL2*, pp. 136, 137.
62. WA to GBS: 25 January 1900. *CL2*, p. 140.
63. GBS to WA: 27 January 1900. *CL2*, pp. 141–3.
64. WA to GBS: 1 February 1900. BL
65. WA: *The World*, 30 December 1900.
66. Siegfried Trebitsch: *Chronicle of a Life*, Heinemann, 1953, p. 95.
67. Op cit, 38, p. 133.
68. WA: *Monthly Review*, November 1901.
69. WA to GBS: 8 December 1894 (unsigned – not sent?). FL.
70. WA to GM: 5 February 1900. WACTM.
71. WA to CA: n/d August 1902. *LWF*, p. 251.
72. WA to GM: 13 February 1900. WACTM.
73. WA to ER: 29 May [1901]. FL.
74. Op cit, 70.
75. CS: *Great Thoughts*, December 1897.
76. WA to Joyce: 25 November 1902. Yale.
77. WA to Whelan: 16 April 1901. PM.
78. WA to GM: 14 May 1901. WACTM.
79. WA to Whelan: 1 July 1901. PM.
80. WA to ERD: 1 July 1902. BL.
81. WA to GPB: 2 June 1902. Harvard.
82. WA: *The World*, 5 November 1902.
83. WA to ER: 30 December 1902. FL.
84. WA to GM: 24 January 1903. WACTM.
85. WA to E. Terry: 25 January 1903. E. Terry Museum.
86. E. Terry to WA: n/d [March? 1903]. BL.
87. E. Terry to WA: 19 February 1903. BL.
88. Op cit, 86.
89. E. Terry to WA: 29 April 1903. BL.
90. Op cit, 86.
91. WA to GM: 16 October 1902. WACTM.
92. WA to ER: 29 April 1903. FL.
93. WA to GM: 21 January 1904. WACTM.
94. *The Tatler*, 10 July 1901.
95. WA to ER: 30 December 1902. FL.

Chapter Ten

1. WA: *The World*, 5 July 1889.
2. HGB to WA: 4 April 1916. BL.
3. Holroyd: *Bernard Shaw*, vol. 2, p. 92.
4. WA: *The World*, 15 November 1889.
5. HGB to WA: 4 April [1900?]. BL.
6. GBS to CC: 11 June 1900. *CL2*, p. 172.
7. GBS to WA: 8 July 1900. *CL2*, p. 175.
8. WA: *The World*, 15 January 1902.
9. WA: *Morning Leader*, 25 September 1909.
10. WA to ER: 13 March 1903. FL.
11. WA to GM: 13 February 1902. WACTM.
12. WA to GM: 2 August 1901. WACTM.
13. WA to ER: 26 September 1902. FL.
14. HGB to WA: 28 April [1903?]. BL.
15. Op cit, 10.
16. Op cit, 3, p. 95.
17. GBS to WA: 1 and 2 March 1902. *CL2*, p. 264.
18. WA to GM: 8 April 1903. WACTM.
19. HGB: *The Exemplary Theatre*, pp. v, viii.
20. WA to Heinemann: 19 February 1904. Octopus.
21. WA/HGB: *Proposals for Privately Printing a Scheme (with Estimates) for a National Theatre*. Leaflet. WACTM.
22. A leaflet. WACTM.
23. WA/HGB: *Scheme & Estimates for a National Theatre*, pp. xix, 62, 36.
24. WA: *The Clarion*, 11 April 1902.
25. Op cit, 23, pp. 36, 37, 44.
26. Op cit, 24.

27. Elsom and Tomalin: *The History of the National Theatre*, p. 36.
28. Irving to WA: 26 July 1904. WACTM.
29. Carton to WA: 3 March 1904. WACTM.
30. AWP to WA: 16 June 1904. BL.
31. WA to GM: 10 August 1904. WACTM.
32. WA: *The World*, 14 June 1904.
33. WA to GPB: 8 November 1904. Harvard.
34. WA: *Daily Chronicle*, 24 May 1906.
35. GBS to WA: 7 June 1906. *CL2*, pp. 627–8.
36. WA: *Fortnightly Review*, July 1906.
37. WA: *G of I*.
38. WA to ER: 9 May 1891. FL.
39. Op cit, 37.
40. Arthur Applin: *The Song of the Ibsenites*, privately printed 1894. WACTM.

41. *Saturday Review*: 15 December 1894.
42. WA: *WHI*, vol. 1, General Preface, p. ix.
43. WA: *International Monthly*, February 1901.
44. WA: *WHI, Peer Gynt*, vol. 4, Introduction, p. xxx.
45. Wicksteed to WA: 17 September 1892. BL.
46. Op cit, 42, p. x.
47. *Daily News*, 8 June 1889. ('On A Doll's House').
48. *Gentlewoman*, 25 February 1893. ('On The Master Builder').
49. *PMG*, 21 November 1896.
50. *The Speaker*, 10 July 1897.
51. WA: *The Speaker*, 24 July 1897.
52. GM to WA: 26 July 1897. WACTM.
53. AS: *Celebrities and Simple Souls*, p. 50.
54. GBS: *HWAIBS*, p. xxv.
55. Meyer: *The Times*, 24 June 1959.
56. Meyer to author: 28 September 1991.
57. Op cit, 42, p. v.

Chapter Eleven

1. HGB to WA: 21 April [1903?]. BL.
2. WA to GPB: 19 May 1903. Harvard.
3. Op cit, 1.
4. WA: *The World*, 15 April 1904.
5. WA: *The World*, 3 May 1904.
6. WA to GM: 22 January 1904. WACTM.
7. WA to Edward Clodd: 19 May 1904. Broth.
8. WA: *Morning Leader*, 21 May 1904.
9. WA: *Morning Leader*, 29 November 1904.
10. WA to Florence Farr: 24 May 1904. Texas.
11. Wilfred Scawen Blunt. Holroyd: *Bernard Shaw*, vol. 2, p. 97.
12. WA: *The World*, 25 October 1904.
13. Op cit, 2.
14. Purdom: *Granville Barker*, p. 21.
15. WA: *The World*, 2 November 1904.
16. WA: *The World*, 7 March 1905.
17. WA: *The World*, 14 February 1904.
18. WA: *The World*, 28 March 1905.
19. Kenneth Tynan: *Curtains*, Longman, 1961, pp. 86, 91.

20. WA to GM: 27 May 1905. WACTM.
21. Op cit, 5.
22. WA: *The World*, 30 May 1905.
23. GBS to WA: 27 August 1903, *CL2*, p. 352.
24. WA to GBS: 1 September 1903. BL.
25. GBS to WA: 2 September 1903. *CL2*, pp. 358, 357.
26. GBS to WA: 16 September 1903. BL.
27. WA: *A Record and Commentary of the Vedrenne-Barker Season*, pp. 6, 10.
28. WA: *The World*, 3 October 1905.
29. WA: *The World*, 24 October 1905.
30. WA: *The World*, 5 December 1905.
31. GBS to WA: 1 January 1906. *CL2*, p. 599.
32. WA: *The World*, 14 November 1905.
33. WA to Mr Thomas: n/d. Beinecke.
34. WA: *The World*, 16 January 1906.
35. Shaw to E. Terry: 16 March 1906. Holroyd: *Bernard Shaw*, vol. 2, p. 31.
36. WA to GM: 25 April 1906. WACTM.
37. WA to GPB: 29 August 1906. Harvard.

38. WA: *The Tribune*, 4 May 1906.
39. WA: *The Tribune*, 18 May 1906.
40. WA: *The Tribune*, 10 June 1906.
41. WA to EL: 27 June 1906. Churchill.
42. *LWF*, p. 281.
43. WA: *The Tribune*, 26 September 1906.
44. WA: *The Tribune*, 20 October 1906.
45. WA: *The Tribune*, 24 October 1906.
46. WA: *The Tribune*, 14 July 1906.
47. GBS to WA: n/d [1906]. BL.
48. GBS to WA: 19 November 1906. BL.
49. WA: *The Tribune*, 20 November 1906.
50. Lillah McCarthy: *Myself and My Friends*, p. 68.
51. Op cit, 49.
52. WA: *The Tribune*, 28 December 1906.
53. HGB: *Drama*, July 1926, p. 176.
54. WA: *The Tribune*, 5 January 1907.
55. HGB to WA: 5 January 1907. BL.
56. WA: *The Tribune*, 5 March 1907.
57. ER to Millicent Fawcett: 1 November 1907. Fawcett.
58. WA: *The Tribune*, 13 May 1907.

59. WA: *The Tribune*, 25 May 1907.
60. BM to WA: 7 February 1907. BL.
61. WA: *The Tribune*, 20 May 1907.
62. WA to W. L. Phelps: 6 April 1907. Beinecke.
63. WA: *The Tribune*, 6 June 1907.
64. WA: *The Tribune*, 5 June 1907.
65. WA: *The Tribune*, 24 June 1907.
66. *The Clarion*, 19 April 1907.
67. *The Referee*, 14 April 1907.
68. WA to LMM: 1 November 1907. WACTM.
69. AWP to WA: 28 February 1908. BL.
70. *The Atheneum*: 30 November 1907.
71. *The Times*, 27 November 1907.
72. WA: *The Tribune*, 27 November 1907.
73. AWP to WA: 27 November 1907. BL.
74. WA: *The Old Drama and the New*, p. 360.
75. Report: *Joint Select Committee of the House of Lords and the House of Commons on the Stage Plays (Censorship)*, 2 November 1909, pp. 375, 376.
76. WA/ HGB: *A National Theatre: Scheme & Estimates*, p. xi.

Chapter Twelve

1. HGB to WA: n/d [1907]. BL.
2. WA: *The Tribune*, 26 November 1907.
3. WA: *The Tribune*, 17 December 1907.
4. WA to GM: 9 May 1907. WACTM.
5. *McClure's Magazine*, February 1913.
6. WA: *Through Afro-America*, pp. 10, 6, 5.
7. Op cit, 4.
8. Op cit, 6, pp. 70, 221, 88, 164–5, 201, 9, 201, 71, 221.
9. Op cit, 4.
10. Op cit, 6, pp. 247, 267.
11. WA to Braekstad: 21 July 1906. Oslo.
12. WA to ER: 30 July 1908. FL.
13. WA: *Morning Leader*, 15 August 1908.
14. WA: *Morning Leader*, 11 April 1908.
15. WA: *New Age*, 3 October, 24 October 1908.
16. Carnegie to WA: 23 September 1908. Simplified Spelling Society.
17. WA: *The Nation*, 7 November 1908.
18. WA to Yeats: 26 April 1904. Nat. Lib. of Ireland.

19. Hankin: *The Nation*, 19 December 1908.
20. WA: *The Nation*, 9 January 1909.
21. WA to GM: 6 May 1909. WACTM.
22. WA: *The Nation*, 13 March 1910.
23. Macqueen-Pope: *Carriages at Eleven*, p. 144.
24. WA: *The Nation*, 26 February 1910.
25. WA: *The Nation*, 12 March 1910.
26. WA: *Morning Leader*, 21 January 1911.
27. WA: *Morning Leader*, 3 July 1910.
28. WA: *Fortnightly Review*, October 1910.
29. Op cit, 24.
30. Op cit, 25.
31. Op cit, 26.
32. WA: *Morning Leader*, 2 April 1910.
33. WA: *The Life, Trial and Death of Francisco Ferrer*, p. 242.
34. WA: *Morning Leader*, 20 August 1910.
35. WA to W. L. Phelps: 2 April 1911. Beinecke.

36. GM to WA: 29 May 1911. WACTM.
37. WA to GM: 16 May 1911. WACTM.
38. WA: *Morning Leader*, 10 June 1911.
39. WA: *Morning Leader*, 17 June 1911.
40. WA to ERD: 17 June 1911. BL.
41. Op cit, 36.
42. WA: *Play-Making*, pp. 17, 307.
43. WA to GM: 1 March 1912. WACTM.
44. WA to ER: 4 April 1912. Texas.
45. WA: *Daily News and Leader*, 1 June 1912.
46. Op cit, 44.
47. WA: *Daily News and Leader*, 10 June 1912.
48. WA to GM: 28 June 1912. WACTM.
49. WA: *Daily News and Leader*, 12 July 1912.
50. WA: *Daily News and Leader*, 14 August 1912.
51. WA: *Daily News and Leader*, 7 August 1912.
52. WA: *Daily News and Leader*, 26 July 1912.
53. WA to GM: 28 June 1912. WACTM.
54. WA to GM: 9 July 1912. WACTM.
55. WA: *Daily News and Leader*, 5 October 1912.
56. Op cit, 54.
57. Op cit, 55.
58. WA: *India and the Future*, p. 28.
59. WA to GBS: 7 August 1912. BL.
60. Op cit, 58, pp. 29, 28.
61. Op cit, 59.
62. WA: *McClure's Magazine*, February 1913.
63. Op cit, 58, p. 33.
64. WA: *Daily News and Leader*, 11 October 1912.
65. WA: *Daily News and Leader*, 19 October 1912.
66. WA to GPB: 3 January 1913. Harvard.
67. WA: *Daily News and Leader*, 1 January 1913.
68. Op cit, 58, p. 276.
69. WA to GM: 14 September 1912. WACTM.
70. Op cit, 58, pp. 274, 279.
71. Forster to Alice Forster: 1 December 1912. *Selected Letters EMF*, Collins, 1983, vol. 1, pp. 166–7.
72. Op cit, 58, p. 104.
73. GBS to WA: 19 April 1919. *CL3*, p. 602.
74. WA: *The Star*, 26 February 1913.
75. WA: *The Star*, 5 June 1913.
76. WA: *The Star*, 2 September 1913.
77. WA: *The Star*, 17 September 1913.
78. WA: *The Star*, 23 September 1913.
79. WA to GM: 10 December 1913. WACTM.
80. WA: *Daily News and Leader*, 24 April 1913.
81. WA: *NY/ 1921*.

Chapter Thirteen

1. WA to Bond: 28 November 1914. KC.
2. WA to ER: 8 August 1908. Texas.
3. WA: *Daily News and Leader*, 5 November 1910.
4. MB to WA: and cutting from *Callaro* n/d [1913?]. BL.
5. WA: *NY/ 1921*.
6. GBS to WA: 19 April 1919. *CL3*, p. 604.
7. WA: *The Nation* (USA) 14 May 1914.
8. WA: *The Star*, 12 May 1914.
9. WA to GM: 13 July 1914. WACTM.
10. WA to Wallas: 30 June 1914. Brit. Lib. Political and Economic Science.
11. Op cit, 1.
12. GBS to WA: 11 November 1914. *CL3*, p. 266.
13. WA to GM: 8 August 1914. WACTM.
14. WA: *Morning Leader*, 31 December 1900.
15. WA to F. Stevenson: 2 May 1887. BL.
16. WA to GM: 15 April 1915. WACTM.
17. WA: *Fighting a Philosophy*, p. 26.

18. WA: *Sunday Pictorial*, 15 December 1918.
19. WA: *The Star*, 25 February 1915.
20. WA: *The Nation* (USA), 6 August 1914.
21. WA: *The Star*, 9 January 1915.
22. WA: *The Star*, 11 December 1914.
23. WA: *The Star*, 16 November 1914.
24. WA: *The Star*, 28 November 1914.
25. WA: *The Star*, 26 November 1914.
26. WA: *The Star*, 16 February 1915.
27. WA to GM: 15 April 1915. WACTM.
28. WA: *The Thirteen Days*, pp. 3, 204, 4.
29. WA to Bond: 18 July 1915. KC.
30. WA to GM: 5 August 1915. WACTM.
31. ER to Vernon Robins: 28 September 1894. FL.
32. ER: diary 5 January, 8 January 1915. FL.
33. ER: diary 18 November 1915. FL.
34. Charles Archer, in *LWF*, naturally breathes no hint of the relationship. Leon Edel to author, 6 October 1991, recalls that while researching his biography of Henry James, he heard vague 'gossip that Robins did have a long affair with Archer and there was even mention of a child'. Thomas Postlewait, in *Prophet of the New Drama*, hazards (erroneously?) ER's possible pregnancy in 1895, but in a letter to the author on 29 May 1992, concedes that 'I am now rather doubtful.'
35. WA to GM: 22 December 1915. WACTM.
36. WA to GM: 23 March 1916. WACTM.
37. WA to GM: 27 June 1916. WACTM.
38. AWP to L. E. Shipman: 6 December 1914. *Collected Letters AWP*, p. 254.
39. WA: *The Nation* (USA), 20 January 1916.
40. Nevinson: *Paint and Prejudice*, p. 87.
41. Gillon, Captain Stair: *The KOSB in the Great War*, Nelson, 1930, p. 341.
42. WA: *The Star*, 26 June 1916.
43. WA: *The Star*, 1 September 1916.
44. WA: *The Nation* (USA), 21 December 1916.
45. WA to Ogden: 20 March 1917. NLS.
46. WA: *The Pirates' Progress*, pp. 27, 2.
47. WA: note, 18 November 1917. Texas.
48. WA: *The Star*, 19 March 1917.
49. Tom Archer to LMM: 27 March 1918. WACTM.
50. WA: *The Star*, 18 April 1918.
51. Caton: *Activity and Rest*, pp. 44–5.
52. WA to ER: 22 July 1918. FL.
53. ER: diary 17 September 1918. FL.
54. FA to LMM: 14 May 1918. WACTM.

Chapter Fourteen

1. WA to ER: 22 July 1918. FL.
2. GBS: *Daily News and Leader*, 9 May 1919.
3. WA: *Colour-Blind Neutrality*, p. 52.
4. Op cit, 1.
5. WA: *War is War*, Preface, p. vii; Act One, p. 8; p. vi.
6. WA: *Play-Making*, p. 13.
7. Op cit, 1.
8. Op cit, 5, Act One, p. 18; Act Two, pp. 38, 39; Act Three p. 80; Preface, p. vi.
9. HGB to WA: 28 June 1918. BL.
10. WA to HGB: 28 June 1918. BL.
11. Op cit, 1.
12. AWP to WA: 13 March 1919. BL.
13. GBS to WA: 19 April 1919. *CL3*, p. 600.
14. Op cit, 2.
15. WA: *Daily News and Leader*, 13 May 1919.
16. Op cit, 2.
17. WA to Bond: 13 January 1919. KC.
18. GBS to GM: 14 July 1915. CL3, p. 301.
19. HGB to WA: 4 April 1916. BL.
20. WA to GM: 7 August 1918. WACTM.
21. WA to GM: 16 August 1918. WACTM.
22. WA to C. Collin: 28 November 1921. Oslo.

23. WA to GM: 3 February 1919. WACTM.
24. WA to GM: 15 January 1919. WACTM.
25. WA to GM: 1 April 1919. WACTM.
26. Skidelsky: *John Maynard Keynes*, vol. 1, p. 256.
27. WA to BM: 28 December 1918. Col.
28. WA to GM: 7 February 1919. WACTM.
29. WA to GM: 1 April 1919. WACTM.
30. WA to GM: n/d. WACTM.
31. WA to GM: 13 March 1919. WACTM.
32. WA to GM: 4 April 1919. WACTM.
33. WA to GM: 11 April 1919. WACTM.
34. WA to GM: 1 July 1919. WACTM.
35. WA to GM: 18 November 1921. WACTM.
36. WA to ER: 25 September 1919. FL.
37. WA to GM: 25 March 1924. WACTM.

38. WA to GM: n/d [10 June 1921?]. WACTM.
39. Tom Archer to LMM: 27 March 1918. WACTM.
40. WA to ERD: 25 September 1921. BL.
41. HGB to WA: 13 May 1921. BL.
42. WA to HGB: 27 December 1919. BL.
43. Op cit, 41.
44. HGB to WA: 1 October 1923. BL.
45. WA to HGB: 11 June 1923. BL.
46. A. A. Milne: *It's Too Late Now*, Methuen, 1939, p. 164.
47. WA: *The Star*, 6 January 1920.
48. WA: *The Star*, 23 April 1920.
49. WA: *The Star*, 23 June 1920.
50. WA: *Illustrated Sporting and Dramatic News*, 24 July 1920.
51. WA: *The Star*, 31 July 1920.
52. WA to ER: 28 September 1922. FL.
53. J Saunders to author: 27 June 1990.
54. FA to ERD: 24 November 1921. BL.
55. WA to MB: 21 March 1921. Merton.

Chapter Fifteen

1. EL: Alfred Lyttelton: *An Account of his Life*, Longmans Green, 1917, p. 381.
2. WBA to WA: 13 November 1918. Cal.
3. WA to GPB: 16 May 1903. Harvard.
4. WBA: *The Shakespeare Country*, Newnes, 1932, p. 5.
5. M. C. Day and J. C. Trewin: *The Shakespeare Memorial Theatre*, Dent, 1932, p. xiii.
6. Op cit, 4, pp. 5, 6.
7. WA to EL: 12 December 1922. WACTM.
8. WA to GBS: 17 May 1919. BL.
9. Op cit, 7.
10. HGB to WBA: 20 August 1919. Cal.
11. Op cit, 5, p. 173.
12. WA to WBA: 12 May 1922. WACTM.
13. WA to HGB: 28 August 1922. WACTM.
14. WA to GBS: 10 June 1922. WACTM.
15. WA: New Shakespeare Company report. TS. WACTM.

16. WA to Lady Meyer: 13 May 1922. WACTM.
17. EL to WA: n/d 1922. WACTM.
18. WA to GM: 11 April 1919. WACTM.
19. GBS to WA: 8 June 1922. WACTM.
20. Op cit, 14.
21. GBS to WA: 13 June 1922. WACTM.
22. HGB to WA: 31 December 1921. BL.
23. WA to HGB: 7 January 1922. BL.
24. WA to HGB: 21 July 1922. WACTM.
25. HGB to WA: 24 July 1922. WACTM.
26. WA to HGB: 25 July 1922. WACTM.
27. WA: TS note on 30-page TS. WACTM.
28. Op cit, 24.
29. WA to EL: 25 August 1922. WACTM.
30. EL to WA: 31 August 1922. WACTM.
31. Op cit, 29.
32. WBA to WA: 11 October 1922. Cal.

33. WA to WBA: 2 December 1922. Cal.
34. WA to WBA: 21 October 1922. WACTM.
35. WA to EL: 18 October 1922. WACTM.

36. WA to EL: 23 October 1922. WACTM.
37. WA to EL: 13 October 1922. WACTM.
38. WA to GM: 27 December 1922. WACTM.

Chapter Sixteen

1. Hannen Swaffer: *My Talks with the Dead*, Spiritualist Press, n/d, p. 4; also HS: *My Greatest Story*, W. H. Allen, 1945, pp. 153–4.
2. WA: *On Dreams*, p. 172.
3. WA to GBS: 6 September 1919. BL.
4. WA to ER: 12 January 1920. FL.
5. WA to GBS: 9 October 1919. BL.
6. Op cit, 3.
7. GBS to WA: 18 October 1919. *CL3*, p. 640.
8. Op cit, 3.
9. Op cit, 7.
10. WA: *The Green Goddess*, Act 1, pp. 17, 20.
11. GM: 29 December 1919. WACTM.
12. WA to ER: 12 January 1920. FL.
13. WA to HGB: 27 December 1919. BL.
14. Ames to WA: 1 March 1920. Shubert.
15. WA to Ames: 4 April 1920. Shubert.
16. Ames to WA: 25 April 1920. Shubert.
17. Op cit, 10, Act 1, p. 13.
18. Ames: TS note n/d [March 1920]. Shubert.
19. WA to GM: 25 December 1920. WACTM.
20. WA to ER: 15 October 1920. FL.
21. WA to GM: 27 December 1919. WACTM.
22. Op cit, 16.
23. Op cit, 19.
24. WA to CA: 31 December 1920. *LWF*, p. 374.
25. WA to GM: 6 February 1921. WACTM.

26. WA to MB: 9 February 1921. Merton.
27. WA to HGB: 21 July 1921. BL.
28. WA to ER: n/d February 1921. FL.
29. *New York Times*, 30 January 1921.
30. Op cit, 25.
31. WA: *Evening Post*, 24 February 1921.
32. WA to HGB: 11 June 1923. BL.
33. Op cit, 19.
34. GBS to WA: 16 March 1921, *CL3*, p. 714.
35. WA to HGB: 21 December 1921. BL.
36. WA: *The Star*, 20 February 1919.
37. WA to GM: 26 October 1922. WACTM.
38. WA to ER: 27 October 1922. FL.
39. WA to GM: 4 January 1923. WACTM.
40. WA to HGB: 30 January 1923. BL.
41. WA to GM: 5 February 1923. WACTM.
42. WA to HGB: 12 April 1923. BL.
43. WA to MB: 28 April 1923. Merton.
44. WA to Amy Corbin: 3 April 1923. *LWF*, p. 386.
45. Op cit, 43.
46. HGB to WA: 5 September 1923. BL.
47. WA to ER: 7 September 1923. Texas.
48. *PMG*; *Evening News*; *Evening Standard*, 7 September 1923; *Observer*, 9 September 1923.
49. Ellen Lancaster-Wallis to WA: n/d [September? 1923]. BL.
50. Ames to WA: 8 September 1923. *LWF*, p. 399.

Chapter Seventeen

1. WA to ER: 23 September 1923. FL.
2. ER: diary 8 November 1925. FL.
3. WA to C. Collin: 15 December 1921. Oslo.
4. Siegfried Sassoon: 11 June 1922. *Diaries* 1920–2, Faber, 1981, p. 171.
5. Victoria Glendinning: *Rebecca West: a Life*, Weidenfeld & Nicolson, 1987, p. 61.
6. WA to Dr Kellner: n/d [1923], *LWF*, p. 369.
7. WA to GBS: 22 June 1921. BL.
8. WA to GBS: 12 June 1923. BL.
9. GBS to WA: 19 June 1923. *CL3*, p. 832.
10. WA to GBS: 20 June 1923. BL.
11. GBS to WA: 22 June 1923. *CL3*, p. 837.
12. WA to GBS: 23 June 1923. BL.
13. WA: *NY/ 1921*.
14. WA: *GBS/ PN*.
15. WA to HGB: 11 June 1923. BL.
16. WA to GM: 31 May 1923. WACTM.
17. Op cit, 15.
18. WA to HGB: 28 September 1923. BL.
19. Op cit, 15.
20. Op cit, 18.
21. HGB to WA: 22 September 1923. BL.
22. HGB to WA: 10 October 1923. BL.
23. Op cit, 15.
24. WA: *The Joy-Ride*: TS Lord Chamberlain's Collection. BL.
25. Unidentified Manchester newspaper. BL.
26. WA to ER: 25 September 1923. FL.
27. WA to HGB: 12 July 1923. BL.
28. WA: *The Samurai*: TS Lord Chamberlain's Collection. BL.
29. WA to ER: 7 December 1923. FL.
30. WA to Harvey: 13 April 1920. NLS.
31. WA to Masefield: 19 January 1924. Edinburgh.
32. WA to GM: 24 August 1924. WACTM.

Chapter Eighteen

1. Michael Meyer to author: 26 September 1991.
2. See key to WACTM in Reference Notes abbreviations.
3. WA: *The Bookman*, December 1924.
4. ER: diary 5 November 1924. FL.
5. WA to HGB: 17 December 1924. BL.
6. GBS to WA: 14 December 1924. *CL3*, p. 895.
7. FA to ERD: 18 December 1924. BL.
8. WA to ER: 17 December 1924. Texas.
9. Jennings to WA: 16th [n/d]. BL.
10. Op cit, 8.
11. WA to GBS: 17 December 1924. Texas.
12. Op cit, 5 and 11.
13. WA to CA: 17 December 1914, *LWF*, p. 402.
14. WA to Jennings: 17 December 1924. Edinburgh.
15. GBS: *HWAIBS*, p. xxxix.
16. Op cit, 7.
17. FA to ERD: 21 December 1924. BL.
18. ER: diary 18 December 1924. FL.
19. CA to ERD: telegram 27 December 1924. BL.
20. CA to ERD: 27 December 1924. BL.
21. ER: diary 29 December 1924. FL.
22. Op cit, 15, p. xxxviii.
23. Holroyd: *Bernard Shaw*, vol. 3, p. 97.
24. Op cit, 15, p. xl.
25. ER: diary 30 December 1924. FL.
26. Ratcliffe to GBS: 1 January 1924 [5]. BL.
27. Op cit, 21.
28. WA: *TP's Weekly*, 21 February 1913.

Select Bibliography

(Unless otherwise specified, place of publication is London.)

Archer, Lieut.-Col. Charles: *William Archer: Life, Work, Friendships*, Allen &
   Unwin, 1931.
Archer, Thomas: *Recollections of a Rambling Life*, ed. Murdoch Wales,
   Boolarong Publications, Brisbane, Australia, 1988.
Beauman, Sally, *The Royal Shakespeare Company*, Oxford, 1982.
Beerbohm, Max: *Around Theatres*, Hart-Davis, 1953.
——: *More Theatres*, Hart-Davis, 1969.
——: *Letters 1892–1956*, ed. Rupert Hart-Davis, John Murray, 1968.
Benson, Frank: *My Memoirs*, Ernest Benn, 1930.
Booth, Michael: *English Melodrama*, Herbert Jenkins, 1965.
Bredsdorff, Elias (ed.): *Sir Edmund Gosse's Correspondence with Scandinavian
   Writers*, Heinemann, 1930.
Buitenhuis, Peter: *The Great War of Words: Literature as Propaganda 1914–18*,
   Batsford, 1989.
Campbell, Mrs Patrick: *My Life and Some Letters*, Hutchinson, 1922.
Caton, A. R.: *Activity and Rest: The Life and Work of Mrs William Archer*, Philip
   Allen & Co, 1936.
Clarke, Ian: *Edwardian Drama*, Faber and Faber, 1989.
Dibdin, James C.: *Annals of the Edinburgh Stage*, Cameron, Edinburgh, 1888.
Downs, Brian W.: *Modern Norwegian Literature 1860–1918*, Cambridge
   University Press, 1966.
Edel, Leon: *Henry James: A Life*, Collins, 1987.
—— (ed.): *The Letters of Henry James*: vol. 3: 1883–1895; vol. 4: 1895–1916;
   Macmillan, 1981, 1984.
Egan, Michael (ed.): *Ibsen: The Critical Heritage*, Routledge & Kegan Paul,
   1972.
Ellmann, Richard: *James Joyce*, Oxford, 1982.
——: *Oscar Wilde*, Hamish Hamilton, 1987.
Elsom, John and Tomalin, Nicholas: *The History of the National Theatre*,
   Jonathan Cape, 1978.

Evans, T. F.: *Shaw: The Critical Heritage*, Routledge & Kegan Paul, 1976.
Findlater, Richard: *Banned! A Review of Theatrical Censorship in Britain*, MacGibbon & Kee, 1967.
Fowell, Frank, and Palmer, Frank: *Censorship in England*, F. Palmer, 1913.
Galsworthy, John: *Letters from John Galsworthy 1900–1932*, ed. Edward Garnett, Jonathan Cape, 1934.
——: *Life and Letters of John Galsworthy*, ed. H. V. Marrot, Heinemann, 1935.
Ganz, Arthur: *George Bernard Shaw*, Macmillan, 1983.
Garnett, Edward: *The Breaking Point: A Censured Play*, Duckworth, 1907.
Granville Barker, Harley: *The Exemplary Theatre*, Chatto and Windus, 1922.
——: Prefaces to *The Player's Shakespeare*: *Macbeth*; *The Merchant of Venice*; *Cymbeline*, Benn, 1923.
——: *A National Theatre*, Sidgwick and Jackson, 1930.
——: 'The Coming of Ibsen' in *The Eighteen Eighties*, ed. Walter de la Mare, Cambridge University Press 1930.
——: *On Dramatic Method*, Sidgwick & Jackson, 1931.
Griffin, Penny: *Arthur Wing Pinero and Henry Arthur Jones*, Macmillan, 1991.
Holroyd, Michael: *Augustus John* (two vols), Heinemann, 1974–5.
——: (ed.) *The Genius of Shaw*, Hodder & Stoughton, 1979.
——: *Bernard Shaw*: *The Search for Love*; *The Pursuit of Power*; *The Lure of Fantasy* (three vols), Chatto and Windus, 1988–91.
Howe, P. P.: *The Repertory Theatre*, Martin Secker, 1910.
Hynes, Samuel: *The Edwardian Turn of Mind*, Oxford University Press, 1968.
——: *A War Imagined*, The Bodley Head, 1990.
Irving, Laurence: *Henry Irving, The Actor and his World*, Faber and Faber, 1954.
Jenkins, Anthony: *The Making of Victorian Drama*, Cambridge University Press, 1991.
Jones, Doris: *The Life and Letters of Henry Arthur Jones*, Gollancz, 1930.
Jones, Henry Arthur: *The Renascence of the English Drama*, Macmillan, 1895.
Kaplan, Fred: *Henry James: The Imagination of Genius*, John Curtis, Hodder & Stoughton, 1992.
Kennedy, Dennis: *Granville Barker and the Dream of Theatre*, Cambridge University Press, 1985.
Lindsay, Lt-Col J. H.: *The London Scottish in the Great War*, Regimental H. Q., 1925.
MacCarthy, Desmond: *The Court Theatre 1904–1907: a Commentary and Criticism*, A. H. Bullen, 1907.
Macqueen-Pope, W: *Carriages at Eleven: The Story of the Edwardian Theatre*: Hutchinson, 1947.
McCarthy, Lillah: *Myself and My Friends*, Thornton Butterworth, 1933.
McDonald, Jan: *The 'New Drama' 1900–1914*, Macmillan, 1986.
Masterman, Lucy: *C. F. G. Masterman: a Biography*, Nicolson & Watson, 1939.
May, Keith: *Ibsen and Shaw*, Macmillan, 1985.

Meyer, Michael: *Henrik Ibsen: The Making of a Dramatist: The Farewell to Poetry; The Top of a Cold Mountain* (three vols), Rupert Hart-Davis, 1967–71.

Milne, A. A.: *Year In, Year Out*, Methuen, 1952.

Morgan, Margery: *A Drama of Political Man*, Sidgwick and Jackson, 1961.

——: *The Shavian Playground: An Exploration of the Art of George Bernard Shaw*, Methuen, 1972.

Murray, Gilbert: *An Unfinished Autobiography*, Allen and Unwin, 1960.

Nilsen, Sidsel Marie, and Reznicek, Ladislav: *Ibsen in Italy*, Biblioscanda, Oslo, 1989.

Orme, Michael (Alice A. Grein): *J. T. Grein: The Story of a Pioneer 1862–1935*, John Murray, 1936.

Pearson, Hesketh: *Bernard Shaw*, Unwin Hyman, 1987.

Peters, Margot: *Bernard Shaw and the Actresses*, Doubleday, New York, 1980.

——: *Mrs Pat: The Life of Mrs Patrick Campbell*, The Bodley Head, 1984.

Pinero, Arthur Wing: *The Collected Letters*, ed. J. P. Wearing, University of Minnesota Press, 1974.

Postlewait, Thomas: (ed.) *William Archer on Ibsen: The Major Essays 1889–1919*, The Greenwood Press, Connecticut 1984.

——: *Prophet of the New Drama: William Archer and the Ibsen Campaign*, The Greenwood Press, Connecticut 1987.

Purdom, C. B.: *Harley Granville Barker*, Rockcliff, 1955.

Ricketts, Charles: *Self Portrait*, comp. T. Sturge Moore, ed. Cecil Lewis, Peter Davies, 1939.

Report from the Select Committee on Theatres and Places of Entertainment, HMSO, 1892.

Report from the Joint Committee of the House of Lords and the House of Commons of The Stage Plays (Censorship), HMSO, 1909.

Robertson, John Mackinnon: *History of Freethought in the Nineteenth Century* (two vols), London, 1929.

Robins, Elizabeth: *Ibsen and the Actress*, Hogarth Press, 1928.

——: *Theatre and Friendship*, Jonathan Cape, 1932.

——: *Both Sides of the Curtain*, Heinemann, 1940.

——: *Whither and How*, unpublished TS, FL.

Rowell, George: *Victorian Theatre Criticism*, Methuen, 1971.

Salmon, Eric: *Granville Barker: A Secret Life*, Heinemann, 1983.

Salter, W. H.: *Trance Mediumship: An Introductory Study of Mrs Piper and Mrs Leonard*, Society for Psychical Research, 1950.

Schmid, Hans: *The Dramatic Criticism of William Archer* (The Cooper Monographs no. 9), Franke Verlag, Bern, 1964.

Scott, Clement: *The Drama of Yesterday and Today* (two vols), Macmillan, 1899.

Shaw, G. Bernard: *The Bodley Head Bernard Shaw: Collected Plays with their Prefaces* (seven vols), supervising ed. Dan H. Laurence, Max Reinhardt, 1970–4.

——: *The Quintessence of Ibsenism*, Walter Scott, 1891.

——: *Our Theatres in the Nineties* (three vols), Constable, 1931.

——: *Sixteen Self-Sketches*, Constable, 1949.

——: *Collected Letters* (four vols), ed. Dan H. Laurence, Max Reinhardt, 1965–88.

——: *An Autobiography 1856–1950* (two vols), ed. Stanley Weintraub, Max Reinhardt, 1969, 1970.

——: *The Diaries 1885–1897* (two vols), ed. Stanley Weintraub, Pennsylvania State University Press, 1986.

Skidelsky, Robert: *John Maynard Keynes* (vols 1 and 2), Macmillan, 1983, 1992.

Sutro, Alfred: *Celebrities and Simple Souls*, Duckworth, 1933.

Thwaite, Ann: *Edmund Gosse: A Literary Landscape 1849–1928*, Secker and Warburg, 1984.

Whitworth, Geoffrey: *The Theatre of My Heart*, Gollancz, 1930.

Wilde, Oscar: *Letters of Oscar Wilde*, ed. Rupert Hart-Davis, Hart-Davis, 1962.

——: *More Letters of Oscar Wilde*, ed. Rupert Hart-Davis, John Murray, 1985.

Wilson, Duncan: *Gilbert Murray OM 1866–1957*, Oxford University Press, 1987.

Woodfield, James: *English Theatre in Transition: 1886–1914*, Croom Helm, 1984.

And newspaper and journal articles by Archer and many others, together with plays by John Galsworthy; Harley Granville Barker; St John Hankin; Henry Arthur Jones; A. A. Milne; Gilbert Murray; Arthur Wing Pinero; Elizabeth Robins; Bernard Shaw; Oscar Wilde and others.

The Principal Works of William Archer

Books, Plays and Pamphlets

Unless otherwise specified, place of publication is London.

Pictor Depictus, or The Daubers Bedaubed, by E. V. Ward (W. A. with E. R. V. Dibdin), 23pp, E. and S. Livingstone, Edinburgh, 1876.

The Fashionable Tragedian, Anon (W. A. and R. Lowe, illustrated by G. Halkett), 24pp, Thos Gray, Edinburgh, 1877.

Blue and Buff, or The Great Muddleborough Election, by E. V. Ward, Enoch & Sons, 1881.

English Dramatists of Today, Sampson Low & Co, 1882.

Henry Irving: Actor and Manager: A Critical Study, Field & Tuer, 1883.

About The Theatre: Essays and Studies, T. Fisher Unwin, 1886.

Masks or Faces? A Study in the Psychology of Acting, Longmans & Co, 1888.

William Charles Macready (Vol. 1 of *Eminent Actors*, ed. W. A.), Kegan Paul and Co., 1890.

The Theatrical 'World' of 1893–1897 (five volumes), Walter Scott, 1894.

Study and Stage: A Year-Book of Criticism, Grant, Richards, 1899.

America Today: Observations and Reflections, Heinemann, 1900.

Real Conversations, Heinemann, 1904.

Scheme & Estimates for a National Theatre (with Harley Granville Barker), privately printed, 1904.

Let Youth But Know: A Plea for Reason in Education, by 'Kappa', Methuen & Co, 1905.

A National Theatre: Scheme & Estimates (with Harley Granville Barker), Duckworth, 1907.

Some Common Objections, Simplified Spelling Society pamphlets nos 2–4, Simplified Spelling Society, 1908–9.

Through Afro-America: An English Reading of the Race Problem, Chapman & Hall, 1910.

Proposals for a Simplified Spelling of the English Language (with W. Rippmann), Simplified Spelling Society, 1911.

The Life, Trial and Death of Francisco Ferrer, Chapman & Hall, 1911.
Art and the Commonweal (1912 Conway Memorial Lecture), 53pp, Watts & Co, 1912.
Play-Making: A Manual of Craftsmanship, Chapman & Hall, 1912.
The Great Analysis: A Plea for a Rational World-Order, Anon, Methuen & Co, 1912.
Fighting a Philosophy, 26pp, Oxford Pamphlets, 1915.
The Thirteen Days: July 23–August 4 1914: A Chronicle and Interpretation, Clarendon Press, Oxford 1915.
To Neutral Peace-Lovers: A Plea for Patience, 16pp, Causton, 1916.
Colour-Blind Neutrality: An Open Letter to Dr Georg Brandes, 53pp, Hodder & Stoughton, 1916.
Knowledge and Character: The Straight Road in Education, 28pp, Allen & Unwin, 1916.
India and the Future, Hutchinson, London, 1917.
God and Mr Wells: A Critical Examination of 'God the Invisible King', Watts & Co, 1917.
501 Gems of German Thought, T. Fisher Unwin, 1917.
Shirking the Issue: A Letter to Dr Georg Brandes, 9pp, Hodder & Stoughton, 1917.
Six of One and Half a Dozen of the Other: A Letter to Mr L. Simon of the Hague, 32pp, T. Fisher Unwin, 1917.
The Villain of the World-Tragedy: A Letter to Prof Ulrich von Wiliamowitz-Moellendorf, 40pp, T. Fisher Unwin, 1917.
A Letter on the Debt of European Literature to Russia, 4pp, 1917.
The Pirates' Progress: A Short History of the U-Boat, Chatto & Windus, 1918.
The Peace President: A Brief Appreciation, Hutchinson, 1918.
War is War; or The Germans in Belgium, Duckworth, 1919.
The Green Goddess, Knopf, New York, 1921; Heinemann, 1923.
The Old Drama and the New: An Essay in Revaluation, Heinemann, 1923.

Selected Ibsen translations

The Pillars of Society in *The Pillars of Society and Other Plays*, Camelot Classics, 1888.
A Doll's House (limited edition), Fisher Unwin, 1889.
Henrick Ibsen's Prose Dramas (five vols), ed. W. A., Walter Scott, 1890–1.
Peer Gynt, trans. W. A. and C. A., Walter Scott, 1892.
The Master Builder, trans. W. A. and E. Gosse, Heinemann, 1893.
Little Eyolf, Heinemann, 1895.
John Gabriel Borkman, Heinemann, 1897.
When We Dead Awaken, Heinemann, 1900.

The Works of Henrik Ibsen (twelve vols), ed. W. A., Heinemann, 1906–12;
  Scriber's, New York, 1906–12.
The Pretenders, trans. W. A. and C. A., Heinemann, 1913.

Other dramatic translations

Gerhart Hauptmann: *Hannele: A Dream Poem*, Heinemann, 1894.
Maurice Maeterlinck: *Interior*, Duckworth & Co., 1899.
Edward Brandes: *A Visit*, 1891.

Posthumous

William Archer as Rationalist, ed. J. M. Robertson, Watts, & Co, 1925.
The Religion of To-Morrow, Correspondence between W. A. and H. H. Powers,
  Watts & Co., 1925.
Three Plays (*Beatriz-Juana*; *Lidia*; *Martha Washington*; with Introduction by
  Bernard Shaw), Constable, 1927.
The Great Analysis, new edition, Williams & Norgate, 1931.
On Dreams, anthology of W. A.'s notes on his dreams, ed. Theodore
  Besterman, Methuen, 1935.
Tourist to the Antipodes: William Archer's Australian Journey 1876–77, ed.
  Raymond Stanley, University of Queensland Press, 1977.

Plays

Plays performed but unpublished (the first two are apparently lost):

Mesmerism or Quits, Edinburgh, 1876.
Rosalind, Edinburgh, 1878.
Australia, or The Bushrangers (with H. Mackenzie, as W. A. and A. G. Stanley),
  1881 (MS at BL).
The Joy-Ride, 1923 (TS at BL).
The Samurai, 1923 (TS at BL).

Plays unperformed and unpublished (unless otherwise noted, all plays
  apparently lost):

The Jeweller's Daughter, 1877.
The Runic Ring, 1877.
Our Special Correspondent, 1878.
Au Revoir, 1878.
The Feast at Felvik, 1878.

Mixed: A Photographic Frenzy, 1879.
Method in his Madness, 1879.
Mandolinata, 1879.
The Khan of Kashgar, 1879 (first act MS at BL).
Auto da Fe, 1879.
(Unidentified *Thackeray* adaptation) 1880.
Irina, 1880.
Clive, 1881.
Votes for Vogan, 188?.
The Mirkwater (with Elizabeth Robins), 1895 (TS at FL).
Benvenuto Cellini (with Elizabeth Robins), 1900 (TS at FL).
Beatriz-Juana, 1920.
Lidia, 1920.
The Magician, 1921.
Martha Washington, 1922.
(Unidentified stock-exchange play), 1923.

As editor and contributor

Actors and Actresses of Great Britain and the United States ed. Brander Matthews
  and Laurence Hutton, Cassell and Co., New York, 1886. Biographical
  articles by W. A.: Vol. 1: Charles Macklin, Tate Wilkinson; Vol. 2: Mrs
  Jordan, Robert Elliston; Vol. 3: J. B. Buckstone; Vol. 4: Samuel Phelps;
  Vol. 5: Mr and Mrs Bancroft, Mr and Mrs Kendal.
Alan's Wife, Anon (Elizabeth Robins and Florence Bell), Grein's Independent
  Theatre Series, 1893. Introduction by W. A.
Dramatic Essays, ed. with R. Lowe; Introductions by W. A.: Vol. 1: 'Leigh
  Hunt'; Vol. 2: 'William Hazlitt'; Vol. 3: 'John Forster and George Henry
  Lewes'; Walter Scott, 1894–6.
Poets of the Younger Generation, ed. W. A., John Lane, 1902.
Charles Lamb: Essays of Elia, ed. W. A., Cassell's National Library, 1904.
William Shakespeare: King Lear, Introduction by W. A., Harrap & Co., 1906.
Plays by George Farquhar, ed. W. A., Fisher Unwin, 1906.
Plays by William Congreve, ed. W. A., American Book Co., New York, 1912.
Harold Chapin: Soldier and Dramatist: Letters, Introduction and ed. W. A., John
  Lane, 1916.
W. S. Gilbert: A Stage Play, Introduction by W. A., Columbia College
  Dramatic Museum Publications, New York, 1916.
The Playhouse: (with W. J. Lawrence) 28pp contribution to *Shakespeare's
  England*, vol 11, Clarendon Press, Oxford, 1916.
Alan Seeger: Poems, Introduction and ed. W. A., Constable & Co., 1917.

Other translations

A. L. Kjelland: *Tales of Two Countries*, Osgood & Co., 1891.

Fritjiof Nansen: *Eskimo Life*, Longmans & Co., 1893.

W. C. Brogger and N. Rolfsen: *Fritjiof Nansen* (a biography), Longmans & Green, 1896.

Fritjiof Nansen: *Furthest North* (trans. revised), Constable & Co., 1897.

Georg Brandes: *William Shakespeare: A Critical Study*, Heinemann, 1899.

——: *Henrik Ibsen, Bjørnsterne Bjørnson: Critical Studies*, Heinemann, 1899.

Index

William Archer is denoted within entries by his initials: WA. Other abbreviations are as follows: Harley Granville Barker: HGB; National Theatre: NT; Elizabeth Robins: ER.

The various newspapers to which WA contributed are indexed beneath the main WA entry. Some may also have separate entries. Plays and other works are indexed as *works* beneath the entries of the appropriate authors.